Enzo Angelucci - Paolo Matricardi

COMPLETE BOOK OF
WORLD WAR II
COMBAT AIRCRAFT
1933-1945

Illustrations by Pierluigi Pinto

MILITARY PRESS
New York

Copyright © 1988 ERVIN s.r.l., Rome
Translation copyright © 1988 ERVIN s.r.l., Rome
All rights reserved.

This 1988 edition
published by Military Press
distributed by Crown Publishers, Inc.,
225 Park Avenue South,
New York, New York 10003

Created by ADRIANO ZANNINO
Editorial assistant SERENELLA GENOESE ZERBI
Editor: Maria Luisa Ficarra
Translated from the Italian by Ruth Taylor

Consultant for color plate Bruno Benvenuti

ISBN 0-517-66475-5
hgfedcba

Color separation SEBI s.r.l., Milan
Typesetting Tipocrom s.r.l., Rome

Printed and bound in Italy by SAGDOS S.p.A., Milan

FIVE YEARS WAR

September 1, 1939: 53 German divisions, backed by an air force consisting of a total of 1,000 bombers and 1,500 fighters, cross the Poland border in several places. This unceasing avalanche, constituting the first application of the Blitzkreig or the "Lightning War", a fundamental part of Third Reich's military strategy, destroyed all of Poland's military resources within a few hours, giving rise to the bloodiest conflict of the modern era. Six years later, on September 2, 1945, with the world shaken by 60 million dead and incalculable destruction, Japan, the last country to lay down its arms, signed its surrender to the Allies on board the American battleship *Missouri*, at anchor in the Bay of Tokyo. The background to the final surrender had been set less than a month earlier, on August 6 and 9, by the two Boeing B-29 bombers that had razed the cities of Hiroshima and Nagasaki to the ground, demonstrating the incredible force of the atomic bomb for the first time.

Apart from their strictly historical significance, these two events marking the beginning and the end of World War II have a single, great protagonist in common: the aircraft. The entire course of the war, its dynamics and its evolution were directly influenced by the weight of aviation and the role which it played between the forces in battle. The aircraft determined all the turning points of the war in Europe, initially with the Battle of Britain, then with the strategic bombing raids on Germany, and finally, with the beginning of the reconquest on the Allies' part after the Normandy landings. In the Pacific, it was essential initially with the Japanese attack on Pearl Harbor, then with Midway and the other great air-sea battles, and lastly with the American bombing raids on Japanese territory.

In six years of fighting, the continuous search for supremacy in the air occupied the belligerent forces fully and in the same way as it had occurred during World War I, the enormous productive, industrial, and organizational effort led to a brusque acceleration in aviation development. In the years between 1939 and 1945, it witnessed an evolution that was so rapid and intense that it could in no way be compared to that of the two previous decades. The best fighters with piston engines were capable of flying at speeds in the region of 465 mph (750 km/h), almost twice that of the last biplanes which still equipped the units of many countries when the war broke out. Furthermore, the most modern and advanced bomber of the conflict (the Boeing B-29) operated at such high speeds and altitudes that it was virtually invulnerable to the enemy defense. As far as the propulsion systems were concerned, the alternative engines reached their maximum potential for development and started to

make way for the jet engine.

This technological evolution involved all the principal protagonists in the conflict to an increasing extent, albeit at different times. Victories and defeats were eventually determined not only by the number of aircraft used in combat, but also and more importantly by their quality.

In fact, in the end the strongest proved to be those who actually had the greatest resources at their disposal, in terms of men and especially productive and industrial apparatus.

The United States was the most obvious example of this. On September 1, 1939, when the German invasion of Poland took place, the American military aviation could be considered unprepared, especially from a quantitative point of view. The U.S. Army Air Corps (USAAC) had at its disposal 2,400 aircraft of all types, 800 of which were front-line. A further 2,500 aircraft were in service with the U.S.Navy, 600 of these being carrier-based. Despite these numbers, it was not a particularly daunting air force. In spite of the presence of 20 or so Boeing B-17s, the standard bomber was still the old two-engine Douglas B-18, while the fighters were mainly Northrop A-17s and Curtiss P-36 Hawks, both transitional aircraft. In the naval aviation, biplanes such as the Grumman F3F and the Curtiss SBC Helldiver continued to serve alongside the first monoplanes such as the Northrop BT and the Douglas TBD Devastator.

The overall inadequacy that characterized the American military aviation when the war broke out in Europe was the result of a series of political, strategic, industrial and economic factors which, during the years of peace, had characterized its evolution, leading it along a path of development that was entirely its own. It had been a slow and complex process and paradoxically, during the 1920s and 1930s, compared to the almost incredible growth in commercial aviation, the military aviation seemed relatively undeveloped and war provided with clearly unsuited means for the new war which was by then brewing on the horizon. At the root of all this lay the conviction that a fresh conflict would affect the United States only from a distance and that it would be of a purely defensive nature.

Following the uncertainties of the years immediately after World War I, it was not until July 2, 1926, that the U.S. Army Air Corps was created on an organizational level, and only then that an initial program of re-equipping and reinforcement was launched. However, the program proceeded very slowly, affected by the political and economic situation of the time and characterized by the great rivalry between the army aviation and that of the navy. This slowed down the expansion still further and hampered the homogeneity between the two armed forces. In fact, unlike the USAAC, the Naval Flying Corps (officially recognized on July 1, 1915) had maintained a reasonably homogenous structure. Its development had been further aided by the creation (August 10, 1921) within the U.S. Navy Department of the Bureau of Aeronautics, a body that was responsible for everything concerning the naval aviation. This close connection had directly linked the development of the air force to programs for the expansion of the fleet. For its part, it was not until March 1, 1935, that the army succeeded in creating a single command for the USAAC. The final process of reorganization took place once the war was under way in June 1941, when the USAAC was provided with an independent general staff, given semi-autonomous status and redesignated the U.S. Army Air Force (USAAF).

The industrial network had also been affected by this complex situation, and due to the lack of a precise impetus, it operated at a rate that was much slower than its enormous potential. In 1938, a total of 1,800 combat planes were built, this figure increasing only slightly the following year (2,195). It was not until 1939, with the nullification of the Neutrality Act of 1935, and the acceptance of the principle of "Cash and Carry", that the American aeronautical industry received a first, decisive push, qualitatively and quantitatively. This was stimulated above all by the orders placed by the French and the British. In 1940, the aircraft production increased remarkably, amounting to 6,028 of all types. Nevertheless, when the United States entered the war, its actual potential had not changed much: the USAAF had 3,305 aircraft ready for service, while the Navy could count on approximately 3,000.

Its awakening occurred with the Japanese attack on Pearl Harbor. The crushing defeat provided a real impetus for the country's war machine, which subsequently began to work at full strength, in an incredible crescendo. In 1942, aeronautical production swiftly rose with regard to the 19,445 aircraft produced in 1941: in all, 47,836 aircraft were built, including 10,769 fighters, 12,627 bombers, and 138,089 engines, compared to the 58,181 of the previous year. At the same time, the 100,000 men in service on December 8, 1941 (comprising both officers and ordinary troops) increased to over a million in the following year.

This effort increased the overall effectiveness of the United States which, in the course of 1943, began to make its presence felt not only in the Pacific, but also in Europe. In that year, 85,898 aircraft of all types were constructed (including 23,988 fighters and 29,355 bombers) as well as 227,116 engines. This extremely high number was accompanied by an equally remarkable rise in quality, especially in the fighter sector. In fact, during this period the best combat planes to be constructed by the American aeronautical industry appeared: the North American P-51 Mustang and the Republic P-47 Thunderbolt in the case of the USAAF, and the Grumman F6F Hellcat and the Vought F4U Corsair in that of the U.S. Navy. Not only did these aircraft make a decisive contribution to the course of the war, but they also went down in the history of aviation as uncontestable champions of aeronautical technology. Like an unstoppable machine, the immense potential of the American industrial system continued to achieve record-breaking quantities. The highest figure was reached in 1944, when 96,318 aircraft (comprising 38,873 fighters and 35,003 bombers) and 256,911 engines were constructed. In 1945, a total of 47,714 aircraft (21,696 fighters and 16,492 bombers), as well as 109,650 engines came off the assembly lines. From 1941 to 1945, production amounted to 297,211 aircraft in all, of which 99,742 were fighters and 97,592 bombers (35,743 four-engined and 35,369 two-engined). The number of engines constructed that year reached 789,947. On January 1, 1945, the United States had a total of 86,000 aircraft at its disposal.

On the other side of the Atlantic, the nation's principal ally was Great Britain, which had declared war on Germany on September 3, 1939. The British air force was undoubtedly the best prepared in Europe to face its direct adversary powerful air force. On October 16, 1939, a total of 1,500 aircraft were ready for service, and these were joined by reserves amounting to a similar figure. From May onward, production had reached a monthly rate of 700 aircraft, while on a strictly qualitative level, the aircraft in service could generally be considered competitive with those of the Luftwaffe. The RAF had excellent monoplane fighters in its front-line, including the Hurricane and the Spitfire, which were to prove to be among the greatest protagonists of the entire conflict. The most representative of the bombers were the two-engined Blenheim, Hampden, Wellington, and Whitley, same of which were already in service, while others were about to enter.

The war's development and its growth to worldwide dimensions subsequently demonstrated the vitality of the British military aviation (the Royal Air Force had been founded on April 1, 1918), as well as the solidity of the tactical and strategical theories that lay at the basis of its formation. It already had a long history, going back to the very period in which aviation was born, and after World War I, it had been consolidated in a constant fashion during the 1920s and 1930s. Its trial by fire began on August 13, 1940 when Hitler initiated the Battle of Britain, and was successfully overcome, although at a high cost. Once the direct threat had been staved off, a second phase in the restrengthening of the military aviation began. The most prestigious of the RAF's aircraft came into being during this period: the Bristol Beaufighter, the de Havilland Mosquito, the increasingly powerful versions of the Supermarine Spitfire, and the large Short Stirling, Halifax, and Lancaster strategic bombers. In the fighter sector in particular, the British aeronautical industry also succeeded in reaching one of its most ambitious aims: the construction of a jet combat plane. Although it did not reach the front until the final months of the war and never confronted its direct German adversary, the Messerschmitt Me.262, the Gloster Meteor was to remain the only aircraft of its kind to serve in the Allied forces before the end of the war. The British effort did not cease until the conflict was over: in 1942, no less than 23,761 aircraft came off the assembly lines, compared to 20,100 in 1941, 15,000 in 1940, 7,000 in 1939, and 4,000 in 1938. In 1943, aeronautical production totaled 26,263 aircraft in all, rising to 29,220 the following year. From 1942 onward, the restrengthening program also affected the "poorer" air force, the Fleet Air Arm, which had not achieved full autonomy until May 1939. By August 1945, it had 11,500 aircraft at its disposal, of which 1,300 were front-line. This was a remarkable step forward, considering that in September 1939 the Royal Navy had been able to count on only 340 aircraft, 225 of which operated from aircraft carriers.

The last of the great powers allied in the struggle against the Third Reich was the Soviet Union. As in the case of the United States, the decisive phase in the restrengthening of this nation's military aviation also began once it found itself directly involved in the conflict. The recovery had been launched in 1918, with the creation of a special organization, the Central Institute of Aerodynamics (TsAGI), with the task of centralizing the design of aircraft and engines, carrying out studies and research, grouping together engineers and technicians, and co-ordinating their efforts. A veritable nucleus which, in the space of a decade, succeeded in equalling and in some cases surpassing the levels reached by similar structures in the rest of Europe. The first high point in this intensive process was achieved during the 1930s, a period in which the Soviet military aviation was considered one of the most powerful in the world. This role had been acquired thanks primarily to the great effectiveness of several aircraft, including the Polikarpov I-16 fighters and the Tupolev SB-2 bombers. These fully demonstrated their superiority as far as the aircraft produced by the most advanced nations in Europe were concerned in the course of the Spanish Civil War.

However, the Soviet Union proved incapable of rising above this level, at least within a short space of time. It found itself in this situation when the German invasion took place in June 1941; the quality of aircraft was unable to compete with their adversary's quality. The units were still in the process of being completely reorganized, and were provided paradoxically with the same aircraft as ten years before, due to the fact that their replacement models were not yet ready. According to an official Soviet report, during the first nine hours of Operation Barbarossa (June 22, 1941) no fewer than 1,200 aircraft were destroyed, 800 of which were on the ground.

However, the counteraction did not take long to materialize.

An enormous effort was put into the recovery and it was aided by the coming of winter. This slowed down the intensity and the effectiveness of German air operations on the one hand. On the other it made it possible to realize one of the most important strategic decisions made by the Soviet Union since 1941: the removal of the war industry away from the front. During the winter months more than 600 factories were transferred to areas that were considered out of danger: the Volga region, the Urals, and Western Siberia. Entire aircraft and engine factories were dismantled and rebuilt, often in emergency conditions, while study and research centers were transferred with them.

This process was long and complex and caused much inconvenience. As far as the latter was concerned, the most significant problem was a great drop in production. Although this had amounted to a total of 15,735 aircraft in 1941, it literally collapsed in the second half of the year and during the early months of 1942: 1,039 aircraft were completed in January, 915 in February, and 1,647 in March. Nevertheless, in the end the results compensated for the tremendous effort. 1942 was the year that marked the beginning of the recovery. Not only from a quantitative point of view (25,400 aircraft and 38,000 engines), but more importantly from a qualitative one, with the appearance of aircraft that were the result of new projects, especially fighters and attack planes. In 1943, progress was even greater with a total of 35,000 aircraft and 49,000 engines being constructed, while 40,300 aircraft of all types were completed in 1944. In the first six months of 1945 alone, 20,900 aircraft were built, at a rate that was equivalent to 41,800 per year, bringing the entire war production to a total of approximately 125,000 aircraft. However, in this process of reinforcement and modernization, an important role was played by the massive contributions made by the others Allies in terms of means and materials. In the aeronautical field, between 1941 and 1945, the United States alone sent approximately 15,000 aircraft of all types to the USSR, as well as 500 million dollars (at that time) in machinery, plants, and raw materials such as steel, copper, and aluminum.

France merits a separate discussion, in that its fate was sealed in the brief space of ten months, between September 3, 1939, when it declared war on Germany, and June 22, 1940, the day of which the armistice was signed. The nation that had been the cradle of aviation in Europe and that had emerged from the World War I among the greatest aeronautical powers, arrived on the threshold of World War II virtually unprepared. The Armée de l'Air, created at an organizational level in 1933, and officially recognized as the third armed force the following year, did not begin to exist as a structure until 1936. It would have had time to become consolidated had its needs been recognized and satisfied quickly, but this did not occur, due to a series of political, strategical, and industrial reasons that in fact diminished its role and potential, especially with regard to the modern and well-organized German war machine. When the war broke out, the Armée de l'Air had only 1,200 modern combat planes at its disposal, of which 826 were fighters, some not yet operative, and approximately 1,500 aircraft (including almost 400 fighters) which dated back to the early 1930s. Despite massive access to foreign aircraft, in the months that followed the situation changed very little. By May 10, 1940, the number of front-line aircraft had reached 1,501, including 784 fighters. In the face of the extremely powerful enemy, the Armée de l'Air fought with great honor and much sacrifice, although it was able to do very little, paying fully for the uncertainties and confusion that had accompanied its development.

On the opposing side, the main elements were the Germans in Europe, and the Japanese in Asia. The Luftwaffe, officially founded on March 1, 1935, suddenly proved to be one of the most powerful and modern air forces in the world. At the end of that year, its potential amounted to 20,000 men and approximately 1,000 front-line aircraft, with production at an extremely high level, averaging 300 aircraft per month. This achievement represented both the climax in a long process of reconstruction and the launching of a subsequent phase of expansion which was to continue without interruption throughout the entire conflict.

Throughout the 1920s and the early 1930s, the rebirth of German military aviation had been smouldering beneath the ashes, despite the severe limitations imposed by the peace treaty after its defeat in the Great War. The definitive turning point occurred in 1926, with the expiration of the Treaty of Versailles and the total recovery of commercial aviation. Paradoxically, in Germany, the symbol of its newly found air power became that of the Deutsche Lufthansa, the new official airline that was formally established on January 6, 1926. Heavily subsidized by the government, the DHL proved to be the most active and enterprising European airline. But its success was not only commercial. In practice, the expansion of activities in the commercial field directly fed the aeronautical industry which, now free from restriction, launched the production of extremely advanced aircraft, and provided the opportunity for the full reconstruction of a technical, organizational, and operative structure which was soon to assume a military aspect.

This ambiguous process had undergone a sudden acceleration after Hitler came to power in 1933. Even after it was founded, the new air force continued to hide behind the mask of civilian activity. Many of the aircraft which were to constitute the very heart of the Luftwaffe in the following years made their debut bearing the insignia of commercial airlines. These included the Junkers Ju.52 and Ju.86, the Heinkel He.111 and the Dornier Do.17. The opportunity to test the potential of this war machine in action was not lacking during the Spanish conflict. A special air force, the Condor Legion, was founded expressly for this purpose and sent to support the Nationalists. In more than two years of fighting, this served to test the entire arsenal of the Luftwaffe and to prove its overall superiority. This experience stimulated preparations for the new conflict, and when the invasion of Poland took place in September 1939, Hitler could count on the most powerful air force in the world (its frontline had 4,840 of the most modern and competitive aircraft at its disposal, including 1,750 bombers and 1,200 fighters). The air force was fed by an industrial network that was already producing 1,000 aircraft per month and which, in 1939 alone, was to complete 8,300 aircraft of all types.

However, the myth of the Luftwaffe's invincibility was not to last beyond the first year of the war, and the Lightning War came to a halt on the shores of the English Channel. The defeat in the Battle of Britain resulted in the sensational emergence of the limitations of the air warfare theories that predominated among the German high command, as well as the limitations of a mainly tactical layout that had been given to the aircraft. The immense potential of the German air force was not weakened in the least by this initial defeat. Although it was affected by its strategic inferiority, and in particular, by the lack of a heavy four-engine bomber in its arsenal, Germany succeeded in making up for these shortcomings by putting an enormous number of combat planes into production and by adapting the principal existing types to the changing operative demands with great flexibility.

Thus the German reaction was a fierce one right up to the finals day of the war, and this effort was sustained perfectly by the nation's industrial network. By mid-1943, the production of fighters alone was going forward at the rate of 700 per month, and this was to increase to 2,500 aircraft per month halfway through the following year. In 1943, the almost incredible total of 25,500 aircraft came off the assembly lines, a remarkable increase compared to the 15,600 aircraft produced in 1942, the 11,800 produced in 1941, and the 10,800 produced in 1940. Furthermore, the highest production rate of the entire conflict was obtained in 1944, with 39,800 aircraft of all types being built that year, while a further 8,000 aircraft were completed in the first five months of 1945. In the light of this enormous effort, Germany also broke a record of historical importance: it was the first nation in the world to build and put into service a jet combat plane. The Messerschmitt Me.262 appeared in the second half of 1944, and was followed shortly afterward by the Arado Ar.234 bomber and the Heinkel He.162 interceptor.

Japan's story was very similar. In 1939, the true extent of the Empire of the Rising Sun's rearmament was still little known in the West, despite the worrisome signs that emerged from the conflict against China. In the aeronautical field especially, there was a widespread conviction that the development of the military aircraft in Japan had been much slower than in the other nations traditionally considered to be in the vanguard in this sector.

Throughout the 1930s, the potential of the Japanese air force had remained practically unnoticed by the rest of the world. What is more, the vast process of reorganization that had taken place within the country's industrial network had also remained unobserved. It had been under way since the end of World War I, and had led to the creation of a massive productive structure that was almost entirely oriented toward military production.

In this phase, a particularly active role was played by the army and the navy, which competed continuously in the building of increasingly improved aircraft that were suited for warfare. The Imperial Navy's aviation corps was the older of the two, having been founded back in 1912, while that of the Army had been established on May 1, 1925. Japan's preparations for World War II are illustrated by the aeronautical production figures during the three years immediately prior to the outbreak of hostilities in Europe. The total of 445 aircraft constructed in 1930, rose to 952 in 1935, to 1,181 in 1936, to 1,511 in 1937, to 3,201 in 1938, to 4,467 in 1939, and to 4,768 in 1940.

The attack on Pearl Harbor revealed for the first time the advanced nature and potential of the Empire of the Rising Sun's air force, as well as its extremely high level of efficiency. The Imperial Army aviation (whose task was to intervene on land) had approximately 1,500 aircraft at its disposal; the Navy aviation (charged with the responsibility of neutralizing the American fleet with its carrier-based units and supporting the invasion of the Pacific islands with those that were land-based) could count on approximately 1,400. Until the second half of 1942, the two air forces carried out their respective tasks with great success. Their continuous series of victories nourished the myth of Japanese invincibility. However, the situation changed during the great air-sea battles that took place in the spring and summer of 1942, in particular during the Battle of Midway. The Imperial fleet lost four of its precious aircraft carriers, all of their aircraft units, and most importantly, many of the most highly trained and effective crews available. This final element was perhaps the most difficult one to replace. Moreover, at a strategic level, the direct consequence was the definitive abandonment of expansion plans toward Australia. In short, the Empire of the Rising Sun found itself forced to abandon the offensive and to take up the defensive much earlier than its strategists had predicted.

Nevertheless, right until the final moment, the war effort remained enormous. The 5,088 aircraft produced in 1941 (including 1,080 fighters and 1,461 bombers) together with 12,621 propellers and 12,151 engines, increased to 8,861 in 1942 (2,935 fighters and 2,433 bombers) as well as 16,999 engines and 22,362 propellers; to 16,693 in 1943 (7,147 fighters and 4,189 bombers) with 28,541 engines and 31,703 propellers and to 28,180 in 1944 (13,811 fighters and 5,100 bombers) with 46,526 engines and 54,452 propellers. Lastly, in the first eight months of 1945, Japan succeeded in producing 11,066 aircraft, including 5,474 fighters and 1,934 bombers, as well as 12,360 engines and 19,922 propellers.

The third of the Axis powers was Italy, which was certainly the weakest and the least prepared to bear the weight of the conflict. When it entered the war on June 10, 1940, the Regia Aeronautica had a total of 3,295 aircraft at its disposal (situated in Italy, the Aegean, and Libya). Of these, 1,796 were frontline: 783 bombers, 594 fighters, 268 observation planes, and 151 reconnaissance planes. Although effective on a quantitative level, from qualitative point of view their potential was remarkably inferior as compared to those of Italy's adversaries, especially in the fighter sector. More than half of these aircraft were Fiat C.R.42 biplanes, which were without a doubt among the best of their kind, although totally inadequate compared to the British and American models of the time. Likewise, the more modern fighters, such as the Fiat G.50s and Macchi M.C.200s, were also inadequate, especially as far as their armament was concerned. The situation was perhaps slightly better in the case of the bombers. The Fiat B.R.20s and the SIAI Marchetti S.M.79s could generally be considered competitive but they were somewhat lacking in defense and were rather vulnerable.

This situation, which was to continue throughout almost the entire first year of the war, was the result of programs that had adopted out-dated criteria and an overall lack of planning and foresight on the part of the high command. Until then the Italian military aviation (founded as an independent armed force on March 28, 1923) had been living in the past, influenced above all by experiences (such as the war in Ethiopia and the Spanish Civil War) carried out in very particular circumstances, which had provided a false picture of the air force and had slowed down its development. The latter conflict especially nourished the conviction that the aircraft which had been so successful in that theater of operations were also capable of effectively bearing the weight of another World War. Consequently, it was from this very conviction that a whole series of decisions were derived. These affected military and industrial planning and led to the excessive continuation of many existing production lines on the one hand, and on the other to the strengthening of inadequate technical, constructive and operative principles in the following years. The clearest proof of this overall inferiority was provided by the disastrous experiences on the English Channel front carried out by the Italian Air Corps at the end of 1940.

An attempt to remedy all this was made once the war had begun. Thanks to the help of Italy's German allies which provided the proper engines, more modern and powerful aircraft were built. It was the fighter sector above all that benefited from this recovery, with the appearance of aircraft that were truly able to face the situation. However, what could not be improved was the production level. In 1940, a total of 3,257 aircraft was built. This figure then rose to 3,503 in 1941. The following year 2,818 aircraft were constructed, and 1,930 were completed in the first eight months of 1943.

September 8, 1943 marked the end of one war for Italy and the beginning of another, which was no less fierce and which saw the country divided into two. The Regia Aeronautica also ceased to exist. On the day of the armistice, 877 aircraft were still in service: 247 reconnaissance planes, 108 bombers, 359 fighters and interceptors, 61 torpedo planes, and 102 light two-engined aircraft. Of these, a couple of hundred succeeded in reaching the South, where they joined the few that remained in the units based in that area and together they constituted the nucleus of a new air force (the Co-belligerent Aviation), which was absorbed into the Allied Balkan Air Force and continued to fight until the end of the war. The situation in the North was similar, although the reverse. In October, the Repubblica Sociale Aviation was founded and immediately afterward it began to fight alongside the Luftwaffe, in the vain attempt to withstand the increasingly frequent raids by the Allied bombers.

AVIA B.534

Fast, easy to handle, and well armed, the Avia B.534 represented one of the best examples of the biplane. Its qualities were fully revealed at the International Aeronautical Meet held in Zurich in 1937, when the Czech team's planes won second, third, and fourth place in the speed competition over 228 mph (367 km/h) with a minimum average difference of barely 7 mph (11 km/h) as compared to the winner, the more modern and powerful German Messerschmitt Bf.109. In the altitude competition, the B.534s came in second, third, and fourth place.

The new aircraft was born at the beginning of the 1930s and was the first to be produced by František Novotny, who had replaced Pavel Beneš and Miroslav Hajn, the two engineers who, up to 1929, had been chief designers at Avia. In fact, their final project, from which the BH.33 fighter had been developed, served initially as the basis of Novotny's work. This began in 1931, with the production of the B.34 model, a single-seater biplane with an all-metal airframe and a fabric skin, powered by a 650 hp Hispano-Suiza Vr 36 engine. Flight tests on the prototype began in 1932, and, after these, the plane was handed over to the military authorities for trials and official flight testing. The verdict was positive and resulted in the ordering of a first series of 12 aircraft.

In the meantime, the designer had continued to develop the basic model with, above all, the use of different types of engine in mind. There were no fewer than seven alternatives, even though only two of them eventually saw the light of day. The first variant (B.234) carried a 580 hp Avia Av 29 engine; however, this power plant did not prove to be very reliable, due mostly to strong vibrations, and the project was abandoned. The second, which used a 750 hp Hispano-Suiza 12 Ydrs, produced better results and culminated in the production of the first B.534 prototype. In August 1933, the new plane's maiden flight took place; and after the initial tests it began its official flight testing. Novotny produced a second prototype with enclosed cockpit and minor modifications and in 1934, with this same plane, one of the test pilots set a new national speed record of 227 mph (365.44 km/h).

The official reply was given on July 17; an order was placed for a first lot of 100 Avia B.534s, followed by a second order for 47. The total requested eventually rose to 447 aircraft. All the planes produced were provided with 850 hp Hispano-Suiza 12 Ydrs maximum power engines built by Avia on license.

Many modifications were introduced in the production of the different variants. The most obvious were the introduction of a sliding canopy, the increase in the number of machine guns installed in the fuselage, from two to four, and the introduction of a metallic propeller and of fairings on the wheels. Also completed were 54 additional examples of a version known as the Bk.534, in which another 7.7 mm machine gun was mounted between the banks of the engine's cylinders in place of the 20 mm cannon that had been planned originally.

During the second half of 1935, the Avia fighters entered service in the units of the Czech air force. The first group to receive them was the 4th Air Regiment, and in 1938 the B.534s became standard equipment for the fighter squadrons. By November 10, 1938, there were 370 of them in front-line duty, as well as 54 of the Bk.534 version.

In March 1939, following the German occupation of Bohemia and Moravia, around 70 B.534s were given to the new Slovak air force. The Avia fighters went into combat bearing these insignia, and they were used on the Russian front from July 1941 to October 1942. The rest of those produced were used by the Luftwaffe for training and for service behind the lines.

---

color plate

Avia B.534 1st Air Regiment Czechoslovakian Air Force - 1939

Aircraft:	Avia B.534
Nation:	Czechoslovakia
Manufacturer:	Avia
Type:	Fighter
Year:	1935
Engine:	Avia-Hispano-Suiza 12 Ydrs, 12-cylinder V, liquid-cooled, 850 hp
Wingspan:	30 ft 10 in (9.40 m)
Length:	26 ft 11 in (8.20 m)
Height:	9 ft 2 in (2.79 m)
Weight:	4,365 lb (1,980 kg) loaded
Maximum speed:	245 mph (394 km/h) at 14,435 ft (4,400 m)
Ceiling:	34,875 ft (10,600 m)
Range:	373 miles (600 km)
Armament:	4 machine guns
Crew:	1

Formation of Slovak air force Avia B.534s bearing the insignia in use in 1940.

Typical example of a fighter that marked the transition between the monoplane and the biplane, the PZL P-24 represented the final stage in the evolution of a successful series of battle planes developed by Zygmunt Pulawski who, up to March 1931, was chief designer at Panstwowe Zaklady Lotnicze, the Polish State aeronautical factory. The founder of the whole series had been the 1929 P-1 model, which was followed in 1930 and 1931 by the P-7 and the P-11 models.

The P-24 was, in fact, the natural development of the P-11 model, produced for the foreign market. The first prototype flew for the first time in May 1933, and, after much further work, the fighter demonstrated its qualities to the full on June 26, 1934, when the second prototype, piloted by Captain Boleslaw Orlinski, touched 257.2 mph (414 km/h) and established an international speed record for its category. At the *Salon Internationale de l'Aéronautique de Paris* (Paris Air Show) in the same year the PZL P-24 was defined unanimously as the world's fastest and best armed interceptor.

The entire production of the P-24 along with nine prototypes, (almost 300 examples of various versions were completed from spring 1935, about half of them on license by Turkey and Romania) was destined for export. The other main users of the plane were Bulgaria and Greece. In 1939, on the eve of the German invasion, there were orders for a total of 190, and among new buyers were Estonia, Finland, Hungary, and Yugoslavia.

The great success of the PZL fighter family was due essentially to the design's originality and to the plane's excellent overall characteristics. These were evident right from the appearance of Pulawski's first ever prototype, the P-1 model, which began flight tests on September 25, 1929. The fighter was provided with a gull-like wing (with the aim of improving the pilot's visibility), an all-metal airframe and skin, and fixed landing gear. It was powered by a 600 hp Hispano-Suiza engine which guaranteed a maximum speed of over 186 mph (300 km/h) at sea level. Both its ease of handling and its climbing qualities were remarkable. The P-1 was presented in 1930, at the Bucharest Air Show and proved to be superior to some of the best fighters of the day, such as the French Dewoitine 27, the Dutch Fokker D.XV, and the British Bristol Bulldog.

However the P-1 never went into production, since the military authorities insisted on the use of radial engines. Therefore, two other prototypes were prepared, the P-6 and the P-7, with the latter (first flight October 1930) ultimately being chosen. Named the P-7a and provided with a Bristol Jupiter VIIF engine built on license by Skoda, 150 aircraft were completed, and they went into service in the second half of 1932.

The wreckage of a Greek air force PZL P-24 following an attack by the Luftwaffe.

A year later, the Polish air force was the first in the world to have its front-line consisting entirely of metallic monoplanes.

Unfortunately, Pulawski met his death in an air accident, on March 31, 1931, and a new designer, Wsiewolod Jakimiuk, was called to develop the P-7's successor. This was the P-11, which made its first flight in September 1931. Modified structurally, better armed, and provided with a more powerful engine (500 hp Bristol Mercury IVS2) the P-11 went into production immediately and, in a series of ever-improved versions, 225 planes were produced by PZL and 70 on license by the Romanian IAR. The Polish air force was founded in 1934, and at the time of the German invasion 12 fighter squadrons were provided with P-11cs. The 114 that were lost shot down approximately 120 enemy planes.

The PZL P-24, on the other hand, saw combat bearing different insignia and was used especially by the Greek air force in the final months of 1940, and at the beginning of 1941 against the *Regia Aeronautica* (Italian Royal air force) and the Luftwaffe.

---

color plate
PZL P-24G Royal Hellenic Air Force - 1940/41

Aircraft:	PZL P-24G
Nation:	Poland
Manufacturer:	Panstwowe Zaklady Lotnicze
Type:	Fighter
Year:	1935
Engine:	Gnome-Rhône 14 N7, 14-cylinder radial, air-cooled, 930 hp
Wingspan:	35 ft 2 $\frac{1}{2}$ in (10.75 m)
Length:	24 ft 7 $\frac{1}{2}$ in (7.52 m)
Height:	8 ft 10 in (2.70 m)
Weight:	4,167 lb (1,890 kg) loaded
Maximum speed:	254 mph (408 km/h) at 14,763 ft (4,490 m)
Ceiling:	29,527 ft (9,000 m)
Range:	497 miles (800 km)
Armament:	2 × 20 mm cannons; 2 machine guns; 220 lb (100 kg) of bombs
Crew:	1

PZL P-24 bearing the insignia of the Turkish air force.

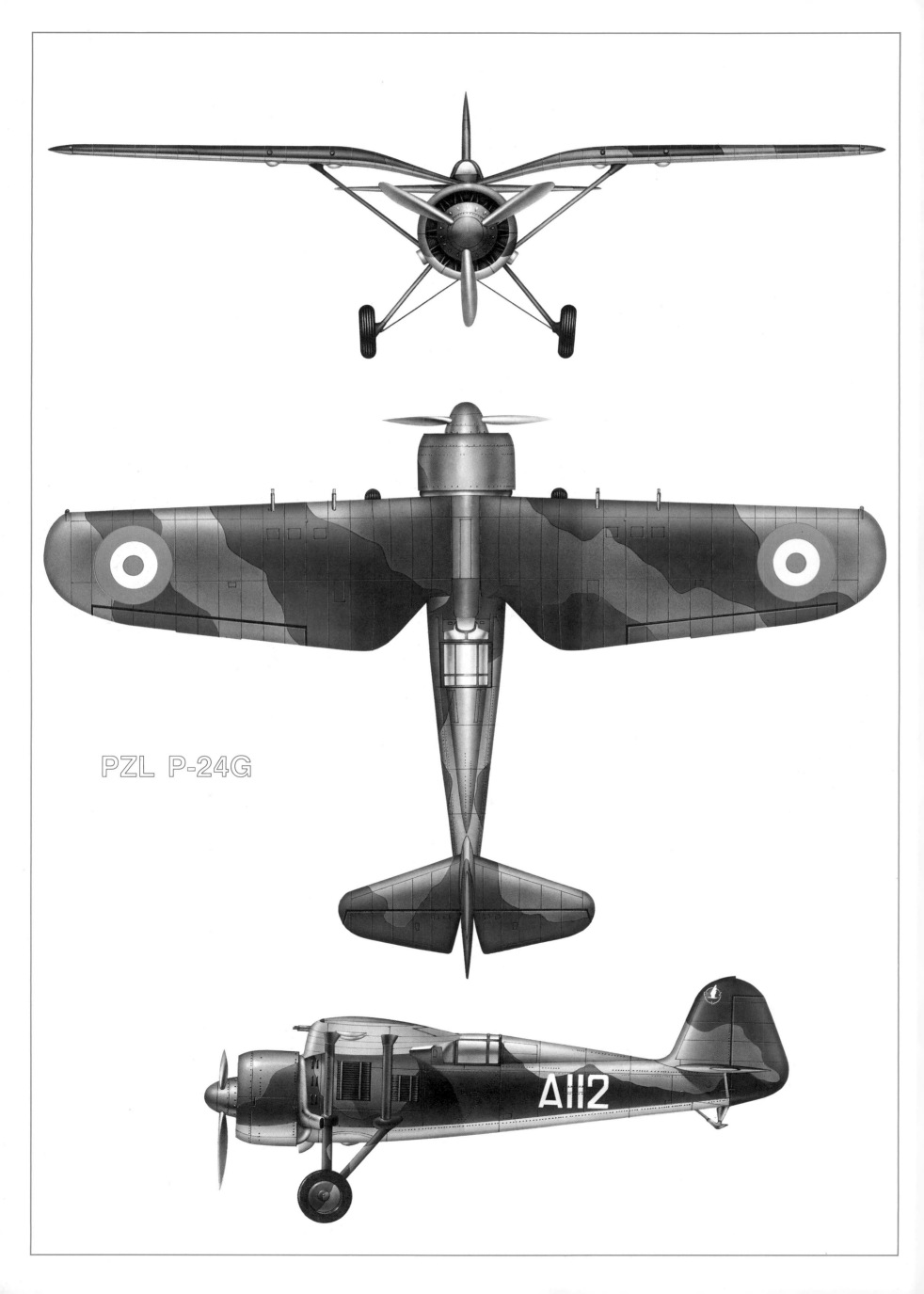

PZL P-24G

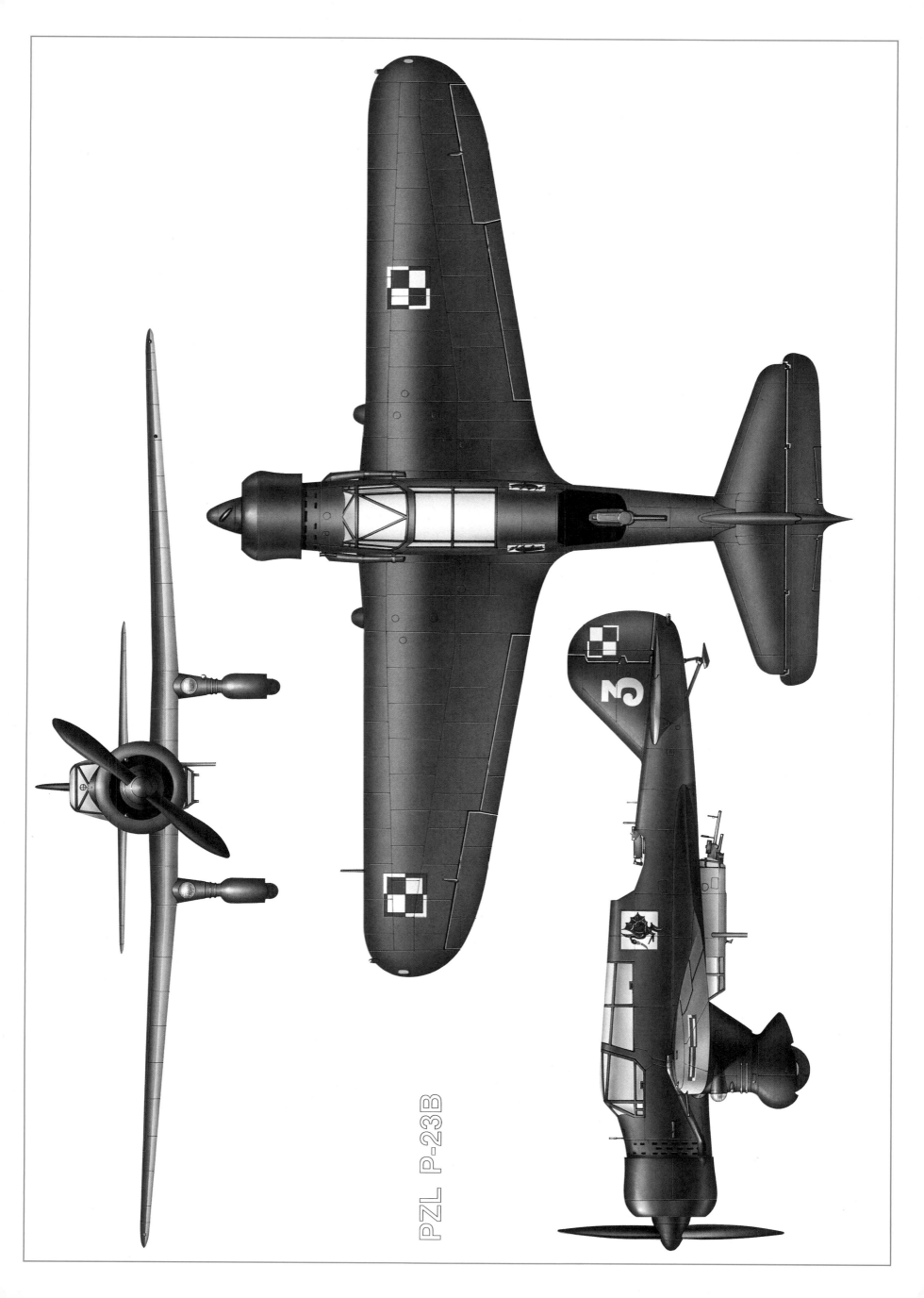

PZL P-23B

In the period between the two wars, the Polish air force attributed as much importance to the tactical support units designed to operate in close cooperation with ground forces, as it did to the fighter units. This practice, which dated back to the experiences of the conflict fought in 1919/20 against the Soviet Union, was maintained throughout the 1930s. The PZL P-23 *Karas* was a typical example of this philosophy: designed in 1932, it entered service toward the middle of 1937, and 250 aircraft were built in two main versions. When World War II broke out, this robust monoplane attack aircraft equipped 12 front-line units and, in the brief period of combat against the Germans, it proved to be an effective weapon.

The specifications that led to the creation of the PZL P-23 were issued by the Polish military authorities in 1931, with the aim of developing a home-produced aircraft to replace those of French origin (especially the Potez and Breguet XIX biplanes) in service in the tactical support units. At that time, PZL designed a single-engine commercial transport plane (designated P-13) that it intended to offer to LOT, the state airline. It was an all-metal low-wing monoplane, capable of carrying six passengers, and its designer (Stanislaw Prauss) intended that it should replace the Junkers F-13 then in service. However, despite the project's promising characteristics, LOT did not show excessive interest, and work on it was abandoned toward the end of 1931.

At this point, Prauss decided to propose his P-13 to the military authorities, offering it as a basis for the development of a new three-seater tactical support plane, and a series of consultations went ahead, culminating in the general approval of the project in the spring of 1932. A Bristol Pegasus radial engine, built on license by Skoda, was chosen, and, in the fall, an order was made for the construction of four prototypes, one of which was to be used for static tests. However, the development phase proved to be rather long, and it was not until August 1934 that the first P-23, powered by a 590 hp engine that drove a two-bladed wooden propeller, was able to make its maiden flight. During a series of tests, it became necessary to carry out a number of modifications (especially of a structural nature) and these were incorporated into the two successive flying prototypes. The definitive configuration was not reached until 1935, when the aircraft went into production on the basis of an order for 40 planes of the initial P-25A version and 210 of the second variant (P-23B). The latter was characterized by the use of a 680 hp Pegasus VIII engine.

The first *Karas* A took to the air in June 1936, but production was slowed down by engine problems, and in the end the aircraft that were completed were destined for use as trainers. In the fall of the same year, deliveries of the more efficient P-23B model began, and it became operative from the middle of the following year. By the end of 1937, 200 of these aircraft had been built, and to these were added another 10 ordered later.

During production of the *Karas*, studies for developing the basic model began. A P-23B was modified structurally (the most obvious variation was the use of a two tail plane empennage) and, redesignated the P-42, it was used for the creation of an even further improved version, the P-46. However, both these aircraft remained at an experimental stage. The same did not occur to a subsequent version (similar to the *Karas* B, but with a more powerful engine and armament) that went into production as the P-43A, on the basis of an order from Bulgaria for 12 aircraft. Another variant was derived from this aircraft (the P-43B, powered by a 980 hp Gnome-Rhône engine), 42 of which were ordered, again by Bulgaria. However, only 33 aircraft had been delivered by August 1939. The rest were requisitioned by the Polish air force when the war broke out.

color plate

PZL P-23B 22nd Bomber Squadron Polish Air Force - Poland 1939

Aircraft:	PZL P-23B
Nation:	Poland
Manufacturer:	Panstwowe Zaklady Lotnicze
Type:	Attack
Year:	1937
Engine:	PZL-Bristol Pegasus VIII, 9-cylinder radial, air-cooled, 680 hp
Wingspan:	45 ft 9 $\frac{1}{2}$ in (13.95 m)
Length:	31 ft 9 $\frac{1}{2}$ in (9.68 m)
Height:	10 ft 10 in (3.30 m)
Weight:	7,773 lb (3,526 kg) loaded
Maximum speed:	198 mph (319 km/h) at 11,975 ft (3,650 m)
Ceiling:	23,950 ft (7,300 m)
Range:	782 miles (1,260 km)
Armament:	2 machine guns; 1,543 lb (700 kg) of bombs
Crew:	3

Rumanian air force PZL P-23 during a combat mission on the Russian front.

Paradoxically, the PZL P-37, the most modern aircraft in service in the Polish air force when the war broke out, was never produced in any great quantity. The fate of this elegant, two-engine bomber was decided by the members of the General Staff who, after heated argument, gave priority to the construction of other types of aircraft. As a result, only a few months before the outbreak of the war, production programs were reduced by a third, and only 36 of the final P-37B version were operational at the time of the German invasion.

In the period between the two wars, the development of a home-produced multiengine bomber had been slowed down in Poland, due mainly to high production costs. At the beginning of the 1930s, the Aeronautical Department had once again rejected a sound proposal presented by PZL (regarding the PZL-3 model) and had preferred to order 20 or so three-engine Fokker F.VIIb/3ms transformed into bombers. It was the need to replace these obsolete aircraft, clearly unsuitable for military duties, that caused PZL to proceed with new studies to be submitted for examination by the Aeronautical Department.

The first proposal was for a bomber version of the PZL 30 civilian transport plane, which had not found any buyers; the second and rather more valid proposal was presented in July 1934 and aroused considerable interest. It was a project for a modern, low-wing monoplane, quite advanced from an aerodynamic and structural point of view and powered by a pair of Bristol Pegasus radial engines. In April 1935, the military authorities gave permission for the construction of three prototypes, the first of which took to the air at the end of June 1936, with the designation P-37/1. The series of flight tests revealed the excellent performance of the aircraft and, after a number of structural modifications, the bomber went into production on the basis of an initial order for 30 aircraft, designated P-37A. The first 10 had a single tail fin empennage, while the remaining 20 were characterized by double tail planes, a configuration similar to that tested on the second prototype (P-37/II), in which a more powerful version of the Pegasus engine had been used (925 hp as compared to 873 hp in the previous series).

The P-37A was presented at the Belgrade Air Show and at the Paris Aeronautical Salon in 1938, and it aroused great interest, orders being obtained from Bulgaria, Yugoslavia, Rumania, and Turkey for a total of 75 aircraft. However, these orders were never fulfilled, due to the outbreak of the war. The P-37As were delivered to the units of the Polish air force from the spring of 1938. In the meantime, from the second prototype a second production variant had been developed (P-37B), characterized by modifications to the canopy and to the landing gear, in addition to the use of more powerful engines. Deliveries of these aircraft (on the basis of an initial order for 150) commenced toward the end of the year, and on consignment the P-37As were relegated to training.

At this point, the contrast of opinions within the General Staff led to the orders being cut drastically and to a consequent slowing down of production. The 150 P-37Bs were reduced to 100, and barely 70 of these had been delivered by the time the war broke out.

The war also halted the development of a more powerful version of the bomber, the P-49, characterized by the use of 1,600 hp engines. A prototype was at an advanced stage of completion, but its construction was suspended because of the advance of the German troops. The aircraft was destroyed.

---

color plate
PZL P-37B Polish Air Force - Poland 1939

Aircraft:	P-37B
Nation:	Poland
Manufacturer:	Panstwowe Zaklady Lotnicze
Type:	Attack
Year:	1938
Engine:	2 PZL-Bristol Pegasus XX, 9-cylinder radial, air-cooled, 918 hp each
Wingspan:	58 ft 10 in (17.93 m)
Length:	42 ft 5 in (12.92 m)
Height:	16 ft 8 in (5.08 m)
Weight:	18,872 lb (8,560 kg) loaded
Maximum speed:	276 mph (445 km/h) at 11,154 ft (3,400 m)
Ceiling:	19,680 ft (6,000 m)
Range:	932 miles (1,500 km)
Armament:	3 machine guns; 5,688 lb (2,580 kg) of bombs
Crew:	4

The prototype of the PZL P-37.

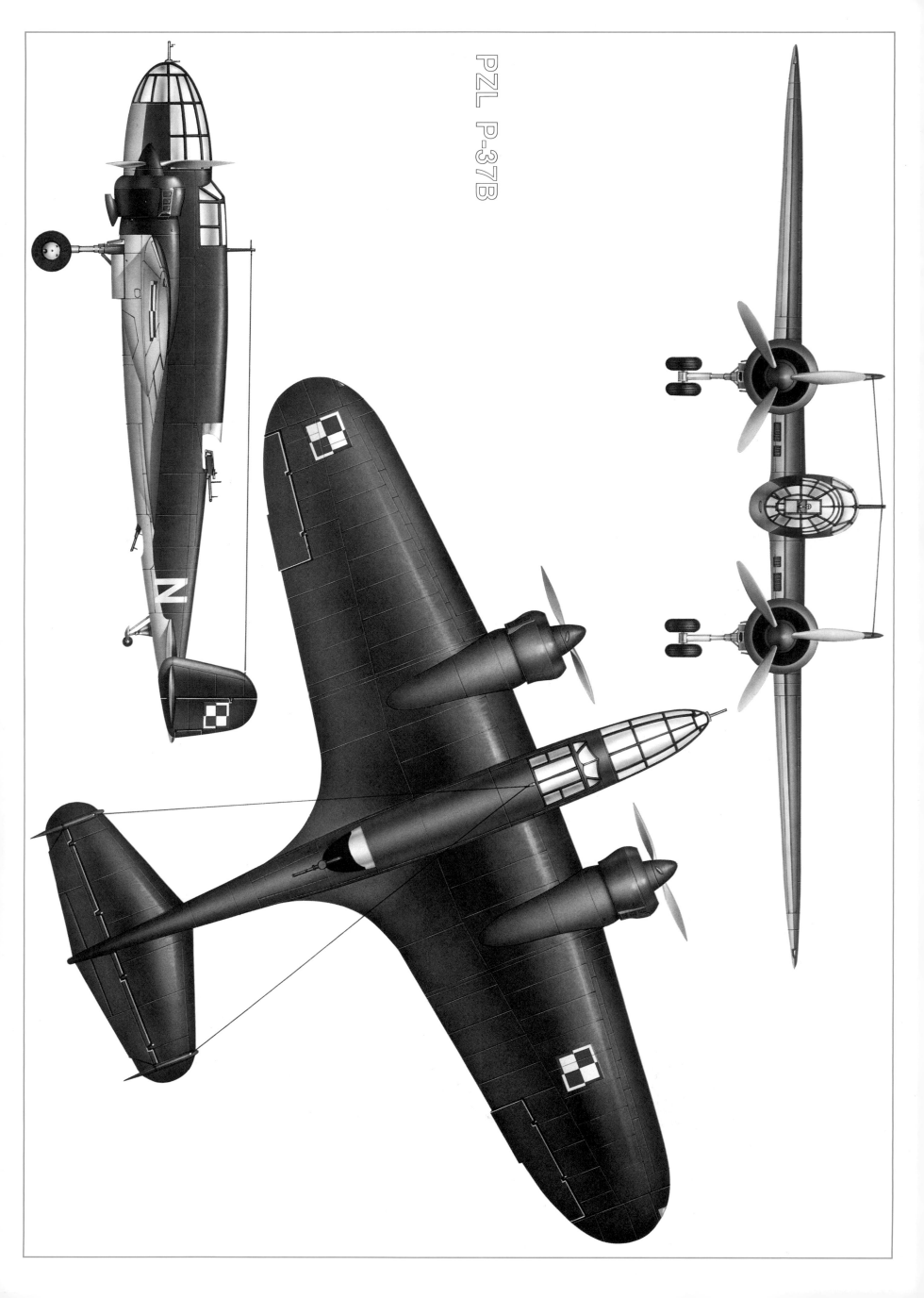

PZL P-37B

FOKKER D.XXI

A Fokker D.XXI license built in Finland with a Pratt & Whitney engine.

A Royal Netherlands air force D.XXI in flight, with prewar colors and insignia.

and the Dutch military authorities ordered a prototype that was to undergo a series of evaluations. This aircraft made its maiden flight on March 27, 1936, powered by a 654 hp Bristol Mercury VI-S radial engine. Although the series of tests confirmed the project's qualities, the passage to the production phase was slowed by lack of official interest. In fact, at the time, the military authorities in the Netherlands were more concerned with developing an effective bomber than a fighter. It was not until the summer of 1937 that an order for 36 aircraft was authorized. Bristol Mercury series VII and VIII engines were chosen.

However, the D.XXI's performance had aroused great interest abroad, and in the same year the Finnish air force signed an order with Fokker for seven production series aircraft. At the same time, an agreement was drawn up for production on license, entrusted to the State Aircraft Factory. From 1938 to 1944, the Finnish industry completed another 93 fighters; of these, the first 38 retained the Bristol engine; the next 50 (built in 1941) were fitted with American Pratt & Whitney Twin Wasp Junior radial engines, generating 836 hp; the last five aircraft were built in 1944 and fitted with Bristol Pegasus engines. Other orders were placed by Denmark, which produced 10 aircraft on license, in addition to some bought in the Netherlands.

The Dutch air force's first D.XXI took to the air on July 20, 1938, and the last was delivered on September 8 the following year. These aircraft's most important victory took place at dawn on May 10, 1940, the first day of Hitler's invasion: they succeeded in shooting down 38 three-engine Junkers Ju.52s out of a group of 55 that was crossing the Dutch border.

A Dutch D.XXI damaged during an attack by the German Luftwaffe.

color plate

Fokker D.XXI 1st Jachtvliegtuigafdeling (1st Fighter Group) Royal Netherlands Air Force - The Netherlands 1940

Among the effective aircraft produced by Fokker in the years immediately prior to the war, the D.XXI fighter deserves a place of honor. It was a transitional plane, still retaining fixed landing gear, although particularly efficient and advanced for its time nevertheless. Above all, it had great potential, and only the course of the war prevented this from being developed. At the time of the German invasion, barely 32 D.XXIs (out of a total order for only 36) were operative in the units of the Dutch air force, and in the few days of combat they fought with great vigor and success, although in the end they were forced to succumb to the overwhelming superiority of the enemy. The fate of 100 or so of these aircraft bearing the Finnish insignia was entirely different: they were used extensively during hostilities against the Soviet Union and stood up admirably to the difficult operative conditions on that front.

The project was launched in 1935, and it was an immediate success when it appeared, due to the advanced nature of its conception. It was a low-wing monoplane with fixed landing gear and composite airframe and covering. It was carefully designed from an aerodynamic point of view, extremely maneuverable, and provided with armament consisting of four machine guns. Compared to the previous high-wing biplanes and monoplanes designed by Fokker, the D.XXI definitely represented an improvement in quality,

Aircraft: Fokker D.XXI	
Nation: The Netherlands	
Manufacturer: Fokker	
Type: Fighter	
Year: 1938	
Engine: Bristol Mercury VIII, 9-cylinder radial, air-cooled, 760 hp	
Wingspan: 36 ft 1 in (11.00 m)	
Length: 26 ft 11 in (8.20 m)	
Height: 9 ft 8 in (2.95 m)	
Weight: 4,519 lb (2,050 kg) loaded	
Maximum speed: 286 mph (460 km/h) at 14,540 ft (4,420 m)	
Ceiling: 36,100 ft (11,000 m)	
Range: 590 miles (950 km)	
Armament: 4 machine guns	
Crew: 1	

Two cannons and two fixed machine guns in the nose, plus another flexible one installed in the rear, as well as performance that included a maximum speed of over 280 mph (450 km/h). Aside from the advanced concept of its general layout, it was these characteristics that most impressed observers when the prototype of the Fokker G.1 appeared at the Paris Aeronautical Salon in 1936.

This was a two-engine middle-wing aircraft with retractable landing gear and an original configuration in the double tail beams and the central fuselage. It was used to best advantage as a fighter, but was created to carry out other roles, such as that of fighter-bomber or reconnaissance plane, with equal efficiency. The Dutch air force received 36 of the G.1A version in 1939, of which 23 were operational on May 10, 1940, when the German invasion began. In the course of five days of combat, these aircraft were destroyed, either in the air or on the ground. However, production of the G.1A also included a variant destined for export (designated the G.1B) and totaled 62 aircraft in all. Twenty or so G.1Bs, which formed part of a lot originally destined for Finland, were requisitioned by the Germans and used for training. In May 1941, one of these allowed two Fokker test pilots to make an adventurous escape from Schipol and to reach the English coast.

With the G.1 project, Fokker had intended to launch an entirely new generation of combat aircraft. Work on the prototype commenced in great secrecy in 1934, and tests began after the Paris show. The prototype took to the air for the first time on March 16, 1937.

The aircraft was of mixed construction: the airframe of the front part of the fuselage consisted of steel tubes with aluminum covering, whereas the central part was built of wood and the rear section (which was widely glazed) of light alloy. The wing was entirely of wood, while the two tail beams were all-metal, except for the vertical rudders, which had a canvas covering. The landing gear retracted into the engine nacelles. The prototype was powered by two Hispano-Suiza 80-02 radial engines capable of generating 750 hp at altitude.

During tests some changes were introduced, and when an order was placed for 36 aircraft in November 1937, the military authorities requested that the engine be replaced by two 830 hp Bristol Mercury VIII engines, which were to drive the three-bladed variable pitch metal propellers, and that the fixed armament be changed to eight 7.9 mm machine guns. In addition, the installation of a bomb load of 660 lb (300 kg) was planned. The standard crew consisted of two men, although the first four aircraft had been built to carry a third crew member.

These aircraft were designated G.1A, and production went ahead at a slow rate, due to delays in engine deliveries. The first of the series was not flight tested until April 11, 1939, and units began to receive the planes in July.

In the meantime, Fokker had developed a second version of the G.1, destined for export. This differed from the first in its slightly reduced dimensions, its armament, and in the adoption of two 750 hp Pratt & Whitney Twin Wasp jr. SB4-G engines. In 1939, Fokker G.1Bs were ordered by Finland (26 aircraft), by Sweden (18), by Denmark (which planned to produce them on license), by Spain, and by Estonia (9). The outbreak of the war halted production: only 12 G.1Bs, part of the Finnish order, had been completed. Three of these were provided with armament and fought against the Luftwaffe. The rest were requisitioned by the Germans.

color plate
Fokker G.1A 4th Fighter Group Dutch Army Air Corps - The Netherlands 1940

A Fokker G.1 adapted for reconnaissance with the addition of a glazed ventral pod.

A Dutch air force Fokker G.1A in prewar camouflage and markings.

Aircraft:	Fokker G.1A
Nation:	The Netherlands
Manufacturer:	Fokker
Type:	Fighter
Year:	1939
Engine:	2 Bristol Mercury VIII, 9-cylinder radial, air-cooled, 830 hp
Wingspan:	56 ft 3 in (17.15 m)
Length:	37 ft 9 in (11.50 m)
Height:	11 ft 2 in (3.40 m)
Weight:	10,582 lb (4,970 kg) loaded
Maximum speed:	295 mph (475 km/h)
Ceiling:	30,500 ft (9,300 m)
Range:	876 miles (1,409 km)
Armament:	8/9 machine guns; 660 lb (300 kg) of bombs
Crew:	2/3

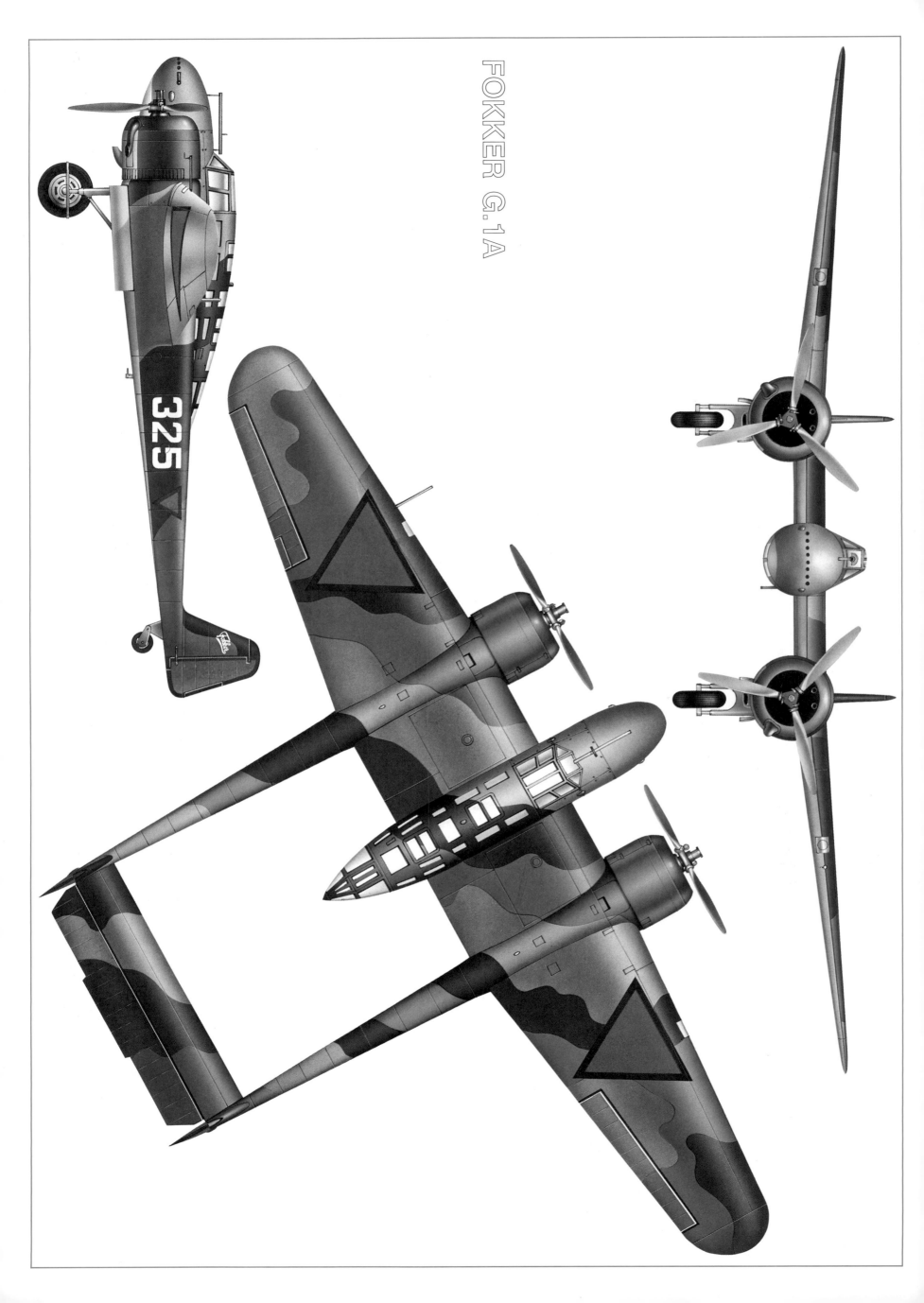

FOKKER G.1A

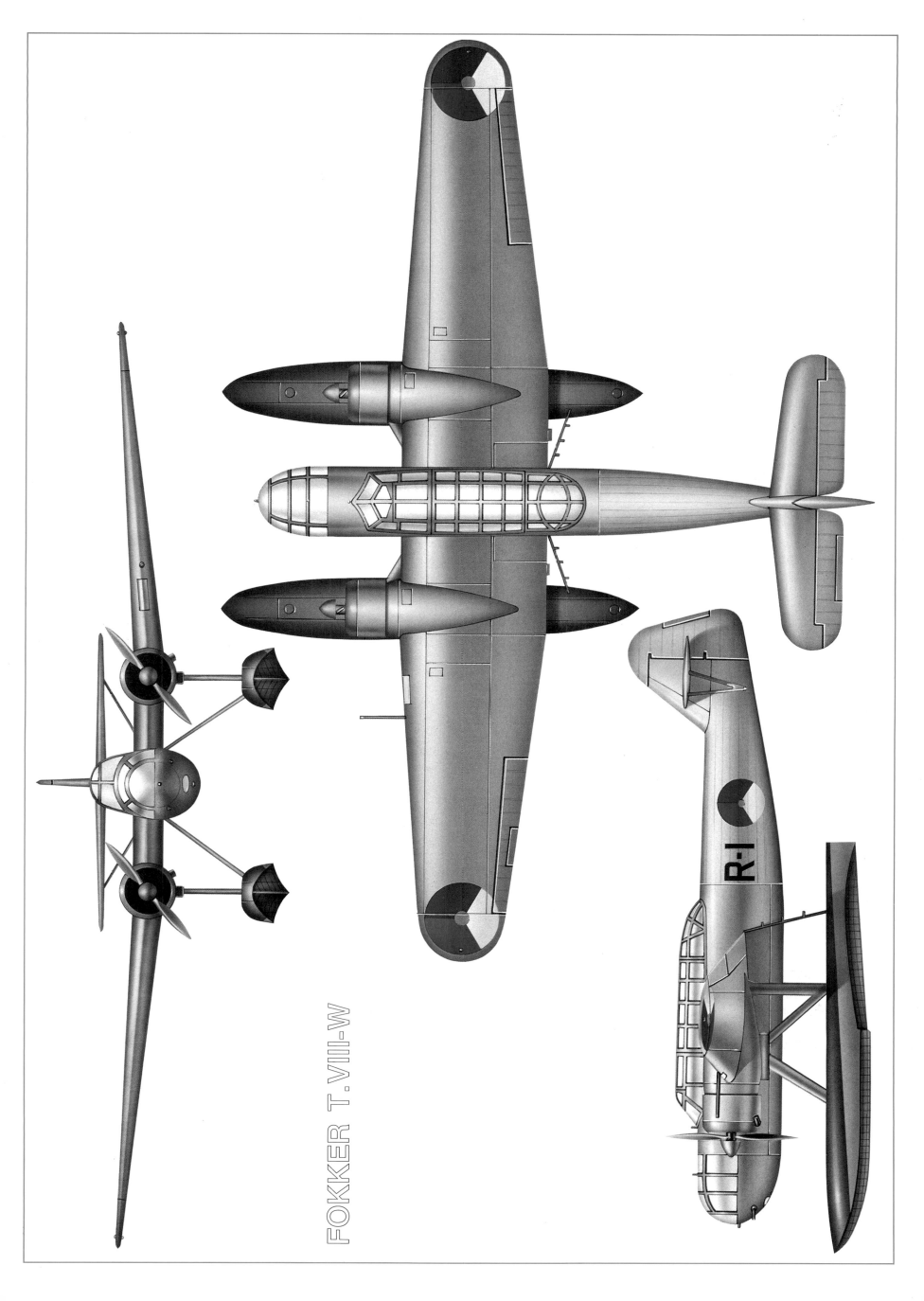

FOKKER T.VIII-W

Fokker's intensive activity in the years prior to World War II led to the creation in 1938 of a twin-engine seaplane for naval use. It was conceived to meet the needs of the Dutch navy but paradoxically ended up being used by the enemy, the Germans. This aircraft was the T.VIII-W: out of a total of 36 planes built, 28 bore the German insignia and served in naval reconnaissance and relief duty mainly in the Mediterranean area and the North Sea.

The T.VIII-W project was launched in 1937 in response to official specifications issued by the Dutch navy calling for a new twin-engine seaplane capable of carrying a torpedo inside its fuselage (with the option of substituting this type of armament with ordinary bombs) to be used principally in coastal defense. Moreover, the aircraft was to have a long range and good cruising speed. In 1938, an order was placed for five production series aircraft, which were completed by June of the following year. Despite the existence of several problems in tuning the aircraft, the Dutch navy was so satisfied with the T.VIII's characteristics that a subsequent order for 26 planes was signed shortly after. These aircraft were to go into service in the East Indies, although none reached this destination. In fact, the outbreak of war halted all plans: the German invasion led to the occupation of the Fokker factory before the lot in production had been completed, and the T.VIII-Ws, once built, were all requisitioned.

The twin-engine Fokkers were built in three versions: the T.VIII-Wg, characterized by its mixed wood and metal structure; the all-metal T.VIII-Wm; and the T.VIII-Wc, with mixed structure and covering but larger overall. Nineteen of the first type were built, 12 of the second, and five of the third. The T.VIII-Wcs were built on the basis of an order issued by the Finnish air force in 1939: they were characterized by a fuselage that was lengthened some 5 ft 11 in (1.80 m) and by wings that were lengthened almost 6 ft 6 in (2 m), as well as by the installation of 902 hp Bristol Mercury XI engines. All the other aircraft were supplied with a pair of American Wright Whirlwind radial engines, generating 450 hp each and driving two-bladed metal propellers.

The Fokker T.VIII-W was a twin-engine mid-wing monoplane, characterized by the presence of two large duralumin floats. The fuselage had an extensively glazed nose that housed the observer's post. Immediately behind the pilot's station was the compartment for the radio operator who had a flexible machine gun at his disposal for the defense of the rear sector. A second fixed weapon, installed in a half-wing, was controlled by the pilot. The bomb load consisted of a maximum of 1,300 lb (600 kg) of bombs or a torpedo.

Apart from its use in the German navy, the Fokker T.VIII-W (in another twist of fate) served in the same roles and in the same theater of war, in the North Sea, in a British Coastal Command unit. This fate awaited eight aircraft that had succeeded in escaping to England on May 14, 1940, and that had been assigned to the 320th Squadron on June 1. The unit, composed of Dutch personnel, was assigned to convoy escort and served in this role for many months, until the lack of spare parts led to this duty being suspended.

---

color plate

Fokker T.VIII-W GVT2 Royal Netherlands Navy - Braassemermeer Lake (The Netherlands) 1940

Aircraft:	Fokker T.VIII-W
Nation:	The Netherlands
Manufacturer:	Fokker
Type:	Bomber
Year:	1940
Engine:	2 Wright Whirlwind, 9-cylinder radial, air-cooled, 450 hp each
Wingspan:	59 ft (17.98 m)
Length:	42 ft 8 in (13.00 m)
Height:	16 ft 5 in (5.00 m)
Weight:	11,030 lb (5,000 kg) loaded
Maximum speed:	177 mph (285 km/h)
Ceiling:	22,300 ft (6,800 m)
Range:	1,710 miles (2,750 km)
Armament:	2/3 machine guns; 1,330 lb (603 kg) of bombs
Crew:	3

Fokker T.VIII-Wm used by the Luftwaffe at a base in the Aegean Sea where the See-Aufklärungsgruppe operated.

The innovative processes that were linked to the change from biplane to monoplane reached the Yugoslavian aeronautical industry, traditionally considered second-rate compared to those of the major European powers, in the first half of the 1930s. The result of this was the Rogozarski IK-3, a small, agile fighter with enclosed cockpit and all retractable landing gear, which proved to be just as reliable and rather more easy to handle than its two more illustrious contemporaries, the British Hawker Hurricane and the German Messerschmitt Bf.109. However, the IK-3 had a relatively short life span, dictated by the events of the war itself: the production program came to a halt when the Germans invaded, by which time only 12 aircraft had been delivered to the units.

In 1933, the idea of developing a modern combat plane came to Ljubomir Ilic and Kosta Sivcev, the two technicians who had produced the first entirely Yugoslavian fighter, the IK-1, a couple of years earlier. Encouraged by this experience, the two designers were convinced that the era of the biplane and the high-wing monoplane was over and that, considering the high-quality performance of the new bombers being developed at the time, only a low-wing monoplane with retractable landing gear possessed the characteristics necessary to guarantee supremacy in the air. The project got under way in great secrecy, and toward mid 1936 all drawings and documentation were handed over to the military authorities for examination.

However, the initial evaluation phase proved to be long, the delay caused to a great extent by official skepticism concerning the new formula. Not until March of the following year was a contract signed for the production of a prototype. The factory that was to supervise its construction was Rogozarski, based in Belgrade. The first aircraft was completed a year later, and the IK-3 made its maiden flight near the end of May 1938. The fuselage had a steel tube airframe with a mixed canvas and metal covering, and the wing was built almost entirely of wood, with only a few steel tube reinforcements. The prototype was powered by a 910 hp "V-12" Hispano-Suiza 12 Y29 engine with supercharger (although in the production series this was replaced by the equally powerful 12 Ycrs model built by Avia on license), which drove a three-bladed variable pitch metal propeller. The armament consisted of a 20 mm cannon installed on the propeller shaft and two fixed machine guns in the fuselage.

During evaluation tests, the concentration of the armament in the nose was one of the most appreciated features, although the aircraft's maneuverability and excellent overall performance also made a good impression. However, flight tests were interrupted suddenly on January 19, 1939, when the prototype crashed to the ground following a deep dive, causing the death of the test pilot, Milan Pokorni. Even though the causes of the accident were not attributed to serious structural problems, this event delayed still further the start of production, which had been planned on the basis of an order for 12 aircraft barely three months earlier.

The first six aircraft were delivered in March 1940, and the others by July. Beginning on April 6, 1941, the date of the German invasion of Yugoslavia, the six operational IK-3s proved their worth in the fierce fighting against the Luftwaffe, and the last two surviving aircraft were destroyed by their Yugoslavian crew during the night of April 11/12. At that time, another 25 aircraft were under construction.

---

color plate

Rogozarski IK-3 51st Fighter Group Yugoslavian Air Force - Belgrade 1941

Aircraft:	Rogozarski IK-3
Nation:	Yugoslavia
Manufacturer:	Rogozarski A.D.
Type:	Fighter
Year:	1938
Engine:	Hispano-Suiza (Avia) 12 Ycrs, 12-cylinder V, liquid-cooled, 910 hp
Wingspan:	33 ft 10 in (10.30 m)
Length:	26 ft 4 in (8.00 m)
Height:	10 ft 8 in (3.25 m)
Weight:	5,796 lb (2,630 kg)
Maximum speed:	326 mph (526 km/h) at 17,700 ft (5,400 m)
Ceiling:	31,000 ft (9,400 m)
Range:	490 miles (785 km)
Armament:	1 x 20 mm cannon; 2 machine guns
Crew:	1

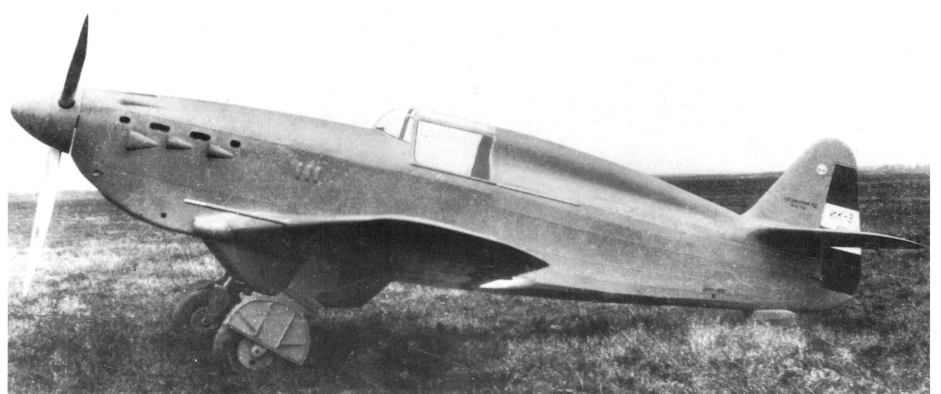

Prototype of the Rogozarski IK-3.

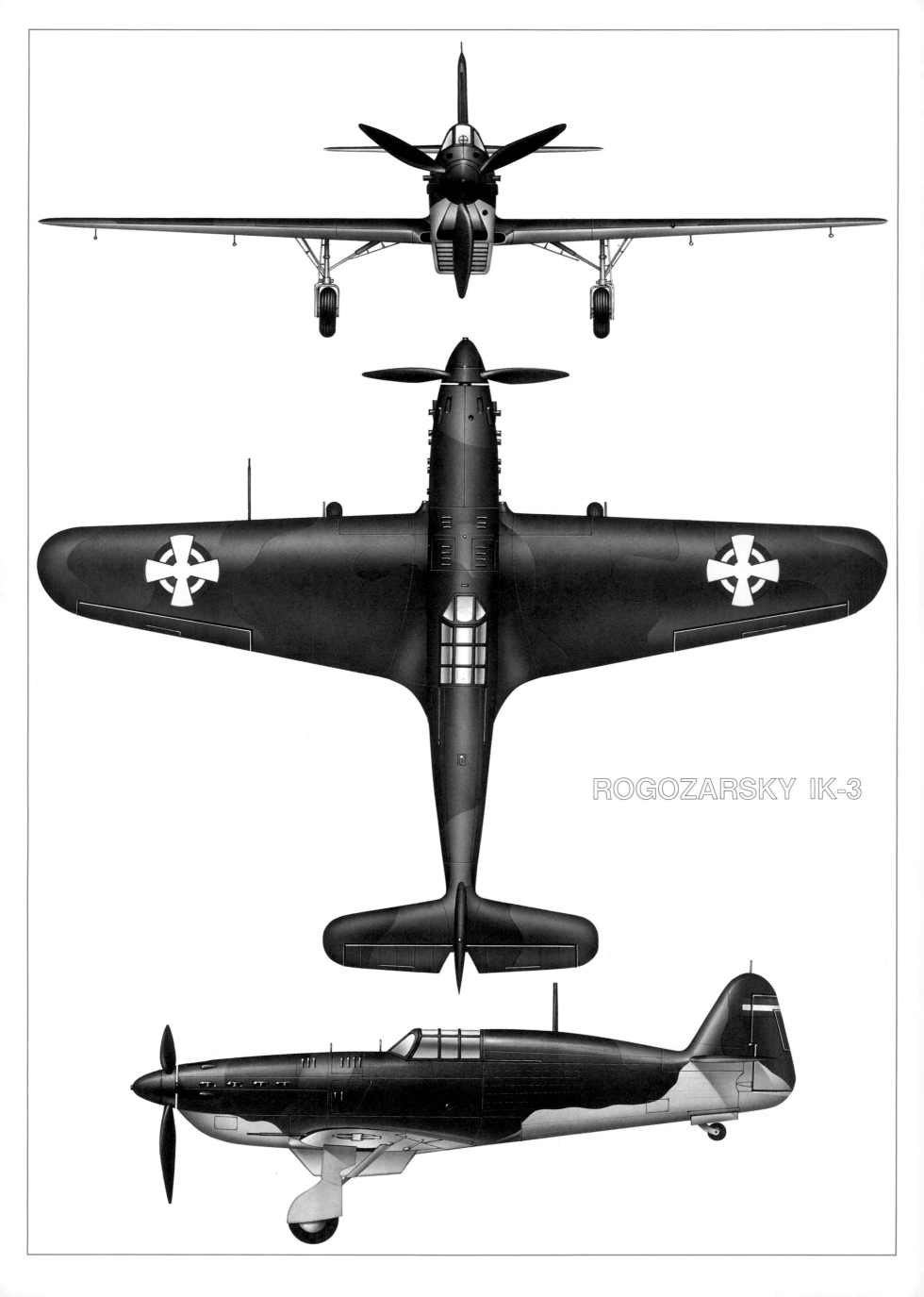

ROGOZARSKY IK-3

ARSENAL VG-33

Among the numerous projects for combat aircraft developed in France in the years immediately prior to the conflict, those designed by the Arsenal de l'Aéronautique beginning in 1936, stand out from the rest. The aim was to develop a monoplane fighter of rather modest size and weight, and several prototypes were prepared. Among these, the VG-33 was the only one to go into production, on the basis of an order that foresaw the completion of no fewer than 820. In practice, however, at the time of the German invasion, only 160 were on the assembly line in various stages of completion, and only a dozen or so were ready to fly. During official flight testing, the performance of this small, all-wood fighter proved to be admirable, in spite of the rather limited power (860 hp) of its engine, especially in terms of speed, at times reaching 347 mph (558 km/h).

The VG-33 derived directly from the VG-30 model, the first of the series. This project, presented in mock-up form in the summer of 1936, made its maiden flight at Villacoublay on October 1, 1938, and proved to be faster than the Morane Saulnier M.S.405. The development phase continued with the designing of the VG-31 model, characterized by reduced wing surface area, and of the VG-32, with a return to the original wing size and in which it was planned to install an American Allison V-1710-C15 engine, generating 1,054 hp and fitted with a supercharger. These prototypes were followed by the first VG-33, marked by a return to the original Hispano-Suiza 12Y31 engine. The aircraft was tested in flight in the spring of 1939, and official tests began on August 11. The Arsenal fighter was a low-wing, single-seater aircraft with retractable landing gear. It was quite light and compact, but heavily armed: a 20 mm cannon and four 7.5 mm machine guns on the wings.

While production of the VG-33 was launched at the Chantiers Aéro-Maritimes de la Seine at Sartrouville, Arsenal went ahead with the development phase of the project, with the aim of improving its potential still further. In the spring of 1940, a prototype ap-

peared, designated VG-34 and provided with a 910 hp Hispano-Suiza engine: this aircraft reached a maximum speed of 327 mph (575 km/h) at an altitude of 20,395 ft (6,200 m). The subsequent VG-35 prototype was characterized by even more powerful engine, while the radiator and landing gear of the VG-36 were modified. The final model was the VG-39, provided with a 1,280 hp Hispano-Suiza 12Z engine and characterized by its redesigned wing, capable of carrying armament consisting of six machine guns. Production programs were also prepared for this variant, which was to be powered by a 1,600 hp engine in the final series. The German invasion put a stop to the project.

color plate
Arsenal VG-33 Armée de l'Air - 1940

Aircraft:	Arsenal VG-33
Nation:	France
Manufacturer:	Arsenal de l'Aéronautique
Type:	Fighter
Year:	1940
Engine:	Hispano-Suiza 12Y31, 12-cylinder V, liquid-cooled, 860 hp
Wingspan:	35 ft 5 in (10.80 m)
Length:	28 ft 4 in (8.64 m)
Height:	10 ft 10 in (3.30 m)
Weight:	6,393 lb (2,896 kg) loaded
Maximum speed:	347 mph (558 km/h) at 17,060 ft (5,200 m)
Ceiling:	36,090 ft (11,000 m)
Range:	745 miles (1,200 km)
Armament:	1 × 20 mm cannon; 4 machine guns
Crew:	1

A French air force Arsenal VG-33.

"The best fighter in the world." In 1937, these words were used at the Brussels Air Show to define the prototype of Morane-Saulnier's latest combat plane, which had recently completed a series of flight tests and official evaluations. Aside from this advertising statement, it became the founder of a long series of over 1,000 aircraft (1,081 to be precise) that were produced up till June 1940 and that earned a prominent place in aviation history for many reasons: the Morane-Saulnier M.S.406 was the first modern aircraft of its category to go into service in the units of the *Armée de l'Air*; it was built in remarkable quantities compared to French production standards of the time, second only to the two-engine Potez 630 series; and, above all, it was the fighter available in the greatest numbers when the war broke out.

The project was launched on the basis of specifications issued in 1934, and the prototype (built in great secrecy) made its first flight on August 8, 1935. Designated the M.S.405, it was a low-wing monoplane with retractable landing gear, powered by an 860 hp Hispano-Suiza 12 Ygrs engine. It had an all-metal airframe with a covering of aluminum, plywood, and canvas, and an enclosed cockpit. The armament consisted of a 20 mm cannon installed in the propeller shaft and two machine guns in the wings.

Right from its first flight, the features of the aircraft proved to be excellent, especially its speed, which reached 303 mph (489 km/h) at 13,200 ft (4,000 m) and just over 250 mph (400 km/h) at sea level. The latter meant that the Morane-Saulnier became the first French fighter to break the 250 mph (400 km/h) barrier. After the initial flight tests, the first prototype was joined by a second (with modifications to the propeller and the wings), and both these aircraft faced a series of official evaluations. At the beginning of 1937, the company received an order for 15 preseries aircraft, and the second of these (which took to the air on May 20, 1938) became the progenitor of the M.S.406: the differences consisted mainly in the use of a different engine, a different type of propeller, and in structural modifications, especially to the wing. The aircraft was chosen for production in this definitive version on the basis of an order that, in March 1938, amounted to 1,000 planes. In order to guarantee this large quantity, assembly lines were set up in several factories and, within a short space of time, the delivery rate was quite high. By September 1939, 572 M.S.406s had already left the factories.

The first unt to receive the new fighter was the 6th *Escadre de Chasse*, in December 1938. Other units followed, and immediately before mobilization in August 1939, 12 groups had been equipped with the aircraft. However, from the beginning of its operational service. it became apparent that the 406 was distinctly inferior to its direct adversary, the Messerschmitt Bf.109E. During the Battle of France, 150 Moranes were lost, as compared to 191 enemy aircraft definitely hit and another 89 probably hit. A further hundred or so Moranes were destroyed on the ground, and about 150 were damaged beyond repair by the French crews to prevent their falling into enemy hands. After the armistice, some Morane 406s remained in service in the Vichy air force (where they were mainly used for training), and others were handed over by the Germans to Finland, which had received 30 aircraft in 1940.

Another foreign buyer was Switzerland, which, after having acquired two M.S.406s, built 82 aircraft on license (designated EFW-3800) as well as 207 of a subsequent home-developed version known as EFW-3801.

Formation of Morane-Saulnier M.S.406s at an airport in Lebanon at the beginning of the war.

An M.S.406, note the cannon in the propeller hub and the retractable radiator.

color plate

Morane-Saulnier M.S.406 1ère Escadrille Groupe Chasse I/2 Armée de l'Air (1st Squadron Fighting Group I/2 *Armée de l'Air*) - France 1940

Aircraft:	Morane-Saulnier M.S.406
Nation:	France
Manufacturer:	SNCAO
Type:	Fighter
Year:	1938
Engine:	Hispano-Suiza 12 Y, 12-cylinder V, liquid-cooled, 860 hp
Wingspan:	34 ft 10 in (10.65 m)
Length:	26 ft 9 in (8.15)
Height:	9 ft 3 in (2.82 m)
Weight:	6,000 lb (2,720 kg) loaded
Maximum speed:	302 mph (486 km/h) at 16,400 ft (5,000 m)
Ceiling:	30,840 ft (9,400 m)
Range:	497 miles (800 km)
Armament:	1 x 20 mm cannon; 2 machine guns
Crew:	1

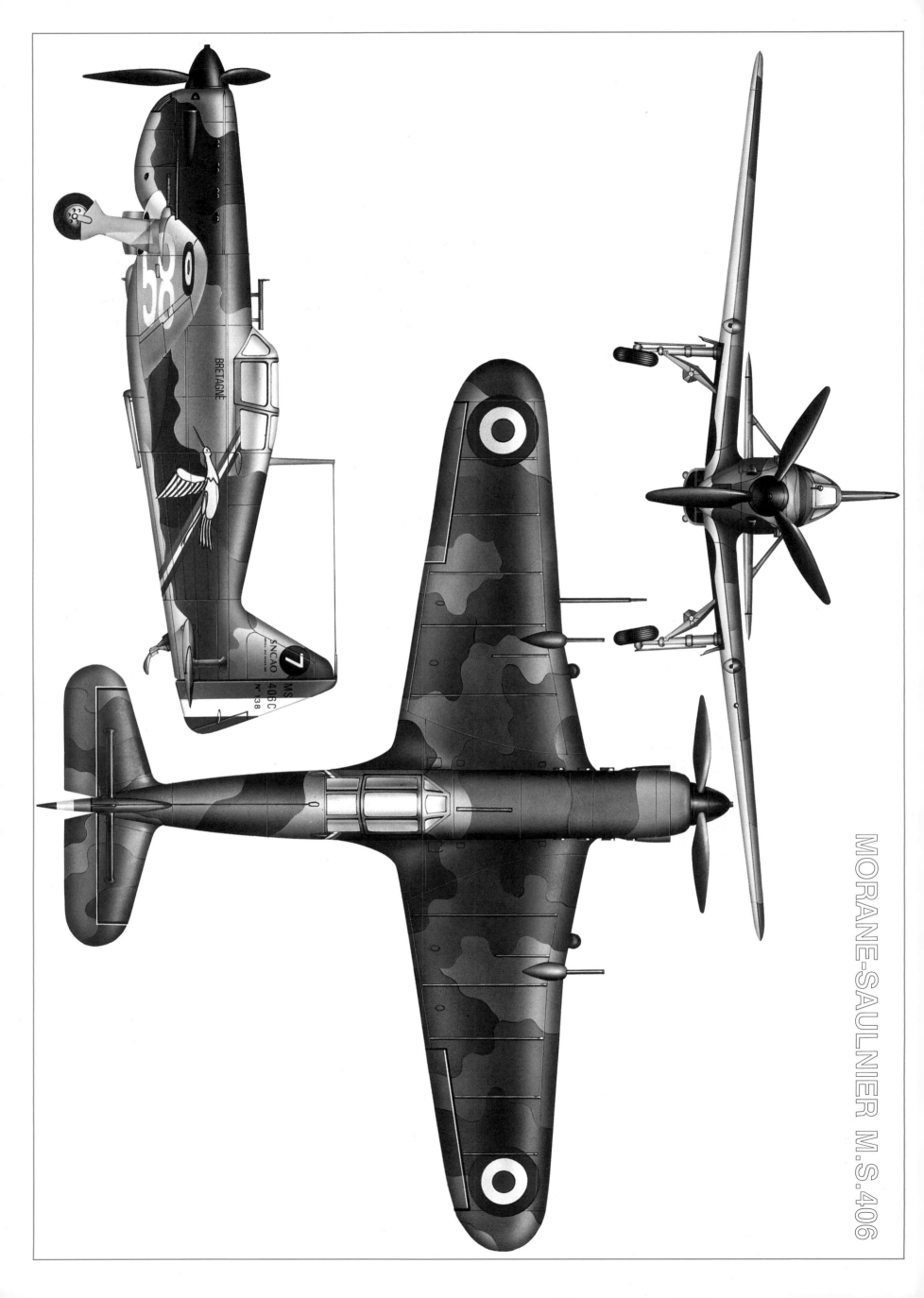

BRETAGNE

SNCAO
406 C
N° 38

MORANE-SAULNIER M.S.406

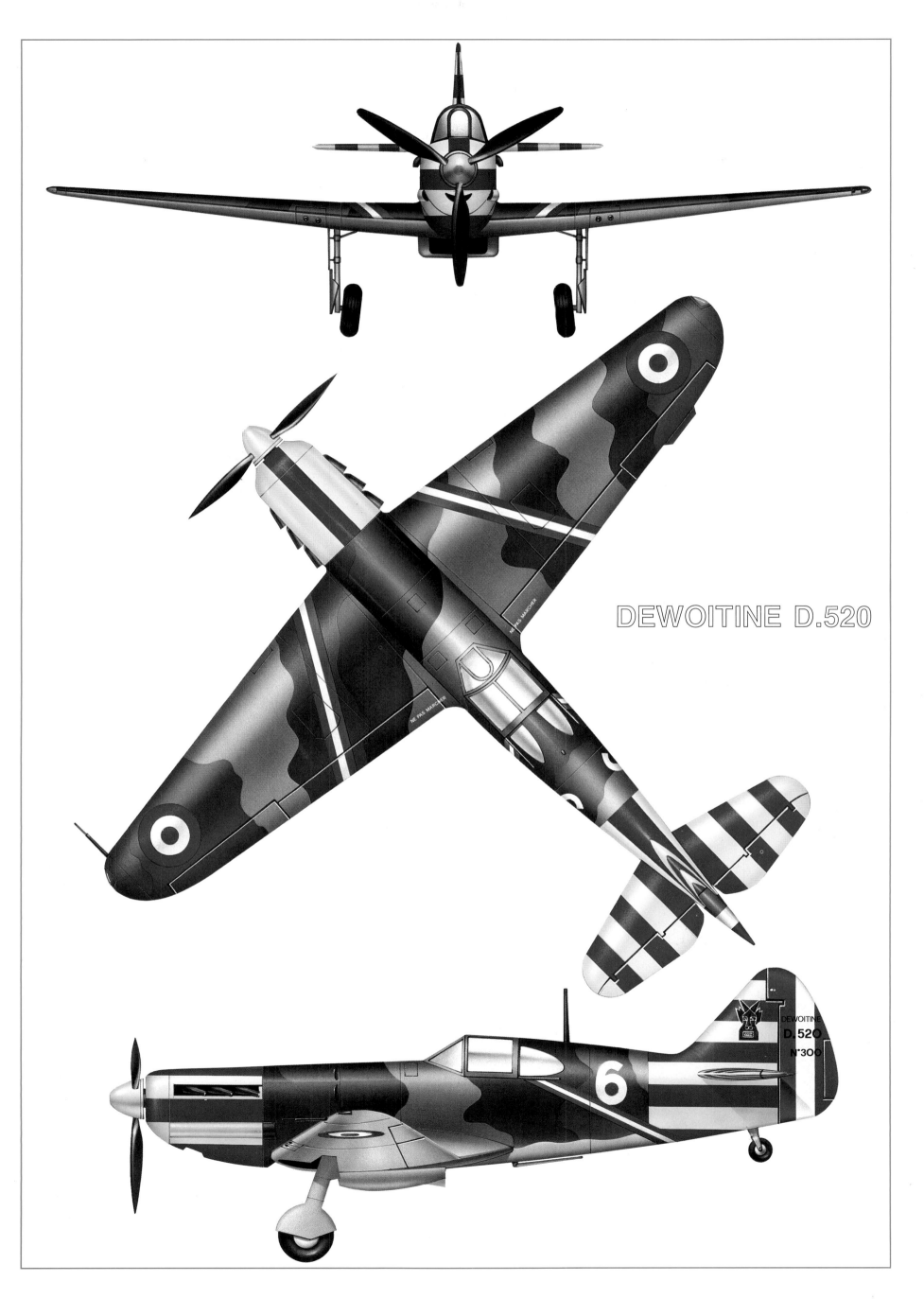

DEWOITINE D.520

The Dewoitine D.520, the best French fighter of the conflict, originated in 1936 as a private enterprise. Paradoxically, its development was forced to wait for two years, since the military authorities preferred to give priority to production of the Morane Saulnier M.S.405, maintaining that the construction of another interceptor was unnecessary. It was not until April 1939 (when the crisis was already imminent and, as it drew closer, the gaps in the *Armée de l'Air*'s rearmament program became more evident) and once the remarkable performance of Emile Dewoitine's fighter had been proved, that the first mass-production orders were placed. Exactly a year later, orders amounted to 2,350 aircraft, with deliveries planned at around 350 a month. In practice, on June 10, 1940, only 36 D.520s could be considered operative; two weeks later, when the armistice was signed, 437 aircraft had been completed. In all, 905 aircraft were built, and production, authorized during the German occupation, continued until 1942.

The project from which the D.520 originated was launched by Emile Dewoitine immediately after he left the Société Aéronautique Française, in June 1936. His studies for a fighter capable of exceeding 325 mph (520 km/h) first found a response at the beginning of the following year, with the (semiofficial) authorization to build two prototypes, plus a third to be used for static tests. Official acceptance was not given until April 3, 1938, and the first prototype took to the air on October 2. The last made its maiden flight on May 5, 1939, and during this period of time the D.520 was forced to undergo a long phase of preparation, necessary in order to eliminate a series of aerodynamic and structural problems. In particular, the radiators had to be repositioned and the engine exhaust modified, while further alterations were carried out on the rudder, the cockpit canopy, and the landing gear.

In its definitive configuration, the D.520 appeared as an elegant low-wing monoplane, powered by an Hispano-Suiza 12Y 31 "V-12" engine with supercharger, driving a three-bladed, variable pitch, metal propeller provided with a 20 mm cannon that fired through its hub. The aircraft's performance was especially noteworthy: during official flight testing it occasionally reached 340 mph (550 km/h) at an altitude of 17,100 ft (5,200 m), climbing to 26,300 ft (8,000 m) in 12 minutes and 53 seconds. On February 7, 1939, proving its remarkable aerodynamic and structural characteristics, the first prototype actually reached 512 mph (825 km/h) in a dive.

An initial order (for 200 aircraft) was placed in April 1939, followed by a second for 510 planes in June. However, production went ahead rather slowly, hampered by difficulties with supplies, in tuning the variant of the engine chosen for the production series (the 935 hp Hispano-Suiza 12Y 45), and with the armament. The first production series D.520 took to the air on October 31. In January 1940, only 13 aircraft had left the assembly lines, and it was not until April that the D.520 could be considered perfectly operational.

However, its brief career bearing the insignia of the *Armée de l'Air* did not limit this brilliant fighter's operative life. In the course of the conflict, the Dewoitine D.520s were used by the Luftwaffe, by the *Regia Aeronautica* (60 aircraft, in 1942-43), by the Bulgarian air force (120 aircraft, from 1943), the Rumanian air force and by the Free French units. At the end of the war, after the French air force had been reestablished, the D.520s were fitted with dual controls and were used as trainers beginning in 1945. The last unit to use the Dewoitine fighter was the *Escadrille de Présentation de l'Armée de l'Air,* that had seven in service. The last flight was carried out by a single-seater D.520 on September 3, 1953.

---

color plate

Dewoitine D.520 5ᵉ Escadrille Groupe de Chasse III/6 Armée de l'Air de l'Armistice (5th Squadron Fighting Group III/6 *Armée de l'Air de l'Armistice*) - Algeria 1941

A D.520 refuels at an Italian airport during a transfer flight from France to Syria after the 1940 armistice.

The second D.520 model.

A D.520 of the 5th Squadron of the III/6 Fighter Group.

Aircraft:	Dewoitine D.520
Nation:	France
Manufacturer:	SNCAM
Type:	Fighter
Year:	1940
Engine:	Hispano-Suiza 12Y 45,12-cylinder, liquid-cooled, 935 hp
Wingspan:	33 ft 6 in (10.20 m)
Length:	28 ft 9 in (8.76 m)
Height:	8 ft 5 in (2.57 m)
Takeoff weight:	6,160 lb (2,790 kg) loaded
Maximum speed:	332 mph (535 km/h) at 18,100 ft (5,500 m)
Ceiling:	34,540 ft (10,500 m)
Range:	552 miles (890 km)
Armament:	1 × 20 mm cannon; 4 machine guns
Crew:	1

BLOCH MB-152

The Bloch MB-152 was one of the most widely used French fighters at the time of the German invasion and during the few weeks prior to the armistice. However, this does not mean that it was a particularly competitive aircraft. With the possible exception of the Dewoitine 520, of which very few existed at the time, the *Armée de l'Air*'s front-line fighters were inferior to those of the Luftwaffe. The major limitations of the Bloch MB-152 were its insufficient range, its awkward handling and its obvious inferiority when compared to its direct adversary, the Messerschmitt Bf.109E.

The Bloch MB-152 was the last operational version of a series of aircraft (none of which was really very successful) that originated in 1934 on the basis of official specifications issued by the French military authorities on June 13. The founder of the whole series was the MB-150, the prototype of which appeared on July 17, 1936. The aircraft's complete inadequacy (on its first flight it did not manage takeoff) led to the project initially being laid aside. At the beginning of the following year, however, work on it resumed, and after a series of substantial modifications, the definitive prototype took to the air successfully on September 29, 1937. In April of the following year, after an initial series of evaluations, an order for 25 preseries aircraft was settled, the confirmation of a further order for 450 planes depending on their success.

It was, in fact, preparations for this mass production that threw light on some serious problems that could be solved only by taking radical measures: the Bloch MB-150's structure proved to be unsuitable for the strict demands of mass production, and it therefore became necessary to redesign it completely. In this revised form the aircraft's designation was also changed to MB-151, and the prototype made its maiden flight on August 18, 1938. While maintaining the general configuration of low-wing monoplane with retractable landing gear, powered by a Gnome-Rhône radial engine that drove a three-bladed variable pitch metal propeller, the MB-151 differed from its predecessor in its modified wing profile and in a general redimensioning of the wing itself. During flight testing and evaluation trials, however, the aircraft still proved to be inadequate and, above all, incapable of achieving the performance desired of the project.

In the meantime, the prototype of an improved version had been prepared, designated the MB-152. This fighter, in its turn, differed from its predecessor, especially in its more powerful engine and armament. Its first flight took place at Villacoublay on December 15, 1938, and was followed by an intensive series of flight tests. However, this aircraft also revealed a lack of preparation.

Nevertheless, production went ahead on the basis of a series of orders for both models: 144 MB-151s were commissioned, along with a total of 482 MB-152s. The Bloch fighter went into operational service in the first units of the *Armée de l'Air* in October and November 1939. Following the armistice, the surviving aircraft (51 Bloch MB-151s and 259 Bloch MB-152s) were taken

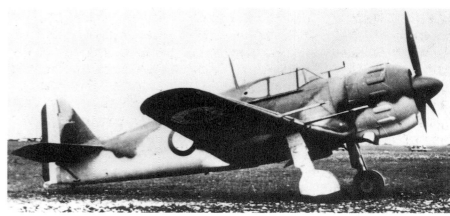

A Bloch MB-152 with 20 mm cannons mounted in the wings.

over by the Germans, and many of them served in the Vichy air force. Further developments to the project (including the more powerful Bloch MB-155, the prototype of which made its first flight on December 3, 1939, and of which nine were built, as well as the MB-157 model of 1942) came to a virtual halt. Lastly, mention should be made of nine MB-151s that were delivered to Greece beginning in April 1940 as part of an order for 25 aircraft.

color plate

Bloch MB-152 Groupe Chasse II/1 Armée de l'Air (II/1 Fighting Group *Armée de l'Air*) - France 1940

Aircraft:	Bloch MB-152
Nation:	France
Manufacturer:	SNCASO
Type:	Fighter
Year:	1939
Engine:	Gnome-Rhône 14 N-25, 14-cylinder radial, air-cooled, 1,080 hp
Wingspan:	34 ft 8 in (10.54 m)
Length:	29 ft 11 in (9.10 m)
Height:	9 ft 11 in (3.03 m)
Takeoff weight:	5,935 lb (2,693 kg)
Maximum speed:	320 mph (515 km/h) at 13,150 ft (4,000 m)
Ceiling:	32,900 ft (10,000 m)
Range:	384 miles (580 km)
Armament:	2 x 20 mm cannons; 2 machine guns
Crew:	1

A Bloch MB-151 during a test flight and still lacking its markings.

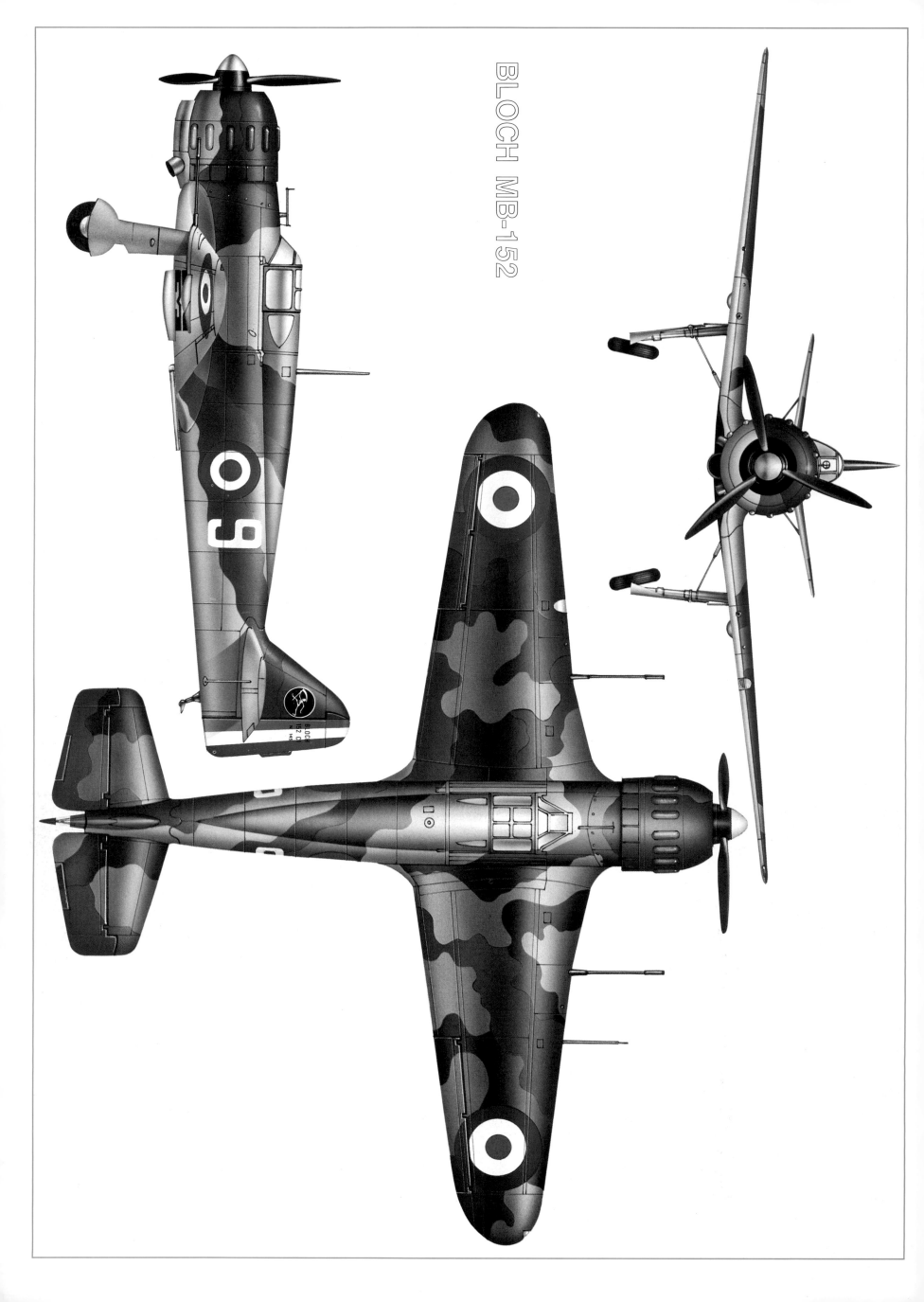

BLOCH MB-152

The Bloch 210 was the *Armée de l'Air*'s first medium "modern" bomber, and with its low-wing and retractable landing gear, it marked the beginning of a transitional phase. This proved to be evident especially with regard to its direct predecessor, the Bloch 200, which had been designed in 1932, completely maintaining the characteristic high-wing and fixed landing gear with heavy struts so typical of aircraft belonging to the generation of the previous decade.

The 210 project got under way in 1933, and the aim was to develop a night bomber that could also serve as a torpedo-bomber. The first prototype took to the air on November 23 the following year, complete with fixed landing gear and two 800 hp Gnome-Rhône radial engines. A second prototype, known as the Bloch 211, was developed at the same time and was powered by two in-line liquid-cooled Hispano-Suiza 12Y engines. It was also provided with retractable landing gear. Of the two prototypes, it was the former that went into production after a long series of flight tests and evaluations, which continued for most of the following year and led to numerous alterations in its structure. Between October and September 1935, many contracts were assigned, not only to Bloch but also to Potez and Hanriot, for the production of an initial lot of 80 aircraft. Further alterations, as compared to the original prototype, were carried out on the assembly line, the most important being the introduction of retractable landing gear and of more powerful Gnome-Rhône engines. The first Bloch 210 model (designated by the military suffix BN4) took to the air on December 12, 1935.

The following year, production was further increased and was distributed among other subcontracting companies, which continued to manufacture it even after the nationalization of the French aeronautical industry. The total number of planes ordered to supply units of the *Armée de l'Air* was 253. After the 51st, these aircraft were redesignated BN5, due to the crew being increased from four men to five. The Bloch 210 was also reasonably successful as an aircraft for export: 45 were built to satisfy orders from

Rumania and from Republican Spain.

At a certain point, in the course of its career with the French air force units, the Bloch proved to be seriously underpowered, and during 1937, a vast remotorization program became necessary, with the introduction of 950 hp Gnome-Rhône 14N engines. The aircraft certainly became more reliable after these modifications, although the increase in power was unable to eliminate the intrinsic limits of the outdated project. When the war broke out, the 210 was considered obsolete and the 150 or so aircraft still in service with the *Armée de l'Air* were used in only a few missions (especially at night) and then withdrawn from front-line duty. In 1942, during the German occupation, several Bloch 210s were used for training.

color plate

Bloch 210 4ᵉ Escadrille Groupe de Bombardement II/23 French Air Force - 1938

Aircraft:	Bloch 210
Nation:	France
Manufacturer:	various
Type:	Bomber
Year:	1935
Engine:	2 Gnome-Rhône 14N, 14-cylinder radial air-cooled, 950 hp each
Wingspan:	74 ft 10 in (22.80 m)
Length:	61 ft 9 in (18.82 m)
Height:	22 ft (6.70 m)
Weight:	22,487 lb (10,190 kg) loaded
Maximum speed:	200 mph (322 km/h) at 11,480 ft (3,500 m)
Ceiling:	32,480 ft (9,900 m)
Range:	808 miles (1,300 km)
Armament:	3 machine guns; 3,527 lb (1,600 kg) of bombs
Crew:	5

French air force Bloch 210 with prewar camouflage.

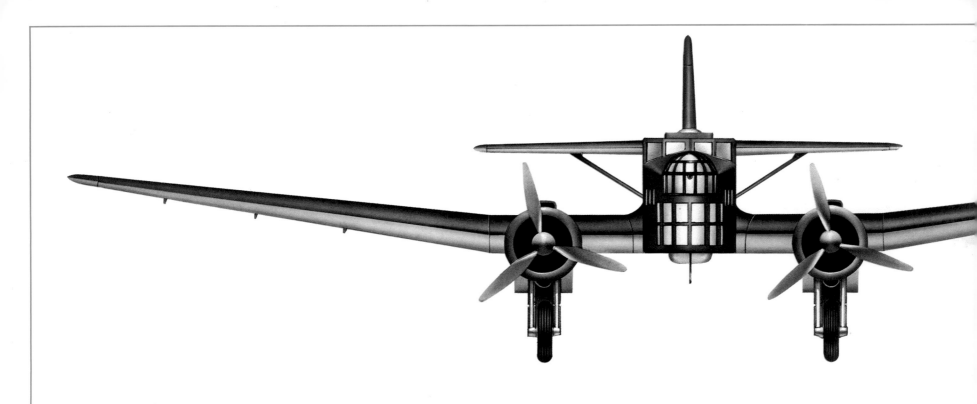

BLOCH 210

Tough and easy to handle, the Latécoère 298 represented the culminating point in the development of a long series of seaplanes produced by the French manufacturer during the 1920s, a series that saw its major exponent in the Latécoère 28 commercial transport model. The project got under way in 1934, based on specifications provided by the *Aéronavale* (French navy air force), which requested a torpedo-bomber with modern features and performance. The prototype was completed in the spring of 1936, and flight testing began on May 8.

The craft was an all-metal low-wing monoplane with two large floats, each housing fuel tanks. It was powered by an 880 hp Hispano-Suiza 12 Ycrs engine, and the armament was contained in a ventral bay; in the case of a torpedo, this was installed in such a way as to project slightly out of the fuselage.

On September 24, 1936, after factory tests, the prototype began official flight testing, which concluded on March 17 of the following year with an initial order for 36 planes to be divided between two versions: 24 of the A type, with fixed wings, and 12 of the B type with folding wings, improved armament and range, and capable of taking on board a fourth crew member. In April 1938, a third order was placed for a further 15 Laté 298Bs and for five D types (similar to the previous ones but lacking the folding wing mechanism). Altogether, production (which, incidentally, recommenced in March 1942, during the German occupation) totaled about 200 aircraft, 80 or so of which were converted (from March

1940) into reconnaissance planes known as the Laté 298E.

Its operational service began in December 1938, and on May 10, 1940, 50 or so aircraft were supplied to five land-based front-line naval units. These planes were used in the attempt to arrest the German invasion and, paradoxically, almost none of their missions were against the naval targets for which they had been conceived. Initially used for daytime ground attack and tactical bombing, the Laté 298s proved to be particularly vulnerable compared to the fighters of the Luftwaffe, and they were subsequently relegated to night missions.

After France's surrender, all production went to equip units of the Vichy government's navy. Later in the war (spring 1944), a Laté 298 unit was incorporated into the Coastal Command of Britain's Royal Air Force for use in antisubmarine defense, cooperating with the two-engine Vickers Wellington.

Some of these versatile planes survived the war and ended their long careers as trainers in the postwar years. The last three were withdrawn in 1950.

color plate
Latécoère 298A Escadrille T.1 French Air Force - 1939

Aircraft:	Latécoère 298D
Nation:	France
Manufacturer:	Latécoère
Type:	Bomber
Year:	1938
Engine:	Hispano-Suiza 12 Ycrs, 12-cylinder V, liquid-cooled, 880 hp
Wingspan:	50 ft 10 in (15.50 m)
Length:	41 ft 2 1/2 (12.59 m)
Height:	17 ft 1 in (5.20 m)
Weight:	9,960 lb (4,500 kg) loaded
Maximum speed:	180 mph (300 km/h) at 6,560 ft (2,000 m)
Ceiling:	19,685 ft (6,000 m)
Range:	932 miles (1,500 km)
Armament:	3 machine guns; 1,477 lb (670 kg) of bombs
Crew:	2/3

Latécoère 298 belonging to the naval aviation of the Vichy government afloat.

The same aircraft in front of a Luftwaffe Dornier Do.24 seaplane.

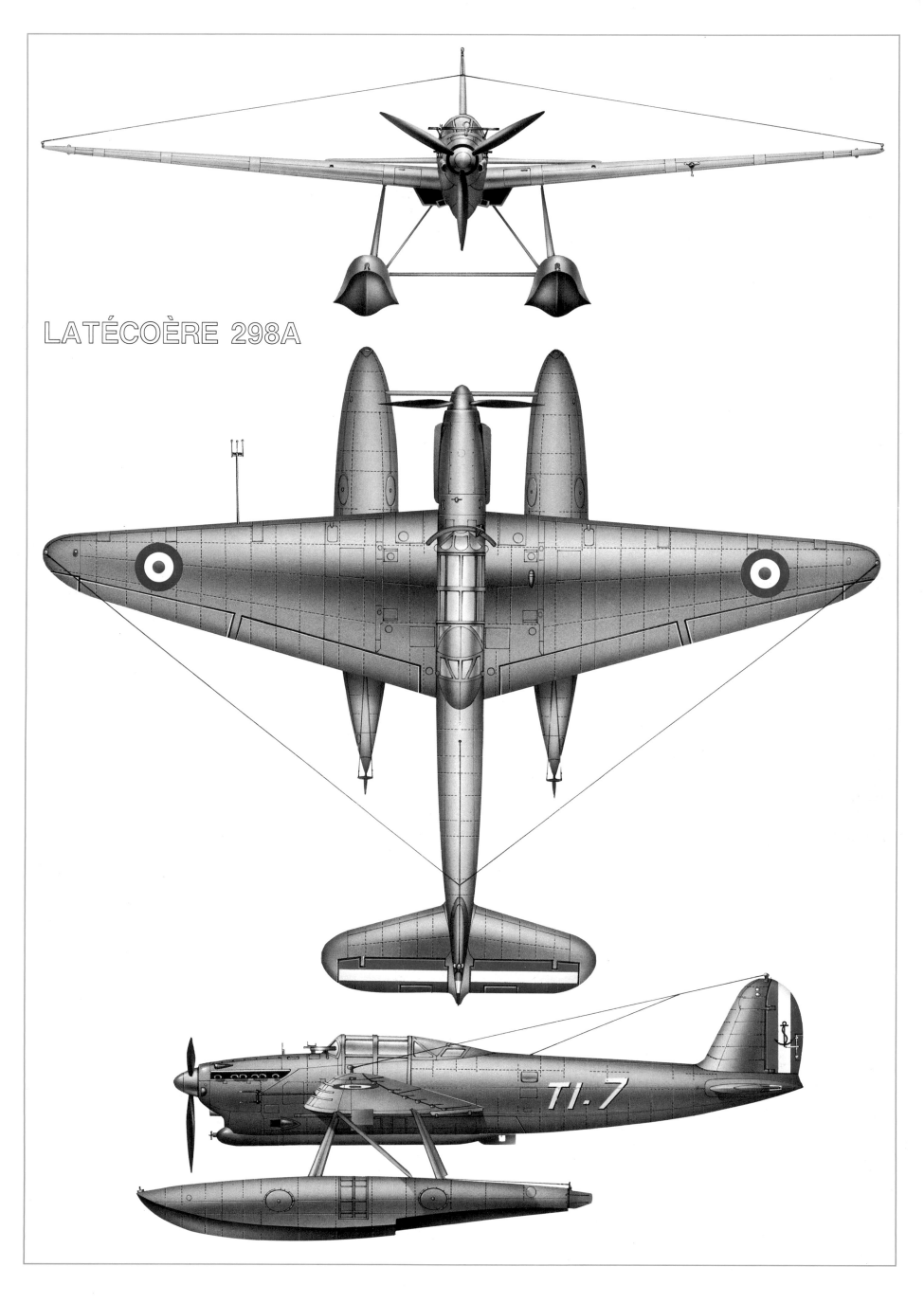

LATÉCOÈRE 298A

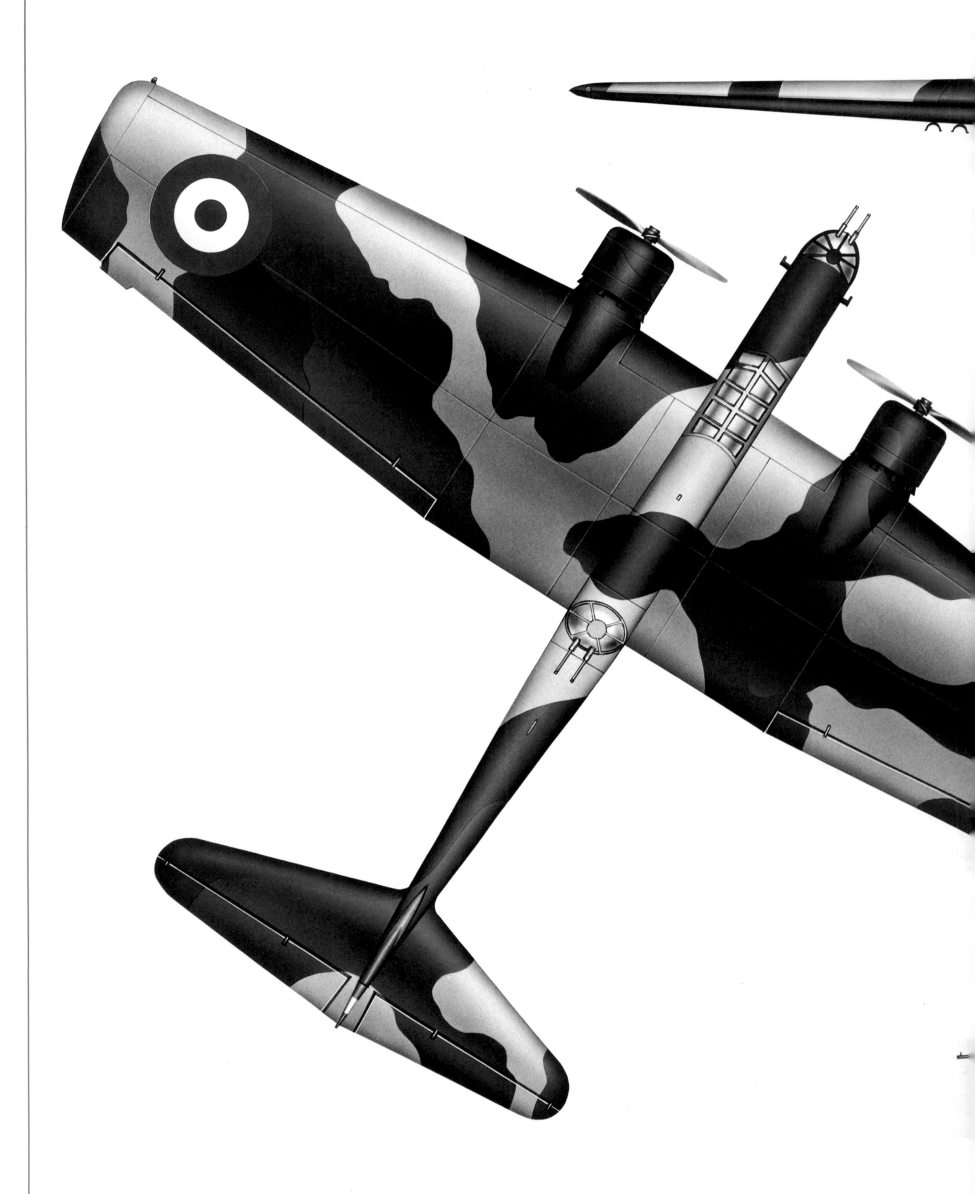

AMIOT 143

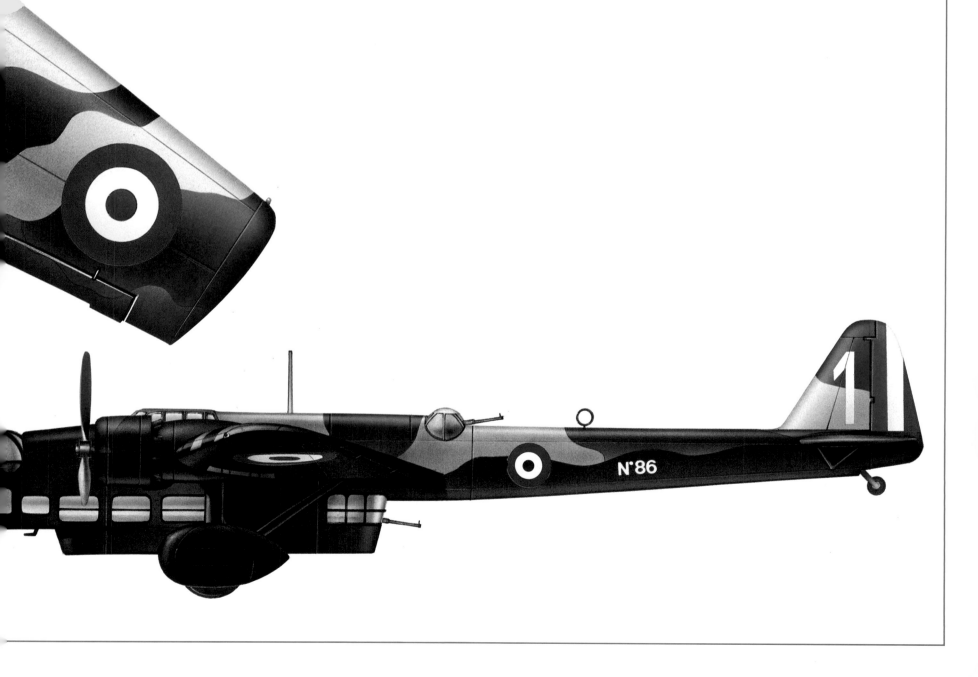

N°86

AMIOT 143

Developed toward the end of the 1920s, the Amiot 143 was still in front-line service at the outbreak of World War II and was one of the few French bombers to go into action in the few days of combat that preceded the armistice.

The origins of this awkward and unattractive two-engine aircraft went back to 1928, the year in which the Air Ministry issued specifications to the aeronautical industry for a day- and night-time bomber. Four manufacturers submitted designs: Blériot with its model 137, Breguet with the 410, SPCA with its model 30, and Amiot with its 140M. The Amiot prototype made its maiden flight in April 1931, and after completing all its flight evaluation test was judged the winner. An order was then placed for an initial delivery of 40 aircraft.

The order was placed in November 1933, but at almost the same time the original specifications were altered, and a request was made for an aircraft able to serve not only as a bomber but also as a long-range heavy fighter and as a reconnaissance plane. Amiot therefore altered the original design and prepared two new and improved prototypes, which were more powerful (thanks to the use of two 740 hp Gnome-Rhône 14K radial engines, provided with superchargers) and were designated 143s. The first of the prototypes flew in August 1934 and was accepted for production after a series of alterations, such as the strengthening of the fuselage, the increasing of the surface area of the fixed tail fins, and the introduction of a new type of gun turret.

The original order was consequently adapted to suit the new variant, and a total of 178 of these were eventually built. The first production series of the Amiot 143 (on the assembly line, the original engine was replaced with a more powerful version, capable of generating 870 hp) flew for the first time in April 1935, and deliveries to the various units began in July. The aircraft was a two-engine monoplane with fixed landing gear, characterized by a widely glazed slab-sided fuselage and armed with four 7.5 mm machine guns, two of which were situated in the gun turret. It had an all-metal structure, and one of its most remarkable features was the unusual thickness of the wings, which allowed direct in-flight access to the engines by means of an internal passage. Variant models included the 143 BN4 and the 143 B5, both produced from 1937 onward and designed specifically for day and night bombing. The crew of the former was reduced to four. One variant that was never followed up was the 142, almost identical to the first models to go into production except for the engines, which were replaced by a couple of liquid-cooled 860 hp Hispano-Suiza 12 Ycrs 12-cylinder Vs. Only one Amiot 142 was built, and after flight tests it was brought up to the standards of the production series.

As production progressed, many units of the *Armée de l'Air* were supplied with Amiot 143s, and at the outbreak of the war six bomber groups were still equipped with this plane, despite the fact that it was clearly obsolete. During the early months of the war, these aircraft were used solely for propaganda flights over German territory. However, beginning on May 10, 1940, their crews were put to the test by the more modern and seasoned planes of the Luftwaffe. The Amiot 143 played a major role in some of the most desperate attempts to defend France. These included the daytime attack on the bridges of Sédan on May 14, 1940: during this mission 11 of the 12 bombers were shot down by their adversaries. Of the planes that survived the armistice, 10 were used by the Germans, mainly for transport duties.

---

color plate
Amiot 143 II/38 Groupe de Bombardement French Air Force - 1940

Aircraft:	Amiot 143
Nation:	France
Manufacturer:	SECM
Type:	Bomber
Year:	1935
Engine:	2 Gnome-Rhône 14 Kirs, 14-cylinder radial, air-cooled, 870 hp each
Wingspan:	80 ft 6 in (24.51 m)
Length:	59 ft 11 in (18.26 m)
Height:	18 ft 8 in (5.68 m)
Weight:	21,385 lb (9,700 kg) loaded
Maximum speed:	193 mph (310 km/h) at 13,120 ft (4,000 m)
Ceiling:	25,920 ft (7,900 m)
Range:	746 miles (1,200 km)
Armament:	4 machine guns; 2,870 lb (1,300 kg) of bombs
Crew:	4/5

The Amiot 143 featured an original structure with notable glazing.

AMIOT 351

The Amiot 354, one of the lesser known combat planes built by the French aeronautical industry just before the war broke out, should be remembered not only as one of the most elegant aircraft of the period but also for its overall performance, which was clearly above average compared to contemporary aircraft in the same category. However, in spite of these merits, this promising twin-engine bomber did not have a great career, being caught up in the confused situation that prevailed in France immediately prior to the war. Only 62 aircraft of the 351 and 354 series were completed and delivered before the armistice, and their career was nonexistent: some of them reached the units without armament, while other were destroyed on the ground by German attacks.

The ancestor of the 350 series was the Amiot 340.01, which took to the air for the first time on December 6, 1937. This aircraft was a transformed version of a prototype (model 341) that had originally been designed as a postal plane and had subsequently been modified to a three-seater bomber, powered by a pair of 920 hp Gnome-Rhône 14N radial engines. A series of official flight tests began in March 1938, and when they had been completed, the project was altered still further in order to make it more suited to operative needs: more powerful engines were adopted, provision was made for a fourth crew member, and twin fins and rudders were introduced. Apart from this, the aircraft retained its overall configuration of mid – wing monoplane with retractable landing gear. It was carefully studied from an aerodynamic point of view and featured a long, completely glazed cockpit, a circular section fuselage, and a "transparent" nose, in which the bombardier's position was situated. In this form, the new prototype, redesignated Amiot 351.01, made its maiden flight at the end of January 1939.

Parallel to the evaluation tests, the designers continued to work on different variants of the basic type, characterized mainly by the installation of different power plants. However, the versions chosen for production were the 351 and the 354. The latter, in particular, once again adopted the original configuration of single fin and rudder and a three-man crew. During the year, orders were placed for a total of 285 of these bombers.

Among the other variants that remained at the prototype, or project stage, mention should be made of the 350 and the 352 (both similar to the 340.01 prototype but fitted with in-line Hispano-Suiza 12Y engines that differed in the power they generated); the 353, in which the fitting of a pair of Rolls-Royce Merlin III engines, each generating 1,030 hp, was planned; the 355.01 (which appeared as a prototype), provided with two Gnome-Rhône 14R engines fitted with turbo-supercharger and capable of generating 1,200 hp; and the 356.01, with two 1,130 hp Merlin X engines. In the final variant to be studied, designated Amiot 357, a pressurized cockpit was planned, thus allowing the bombardier to operate at high altitudes, as was the installation of a pair of turbo-supercharged Hispano-Suiza 12Z engines.

During the German occupation, some Amiot 354s were converted and transformed into fast transport planes, following the removal of the armament and the installation of extra fuel tanks in the bomb hold. In the course of the war, these aircraft were used by Air France for flights to the overseas territories. One aircraft survived the war and went into service again in 1946 as a liaison plane.

color plate

Amiot 351 Groupe de Bombardement II/34 Armée de l'Air (Bomber Group II/34 *Armée de l'Air*) - Orano-La Sénia (Algeria) 1940.

Aircraft:	Amiot 351
Nation:	France
Manufacturer:	SECM
Type:	Bomber
Year:	1940
Engine:	2 Gnome-Rhône 14N, 14-cylinder radial, air-cooled, 920 hp each
Wingspan:	74 ft 11 in (22.83 m)
Length:	47 ft 7 in (14.50 m)
Height:	13 ft 4½ in (4.06 m)
Weight:	24,912 lb (11,285 kg) loaded
Maximum speed:	298 mph (479 km/h) at 13,120 ft (4,000 m)
Ceiling:	32,810 ft (10,000 m)
Range:	1,535 miles (2,470 km)
Armament:	1 × 20 mm cannon; 2 machine guns; 2,200 lb (1,000 kg) of bombs
Crew:	4

An Amiot 354 transformed in civil aircraft during the German occupation of France.

Judged to be one of the best medium bombers in service in the world at the time, the Lioré et Olivier aircraft of the LeO 45 series represented a true evolutionary leap in the *Armée de l'Air*'s equipment. Reasonably advanced in concept, powerful, well armed, and with a performance equal to that of any contemporary fighter, these excellent two-engine aircraft nevertheless appeared too late to make a significant contribution to the course of the war. On May 10, 1940, out of a total of 222 planes forming part of the units, only about half could be considered operational. However, with a total of 452 built up to the time of the armistice and a further 150 built during the German occupation, the LeO 45s served in the Vichy air force and in the navy for the duration of the war, and many of the 67 survivors remained in service after the conflict. The last two LeO 453s (a variant fitted with Pratt & Whitney engines) were not withdrawn until September 1957. From many points of view, this long career can be considered the best recognition of the merits of this bomber, which was the only French aircraft used in the 1939/1940 campaign to remain in active service for no fewer than 12 years after the war ended.

The project originated in response to official specifications issued on November 17, 1937, requesting the aeronautical industry to produce a fast, modern medium bomber to replace the by then obsolete aircraft that constituted the *Armée de l'Air*'s standard equipment. More particularly, the new aircraft was to be capable of carrying up to 3,300 lb (1,500 kg) of bombs at a speed of 250 mph (400 km/h) and have an active range of about 560 miles (900 km). It was to have a four-man crew, and the defensive armament was to include a 20 mm cannon.

Several manufacturers responded to the specifications (including Amiot and Latécoère), but Lioré et Olivier's proposal immediately appeared the most competitive. The prototype (LeO 45-01) made its first flight on January 16, 1937, and apart from some stability problems, its overall performance proved to be excellent. During official evaluations, which commenced on September 2, the aircraft achieved a maximum horizontal speed of 278 mph (480 km/h) at 13,150 ft (4,000 m), while following a dive from 16,500

ft (5,000 m) the aircraft touched 387 mph (624 km/h), demonstrating remarkable qualities of structural strength and streamlining. The LeO 45 was an all-metal low-wing monoplane with retractable landing gear. Its bomb load was completely contained in the fuselage, and the defensive armament consisted of a 20 mm cannon on the aircraft's back, a retractable 7.5 mm machine gun in the belly, and another fixed one in the front of the aircraft.

However, evaluation tests revealed a series of deficiencies in the original engines (Hispano-Suiza 14AA, generating 1,078 hp at takeoff), and when the first contract was drawn up for the production of 20 aircraft in January 1938, a request was made for the installation of equally powerful Gnome-Rhône 14N engines. The prototype was renamed LeO 451-01, and flight testing resumed on October 21, 1938. Meanwhile, orders had been placed for a total of 145 aircraft. The first LeO 451-01 of the series made its maiden flight on March 24, 1939, following schedule delays and by September only five aircraft could be considered operational.

During the occupation, the Germans did not show any particular interest in the bomber. Some were converted for transport, others were assigned to the *Regia Aeronautica*, which incorporated them into the 51st Autonomous Bomber Group. Among the variants in production after the 451, as well as the LeO 453, were the 452, fitted with different Gnome-Rhône engines; the 454, with two Bristol Hercules engines; and, lastly, the 458, with Wright R-2600 engines.

---

color plate

Lioré et Olivier LeO 451 Groupe Reconnaissance II/31 Armée de l'Air (II/31 Reconnaissance Group *Armée de l'Air*) - France 1940

Aircraft:	Lioré et Olivier LeO 451
Nation:	France
Manufacturer:	SNCASE
Type:	Bomber
Year:	1939
Engine:	2 Gnome-Rhône 14N, 14-cylinder radial, air-cooled, 1,140 hp each
Wingspan:	73 ft 10 ½ in (22.50 m)
Length:	56 ft 4 in (17.17 m)
Height:	17 ft 2 in (5.23 m)
Weight:	25,133 lb (11,385 kg) loaded
Maximum speed:	307 mph (494 km/h) at 15,748 ft (4,800 m)
Ceiling:	29,530 ft (9,000 m)
Range:	1,430 miles (2,300 km)
Armament:	1 x 20 mm cannon; 2 machine guns; 4,400 lb (2,000 kg) of bombs
Crew:	4

The prototype of the LeO 451 with Gnome-Rhône engines.

The prototype of the LeO 451 in its original configuration with Hispano-Suiza engines.

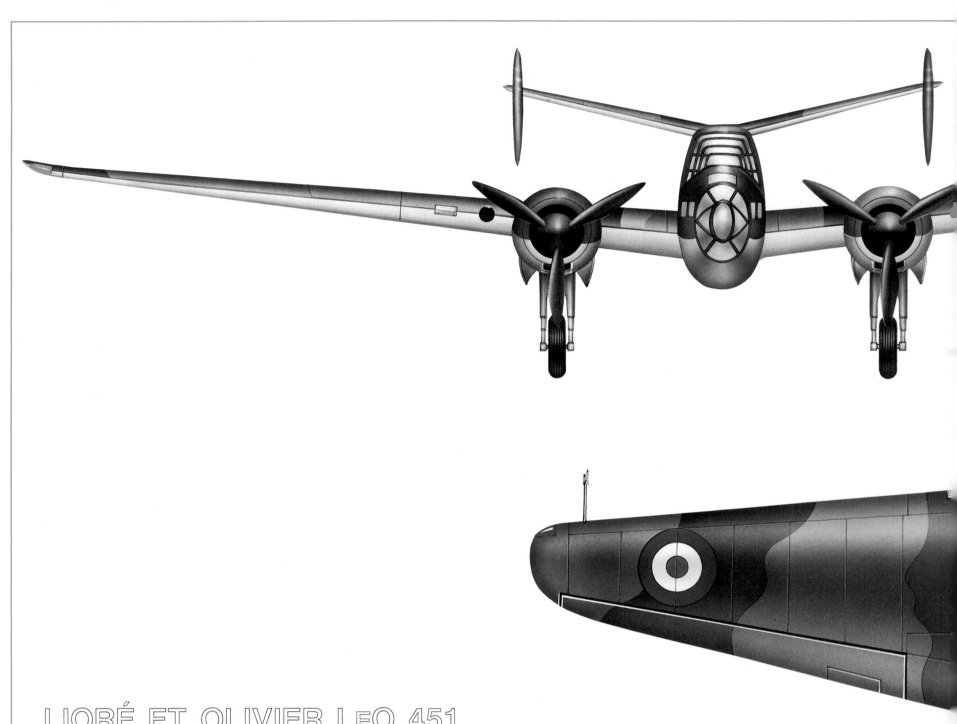

LIORÉ ET OLIVIER LeO 451

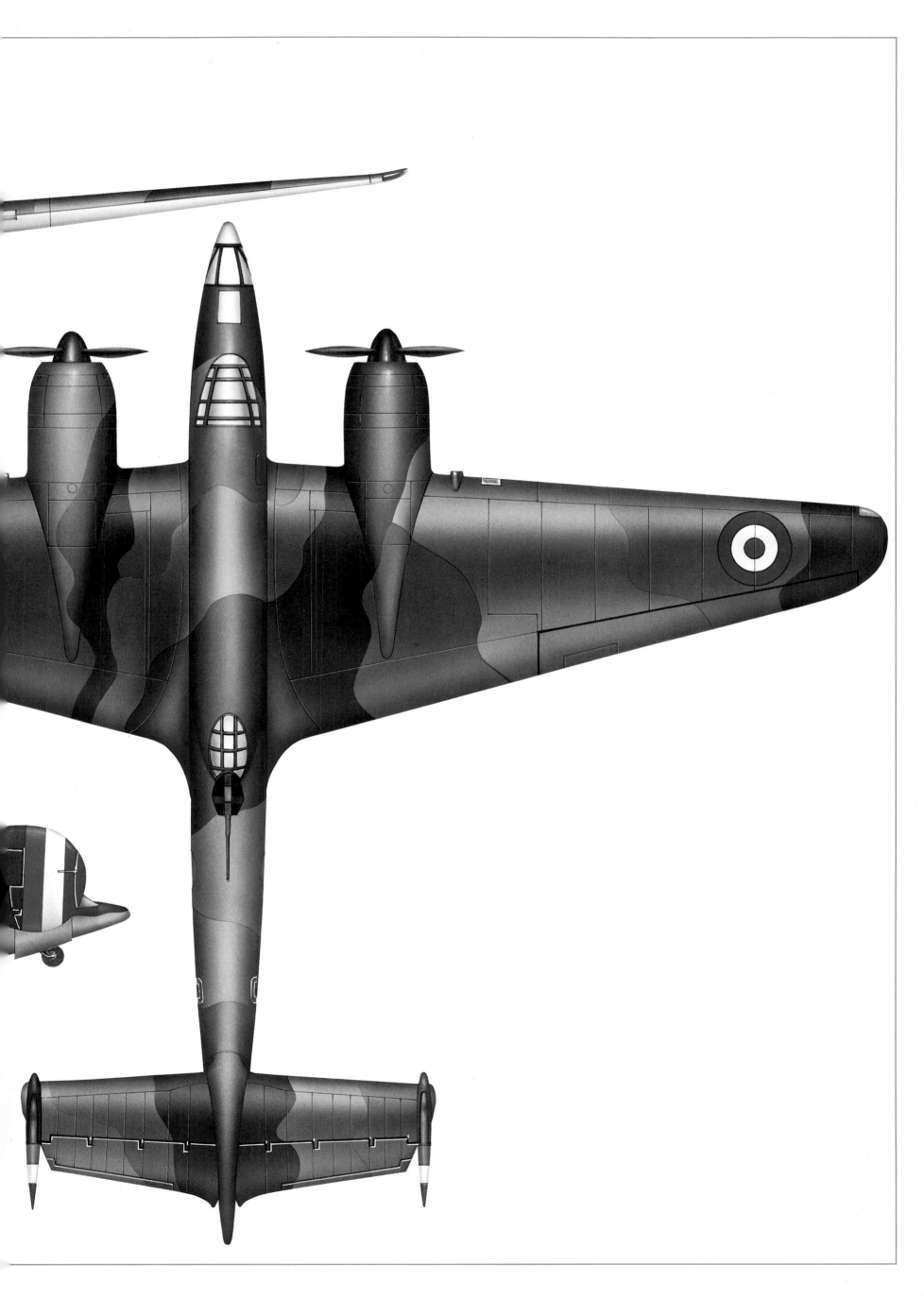

Created with the production of a modern heavy fighter in mind, the Potez 63 project eventually gave rise to one of the most prolific and versatile series of combat aircraft to be built by the French aeronautical industry at the time of the conflict. The 63 series, conceived near the end of 1934, generated not only strategic fighters, but also light bombers as well as attack and reconnaissance planes, and by June 1940 a total of more than 1,100 aircraft had been produced. Moreover, this elegant two-engine aircraft remained in active service during the German occupation, and approximately 250 additional planes built in that period served bearing the insignia of the Luftwaffe (which used them for transport and liaison), of the Vichy air force, of the Italian *Regia Aeronautica* (which received 15 aircraft) and of the Rumanian air force.

The project got under way on the basis of precise official specifications issued in October 1934, calling for the construction of an aircraft capable of carrying out three main roles: a two-seater interceptor and escort fighter; a two-seater night fighter; and a three-seater fighter to be used as a controller for directing, via radio, operations carried out by single-seater fighter units. Work began in April of the following year, and the first prototype (the 63.01) took to the air on April 25, 1936, almost a year later. The aircraft was an all-metal low-wing monoplane with retractable landing gear and double rudders. It was powered by a pair of 580 hp Hispano-Suiza 14Hbs radial engines. Following an accident that occurred during landing, which led to the tail fins being redesigned and to the engines being substituted, the prototype was renamed the 630.01 and flight testing resumed on August 3, 1936. In the meantime, a second prototype had been completed, fitted with Gnome-Rhône 14 Mars engines and designated the 631.01. It made its first flight on March 15, 1937. After a series of evaluation tests, production was launched on the basis of an order for 80 Potez 630s and 90 Potez 631s. Delivery to the units began toward the end of 1938, and a total of 207 631s were eventually built.

Meanwhile, the basic project had been amplified, with other variants destined to carry out different roles being produced. The two-seater day bomber, the Potez 633, took to the air at the end of 1937; the first Potez 637, a three-seater reconnaissance plane also used in cooperation with the army, appeared in the summer of 1938; on December 31 of the same year, the prototype of the Potez 63.11, a three-seater tactical reconnaissance plane, took to the air, the last version to go into mass production.

Initially 125 of the Potez 633 version, distinguished by glazing on the front part of the fuselage and by its capacity to transport eight 110 lb (50 kg) bombs internally, were ordered. However, this order was subsequently canceled, although 21 aircraft were exported to Rumania and 10 to Greece, while another 40 were requisitioned by the *Armée de l'Air*. The Potez 637, similar to the 631 but with a glazed central pod for an observer, was considered a transitional model and only 60 were built while awaiting replacement by the more effective Potez 63.11. In this final variant the front and central part of the fuselage and the cockpit were substantially redesigned. By May 31, 1941, 702 of these aircraft had been built, and total production amounted to over 850.

Among the experimental versions that were never followed up, mention should be made of the 635, which derived from the 631 and was intended as a two-seater night bomber armed with two 20 mm cannons installed in the fuselage and pointing upward at a 20 degree angle; the 639, intended for ground attack and featuring a fixed cannon in the belly pointing downward at a 14 degree angle; and the 63.12, which was derived from the 633 and intended for dive-bombing.

color plate

Potez 631 3ème Escadrille Groupe Chasse II/1 Armée de l'Air (3rd Squadron II/1 Fighting Group *Armée de l'Air*) - France 1939

Aircraft:	Potez 631
Nation:	France
Manufacturer:	SNCAN
Type:	Night fighter
Year:	1938
Engine:	2 Gnome-Rhône 14 M6/7, 14-cylinder radial, air-cooled, 660 hp each
Wingspan:	52 ft 8 in (16.00 m)
Length:	36 ft 5 in (11.07 m)
Height:	11 ft 10 in (3.61 m)
Takeoff weight:	9,920 lb (4,500 kg)
Maximum speed:	276 mph (445 km/h) at 13,150 ft (4,000 m)
Ceiling:	29,600 ft (9,000 m)
Range:	760 miles (1,225 km)
Armament:	2 x 20 mm cannons; 8 machine guns
Crew:	2/3

A Potez 63.11 in Syria in 1941. This was one of the aircraft that fought alongside the British, rebelling against the Vichy government.

POTEZ 631

VICKERS WELLINGTON Mk.I

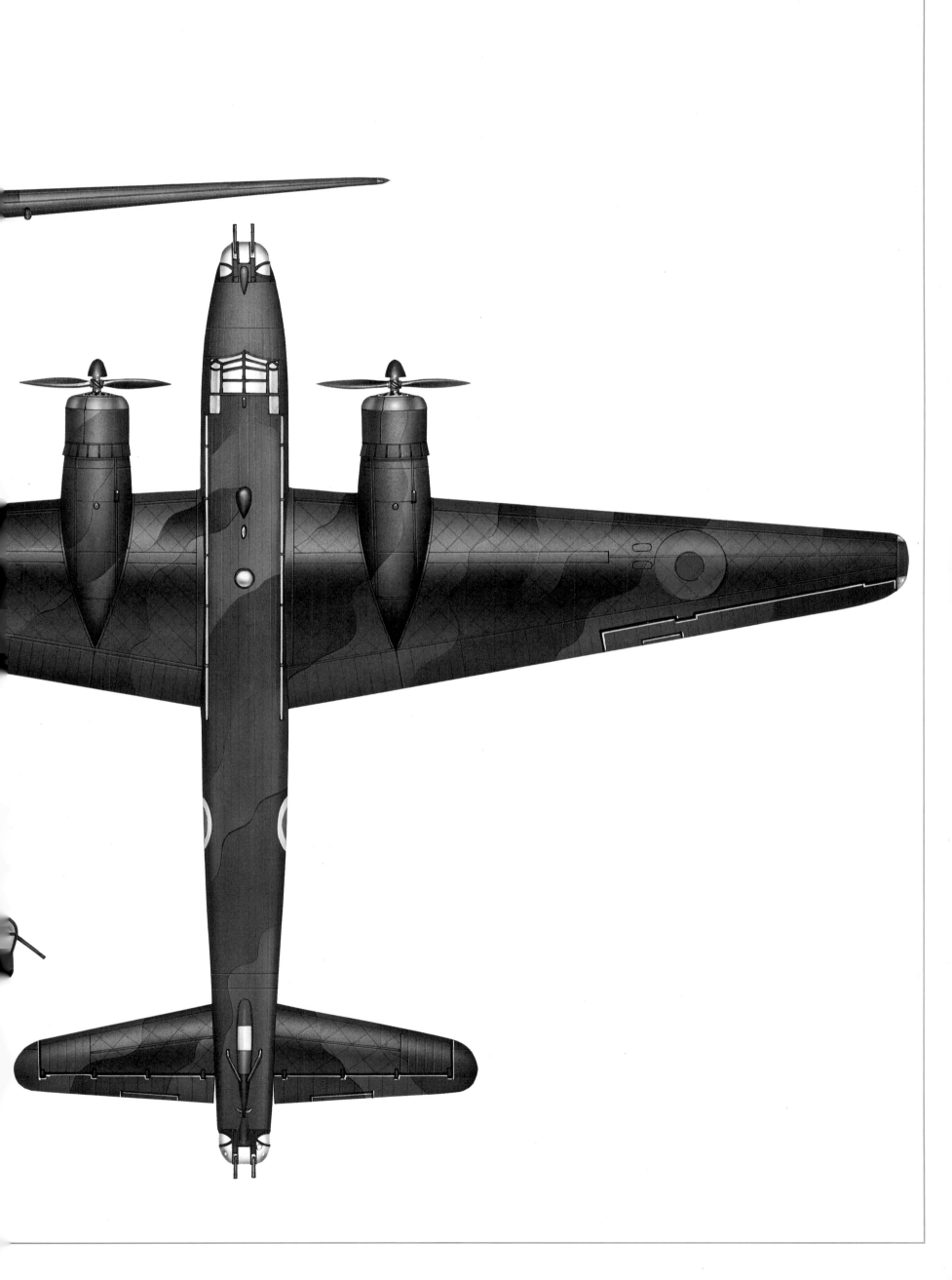

A Vickers Wellington Mk.I of the 214th Squadron in flight before the start of the conflict. The crosses on the insignia are identification marks for use during exercises.

The Wellington was one of the best known and most widely used of the British bombers and, until the appearance of the first heavy bombers, such as the Short Stirling, the Handley Page Halifax, and the Avro Lancaster, it constituted the strong point of the RAF's Bomber Command. In a certain sense, the Wellington was one of the last representatives of a generation of aircraft that characterized military aviation in the 1930s and that were the typical expression of the biplane formula. Although it shared the characteristics of many other models designed in various countries, the Vickers bomber stood out for a technological feature that was to remain unique: its geodetic structure, which combined relative lightness with almost incredible strength. Although it was canvas covered, the Wellington proved capable of standing up to a remarkable amount of punishment and damage while still remaining airborne. Its importance in the RAF's arsenal can be illustrated by a few figures: from 1937 to 1945, 11,461 of this versatile aircraft were built in several versions, serving brilliantly in many roles, from transport to reconnaissance, and in Coastal Command they were used in naval reconnaissance, submarine warfare, and as bombers specialized in mine-laying. Lastly, as a trainer, the Wellington was not withdrawn until 1953.

The prototype made its maiden flight on June 15, 1936, three and a half years after the project had got under way, and a series of flight tests fully confirmed the aircraft's potential. By the end of the year, an order had been placed for 180 planes, and the first Wellington of the initial production series (Mk.I) appeared on December 23, 1937. The two-engine aircraft was immediately christened Wimpey (after a popular cartoon character). It was a mid-wing monoplane with retractable landing gear, powered by a pair of 1,000 hp Bristol Pegasus radial engines and capable of carrying 4,408 lb (2,000 kg) of bombs in its hold. Its defensive armament was particularly powerful and consisted of six 7.7 mm machine guns installed in two turrets in the nose and the tail and in two lateral positions.

Once production of the first series was complete, other variants soon followed. Among the principal variants, after the Wellington Mk.IA and Mk.IC, which were mainly strengthened in armament (187 Mk.IAs and 2,685 Mk.ICs were built), the prototype of the Mk.II series appeared on March 3, 1939. This was powered by a pair of 1,145 hp Rolls-Royce Merlin X liquid-cooled engines, chosen because of the prospect of the Bristol radials becoming unavailable. On May 16 of the same year, the prototype of the Mk.III series appeared (of which 1,517 were built), marking a return to the use of air-cooled engines with a pair of 1,389 hp Bristol Hercules. Following the Mk.IV (200 of which were built and fitted with Pratt & Whitney Twin Wasp engines), another major production variant was the Mk.X (in fact, the most widely used of all, with 3,803 aircraft being built), fitted with more powerful Bristol Hercules engines.

On the European front, the Wellington's career in the units of Bomber Command came to an end in October 1943. However, it was used extensively in other theaters of war and in the units of Coastal Command, for which variants for naval use had been purposely built. The Mk.VIII series (of which 397 were built) specialized in reconnaissance. This was followed by the Wellington Mk.XI series (numbering 180 aircraft) and the Mk.XII (58), Mk.XIII (844), and Mk.XIV (841) series. The latter aircraft, differing mainly in their engines and armament, were used in a great variety of roles. The final production series (Mk.XV and Mk.XVI), however, were altered as compared to the initial variants and destined for transport: the main modifications consisted in their carrying no armament and in the transformation of the bomb compartment into a hold. The last Wellington, a Mk.X, came off the assembly lines in October 1945.

color plate
Vickers Wellington Mk.I 115th Squadron RAF - Great Britain 1940

A Wellington Mk.II during refuelling prior to a mission in North Africa.

A Vickers Wellington modified with electronic equipment for training.

Aircraft:	Vickers Wellington Mk.III
Nation:	Great Britain
Manufacturer:	Vickers-Armstrong Ltd.
Type:	Bomber
Year:	1939
Engine:	2 Bristol Hercules XI, 14-cylinder radial, air-cooled, 1,389 hp each
Wingspan:	86 ft 4 in (26.26 m)
Length:	60 ft 11 in (18.54 m)
Height:	17 ft 5 in (5.31 m)
Takeoff weight:	29,538 lb (13,381 kg)
Maximum speed:	254 mph (410 km/h) at 12,530 ft (3,810 m)
Ceiling:	19,050 ft (5,790 m)
Range:	1,539 miles (2,478 km)
Armament:	8 machine guns; 4,408 lb (2,000 kg) of bombs
Crew:	6

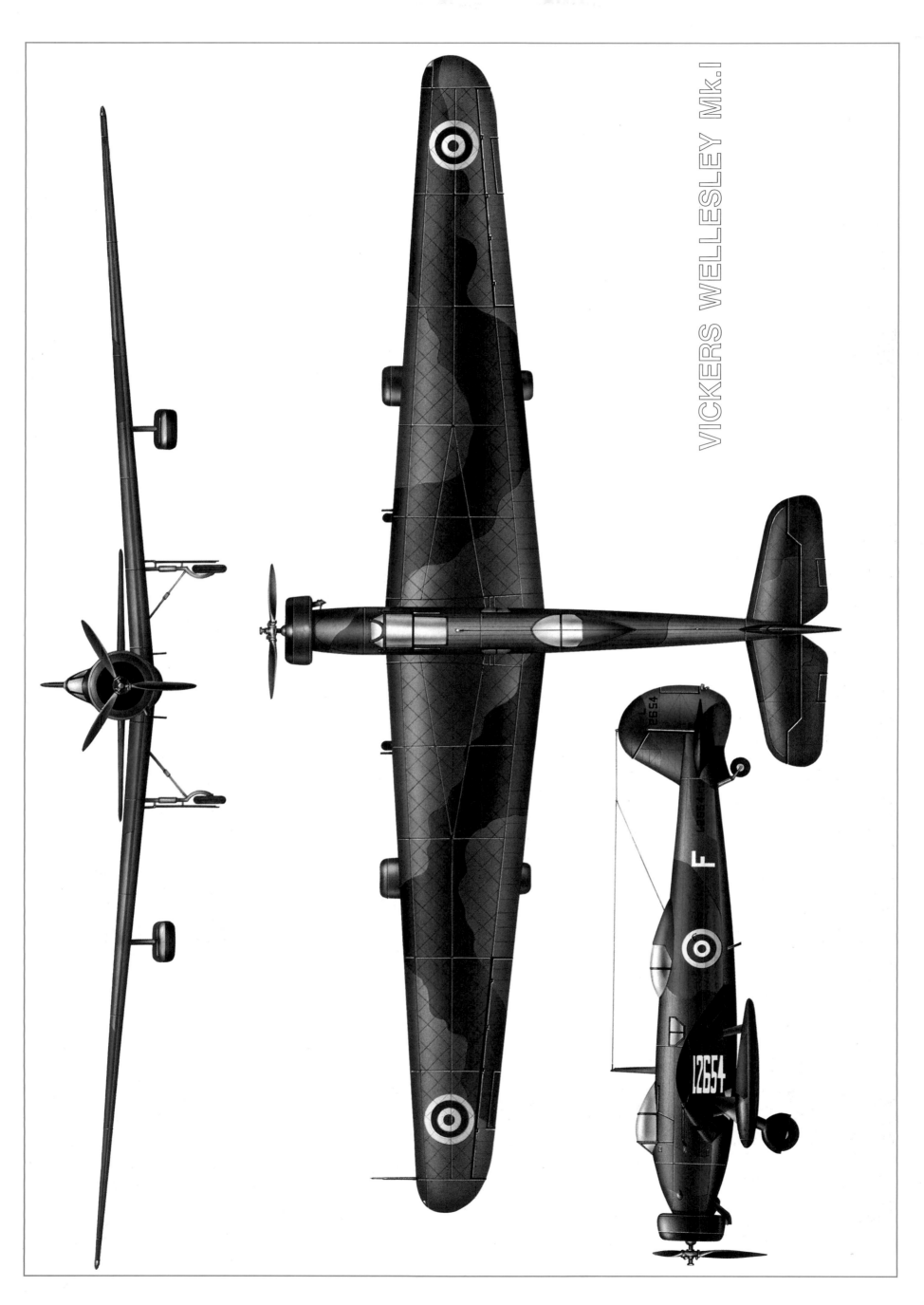

VICKERS WELLESLEY Mk.I

Of remarkably advanced conception for its time, the Vickers Wellesley nevertheless remained a transitional aircraft and was soon replaced in service by new, more modern bombers when the war broke out. However, this elegant monoplane should be remembered for a series of merits, mainly of a technical and design nature, that from many points of view made the aircraft unique among its kind. In an era still dominated by the biplane, the Wellesley (conceived in 1934), was remarkable for some innovative features that were to gain ground only in later years. These included its cantilever wings, retractable landing gear, enclosed cockpit, and, in particular, its geodetic structure (later to become famous in the Vickers Wellington bomber), which was able to guarantee great strength at the same time as minimum weight.

This project technique, derived directly from that used on the airships built by Vickers, was applied for the first time at the beginning of the 1930s by Barnes Wallis and Rex Pierson in the construction of the prototype of a single-engine biplane. Later, on the basis of the results achieved and in response to official Air Ministry specifications, Wallis designed a new model, conceived as a torpedo-bomber, which was chosen in 1934 and then went into production. At the same time, however, Vickers had developed another project in which all the technical innovations of the previous model had been finalized for the construction of a cantilever wing monoplane. This prototype made its maiden flight on June 19, 1935, and right from the start it gained the upper hand over its rival in terms of overall performance. Consequently, the order that had already been placed for the biplane model was cancelled and replaced by a request for 96 of the new aircraft, which was officially named the Wellesley. Subsequent orders brought the total number of aircraft produced up to 176.

One of the Wellesley's most remarkable external features was its wings, which were exceptionally long and thick and beneath which two carefully designed aerodynamic containers were installed to carry the bomb load. Internally, the geodetic structure was adopted for the whole wing and the part of the rear fuselage on the main longeron. The covering was in fabric, and the pilot and the observer were installed in two distinct cockpits, enclosed by a transparent cowling. The aircraft was powered by a Bristol Pegasus radial engine, which, in the production model, was able to generate 925 hp.

The first Wellesley Mk.Is came off the production line early in 1937, and RAF units began to receive the aircraft in April of the same year. Even though the squadrons in national territory were reequipped with new, two-engine bombers during 1939, those based in Africa kept the Wellesley until the early months of the war, when the aircraft took part in many bombing missions.

Although the Wellesley certainly cannot be remembered for the intensity of its war action, an assignment that the monoplane brought to a brilliant conclusion in 1938 is of some significance. In that year, five planes were modified by the RAF in an attempt to break the straight long-distance flight record. The planes were stripped of all their military equipment, supplied with more powerful Pegasus XXII engines, and adapted to carry 1,550 USgal (5,864 l) of fuel instead of the usual 510 USgal (1,932 l). After a test flight, this assignment was carried out by two Wellesleys that left Ismailia in Egypt on November 5, 1938, and succeeded in reaching Australia 48 hours later, after a 7,158.6 miles (11,520.4 km) non-stop flight.

color plate
Vickers Wellesley Mk.I 14th Royal Air Force Squadron - Sudan 1940

Aircraft:	Vickers Wellesley Mk.I
Nation:	Great Britain
Manufacturer:	Vickers Ltd.
Type:	Bomber
Year:	1937
Engine:	Bristol Pegasus XX, 9-cylinder radial, air-cooled, 925 hp
Wingspan:	74 ft 7 in (22.73 m)
Length:	39 ft 3 in (11.96 m)
Height:	12 ft 4 in (3.76 m)
Weight:	11,100 lb (5,028 kg) loaded
Maximum speed:	228 mph (367 km/h) at 19,680 ft (6,000 m)
Ceiling:	33,000 ft (10,000 m)
Range:	1,110 miles (1,786 km)
Armament:	2 machine guns; 2,000 lb (905 kg) of bombs
Crew:	2

A close up detail of the original structure of the Vickers Wellesley.

BRISTOL BLENHEIM Mk.I

A Blenheim Mk.I at Addis Abeba airport in front of *Ala Littoria*'s destroyed air terminal.

A Blenheim Mk.I of the 211th Squadron ready for takeoff from a Greek airport in 1941.

generating 608 hp) in the airframe then in construction and, in this configuration, the prototype (designated Type 142) made its maiden flight on April 12, 1935. It was an elegant all-metal, low-wing aircraft, with retractable landing gear. It was particularly impressive as far as speed was concerned: during flight tests it reached almost 307 mph (495 km/h), a performance superior to that of any other British fighter at the time.

Two months later, impressed by the aircraft's remarkable qualities, Lord Rothermere presented it to the nation. The Air Ministry lost no time in evaluating the transformation of the prototype into a bomber and, in September, placed an initial order for 150 production series aircraft. However, adapting the aircraft for military use did not prove to be a simple task. The Blenheim had to be substantially modified, especially the wing structure (the wings were, in fact, raised to provide bomb housing) and the fuselage, in order to provide positions for the armament.

The first prototype of the series took to the air on June 25, 1936, and deliveries of the aircraft to the units commenced in January 1937. Production was soon going ahead at a great pace and, before passing to the subsequent major production variant, the Mk.IV (built toward the end of 1938), no fewer than 1,552 Blenheim Mk.Is came off the assembly lines. In the new version the designers had taken the operative experiences of the aircraft into account, for these had revealed a certain inadequacy. In fact, as well as being provided with additional armament, the machine guns being increased to five and the bomb load reaching 1,325 lb (600 kg), and more powerful engines (920 hp Bristol Mercury XVs), the Blenheim Mk.IVs also featured modifications to the fuselage (with a different nose structure) and to the wings (containing larger fuel tanks). The first units began to receive the new variant in March 1939, and 168 Blenheim Mk.IVs were operative when the war broke out. Production continued until a total of 3,983 had been completed, including those of a version (Type 149) rejected by the RAF but used by Canada, where they were built on license under the name of Bolingbroke (similar overall to the Blenheim Mk.I but powered by different engines), and 945 Mk.Vs (Type 160), modified above all in their armament and fuselage. However, the latter aircraft never proved to be particularly effective.

Among the minor variants, mention should be made of 200 or so aircraft (Mk.IF) that were converted into heavy fighters and provided with four forward machine guns.

On September 3, 1939, the RAF carried out its first operative mission of World War II (a reconnaissance flight over Germany). The protagonist of this historical event was a small and fast medium bomber, the Bristol Blenheim, and, although not an outstanding combat plane, it proved to be indispensable in its role during the first three years of the war. More than 5,500 Blenheims were built in two major production versions, and they fought on almost all fronts, also bearing the insignia of the Canadian and South African air forces.

The origins of the twin-engine Bristol still constitute an original part of British aviation history. In fact, the Blenheim came into being in 1934, on the initiative of a newspaper magnate, Lord Rothermere, owner of the *Daily Mail,* who asked manufacturers to design a fast, modern twin-engine private transport plane, capable of carrying six passengers and two crew members. Lord Rothermere was very explicit in his request: the aircraft was to be "the fastest commercial plane in Europe, if not the world."

This proposal attracted the attention of the Bristol company, which happened to be working on studies for an aircraft of this type at the time. Frank Barnwell, the designer, had no hesitation in installing two powerful Bristol Mercury radial engines (each

color plate
Bristol Blenheim Mk.I 211th Squadron RAF - Greece 1940

Aircraft:	Bristol Blenheim Mk.I
Nation:	Great Britain
Manufacturer:	Bristol Aeroplane Co. Ltd.
Type:	Bomber
Year:	1937
Engine:	2 Bristol Mercury VIII, 9-cylinder radial, air-cooled, 840 hp each
Wingspan:	56 ft 4 in (17.17 m)
Length:	39 ft 9 in (12.12 m)
Height:	9 ft 10 in (2.99 m)
Weight:	12,500 lb (5,670 kg) loaded
Maximum speed:	260 mph (418 km/h) at 11,800 ft (3,600 m)
Ceiling:	27,280 ft (8,315 m)
Range:	1,215 miles (1,810 km)
Armament:	2 machine guns; 1,000 lb (454 kg) of bombs
Crew:	3

A Beaufighter in service with the Browdy Station Flight, armed with rockets.

Powerful and versatile, the Bristol Beaufighter proved to be unmatchable in a great number of roles: conceived as a heavy fighter, it was used for the duration of the war and on all fronts as a night fighter, a fighter-bomber, a torpedo-bomber, a ground attack plane, and an antishipping aircraft. No fewer than 5,562 of these aircraft in numerous versions came off the assembly lines from 1940 to September 1945, and their operative career continued well beyond the end of World War II: they were active in the front line of the RAF up to 1950, while the last ones, used for target towing, remained in service for another ten years.

The project (initially designated Type 156) originated toward the end of 1938, and the Air Ministry immediately gave it a good reception, thanks to the limited development times guaranteed by the Bristol company's technicians. In fact, the airframe of the new aircraft was fundamentally based on that of the Beaufort torpedo plane (Type 152), at that time already at the prototype stage, and it retained the wings, the tail fins, and the landing gear. On the other hand, the front part of the fuselage (carefully studied to contain the heavy armament consisting of four 20 mm cannons) was entirely different, while two Bristol Hercules radial engines were chosen as power plants.

This proposal, presented in October, resulted in a request for four prototypes, the first of which took to the air on July 17, 1939. The aircraft was an all-metal, cantilever, mid-wing monoplane with retractable rear tricycle landing gear. Flight testing revealed its excellent overall performance, especially its speed, the first prototype reaching 335 mph (539 km/h) at an altitude of 16,500 ft (5,000 m). However, a series of problems emerged in the operation of the first versions of the Hercules engines. These were overcome after it was decided to adopt the more powerful XI version in the production series.

A great number of Beaufighters (300 aircraft) were ordered before it had even made its maiden flight and the aircraft of the initial Mk.IF variant began to equip the units of Fighter Command on September 2, 1940. The first Mk.ICs were delivered beginning in the spring of 1941, destined to equip Coastal Command,

and total production of the first series amounted to 910 aircraft, including 54 destined for Australia. The Beaufighter Mk.IFs were used mainly as night fighters, although 80 or so were modified (increased fuel capacity, elimination of the armament on the wings and of the desert equipment) for use as daylight fighters and served mainly in the Mediterranean area and Africa.

The great demand for Hercules engines for the heavy bombers led to the construction of a second production variant, the Mk.II, characterized by the installation of two in-line 1,280 hp Rolls-Royce Merlin engines. The 450 aircraft built (the first took to the air on March 22, 1941) were all of the fighter version (Mk.IIF) and were used for the defense of national territory at night.

Fortunately, the lack of radial engines that had been feared never arose, and the appearance of new and more powerful versions of the Hercules stimulated further development of the Beaufighter. The third major production variant (the 1942 Mk.VI) was built adopting Hercules XVI radial engines, capable of generating 1,693 hp at 7,545 ft (2,300 m), as standard. The increase in power not only improved the aircraft's performance, but also made it possible to carry more armament. In the anti-shipping versions (Mk.VIC) this included torpedoes and rockets. The Beaufighter torpedo planes' first missions took place in April 1943 and continued with growing success for almost the entire duration of the war. The fighter variant (Mk.VIF), in particular, was the first to be used in India and Burma. Before passing to the final production variant (the Mk.X), a total of 1,832 Beaufighter Mk.VIs came off the assembly lines.

color plate

Bristol Beaufighter Mk.IF 600th Night Fighter Squadron Royal Air Force - Great Britain 1941

Aircraft:	Bristol Beaufighter Mk.IF
Nation:	Great Britain
Manufacturer:	Bristol Aeroplane Co.Ltd.
Type:	Fighter
Year:	1940
Engine:	2 Bristol Hercules XI, 14-cylinder radial, air-cooled, 1,400 hp each
Wingspan:	57 ft 10 in (17.63 m)
Length:	41 ft 4 in (12.50 m)
Height:	15 ft 10 in (4.83 m)
Weight:	21,000 lb (9,500 kg) loaded
Maximum speed:	321 mph (516 km/h) at 15,800 ft (4,800 m)
Ceiling:	26,500 ft (8,000 m)
Range:	1,170 miles (1,890 km)
Armament:	4 × 20 mm cannons; 6 machine guns
Crew:	2

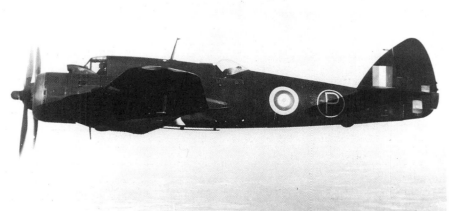

The prototype of the Beaufighter night fighter.

A Beaufighter light bomber taking off in Malta for a combat mission.

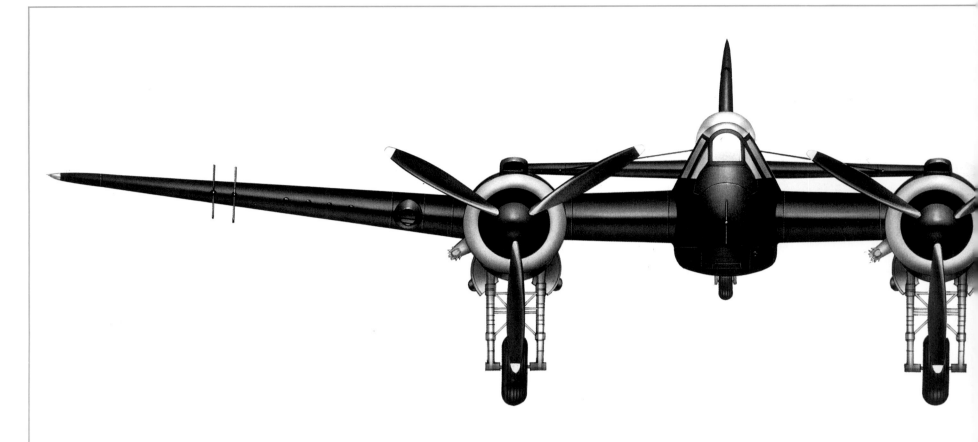

BRISTOL BEAUFIGHTER Mk.IF

BQ◉F R2256

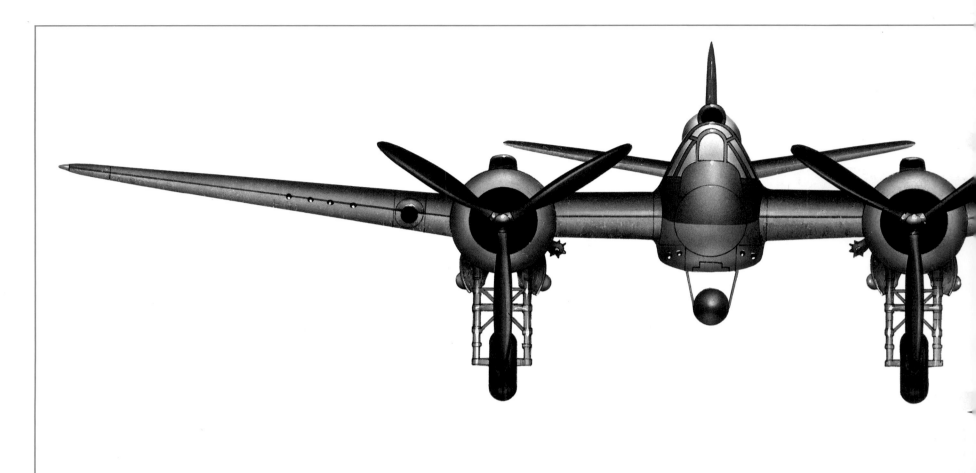

BRISTOL BEAUFIGHTER Mk.X

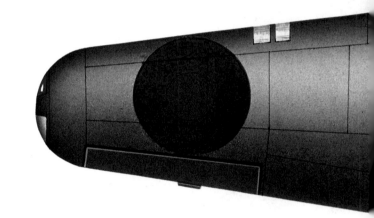

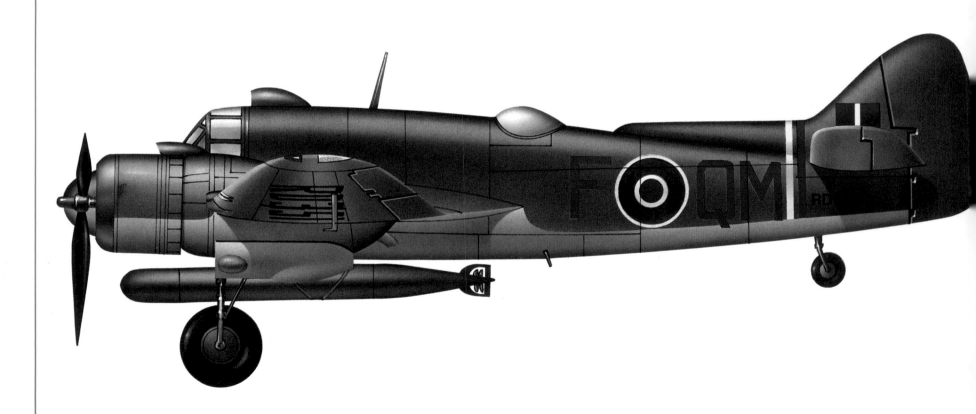

Although conceived back in 1938, the Bristol Beaufighter proved invincible in a great number of roles right until the end of the war. In fact, it served as a heavy fighter, night fighter, fighter-bomber, ground attack plane, torpedo plane, and in anti-submarine and anti-shipping attacks. The final version, the Mk.X, was prepared expressly for anti-shipping use. In all, 2,205 of this version were constructed and were intended almost exclusively for the units of the Royal Air Force Coastal Command. They had started to use the Beaufighters in the spring of 1941, with the Mk.IC series. Their career became increasingly intensive with the use of the more powerful Mk.VICs of 1942, in which rockets and torpedoes were adopted for the first time. The combat missions of the Beaufighter torpedo planes (officially christened Torbeau) began in April 1943, and continued successfully for practically the entire duration of the conflict.

In 1943, these aircraft were joined by the first of the new variant. The Beaufighter Mk.X was fitted with XVII series Bristol Hercules radial engines (generating 1,795 hp), designed to supply maximum power at low altitudes. Its armament included virtually the entire range of weapons tested in the previous versions: rockets, a torpedo and bombs could be carried with equal ability and in various combinations. In addition, an AI Mk.VIII research radar was installed in the nose. However, the greater weight of the radar affected both its directional and longitudinal stability, and made it necessary to increase the balances' surface area and to fit the aircraft with a large fin on its back. Despite this, and thanks to the great firing power of the arms on board, the Mk.Xs proved to be deadly and an extremely efficient aircraft, especially against submarines. In March 1945, aircraft of the 236th and 254th Squadrons of Coastal Command located and destroyed no fewer than five German U-Boots within 48 hours. These Beaufighters had a particularly intensive career in northern Europe and the Mediterranean.

The last production series, designated Mk.XIC, also went to Coastal Command. These aircraft were basically Mk.Xs without torpedo launching equipment and 163 were completed. About 50 of them were supplied to the Royal Australian Air Force. Moreover, between 1944 and 1945, Australia built a further 364 on license, which were designated Beaufighter Mk.21. They carried out an important role in the Pacific: continuous attack missions against Japanese shipping.

In fact, it was in this role that the "Beau" earned perhaps the

A Beaufighter T.F.X. in flight over the North Sea.

most significant nick-name of its career: Whispering Death.

Another variant is also worthy of mention. Designated Mk.XII, it never went beyond the project phase: the aircraft's frame was notably reinforced, in order to allow an increase in the bomb load, while its power was entrusted to a pair of Bristol Hercules 27 radial engines.

color plate
Bristol Beaufighter Mk.X 254th Squadron - Coastal Command Royal Air Force - Great Britain 1943

Aircraft:	Bristol Beaufighter Mk.X
Nation:	Great Britain
Manufacturer:	Bristol Aeroplane Co. Ltd.
Type:	Fighter-bomber
Year:	1943
Engine:	2 Bristol Hercules XVII, 14-cylinder radial, air-cooled, 1,795 hp each
Wingspan:	57 ft 11 in (17.63 m)
Length:	41 ft 9 in (12.70 mm)
Height:	15 ft 10 in (4.83 m)
Weight:	25,231 lb (11,430 kg)
Maximum speed:	303 mph (488 km/h) at 1,315 ft (400 m)
Ceiling:	15,049 ft (4,575 m)
Range:	1,469 miles (2,367 km)
Armament:	4 x 20 mm cannons; 7 machine guns; 2,132 lb (966 kg) of bombs
Crew:	2

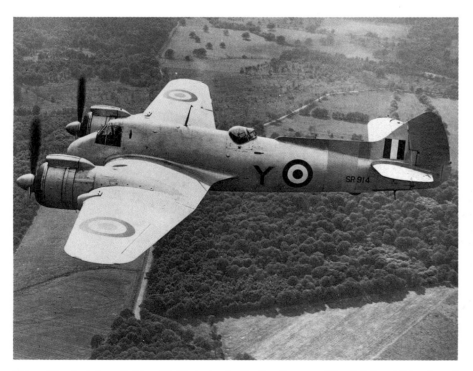
One of the last Beaufighter Mk.Xs to be built after the war. The tail fin of this aircraft is connected to the fuselage.

A Beaufighter during a rocket attack on German shipping targets.

As well as the effective Beaufighter, another aircraft built by the Bristol company had long been the standard torpedo plane in service in the Royal Air Force's Coastal Command. This was the Beaufort, a sturdy and fast aircraft that for three years (from 1940 to 1943) carried out its role in an excellent manner, being used mainly in the North Sea, the Atlantic and the Mediterranean. Total production in Great Britain amounted to 1,121 aircraft in two series, characterized mainly by the adoption of different types of engine. To these were added a further 700 aircraft built in Australia.

The specifications that gave rise to the Beaufort were issued by the British Air Ministry in 1935. There were two distinct requests: the first for a monoplane torpedo aircraft powered by two Bristol Perseus radial engines; the second for a bomber reconnaissance aircraft. Both sets of specifications were fulfilled by Bristol with the creation of derivatives from the excellent project that had led to the Type 142 Blenheim: the first with the development of the Type 152, the second with the Type 149 Bolingbroke, which was built in Canada.

Work on the Type 152 began in the summer of 1936, on the basis of an initial contract for 78 production series aircraft, and the prototype of the Beaufort took to the air for the first time on October 15, 1938. It was an all-metal mid-wing monoplane that closely resembled the Blenheim Mk.IV, retaining its layout and general structure. The main difference lay in the fuselage, which was noticeably higher and ended in a turret on its back provided with two machine guns. Another turret, provided with two similar weapons, was situated in the front part of the nose. The offensive armament consisted of a 1,325 lb (600 kg) bomb load, although this could be increased to 1,986 lb (900 kg) in exceptional circumstances, or a 1,611 lb (730 kg) torpedo. It was powered by a pair of Bristol Taurus 14-cylinder radial engines, whose potential increased from 1,010 hp in the initial production series aircraft to 1,130 hp in the subsequent ones. The change to this power plant instead of the one planned originally was made necessary by the remarkable increase in weight (approximately 25 percent) that occurred during the development of the project.

The new engines actually contributed to slowing down preparation of the aircraft, already hampered by many problems. In fact, the series of flight tests and operative evaluations was particularly long, and it was not until the beginning of 1940 that the first Beaufort Mk.Is (955 built in all) began to equip the 22nd Squadron of Coastal Command. The aircraft's operational debut took place on the night of April 15-16, with a mine-laying mission.

Production went ahead with the Beaufort Mk.II, in which 1,200 hp American Pratt & Whitney Twin Wasp radial engines were adopted. The first of the 166 built took to the air in September 1941. Two other versions were proposed but never followed up: the Mk.III, with a pair of 1,280 hp Rolls-Royce Merlin XX engines,

A Beaufort employed by the Kemley Station Flight.

and the Mk.IV, with two 1,267 hp Bristol Taurus XX engines.

The adoption of American engines characterized an interesting production series of Beauforts built in Australia from 1940. There were several versions, and all were entirely different due to the characteristics of the engine and the propellers: the first was the Mk.V (which took to the air in May 1941, a total of 50 being built in all), that was followed by 30 Mk.VAs, by 60 Mk.VIs, by 40 Mk.VIIs, and by 520 Mk.VIIIs. The final variant remained in production until August 1944 and was characterized by improvements to the fuel tanks, armament, and navigation system.

---

color plate

Bristol Beaufort 42nd Squadron Royal Air Force - Thorney Island, Great Britain 1940

Aircraft:	Bristo Beaufort Mk.I
Nation:	Great Britain
Manufacturer:	Bristol Aeroplane Co. Ltd.
Type:	Torpedo-bomber
Year:	1940
Engine:	2 Bristol Taurus VI, 14-cylinder radial, air-cooled, 1,130 hp each
Wingspan:	57 ft 10 in (17.62 m)
Length:	44 ft 7 in (13.59 m)
Height:	12 ft 5 in (3.79 m)
Weight:	21,223 lb (9,630 kg) loaded
Maximum speed:	265 mph (426 km/h) at 6,000 ft (1,800 m)
Ceiling:	16,500 ft (5,050 m)
Range:	1,600 miles (2,575 km)
Armament:	4 machine guns; 1 × 1,611 lb (730 kg) torpedo
Crew:	4

An Australian built Bristol Beaufort Mk.VI. The aircraft produced in Australia were fitted with engines made in the United States.

BRISTOL BEAUFORT Mk.I

BOULTON PAUL DEFIANT Mk.I

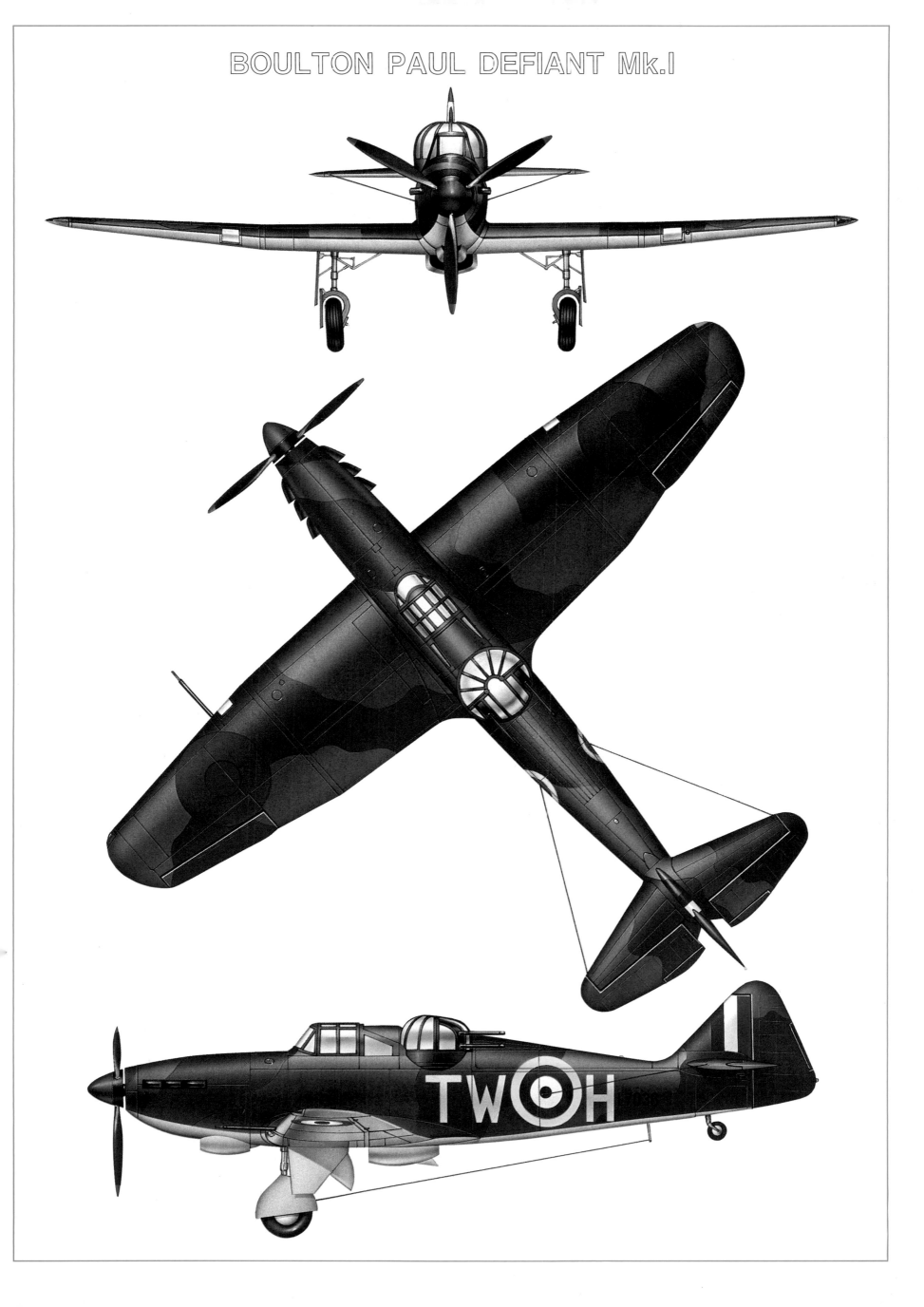

The Boulton Paul Defiant proved, on the whole, to be a rather unsuccessful aircraft. This was due not so much to the value of the project (modern and quite advanced for the time) as to the inadequacy of the operative concept that led to its being built. This foresaw the use of a daylight fighter armed in an entirely unconventional manner, with four machine guns concentrated in a turret on the aircraft's back and hydraulically controlled in place of the fixed ones traditionally installed on the wings or in the nose. In practice, operative experiences fully revealed the unsatisfactory nature of this solution: not only was the aircraft hampered by serious limitations in handling and overall performance due to the additional weight of the second crew member and the turret, but it was also particularly vulnerable in pure combat. Its only successes occurred during the first weeks of fighting and were due mainly to the element of surprise. After a brief operational career in the summer of 1940, the Defiants were relegated to the role of night fighters, in which they proved to be somewhat more effective, and eventually they were used for target towing.

In Britain, the installation of a turret on a fighter had already been carried out, in 1934, on several Hawker Demon biplanes, in which Frazer-Nash type turrets had been fitted. The experience proved, on the whole, to be satisfactory, and the following year the Air Ministry issued specifications calling for the development of a two-seater monoplane fighter provided with similar armament. Prototypes were prepared both by Hawker and Boulton Paul, and the latter was eventually chosen, in consideration above all of the heavy commitments that already saturated Hawker's productive capacity.

The first prototype (designated P.82) made its maiden flight on August 11, 1937. It was a modern all-metal low-wing monoplane with retractable landing gear. It was powered by a Rolls-Royce Merlin I engine that drove a three-bladed, variable pitch, metal propeller. The turret with the four machine guns was situated behind the pilot's cockpit, and its installation was carefully blended from an aerodynamic point of view. Following a series of flight tests and operative evaluations, the aircraft was accepted and went into production. The first Defiant Mk.I took to the air on July 30, 1939, and deliveries to the units began at the end of the year. Its operative debut took place on May 12, 1940, at Dunkirk, where the new fighters enjoyed a brief period of success.

In the meantime, a second production variant, the Mk.II, had been prepared with the aim of improving the Defiant's unsatisfactory performance. It flew for the first time on June 20, 1940, and 210 were built. Two aircraft of the first series served as prototypes: the most obvious variation lay in the fitting of a more powerful Merlin XX engine, while other minor modifications concerned the vertical rudder (greater surface area), the engine feeding and cooling systems, and the capacity of the fuel tanks (which was increased).

In practice, however, these modernizations served little purpose. Apart from its use as a night fighter, the Defiant Mk.II (like its predecessors) was also relegated to the role of target towing in the end. For this specific task, 140 new planes were built. A total of 1,064 Defiants came off the assembly lines, and production ceased in 1943.

---

color plate

Boulton Paul Defiant Mk.I 141st Fighter Squadron Royal Air Force — West Malling (Great Britain) 1940 — Battle of Britain

---

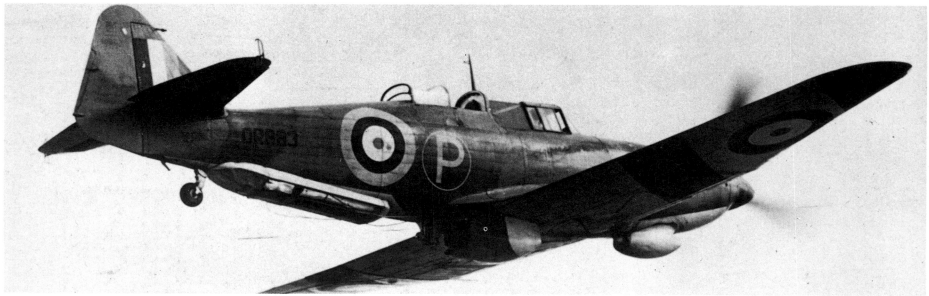

Defiant transformed into a target tug, with typical yellow and black markings on the belly.

Boulton Paul Defiant with tropical filter over the oil-cooler air intakes.

Aircraft:	Boulton Paul Defiant Mk.I
Nation:	Great Britain
Manufacturer:	Boulton Paul Aircraft Ltd.
Type:	Fighter
Year:	1940
Engine:	Rolls-Royce Merlin III, 12 cylinder V, liquid-cooled, 1,030 hp
Wingspan:	39 ft 4 in (11.99 m)
Length:	35 ft 4 in (10.77 m)
Height:	12 ft 2 in (3.70 m)
Weight:	8,350 lb (3,785 kg) loaded
Maximum speed:	303 mph (487 km/h) at 16,500 ft (5,000 m)
Ceiling:	30,350 ft (9.250 m)
Range:	465 miles (748 km)
Armament:	4 machine guns
Crew:	2

The first great air battle of World War II was fought in the skies over England from August 13 to October 31, 1940. During these months, which proved to be decisive in the outcome of the war, one of the immortal protagonists of the bitter confrontation between the Royal Air Force and the Luftwaffe was the Hawker Hurricane. In fact, it was the task of this monoplane fighter (the first of its kind to be supplied to the British units) to bear much of the initial brunt of the German attack until a sufficient number of the more reliable Spitfires became available. Although generally inferior to the Messerschmitt Bf.109Es, the RAF Fighter Command's Hurricanes fought with great courage and determination.

Leaving aside the events linked with the Battle of Britain, the Hurricane was respected for many other reasons: it was the first British interceptor to carry eight machine guns; the first to exceed the 300 mph (480 km/h) barrier; and it was the fighter most widely used by the RAF during the first two years of the war (in 1940, in particular, more than half the German planes shot down were destroyed by Hurricanes). Its operational career (which began at the end of 1937 and continued up till the end of the war on virtually all battlefronts) was enviable, as was the quantity of aircraft built. Production continued without interruption from 1936 to the end of 1944, and a total of 14,233 were built in three separate basic versions, which were in turn developed into numerous other sub-series for naval use too. At a practical level, it was thanks to the great versatility that was one of its main features that the Hurricane was able to play such an important role in the war: initially conceived purely as an interceptor, it provided excellent service as a night fighter, a fighter-bomber, or a ground attack plane.

Sydney Camm, who was already famous for having designed some of Britain's most ''classic'' fighters during the late 1920s, started work on the Hurricane project in January 1934. Previously, he had worked on the design of another monoplane, which was to have been provided with a Rolls-Royce Goshawk engine, but as soon as he heard of the newly developed Merlin engine, he modified his design in order to accommodate this more reliable power plant. The prototype made its maiden flight on November 6, 1935, and immediately produced excellent results, especially in terms of pure speed — 314 mph at 16,450 ft (506 km/h at 5,000 m) — and climb, reaching 14,800 ft (4,500 m) in 5 minutes and 7 seconds after take off. The Hurricane was a low-wing monoplane with retractable landing gear. It had an all-metal airframe and was entirely covered in fabric, apart from the front part of the fuselage, which had a metal covering. The original two-bladed wooden propeller was replaced later by a metal three-bladed one with variable pitch.

The Hawker company was already preparing to put the plane into mass production, convinced of the project's great potential. The official reply was not long in coming: on June 3, 1936, an order was placed for an initial lot of 600 planes. The first Hurricane

Tropical version Hurricanes from a North African airport.

Factory fresh Hawker Hurricane Mk.I with three-bladed propeller, still lacking the Bomber unit codes.

Mk.Is came off the production line in October, and were delivered to the First Squadron of the Fighter Command two months later. A few of these planes' features differed from those of the prototype: the introduction of a 1,030 hp Merlin engine, and alterations of the exhaust, the canopy, and the landing gear fairings.

When the war broke out, 497 Hurricanes were in service in 18 squadrons, which had become 24 by the eve of the Battle of Britain. In August, 32 squadrons were equipped with Hurricanes, as compared to 19 with Spitfires. This disparity, but most of all the inherent differences in the two planes, led Fighter Command to use the Spitfires against the German fighters and the Hurricanes to block the daily incursions of the German bombers.

color plate

Hawker Hurricane Mk.I 601st Royal Air Force Squadron - Battle of Britain - 1940

Aircraft:	Hawker Hurricane Mk.I
Nation:	Great Britain
Manufacturer:	Hawker Aircraft Ltd.
Type:	Fighter
Year:	1937
Engine:	Rolls-Royce Merlin II, 12-cylinder V, air-cooled, 1,030 hp
Wingspan:	40 ft (12.19 m)
Length:	31 ft 5 in (9.55 m)
Height:	13 ft 1 in (3.99 m)
Weight:	6,600 lb (2,993 kg) loaded
Maximum speed:	320 mph (515 km/h) at 20,000 ft (6,100 m)
Ceiling:	33,200 ft (10,120 m)
Range:	460 miles (740 km)
Armament:	8 machine guns
Crew:	1

Hawker Hurricane Mk.I of the initial production series, with two-bladed propeller, at a Belgian airport during the early days of the war.

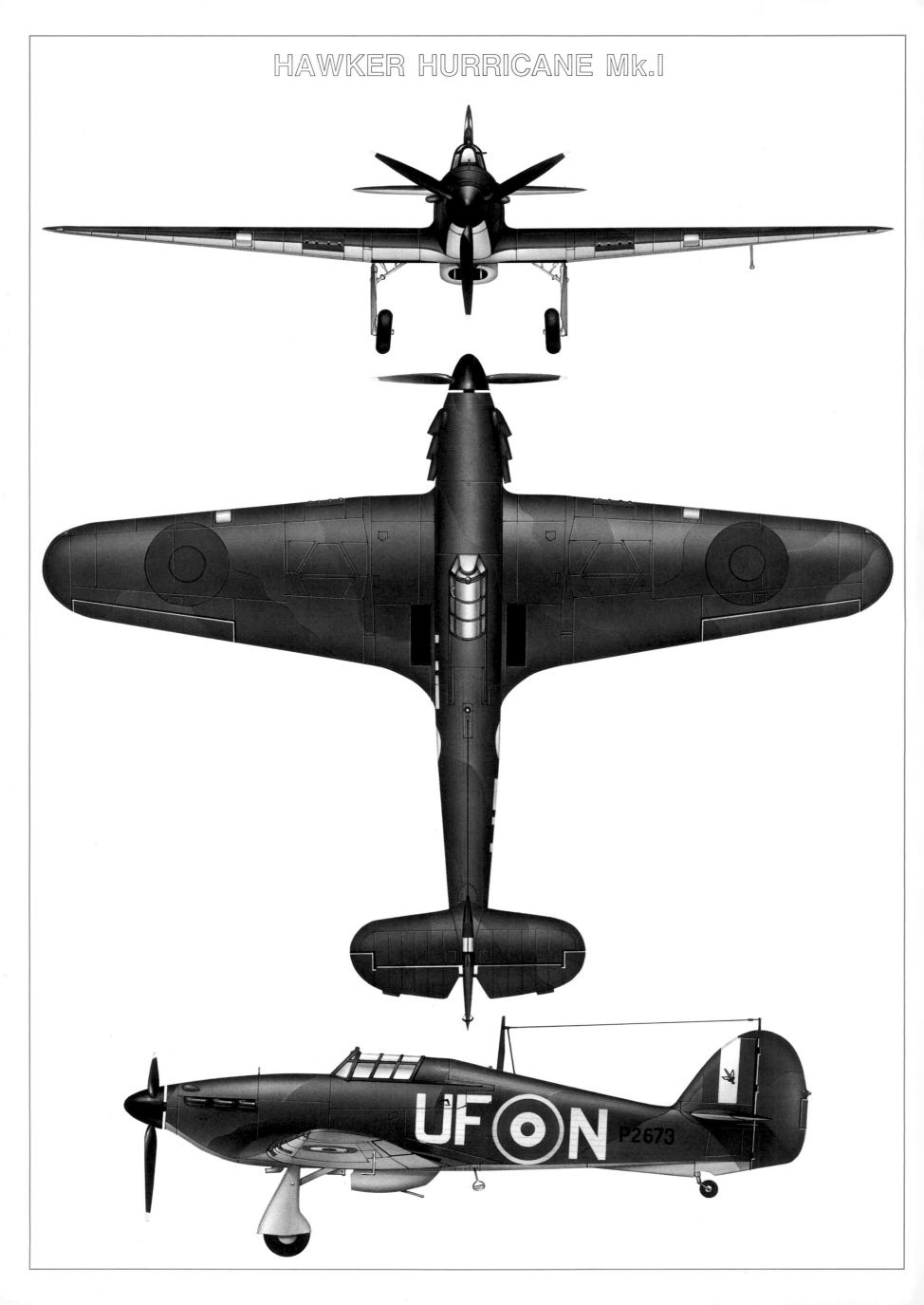

HAWKER HURRICANE Mk.I

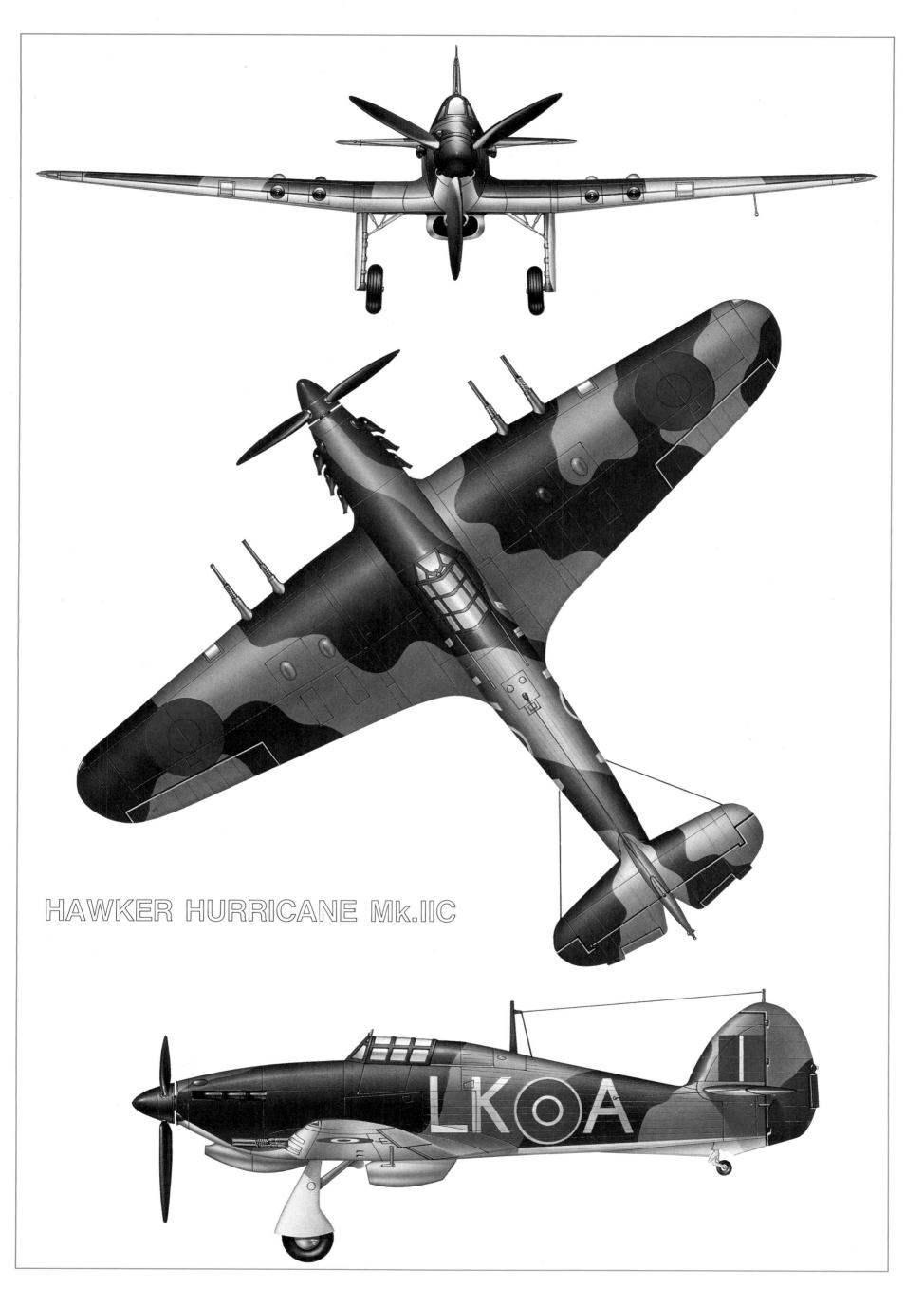

HAWKER HURRICANE Mk.IIC

As the war advanced it gave a great impetus to the production of the first version of the Hurricane. Hawker alone built 1,924 of the Mk.I series, to which were added another 1,850 completed by Gloster. In the meantime, production on license had begun in Canada (by the Canadian Car & Foundry), where no fewer than 1,451 Hurricanes were to be built. However, this quantity did not prevent Sydney Camm's fighter from being developed at a qualitative level also. In fact, in September 1940, the first aircraft of the second major production variant, the Mk.II, appeared. This was the series that was eventually built in the greatest number, a total of approximately 7,300 aircraft being completed in all.

The Hurricane Mk.II was initially developed by installing a 1,280 hp Rolls-Royce Merlin XX engine on the airframe of the first series. Thus modified, the fighter assumed the designation of Mk.IIA Series 1. At the same time, two new interchangeable wings were designed: the first was capable of housing twelve 7.7 mm Browning machine guns, and the second four 20 mm Oerlikon/Hispano cannons. Moreover, both wing types allowed for the installation and the transportation of two bombs, weighing either 250 lb (113 kg) or 500 lb (227 kg), thus intensifying the role of fighter-bomber that was to become dominant in the subsequent phases of the Hurricane's operative career.

The aircraft of the initial subseries were followed by a few belonging to a second, temporary version (the Mk.IIA Series 2), the fuselage of which was lengthened and strengthened, to allow for the installation of the new wing. These Hurricanes maintained the original wing and armament, but it was not long before the definitive versions began to come off the assembly lines. The first of these was the Mk.IIB, characterized by armament consisting of 12 machine guns; the second was the Mk.IIC, provided with four cannons.

Hawker, Gloster, and Austin built 3,100 Hurricane Mk.IIBs, while production of the Mk.IIC series was higher still, amounting to 3,400 aircraft. These two subvariants equipped no fewer than 96 RAF units between 1941 and 1944 and were widely used on all fronts, especially in North Africa and the Far East.

More powerful armament also characterized the final variant of the Mk.II series, the D, which appeared in 1942. The fitting of a new wing allowed for the airframe to be noticeably rejuvenated (its design dated back to 1934) and for full advantage to be taken of the aircraft's performance in the role of ground attack. The Hurricane Mk.IIDs (approximately 800 of which were built) were armed with four 40 mm Vickers or Rolls-Royce cannons, in addition to one or two 7.7 mm machine guns to facilitate the aim of the prin-

A pair of tropical-version Hurricane Mk.IICs in flight over the Libyan desert.

cipal weapons. This firepower proved to be deadly in antitank attack and was exploited mainly in North Africa and the Far East.

From the Mk.II series were derived the most widely used variants of the Sea Hurricane, the naval version of the fighter which beginning in 1941, operated on board convoys in the Atlantic in order to protect them from the threat of the four-engined German FW 200 Condors. Approximately 50 Sea Hurricane Mk.IAs, developed from the Hurricane Mk.I, were followed by about 340 Sea Hurricane Mk.IBs (derived from the Mk.IIA Series 2 aircraft) and 400 Sea Hurricane Mk.ICs (derived, in their turn, from the similar Mk.IIB and IICs and armed with four 20 mm cannons). The final variant was the Sea Hurricane Mk.IIC (approximately 400 of which were built), a direct transformation of the Mk.IIC land version. Their use in a naval context was particularly intense during the middle years of the war. The Sea Hurricanes' most famous mission took place in the summer of 1942, on board the aircraft carriers *Indomitable, Eagle,* and *Victorious,* while protecting a convoy heading for Malta: in three days of fighting against the air forces of the Axis, 39 enemy aircraft were destroyed with the loss of only eight fighters.

color plate

Hawker Hurricane Mk.IIC 87th Fighter Squadron Royal Air Force - Western Desert (North Africa) 1941-42

Aircraft:	Hawker Hurricane Mk.IIC
Nation:	Great Britain
Manufacturer:	Hawker Aircraft Ltd.
Type:	Fighter-bomber
Year:	1941
Engine:	Rolls-Royce Merlin XX, 12-cylinder V, liquid-cooled, 1,280 hp
Wingspan:	40 ft (12.19 m)
Length:	32 ft 2 in (9.80 m)
Height:	13 ft 1 in (3.99 m)
Takeoff weight:	7,800 lb (3,533 kg) loaded
Maximum speed:	339 mph (545 km/h) at 22,000 ft (6,700 m)
Ceiling:	35,600 ft (10,850 m)
Range:	460 miles (740 km)
Armament:	4 × 20 mm cannons; 1,000 lb (454 kg) of bombs
Crew:	1

A formation of Hurricane Mk.IICs, with 20 mm cannons on the wings.

The second major production variant of the Hawker Hurricane was the Mk.II, the first of which appeared in September 1940. In this series (which was also the one of which most aircraft were produced, amounting to approximately 7,300) Sydney Camm's project was definitively adapted for the role of fighter-bomber. The final version (the Mk.IID of 1942) had a new wing, which remarkably renewed the airframe, whose design dated back to 1934, as well as allowing for further improvements in the aircraft's performance in ground attack. The Hurricane Mk.IIDs (of which approximately 800 were built) were armed with four Vickers or Rolls-Royce 40 mm cannons, in addition to one or two 7.7 mm machine guns to facilitate the aim of the more powerful weapons. This firing power proved to be deadly in antitank attack and was exploited mainly in North Africa and the Far East.

In fact, it was the success of this configuration that led to the creation of the third and final major production variant of the Hurricane, the Mk.IV, initially designated Mk.IIE (the first 270 aircraft were delivered with this designation) the new Hurricane differed from its predecessors in the adoption of a «universal wing,» which made the potential of the aircraft's armament particularly flexible. In fact, as well as the two 7.7 mm machine guns for taking aim, it was possible to install two 40 mm antitank cannons and two bombs weighing 250 lb (113 kg) or 500 lb (227 kg) each, or, alternatively, extra ejectable fuel tanks or eight 60 lb (27 kg) rockets. Experiments using the latter weapon had been under way since February 1942 on a Hurricane in which two pairs of supports for launching three rockets each had been installed beneath the wings, and the final results had been particularly encouraging. With the definitive adoption of this deadly weapon, the Hurricane thus became the first Allied aircraft to use air-land rockets, making a remarkable increase in its operative activity possible. In addition to the new wing and the increase in armor, the Hurricane Mk.IV was fitted with one of the most powerful versions of the Rolls-Royce Merlin engine, built for use at low altitude and capable of generating a maximum of 1,298 hp. The first prototype of the Mk.IV appeared on March 14, 1943, and units of the RAF soon began to receive the 524 production series aircraft, in addition to the initial 270 Mk.IIEs. Their operative career was long and extensive, and these Hurricanes distinguished themselves particularly on the Tunisian front and in Burma. Moreover, the 6th Squadron remained in action in Italy until the end of the war and was subsequently sent to Palestine where, until January 1947, it had the honor of being the last RAF unit to be equipped with Sydney Camm's fighter.

A final attempt to strengthen the airframe still further was made in 1943, with the construction of two prototypes that were designated Hurricane Mk.V. They were fitted with an even more powerful version of the Merlin engine (the 32 generating 1,635 hp at takeoff), which was particularly suitable for use at low altitudes and drove a four-bladed propeller. The first prototype took to the air on April 3, 1943, but after a series of tests it was decided to abandon the program, and the two aircraft were reconverted into the Mk.IV configuration.

---

color plate

Hawker Hurricane Mk.IV 60th Squadron Royal Air Force - Far East

---

Aircraft:	Hawker Hurricane Mk.IV
Nation:	Great Britain
Manufacturer:	Hawker Aircraft Ltd.
Type:	Fighter-bomber
Year:	1943
Engine:	Rolls-Royce Merlin 24, 12-cylinder V, liquid-cooled, 1,298 hp
Wingspan:	40 ft 1 in (12.19 m)
Length:	32 ft 2 in (9.80 m)
Height:	13 ft 1 in (3.99 m)
Weight:	8,512 lb (3,856 kg)
Maximum speed:	283 mph (457 km/h) at 13,536 ft (4,115 m)
Ceiling:	35,690 ft (10,850 m)
Range:	480 miles (772 km)
Armament:	2 × 40 mm cannons, 2 machine guns, 1,002 lb (454 kg) of bombs
Crew:	1

A Hawker Hurricane Mk.IV equipped with auxiliary fuel tank taking off from a Balkan airport.

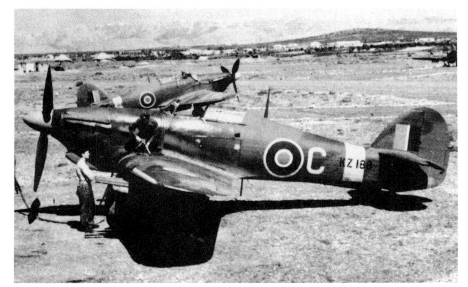

A Hurricane Mk.IV in Yugoslavia in 1944.

A Hurricane Mk.IV armed with rockets under the wings.

HAWKER HURRICANE Mk.IV

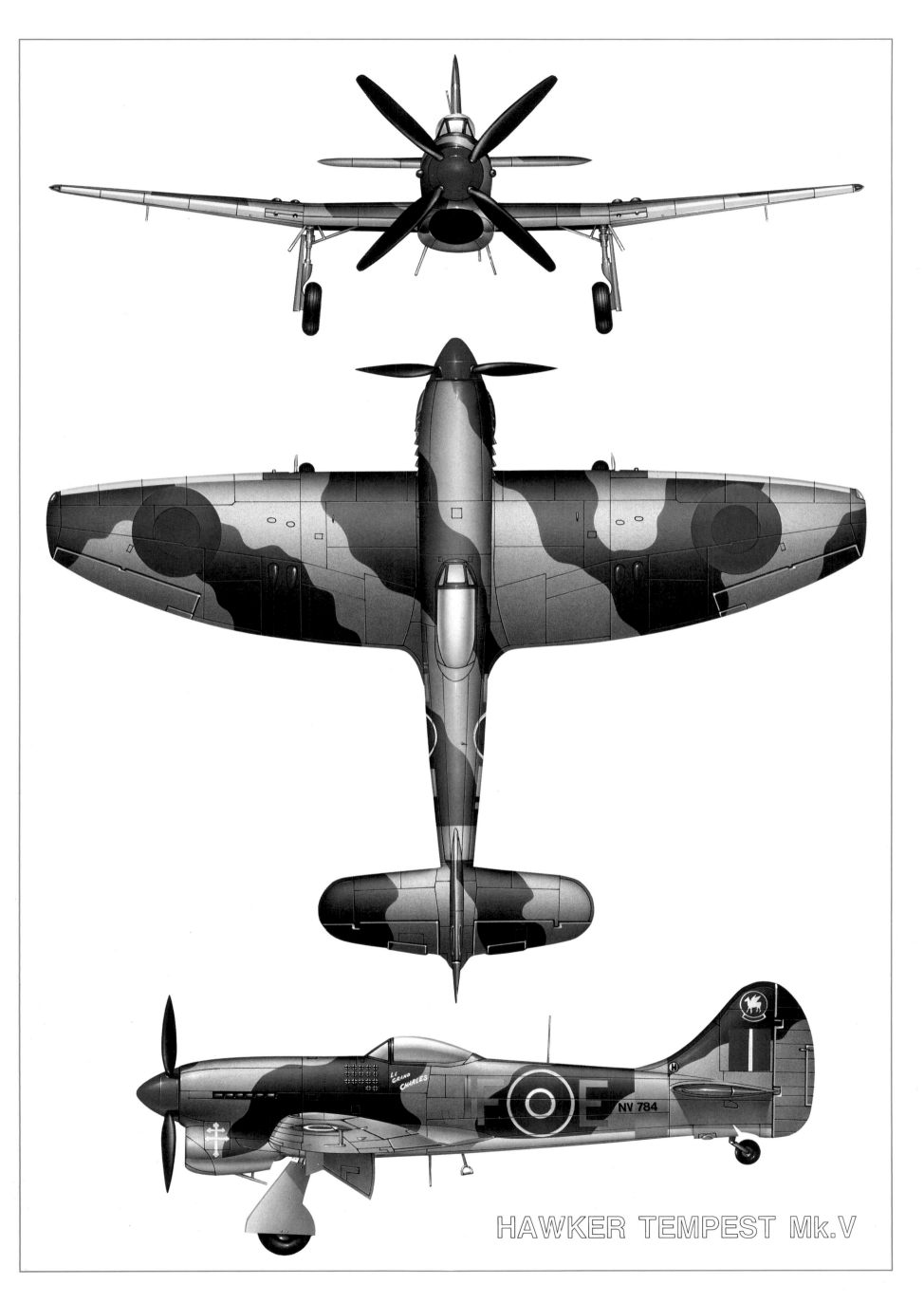

HAWKER TEMPEST Mk.V

In 1940, the Hawker Tempest represented the optimal development of the project which had given rise to the Typhoon, an aircraft that had proved to be disappointing as an interceptor, although formidable as an attack plane. Among the fastest of the propeller-driven combat planes sent into action by the RAF during the last year of the war, the Tempest distinguished itself in two particular tasks (also true of the Spitfire Mk.XIV): the pursuit of German V-1 flying bombs and the interception of the Luftwaffe's revolutionary Me.262 jet. The principal production variant during the war was the Mk.V. Up till August 1945 800 were built. The Tempest Mk.VI (142 built, differed mainly in the adoption of a 2,300 hp Napier Sabre engine) and those of the Mk.II series (764 of these were built, differing radically in that they were fitted with a 2,526 hp Bristol Centaurus radial engine) were not ready in time to participate in the war. Nevertheless, the last Tempests remained in service until 1949 and 1951, respectively.

Sydney Camm, the Hawker's chief designer, had set to work on the new project at the time of the Typhoon's first tests, with the aim of improving it. The modifications were concentrated above all on the wing, whose structure, profile and shape were completely redesigned. Different engines were chosen for the new fighter (originally designated Typhoon Mk.II, and subsequently rechristened Tempest): the 24-cylinder Napier Sabre for the Mk.I and Mk.V series; the "V-12" Rolls-Royce Griffon for the Mk.III series; and the 18-cylinder Bristol Centaurus for the Mk.II series. After the Tempest Mk.I remained at the prototype stage and following the abandonment of the project powered by the Rolls-Royce Griffon, the only basic variants that eventually went into production were the Mk.V, fitted with a Napier Sabre engine, and the Mk.II, with the Centaurus radial.

The first prototype of the family to take to the air was the Mk.V, on September 2, 1942, and the first production series aircraft appeared on June 21 of the following year. This aircraft went into service in April 1944, and right from its first missions it proved to have an outstanding performance, not only interception and altitude combat, but also in ground attack. The Tempest Mk.V was much faster than almost all its adversaries and many of its Allied counterparts. This characteristic immediately rendered it indispensible in facing the threat posed by the German V-1 flying bombs.

Its success in this particular role can be seen with the aid of a few figures. From June 13 to September 5, 1944, the merit for no fewer than 638 of the 1,771 V-1s destroyed by the British air defense was due to the Tempests. A precise combat tactic was prepared. Provided with supplementary fuel tanks that permitted

A Tempest Mk.V in flight; it has supplementary fuel tanks below the wings.

A Tempest Mk.II with Bristol Centaurus radial engine.

a maximum of four and a half hours patrolling time, the fighters flew at 9,868 ft (3,000 m), maintaining constant contact with the radar stations on the ground, which quickly supplied them with details of the paths of the V-1s. The attack was generally carried out during a dive, in that the bombs flew at altitudes ranging from 986 ft (300 m) to 7,894 ft (2,400 m), allowing the Tempests to acquire notable advantages in speed. The heavy armament on board did the rest. Although in some cases, once the ammunition was finished, many pilots succeeded in arriving alongside the V-1s and making them plunge into the sea by tipping them over with the tips of their wings.

As for the Tempest Mk.II, this prototype took to the air for the first time on June 28, 1943, and the first production series aircraft was completed on October 4 of the following year. The prototype of the Mk.VI version made its maiden flight on May 9, 1944.

A Hawker Tempest pictured at the time of the Normandy landings with invasion stripes.

color plate

Hawker Tempest Mk.V 3rd Squadron Royal Air Force - Belgium 1944. Personal aircraft of Wing Commander Pierre Clostermann

Aircraft:	Hawker Tempest Mk.V
Nation:	Great Britain
Manufacturer:	Hawker Aircraft Co. Ltd.
Type:	Fighter-bomber
Year:	1944
Engine:	Napier Sabre 11A, 24-cylinder H, liquid-cooled, 2,210 hp
Wingspan:	41 ft 1 in (12.50 m)
Length:	33 ft 9 in (10.26 m)
Height:	16 ft 1 in (4.90 m)
Weight:	13,558 lb (6,142 kg)
Maximum speed:	435 mph (702 km/h) at 18,552 (5,640 m)
Ceiling:	36,595 ft (11,125 m)
Range:	738 miles (1,190 km)
Armament:	4 x 20 mm cannons; 2,004 lb (908 kg) of bombs
Crew:	1

The Hawker Typhoon never succeeded in becoming the powerful interceptor fighter that its designers had intended. However, it did become a formidable tactical support plane, perhaps the most famous to be used in combat by the Allies during the conflict. A total of 3,330 was built in all, and production ceased in 1944.

The specifications that gave rise to the Typhoon were issued by the British Air Ministry in 1937. They called for a fighter powered by the new 2,000 hp engines that were being developed at the time: the Rolls-Royce Vulture and the Napier Sabre. The two engines were very innovative: the former consisted of 24 cylinders arranged in an X formation (in practice, two cylinder blocks from the Peregrine V-12 united on a single base); the latter consisted of 24 cylinders arranged in an H formation (two blocks of 12 horizontal cylinders placed opposite one another, each with its own shaft driving a common reducer). The program was entrusted to the Hawker Company, and Sydney Camm, its chief designer and the "inventor" of the famous Hawker Hurricane, decided to develop four prototypes: two type Rs (known as Tornadoes) with the Vulture engine, and two type Ns (Typhoons) powered by the Sabre.

The first to take to the air was the Tornado, on October 6, 1939, followed by the Typhoon prototype on February 24, 1940. The tests that followed were not particularly successful. There were continuous problems in the functioning of the power plants, as well as by serious structural weaknesses, and the preparatory phase for the two aircraft proved to be extremely long. In 1941, the program for the production of the Vulture engine was abandoned, leaving only the Typhoon in the running. However, even after production had got under way (the first aircraft of the initial Mk.IA series, with armament consisting of 12 machine guns, took to the air on May 27), the fighter continued to be plagued by serious problems that were to last throughout its operative career (deliveries to the RAF units began in September). In fact, the problems concerning weaknesses in the rear section of the fuselage and the functioning of the engines persisted: continuous mechanical breakdowns and an inability to generate the required power clearly demonstrated that the Sabre engine was still far from reaching its definitive stage. The engine's inadequacy was the main reason for the Typhoon's failure as an interceptor, and numerous accidents that led to the loss of many pilots made the Air Ministry begin to seriously consider withdrawing the aircraft from service.

It was not until the second half of 1942 that Hawker entirely managed to solve the problems that plagued the Typhoon. Consequently, having realized the aircraft's limitations and its true capacities, it was decided to use it in the role of ground attack and tactical support and no longer as an interceptor. Thus Sydney Camm's fighter began its "second career," a career that was to be brilliant and intensive for the entire duration of the conflict and in roles that were to prove entirely suited to the Typhoon's characteristics. In fact, the aircraft was extremely fast at low altitudes (in horizontal flight its performance was superior to that of the German Focke Wulf Fw.190 and even to that of the Spitfire), while its heavy armament made it extremely effective against ground targets, especially armored vehicles.

Following the construction of approximately one hundred Mk.IAs, the major production series was the Mk.IB (the prototype made its maiden flight on May 3, 1941) in which the 12 machine guns were replaced by four 20 mm cannons. These Typhoons went into service on August 19, 1942, and their bomb load was gradually increased, until it included eight rockets and a maximum of 2,004 lb (908 kg) of bombs. More powerful versions of the Sabre engines were fitted in the subsequent subseries. The Typhoon scored its greatest successes during the final year of the war, being widely used initially during the Normandy landing and then in the dramatic operations to reconquer Europe.

A formation of Hawker Typhoon Mk.IBs armed with cannons. These aircraft have the old canopy of the earlier model.

A Typhoon Mk.IB, armed with rockets beneath the wings, while taxiing. The aircraft is fitted with the new bubble canopy.

color plate

Hawker Typhoon Mk.IB 609th Squadron RAF - Biggin Hill, Great Britain 1943

Aircraft:	Hawker Typhoon Mk.IB
Nation:	Great Britain
Manufacturer:	Hawker Aircraft Co. Ltd.
Type:	Fighter
Year:	1942
Engine:	Napier Sabre IIa, 24-cylinder H, liquid-cooled, 2,210 hp
Wingspan:	41 ft 8 in (12.67 m)
Length:	32 ft 0 in (9.73 m)
Height:	14 ft 10 in (4.52 m)
Weight:	13,267 lb (6,010 kg)
Maximum speed:	404 mph (652 km/h) at 18,025 ft (5,480 m)
Ceiling:	35,100 ft (10,670 m)
Range:	608 miles (980 km)
Armament:	4 × 20 mm cannon; 2,004 lb (908 kg) of bombs
Crew:	1

HAWKER TYPHOON Mk.IB

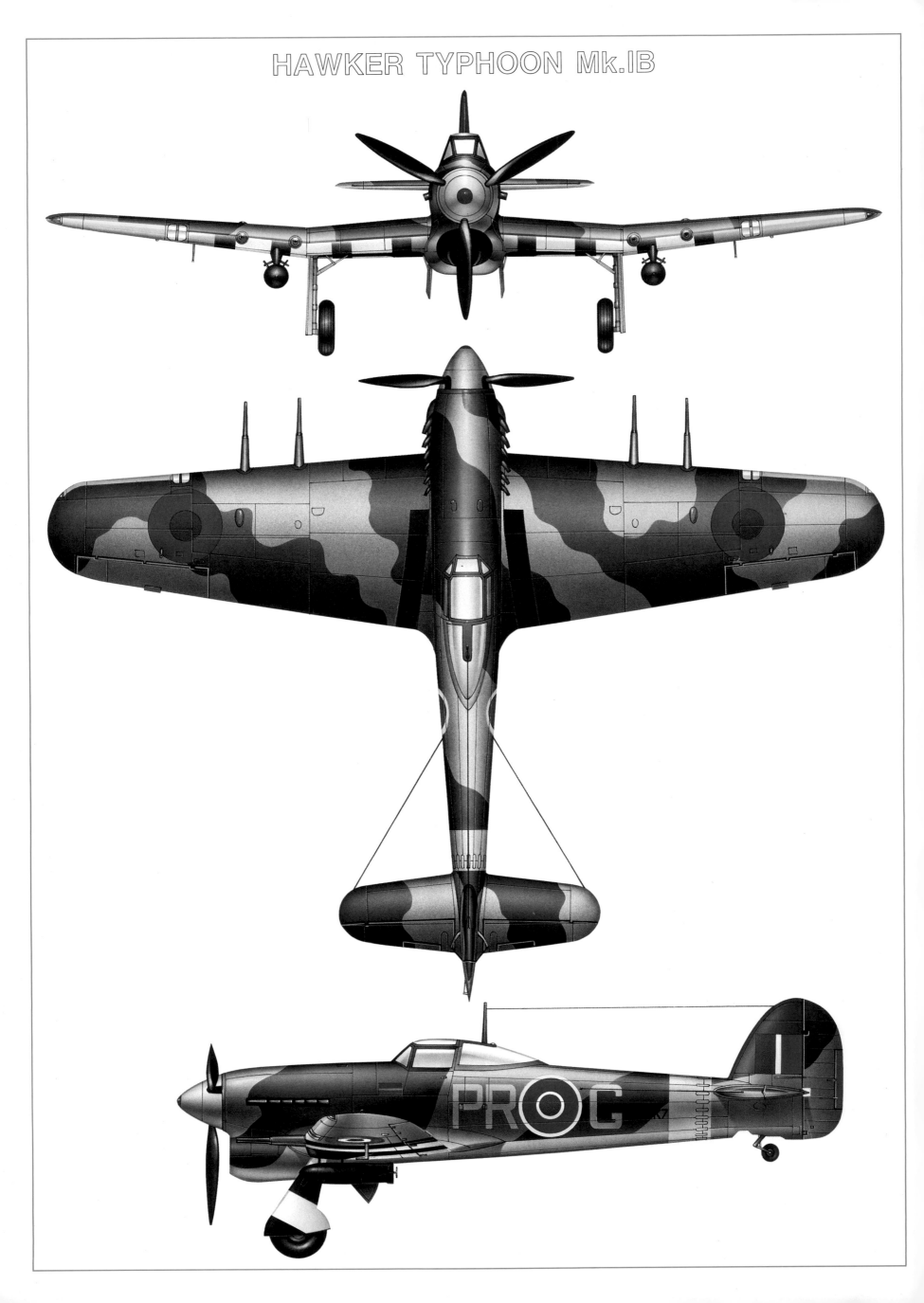

SUPERMARINE SPITFIRE Mk.I

Like the great Messerschmitt Bf.109, its direct adversary, the Supermarine Spitfire gained fame as a fighter par excellence. In the two opposing camps for which they fought, both of these aircraft became the very symbols of the nations in which they had originated. From many points of view, the development of each was conditioned by the existence of the other, by the continuous search for a margin of superiority that would lead to the gaining and maintaining of air supremacy. This confrontation began during the Battle of Britain and continued without interruption throughout World War II.

The Spitfire proved to be an aircraft that was potentially more powerful than its counterpart. This is demonstrated by the fact that, by means of a series of constant improvements, Reginald J. Mitchell's project always remained highly competitive — so much so, in fact, that its final variants remained in front-line service with the RAF well into the 1950s, when the propeller and piston engine had already been superseded by the jet. No fewer than 20,531 Spitfires, in approximately 40 versions, came off the assembly lines — the highest number of any British aircraft. The development of this remarkable series can be appreciated with the help of a few figures: the first prototype had a 990 hp Rolls-Royce Merlin C engine and was capable of reaching a maximum speed of 350 mph (562 km/h); the aircraft belonging to the F.XVIII series were powered by 2,375 hp Rolls-Royce Griffon 67s, while the 1945 Spitfire F.22 could reach a maximum speed of 450 mph (725 km/h). In the course of production, firepower (an element of prime importance in a fighter, since the quality and type of armament adopted had a direct influence on the aircraft's performance) was actually tripled, from 1,800 grams per minute to 5,400 grams.

The origins of the Spitfire provide what may be the clearest indication of the great influence that racing events had on the development of aeronautical technology in the period between the two wars. Its origins can be traced back to the series of racing seaplanes created by Mitchell in the late 1920s for the Schneider Cup, a series that culminated in the Supermarine S.6B,

Spitfire Mk.I of the initial production series, with two-bladed wooden propeller.

which won the coveted trophy outright on September 13, 1931, with a speed of 339.82 mph (547.22 km/h). Many of the technical and technological characteristics of these aircraft were adopted once again in the Spitfire, including the power plant developed by Rolls-Royce from the 2,350 hp R type engine that had made victory possible.

The prototype of the Spitfire took to the air for the first time on March 5, 1936. The fighter represented the culmination of a long study phase that had begun in 1934. It was a small, all-metal single-seater with retractable landing gear, and it had carefully studied aerodynamic lines and characteristic, elliptical wings. Moreover, its armament was to be especially powerful, considering that it included eight machine guns.

Flight tests and evaluations exceeded even the most optimistic expectations, and an initial order was placed in June for 310 aircraft. Production began in 1937, with the Mk.I series, and was soon going ahead at a great pace. By October 1939, total orders already amounted to over 4,000 aircraft. Nevertheless, reequipping was relatively slow: the Spitfire Mk.Is (of which 1,583 were built before giving way to the 1940 Mk.II version) went into service in June 1938, and barely nine squadrons were operational when the war broke out. However, this number had increased to 19 in the period immediately prior to the Battle of Britain.

A Spitfire Mk.IB with three-bladed propeller and wing armament consisting of cannons and machine guns.

A Supermarine Spitfire Mk.IIB with cannons on the wings.

color plate
Supermarine Spitfire Mk.I 610th Fighter Squadron (County of Chester) - Battle of Britain England 1941

Aircraft:	Supermarine Spitfire Mk.I
Nation:	Great Britain
Manufacturer:	Supermarine Division of Vickers-Armstrong Ltd.
Type:	Fighter
Year:	1938
Engine:	Rolls-Royce Merlin II, 12-cylinder V, liquid-cooled, 1,030 hp
Wingspan:	36 ft 10 in (11.22 m)
Length:	29 ft 11 in (9.12 m)
Height:	11 ft 5 in (3.48 m)
Weight:	5,332 lb (2,415 kg) loaded
Maximum speed:	355 mph (571 km/h) at 19,000 ft (5,800 m)
Ceiling:	34,000 (10,360 m)
Range:	500 miles (805 km)
Armament:	8 machine guns
Crew:	1

The evolution of the Supermarine Spitfire, the best British fighter of the conflict and among the best of those of all the nations at war, proceeded at a similar rate to that of its principal and immediate German adversaries: first, the Messerschmitt Bf.109 and subsequently the Focke Wulf Fw.190. There was a continuous search for a margin of superiority in order to conquer and retain, time after time, supremacy in the air, and the confrontation that began during the Battle of Britain went ahead without interruption for the entire duration of World War II.

Following the construction of 1,583 Spitfire Mk.Is (in service since June 1938), the assembly lines began to produce the first aircraft of the second production variant, the Mk.II. These fighters, which went into service toward the end of 1940, differed in the adoption of a 1,175 hp Rolls-Royce Merlin XII engine. Two main versions were completed: the Mk.IIA (750 aircraft), provided with eight machine guns, and the Mk.IIB (170 aircraft), armed with four machine guns and two 20 mm cannons. Although the search for greater power and heavier armament was apparent, the Spitfire Mk.IIs were still a transitional variant. In the subsequent Mk.V series, the first optimum compromise between performance, flexibility of use, and firepower was reached. In these Spitfires, (which began to come off the assembly lines in March 1941) two types of wing were adopted: a standard one, identified by the prefix F; and a shorter one that was clipped at the end (prefix LF) and particularly suited to flying at low altitudes. In addition, the aircraft's armament also became more articulated and flexible, varying from the eight machine guns of the subseries Mk.VA to the four machine guns and two 20 mm cannons of the Spitfire Mk.VB and the four 20 mm cannons of the Mk.VC. The last, in particular, was provided with a so-called universal wing, capable of housing all the possible armament configurations. As for the power plants, Merlin 45 and 50 engines were chosen, generating 1,440 hp and 1,490 hp respectively. Production of the Spitfire Mk.Vs was enormous, amounting to 94 of the Mk.VA variant, 3,923 of the MK.VB and 2,447 of the Mk.VC. In addition, 229 aircraft designated Spitfire Mk.IV were completed in the PR (photographic reconnaissance) configuration. In these aircraft the machine guns were replaced by an additional fuel tank with a capacity of 121 USgals (320 liters) on the leading edge of the wing, while two cameras were installed in the rear part of the fuselage in such a way as to be able to operate on both sides of the aircraft. Moreover, the cockpit was pressurized and, in order to improve the aircraft's aerodynamics at great altitudes, the wingspan was increased, up to 40 ft 5 in

A Spitfire Mk.V adapted for photographic reconnaissance.

(12.24 m) and was characterized by rounded wing tips.

In May 1941 the first clashes in combat with its immediate German adversary the Messerschmitt Bf.109 took place, although the Supermarine fighters always retained a slight overall advantage, except at altitudes over 19,735 ft (6,000 m). Use of the fighter rapidly spread and, in September, 27 units were equipped with Mk.VA aircraft; this figure had risen to 47 units three months later. In the meantime, production had reached remarkable levels: at the beginning of 1942 more than 1,700 Spitfire Mk.VS had been completed, and during the same year more than 3,300 aircraft were to come off the assembly lines.

The Mk.V series Spitfires were the first to be widely used overseas, from Malta in March 1942 to the Middle East and, from the beginning of 1943, in the Pacific. Moreover, these aircraft were also the first to be used as fighter-bombers, due to their being able to carry 498 lb (226 kg) of bombs.

The balance as compared to the German fighter was upset in September 1941, with the appearance of the new Focke Wulf Fw.190. During the first clashes (over France), it was evident that the Spitfire Mk.V was markedly inferior to its adversary: its only advantage lay in the fact that it was able to make tighter turns. The response to this new threat was not long in coming and arrived in July of the following year with the first Spitfire Mk.IXs, which were really a combination of the Mk.V airframe and the most powerful Merlin engine in the 1,565 hp version.

color plate

Supermarine Spitfire Mk.V tropicalized model of the 81st Fighter Squadron Royal Air Force - Scily (Italy) 1943

Aircraft:	Supermarine Spitfire Mk.VB
Nation:	Great Britain
Manufacturer:	Supermarine Division of Vickers-Armstrong Ltd.
Type:	Fighter
Year:	1941
Engine:	Rolls-Royce Merlin 45, 12-cylinder V, liquid-cooled, 1,440 hp
Wingspan:	36 ft 10 in (11.22 m)
Length:	29 ft 11 in (9.12 m)
Height:	11 ft 5 in (3.43 m)
Weight:	6,417 lb (2,911 kg) loaded
Maximum speed:	374 mph (602 km/h) at 13,000 ft (4,000 m)
Ceiling:	37,000 ft (11,280 m)
Range:	470 miles (750 km)
Armament:	2 × 20 mm cannons; 4 machine guns
Crew:	1

A Turkish Air Force Spitfire Mk.V with tropical filter.

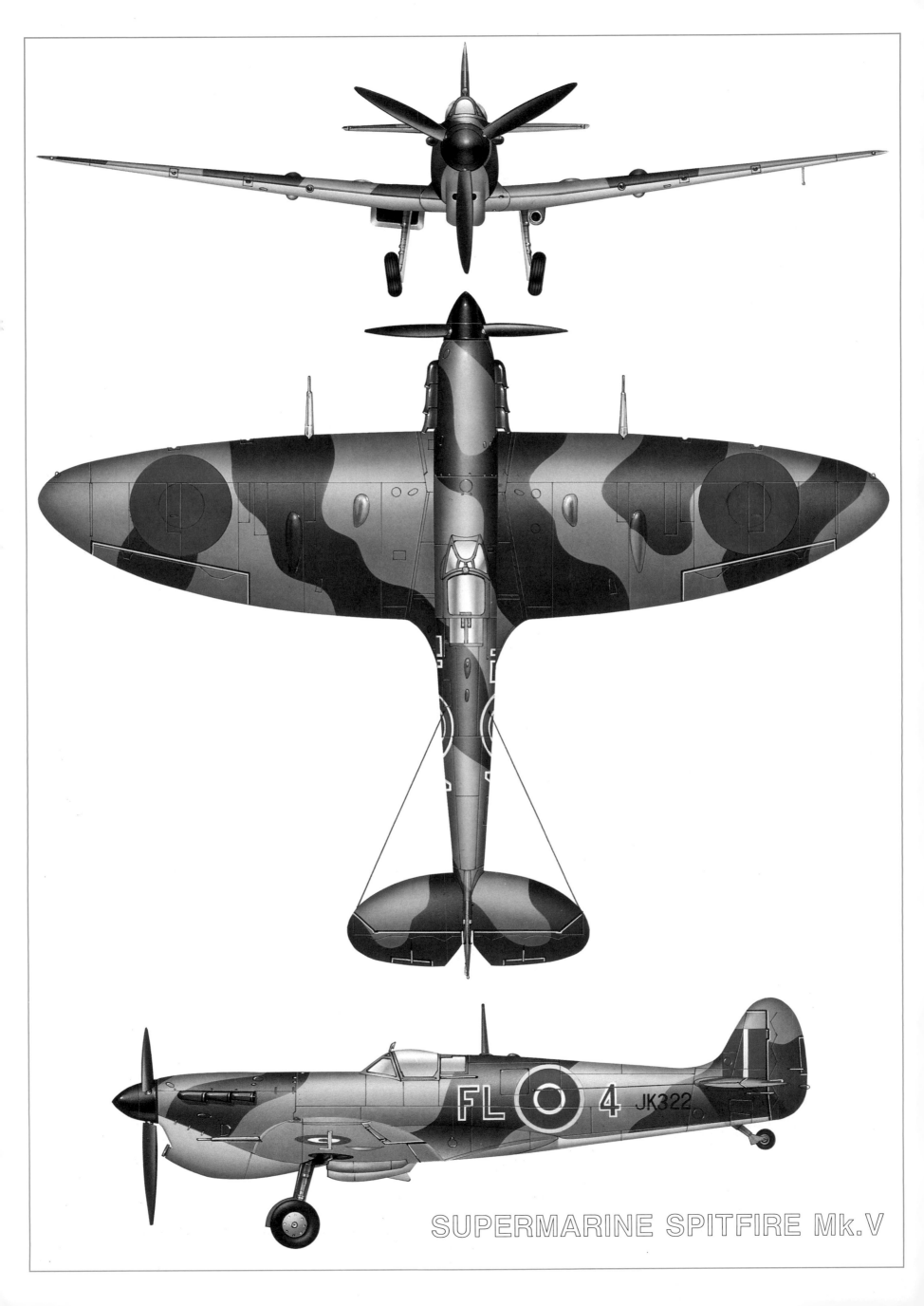

SUPERMARINE SPITFIRE Mk.V

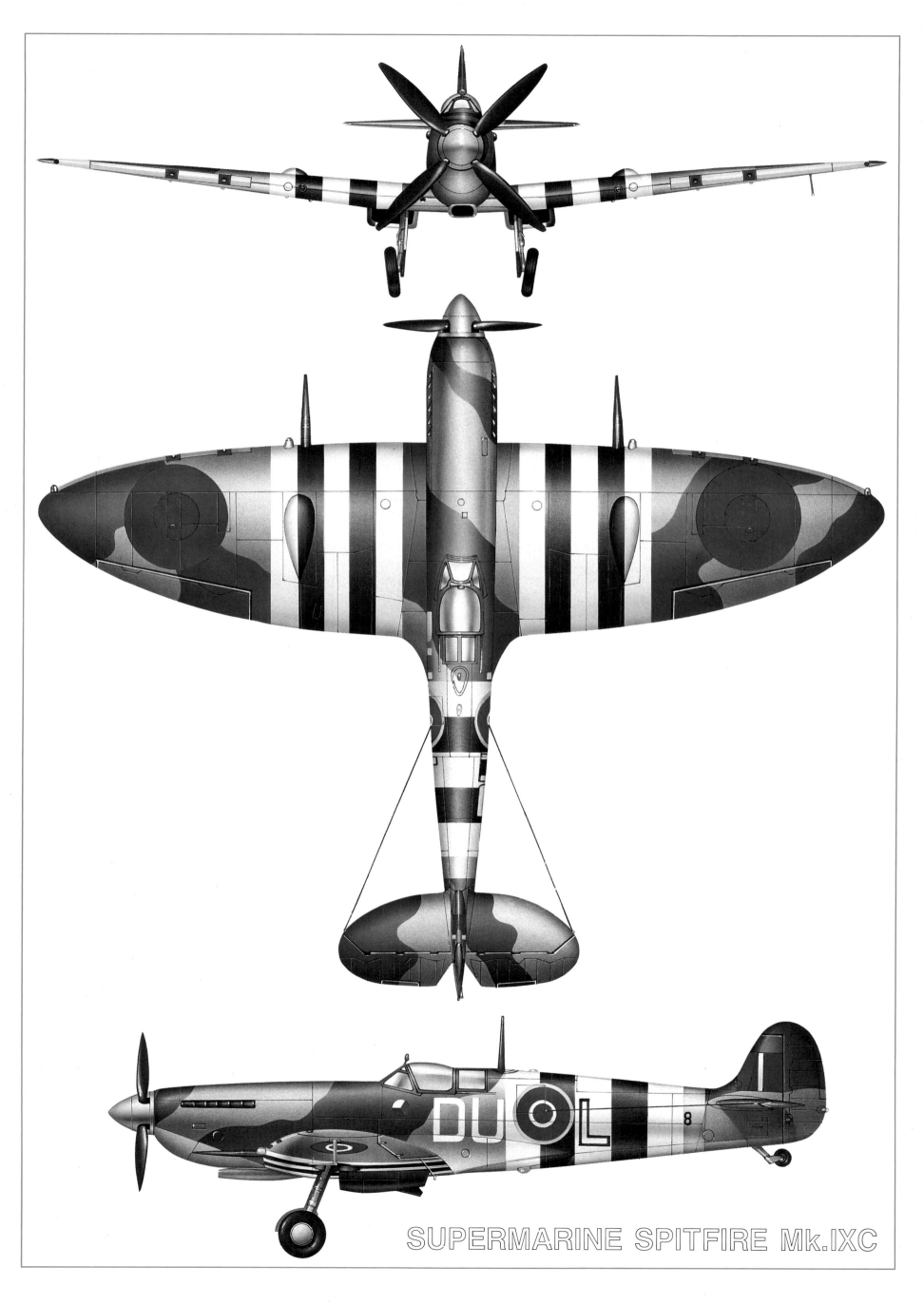

SUPERMARINE SPITFIRE Mk.IXC

Two Spitfire Mk.IXs in flight over Mount Vesuvius, near Naples.

cabin. In 1943 the Spitfire airframe was substantially improved, with the appearance of the first Mk.XIIs fitted with the new Rolls-Royce Griffon engine. As well as seeing the creation of more powerful and prestigious versions of the Spitfire, the same year also marked the beginning of the second phase of Reginald J. Mitchell's fighter's operative career, which was to continue well into the 1950s.

color plate
Supermarine Spitfire Mk.IXC 312th (Czech) Squadron RAF - Operation Overload, June 1944

Aircraft:	Supermarine Spitfire Mk.IX
Nation:	Great Britain
Manufacturer:	Supermarine Division of Vickers-Armstrong Ltd.
Type:	Fighter
Year:	1942
Engine:	Rolls-Royce Merlin 61, 12-cylinder V, liquid-cooled, 1,565 hp
Wingspan:	36 ft 10 in (11.22 m)
Length:	30 ft 6 in (9.30 m)
Height:	11 ft 5 in (3.48 m)
Weight:	7,500 lb (3,400 kg) loaded
Maximum speed:	408 mph (656 km/h) at 25,000 ft (7,620 m)
Ceiling:	44,000 ft (13,400 m)
Range:	434 miles (700 km)
Armament:	2 × 20 mm cannon; 4 machine guns
Crew:	1

The continuous search for supremacy over the German fighters led, in 1942, to the development of a new variant of the Supermarine Spitfire, the best British fighter of the conflict and among the best of those of all the countries taking part in the war. This version, built specially to contest the superiority of the Focke Wulf Fw.190 over the Spitfire Mk.V, was the Mk.IX, which appeared in July and was basically a combination of the airframe of the Mk.V with a more powerful version of the Merlin engine, generating 1,565 hp. A total of 5,665 Spitfire Mk.IXs was built in all, in numerous subseries. These differed in their employment at low, medium, and high altitude (with wings type LF, F, and HF respectively) and in their armament (type B, C, or E, the latter suffix indicating two 12.7 mm machine guns, two 20 mm cannons, and a bomb load of up to 1,002 lb - 454 kg).

The Spitfire Mk.IX began to reequip the units of the RAF's Fighter Command from July 6, 1942 (the first unit to receive the new fighter was the 64th Squadron), but it was soon widely used. One of the greatest employers of the aircraft, apart from the RAF, was the Soviet Union, which received no fewer than 1,188 Mk.IXs within the context of the military aid program from mid-1944 until April 1945.

Among the numerous variants of the Spitfire Mk.IX, mention should be made of the one designated Mk.XVI (of which 1,054 were built), which differed from the basic model mainly in the adoption of a Merlin engine built on license in the United States by Packard. This decision was taken in 1943 in order to increase production of the Spitfire to a maximum: the engine built in the United States was a Merlin 66, capable of generating 1,705 hp, and when exportation to Great Britain commenced at the beginning of the following year (with the designation Merlin 266), it was installed in the new version of the fighter. The Spitfire Mk.XVI was constructed with armament of type C or type E, and with F or LF type wings. In the final production series the famous canopy was replaced by another "drop-shaped" one, providing the pilot with greater visibility over 360 degrees. This modification made it necessary to alter the rear part of the fuselage, which was lowered.

The evolution of the prolific series of Spitfires continued. Further variants were developed as well as the Mk.IX. These included the Mk.VI and Mk.VII (100 and 140 built respectively) with improvements for interception at high altitudes: the former was fitted with a 1,435 hp Merlin engine and had a pressurized cabin and pointed type HF wings; the latter was fitted with a Merlin 61, 64, or 71 engine with two-stage supercharger, pressurized cabin, retractable tail wheel, and a larger vertical rudder with a characteristically pointed shape. The Spitfire Mk.VIII should also be mentioned. A total of 1,658 was built, and they were provided with Merlin 61, 63, 66, or 70 engines with two-stage supercharger. The Mk.X and Mk.XI series (16 and 471 aircraft built respectively) were constructed for photographic reconnaissance. They were both unarmed, and the former was provided with a pressurized

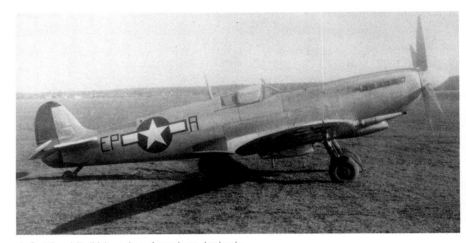

A Spitfire Mk.IX bearing American insignia.

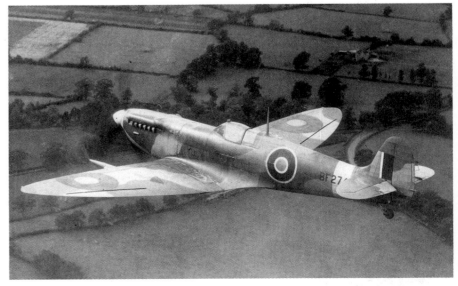

A Spitfire Mk.IX during a test flight. The aircraft bears national insignia but still lacks its unit code.

It was once again the need to contest the superiority of the German Focke Wulf Fw.190 that led to the creation of an umpteenth variant of the Spitfire, the Mk.XII, in 1943. This aircraft was not particularly significant from a strict production point of view, considering that barely 100 were built, an extremely small number compared to the 20,531 aircraft that came off the assembly lines in all. However, their construction marked an important step in the evolution of Reginald J. Mitchell's fighter, in that it saw the installation of the new Rolls-Royce Griffon engine in an operative version for the first time. In fact, it was this very engine that characterized the second phase of the Spitfire's career, which was to continue well into the 1950s.

The Rolls-Royce Griffon was tested for the first time in 1941 on a prototype that had originated as the Spitfire Mk.III, powered by a 1,298 hp Merlin XX engine. Following the installation of the new engine, this aircraft was redesignated Spitfire Mk.XX and became the ancestor of the Mk.XII version (designated Type 366 in the factory), built for interception at low altitude. In fact, the engine generated maximum power at about 985 ft (300 m) and was thus particularly suitable for a fighter meant to withstand the attacks of the German Fw.190s, which became an increasing threat in their raids along the south coast of England.

The Spitfire Mk.XIIs went into service in the spring of 1943 in two units assigned to territorial defense, and they remained operative throughout the following year. These aircraft proved to be perfectly suited to the specific tasks required of them, and (together with the Hawker Typhoons) their career was marked by notable success. Their speed in horizontal flight was particularly remarkable, reaching 368 mph (593 km/h) at sea level, compared to the Spitfire Mk.IX's 311 mph (502 km/h).

Although the Rolls-Royce Griffon adopted in the Spitfire Mk.XIIs was capable of generating 1,750 hp, at its initial stages it was fitted with a single-stage supercharger that limited its performance at altitude. Thus, these aircraft represented a transition before the preparation of the definitive version of the power plant, which fitted with a two-stage two-speed supercharger and capable of generating over 2,050 hp, subsequently made possible the construction of the Spitfire Mk.XIV, the most important variant of the last year of the war and the one that in its turn, led to the final series of the fighter.

However, the Spitfire Mk.XIVs were also transitional aircraft, derived as they were from the airframe of the Mk.VIII series. The «definitive» version with the Rolls-Royce Griffon, completely redesigned, was the Mk.XVIII, which went into service when the war was over.

---

color plate

Supermarine Spitfire Mk.XII 41st Fighter Squadron Royal Air Force - Great Britain 1943

Aircraft:	Supermarine Spitfire Mk.XII
Nation:	Great Britain
Manufacturer:	Supermarine Division of Vickers Armstrong Ltd.
Type:	Fighter
Year:	1943
Engine:	Rolls-Royce Griffon IV, 12-cylinder V, liquid-cooled, 1,750 hp
Wingspan:	32 ft 7 in (9.93 m)
Length:	31 ft 10 in (9.70 m)
Height:	11 ft (3.35 m)
Weight:	7,408 lb (3,356 kg)
Maximum speed:	392 mph (632 km/h) at 18,046 ft (5,486 m)
Ceiling:	40,105 ft (12,192 m)
Range:	492 miles (793 km)
Armament:	2x20 mm cannons, 4 machine guns, 500 lb (227 kg) of bombs
Crew:	1

Prototype of the "Low flight" Spitfire Mk.XII with clipped wings and retractable tail wheel

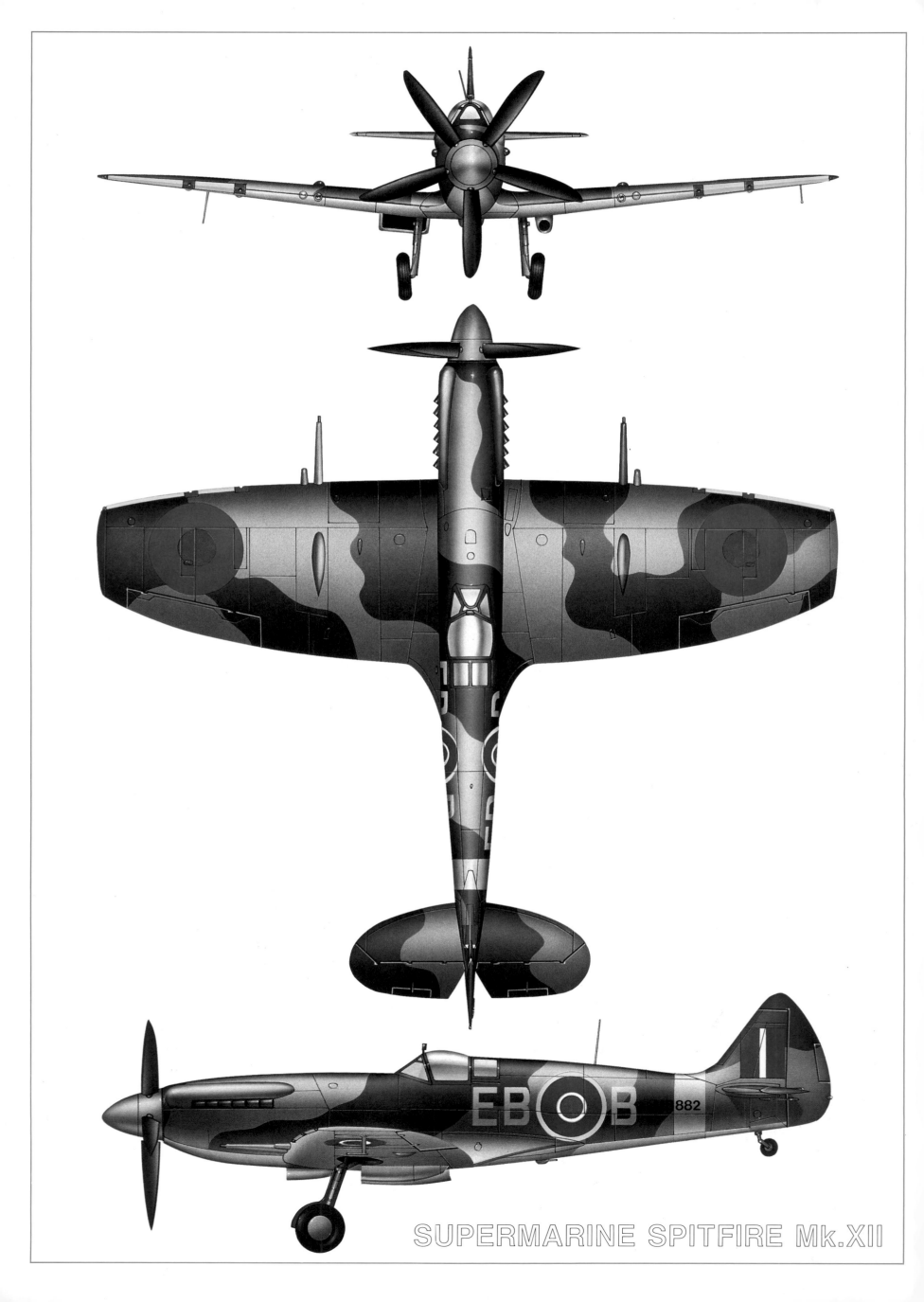

SUPERMARINE SPITFIRE Mk.XII

Following the experiences with the initial versions of the Rolls-Royce Griffon engine (which had led to the construction of the Spitfire Mk.XII in 1943), the second phase in the career of Reginald J. Mitchell's immortal fighter proceeded rapidly, developing alongside the evolution of the engine. The new variant, the Mk.XIV became the most important in the last year of the conflict. 957 aircraft came off the assembly lines before making way for the "definitive" version with the Griffon engine, the Mk.XVIII, which went into service once the war was over.

The Spitfire Mk.XIIs went into service in the spring of 1943, and their career was marked by notable successes. Their performance was remarkable as far as horizontal speed was concerned, reaching 368 mph (593 km/h) at sea level, compared to the Spitfire Mk.IX's 311 mph (502 km/h). In fact, it was these outstanding results, together with the availability of a stronger and improved versions of the power plant, that led to the creation of the new variant.

The Mk.XIVs were also transitional aircraft. In fact, the prototypes of these aircraft were obtained by modifying six Mk.VIIIs taken directly from the assembly lines. Apart from the installation of a Rolls-Royce Griffon 65 fitted with a two-stage two-speed supercharger (capable of generating more than 2,050 hp and controlling a five-bladed propeller) the basic differences lay in the aircraft's general reinforcement and in the enlargement of the tail planes' surface area.

Deliveries of the first production series aircraft began in October 1943. After an intensive series of tests, the first unit to receive the

401st Squadron, shot down the first Messerschmitt Me.262 of the war.

The evolution of the aircraft proceeded without interruption, although the final variants of the Spitfire were not ready in time to be used in combat. The subsequent series was the Mk.XVIII (300 of which were completed), which was basically redesigned, fitted with reinforced wings and landing gear, and provided with larger fuel tanks and a drop canopy. The power plant was a 2,375 hp Griffon 67.

Some 225 Spitfire Mk.XIXs were built exclusively for use as high altitude photoreconnaissance planes. They lacked armament and were provided with a pressurized cockpit. The original airframe reached its final development in these variants and the three subsequent models built immediately after the war (F.21, F.22, and F.24) were subjected to substantial restructuring, especially in regard to the wings, tail planes, and landing gear. With the production of these aircraft, the total number of Spitfires with Griffon engines delivered to the Royal Air Force reached 2,053. The aircraft's last flight in a front-line unit took place on April 1, 1954, carried out by a PR 19 in service with the 81st Squadron. This was approximately 18 years and one month after the original prototype had made its maiden flight.

color plate

Supermarine Spitfire Mk.XIV 610th Fighter Squadron Royal Air Force - England, 1944. Personal plane of Squadron Leader R.A. Newbury, Commanding officer of the Squadron

Aircraft:	Supermarine Spitfire Mk.XIV
Nation:	Great Britain
Manufacturer:	Supermarine Division of Vickers-Armstrong Ltd.
Type:	Fighter
Year:	1944
Engine:	Rolls-Royce Griffon 65, 12-cylinder V, liquid-cooled, 2,078 hp
Wingspan:	36 ft 10 in (11.22 m)
Length:	32 ft 8 in (9.95 m)
Height:	12 ft 8 in (3.87 m)
Weight:	8,509 lb (3,855 kg)
Maximum speed:	450 mph (724 km/h) at 26,069 ft (7,925 m)
Ceiling:	44,615 ft (13,563 m)
Range:	459 miles (740 km)
Armament:	2 x 20 mm cannons; 4 machine guns; 500 lb (227 kg) of bombs
Crew:	1

A Spitfire Mk.XIV with canopy linked to the fuselage.

new Spitfires was the RAF's 610th Squadron in January of the following year.

The Mk.XIVs of the initial production lot had wings with two 20 mm cannons, four 7.7 mm machine guns and a support for a 500 lb (227 kg) bomb. Subsequently, however, an "E" type universal wing was adopted, with standard armament consisting of two 12.7 mm machine guns, two 20 mm cannons and up to 1,002 lb (454 kg) of bombs. Two subseries were built by the assembly lines: the first in a fighter structure (527 built) and the second for low altitude photoreconnaissance (FR Mk.XIV, of which 430 were built). Both could be fitted with F or LF wings, depending upon the type of mission to be carried out. The final production series aircraft were fitted with a drop canopy, instead of the traditional kind.

The Mk.XIVs' great qualities of speed proved valuable not only in opposing the latest German fighters (also those with rocket engines), but also the threat posed by the V-1 flying bombs. During the last phase of the conflict in Europe, these Spitfires succeeded in destroying no less than 300 of these deadly German weapons.

Moreover, on October 5, 1944, a Mk.XIV, in service with the

The prototype of the Spitfire Mk.XIV, built using the airframe of the Spitfire Mk.VIII.

Although the Royal Air Force was one of the world's most modern and powerful military Air Force at the time the war broke out, the same could not be said of its naval couterpart, the Fleet Air Arm. During the period in which the RAF's fighter front-line consisted of aircraft such as the Hawker Hurricane and the Supermarine Spitfire, among the best of their kind, the Royal Navy still remained in the era of the biplane. In 1941, due to the changing needs of marine warfare, it was decided to repeat the success already experienced with the «navalized» versions of the Hurricane in the case of the Spitfire too. Thus Reginald J. Mitchell's fighter began a second career that although launched with some delay soon evolved alongside those of the land-based variants and had equal success. The final version of the Seafire (the F.47, built immediately after the war) was also the last to see combat, in Korea in 1950, well into the jet age.

The experiences that led to the creation of the Seafire took place toward the end of 1941, with a production model of the Spitfire Mk.VB. This aircraft, which had a reinforced fuselage and was modified by the addition of an arrester hook, was tested for a long period on board the aircraft carrier *Illustrious*, dispelling all fears concerning its employment on ship, especially those deriving from its high landing speed. Immediately after the completion of test it was decided to convert another 48 Mk.VBs, and a further 118 aircraft were soon added to this initial quantity. The new fighters went into service in June 1942, as Seafire Mk.IBs, in time to take part in the invasion of North Africa in November, based on the aircraft carrier *Furious*.

This initial production series, obtained by converting an aircraft already in existence, was followed by a second (Seafire Mk.IIC) constructed for naval use right from the start: these aircraft had a reinforced fuselage and Type C «universal» wing (capable of housing all the various types of armament planned, from eight machine guns to two 20 mm cannons plus four machine guns, to four 20 mm cannons), strengthened in order to allow for catapult take off. In all, 372 were built, of which 110 of the low-altitude version (LF).

However, the major production series was the Mk.III, which appeared in 1943, in which the Seafires were finally provided with folding wings in order to facilitate their storage in the aircraft carriers hangars and operations on the flight deck: the mechanism was manual, and the wing could be folded in two sections. From April 1943 to July 1945 a total of 1,220 aircraft was completed in various series, also built for photo reconnaissance, use at low altitude, and as fighter-bombers. The Seafire Mk.IIIs took part in

A Seafire Mk.IIC awaiting takeoff from the flight-deck of *H.M.S. Formidable*.

all air-sea operations, including those in the Far East, until the end of the war.

As in the case of the Spitfire, the Seafire also benefitted from the enormous improvements that derived from the adoption of the Griffon engine, although the end of the conflict prevented the «second generation» versions from taking an active part in warfare. The prototype of the Mk.XV series (powered by a Griffon with a 1,876 hp single-stage supercharger) appeared in 1944, although it did not go into front-line service until May of the following year. A total of 390 of this variant were built, and were followed by 232 Seafire Mk.VIIs, in which the main differences consisted in the adoption of a drop canopy and the consequent modifications to the fuselage.

The final versions appeared in the years immediately after the war and followed the evolution of the Spitfire: the Seafire F.45 (50 built in all, in service from the end of 1946) corresponded to the F.21; the Seafire F.46 (24 built) was derived from the F.22; the Seafire F.47 (140 built in all), completely «navalized» with the adoption of folding wings, was derived from the F.24.

---

color plate

Supermarine Seafire Mk.IIC 899th Squadron Royal Navy - H.M.S. *Indomitable*, 1943

Aircraft:	Supermarine Seafire Mk.III
Nation:	Great Britain
Manufacturer:	Supermarine Division of Vickers Armstrong Ltd.
Type:	Fighter
Year:	1943
Engine:	Rolls-Royce Merlin 55, 12-cylinder V, liquid-cooled, 1,490 hp
Wingspan:	36 ft 10 in (11.22 m)
Length:	30 ft 3 in (9.20 m)
Height:	11 ft 2 in (3.40 m)
Weight:	7,108 lb (3,220 kg)
Maximum speed:	351 mph (566 km/h) at 12,282 ft (3,734 m)
Ceiling:	33,888 ft (10,302 m)
Range:	725 miles (1,167 km)
Armament:	2 × 20 mm cannons, 4 machine guns, 500 lb (227 kg) of bombs
Crew:	1

A Seafire Mk.III, basically a «navalization» of the Spitfire Mk.V, with arrester hook and folding wings.

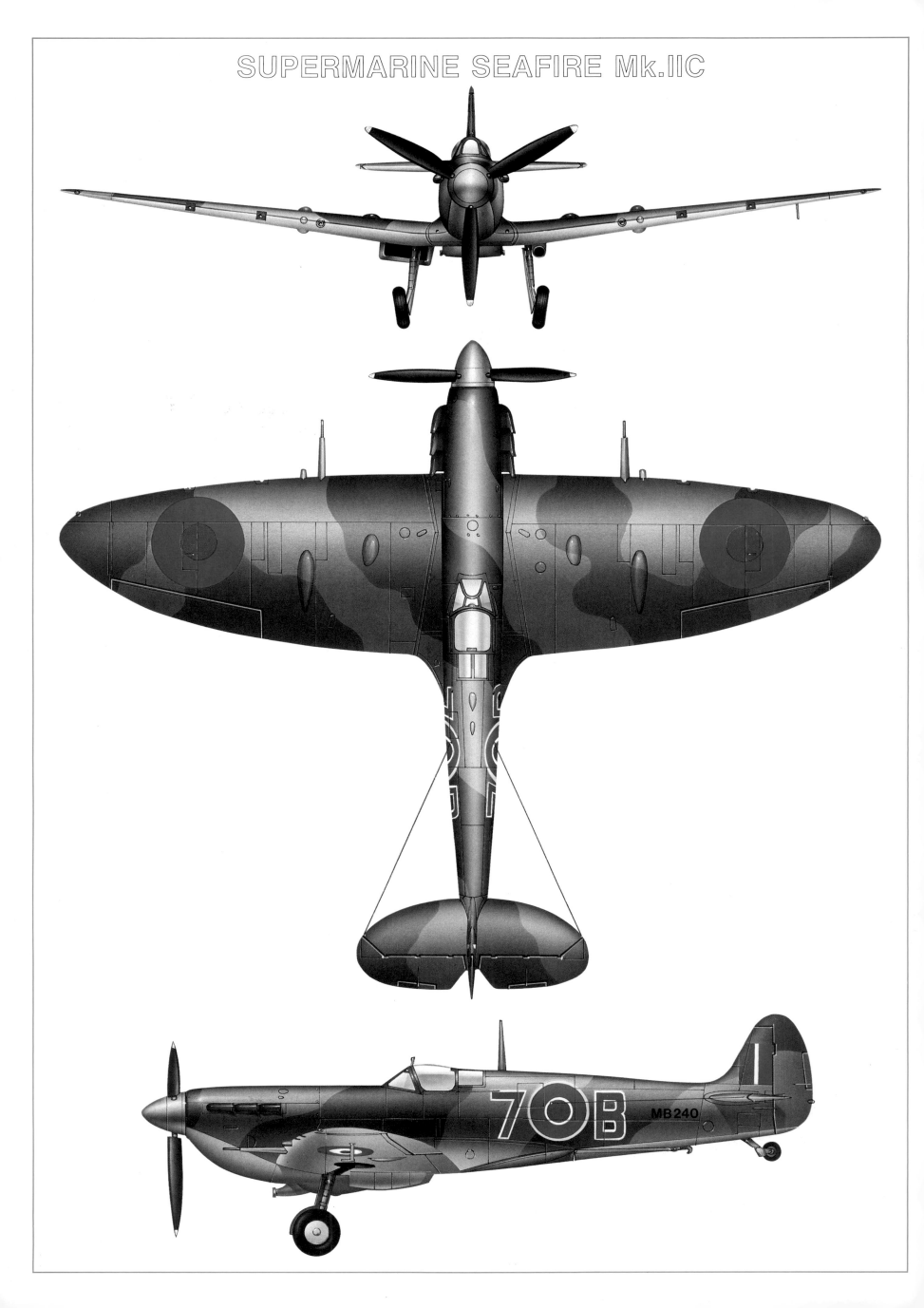

SUPERMARINE SEAFIRE Mk.IIC

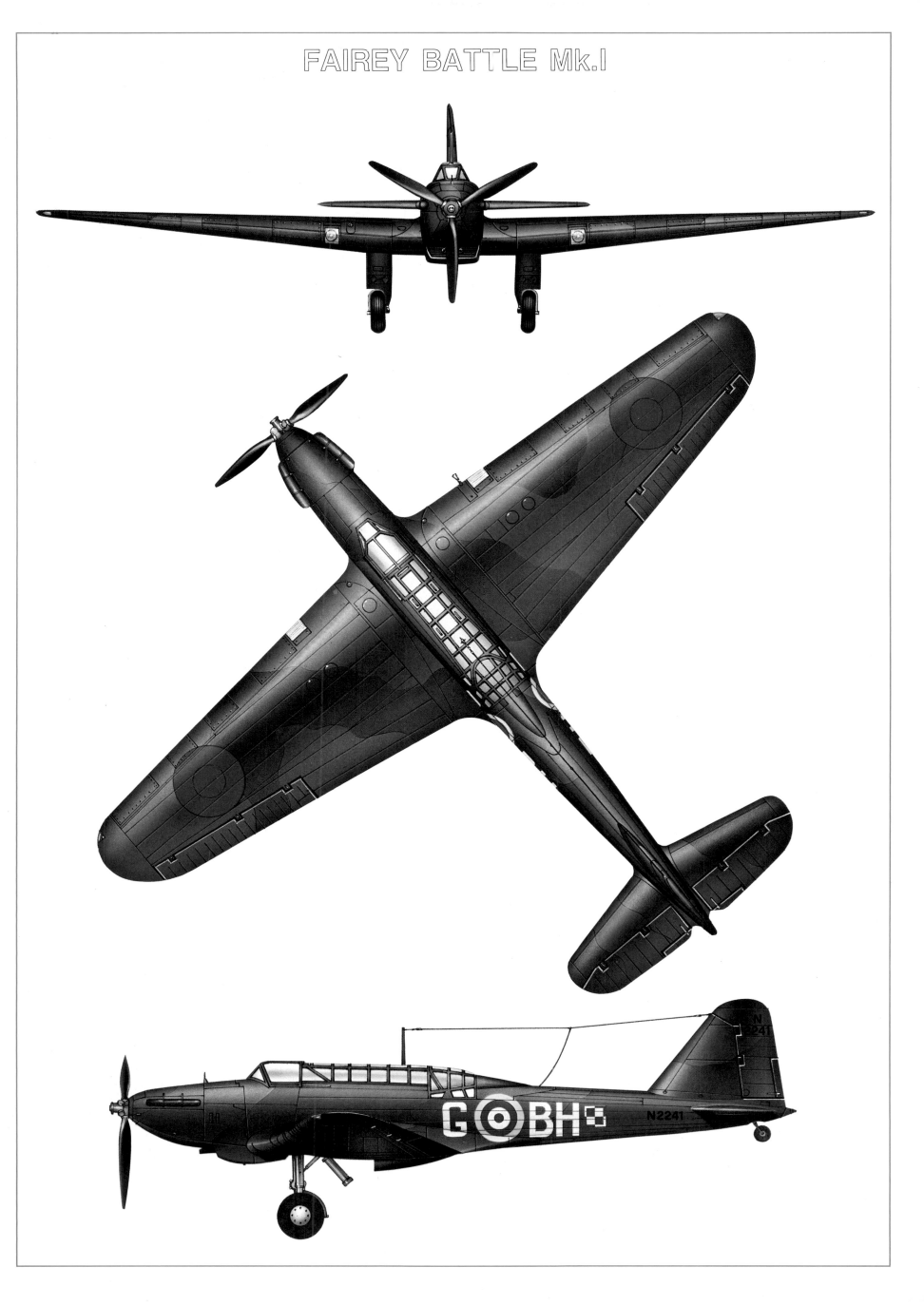

FAIREY BATTLE Mk.I

The Fairey Battle was designed in 1933 to replace the biplane light bombers that were still in service in the RAF at the time. It was clearly a transitional aircraft and, as such, proved to be unsuited to the new, more aggressive roles imposed by World War II. Although modern in concept, with an all-metal airframe and retractable landing gear, the Fairey was already out-of-date by the time the war began, and its front-line career lasted approximately a year, up to September 1940. In fact, this date marked the end of production (amounting to 2,185 aircraft out of total orders for 2,419) and virtually coincided with the beginning of the aircraft's withdrawal from front-line duty and its being assigned to less demanding roles, such as training and target towing. Nevertheless, the Fairey bomber was widely used, especially during the early months of the war and especially in the Battle of France, during which it suffered heavy losses.

The prototype of the Battle took to the air for the first time on March 10, 1936. The aircraft had been designed in response to Air Ministry specifications issued in April 1933, calling for a single-engine two-seater bomber capable of carrying a bomb load of 1,000 lb (454 kg) over a distance of 1,050 miles (1,690 km) at a speed of 200 mph (322 km/h). The prototype more than fulfilled these requirements, and, following a series of flight tests and official evaluations, it was accepted by the RAF. It then went into production on the basis of a series of orders amounting to no fewer than 655 aircraft. This number soon increased, so much so that the participation of other manufacturers in the production program became necessary.

The Fairey Battle was a large, low-wing, single-engine aircraft. Its three-man crew (pilot, gunner and radio operator) was housed in a large, completely glazed cockpit; the bomb load was completely contained inside the wings, while the defensive armament consisted of a fixed machine gun in a half-wing and another flexible one in the rear. The aircraft was powered by an engine that was to become famous, the Rolls-Royce Merlin Mk.I generating 1,030 hp and driving a three-bladed, variable pitch metal propeller.

The first Battle Mk.I was delivered to an operative unit in March 1937, and by the end of the year 85 aircraft had been completed. However, by the time the war broke out, this figure had increased and amounted to more than 1,000 (the production series differed above all in the adoption of successive versions of the Merlin engine).

The Fairey bombers had the honor of carrying out the first missions of the war and, having been sent to France on September 2, 1939, as part of the British Advanced Air Striking Force, one of these aircraft shot down the first German aircraft of the conflict, on September 20. On this occasion, however, the aircraft's limitations became apparent, especially its inability to defend itself when attacked by enemy fighters. Although the Battles were therefore withdrawn from daylight operations, the developments of the war soon caused this decision to be changed and, in the spring of 1940, the aircraft were sent, almost at their own risk, to oppose the German advance. The most tragic date was May 14, 1940, during an attack on bridges and a concentration of troops at Sedan, when 40 of the 71 Battles taking part were shot down. During the next few weeks, the units were recalled to Great Britain, and the gradual withdrawal of the bomber from front-line duty began.

Within the context of Commonwealth training programs, many Battles were sent to Australia and Canada. The Royal Australian Air Force used 364, and the Royal Canadian Air Force no fewer than 739.

color plate

Fairey Battle Mk.I 300th (Masovian) Polish Squadron RAF - 1940

Aircraft:	Fairey Battle
Nation:	Great Britain
Manufacturer:	Fairey Aviation Co. Ltd.
Type:	Bomber
Year:	1937
Engine:	Rolls-Royce Merlin Mk.I, 12-cylinder V, liquid-cooled, 1,030 hp
Wingspan:	54 ft (16.46 m)
Length:	52 ft 1 in (15.87 m)
Height:	15 ft 6 in (4.72 m)
Weight:	10,792 lb (4,895 kg) loaded
Maximum speed:	241 mph (388 km/h) at 13,000 ft (3,960 m)
Ceiling:	23,500 ft (7,160 m)
Range:	1,050 miles (1,690 km)
Armament:	2 machine guns; 1,000 lb (454 kg) of bombs
Crew:	3

A Fairey Battle serving in the British Advanced Air Striking Force, stationed in France in September 1939.

Although great technological advances were made in aviation under the impetus of the war, some notable exceptions proved how specific needs could be fully satisfied by planes that seemed totally out of date. The fighting in the Mediterranean and the Atlantic, with its special operational conditions, included among its major protagonists the Fairey Swordfish, a slow and awkward biplane. Despite this apparent handicap, the Swordfish proved to be one of the finest torpedo-bombers in history. The Swordfish's qualities can be appreciated with the help of a few figures: for nine years, from July 1936 to May 1945, this airplane was used in service by the units of the British Fleet Air Arm, and a total of 2,391 were built.

The Swordfish's origins went back to 1932, the year in which the Fairey Aviation Company had begun to develop privately a torpedo biplane, with the aim of selling it to the Fleet Air Arm. Designated T.S.R.I. the prototype of this plane took to the air the following year on March 21 but was destroyed six months later during a test flight. Despite this accident, the original design was not abandoned, and in 1933 Fairey prepared a new model in response to an official request. This model, designated T.S.R.II, made its maiden flight on April 17, 1934, and official flight testing began immediately after. As compared to its direct predecessor, its main differences lay in the lengthened fuselage, the enlarged vertical fin, and in alterations to the forward landing gear. After tests, including being launched by catapult from the deck of the aircraft carrier H.M.S. *Repulse*, the prototype was officially approved and named Swordfish; an initial order was placed for 86 planes.

Built with a metal airframe and covered with a fabric skin, the Swordfish had wings that could be folded backwards to make storage on-board ship easier, while its landing gear could be replaced by a pair of floats, for use on major warships. The earliest models relied for their power on a 690 hp Bristol Pegasus radial engine (this power was increased in the later versions), which worked a three-bladed, fixed-pitch metal propeller. On reconnaissance missions, the plane carried a crew of three men, while in the case of a torpedo-launching mission this was reduced to two. Its defensive armament consisted of a fixed forward synchronized machine gun and another flexible one mounted in the observer's cockpit. It also carried either 1,500 lb (680 kg) of bombs or a 1,610 lb (730 kg) torpedo or (from the second version onward) eight rockets, which were installed under the wings.

The first Swordfish Mk.Is were delivered from February 1936 and went into service on board the aircraft carrier H.M.S. *Glorious* in the following July. Production was divided among three other versions: the 1943 Mk.II (strengthened wings and more powerful engine); the Mk.III of the same year, which had a radar unit installed under the fuselage; and the Mk.IV which had an enclosed cockpit and was made for Canada.

When war broke out, the Swordfish was operational on 13 Royal Navy ships and on five aircraft carriers: the *Ark Royal*, the *Courageous*, the *Eagle*, the *Glorious*, and the *Furious*. It continued to serve as a torpedo-bomber until early 1942, and during this period it played a distinguished role in many major combat operations, including the attack on the Italian fleet at Taranto (November 10/11, 1940) and the sinking of the *Bismarck*. Swordfish were later assigned to antisubmarine warfare, operating from on-board convoy escort aircraft carriers in the Atlantic, and in this role, too, they proved to be particularly effective.

---

color plate

Fairey Swordfish Mk.I 815th Squadron based on the aircraft carrier H.M.S. *Illustrious* Fleet Air Arm - 1940

Aircraft:	Fairey Swordfish Mk.I
Nation:	Great Britain
Manufacturer:	Fairey Aviation Co. Ltd.
Type:	Torpedo-bomber
Year:	1936
Engine:	Bristol Pegasus III M3, 9-cylinder radial, air-cooled, 690 hp
Wingspan:	45 ft 6 in (13.87 m)
Length:	36 ft 4 in (11.07 m)
Height:	12 ft 10 in (3.91 m)
Weight:	9,250 lb (4,190 kg) loaded
Maximum speed:	139 mph (224 km/h) at 4,750 ft (1,450 m)
Ceiling:	10,700 ft (3,260 m)
Range:	546 miles (879 km)
Armament:	2 machine guns; 1 × 1,610 lb (730 kg) torpedo
Crew:	2/3

Fairey Swordfish with 1,610 lb torpedo.

FAIREY SWORDFISH Mk.I

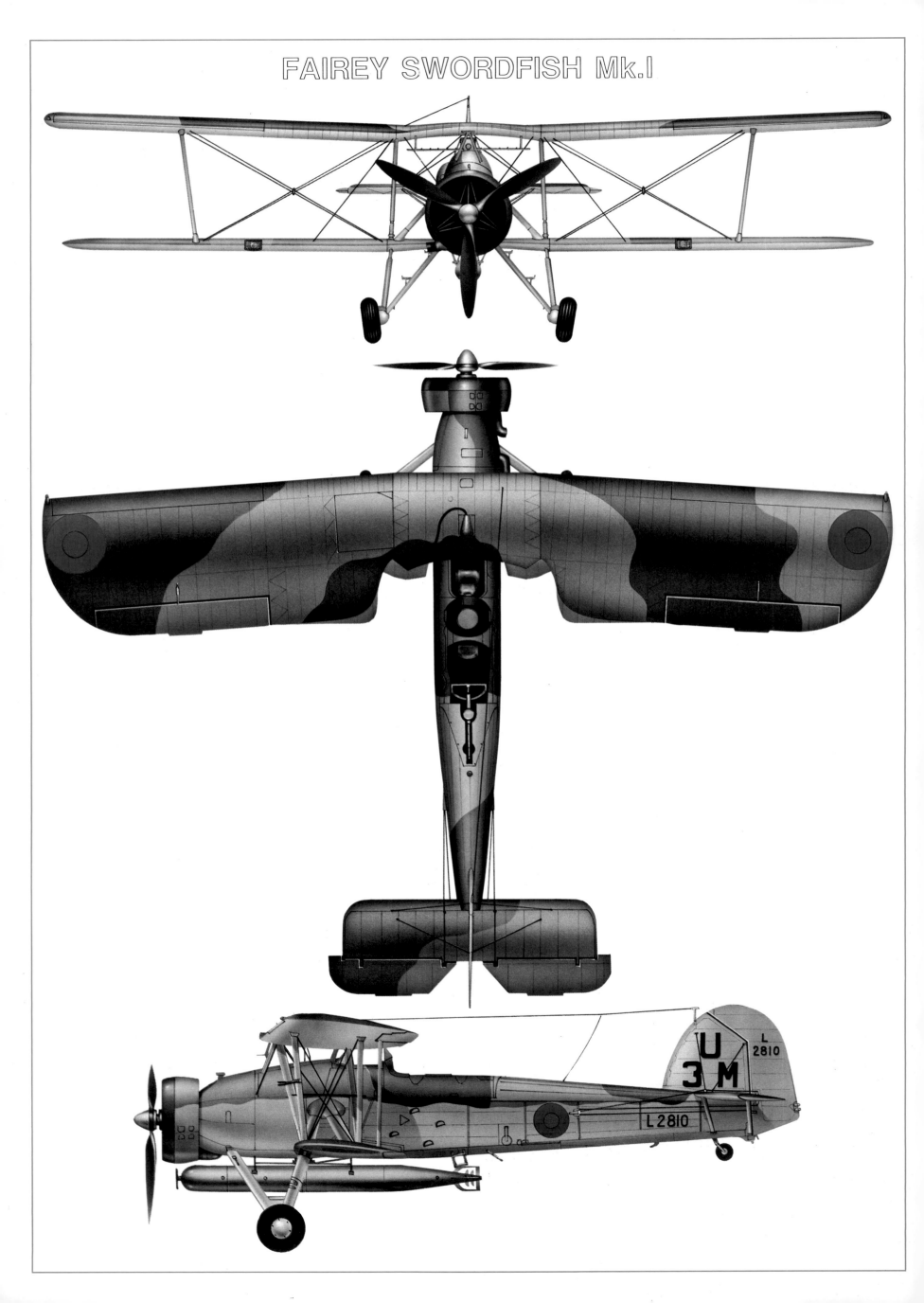

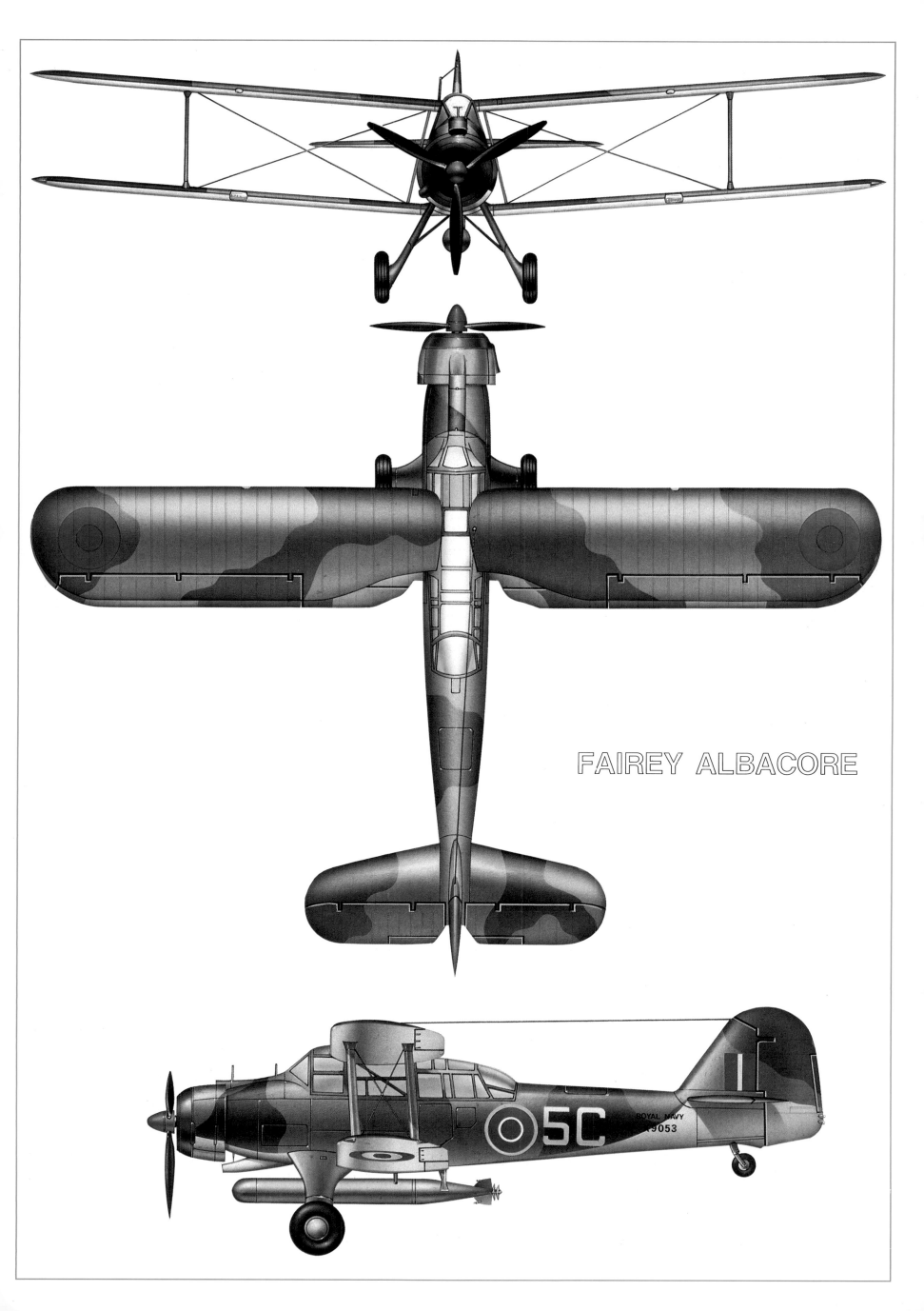

FAIREY ALBACORE

The idea that lay behind the construction of the Albacore, in 1936, was that of creating a carrier-based torpedo-bomber capable of replacing the older Swordfish, also built by Fairey. This intention was never actually fulfilled, since the more modern biplane did not come up to expectations: only slightly faster than the Swordfish, it also proved to be somewhat less maneuverable. In practice, although 800 Albacores were built in all from 1939 to 1943, they ended up simply supporting their older rival, which even outlived them in service: the last Albacores were withdrawn from the units in November 1943, while the Swordfish remained in action up to the end of the conflict.

The project originated on the basis of specifications issued by the Air Ministry in 1936, and 98 production series aircraft were ordered even before the prototype was completed. The first of these took to the air on December 12, 1938 and production was launched at the beginning of the following year. The Albacore was a biplane with all-metal airframe, mixed fabric (the wings) and metal covering, and completely enclosed cockpit. The defensive armament consisted of a fixed machine gun in the right half-wing and of a pair of flexible ones installed in the rear, for use by the observer. The offensive armament consisted of a 1,610 lb (730 kg) torpedo installed between the landing gear legs or, alternatively, of up to six 250 lb (113 kg) bombs that could be carried on the wings. The aircraft was powered by a Bristol Taurus radial engine (initially in the 1,080 hp Mk.II version, later substituted by a 1,146 hp Mk.XII model), that drove a three-bladed, variable pitch, metal propeller.

The Albacore was used initially by ground-based units. The first was the 826th Squadron, established for this purpose, which began to receive deliveries of the aircraft on March 15, 1940. The biplanes had their baptism of fire on March 31, during an attack on German torpedo boats off Zeebrugge and against targets on Belgian territory. The Albacores were not used on board ship until the end of the year (November 20, to be precise) when two units were assigned to the aircraft carrier *Formidable*. The first mis-

sion of note took place in March 1941, during the Battle of Cape Matapan.

The high point in the Albacore's career occurred in 1942, the year in which it equipped no fewer than 15 Fleet Air Arm squadrons, and was used in action in areas stretching from the Atlantic to the Mediterranean. The following year, with the appearance of the Fairey Barracuda, the biplanes started to be withdrawn from the carrier-based front line to be relegated to secondary roles. Some of them were ceded to the Canadian Royal Air Force and used during the Normandy landing.

color plate

Fairey Albacore 820th Squadron Fleet Air Arm *HMS Formidable* - Mediterranean Sea 1942

Aircraft:	Fairey Albacore
Nation:	Great Britain
Manufacturer:	Fairey Aviation Co. Ltd.
Type:	Torpedo-bomber
Year:	1940
Engine:	Bristol Taurus XII, 14-cylinder radial, air-cooled, 1,146 hp
Wingspan:	50 ft (15.24 m)
Length:	39 ft 11 in (12.14 m)
Height:	14 ft 2 in (4.32 m)
Takeoff weight:	10,475 lb (4,745 kg) loaded
Maximum speed:	161 mph (259 km/h) at 4,000 ft (1,200 m)
Ceiling:	20,700 ft (6,300 m)
Range:	930 miles (1,500 km)
Armament:	3 machine guns; 1,610 lb (730 kg) of torpedo
Crew:	3

Fairey Albacore equipped with bombs

The Fairey Fulmar was the first Fleet Air Arm fighter that, from the point of view of firepower, could be considered equal to the Royal Air Force's Spitfires and Hurricanes. Until the appearance of the naval versions of these two combat planes, it formed the front line of the units based on board ship, proving to be an effective aircraft overall, although not very fast and difficult to handle. From 1940 to 1943, a total of 602 Fulmars were built in two main versions, many of which were converted for the role of night fighter.

Toward the mid 1930s, the need to replace the biplanes that were by then obsolete was strongly felt in the Fleet Air Arm. In 1938, to satisfy this need Fairey responded to official specifications and prepared a prototype derived from that of a light bomber built a couple of years earlier. The request was not long in coming, with an initial order for 127 aircraft, and the first definitive prototype made its maiden flight on January 4, 1940. About four months later (April 6) a second prototype appeared, fitted with the engine that was to characterize the first production series, the 1,080 hp Rolls-Royce Merlin VIII. The aircraft was an all-metal low-wing monoplane with retractable landing gear, in which the two-man crew was housed in a separate, long cockpit. The armament was especially heavy, consisting of eight 7.7 mm machine guns on the wings. Right from the start the structure had been conceived for use on board ship: it was provided with folding wings to facilitate storage on board, with landing hook, and with reinforcements for catapult launching.

Delivery to the units commenced at the beginning of June 1940, and after 250 aircraft belonging to the first series had been built, the assembly lines completed production with the Mk.II version, with substantial modifications to the engine (1,300 hp Rolls-Royce Merlin XXX), to the propeller, and to the equipment (tropical type). The last of these aircraft was delivered in February 1943.

These versatile aircraft had a particularly intense career in the Mediterranean area, where they began to be used in the less demanding role of night fighter, for which approximately 100 aircraft of the second series were modified. In 1943, the Fulmars started to be withdrawn from front line service and replaced by the more modern and powerful Supermarine Seafire and Fairey Firefly.

The Fulmars were also used in an unusual role, that of a "sacrificed" catapulted fighter, justified by the desperate need to protect convoys crossing the Atlantic from the threat of attack by the Germans at any cost. The aircraft were loaded on board armed cargo ships and were launched at times of need. This inevitably led to the aircraft being destroyed, since there was no way in which they could return to base. This represented a veritable suicide mission for the pilots. In fact, their only hope for salvation after combat consisted in abandoning the aircraft and being picked up in the sea. However, this did not always prove to be possible. Rescue was often prevented not only by operative needs of the convoy, but also by weather conditions.

A Fairey Fulmar transformed in target tug.

A Fulmar Mk.II equipped with ice guard on the ventral air intake.

color plate
Fairey Fulmar Mk.II 809th Squadron Fleet Air Arm *HMS Victorious* - Mediterranean Sea 1942

Aircraft:	Fairey Fulmar Mk.II
Nation:	Great Britain
Manufacturer:	Fairey Aviation Co. Ltd.
Type:	Fighter
Year:	1940
Engine:	Rolls-Royce Merlin XXX, 12-cylinder V, air-cooled, 1,300 hp
Wingspan:	46 ft 5 in (14.13 m)
Length:	40 ft 3 in (12.24 m)
Height:	14 ft (4.27 m)
Takeoff weight:	10,350 lb (4,695 kg) loaded
Maximum speed:	259 mph (416 km/h) at 9,000 ft (2,743 m)
Ceiling:	16,000 ft (4,877 m)
Range:	783 miles (1,260 km)
Armament:	8 machine guns; 250 lb (113 kg) of bombs
Crew:	2

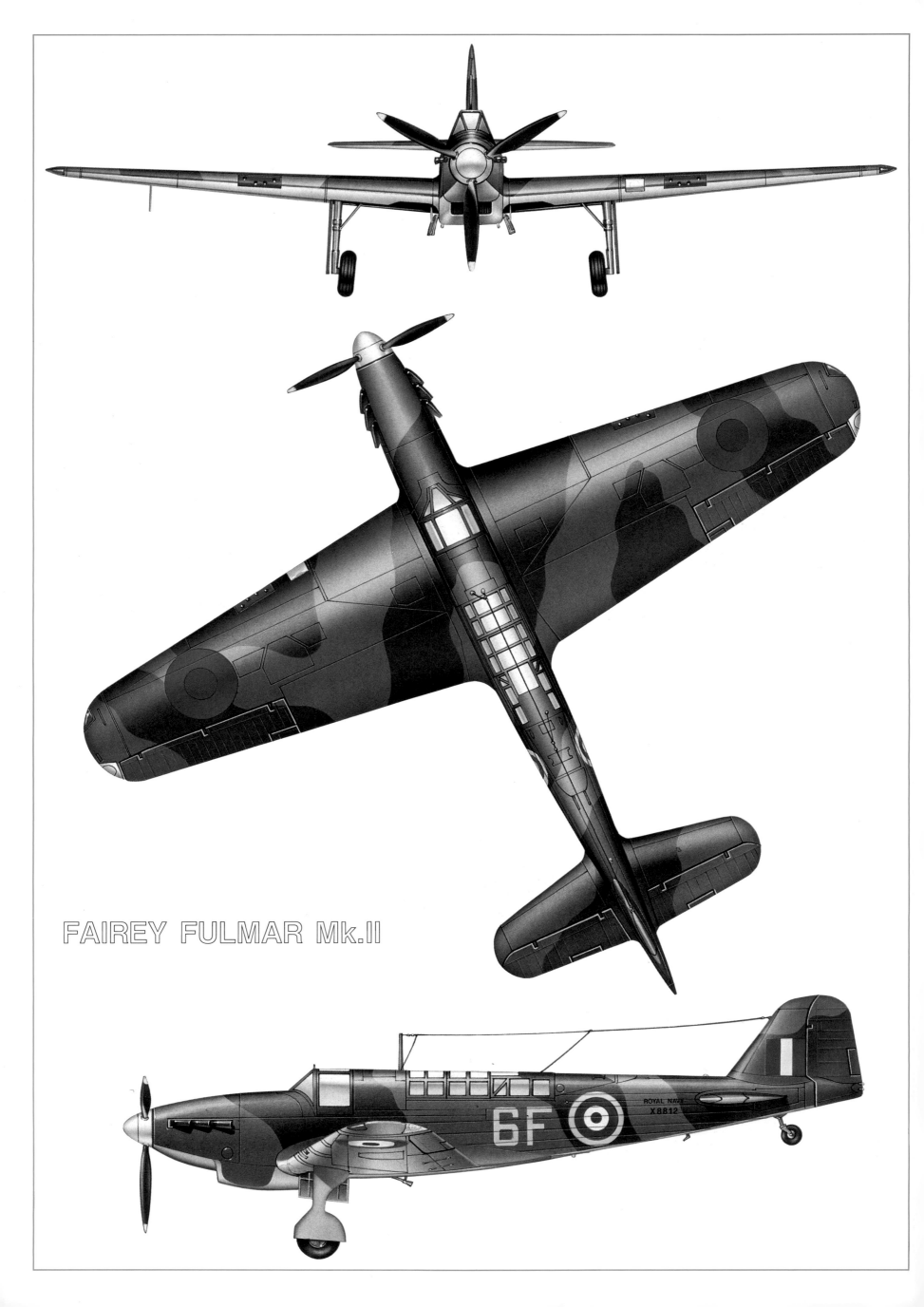

FAIREY FULMAR Mk.II

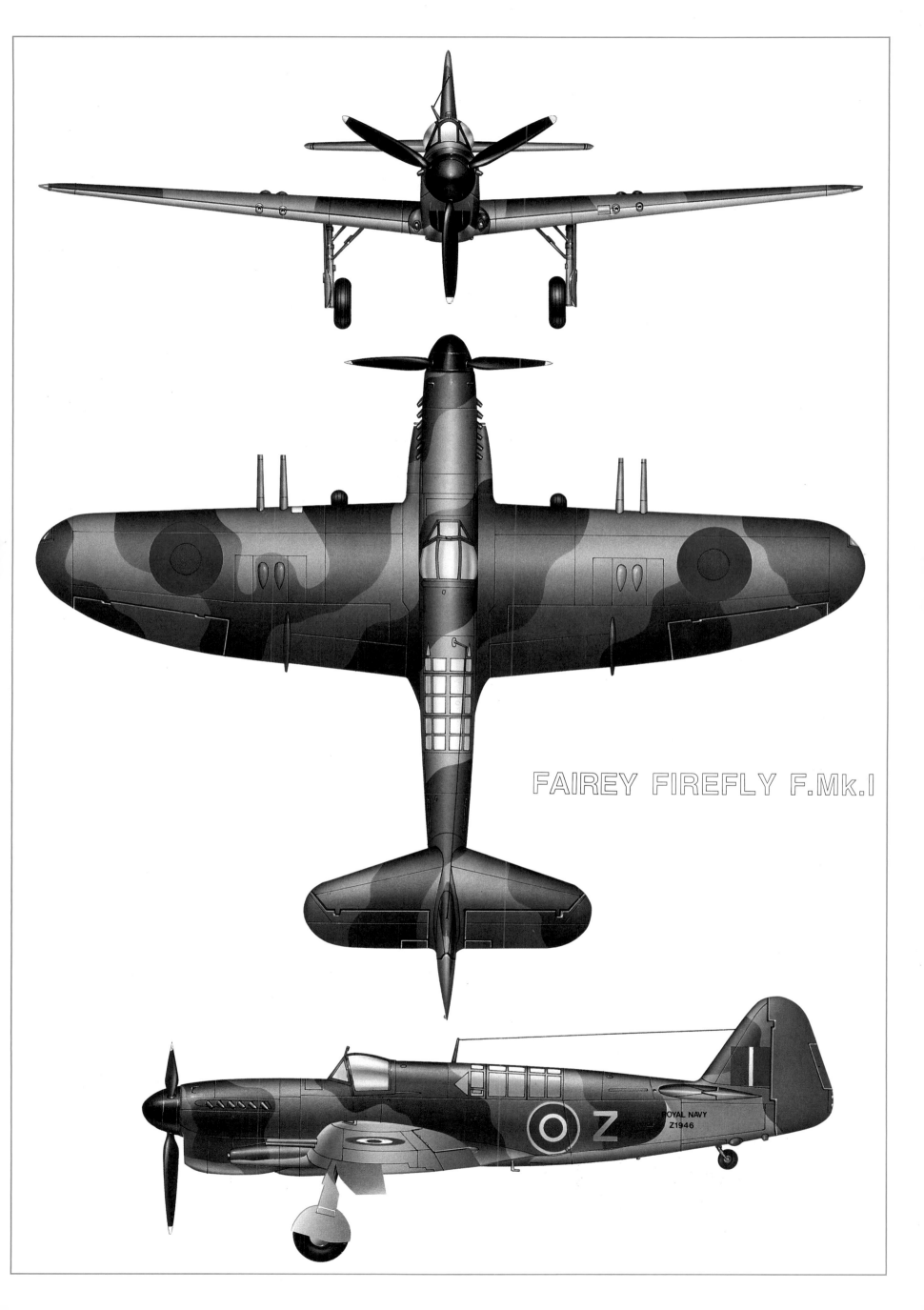

FAIREY FIREFLY F.Mk.I

A Fairey Firefly Mk.I in flight. An aircraft of this type was the first British plane to fly over Tokyo during the war.

In the autumn of 1943, the equipment of British carrier-based aviation improved remarkably as far as quality was concerned when the first Fairey Firefly fighter-reconnaissance aircraft went into service. Compared to its predecessor, the Fulmar (with which, in 1940, the Royal Navy had been provided for the first time with a combat plane with firing power equal to that of the Royal Air Force's contemporary land-based fighters), Fairey's new project proved to be much faster, better armed, and extremely versatile. In fact, the Fireflies were used not only in the traditional role of two-seater fighter-reconnaissance, but also as a bomber and a night fighter. Their overall effectiveness is demonstrated by the fact that the aircraft of the initial Mk.I series remained in front-line service throughout 1946, and those of the final variants built after the war served until the late 1950s. Production came to a halt on April 20, 1956, after a total of 1,702 aircraft had been built, many of which were destined for export.

The project was launched by Fairey in 1940, and the first of the four prototypes took to the air on December 22, 1942. The aircraft's layout was similar to that of the Fulmar: it was an all-metal low-wing monoplane with retractable rear tricycle landing gear. The two crew members were housed in separate cockpits. It was powered by a Rolls-Royce Griffon engine, which in the original version, was capable of generating up to 1,735 hp at an altitude of 980 ft (300 m). The fixed armament consisted of four 20 mm cannons installed in the half-wings. The initial flight and evaluation tests revealed the excellent qualities of the aircraft, especially at low speed, and soon the other three prototypes followed the first (they made their respective maiden flights in March, August, and September). Production was launched at the same time on the basis of an initial order for 300 aircraft, which was doubled in June 1942. The total number of aircraft ordered subsequently rose to 800, although the assembly lines actually completed 459 fighter version Fireflies (F.Mk.I) and 236 of the photo reconnaissance version (FR.Mk.I), characterized by the adoption of a radar apparatus installed in fairing beneath the engine. As for the second production series (NF.Mk.II), conceived as night fighters, only 37 of the 328 aircraft foreseen in the original order were built: it was considered preferable to convert another 140 Firefly FR.Mk.Is for this role.

The first Fireflies became operative on October 1, 1943, on board the aircraft carrier *Indefatigable*, although their debut in combat took place in July of the following year in Norway, during operations against the German battleship *Tirpitz*. However, the main theater of action was the Pacific where, from January 1945 until the Japanese surrender, the Fireflies were used with remarkable success, in all major air-sea operations.

The versions developed after the war deserve to be mentioned; the aircraft was fitted with still more powerful power plants, heavier armament, and was adapted for use in antisubmarine attack. The most important of these included the Mk.IV, powered by a 2,129 hp Griffon 74 engine, of which 160 were built; the Mk.5 (approximately 352 built, taking to the air for the first time on December 12, 1947); the Mk.6 of 1949 (133 built); and the final Mk.7 variant (October 16, 1951, 151 built in all). Lastly, numerous subseries destined for training and target towing were recovered for conversion.

color plate

Fairey Firefly F.Mk.I 1772nd Squadron Royal Navy - H.M.S. *Indefatigable*, Great Britain 1944

Aircraft:	Fairey Firefly Mk.I
Nation:	Great Britain
Manufacturer:	Fairey Aviation Co. Ltd.
Type:	Fighter-bomber
Year:	1943
Engine:	Rolls-Royce Griffon IIB, 12-cylinder V, liquid-cooled, 1,735 hp
Wingspan:	44 ft 6 in (13.56 m)
Length:	37 ft (11.28 m)
Height:	15 ft 5 in (4.74 m)
Weight:	14,288 lb (6,481 kg)
Maximum speed:	319 mph (513 km/h) at 17,000 ft (5,180 m)
Ceiling:	29,000 ft (8,840 m)
Range:	1,364 miles (2,195 km)
Armament:	4×20 mm cannons, 2,002 lb (907 kg) of bombs
Crew:	2

A Fairey Firefly adopted as a fighter-bomber, with bombs beneath the wings.

Considered one of the British Fleet Air Arm's most versatile combat planes during the last years of the war, the Fairey Barracuda was also the first all-metal carrier-based monoplane torpedo plane to be built in Great Britain. These aircraft, used as torpedo planes, bombers, and dive-bombers, went into front-line service early in 1943, ant took part in all subsequent air-sea operations. Many of the approximately 2,600 Barracudas survived the war and remained in active service until 1953, when they were replaced by the American Grumman Avengeres.

The project was launched back in 1937, on the basis of specifications issued by the British Air Ministry that called for the construction of a carrier-based torpedo plane to replace the Albacore biplanes. Six companies participated and eventually, in July 1938, Fairey obtained an order for two prototypes. Initially the choice of engine fell on the new Rolls-Royce Exe (24-cylinders, generating 1,207 hp), but when the program for its development was abandoned, it was decided to install a Merlin 30 engine in the Mk.I production version. The first prototype made its maiden flight on December 7, 1940, and was followed by the second experimental aircraft on June 29, 1941. The aircraft was an all-metal mid-cantilever wing three-seater monoplane, fitted with Fairey-Youngman high lifting devices which remarkably improved its performance at low speed. The cycle of evaluation tests was not completed until February 1942. Production, soon after, went ahead at full speed.

However, only 30 Barracuda Mk.Is came off the assembly lines before the second Mk.II variant was prepared. This differed mainly in its more powerful engine. In order to face the substantial demand, other aeronautical companies were called upon to participate in the program. These included Blackburn, Boulton Paul and Westland. A total of 1,688 aircraft were built.

The Barracuda Mk.II went into service in January 1943, with the 827th Squadron, although it did not receive its baptism of fire until eight months later, in September, during the Allied landings at Salerno. This aircraft's most memorable endeavour took place on April 3, 1944, off the northern coast of Norway, when 42 Barracudas stationed on the aircraft carriers *Victorious* and *Furious* (escorted by Hellcat, Seafire, Wildcat and Corsair fighters) attacked in two waves the German battleship *Tirpitz*, which had taken shelter in a fjord. They inflicted damage that was not irreparable, but which seriously diminished the vessel's capacities. Similar missions were

carried out in the next four months, until the *Tirpitz* was eventually sunk by Lancaster bombers on November 12. In April 1944, the Barracudas also appeared in the Pacific, operating from on board the aircraft carrier *Illustrious*.

The next production variant, the Mk.III, was developed in 1943, expressly for antishipping and anti-submarine attacks. With this aim in mind, radar research apparatus was installed in a radome beneath the rear section of the fuselage. The Barracuda Mk.III went into production in 1944, and 852 were completed.

The last version of the series was the Mk.V, characterized by the adoption of a 2,058 hp Rolls-Royce Griffon 37 engine and by consequent structural modifications (greater wingspan, increase in fuel capacity, and tail fins with a larger surface area). However, its development was very slow, and the first production series aircraft did not appear until November 16, 1944. Of the 140 aircraft ordered, only 30 were delivered before the end of the war. These aircraft never went into service and served as trainers until 1950.

color plate

Fairey Barracuda Mk.II 715th Squadron Royal Navy Air Service - Yeovilton/St. Merryn, 1943-1944

Aircraft:	Fairey Barracuda Mk.II
Nation:	Great Britain
Manufacturer:	Fairey Aviation Co. Ltd.
Type:	Torpedo plane
Year:	1943
Engine:	Rolls-Royce Merlin 32, 12-cylinder V, liquid-cooled, 1,663 hp
Wingspan:	49 ft 3 in (14.99 m)
Length:	39 ft 10 in (12.12 m)
Height:	15 ft 1 in (4.60 m)
Weight:	14,119 lb (6,396 kg)
Maximum speed:	240 mph (386 km/h) at 1,809 ft (550 m)
Ceiling:	16,447 ft (5,000 m)
Range:	683 miles (1,100 km)
Armament:	2 machine guns; 1,642 lb (744 kg) of bombs
Crew:	3

A Fairey Barracuda Mk.II in flight.

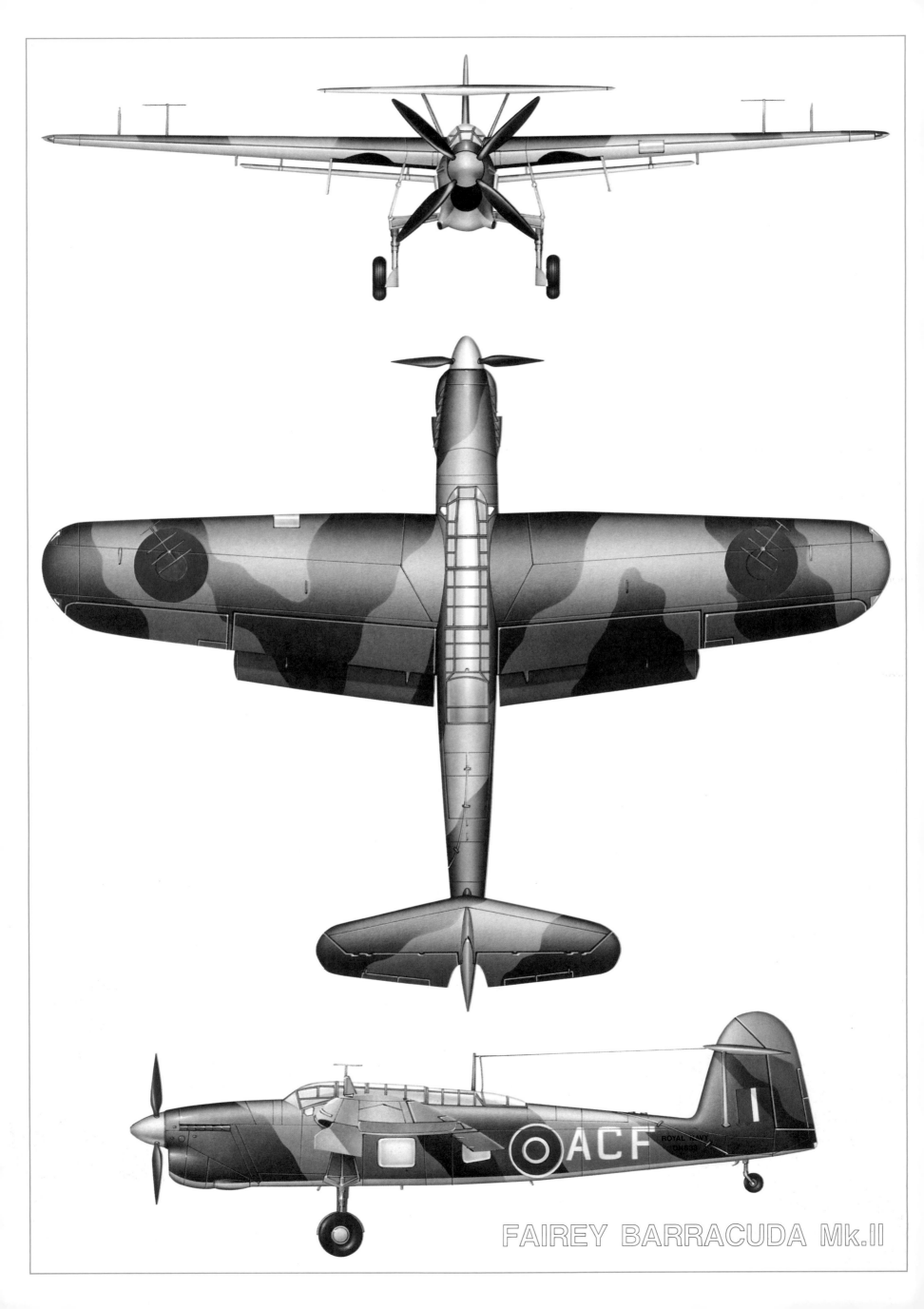

FAIREY BARRACUDA Mk.II

The Royal Air Force's second heavy bomber, the Handley Page Halifax, went into service only three months after the Short Stirling. However, despite this brief space of time, the new aircraft proved to be greatly superior to the previous one. This was due not only to its overall performance, which classified the Halifax as one of the best combat planes of its kind in the entire war, but also to its remarkable versatility, in addition to the role of night bomber, the large four-engine aircraft was used successfully in the roles of transport plane, air ambulance, glider-tower and naval reconnaissance. In all, 6,176 aircraft in a dozen production series came off the assembly lines, and after having been in service from November 1940 until the end of the war, the last of them were not withdrawn until the beginning of 1952. An idea of the importance of the Halifax's operative career in the events of the war can be appreciated with the help of a few figures: from March 11, 1941 (date of the first bombing raid carried out on Le Havre by the aircraft in service with the 35th Squadron of Bomber Command) to April 25, 1945, the four-engine Handley Pages carried out no fewer than 75,532 missions and dropped more than 227,000 tons of bombs on European targets. This career was obscured only by that of the aircraft's direct successor, the Avro Lancaster, the best of the trio of British strategic bombers.

The project for the Halifax originated on the basis of specifications issued by the British Air Ministry in 1935, requesting the creation of a two-engine bomber. Handley Page responded to this request with a project (HP 55) that was rejected. A year later, in September 1936, a second set of specifications was issued, regarding a medium-heavy bomber that was to be powered by a pair of Rolls-Royce Vulture engines that were being developed at the time. Once again, Handley Page responded and its project (HP 56) was judged valid. Subsequently, the project was substantially revised, with the adoption of four Rolls-Royce Merlin engines being foreseen. The construction of two prototypes (HP 57) was authorized on September 3, 1937, and the first of these took to the air on October 25, 1939. Compared to the original specifications, the new aircraft was much larger, and its total weight had more than doubled.

The first Halifax of the initial Mk.I series took to the air almost a year later, on October 11, 1940. It was an all-metal mid-wing monoplane powered by four Rolls-Royce Merlin X engines, each generating 1,280 hp and driving three-bladed variable-pitch metal propellers. The defensive armament consisted of six machine guns, two in a nose turret and four in a rear position; the bomb load totaled 13,000 lb (5,890 kg) and was completely housed inside the fuselage. Following the construction of 2,050 Mk.I and Mk.II series aircraft (the latter was provided with more powerful engines and armament and was characterized by a substantial improvement in performance), toward the middle of 1943, the Mk.III, the second major production variant, appeared and with it the Halifax underwent a radical change: in place of the four liquid-cooled Rolls-Royce engines, Bristol Hercules XVI radials were installed, each generating 1,615 hp. The Halifax Mk.III went into service in February 1944, and 2,060 were built. The final bomber versions were the Mk.VI and Mk.VII, characterized by the adoption of more powerful engines and overall improvements, especially as far as range was concerned.

Among the series not realized for land bombing, mention should be made of the Mk.V, destined for Coastal Command, and the Mk.VII, used for launching paratroops. Immediately after the war, two other variants were built for this particular role: the Mk. VIII (more than 100) and the Mk.IX (approximately 400).

color plate

Handley Page Halifax Mk.III 158th Bomber Squadron Royal Air Force - Lissett, Yorkshire, Great Britain 1945.
One of the four Halifax that exceeded 100 war missions, carrying out 128 raids

Aircraft:	Handley Page Halifax Mk.I
Nation:	Great Britain
Manufacturer:	Handley Page Ltd.
Type:	Bomber
Year:	1940
Engine:	4 Rolls-Royce Merlin X, 12-cylinder V, liquid-cooled, 1,280 hp each
Wingspan:	98 ft 10 in (30.12 m)
Length:	70 ft 1 in (21.36 m)
Height:	20 ft 9 in (6.33 m)
Weight:	55,000 lb (24,947 kg) loaded
Maximum speed:	265 mph (426 km/h) at 17,500 ft (5,300 m)
Ceiling:	22,800 ft (6,950 km)
Range:	1,860 miles (3,000 km)
Armament:	6 machine guns; 13,000 lb (5,890 kg) of bombs
Crew:	7

A Handley Page Halifax Mk.III with fuselage roundels and fin flashes of the type used in the final stages of the war.

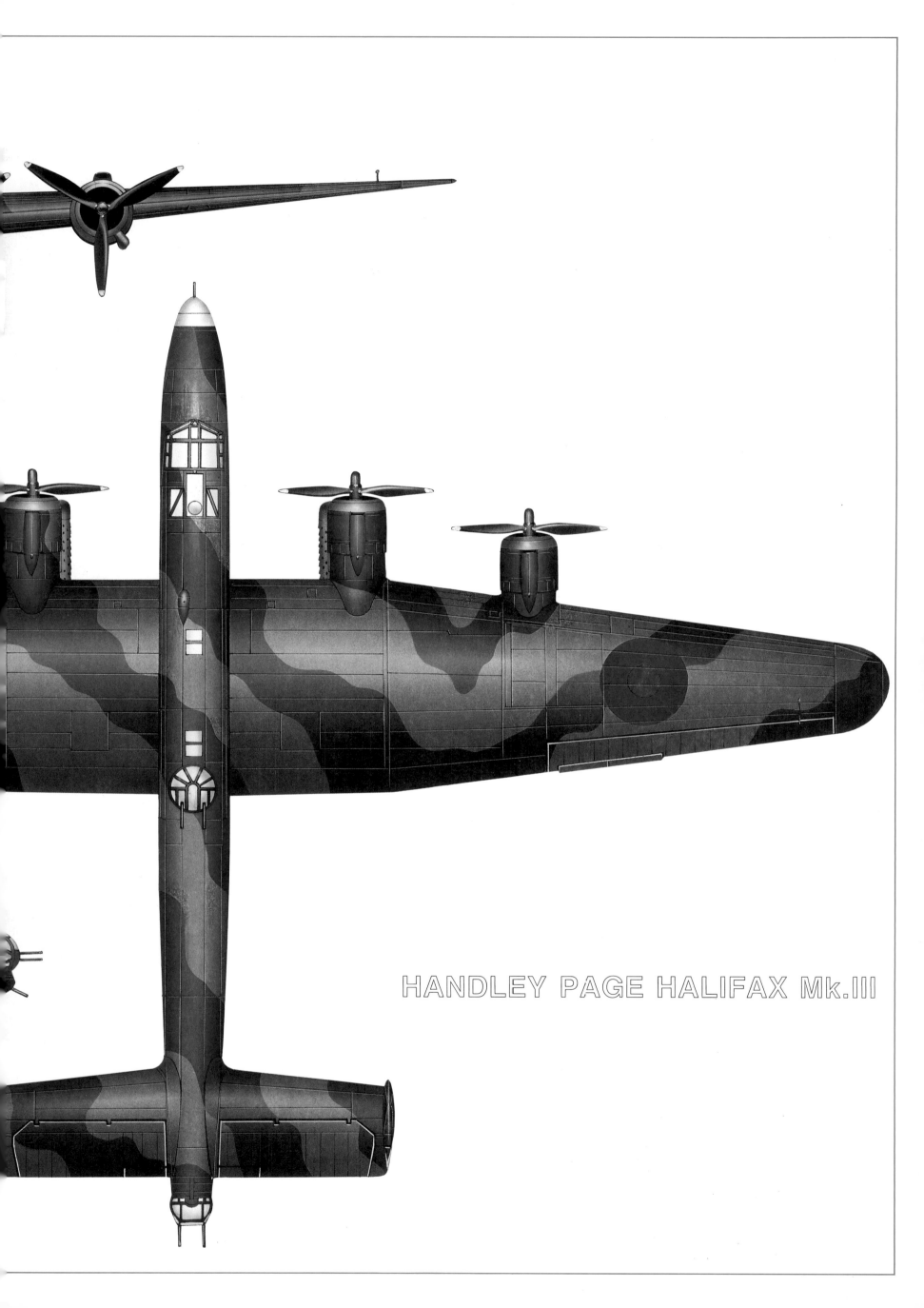

HANDLEY PAGE HALIFAX Mk.III

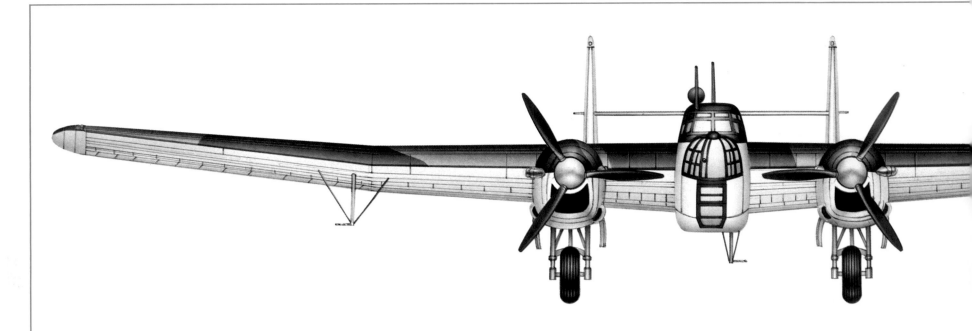

ARMSTRONG WHITWORTH WHITLEY Mk.VII

One of the oldest medium bombers in service in the units of the RAF when the war broke out, the Armstrong Whitworth Whitley was clearly a transitional aircraft, the first of the trio of planes of this type (which included the Vickers Wellington and the Handley Page Hampden) built in Great Britain in the period immediately prior to the war. Although outdated by the time the war broke out, and therefore relegated to night missions, the Whitley nevertheless had a long and extensive operative career, considering that a total of 1,814 were built. They remained in front-line service with the units of Bomber Command until the spring of 1942, while those in Coastal Command were withdrawn almost a year later. They were subsequently relegated to secondary roles.

The Whitley originated on the basis of official specifications issued in July 1934, and an initial production order (for 80 aircraft) was placed before the prototype even took to the air. This made its maiden flight on March 17, 1936, powered by a pair of 795 hp Armstrong Siddeley Tiger X radial engines that drove three-bladed, variable pitch metal propellers. It was a large, middle-wing, twin-engine aircraft, with retractable landing gear and vertical twin rudders, in which the most characteristic feature was the wing. This was quite thick, with a large surface area, and was installed in the fuselage at a sharp angle of incidence, which was transformed into a characteristic "nose down" attitude during flight.

Operative tests and evaluations were completed in the fall, and the first Mk.I series aircraft were delivered at the beginning of 1937. However, only very few (34 in all) of these aircraft were built, and they ceded their place on the assembly lines to 46 Whitley Mk.IIs and 80 Mk.IIIs. The difference between these production variants lay mainly in the armament and in the power of the engines (795 hp and 920 hp Tigers, respectively).

In the following version, the Mk.IV (which made its maiden flight on April 5, 1939, and 40 of which were built), the power plants were radically changed, and a pair of 1,030 hp Rolls-Royce Merlin V-12, were fitted, while the defensive armament was strengthened still further, thanks to the installation of a four-machine-gun tail turret. From this series the major production variant (the Mk.V, of which 1,466 were built) was then derived, featuring the installation of more powerful Merlin engines, as well as modifications to the tail fins and the fuselage. The fuel capacity was also increased, thus providing the aircraft with a greater range. Deliveries of the Whitley Mk.V began in 1939 and terminated in the summer of 1943.

The final variant was the Mk.VII, built expressly for Coastal Command and for the role of naval bomber and antisubmarine fighter. Although the 1,145 hp Merlin engines of the Whitley Mk.Vs were retained, the weight of these aircraft increased notably, considering that they were provided with extra tanks, increasing their fuel capacity from 1,005 USgal (3,805 liters) to 1,320 USgal (5,000 liters) and providing them with a range of 1,676 miles (2,700 km). This resulted in an overall reduction in performance, especially as far as speed was concerned. Nevertheless, the Whitley Mk.VIIs proved to be particularly suited to their role: they went into service toward the end of 1941, and were the first Coastal Command bombers to be provided with long-range submarine tracking radar equipment.

The Whitleys took part in all the major combat operations during the early years of the war. Moreover, they were the first British bombers to fly over Berlin (on October 1, 1939, although only to drop leaflets) and the first to drop bombs on Italian territory, over Turin and Genoa, on June 11, 1940.

color plate
Armstrong Whitworth Whitley Mk.VII 612th Squadron Coastal Command Royal Air Force - 1941

Aircraft:	Armstrong Whitworth Whitley Mk.VII
Nation:	Great Britain
Manufacturer:	Armstrong Whitworth Aircraft Ltd.
Type:	Bomber
Year:	1941
Engine:	2 Rolls-Royce Merlin X, 12-cylinder V, liquid-cooled, 1,145 hp each
Wingspan:	84 ft (25.60 m)
Length:	70 ft 6 in (21.49 m)
Height:	15 ft (4.57 m)
Weight:	28,200 lb (12,792 kg) loaded
Takeoff weight:	34,190 lb (15,488 kg)
Maximum speed:	215 mph (346 km/h) at 14,795 ft (4,498 m)
Ceiling:	17,600 ft (5,365 m)
Range:	1,676 miles (2,700 km)
Armament:	5 machine guns; 6,000 lb (2,718 kg) of bombs
Crew:	5/6

An Armstrong Whitworth Whitley. On October 1, 1939, bombers of this type carried out the first daylight raid on Berlin.

After the Short Stirling and the Handley Page Halifax, the Lancaster was the last heavy bomber model to go into front-line service with the RAF during the war. However, although it went into service almost a year and a half after its predecessors, the four-engine Avro was clearly superior. Some idea of the importance this aircraft had in the Allied arsenal can be gained from a few figures: from the end of 1941 to the beginning of 1946, a total of 7,366 Lancasters was built; they completed 156,000 missions in the course of the conflict, dropping a total of 608,612 tons of bombs. In comparison, a total of 6,176 Halifaxes was built, and between March 11, 1941 (the date of their first bombing mission), and April 25, 1945, they carried out 75,532 missions, dropping more than 227,000 tons of bombs on European targets.

The specifications that gave rise to the Lancaster were the same as those from which the Halifax project originated in September 1936. The Air Ministry requested the construction of a bomber powered by two Rolls-Royce Vulture engines that were being developed at the time. Avro proposed its model 679 Manchester, which took to the air in the form of a prototype on July 25, 1939, going into production at the end of a series of evaluation tests. The new bomber went into service in November 1940, but right from the start of its operative career the inadequacy of its engines became apparent. They proved to be incapable of providing the aircraft with a performance that could be considered acceptable, especially at altitude. The program seemed destined to fail, considering that Rolls-Royce was too busy with production of the Merlin engine to find time to improve the Vulture, an especially complex power plant. A solution was found in the summer of 1940. This consisted in modifying the Manchester in such a way that it could be fitted with four Merlin engines. Roy Chadwick, the designer, immediately started work on a Manchester taken from the assembly lines, and on January 9, 1941, the new prototype (designated Manchester Mk.III) took to the air. It was followed on May 13 by a second aircraft, and flight tests went beyond even the most optimistic expectations, revealing excellent general characteristics. It was therefore decided to put the four-engine aircraft (officially designated Lancaster Mk.I) into production, replacing the Manchester on the assembly lines as soon as the 200th aircraft had been completed. The first production series Lancaster took to the air on October 31: it differed from the prototype above all in the adoption of more powerful Merlin engines and the installation of turrets on the aircraft's back and in the belly, a considerable increase in weight when fully loaded that also penalized its performance as far as speed was concerned.

Nevertheless, the new bomber was still an excellent aircraft, and production was soon proceeding at a great rate, using assembly lines belonging to other aeronautical manufacturers, such as Austin Motors, Vickers-Armstrong, and Armstrong Whitworth. In all, 3,425 Lancaster Mk.Is were completed, and their operative career (which commenced at the beginning of 1942) was intensive for the entire duration of the conflict. Apart from its excellent flying characteristics and overall performance, the Lancaster's success was also due to its great capacity, which allowed it to carry bombs of increasing size and weight. Many Mk.Is were specially modified to drop bombs weighing over 12,015 lb (5,443 kg), even managing to carry the "Grand Slam," which, at 22,028 lb (9,979 kg), was the heaviest bomb to be carried by an aircraft in the course of the war. The first of these was released on March 14, 1945. Among the numerous missions in which the Lancasters played a leading role, mention should be made of the attack to the Moehne, Eder, and Sorpe dams in the Ruhr Valley on the night of May 16/17, 1943. The four-engine aircraft were modified for the occasion in order to carry the special rotating bombs developed by Barnes Wallis.

The high production rate of the Mk.I soon led to a shortage in Merlin engines, and the need to find alternative engines led to the construction of the next variants, the Mk.II and Mk.III.

color plate

Avro Lancaster Mk.I 106th Bomber Squadron RAF - Conningsby, Great Britain 1943

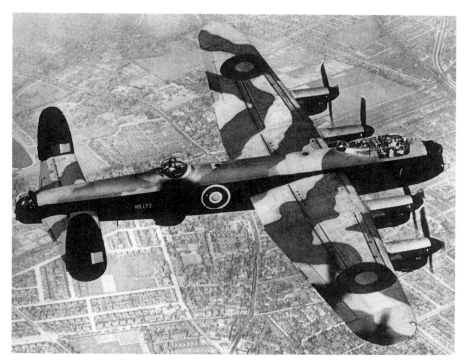

An Avro Lancaster in flight. The aircraft is equipped with an H25 radar beneath the fuselage.

A Lancaster expressly modified for launching the special bombs meant to destroy the dams on the Ruhr. The mission was carried out by the RAF's 617th Bomber Squadron, known as the "Dam Busters".

Aircraft:	Avro Lancaster Mk.I
Nation:	Great Britain
Manufacturer:	A.V. Roe & Co. Ltd.
Type:	Bomber
Year:	1942
Engine:	4 Rolls-Royce Merlin XXIV, 12-cylinder V, liquid-cooled, 1,620 hp each
Wingspan:	102 ft 3 in (31.09 m)
Length:	69 ft 8 in (21.18 m)
Height:	20 ft 0 in (6.10 m)
Weight:	70,092 lb (31,752 kg)
Maximum speed:	286 mph (462 km/h) at 11,513 ft (3,500 m)
Ceiling:	24,671 ft (7,500 m)
Range:	2,527 miles (4,070 km)
Armament:	8 machine guns; 22,046 lb (9,987 kg) of bombs
Crew:	7

AVRO LANCASTER Mk.I

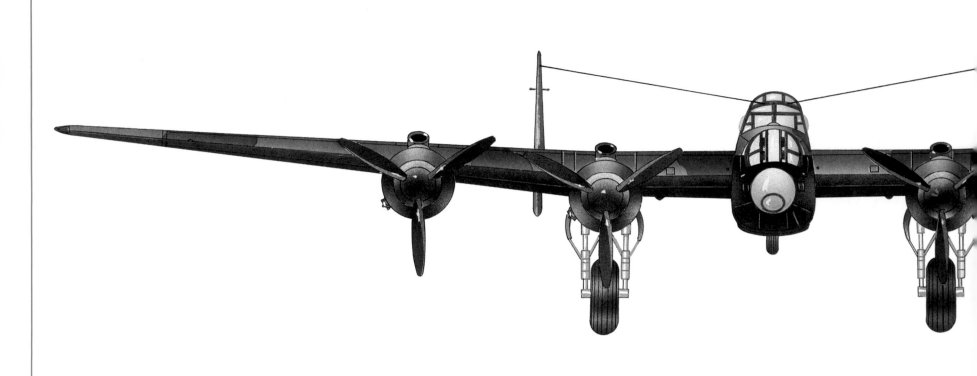

AVRO LANCASTER Mk.II

KD⊙A   DS685

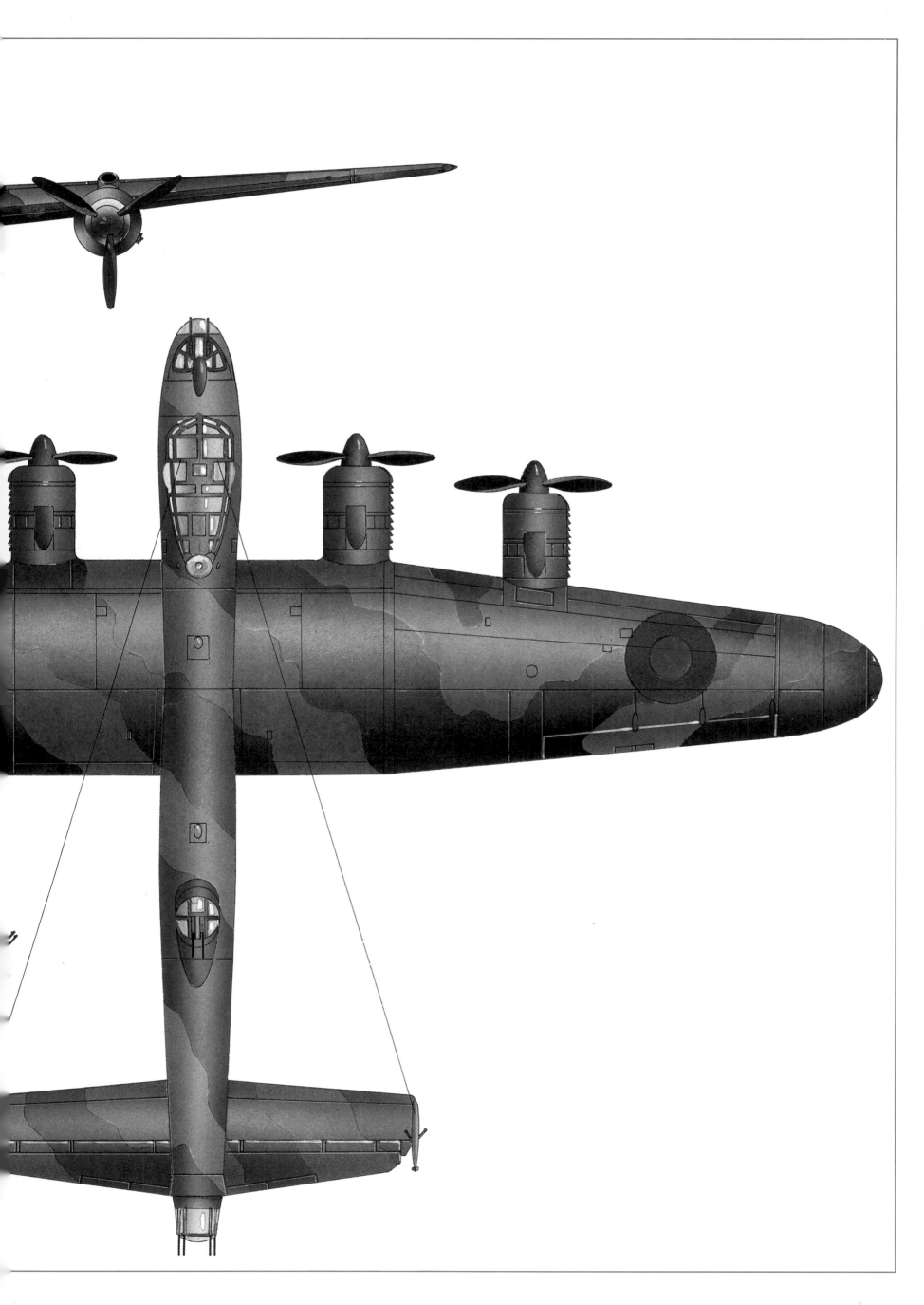

The Lancaster's great success and the high production rate that had been imposed back in 1941, soon created a shortage of Rolls-Royce Merlin engines. In fact, this prestigious engine equipped practically all of the most successful aircraft built by the British aeronautical industry (from the Spitfire to the Hurricane, from the Mosquito to the numerous types of aircraft in the Fleet Air Arm, as well as the Lancaster itself) and its assembly lines went ahead at full speed in order to satisfy the increasing demand. It was therefore the actual need to compensate for possible deficiency in the supply of the engine that led to the construction of a second production variant of the bomber, fitted with an alternative engine. The 1,735 hp Bristol Hercules radial (the VI and XVI versions) was selected and installed on a Lancaster prototype in the second half of 1941.

The aircraft was flown for the first time on November 26, and at the beginning of the following year, together with another two experimental aircraft, it was submitted to an intensive cycle of evaluations. The results were satisfactory, and production was launched immediately afterwards, with the designation Lancaster Mk.II. The new bombers went into service in March 1943, and they gradually began to re-equip several units of Bomber Command.

However, despite its good overall characteristics, the Lancaster Mk.II never succeeded in equaling those fitted with Merlin engines. Although its performance in takeoff, ascent and at low altitude was better, it was slower in flight and consumed more fuel. Production ceased after 301 had been completed. The decision to abandon the radial engines also occurred due to the arrival in Great Britain of the first Rolls-Royce Merlin engines built in the United States by Packard. This new and plentiful supply eventually dispelled all fears of a shortage of these plants.

The subsequent Mk.III version was in fact fitted with American engines, and, apart from this and slight modifications to the tip of the nose, it was practically identical to the first production variant. A total of 3,039 were built in all. The final version was designated Mk.VII (180 built). The American Martin turret on the aircraft's back was its only major difference. Moreover, 430 Lancasters were built in Canada by the Victory Aircraft company and designated Mk.X. They were fitted with Packard-Merlin engines. The first was completed on August 6, 1943.

Lastly, mention should be made of a special subseries (very few were built) created by the conversion of several Lancaster Mk.Is and Mk.IIIs. This was the Mk.VII, which appeared toward the end of 1944, and was characterized by Merlin engines generating 1,635 hp and each controlling four-bladed propeller instead of a three-bladed one. These aircraft, which lacked armament, apart from the turret on their back, carried electronic ap-

A line up of Lancasters at Waterbeach, in 1944.

paratus, thus creating disturbance in the enemy's radar.

The end of the war did not mark the end of the Lancaster's career. These four-engine aircraft remained in front-line service with Bomber Command for a long period, until the arrival of the Avro Lincoln immediately after the war. Many were subsequently modified for photoreconnaissance and remained in service until the 1950s.

---

color plate

Avro Lancaster Mk.II 115th Squadron Royal Air Force. This aircraft was shot down on the night of August 2-3, 1944, during a raid on Hamburg

---

Aircraft:	Avro Lancaster Mk.II
Nation:	Great Britain
Manufacturer:	A.V. Roe & Co. Ltd.
Type:	Bomber
Year:	1943
Engine:	4 Bristol Hercules VI, 14-cylinder radial, air-cooled, 1,735 hp each
Wingspan:	102 ft 3 in (31.09 m)
Length:	69 ft 8 in (21.18 m)
Height:	20 ft (6.10 m)
Weight:	63,083 lb (28,577 kg)
Maximum speed:	264 mph (426 km/h) at 14,036 ft (4,267 m)
Ceiling:	18,552 ft (5,640 m)
Range:	2,547 miles (4,103 km)
Armament:	10 machine guns; 14,017 lb (6,350 kg) of bombs
Crew:	7

A Lancaster flying with only one engine working.

This Lancaster is one of the thirty aircraft shot down during the raid against Hamburg.

Among the countries involved in the conflict, Great Britain was the first to feel the need for a four-engine heavy bomber. The first aircraft of this type was the Short Stirling, although, unlike its successors, the Handley Page Halifax and the Avro Lancaster, it did not prove to be particularly effective in the role for which it had been conceived, especially as far as its performance at high altitude was concerned. Nevertheless, the Stirling remained in front-line service until the middle of 1943, when it was gradually used for less important missions and relegated to secondary roles, such as transport and glider-towing, for which the last two production series, the Mk.IV and the Mk.V, were purposely built. A total of 2,371 aircraft in four major production versions came off the assembly lines.

The Stirling originated in 1936, when the British Air Ministry issued specifications for a heavy bomber with a seven- or eight-man crew. Short traditionally specialized in the construction of seaplanes, and the Stirling was its first large land aircraft with retractable landing gear. Its designers therefore preferred to study suitable solutions on a reduced-scale model before building the actual prototype. Designated Short S.31 and powered by four 91 hp Pobjoy Niagara engines, this experimental aircraft was a half-scale version of the four-engine aircraft. It was flown for the first time in great secrecy on September 19, 1938 and the experiences that followed were considered extremely useful as far as the development of the real project was concerned. Nevertheless, following its maiden flight on May 14, 1939, the first ''real'' prototype, the Short S.29 Stirling, was totally destroyed while landing. It was therefore necessary to build a second experimental aircraft with which to complete the series of flight tests and evaluations. The aircraft went into production sometime after and the first Stirling Mk.I took to the air on May 7, 1940. Three months later, deliveries to the units of Bomber Command commenced, and the aircraft made its operational debut on the night of February 10-11, 1941 in an air raid on Rotterdam.

This mission was the first of a long series of bombing attacks, first in daylight and then solely at night, in which the Short Stirling was used until the more effective Halifax and Lancaster bombers became available in greater numbers. In fact, the Stirling had an insufficient operative ceiling (mainly due to its wings being too short, although this had specifically been requested by the Air Ministry at the start so that the aircraft would fit existing hangars), and it was incapable of carrying large, high-potency bombs. It carried out its last mission in the units of Bomber Command on September 8, 1944, although halfway through the previous year

the Stirling had virtually been withdrawn from front-line duty, gradually being assigned to glider-towing and transport.

In 1942, the initial production series was followed by aircraft of the Mk.III variant, which featured heavier armament, with a new type of turret on the aircraft's back, and more powerful engines, the 1,650 hp Hercules XVI. Previously, the construction of a version built on license in Canada had been planned. This was designated Mk.II and fitted with American Wright-Cyclone R-2600 engines, but only very few had been completed. The next series, the Mk.IV, was developed specifically for glider-towing: deprived of two-thirds of its defensive armament and provided with the appropriate equipment, it proved to be very effective, and the 450 aircraft of this type built took part in all the major operations during the last two years of the conflict, making their debut on June 6, 1944, during the Allied invasion of Normandy. The last Stirlings to be built were 160 Mk.Vs that were transformed into transport planes and were in service from January 1945 throughout the whole of the following year, when they were replaced by the Avro York.

color plate

Short Stirling Mk.I 7th Bomber Squadron Royal Air Force - Oakington, Great Britain 1941

Aircraft:	Short Stirling Mk.I
Nation:	Great Britain
Manufacturer:	Short Brothers Ltd.
Type:	Bomber
Year:	1940
Engine:	4 Bristol Hercules XI, 14-cylinder radial, air-cooled, 1,590 hp each
Wingspan:	99 ft 1 in (30.21 m)
Length:	87 ft 3 in (26.60 m)
Height:	22 ft 9 in (6.93 m)
Weight:	59,400 lb (26,943 kg) loaded
Maximum speed:	260 mph (418 km/h) at 10,500 ft (3,200 m)
Ceiling:	17,000 ft (5,180 m)
Range:	2,330 miles (3,750 km)
Armament:	8 machine guns; 14,000 lb (6,350 kg) of bombs
Crew:	7-8

A Short Stirling Mk.III adopted by the 214th Squadron of the Royal Air Force.

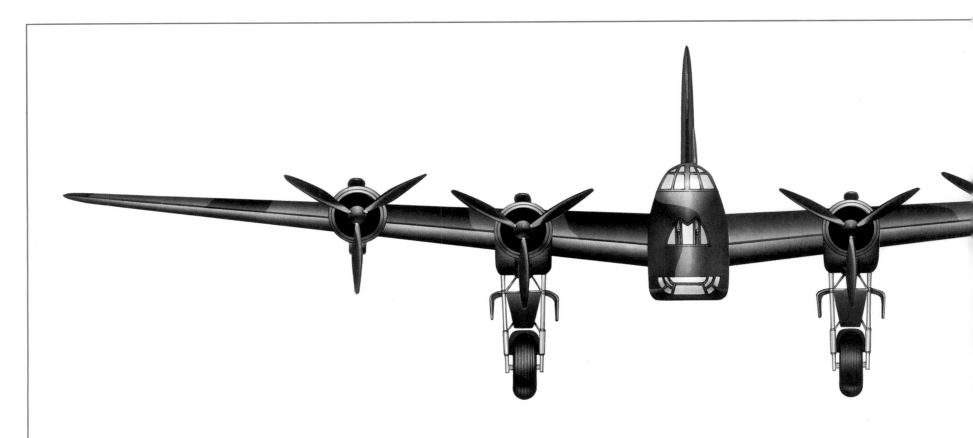

SHORT STIRLING Mk.I

Unanimously recognized as one of the most versatile and effective combat planes built in the course of the war, the de Havilland Mosquito has rightly earned a prominent position among the "immortals" of aviation history. Fighter, reconnaissance plane, bomber: in virtually every role this elegant all-wood two-engine aircraft proved to be remarkable. Its performance was unsurpassable, and it was a deadly weapon, so much so that the final versions remained in service long after the war was over. It was not until 1951 that the units of Bomber Command replaced the old "Mossie" with the twin-jet English Electric Canberra. From 1941 to 1950, no fewer than 6,439 Mosquitos in a dozen variants were built in Great Britain, while a further 1,342 aircraft were constructed in Canada and Australia.

The DH 98 project was launched privately by de Havilland in 1938. The aim was to construct a bomber-reconnaissance plane capable of flying at such a high altitude and at such a great speed that it would not need defensive armament. It was undoubtedly an original beginning, and it was perhaps for this very reason that the project was not initially accepted by the official authorities. It was not until World War II had begun that the Air Ministry began to reconsider de Havilland's proposal, especially since it was planned to build the aircraft entirely in wood, a feature that would have proved invaluable should a shortage of strategic materials have arisen. Work began in great secrecy at the end of December 1939, and just under a year later, on November 25, 1940, the first prototype took to the air.

Right from the start it became apparent that the Mosquito was a "thoroughbred," provided with exceptional maneuverability as well as being extremely fast both in horizontal flight and in ascent (during tests it reached 397 mph - 640 km/h). The key to this success lay in a fortunate combination of several factors: the carefully studied aerodynamic lines; the high weight/power ratio; the pairing of an extremely valid airframe with two equally excellent engines, in this case the Rolls-Royce Merlin. Official skepticism turned to interest, and it was decided to give immediate priority to production. The series of official evaluations began on February 19, 1941, and the first prototype was followed by a second fighter version (on May 15) and by a third reconnaissance version (on June 10). This variant (PA Mk.I) was the first to go into service, in September, as well as to confirm the validity of the theory that had given rise to the project: on September 17, during a daytime reconnaissance mission in France, a Mosquito PA Mk.I easily managed to escape three Messerschmitt Bf.109s that had attacked it by climbing to an altitude of 23,066 ft (7,000 m).

In May 1942 the first Mosquito bomber went into service (241 of this series, the Mk.IV, were built, in two subseries), almost at the same time as the night fighter variant (the Mk.II, of which 467 were built). Many other series were derived from these three initial ones, characterized by constant improvements and up-datings.

A detail showing the position of the Mosquito's armament, concentrated in the nose, and the door by which the crew entered the aircraft.

The reconnaissance versions were almost always derived from bomber variants, the second version of which was the Mk.IX, which appeared in the spring of 1943: it had more powerful engines, and its bomb load was doubled. Toward the end of the same year, the major production series of bombers followed (known as the Mk.XVI, 1,200 were built). These aircraft were provided with a pressurized cockpit, and their bomb load was increased to 3,973 lb (1,800 kg). As for the night fighters, following the construction of 467 Mosquito Mk.IIs, 97 Mk.XIIs and 270 Mk.XIIIs were built from March 1943 and February 1944 respectively.

However, the Mosquito was most widely employed in the role of fighter-bomber. The Mk.VI series was derived directly from the Mk.II adding to the already heavy armament of the fighter two 254 lb (115 kg) bombs in the fuselage and another two beneath the wings; this load was subsequently doubled. This series was the most numerous of all, with a total of 2,584 aircraft being constructed. These Mosquitos went into service in 1943, also being employed by Coastal Command in the role of antishipping attack. They were mainly armed with eight rockets, although a 57 mm cannon was installed for antisubmarine attack. This modification was carried out on 25 aircraft designated Mk.XVIII.

color plate
de Havilland Mosquito Mk.IV 139th Bomber Squadron RAF - Great Britain 1943

Aircraft:	de Havilland Mosquito Mk.IV
Nation:	Great Britain
Manufacturer:	de Havilland Aircraft Co. Ltd.
Type:	Bomber
Year:	1942
Engine:	2 Rolls-Royce Merlin XXI, 12-cylinder V, liquid-cooled, 1,250 hp each
Wingspan:	54 ft 3 in (16.51 m)
Length:	40 ft 10 in (12.42 m)
Height:	15 ft 3 in (4.65 m)
Weight:	21,823 lb (9,886 kg)
Maximum speed:	380 mph (612 km/h) at 21,052 ft (6,400 m)
Ceiling:	31,082 ft (9,449 m)
Range:	1,219 miles (1,963 km)
Armament:	2,002 lb (907 kg) of bombs
Crew:	2

A de Havilland Mosquito in flight. The photo shows the bomber version with glazed nose.

DE HAVILLAND MOSQUITO Mk.IV

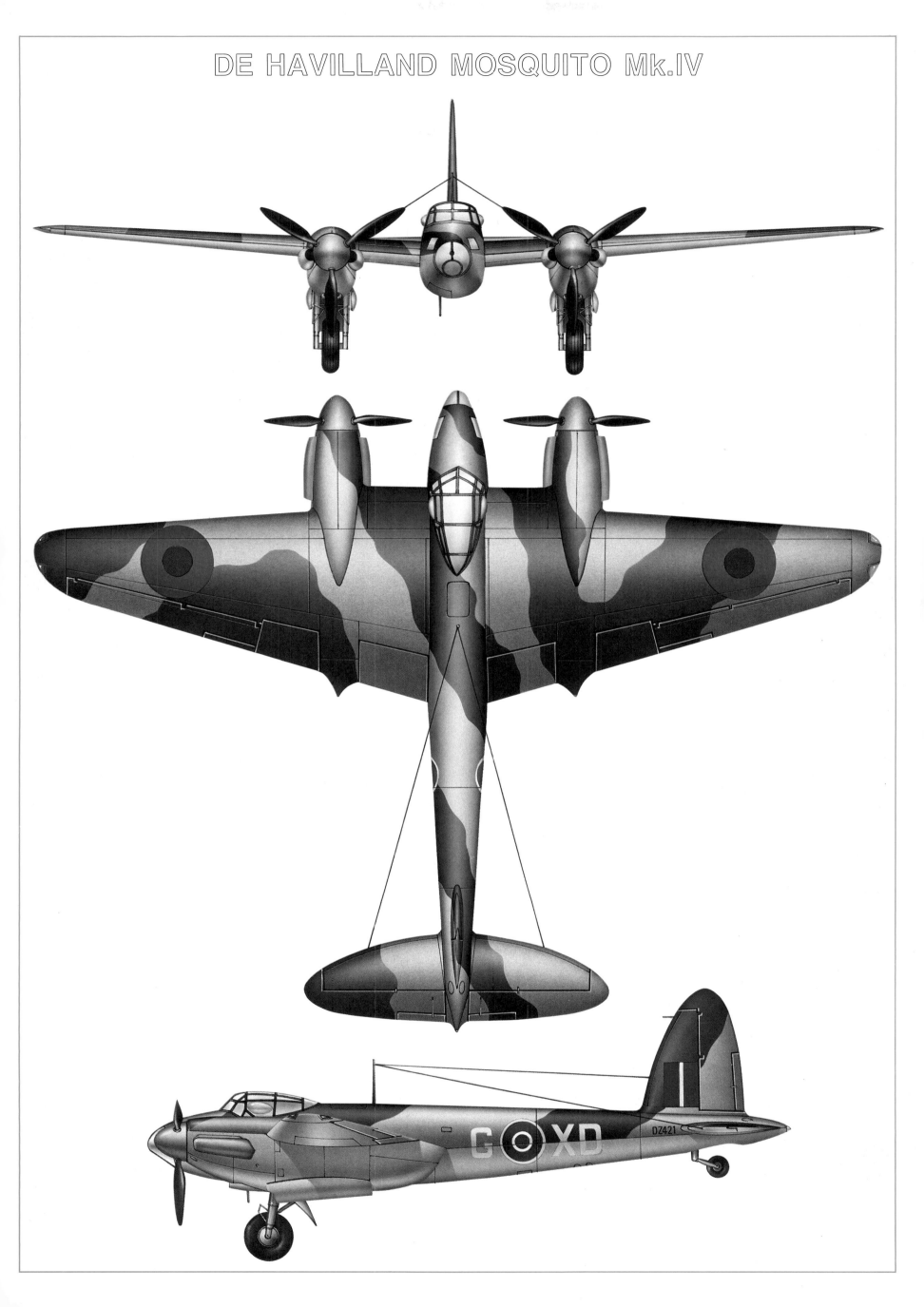

The RAF's last biplane fighter, the Gladiator marked the final stage in the development of a series of combat planes of which the Grebe, the Gamecock, and the Gauntlet were the best examples produced by the Gloster Company during the 1920s, and 1930s. Moreover, at a time when the monoplane dominated the international aeronautical scene, this agile biplane shared with the Italian Fiat C.R.42 and the Russian Polikarpov I-153 the honor of being the last plane of this type to see combat duty. In the first two years of the war, although it was clearly a transition plane, the Gladiator performed valiantly on both the European and African fronts and in the Mediterranean. By the spring of 1940, production reached a total of 746 aircraft, 165 of which were exported to several countries (including Sweden, Belgium, China, Norway, and Ireland), guaranteeing the project's success well beyond British territory.

The specifications that gave birth to the Gladiator were issued in 1930. These requested a new fighter, faster and more heavily armed than other planes then in service. More particularly, the maximum speed was to be 248 mph (400 km/h) and the aircraft was to carry four machine guns instead of the standard two. The building of the prototype was entrusted to a team headed by H.P. Folland, and work began in the spring of 1934. The plane, known as the SS.37, made its first flight in September, with results that were remarkable right from the start. Powered by a 645 hp Bristol Mercury VIS radial engine (its power was to increase notably once production began), the prototype reached 242 mph (390 km/h) at an altitude of 11,500 ft (3,500 m). Official testing began on April 3, 1935, and three months later a first order was placed for 23 aircraft. The Gladiator prototype was a more advanced version of its direct predecessor, the Gauntlet, and although it maintained its general structure, it was more aerodynamic and robust. It also featured landing gear without additional struts. The production models differed in that they were fitted with an 840 hp Mercury engine and carried four Browning machine guns (as opposed to the prototype, which carried two Vickers guns and two Lewises). Their cockpit was also provided with a sliding canopy. The first planes of the Mk.I series were delivered in July 1936 and went into service in February, the following year. Altogether, 378 of these aircraft were built.

Soon after (in 1938), a second production series, known as the Mk.II, appeared. This was virtually identical except for its engine and its propeller, the original wooden two-bladed one being replaced by a three-bladed, fixed-pitch metal one. A seagoing variant of this version was also produced, and featured a landing hook, reinforcements for catapult launching, and an inflatable dinghy in a streamlined housing under the fuselage. Christened the Sea Gladiator, 98 of these models were produced.

A Gloster Gladiator Mk.I in flight over the English countryside.

When the war broke out, the Gladiator was in use in 13 Fighter Command squadrons. In November 1939, two units were sent to France, where they were involved in heavy combat until May, of the following year, while in April 1940, another squadron was sent to Norway. These early missions soon proved that the Glosters were clearly inferior compared to the more modern German aircraft, and from the Battle of Britain onward, the Gladiators were assigned to lighter duty: only one Squadron remained in Britain, the rest were sent to Africa and the Mediterranean area, where they were involved in combat until the fall of 1941. Their career on these fronts was undoubtedly aided by the overall mediocrity of the Italian fighters, their principal adversaries.

color plate
Gloster Gladiator Mk.I 73rd Royal Air Force Squadron - 1938

Aircraft:	Gloster Gladiator Mk.II
Nation:	Great Britain
Manufacturer:	Gloster Aircraft Co. Ltd.
Type:	Fighter
Year:	1938
Engine:	Bristol Mercury VIII A, 9-cylinder radial, air-cooled, 840 hp
Wingspan:	32 ft 3 in (9.83 m)
Length:	27 ft 5 in (8.36 m)
Height:	10 ft 2 in (3.10 m)
Weight:	4,850 lb (2,200 kg)
Maximum speed:	257 mph (414 km/h) at 14,500 ft (4,420 m)
Ceiling:	33,490 ft (10,210 m)
Range:	444 miles (715 km)
Armament:	4 machine guns
Crew:	1

A Gloster Gladiator Mk.II with three-bladed metal propeller.

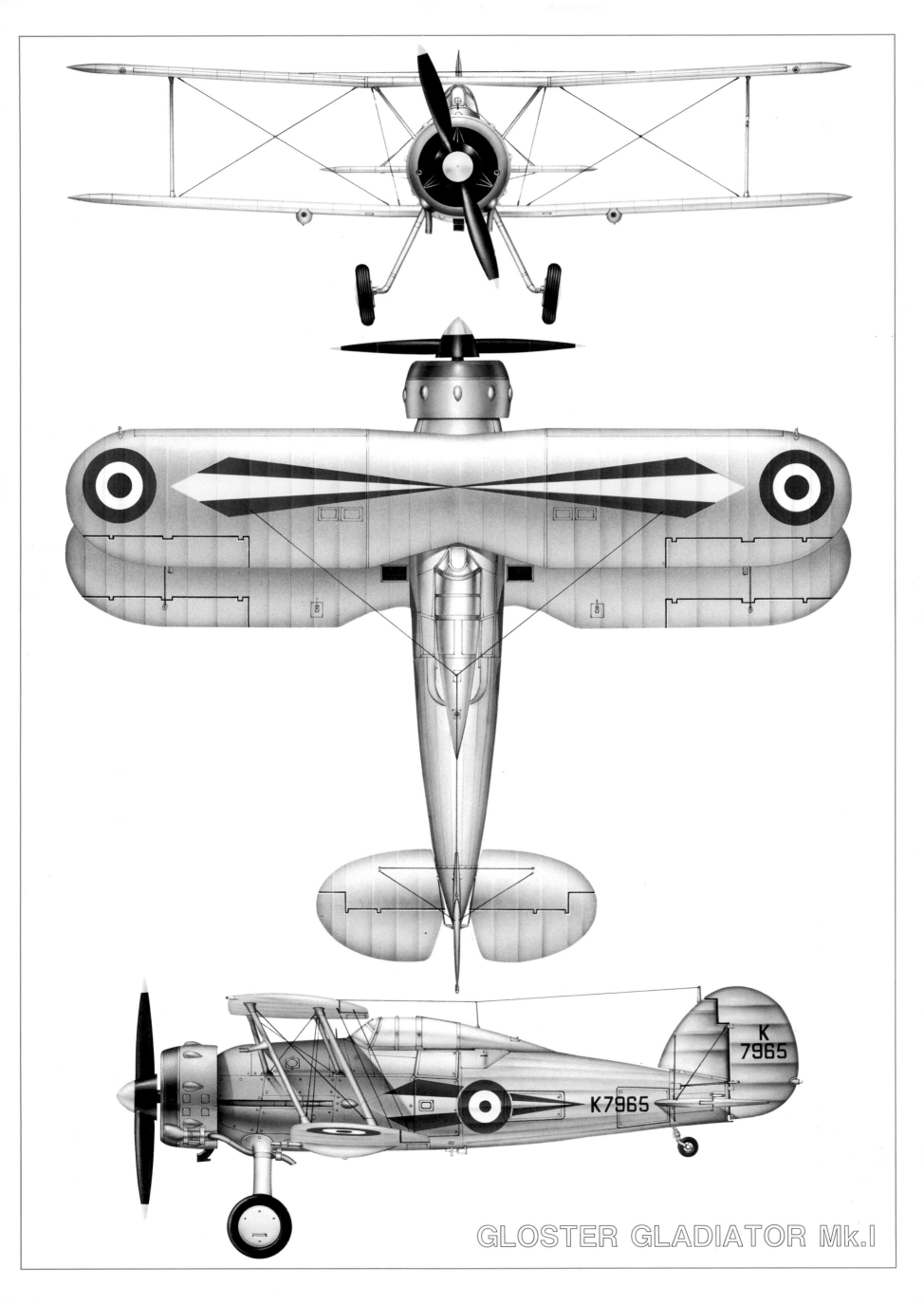

GLOSTER GLADIATOR Mk.I

GLOSTER METEOR Mk.III

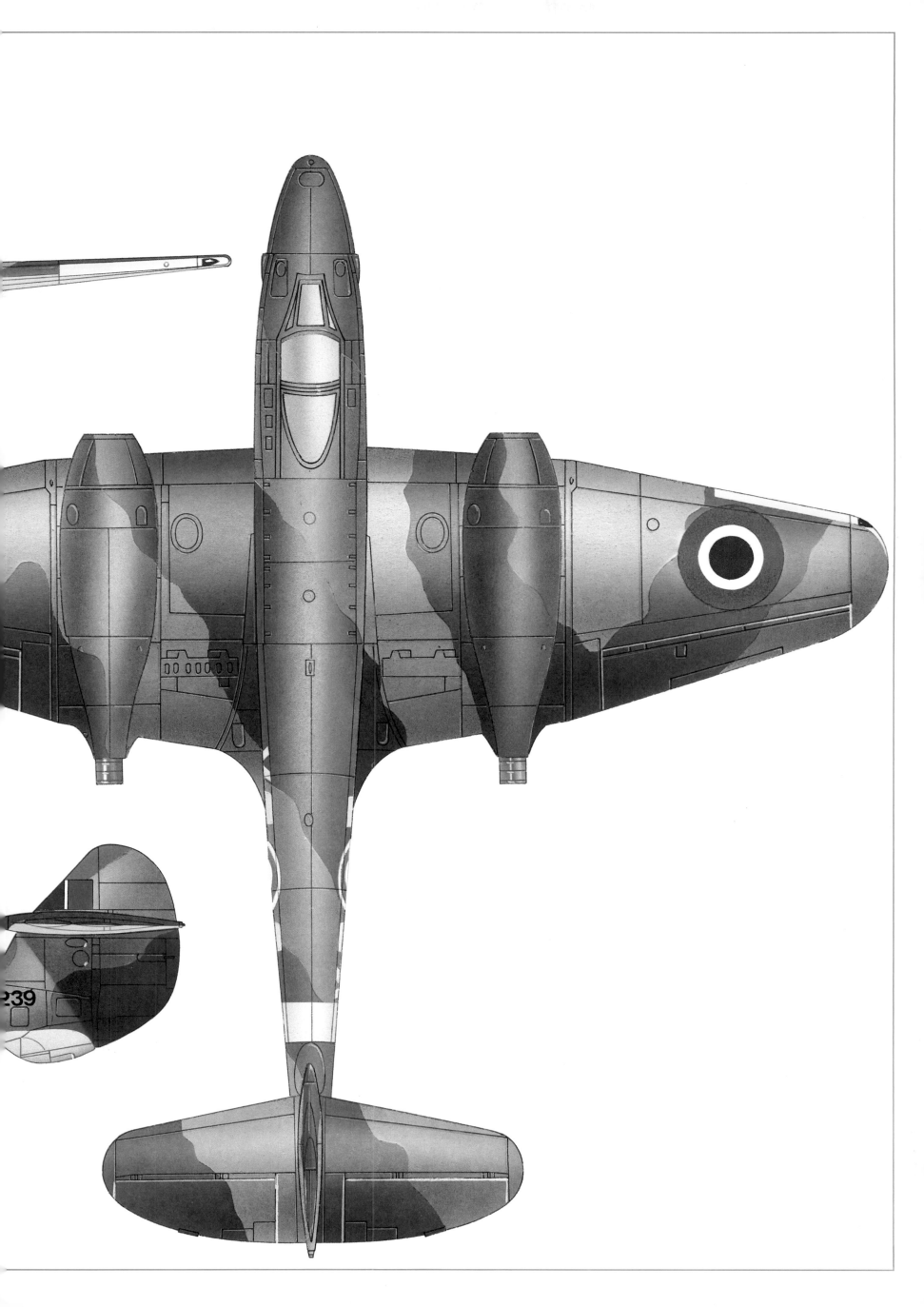

In the close race for the construction of a jet fighter, Great Britain took second place, following Germany. Nevertheless, its Gloster Meteor had the honor of going down in history as the only Allied aircraft of the new generation to go into service before the end of World War II. Despite its limited career during the final months of the war in Europe (in which it did not have the chance of measuring itself against its great rival, the Messerschmitt Me.262), the Meteor also marked the end of an era in the British Royal Air Force and the beginning of a phase that was to see rapid developments in the immediate postwar years. Production of these aircraft continued until 1954, almost 3,900 were completed, the last of which remained in frontline service until August 1951.

The program was launched in August, 1940, while the Battle of Britain was in progress, on the basis of official specifications coded F.9/40. George Carter, the technicians charged with the project, chose a two-engine configuration. This was due to the fact that the earliest types of turbojets were at an experimental phase at the time and were not yet capable of providing the thrust necessary to guarantee the desired performance alone. In February 1941, 12 prototypes were ordered (although only eight were completed) and the first (equipped with W.2B engines with 205 lb — 454 kg — thrust) began tests on the ground in July of the following year. Delays in tuning the engine led to the installation of different engines in the remaining experimental aircraft, and the first to take to the air was the fifth prototype, powered by a pair of Halfors H.1 turbojets with 2,302 lb (1,403 kg) thrust, on March 5, 1943. It was an historical date, although the first flight by a jet-propelled aircraft had taken place in Britain on May 15, 1941, carried out by an experimental model of the Gloster (designated E. 28/39) powered by a single Whittle W.1 engine with 860 lb (390 kg) thrust.

The initial production series Meteors (Mk.I) were in fact provided with turbojets derived from the Whittle W.I, the W.2B/23 model with 1,700 lb (770 kg) thrust, which Rolls-Royce had prepared and constructed under the name of Welland. The launching of series production was marked by an order for 20 fighters and the first of these (which took to the air on January 12, 1944) was delivered to the United States in February, in exchange for a pre-series Bell YP-59A Airacomet, the first jet plane to be built on the other side of the Atlantic. Other Meteor Mk.Is were used for the development of the airframe and the engine unit, and the remaining aircraft were delivered to the RAF by June.

The first unit to receive the new fighters was the 616th Squadron, which entered service in July. On the 27th, the first mission was carried out against the German flying bombs and on August 4, one of these was shot down. The missions against the V-1s continued throughout the summer and, apart from their reasonable success, they served mainly to train pilots and ground staff in us-

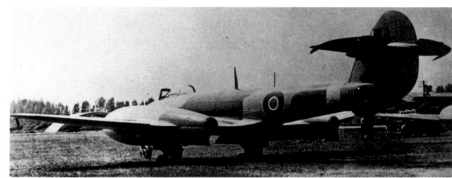

A Meteor Mk.I. This version was employed by the RAF in combat, also operating from bases on the Continent.

ing the new aircraft, as well as to study particular tactics and combat techniques.

In the meantime, a new variant of the Meteor had been prepared, the Mk.III, of which about 200 were to be produced, 15 with Welland engines and 195 with Rolls-Royce Derwent engines, with 1,997 lb (905 kg) thrust. These aircraft formed part of the second and final version to enter service in World War II. They were also characterized by their greater fuel capacity and a sliding drop canopy, instead of the Meteor Mk.I's canopy which was hinged to the side. The first was delivered on December 18, 1944 to the 616th Squadron and in January 1945, these aircraft were sent to Belgium, thus becoming the first Allied jet fighter to serve on the Continent.

---

color plate
Gloster Meteor Mk.III 616th Squadron Royal Air Force - England, 1944

Aircraft:	Gloster Meteor Mk.III
Nation:	Great Britain
Manufacturer:	Gloster Aircraft Co. Ltd.
Type:	Fighter
Year:	1945
Engine:	2 Rolls-Royce Derwent 1, turbojet with 1,997 lb (905 kg) thrust
Wingspan:	43 ft 1 in (13.11 m)
Length:	41 ft 4 in (12.57 m)
Height:	13 ft (3.96 m)
Weight:	13,818 lb (6,260 kg)
Maximum speed:	492 mph (793 km/h) at 30,098 ft (9,150 m)
Ceiling:	44,078 ft (13,400 m)
Range:	1,338 miles (2,156 km)
Armament:	4 × 20 mm cannons
Crew:	1

A Gloster Meteor Mk.III. The aircraft went into service during the final days of the conflict.

One of the Henschel Hs.123 prototypes.

Aircraft:	Henschel Hs.123A-1
Nation:	Germany
Manufacturer:	Henschel Flugzeugwerke AG
Type:	Ground attack fighter
Year:	1936
Engine:	BMW 132 Dc, 9-cylinder radial, air-cooled, 880 hp
Wingspan:	34 ft 5 in (10.50 m)
Length:	27 ft 4 in (8.33 m)
Height:	10 ft 6 in (3.21 m)
Weight:	4,888 lb (2,200 kg) loaded
Maximum speed:	212 mph (317 km/h) at 3,940 ft (1,200 m)
Ceiling:	29,525 ft (9,000 m)
Range:	534 miles (860 km)
Armament:	2 machine guns; 440 lb (200 kg) of bombs
Crew:	1

A Henschel Hs.123A forming part of the Condor Legion during the Spanish Civil War.

A Luftwaffe Hs.123 with civilian registration, prior to the expiring of the Treaty of Versailles and German rearmament.

The Luftwaffe's first dive-bomber, this was also the last biplane to serve in the German air force. The Henschel Hs.123 was produced under the initiative of General Ernst Udet — one of the protagonists in the revival of aeronautics in Germany in the period between the two wars — on the basis of official specifications issued in 1933. It appeared two years later, and although it was obviously out-of-date by the time World War II broke out, the Hs.123 was nevertheless used extensively in action during the early months of the conflict.

In response to the specifications in 1933, both Henschel and Fieseler (the latter produced the Fi.98) submitted designs that were rather similar in their overall configuration: a single-seater biplane with metal fuselage. Both prototypes were completed early in 1935, but right from the time of the first tests, the general superiority of the Hs.123 V1's performance became apparent. It had made its maiden flight on May 8, piloted by Udet himself. The aircraft was favored above all by its greater aerodynamic efficiency, guaranteed by the clear and simple structure of its sesquiplane wings, provided with only a single interplane strut and totally free of metal bracing.

The first prototype was followed by another two experimental aircraft and official testing started at the beginning of June. During the tests, however, two planes were lost in circumstances that threw doubts on the strength of the aircraft: in both cases, the Hs.123's structure had broken down during the recovery phase following a deep dive, with disastrous results. Investigation revealed that the central wing section had given way. The design was therefore reexamined, and all the modifications were incorporated into a fourth prototype. This passed a series of evaluation tests with positive results and went into production. The first production series, known as the Hs.123A-1 and provided with a more powerful version of the BMW 132 radial engine that had powered the prototypes, were delivered to units from the middle of 1936.

The military potential of the new aircraft was soon put to the test in action: in December 1936, five Hs.123s were sent to Spain as part of the Condor Legion. Their missions began early in the following year and revealed that the aircraft's qualities made it suited not so much for the role of dive-bomber (as had been the original intention) as for use in ground attack working in cooperation with land forces.

However, the Hs.123's active career began to draw slowly to a close with the appearance of the Ju.87 Stuka and the subsequent decision by the Luftwaffe to standardize its dive-bomber units with the more effective and advanced Junkers design. Production ceased in the fall of 1938, despite the fact that two other prototypes had been prepared in the meantime with the intention of producing two further variants: the first (Hs.123B) was provided with a 960 hp BMW 132K engine that drove a three-bladed, variable-pitch, metal propeller; the second variant (Hs.123C) was for use in ground attack and was provided with another pair of machine guns installed in the lower wing. However, neither of these variants was ever followed up.

At the outbreak of war, all the Hs.123s were relegated to training or to secondary roles, and only one unit remained in front-line action. On September 1, 1939 these planes carried out in Poland the first ground attack of World War II, and they remained in service, in a tactical support role, up to the conclusion of the French campaign. They continued to be used, although on increasingly rare occasions, up to the summer of 1944.

color plate

Henschel Hs.123A-1 Grupo 24 Aviaciòn del Tercio (24th Group of the Spanish Nationalist Air Force) - 1939

HENSCHEL Hs.123A-1

HENSCHEL Hs.129 B-2/R-2

Experiences in Spain with attack aircraft of the Henschel Hs.123 and Junkers Ju.87 type led the German Air Ministry (RLM or *Reichluftfahrtministerium*) to request manufacturers to build a heavier aircraft, conceived expressly for the role of ground attack, antitank attack in particular, heavily armored and powered by two engines to guarantee greater reliability in the case of enemy attack. The model that emerged as the winner was the Henschel Hs.129, a veritable "flying tank". A total of 879 of these aircraft was eventually produced, and in the final subseries it was even armed with a 75 mm cannon installed in a container in the belly. Although these aircraft were difficult to handle and did not have a particularly outstanding performance record, they proved to be extremely effective in their role. They were used mainly on the eastern front and, to a lesser extent, in North Africa, Italy, and France.

The project, whose development was followed by Henschel's technical director Friedrich Nicolaus, was completed during 1938, and the first of the three prototypes (Hs. 129 V-1) took to the air at the beginning of the following year. It was a compact, low-wing monoplane with retractable landing gear and was powered originally by a pair of Argus As.410 12-cylinder V air-cooled engines, each generating 465 hp. Its main feature was the heavy armor on the fuselage: in particular, the pilot was virtually enclosed in a capsulelike structure of steel varying in thickness between 0.2 and 0.4 in (6 mm and 12 mm) and weighing almost half a ton on its own, while the windscreen was in 3 in (75 mm) thick reinforced glass. The aircraft's armament was to consist of two 20 mm MG 151 cannons and two 7.9 mm MG 17 machine guns, all installed on either side of the nose.

However, during flight tests and a series of operative evaluations, the Hs.129's performance proved to be inadequate, while the cramped cockpit and, in particular, the poor visibility available to the pilot were severely criticized by the test pilots. In spite of this negative judgment, the Hs.129 went into production with an order for eight preseries aircraft designated A-0.

The A-1 series version was never built. Henschel (which in the meantime had prepared a new project that was larger and provided with more powerful engines) was asked to install two Gnome-Rhône 14M 14-cylinder radial engines generating 700 hp each on the Hs.129. Toward the end of 1940, a small series of seven Hs.129 B-0s modified in this way was built. In addition, the pilot's cockpit was restructured, and although still cramped it was provided with a larger canopy. Production was launched in December 1941, with the B-1/R-3 series, and deliveries to the units began on March 28 of the following year. The aircraft made its operational debut at the beginning of May on the eastern front.

The Hs.129 was subject to continuous updating that was almost exclusively concerned its armament. The 1942 B-1/R-2 series was provided with a third cannon, a 30 mm MK.101 type, installed

beneath the fuselage; another four MG 17-type machine guns were added to the B-1/R-3; the bomb load of the B-1/R-4 reached 551 lb (250 kg); and the aircraft of the B-1/R-5 series were adapted for photo reconnaissance. The subvariants of the 1943 B-2 series were characterized by their greater efficiency in the role of antitank attack: in the B-2/R-1, the pair of 7.9 mm machine guns were replaced by two 13 mm weapons of the MG 131 type; in the B-2/R-2 a 30 mm MK 103 ventral cannon was added, which became a 37 mm BK 3.7 in the B-2/R-3 variant and a 75 mm PaK 40 in the B-2/R-4. This armament also characterized the last of the series, the Hs.129 B-3, in which the 75 mm cannon was a BK 7.5 type worked by electropneumatic controls. This aircraft, of which approximately 25 were built, was tested in May 1944 and went into service on the eastern front in September, proving to be a formidable weapon against the heavy Russian tanks.

color plate
Henschel Hs.129 B-2/R-2 8 (Pz)/Sch. G1 Luftwaffe - Russian front 1943

A Hs.129 A characterized by inline engine.

A Hs.129 B captured by the Allies during evaluation tests.

Rear view of a Hs.129 B. The fully enclosed blast troughs for the guns are clearly seen.

Aircraft:	Henschel Hs.129 B-2/R-2
Nation:	Germany
Manufacturer:	Henschel Flugzeugwerke AG
Type:	Ground attack
Year:	1942
Engine:	2 Gnome-Rhône 14M, 14-cylinder radial, air-cooled, 700 hp each
Wingspan:	46 ft 7 in (14.20 m)
Length:	32 ft (9.73 m)
Height:	10 ft 8 in (3.25 m)
Weight:	11,574 lb (5,243 kg) loaded
Maximum speed:	253 mph (407 km/h) at 12,570 ft (3,800 m)
Ceiling:	29,530 ft (9,000 m)
Range:	428 miles (690 km)
Armament:	2 × 20 mm cannons; 1 × 30 mm cannon; 6 machine guns
Crew:	1

Designed in 1933, the Junkers Ju.87 Stuka remained in production until 1944. More than 5,700 of these aircraft were completed in a dozen versions, and it went down in history as one of the most widely used combat planes in the entire German aeronautical arsenal. However, apart from this purely quantitative aspect, this ugly and awkward aircraft played a primary role in the gloomy events of World War II, more particularly so because it became (at least in the early years of the conflict) the true symbol of the Luftwaffe's strength. The Stuka (short for *Sturzkampfflugzeug*, the word for dive-bomber used in Germany to indicate all aircraft of this type) was the real protagonist of Germany's lightning war; and it was the Stuka, apart from its actual fighting potential, that sowed terror among its adversaries with the characteristic whistling sound that accompanied its rapid dive toward its target. Even when the myth surrounding this aircraft slowly began the fade (and this commenced during the Battle of Britain), it remained virtually irreplaceable in its role, so much so that the German aeronautical industry proved incapable of producing a substitute of equal value, despite the great progress it made during the war.

The Ju.87 project was launched in 1933, in response to a request from the German military authorities for the construction of an aircraft for use as a dive-bomber. Four manufacturers answered the call (Arado, Blohm und Voss, Heinkel, and Junkers), and in March 1936, after an extensive series of comparative tests, the Junkers prototype was chosen. The aircraft, designed by Hermann Pohlmann, had made its maiden flight at the beginning of 1935, but during the months that followed it had been substantially modified. In fact, the original prototype had been characterized by double tail planes and the use of a British Rolls-Royce Kestrel engine, generating 525 hp at take-off, that drove a two-bladed wooden propeller. The tests brought to light problems in the engines, which had a tendency to overheat, as well as symptoms of structural weakness, and in the second prototype, therefore, a 610 hp Junkers Jumo engine was chosen, and this drove a three-bladed variable pitch metal propeller. More particularly, a single tail plane configuration was adopted. All these modifications, as well as other details, were incorporated into a third prototype, which provided the basis for the first production version.

The Ju.87 had an all-metal airframe and covering, wings of the characteristic "inverted gull" shape, and fixed landing gear housed in large fairings. The main bomb load was installed in a support at the center of the fuselage, while the initial defensive armament consisted of a fixed 7.9 mm machine gun in a half-wing and a similar flexible weapon in the rear of the completely glazed cockpit.

The first production variant (Ju.87 A-1) appeared at the beginning of 1937 and was used mainly as a trainer. Later, these aircraft saw limited combat duty during the Spanish Civil War. In 1938, the initial version was followed by the first variant of the B series (the Ju.87 B-1), characterized by the use of a more powerful Jumo engine and by modifications to the fuselage and empennage. This was the first version to be built in any great number; the second most produced was the D series, in which the aircraft was further improved from a structural and aerodynamic point of view and was provided with more powerful power plants and armament. Deliveries of the first series (Ju.87 D-1) to the units of the Luftwaffe commenced in the spring of 1941; the following year, the final G version was developed from this basic variant and specialized in antitank attack.

color plate

Junkers Ju.87 B-2 Trop. Luftwaffe Gruppe 1/Stukageschwader 1 - North Africa 1941

Aircraft:	Junkers Ju.87 B-1
Nation:	Germany
Manufacturer:	Junkers Flugzeug und Motorenwerke AG
Type:	Attack
Year:	1938
Engine:	Junkers Jumo 211, 12-cylinder V, liquid-cooled, 1,200 hp
Wingspan:	45 ft 3 in (13.79 m)
Length:	36 ft 5 in (11.10 m)
Height:	13 ft 2 in (4.01 m)
Weight:	9,560 lb (4,330 kg) loaded
Maximum speed:	238 mph (383 km/h) at 13,410 ft (4,090 m)
Ceiling:	26,250 ft (8,000 m)
Range:	490 miles (788 km)
Armament:	3 machine guns; 1,100 lb (500 kg) of bombs
Crew:	2

A Ju.87 B belonging to the Stukageschwader 1, damaged and captured by the British in North Africa. Its camouflage is unusual for a German aircraft.

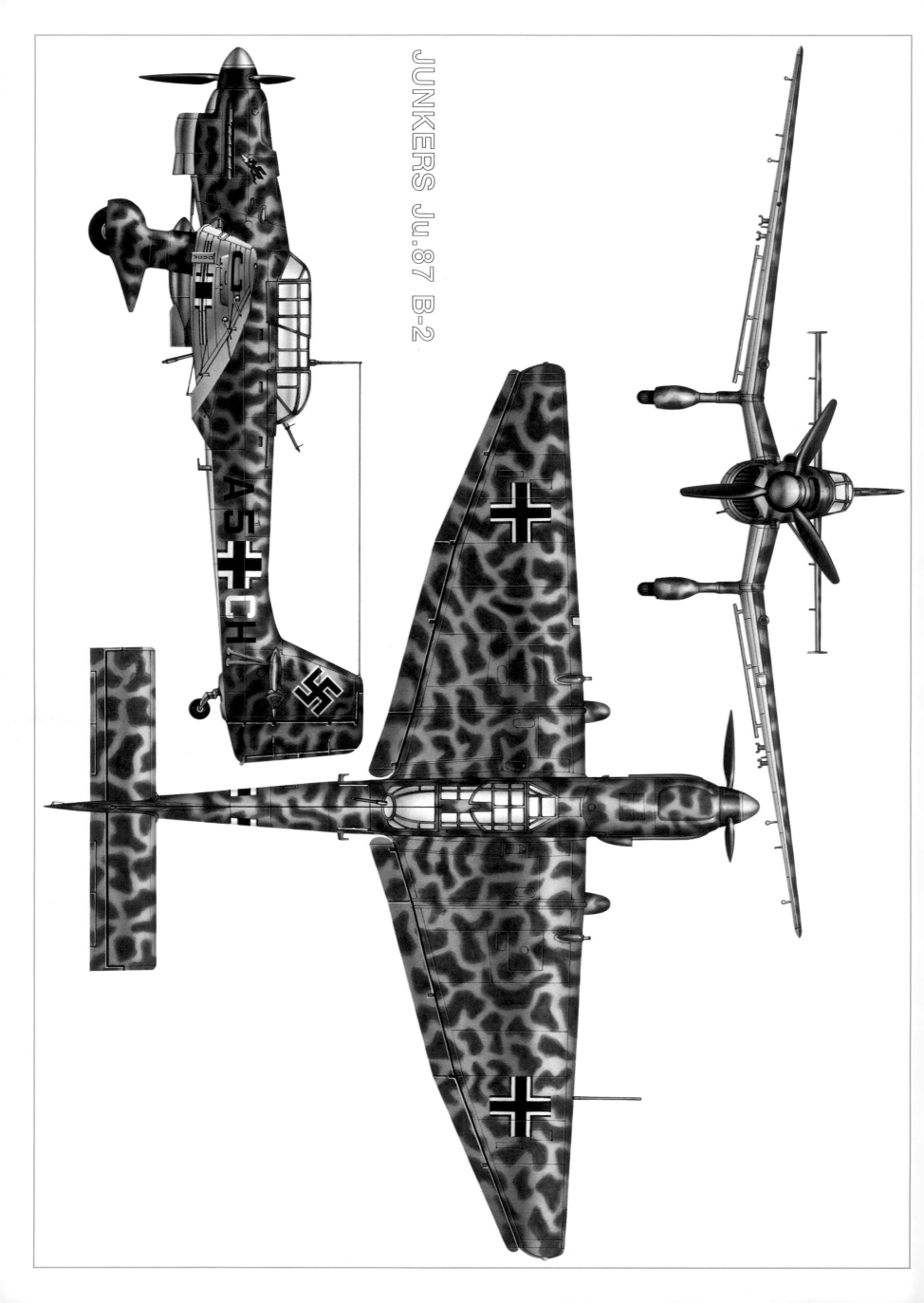

JUNKERS Ju.87 B-2

JUNKERS Ju.87 G

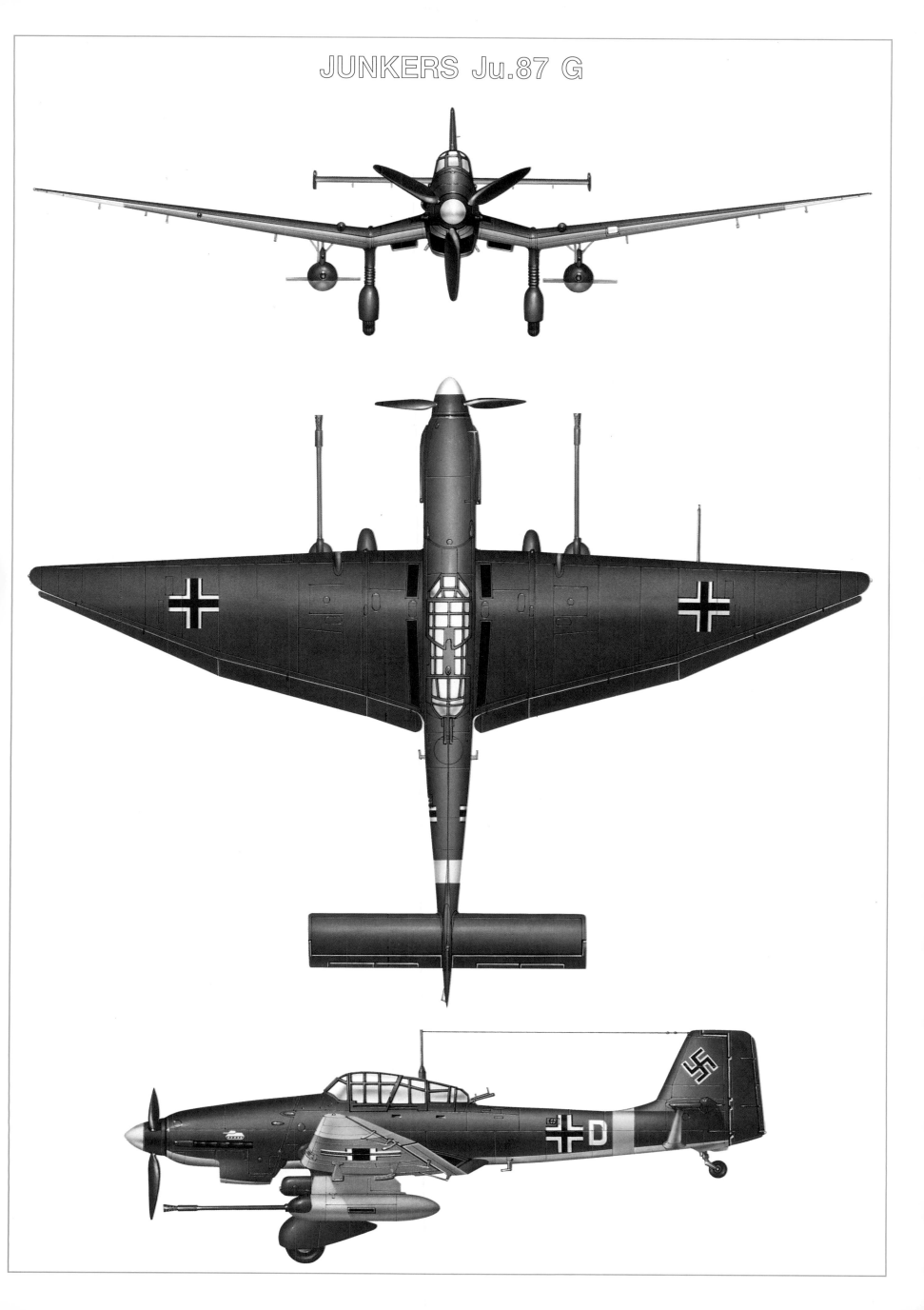

The *Stuka-Kanone*, a Junkers Ju.87 D armed with two cannons below the wings, intended to operate in the intercepting of flying tanks.

Despite the fact that it had been designed in 1933, the Junkers Ju.87 Stuka was one of the most active combat planes to be built in Germany during the conflict. The Stuka remained in production until 1944, a total of more than 5,700 being constructed in all, and it was virtually irreplaceable. In fact, despite numerous projects drawn up with the aim of substituting it, the aircraft remained in front-line service on all fronts until the last day of the war, even after the myth surrounding it as a war machine had greatly declined. Following the initial A and B variants, the most widely used was the D, which appeared in 1941 and represented the maximum development of the airframe.

Compared to its predecessors, the overall performance of the Ju.87 D was remarkably improved (thanks to the adoption of a more powerful Junkers Jumo engine and more carefully studied aerodynamics). It also had better defense (with four machine guns and increased protection for the crew) and was better armed, with the bomb load being increased to 3,973 lb (1,800 kg). The first series (Ju.87 D-1) began to equip the Luftwaffe units in the spring of 1941 and was gradually joined by other subseries that differed from one another mainly in their armament and the power of their engines. The most widely used of these was the D-3, built for ground attack and provided with better armor. A variant specialized in night missions (the D-7) was derived both from it and the subsequent Ju.87 D-5 and was powered by a 1,500 hp Jumo 211P engine. Moreover, 20 mm cannons replaced the machine guns situated on the wings.

It was difficult to find a role for which the Stuka had not been widely tested. Nevertheless, in 1942, the need for an effective antitank weapon led to the construction of a new version, specialized in this very role. This was the Ju.87 G, the last of the long series to go into service and characterized by the installation of two 37 mm BK 3.7 cannons beneath the wings.

The idea of strengthening the offensive armament to a maximum was not new, although up till then all attempts at this had not proved to be a great success in Germany (as, for example, in the case of the Henschel Hs.129). However, in the case of the Ju.87, the result proved without a doubt to be better: although the overall weight of the aircraft increased remarkably, thus affecting its performance (especially as far as speed, altitude, and range were concerned), it proved to be particularly effective. The 37 mm cannon was already used in antiaircraft attack on the ground, weighed 801 lb (363 kg), and was fed by six-shot loaders. It was a deadly weapon in antitank attack, thanks above all to its great initial firing speed, which was more than 2,796 ft (850 m) per second. The Junkers Ju.87 G-1 (the only series to be built) was obtained by modifying the D-5 airframe, on which the experimental installa-

tion was successfully tested in the summer of 1942. These aircraft were employed almost exclusively in Russia and on the eastern front, and it was at the controls of these aircraft that Hans Ulrich Rudel scored his remarkable record, unique among all the pilots who took part in the war: no fewer than 519 Soviet tanks destroyed during 2,530 combat missions, in the course of which he was shot down no fewer than 30 times.

In order to complete the long production of the Ju.87, mention should also be made of another variant that derived directly from the D version.

This was the H, destined for training and built with the aim of speeding up to a maximum the preparation of fighter and bomber pilots in order to replace the heavy losses suffered by the units on the eastern front. Five subseries of the Ju.87 H were built, and the aircraft differed from its predecessors solely due to the presence of dual controls, lack of armament, and a modification to the rear part of the canopy in order to improve the instructor's visibility.

color plate
Junkers Ju.87 G 10 (Pz)/SG1 Luftwaffe - Eastern front 1944

Aircraft:	Junkers Ju.87 G-1
Nation:	Germany
Manufacturer:	Junkers Flugzeug und Motorenwerke AG
Type:	Attack
Year:	1942
Engine:	Junkers Jumo 211J, 12-cylinder V, liquid-cooled, 1,400 hp
Wingspan:	49 ft 3 in (15.00 m)
Length:	37 ft 9 in (11.50 m)
Height:	12 ft 9 in (3.90 m)
Weight:	14,569 lb (6,600 kg)
Maximum speed:	195 mph (314 km/h)
Range:	198 miles (320 km)
Armament:	2×37 mm cannon; 1 machine gun
Crew:	2

A Ju.87 D in service with the *Regia Aeronautica*, photographed at an airport in Sardinia in the spring of 1943.

In the ambiguous rearmament policy carried out by Germany in the early 1930s, almost all of the bombers that would later equip the Luftwaffe once the war broke out (with the exception of the Junkers Ju.88) had originated as civilian transport planes. In the case of the Junkers Ju.86, its design gained its fame thanks to the aircraft's commercial career: 50 or so of this modern, two-engine aircraft were used by no fewer than eight airlines throughout the world, including Swissair, South African Airways, and, obviously, the German airline Deutsche Lufthansa. However, in the end, military production gained the upper hand, and although the bomber started to be withdrawn from front-line duty in the fall of 1938 and was replaced by the more modern and reliable Heinkel He.111s and Dornier Do.17s, altogether almost 1,000 of these aircraft were built.

The project got under way in the summer of 1934, headed by Ernst Zindel, "father" of the immortal Junkers Ju.52/3m. It was based on specifications that expressly requested a two-engine aircraft that could serve as both civilian transport and medium-bomber. Initially, five prototypes were ordered, and the first of these was produced in record time, managing to make its maiden flight on November 4, 1934. An unusual technical feature of this project was the use of two 600 hp Junkers Jumo 205C diesel engines. According to the technicians, these engines offered the double advantage of using a fuel that was less dangerous than petrol and of consuming 25 percent less than the equivalent conventional aeronautical engine. However, when put into practice, this choice proved to be of limited value, not only due to difficulties in tuning the engine but also to the general inadequacy of its performance. The first series, known as the A-1, was delivered starting in the spring of 1936 and was followed by a second military version, known as the D-1, characterized particularly by its greater fuel capacity. At the same time, the B and C civilian versions were developed.

The limitations of the engines became obvious during the bomber's first use in action (in Spain, where five Ju.86D-1s were utilized by the Condor Legion), and the Junkers Company decided to remedy these serious problems. The E-1 version (whose delivery began in the summer of 1937), was powered by two 810 hp BMW radial engines, and production was subsequently concentrated on this by now definitive solution. Later, the G model appeared on the production line, with modifications to the front part of the fuselage aimed at improving the pilot's visibility.

By the end of 1938, the Luftwaffe had 235 Ju.86 bombers in service, although their career in front-line action was drawing to a close. However, following the outbreak of the war, Junkers proposed yet another version of the aircraft for use as high-altitude photo reconnaissance. This plane, known as the Ju.86P, featured greatly lengthened wings, modifications to the prow, and was powered by two Junkers Jumo 207A supercharged diesel engines able to generate 750 hp at an altitude of 32,000 ft (9,750 m). These planes proved to be reasonably reliable and were used successfully up to the summer of 1942. The final version was the R, provided with two even more powerful Jumo 207B engines and with longer wings, capable of operating at 46,000 ft (14,000 m).

As well as its service in the Luftwaffe (which continued up to the beginning of 1944, mostly in the flying schools), the Ju.86 was also supplied to Sweden, South Africa, Chile, Portugal, and Hungary.

color plate

Junkers Ju.86E Civilian registration numbers prior to the reestablishment of the Luftwaffe - Germany 1937

Aircraft:	Junkers Ju.86E-1
Nation:	Germany
Manufacturer:	Junkers Flugzeug und Motorenwerke AG
Type:	Bomber
Year:	1937
Engine:	2 BMW 132F, 9-cylinder radial, air-cooled, 810 hp each
Wingspan:	73 ft 10 in (22.47 m)
Length:	58 ft 7 1/2 in (17.85 m)
Height:	16 ft 8 in (5.05 m)
Weight:	18,078 lb (8,190 kg) loaded
Maximum speed:	224 mph (360 km/h) at 13,120 ft (4,000 m)
Ceiling:	24,610 ft (7,500 m)
Range:	870 miles (1,400 km)
Armament:	3 machine guns; 1,760 lb (798 kg) of bombs
Crew:	4

A formation of Junkers Ju.86 bombers belonging to the Hungarian air force.

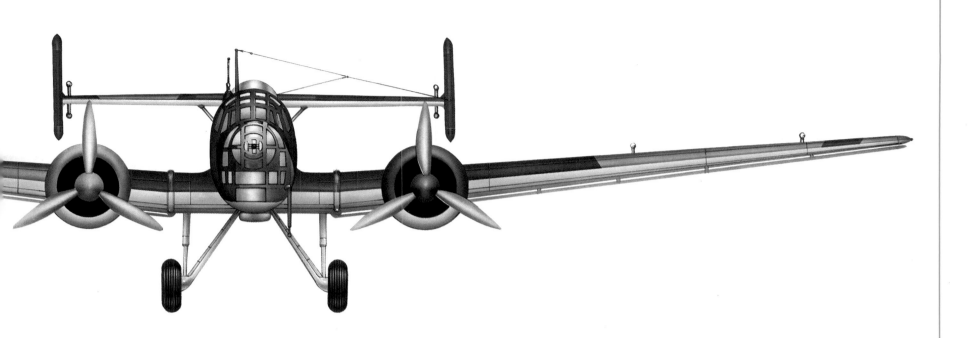

JUNKERS Ju.86E

D-ALOH

JUNKERS Ju.88 A-14

3Z+DK

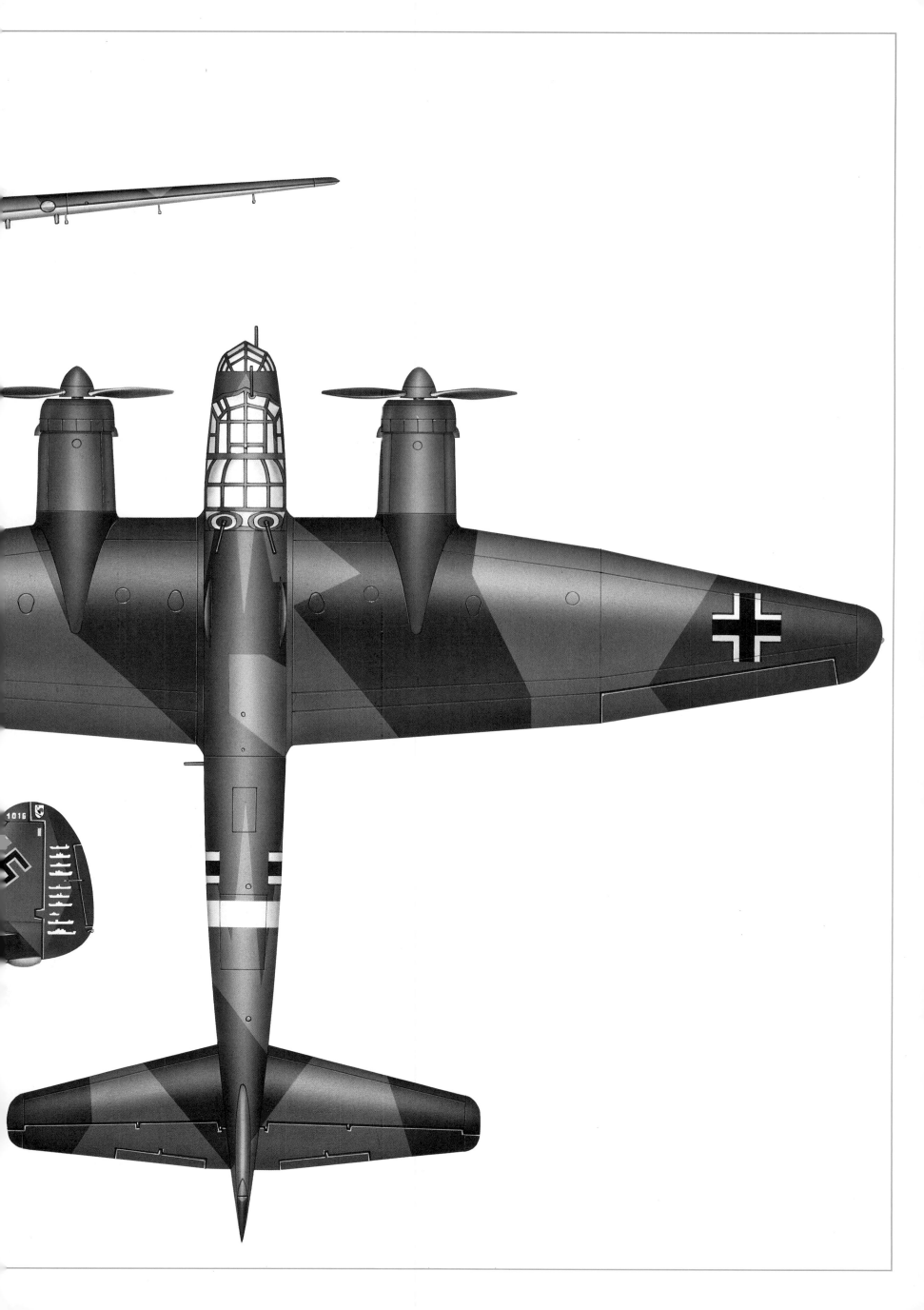

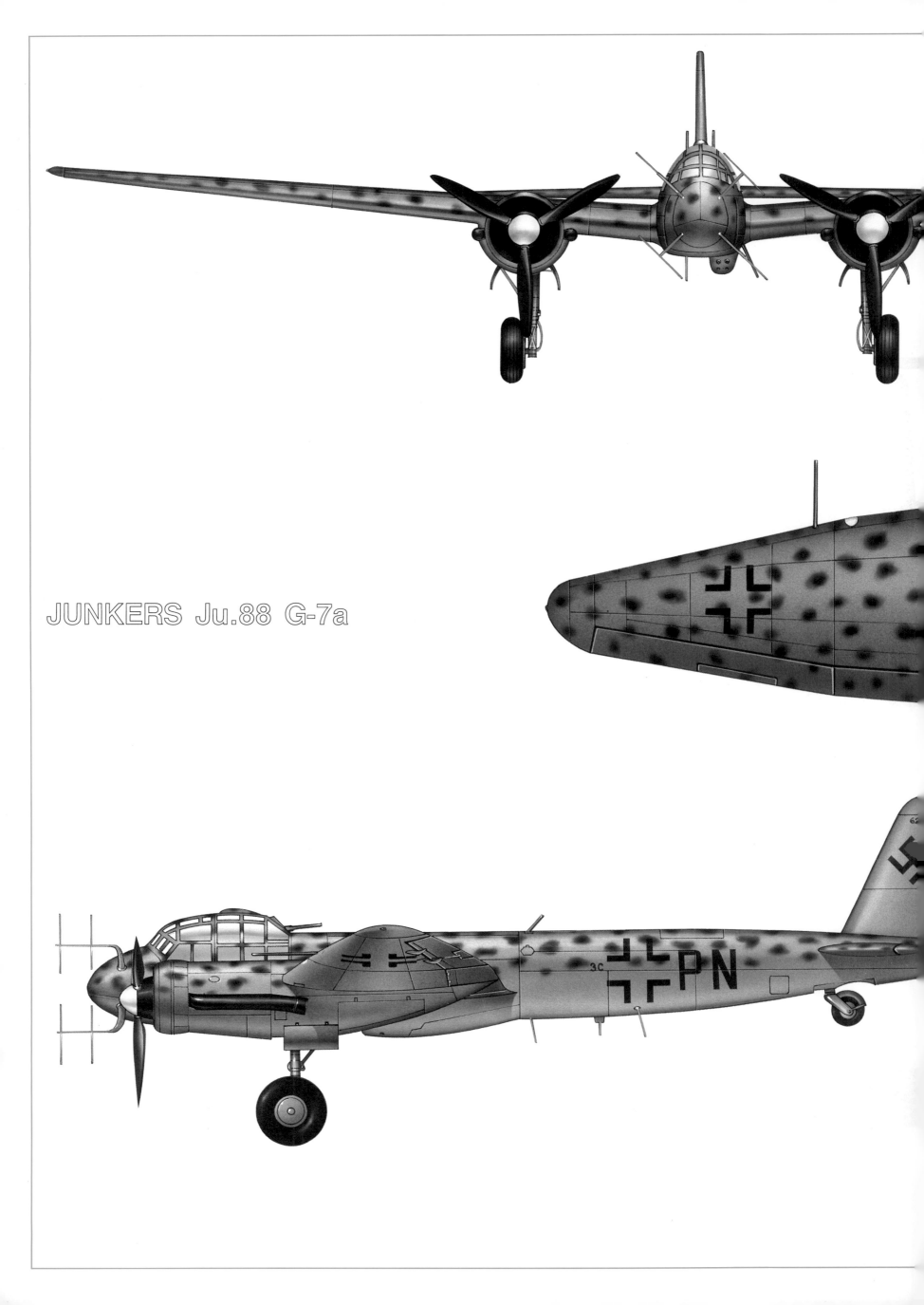

JUNKERS Ju.88 G-7a

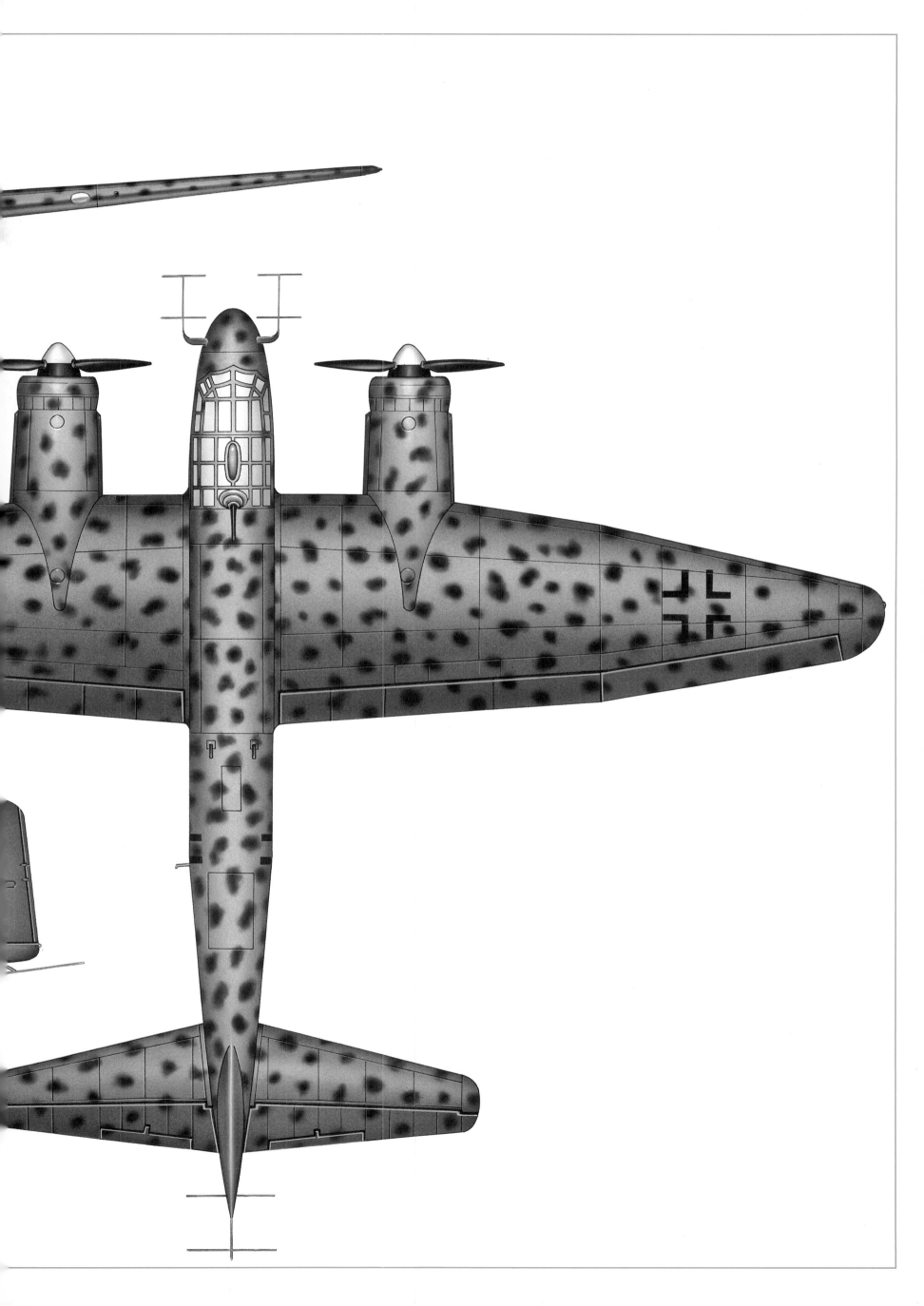

Undoubtedly the Luftwaffe's most versatile aircraft, the Junkers Ju.88 originated in 1936 and remained in production for the entire duration of the war. Proof of the project's remarkable qualities can be demonstrated by a few figures: from early 1939 up to 1945, more than 16,000 of these aircraft came off the assembly lines, being built in an innumerable sequence of versions increasingly improved for specific roles. In this constant evolution (in which the two-engine Junkers passed from its initial role of fast bomber to that of night fighter, reconnaissance plane, dive-bomber, ground attack aircraft, and torpedo bomber) the aircraft's basic structure remained virtually unchanged. It even constituted the starting point for the development of two subsequent models (the Ju.188 and the Ju.388 which appeared in the final years of the war), which exploited the potential of the airframe to the full. In all, the prototypes numbered more than 100.

The Ju.88 project was launched on January 15, 1936, by W.H. Evers and Alfred Gassner, in response to a request from the German Air Ministry that specified requirements for a fast, three-seater medium bomber, capable of carrying a maximum bomb load of 1,765 lb (800 kg) at a speed of 280 mph (450 km/h). Junkers presented two models in the competition, the Ju.88 and the Ju.85 (the latter characterized by twin fin and rudder), which competed with prototypes prepared by Henschel (Hs.127) and by Messerschmitt (Bf.162). In the end, the Ju.88 emerged as the winner, and the first prototype (Ju.88 V-1, registered D-AQEN) made its maiden flight on December 21, 1936. It was an all-metal low-wing monoplane with retractable landing gear, powered by two Daimler-Benz DB 600 Aa engines, each generating 1,000 hp. This was followed by another two experimental versions, the third of these (in September 1937) incorporating a modification that was to prove fundamental to the future of the aircraft: the installation of a pair of 1,000 hp Junkers Jumo 211A engines. With these power plants, the already remarkable performance of the Ju.88 V3 improved still further, and more particularly it reached 323 mph (520 km/h) during testing.

Mass production was ordered immediately, and before the first 10 preseries aircraft were built another seven prototypes were constructed and tested. In March 1939, the fifth of these set a record on a closed circuit of 620 miles (1,000 km), flying at an average speed of 320.98 mph (516.89 km/h) with a load of 4,415 lb (2,000 kg). The others served to establish the optimal configuration of the bomber for production.

The first production series version was the Ju.88 A-1, which went into service in August 1939 and was used in operations beginning in September 26. However, early experiences proved that the aircraft's defensive armament was totally inadequate, and the more important subsequent variant, the Ju.88 A-4, originated from the need to correct this deficiency. In this aircraft the crew's protection was also increased, while at a structural level the wings were lengthened and the landing gear strengthened. The Ju.88 A series amounted to no fewer than 17 variants, although this did not prevent the evolution of the basic project from continuing during their production.

The principal versions were the Ju.88 B of 1940 (which served for the development of the future Ju.188), the C, and the G, in which the bomber was transformed into a night fighter, while the D variant aircraft were destined for use as reconnaissance planes. The Junkers Ju.88 G-1 appeared in the spring of 1944 and proved to be especially efficient in its role, due mainly to the heavy armament concentrated in the nose and to the radar that was linked to an excellent ground control system and allowed the aircraft to achieve remarkable success against enemy bomber formations.

In the constant and continuous evolution of the two-engine Junkers, the last two production versions deserve to be remembered because, although they were built in relatively small numbers, they exploited the aircraft's potential to the maximum:

the S of 1943, once again a bomber, remarkably improved from the point of view of aerodynamics and performance (it had two BMW 801 D engines generating 1,700 hp each) and the T derivative, destined for photo reconnaissance. The Ju.88 T-3 was capable of reaching 410 mph (660 km/h) in its "cleanest" configuration.

---

color plate
Junkers Ju.88 A-14 1/KG 77 Luftwaffe - Libya 1942

A Ju.88 captured by the British during testing trials carried out by the RAF.

A Ju.88 with white overpaint covering the original camouflage and insignia.

Aircraft:	Junkers Ju.88 A-1
Nation:	Germany
Manufacturer:	Junkers Flugzeug und Motorenwerke AG
Type:	Bomber
Year:	1939
Engine:	2 Junkers Jumo 211B, 12-cylinder V, liquid-cooled, 1,200 hp each
Wingspan:	60 ft 3 in (18.38 m)
Length:	47 ft 1 in (14.36 m)
Height:	17 ft 6 in (5.32 m)
Weight:	22,840 lb (10,360 kg) loaded
Maximum speed:	280 mph (450 km/h) at 18,050 ft (5,500 m)
Ceiling:	26,250 ft (8,000 m)
Range:	1,056 miles (1,700 km)
Armament:	3 machine guns; 3,960 lb (1,800 kg) of bombs
Crew:	4

In the long career of the Junkers Ju.88, the night fighter versions held a special importance. Not only because they, perhaps more than any other variant, testified to the great versatility of an aircraft conceived back in 1936 as a fast bomber, but also because in the specific role of night fighters the two-engine Junkers had an intensive and effective operative career, eventually emerging among the best in their category.

The first major production version intended as a night fighter was the Ju.88 C, which went into service in July 1940, in the newly founded *Nachtjagdgeschwader* 1. It was established at the request of Goering himself to oppose the raids carried out by the RAF's Bomber Command. The transformation of the bomber had been carried out on the Ju.88 V-7 prototype. The changes basically consisted of the adoption of a ''solid'' nose instead of a glazed one, and in the installation of heavy armament in the nose (two 20 mm MG FF cannons and two 7.9 mm MG 17 machine guns). This innovation produced positive results. Although no official request had been made by the Luftwaffe, during 1940, several Ju.88 A-1s were altered in a similar way and they went into production as the Ju.88 C. In addition, 3,200 aircraft were produced in numerous subseries. They differed from each other basically by the type of their radar, the engine, and armament. Mention should be made of the most important of these among which was the Ju.88 C-4 that began production in 1941. This fighter was characterized by an increased wingspan and greater protection. In terms of armament it possessed three 20 mm cannons and three machine guns in the nose.

However, the C series Ju.88s soon proved to be unsuited to their role, weighed down by the large antennae of the radar and the increasingly heavy armament which notably damaged the aircraft's maneuverability at low altitude. In 1943, in order to overcome these limitations, a new prototype was prepared. It adopted the Ju.188's empennages which offered larger surface area, and, in addition, installed a pair of BMW 801 radial engines. This prototype later gave rise to the subsequent G variant.

In the prototype the armament was completely revised. The new features included six 20 mm MG 151 cannons, two installed on the right side of the nose and four in a pod on the left of the belly, and an MG 131 machine gun placed at the second crew member's disposal for the rear defense.

However, in the production series, the two side cannons were removed, and many aircraft retained only those in the belly, with another two similar weapons on their backs.

The latter were installed in a vertical position and slanted in such a way as to fire upward (*Schräge Musik*).

The initial Junkers Ju.88 G-1 variant appeared in the spring of 1944, and was followed by the G-4 (standard avionics), the G-6 (developed in subseries provided both with BMW 801 radials and

A Junkers Ju.88 G-7 with the antennae of the radar apparatus in the nose contained in a conical-shaped wooden fairing.

in-line Jumo 213As), and the final G-7 version, which went into service toward the end of the year. Three subtypes of the latter aircraft (provided with Jumo engines, a water and gas injection system, and larger fuel tanks) were built, and differed basically in their radar systems.

The Junkers Ju.88 Gs proved to be particularly effective in their role and scored notable successes against the formations of enemy bombers. In all, 800 were built before the collapse of the Third Reich.

color plate

Junkers Ju.88 G-7a Nachtjagdgeschwader 5 Luftwaffe - Copenhagen-Kastrup, 1945

Aircraft:	Junkers Ju.88 G-7b
Nation:	Germany
Manufacturer:	Junkers Flugzeug und Motorenwerke AG
Type:	Night fighter
Year:	1944
Engine:	2 Junkers Jumo 213E, 12-cylinder V, liquid-cooled, 1,725 hp each
Wingspan:	65 ft 9 in (20.00 m)
Length:	47 ft 9 in (14.53 m)
Height:	15 ft 11 in (4.85 m)
Weight:	28,938 lb (13,109 kg)
Maximum speed:	401 mph (647 km/h) at 29,878 ft (9,083 m)
Ceiling:	32,889 ft (9,997 m)
Range:	1,398 miles (2,252 km)
Armament:	6 x 20 mm cannons; 1 machine gun
Crew:	4

A Junkers Ju.88 G-6 in flight following its capture by the British.

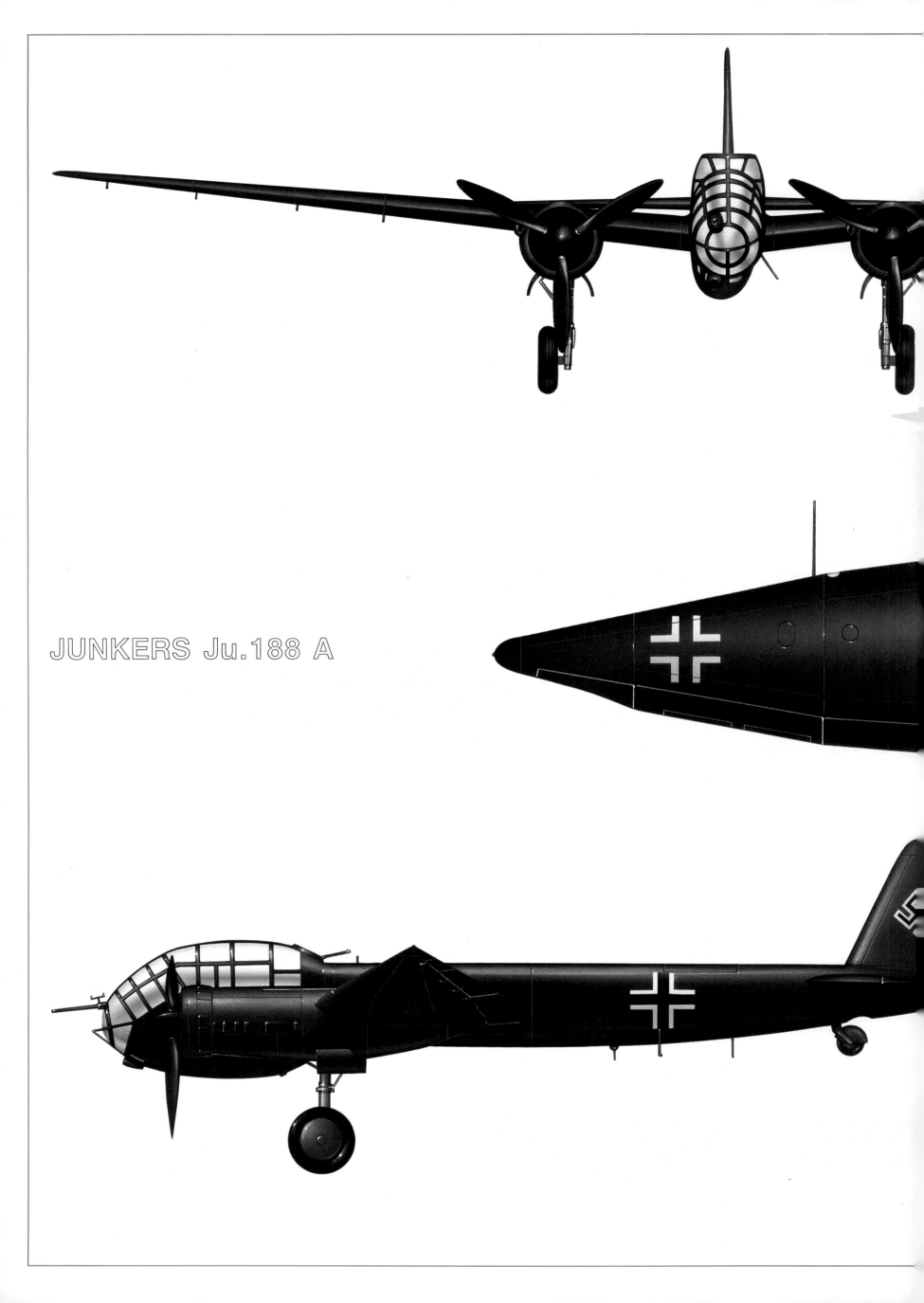

JUNKERS Ju.188 A

In 1942, the prolific family of the Junkers Ju.88 (which originated in 1936 and remained in production for the entire duration of the war, providing the Luftwaffe's arsenal with its most versatile combat plane) was enriched by a new model, the Ju.188, which started to come off the assembly lines in February of the following year. Developed initially as a transitional aircraft, the umpteenth variant of the seasoned two-engine aircraft eventually became a definitive aircraft and marked the project's maximum evolution. In all, 1,076 were built, and over half of these remained in service as reconnaissance planes until the end of the war.

The basic failure of the program to build a more modern substitute for the bomber led to the creation of the Ju.188. This project, designated Ju.288, was already at quite an advanced stage when the war broke out, although a series of delays was subsequently to accumulate, making its going into service within a short space of time appear problematic. In the autumn of 1941, this led Junkers to modify a Ju.88 series B aircraft, which was redesignated Ju.88 E-0 and which it used to develop the new version. The main changes with respect to the initial A variant consisted in the adoption of a different front section on the fuselage, in the lengthening of the wings, and in the adoption of new streamlined tips, as well as in the different surface area and structure of the tail fins and the option of fitting Junkers Jumo 213 engines (1,600 hp V-2, liquid-cooled) or BMW 801s (1,700 hp, 14-cylinder radial, air-cooled). The Ju.188 V-1 and Ju.188 V-2 prototypes appeared in the spring of 1942 and in January 1943, respectively, and following a series of tests, the aircraft went into production.

The first series, designated Ju.188 E and fitted with a pair of BMW engines, went into service in October 1943. It was subsequently followed by the F series specialized in reconnaissance, by the G series of bombers, and by the H series, once more for reconnaissance. The variants powered by Jumo engines were developed following a slight delay. The first was the Ju.188 A, delivered from mid-1943, followed by the A-2 subseries (January 1944, with more powerful engines capable of generating 2,240 hp in case of emergency) and the A-3 subseries, modified to serve as a torpedo plane. The second was the Ju.188 D, adapted for reconnaissance, built in two subseries, the D-1 and D-2. Experimental variants included the R, the S, and the T. Three of the first were built for use as night fighters. The second and third (of which very few were built too) were built for attack and high-altitude reconnaissance respectively: both were provided with a pressurized cockpit, fitted with Jumo engines generating 2,168 hp at takeoff, and lacked defensive armament. These last two variants were outstanding due to their excellent performance: the Ju.188 S-1, with a bomb load of 1,766 lb (800 kg) reached 426 mph (686 km/h); the Ju.188 T-1 had a speed of 434 mph (700 km/h).

In fact, the final version of the original model, the Ju.388, was derived from the Ju.188, and appeared toward the end of 1943. The production program for this aircraft provided for three variants, the 388 J (all-purpose high-altitude fighter), the 388 K (high-altitude bomber), and the 388 L (high-altitude photo reconnaissance), although of the few dozen aircraft completed before the end of the war, most were of the reconnaissance type, which had a virtually nonexistent operative career. The Ju.388 L prototype was obtained by altering a Ju.188 T, and the first of the 47 aircraft completed were delivered from October 1944 onward. As for the Ju.388 J, only three prototypes were completed, while ten preseries and five aircraft of the bomber variant were built.

---

color plate

Junkers Ju.188 A 2nd Gruppe Kampfgeschwader 2 Luftwaffe - Norway 1944

Aircraft:	Junkers Ju.188 E-1
Nation:	Germany
Manufacturer:	Junkers Flugzeug und Motorenwerke AG
Type:	Bomber
Year:	1943
Engine:	2 BMW 801 D-2, 14-cylinder radial, air-cooled, 1,700 hp each
Wingspan:	72 ft 4 in (22.00 m)
Length:	49 ft 1 in (14.94 m)
Height:	14 ft 7 in (4.44 m)
Weight:	31,988 lb (14,491 kg)
Maximum speed:	309 mph (499 km/h) at 19,736 ft (6,000 m)
Ceiling:	30,756 ft (9,350 m)
Range:	1,210 miles (1,950 km)
Armament:	1 × 20 mm cannon, 3 machine guns, 6,622 lb (3,000 kg) of bombs
Crew:	4

A Junkers Ju.188 D2 during operative evaluations carried out by the Allies after the war.

Ju.188s in service with the K.G.26 at an airport near Oslo. These aircraft were used in attacks on naval convoys and the first plane has supports on the nose for radio antennae.

From 1936 to 1945, almost 35,000 of these aircraft were built. This figure alone gives an indication of the importance of the Messerschmitt Bf.109 in the German aeronautical arsenal during World War II. However, in the course of its long and extensive career on all fronts, this small, agile, and powerful aircraft acquired a role that went well beyond the purely quantitative dimensions of its production (the highest, without exception, of the entire war), and it fought its way into the ranks of the greatest protagonists of aviation history.

In fact, the appearance of the Bf.109 brought the era of the biplane to a definitive close, imposing qualitative standards that sooner or later were to serve as reference points for aircraft manufacturers throughout the world. From this point of view, Willy Messerschmitt's fighter not only placed Germany suddenly in the vanguard in the field of military aviation, but it also became the progenitor of all the pure combat planes that were to emerge from the conflict. In this latter role, the Bf.109 had a fierce adversary (and not only in the skies over Europe) in another "immortal," the British Supermarine Spitfire, with which it participated in a continuous technological chase, aimed at gaining supremacy in the air and leading to the continuous strengthening and improving of both aircraft.

The Bf.109 originated in the summer of 1934, in response to an official request for a monoplane interceptor with which to replace the Heinkel He.51 and the Arado Ar.68 biplanes. Its designers, Willy Messerschmitt and Walter Rethel, took the excellent features of the four-seater Bf.108 *Taifun* commercial aircraft as their basis and created the smallest possible structure compatible with the most powerful engine then available. The fighter thus took the form of a compact, all-metal, low-wing monoplane with retractable landing gear and an enclosed cockpit. Originally, it had been planned to install the new 610 hp Junkers Jumo 210A engine, but because this power plant was unavailable, the prototype was fitted with a Rolls-Royce Kestrel V engine, generating 695 hp at takeoff and driving a two-bladed wooden propeller.

The aircraft was completed in September 1935, and a month later it began comparative tests together with the other prototypes created in response to the same specifications: the Arado Ar.80, the Heinkel He.112, and the Focke Wulf Fw.159. The final choice left the He.112 and the Bf.109 in the running, and both manufacturers received an order for 10 preseries aircraft. In practice, however, the Messerschmitt project proved to be the best and, in the course of its development, the aircraft was substantially modified, especially in its armament and its engine, which now became the Jumo 210A. The first aircraft of the initial production

Cleaning the armament of a Bf.109E at an airport in the Libyan desert.

series, the Bf.109B, appeared in February 1937, and four months later they were sent to Spain. Experiences in combat removed any remaining doubts concerning the aircraft's remarkable capabilities, and this success was further increased by a series of sporting performances in which, propaganda aside, the Bf.109 was judged the best fighter of the time. In November 1937, a prototype fitted with an engine capable of generating 1,650 hp over short distances broke the world speed record, setting a new one of 379.07 mph (610.43 km/h).

The B variant was followed by the C, with strengthened armament, and then by the D, fitted with Daimler Benz DB 600 engines. This marked the transition toward the first mass-produced version, the Bf.109E, characterized by the use of the more powerful and reliable Daimler Benz DB 601 engine. The first Bf.109E-1s were completed at the beginning of 1939, and total production of the various subseries reached 1,540 within a year. In 1940, 1,868 of these aircraft were built and, with the gradual withdrawal of the previous variants, the fighter assumed the leading role in all the Luftwaffe's operations, especially in the Battle of Britain.

Aircraft:	Messerschmitt Bf.109E-1
Nation:	Germany
Manufacturer:	Messerschmitt AG
Type:	Fighter
Year:	1939
Engine:	Daimler Benz DB 601D, 12-cylinder V, liquid-cooled, 1,050 hp
Wingspan:	32 ft 4 1/2 in (9.87 m)
Length:	28 ft 4 in (8.65 m)
Height:	8 ft 2 in (2.50 m)
Weight:	4,431 lb (2,010 kg) loaded
Maximum speed:	342 mph (550 km/h) at 13,120 ft (4,000 m)
Ceiling:	34,450 ft (10,500 m)
Range:	410 miles (660 km)
Armament:	2 x 20 mm cannons; 2 machine guns
Crew:	1

color plate
Messerschmitt Bf.109E JG.26 Schlageter Kdz. Adolf Galland's plane - France 1940

A Bf.109E returns for dispersal in a Libyan airport.

MESSERSCHMITT Bf.109 E

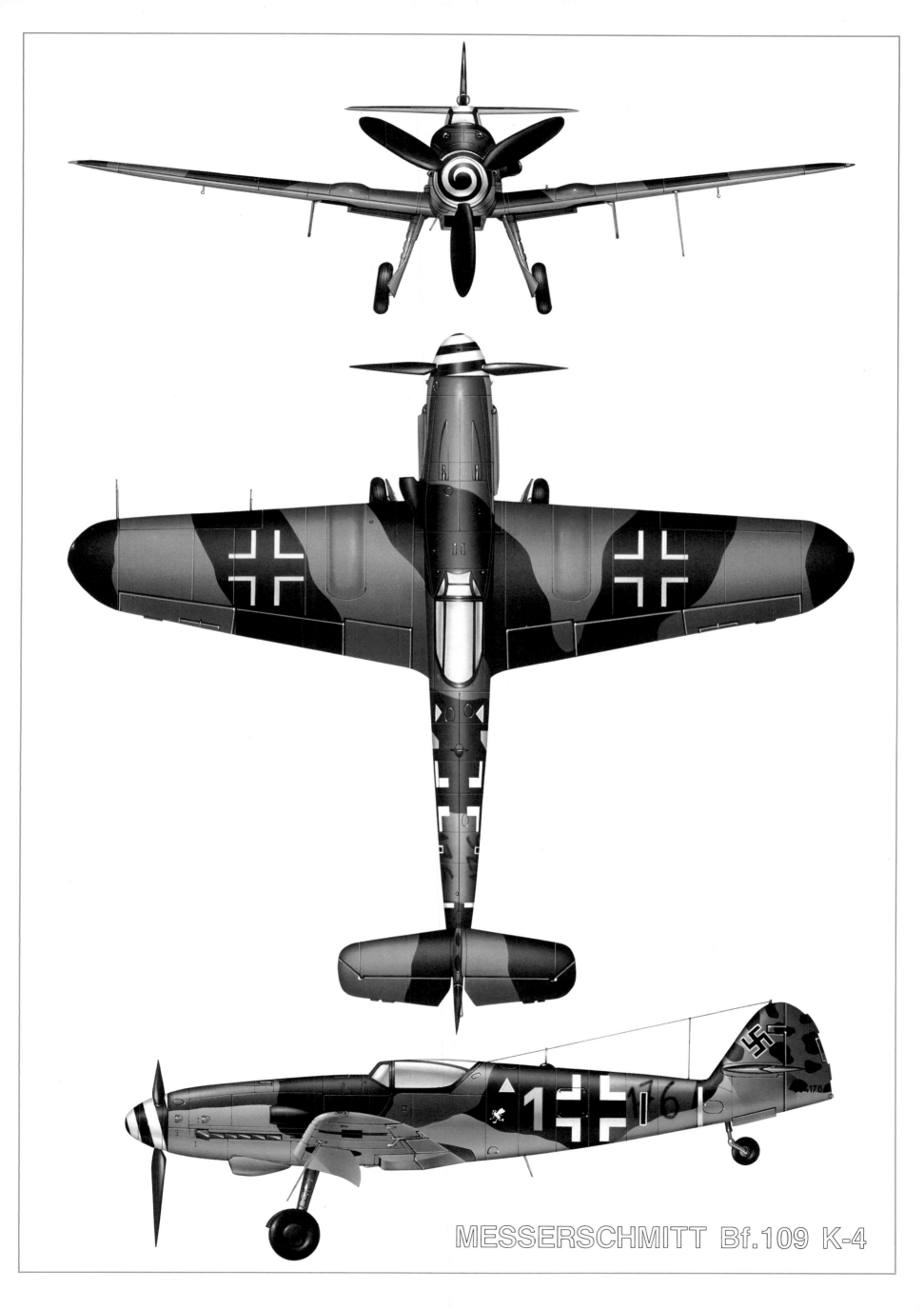

MESSERSCHMITT Bf.109 K-4

For the conflict's entire duration the evolution of the Messerschmitt Bf.109 remained constant in an effort to fully improve the great potential of its airframe. The final production variants were the H and the K, derived respectively from the F and the G. The Bf.109 Hs were developed in 1943 with the aim of building a fighter suitable for high altitude use. They were characterized by a larger wingspan and by a Daimler Benz DB 601 E engine with GM-1 superpower device. The aircraft proved to have a maximum speed of about 465 mph (750 km/h) at an altitude of 32,894 ft (10,000 m); however in spite of this brilliant performance, its preparation was abandoned following the appearance of serious signs of vibration on the wings. The Bf.109 K was more successful. Built during the last year of the war, it was the last operative variant of Willy Messerschmitt's fighter, and can be considered without doubt one of the best of the entire family.

The first pre-series K-0 appeared in September 1944, and compared to the model from which it was derived, it differed in a series of aerodynamic and structural modifications. These included the altered shape of the engine housing, a longer spinner, a larger rudder-tail fin unit, and a ''Galland'' type canopy in the cockpit, which allowed the pilot a greater field of vision. In these pre-production aircraft, the 30 mm cannon installed in the propeller axis was eliminated and replaced by a pair of 15 mm caliber MG 151 type weapons in the fuselage. As for the engines, although a Daimler Benz DB 605 D was going to be installed, the more powerful DB 605 ASCM was later adopted for the production series aircraft. This engine was capable of generating 2,000 hp at takeoff and 1,800 hp at an altitude of 16,450 ft (5,000 m).

Two months later, in November 1944, the assembly lines began to complete the first production series aircraft, the K-2 and K-4 (which differed from each other in that the latter was provided with a pressure system), and these aircraft went into service during the first few days of 1945. However, it was not long before operative needs made it necessary to strengthen the offensive armament. Therefore, in the final production variant, the Bf.109 K-4, the 30 mm cannon was reinstalled in the propeller axis. Even heavier armament was installed in the subsequent K-6 series, which was built for the role of bomber pursuit. In addition to the cannon in the nose, two similar weapons were installed in pods below the wings, while the 15 mm MG 151 cannons in the fuselage were replaced by two 13 mm MG 131 caliber machine guns. These aircraft were delivered to the units of the Luftwaffe beginning in January 1945, although only a few of them were used before the fall of the Third Reich.

The final subseries was the K-14, deliveries of which began in the last two weeks of the war. These Bf.109s, rendered more powerful by the new DB 605L engine fitted with mechanical two-stage compressor and capable of generating 1,700 hp at takeoff and 1,350 hp at 31,250 ft (9,500 m), proved to possess an outstan-

A Messerschmitt Bf.109 K's incomplete fuselage photographed at Plauen railyard in 1945.

ding performance at extremely high altitude, with a maximum speed of 451 mph (727 km/h) at no less than 37,500 ft (11,400 m). This was the same speed reached by the Bf.109 K-4 at 19,736 ft (6,000 m). As for the armament, this consisted of a 30 mm caliber cannon in the nose and two 13 mm MG 131 machine guns in the fuselage. However, only very few K-14s managed to go into combat before Germany surrendered.

Despite Germany's desperate situation in the final months of the war, production of Willy Messerschmitt's fighter went ahead unceasingly, eventually totaling about 35,000 aircraft, the highest number of the entire conflict.

---

color plate

Messerschmitt Bf.109 K-4, II Gruppe Jagdgeschwader 3, Luftwaffe - Pasewalk, Germany, 1945

Aircraft:	Messerschmitt Bf.109 K-4
Nation:	Germany
Manufacturer:	Messerschmitt A.G.
Type:	Fighter
Year:	1945
Engine:	Daimler Benz DB 605 ASCM, 12-cylinder, liquid-cooled, 2,000 hp
Wingspan:	32 ft 9 in (9.97 m)
Length:	29 ft (8.84 m)
Height:	8 ft 2 in (2.49 m)
Weight:	7,448 lb (3,374 kg)
Maximum speed:	451 mph (727 km/h) at 19,736 ft (6,000 m)
Ceiling:	41,118 ft (12,000 m)
Range:	355 miles (573 km)
Armament:	1 × 30 mm cannon; 2 × 15 mm cannons
Crew:	1

The Messerschmitt Bf.109 K was the best of its family.

A Bf.109 G-6 in flight. The white band on the fuselage indicated the aircraft in service in the Mediterranean.

Like Great Britain's Supermarine Spitfire, Germany's Messerschmitt Bf.109 underwent almost constant improvement. Following the first mass-produced version (the E, which appeared at the beginning of 1939 and was one of the great protagonists of the Battle of Britain), in January 1941 the first aircraft of a notably improved variant, the F, started to go into service. They were considered by many to be the most brilliant aircraft of the series. The main modifications consisted in the adoption of a more powerful Daimler Benz engine and in an overall improvement to the aircraft's aerodynamic characteristics, thanks to the installation of a large spinner in the fuselage, a retractable rear wheel, and the rounding of the wing tips. Moreover, the wings were provided with high lift devices and a different type of aileron.

The first preseries Bf.109 F-0s were tested by the Luftwaffe in the second half of 1940, and after the initial F-1 series had gone into service, mass production went ahead at a great rate with the construction of numerous subvariants, which differed from one another mainly in the type of armament and the engine adopted. Among the most important of these, mention should be made of the F-3 (which appeared at the beginning of 1942) capable of reaching a speed of 389 mph (628 km/h) at an altitude of 22,040 ft (6,700 m); the F-4/B, capable of carrying 1,103 lb (500 kg) of bombs; the F-5 and F-6 (which appeared toward the end of 1942), which were adapted for the role of fighter-reconnaissance and armed with only two 7.92 mm machine guns. The Bf.109s had a brilliant operative career, especially during the first months in which they were in service, when in some cases the Messerschmitt fighter proved to be superior even to the RAF's Spitfire Mk.V.

It was in fact due to the need to strengthen this superiority (already obtained by the Luftwaffe with the Focke Wulf Fw.190) that the next variant, the Bf.109 G, was built in 1942. This was also the variant of which the greatest number of aircraft was built. The main difference compared to its immediate predecessor lay

in the adoption of a Daimler Benz DB 605 engine, capable of generating 1,475 hp. The notable increase in power (the DB 601 installed in the Bf.109 F generated 1,200 hp) allowed for an increase in armament, although this was to the detriment of the aircraft's overall performance.

The first Bf.109 Gs (christened Gustav) went into service in the late summer of 1942, and once again their production was characterized by the construction of numerous series and subseries. Among the most important of these were the G-1, which was provided with a pressurized cockpit and a supercharged DB 605 A-1 engine; the G-2, similar to the previous series but lacking the pressurized cockpit; the G-5, with a DB 605 D engine capable of generating 1,800 hp of power in case of emergency, thanks to a device for water and methyl alcohol, injection as well as a larger rudder; the G-6, whose armament included the installation of a 30 mm Mk.108-type cannon that fired through the propeller hub, two MG 131 machine guns in the nose, and two 20 mm MG 151/20 cannons housed beneath the wings. The final series of Gustavs to go into service was the G-14, provided with external supports for machine guns, rockets, or bombs.

In 1943 the Messerschmitt company began to develop a high altitude version of its fighter. This was the Bf.109 H, which was derived from the F variant and was characterized by a larger wingspan and a Daimler Benz DB 601E engine with a GM-1 supercharging device. The aircraft proved to have a maximum speed of about 465 mph (750 km/h) at an altitude of 32,894 ft (10,000 m), but despite this brilliant performance its development was abandoned following the appearance of serious tail vibrations. However, in the last year of the war the final variant of Messerschmitt's fighter to go into service was derived from the Bf.109 G. In this aircraft, the Bf.109 K, the airframe was developed to a maximum.

color plate

Messerschmitt Bf.109 G-6/R6 II Staffel/JG 53 Jagdgeschwader Luftwaffe - Eastern front 1943

A Bf.109 G equipped with *Ofenrohr*, 21 mm rocket launchers installed below the wings and employed against the formations of Allied bombers.

Aircraft:	Messerschmitt Bf.109 G-2
Nation:	Germany
Manufacturer:	Messerschmitt AG
Type:	Fighter
Year:	1942
Engine:	Daimler Benz DB 605 A-1, 12-cylinder V, liquid-cooled, 1,475 hp
Wingspan:	32 ft 6 1/2 in (9.90 m)
Length:	29 ft (8.84 m)
Height:	8 ft 2 in (2.49 m)
Weight:	6,834 lb (3,095 kg) loaded
Maximum speed:	406 mph (653 km/h) at 28,540 ft (8,700 m)
Ceiling:	39,370 ft (12,000 m)
Range:	528 miles (850 km)
Armament:	1 × 20 mm cannon; 2 machine guns
Crew:	1

A Bf.109 G preparing for takeoff during a mission on the Russian front at the beginning of Operation Barbarossa.

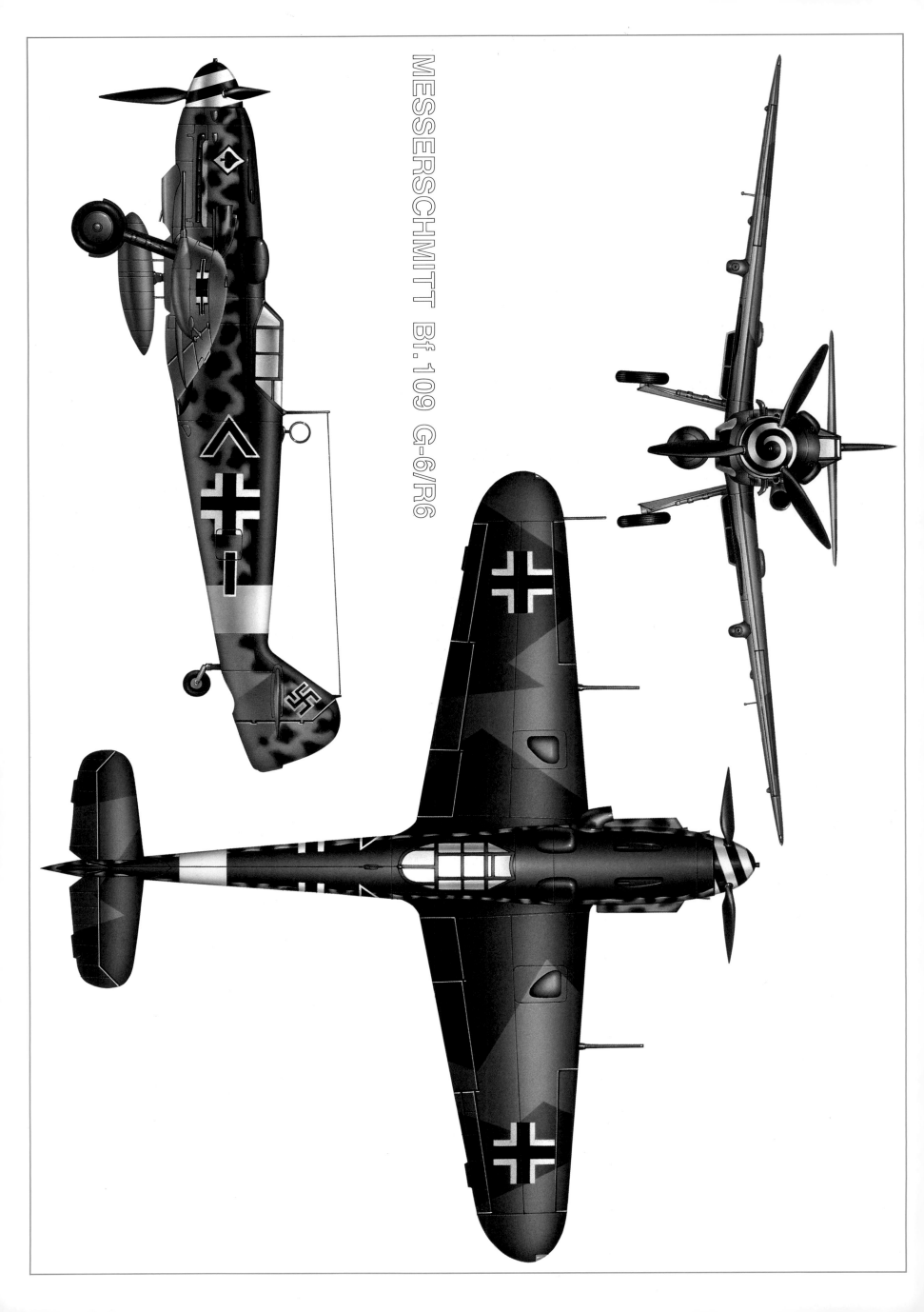

MESSERSCHMITT Bf.109 G-6/R6

MESSERSCHMITT Bf.110 C

The failure of the Messerschmitt Bf.110 as a heavy fighter was dramatically demonstrated during the Battle of Britain, in which Willy Messerschmitt's two-engine aircraft proved to be pitifully awkward and defenseless when faced with the fast and maneuverable Spitfires and Hurricanes. However, once the limitations of its design (so praised by Goering, who nicknamed the aircraft *Zerstörer*, or "Destroyer") had been accepted, the Bf.110 remained as an irreplaceable weapon in the Luftwaffe's arsenal. It achieved success in the role of fighter-bomber, reconnaissance plane, and, particularly, as a night fighter. From 1938 to 1945, a total of approximately 6,050 were built in numerous versions, and they served on practically all fronts from the beginning of the war to the end.

The Bf.110 was designed in 1934, in response to a request by the Luftwaffe for a long-range strategic fighter that could also be used as a fast bomber. The first of three prototypes took to the air on May 12, 1936, powered by a pair of 910 hp Daimler-Benz DB 600 A engines. It was a slender, all-metal, low-wing two-engine aircraft with retractable landing gear, characterized by twin-rudder and a long glazed cockpit that housed the three-man crew. The three prototypes were plagued by problems regarding the reliability of the power plants and proved to be rather difficult to handle. Although the first problems were solved with the appearance of the DB 601A engine, the lack of maneuverability was to remain a negative characteristic of the project throughout its evolution.

In March 1938, following the construction of another two prototypes and some preseries aircraft, the first Bf.110 Bs appeared (45 were completed in all). Although improved aerodynamically and in their armament, these were still powered by 680 hp Junkers Jumo 210D engines. Not until the following year, when the direct-injection DB 601 A engines became available, was the first major version, the Bf.110 C, built. After 10 preseries aircraft, mass production of the C-1 variant began immediately with maximum priority: 315 came off the assembly lines in the course of the year. The aircraft's operational debut coincided with the outbreak of the conflict, during the invasion of Poland.

The disappointing experiences of the summer of 1940 on the English Channel front led to a reconsideration of the development of the Bf.110 as a fighter and, in the same period, the first variants specialized in the role of fighter-bomber and ground attack aircraft appeared. The main ones were the E and the F, while with the D series the first experiences in the role of night fighter were tried. In the course of this development, the aircraft's power was increased continually: the Bf.110 Fs were powered by 1,350 hp Daimler Benz DB 601 F engines, and the Bf.110 Gs by 1,475 hp DB 601 B-1 type engines (the final production version, the H, was derived from the latter).

The first subvariant built expressly for use as a night fighter was the G-4 of 1942. In this role the two-engine Messerschmitts achieved considerable success, and this was increased still further with the introduction of Liechtenstein-type interceptor radars. Although this equipment affected the aircraft's performance due to the bulky antenna installed on the nose, it contributed to making the Bf.110 a particularly effective weapon against the massive raids carried out by Allied bombers on German territory. The aircraft's use in this role culminated at the beginning of 1944, when 60 percent of the night fighters at the Luftwaffe's disposal consisted of Messerschmitt Bf.110s: the front line amounted to approximately 320 of these aircraft. With the appearance of more efficient aircraft, its use in this role gradually diminished.

Aircraft:	Messerschmitt Bf.110 C-1
Nation:	Germany
Manufacturer:	Messerschmitt AG
Type:	Fighter
Year:	1939
Engine:	2 Daimler Benz DB 601 A-1, 12-cylinder V, liquid-cooled, 1,050 hp each
Wingspan:	53 ft 4 in (16.25 m)
Length:	39 ft 7 in (12.07 m)
Height:	13 ft 6½ in (4.12 m)
Weight:	13,289 lb (6,028 kg) loaded
Maximum speed:	336 mph (540 km/h) at 19,685 ft (6,000m)
Ceiling:	32,810 ft (10,000 m)
Range:	680 miles (1,094 km)
Armament:	5 machine guns; 2×20 mm cannons
Crew:	2/3

color plate
Messerschmitt Bf.110 C 5/ZG 26 Luftwaffe - France 1940

A "factory fresh" Bf.110 at the Messerschmitt factory.

A Bf.110 C in service with the ZG 1 "Wespen Geschwader".

The Luftwaffe high command was so enthusiastic about the concept of the «heavy fighter» that, even during the initial phase of the development of the Bf.110, Messerschmitt was asked to design its successor. Thus, the Me.210 came into being. It was a new two-engine aircraft, and although it had features that were more advanced than those of the previous model (especially as far as the armament was concerned, with the adoption of two remote-controlled turrets on the sides of the fuselage), it proved to be difficult to tune. The aircraft made its maiden flight on September 5, 1939, and right from the start the prototype proved to be particularly unstable. The numerous modifications carried out in the course of the lengthy cycle of evaluation tests did nothing to correct the dangerous tendency to stall and go into a spin. Nevertheless, the Me.210 went into production and 200 aircraft came off the assembly lines before the program was suspended in April 1942.

Because there was strong pressure to salvage the project, Messerschmitt proposed two alternative models: the first, known as the Me.310, maintained the formula of its precedessor, although the installation of a pair of Daimler Benz DB 603A engines generating a maximum of 1,850 hp at altitude and a pressurized cockpit were foreseen. The second (the Me.410) foresaw the use of the same power plants in a more simple aircraft, lacking pressurization and with improvements to the structure of the wings and the fuselage. In the end, the second project was chosen, and the prototype of the Me.410 *Hornisse* (Hornet), obtained by modifying a Me.210 A-0, took to the air toward the end of 1942.

In January of the following year, the Luftwaffe began to receive the first aircraft of the two initial production variants, the Me.410 A-1 fighter-bomber, and the Me.410 A-2 heavy bomber. The two types had very similar offensive armament, consisting of a pair of 20 mm cannons and two 7.9 mm machine guns installed in the nose, plus two 13 mm machine guns in the remote-controlled turrets on the sides of the fuselage for the defense of the rear section. By April, 48 aircraft had reached the units, where they replaced the Dornier Do.217 and the Junkers Ju.88, and by the end of 1943 deliveries amounted to 457 aircraft. Numerous subseries were developed, including the remarkable Me.410 A-1/U4, armed with a 50 mm cannon for attacking bombers.

Although the serious problems that afflicted its direct predecessor had been overcome, the Me.410 never proved to be an outstanding aircraft, and, what is more, it never proved to be superior to the more reliable Bf.110, which it was supposed to replace. An attempt was made to improve its overall performance in the spring of 1944, with the appearance of the first aircraft of the B series, which differed above all in the adoption of a pair of Daimler Benz DB 603G engines generating a maximum of 1,900 hp. The initial subseries, B-1 and B-2, were destined for the roles of fighter-bomber and heavy bomber respectively, and various armament combinations were tested in them, including rockets. These were followed by the B-3 subseries (the same as the A-3), prepared for photo reconnaissance, and the B-6, for use in an antishipping role, provided with radar and more heavily armed. Production ceased in September 1944, after 1,160 aircraft had been completed.

During the last year of the war and right up to the end of hostilities, the Me.410s were used mainly in the defense of German territory, in the valiant attempt to stem the incessant raids of the Allied bombers.

---

color plate

Messerschmitt Me.410 A-3 2nd Staffel 122nd Aufklarungsgruppe Luftwaffe - Italy 1944

Aircraft:	Messerschmitt Me.410 A-1
Nation:	Germany
Manufacturer:	Messerschmitt AG
Type:	Fighter-bomber
Year:	1943
Engine:	2 Daimler Benz DB 603A, 12-cylinder V, liquid-cooled, 1,850 hp each
Wingspan:	53 ft 9 in (16.35 m)
Length:	41 ft (12.48 m)
Height:	14 ft (4.28 m)
Weight:	21,276 lb (9,638 kg)
Maximum speed:	387 mph (624 km/h) at 22,040 ft (6,700 m)
Ceiling:	23,026 ft (7,000 m)
Range:	1,050 miles (1,690 km)
Armament:	2 × 20 mm cannons, 4 machine guns, 2,205 (1,000 kg) of bombs
Crew:	2

An Me.410 A-1/U2 equipped with radar apparatus. The aircraft bears the British insignia adopted during flight tests carried out in England following its capture.

A Messerschmitt Me.410 during takeoff.

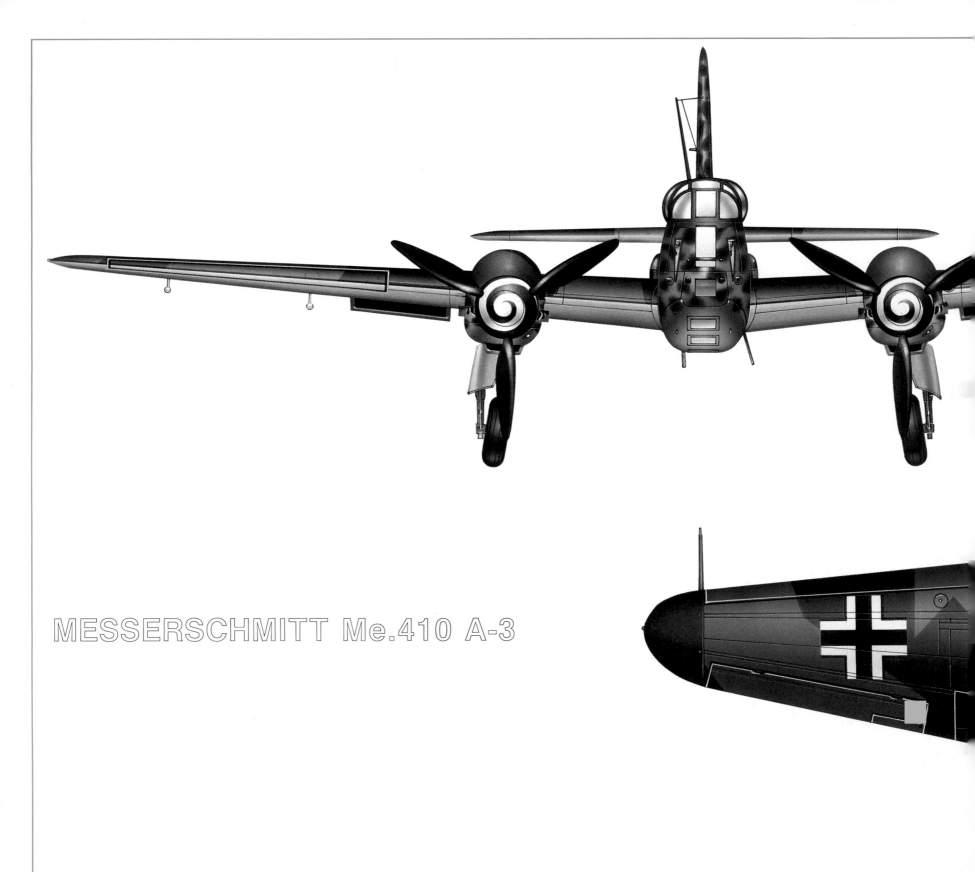

MESSERSCHMITT Me.410 A-3

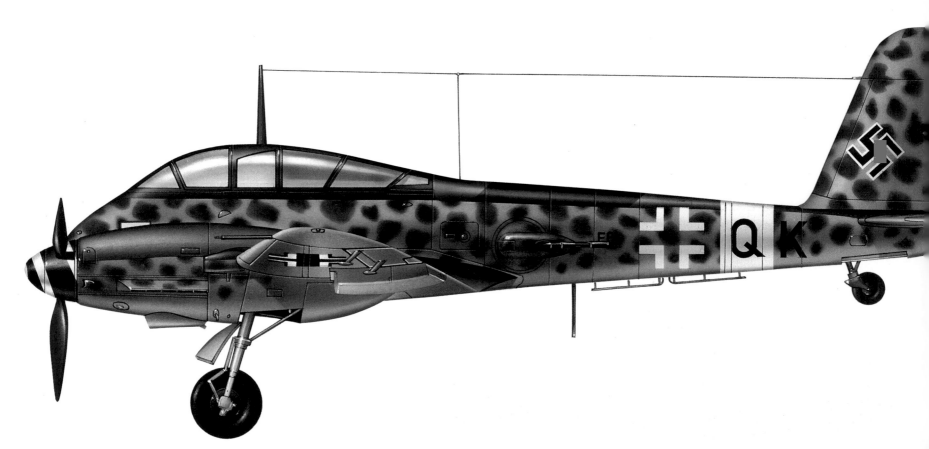

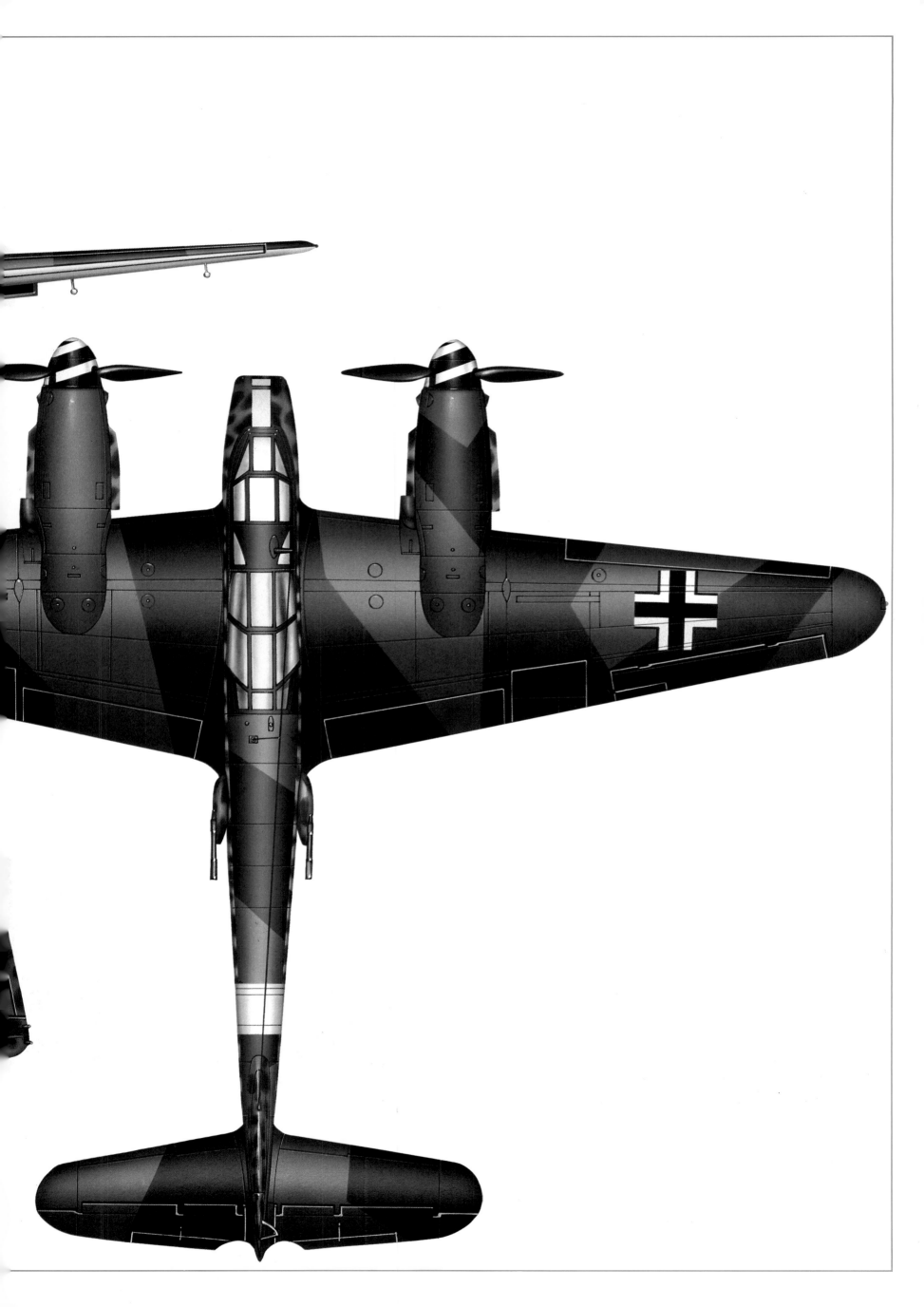

Beyond doubt, the Messerschmitt Bf.110, which was a sensational failure as a heavy fighter, redeemed itself especially in the role of night fighter, in which it served from 1941 until the end of the war. The two-engine Messerschmitts scored considerable success in this speciality, and this success increased with the introduction of Liechtenstein interception radar. Although this apparatus penalized the aircraft's performance because of the large antennae installed on the nose, it contributed to rendering the Bf.110 a particularly effective weapon against the massive raids carried out by Allied bombers on German territory.

The first experiences in this role were carried out by several series of the D and F versions, and in particular by the Bf.110 F-4. These aircraft (which went into production from 1941) were provided with two Daimler Benz DB 601F engines generating 1,350 hp, while the already heavy standard armament, consisting of two 20 mm cannons and four 7.9 mm machine guns, was strengthened in some cases by the addition of two 30 mm cannons in fairings below the fuselage. Radar apparatus was also installed in the next subseries, and despite a decrease in the aircraft's performance due to the increase in overall weight and greater aerodynamic resistence, they scored some notable successes. The fighter was made even more effective against the Allied bomber formations by the installation of two fixed cannons on the aircraft's back positioned to fire upward at a 60 to 70 degree angle (Schräge Musik).

Toward the end of 1941, when it became clear that the program for the Messerschmitt Me.210 (designed as the Bf.110's successor) still had a long way to go, it became necessary to construct a new and more powerful variant of the two-engine aircraft. This was the Bf.110 G, fitted with a pair of 1,475 hp Daimler Benz DB 605 B engines and with substantial improvements from an aerodynamic point of view. The definitive night fighter version, the G-4, was developed from it and went into production in June 1942. Another variant to serve as a night fighter (the H-4) was also derived from the final production version, the Bf.110 H, a small number of which were built from 1942 onward, at the same time as the G version. The differences between the two were minimal and consisted mainly in the H series being fitted with two Daimler-Benz DB 605 E engines and in an overall structural strengthening.

It was these aircraft that bore the brunt of the defense of German territory throughout 1943, and the use of the Bf.110s in this role reached a climax at the beginning of the following year, when 60 percent of the night fighters at the Luftwaffe's disposal consisted of the two-engine Messerschmitts. In all, the front-line reached a maximum of almost 320 of these aircraft. Their operative career was very extensive and was marked by continuous success, due also to the increasingly sophisticated tactics of flying and approach adopted by the units and the ground controllers: between November 18, 1943, and March 31, 1944, RAF Bomber Command's losses amounted to 1,047 aircraft, almost three-quarters of which were victims of the Luftwaffe's night fighters. In fact, on January 21, 1944, no fewer than 55 bombers out of a total of 648 were lost during a raid on Magdeburg, and the same fate awaited a further 43 aircraft a week later during a raid on Berlin. Among the Bf.110 G-4 pilots, the greatest number of victories was scored by Major Heinz-Wolfgang Schnaufer, who shot down 121 planes. In second place was Major Helmut Lent, with a total of 102.

Detail of the antenna of the Liechtenstein SN2 radar. The small antenna in the center of the nose is that of the Liechtenstein C1 radar.

A Bf.110 G-4 that was captured and evaluated in Great Britain after the war. The aircraft is provided with radar and supplementary fuel tanks.

Aircraft:	Messerschmitt Bf.110 G-4
Nation:	Germany
Manufacturer:	Messerschmitt A.G.
Type:	Night fighter
Year:	1942
Engine:	2 Daimler Benz DB 605 B, 12-cylinder in-line, liquid-cooled, 1,475 hp each
Wingspan:	53 ft 5 in (16.25 m)
Length:	41 ft 7 in (12.65 m)
Height:	13 ft 1 in (3.99 m)
Weight:	20,728 lb (9,390 kg)
Maximum speed:	341 mph (550 km/h) at 22,998 ft (7,010 m)
Ceiling:	26,069 ft (7,925 m)
Range:	1,309 miles (2,100 km)
Armament:	2 x 30 mm cannon; 2-4 x 20 mm cannon; 2 machine guns; 1,540 lb (698 kg) of bombs
Crew:	2-3

color plate

Messerschmitt Bf.110 G-4/R3 8th Staffel 3rd Nachtjagdgeschwader Luftwaffe - Belgium 1944

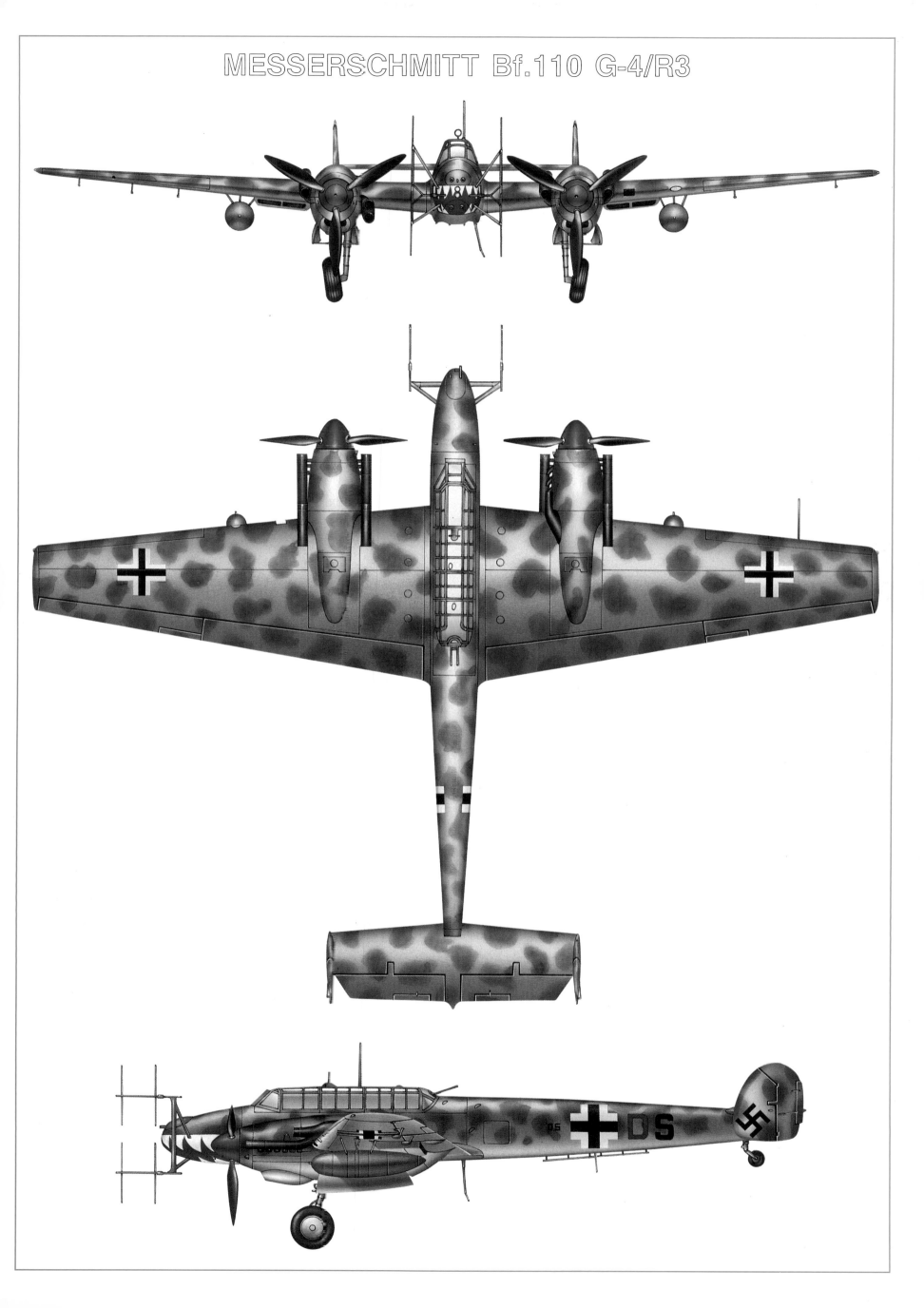

In the forefront of aeronautical production throughout the world, at the time the Messerschmitt Me.163 Komet marked the beginning of a new phase in air warfare. In fact, this revolutionary interceptor was the first aircraft in the world to be powered by a rocket engine, and had it arrived on the scene of the conflict a year earlier, it would certainly have altered the balance between the adversaries. This small and fast combat plane's first mission took place on May 13, 1944. The plane was piloted by Wolfgang Späte over Bad Zwischenahn, the base of the first Luftwaffe unit (the 16th *Erprobungscommando*). This mission, carried out by a preseries aircraft entirely painted in red, came to an end without casualities. It marked the beginning of an intense flying career that was to continue throughout the last year of the war. Nevertheless, the Me.163's career was largely influenced by Germany's critical situation: shortage of fuel, production difficulties due to the continuous and devastating Allied bombing raids, lack of time to prepare the aircraft definitively, and to train the pilots. In all, just over 300 Me.163s were completed before production was interrupted in 1945. Most of these were of the B-1a version (237 aircraft built in 1944, and 42 in January of the following year), the only one to be used in combat.

The Komet was the result of the work of two great aeronautical technicians. The first, Alexander Lippisch, who started to work on the development of all-wing gliders in 1926, developed and perfected the formula, overcoming all problems concerning stability and control. The second, Helmuth Walter, was the designer of the first rocket engine fed by combustible liquids. In fact, the Me.163 was simply a glider which used the revolutionary form of propulsion only for a few moments: the time necessary for takeoff, ascent, attacking, and carrying out escape maneuvers before returning to the ground. Structurally, the aircraft was a small monoplane, built of several materials; the pilot, rocket engine, and fuel were installed in the fuselage, and the armament was located on the half-wing root.

The project was launched at the beginning of 1939, when Lippisch and his work team started to collaborate in great secrecy with the Messerschmitt company in Augsburg. Work went ahead very slowly and the first prototype without an engine was tested at the beginning of 1941. It was towed and then released at altitude by a two engine Messerschmitt Bf.110.

On August 13, Heini Dittmar, the chief test pilot, carried out the first flight with an engine, and on October 2 for the first time ever, he reached Mach 0.84: the recorded speed was 623.4 mph (1,003.9 km/h), about 155 mph (250 km/h) above the official world record. The tests continued, above all to perfect the takeoff procedure (carried out by means of an unhookable under-carriage, while landing took place on a belly skid) and the functioning of the propellers, which were extremely delicate and unstable. This

An Me. 163 B that was captured and tested by the British.

process was not without problems, and many disasters clouded the long cycle of preparations.

Following the construction of ten preseries Me.163 A-0s, the Me.163 B prototype took to the air on February 21, 1943, while deliveries of the first aircraft of the initial production series, the Me.163 B-1a, began in May 1944. The first encounter with the Allied bombers took place on July 28, near Merseburg.

Five Komets of the 1/JG 400 attacked a formation of American B-17s. However, their combat activity threw light on a series of defects: firing difficulties, caused by the high speed at which the Me.163s approached the bombers (making it possible only to fire in 3 seconds); problems with controlling the engine (which had a duration of seven and a half minutes) that could only be turned off. Production of the Me.163 B-1 ceased in February 1945, before the aircraft could be tuned definitively. Other projects included the Me.163 C-1a version (three of which were built), with a modified airframe and engine to increase the duration of the thrust and the Me.163 D, provided with retractable forward tricycle landing gear and further improvements. Only one prototype was built which, in the end, was redesignated Me.263.

---

color plate

Messerschmitt Me.163 B-1 2nd Staffel Jagdgeschwader 400 Luftwaffe - Germany, 1944-1945

Aircraft:	Messerschmitt Me.163 B-1a
Nation:	Germany
Manufacturer:	Messerschmitt AG
Type:	Fighter
Year:	1944
Engine:	Walter HWK 509 A-2 (rocket)
Potency:	3,752 lb (1,700 kg)
Wingspan:	30 ft 7 in (9.32 m)
Length:	19 ft 3 in (5.84 m)
Height:	9 ft 1 in (2.77 m)
Weight:	9,072 lb (4,110 kg)
Maximum speed:	596 mph (960 km/h) at 9,868 ft (3,000 m)
Ceiling:	39,802 ft (12,100 m)
Range:	80 miles (130 km)
Armament:	2 x 30 mm cannons
Crew:	1

The Me.163 seen from the front with the landing gear that was released after take-off.

MESSERSCHMITT Me.163 B-1

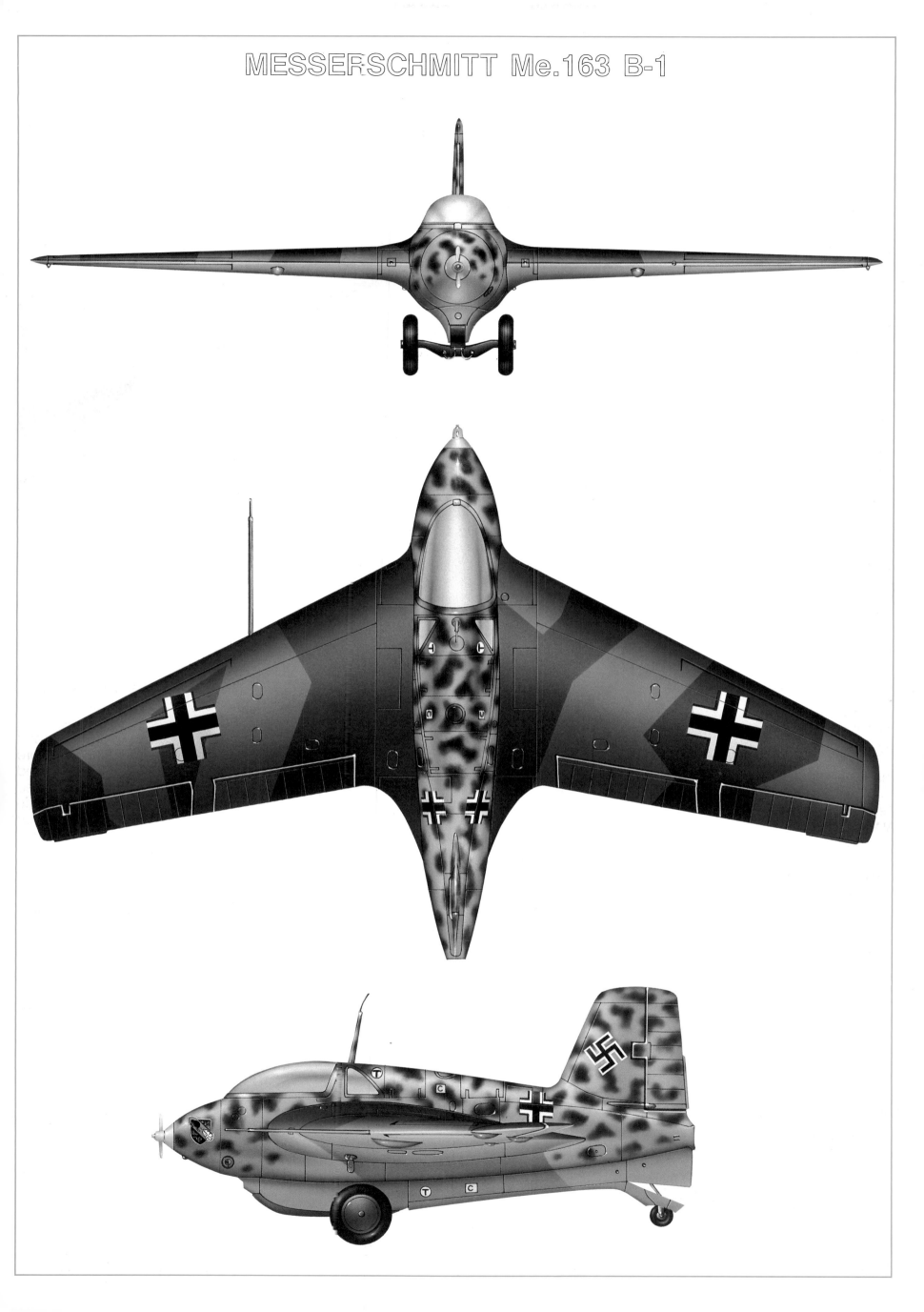

MESSERSCHMITT Me.262 A-1

In the history of aviation, the Messerschmitt Me.262 marked at the same time the end of an era and the beginning of a new one. In fact, with this elegant and powerful combat plane, the jet engine made its forceful debut in a field that had up till then been dominated by the traditional engines. In the turmoil of World War II, the results of the plane were sensational. With its remarkable performance in terms of speed, superior to that of any other aircraft in existence at the time, and its heavy armament, the Me.262 proved to be a formidable threat to the enemy right from its combat debut in the autumn of 1944. However, fortunately for the Allies, the enormous potential of this aircraft was only partially exploited by Germany. Several historians have written that, had the Messerschmitt Me.262 been available earlier and had it been employed immediately in the role to which it was most suited (that of pure fighter), it is highly probable that it would have altered the course of World War II. However, production was dissipated in a series of variants in which it was attempted to adapt the aircraft to various roles, first of all bomber, then that of night fighter. The result was that the 1,430 aircraft built during the last months of the war went into service too late and in too small a number to have any effect on the course of events. Nevertheless, the Me.262 fought tenaciously until the cease of hostilities in Europe, and its career truly represented the swan-song of the Luftwaffe.

The Me.262 project was launched toward the end of 1938, following specifications which called for the installation of the two new gas turbines being developed at the time by BMW and Junkers. It was in fact the delay in preparing these revolutionary engines that led to the development of the program being affected for the first time. In March 1940, Messerschmitt completed a mock-up of the aircraft and received an order for the construction of three prototypes. However, the preparation of the engines continued to call for more time than had been foreseen, and in order to speed up the initial flight tests and begin the study of the airframe's behavior, in March 1941, the first aircraft was fitted with a traditional Junkers Jumo 210 G engine installed in the nose. This structure took to the air for the first time on April 18, with satisfactory results, but it was not until November, when the first BMW 003 turbojets became available, that the definitive prototype could be prepared. During the first flight test (March 25, 1942) the piston engine was also retained and this proved to be a lucky foresight considering that, immediately after takeoff, the two turbojets stopped working due to the breakage of the compressor blades and the pilot, Fritz Wendel, managed to land thanks entirely to the "old" propeller.

Development continued with the more reliable Junkers Jumo 004 A, and restructured in this manner, the third prototype managed to complete its first test flight successfully on July 18, 1942. A long preparation phase followed with other experimental air-

One of the Me.262 prototypes during flight tests. The aircraft has traditional type landing gear, fitted with tail wheel.

craft and a year later (July 23, 1943), the new aircraft was presented to Hermann Goering. On November 26, this was followed by its presentation to Hitler, who was very impressed and ordered that the aircraft go into production immediately as a bomber. This decision was the cause of further delays in the program and it was not until April, 1944, that the first of the 23 pre-series Me.262 A-0 appeared.

The first production series version was the A-1a fighter, armed with four 30 mm cannons, and it was followed by the A-2a bomber variant, capable of carrying a maximum bomb load of 2,207 lb (1,000 kg). Several experimental subseries were built in order to test different types of armament and on board equipment (these included the Me.262 A-3a for tactical support and the A-5a fighter-reconnaissance plane), although in October, 1944, it was from the two-seater Me.262 B-1a trainer variant that the first night fighter version (designated B-1a/U1) was derived. This was followed by the definitive B-2a version. Despite the fact that it was penalized as far as speed was concerned by the large radar antennae on the nose, this Me.262 had great potential for development. However, only very few B-1a/U1s were delivered in 1945, while the B-2as never went beyond the prototype stage.

---

color plate

Messerschmitt Me.262 A-1 III Gruppe Ergangzungs Jagdgeschwader 2 (III/EJG 2) Luftwaffe - Lechfeld, January, 1945

A Messerschmitt Me.262 in service with the Sonderkommando Nowotny, the first German unit to employ the jet fighter.

Aircraft:	Messerschmitt Me.262 A-1a
Nation:	Germany
Manufacturer:	Messerschmitt AG
Type:	Fighter
Year:	1944
Engine:	2 Junkers Jumo 004 B-1, turbojets with a thrust of 1,986 lb (900 kg) each
Wingspan:	41 ft 1 in (12.50 m)
Length:	34 ft 9 in (10.58 m)
Height:	10 ft 10 in (3.83 m)
Weight:	14,099 lb (6,387 kg)
Maximum speed:	539 mph (869 km/h) at 13,245 ft (6.000 m)
Ceiling:	37,664 ft (11,450 m)
Range:	652 miles (1,050 km)
Armament:	4 × 30 mm cannons
Crew:	1

FOCKE WULF Fw.190 A-4

A Focke Wulf Fw.190 A5 with supplementary fuel tanks on the wings and 1,100 lb (500 kg) of bombs beneath the belly.

An Fw.190 A3 in service with the I/SG 1 during takeoff from an airport in occupied France.

An Fw.190 used to launch a Mistel flying bomb.

Considered by many as the best German fighter of World War II, the Focke Wulf Fw.190 was created to flank the already excellent Messerschmitt Bf.109, although it eventually proved to be superior even to its direct rival. Powerful, agile, and versatile, more than 20,000 of this small and compact combat plane were constructed, 13,367 of which were interceptors while the rest were fighter-bombers, from the summer of 1941 up to the end of the war, sharing with the Bf.109 the honor and the burden of constituting the Luftwaffe's front line. From many points of view the careers of the two aircraft were very similar: like the Messerschmitt fighter, the one developed by Focke Wulf was continuously updated and improved in the course of production, exploiting to the full the excellent qualities of the airframe and making the aircraft constantly competitive.

The project was launched in the autumn of 1937, when the German Air Ministry proposed that Focke develop a fighter-interceptor to be produced alongside the Messerschmitt Bf.109. The design team, headed by Kurt Tank, prepared two alternative proposals which differed basically in the type of engine adopted: the first foresaw the use of an in-line Daimler Benz DB 601, while the second was to be fitted with a BMW 139 18-cylinder radial engine, then in the final stages of development. In Germany at that time, designers tended to favor the adoption of liquid-cooled in-line engines for fighters, not only for their great aerodynamic advantages, but above all due to the availability of excellent power plants that had been widely tested and that would probably be developed further in the future. Nevertheless, Kurt Tank managed to convince the ministerial authorities of the effectiveness of the choice of a radial engine for his project. Three principal factors acted in his favor: the fact that the Daimler Benz DB 601 was likely to become less available in the future, as there was already great demand for those produced; the great and promising potential of the new BMW engine; and last but not least, the fact that the radial engine was less vulnerable than the liquid-cooled one, which needed radiators and piping that were easily damaged in combat.

The construction of three initial prototypes was authorized, and the first of these took to the air on June 1, 1939. Despite problems

in overheating, the aircraft proved to have excellent flying characteristics and an impressive performance, especially as far as speed was concerned. However, a long time was necessary for the development of the aircraft. It was not until the fifth prototype that the Fw.190 assumed its definitive configuration, following substantial modifications to the fuselage and wings and, above all, the installation of a different engine. In fact, development of the BMW 139 had been abandoned in favor of a 14-cylinder model designated 801. The successful combination of a large radial engine and a slender fuselage, particularly advanced from an aerodynamic point of view, constituted the most striking aspect of the new fighter. Otherwise, the Focke Wulf Fw.190 was an all-metal low-wing monoplane with retractable landing gear, characterized by an almost entirely transparent cockpit that provided the pilot with a remarkable field of vision. The armament initially consisted of four machine guns, two of which were installed in the upper part of the fuselage.

After flight testing, 40 preseries aircraft were ordered, followed by 100 aircraft of the initial variant, the Fw.190 A-1, which went into service in July 1941. In September, the first confrontation with the RAF's Spitfire Mk.Vs took place, and the German fighter proved to be generally superior to the British one, apart from its armament. This was strengthened, together with the engine, in the subsequent A-2 and A-3 series, and updating continued throughout the numerous subseries that followed. Some of the best known were the A-4 of 1942, and the A-5, the A-6, the A-7, and the A-8 of 1943. In these variants, the aircraft was also adapted to the role of fighter-bomber, although this use was explicitly planned for the subsequent versions.

color plate

Focke Wulf Fw.190 A-4 personal aircraft of the Commander of the I/JG 54 (1st Group 54 Flight Wing) Luftwaffe - Russian Front 1943-44

Aircraft:	Focke Wulf Fw.190 A-1
Nation:	Germany
Manufacturer:	Focke Wulf Flugzeugbau GmbH
Type:	Fighter
Year:	1941
Engine:	BMW 801C-1, 14-cylinder radial, air-cooled, 1,600 hp
Wingspan:	34 ft 5 1/2 in (10.50 m)
Length:	29 ft (8.84 m)
Height:	12 ft 11 1/2 in (3.94 m)
Weight:	8,770 lb (3,973 kg) loaded
Maximum speed:	389 mph (626 km/h) at 18,045 ft (5,500 m)
Ceiling:	34,775 ft (10,600 m)
Range:	497 miles (800 km)
Armament:	4 machine guns
Crew:	1

FOCKE WULF Fw.190 D-9

In the long evolution of the Focke Wulf Fw.190 while the final Ta.152 (the last project of Kurt Tank in 1937) was being developed, the D variant of 1944 represented a transitional phase. Despite this, from many points of view, the Long-nose Dora (the Fw.190 D became known by this nick-name in the Luftwaffe, due to the lengthening of the front section caused by the installation of the large Junkers Jumo 213A V-12 engine in place of the usual BMW 801 radial) was the most successful version of the entire family. This was mainly due to the engine itself, which was capable of generating no less than 2,240 hp in case of emergency and guaranteed the fighter an excellent performance. The Fw.190 D-12/R21 (one of the numerous subseries developed in the course of production, amounting to a total of almost 700 aircraft) proved to be the fastest of all the Fw.190s, reaching speeds of about 453 mph (730 km/h) at altitude.

Kurt Tank first used an in-line Junkers Jumo engine at the beginning of 1942, when he transformed six Fw.190 A airframes into prototypes. The second phase of evaluations by the Luftwaffe began toward the end of 1943, when some A-7 series aircraft were modified in a similar way to Fw.190 D-0s. Through gradual improvements, the definitive structure was eventually finished and the first Fw.190 D-9 took to the air in May, 1944. Apart from the installation of the in-line engine with a characteristic circular radiator, the most obvious feature of the aircraft was the remarkable lengthening of its fuselage. This together with larger vertical tail planes, made it an aircraft that was noticeably different from its predecessors.

The Fw.190 Ds were initially regarded with suspicion by the Luftwaffe pilots. Eventually, once the crews were familiar with it and the fighter was able to express its true potential, this attitude radically changed. The Dora maintained a remarkable performance, especially in its speed in ascent. It was clearly superior to the aircraft that had radial engines. Its maneuverability and turning radius were also superior. It began its service in September 1944 with the units of the III/JG 54, defending the airports of Hesepe and Achmer, near the Dutch border. It was here that the Nowotny Command, which was evaluating the new Messerschmitt Me.262 jets, was based. Protection was vital, considering that the revolutionary

fighters were particularly vulnerable during takeoff and landing, and the Fw.190 D-9s soon proved to be competitive with the North American P-51D and Supermarine Spitfire Mk.XIVs were concerned. These were two of the Luftwaffe's most feared adversaries.

The Dora equipped many fighter units until the end of the war and several subseries were built, differing from each other mainly in their armament and engines. In addition, numerous experimental versions were studied, most of which would have used new engines, such as the 2,400 hp BMW 802 radials, the 3,900 hp BMW 803 (the latter was a large 28-cylinder engine), and the Daimler Benz DB 609, DB 614 and DB 623. They generated 2,660, 2,020, and 2,400 hp respectively. However, the aircraft's great effectiveness was not very useful during the final, desperate months of the war, when Luftwaffe was hampered by a lack of skilled pilots and a shortage of fuel.

color plate

Focke Wulf Fw.190 D-9 II Jagdgeschwader 4, Reichsverteidigung (Defense of the Reich), Luftwaffe - Germany, 1945

Aircraft:	Focke Wulf Fw.190 D-9
Nation:	Germany
Manufacturer:	Focke Wulf Flugzeugbau GmbH
Type:	Fighter-bomber
Year:	1944
Engine:	Junkers Jumo 213A-1, 12-cylinder V, liquid-cooled, 1,700 hp
Wingspan:	34 ft 6 in (10.50 m)
Length:	33 ft 6 in (10.20 m)
Height:	11 ft 0 in (3.35 m)
Weight:	10,684 lb (4,840 kg)
Maximum speed:	425 mph (685 km/h) at 21,710 ft (6,600 m)
Ceiling:	39,473 ft (12,000 m)
Range:	521 mph (840 km/h)
Armament:	2 x 20 mm cannons; 2 machine guns; 1,103 lb (500 kg) of bombs
Crew:	1

A Focke Wulf Fw.190 D-9 with supplementary fuel tank in the belly.

FOCKE WULF Fw.190 F-8

The long evolution of the Focke Wulf Fw.190, considered by many the best German fighter of World War II, continued for practically the entire duration of the conflict. This constant task of updating and strengthening succeeded in keeping the aircraft competitive and by exploiting the great qualities of the airframe in making it effective in roles that differed from its original one of interceptor. In the Fw.190's intensive career, its use as a fighter-bomber came second in order of importance, and following the brillant results recorded by some of the numerous subseries of the initial A variant, late in the autumn of 1943 it was decided to build a new, improved version for tactical support. This was the Fw.190 F, which was developed alongside the similar G series.

The Focke Wulf Fw.190 Fs were basically derived from the A series aircraft, differing only in the elimination of part of the fixed armament on the wing and in the adoption of racks to carry the bomb load. In addition, the landing gear was strengthened and the armoring protecting the pilot and the engine was increased, while a characteristic bulged canopy was installed in the fuselage to overcome the problem of visibility during low-altitude operations of which many units complained. The initial F-1 variant, of which 30 or so were completed, obtained by converting a similar number of A-4s, was delivered for evaluation tests toward the end of the year. It was followed, during 1943, by the two F-2 and F-3 subseries (the first to be built on independent assembly lines) in which the aircraft assumed its definitive form. However, production was suspended halfway through the following year, after some

550 aircraft had been completed to give priority to the construction of the more powerful G version, and did not recommence until the spring of 1944, with the final two subseries, F-8 and F-9, in which the fighter-bomber was further improved. The Fw.190 F-8 proved to be particularly effective in the role of antitank attack, capable as it was of carrying fourteen 210 mm rockets, or six 280 mm rocket launchers, or twenty-four 50 mm unguided rockets. This type of armament was tested on the eastern front in October 1944 and adopted toward the end of the year. As for the aircraft belonging to the F-9 subseries, their main characteristic was the adoption of a BMW 801 TS engine.

The Focke Wulf Fw.190 F's already remarkable characteristics were improved still further in the G variant aircraft, which differed basically in their greater fuel capacity and the increased bomb load. These characteristics were obtained by eliminating the two machine guns installed in the fuselage and limiting the armament to two 20 mm cannons on the wings. The initial G-1 subseries (derived from the A-4 and of which only 50 were produced) was followed on the assembly lines by the G-2 (based on the airframe of the Focke Wulf Fw.190 A-5) and by the G-3 (delivered from the late summer of 1943, and provided with a 1,870 hp BMW 801 D-2 engine). This power plant was also used for the final G-8 variant, basically derived from the A-8, which was built from September 1943 until February 1944. The G series Focke Wulfs became operative toward the end of 1942 in North Africa, although most of them were used on the eastern front.

A Focke Wulf Fw.190 G equipped with supports on the belly for carrying a bomb load.

color plate
Focke Wulf Fw.190 F-8 1/SG4 Luftwaffe - Italy 1944

Aircraft:	Focke Wulf Fw.190 F-3
Nation:	Germany
Manufacturer:	Focke Wulf Flugzeugbau GmbH
Type:	Fighter-bomber
Year:	1943
Engine:	BMW 801 D-2, 14-cylinder radial, air-cooled, 1,700 hp
Wingspan:	34 ft 8 in (10.50 m)
Length:	30 ft (9.12 m)
Height:	12 ft 11 in (3.94 m)
Weight:	10,843 lb (4,921 kg)
Maximum speed:	393 mph (694 km/h) at 18,092 ft (5,550 m)
Ceiling:	34,868 ft (10,600 m)
Range:	465 miles (750 km)
Armament:	2 × 20 mm cannons, 2 machine guns, 551 lb (250 kg) of bombs
Crew:	1

A pair of Focke Wulf Fw.190 F fighter-bombers in service on the Russian front.

FOCKE WULF Ta.152 H-1

The Focke Wulf Ta.152 with "tropical-type" filter on the air inlet of the carburetor.

The agile and penetrating shape of the Focke Wulf Ta.152 H.

The final expression of the Focke Wulf Fw.190, considered by many as the best German fighter of World War II, was the Ta.152, an aircraft that was rather different from that designed by Kurt Tank back in 1937; however it was representative nevertheless of the lengthy evolution that the basic model had undergone during the various periods of the conflict. The Ta.152 was created to act as an interceptor at high altitude, and as such, it proved to be capable of an outstanding performance, especially as far as speed was concerned, being superior to that of any other enemy fighter. The H version could reach no less than 464 mph (748 km/h) at 30,098 ft (9,150 m) and 471 mph (759 km/h) at 41,118 ft (12,500 m). However, relatively few of these remarkable combat planes came off the assembly lines during the last months of the war and their career was rather limited, and almost non-existent in the role for which they had been conceived.

In 1940, Focke Wulf had begun to study variants of its Fw.109 capable of operating well at altitudes much greater than those reachable by the versions in production. These attempts had been hampered by the lack of a suitable engine at the time. However, the need for a high altitude fighter became more pressing toward the end of 1942, above all following the news concerning the building of the new Boeing B-29 strategic bomber by the Americans. Consequently, the German Air Ministry began to press Messerschmitt and Focke Wulf to prepare specific projects for an interceptor capable of being used also as a reconnaissance plane.

Kurt Tank presented two proposals, both derived from the Fw.190 D model (the variant characterized by the adoption of the large Junkers Jumo 213 A "V-12" engine instead of the usual BMW 801 radial), designated respectively Fw.190 Ra-2 and Fw.190 Ra-3. The two projects were accepted, and in honor of the designer, their code was characterized by the first two letters of Tank's surname: Ta.152 B and Ta.152 H. Moreover, the suffixes indicated the roles which Tank himself intended for the aircraft: Begleitjäger (escort fighter) and Höhenjäger (high altitude fighter). In both aircraft, the power was entrusted to a Junkers Jumo 213 E "V-12" engine capable of generating in the region of 1,750 hp and provided with a three-speed two-stage compressor. The cockpit was pressurized and the basic armament consisted of a 30 mm Mk.108 cannon in the propeller axis and two 20 mm caliber weapons (MG 151/20) in the wings.

The H variant was chosen to go into service and the first prototype was ready in the autumn of 1944. This was followed by 20 pre-series Ta.152 H-0s (the first of which took to the air in October of the same year) which were used to carry out flight tests and service evaluations. The production series Ta.152 H-1s began to come off the assembly lines toward the end of the year, and approximately 150 were completed before production was halted. However, not one fighter unit was completely equipped with the new aircraft and its only role of any importance was in the protec-

tion of the landing fields used by the Messerschmitt Me.262s, with the aim of keeping away the enemy fighters which exploited this delicate flight phase in order to shoot down the German jet planes.

The Ta.152 H's outstanding performance was tested personally by the designer himself. In December, 1944, while flying between Lagenhagen and Cottbus at the controls of one of the first aircraft, Kurt Tank was intercepted by a pair of American P-51 Mustangs. His tactics for escape were extremely simple. Pulling out the throttle to the full, he literally left the enemy fighters behind, and there was nothing they could do to pursue him.

color plate
Focke Wulf Ta.152 H-1 Staff Flight of JG 301, Defense of the Reich - Germany, 1945

Aircraft:	Focke Wulf Ta.152 H-1
Nation:	Germany
Manufacturer:	Focke Wulf Flugzeugbau GmbH
Type:	Fighter
Year:	1945
Engine:	Junkers Jumo 213 E-1, 12-cylinder V, liquid-cooled, 1,750 hp
Wingspan:	47 ft 8 in (14.50 m)
Length:	35 ft 6 in (10.80 m)
Height:	13 ft 1 in (4.00 m)
Weight:	10,485 lb (4,750 kg)
Maximum speed:	471 mph (759 km/h) at 41,118 ft (12,500 m)
Ceiling:	48,684 ft (14,800 m)
Range:	745 miles (1,200 km)
Armament:	1 × 30 mm cannon; 2 × 20 mm cannons
Crew:	1

A Ta.152 H that fell into French hands at the end of the war.

HEINKEL He.111

Officially designed as a civilian aircraft (in the same way as its contemporaries, the Junkers Ju.86 and the Dornier Do.17), the Heinkel He.111 was perhaps the best representative of the deceptive rearmament policy carried out by Germany in the early 1930s. Like the other two aircraft, it was created to fulfill the double role of fast commercial transport plane and bomber, but it was eventually to stand out for its true qualities as a combat plane more than the other two. This occurred especially at a quantitative level, considering that production of this elegant two-engine aircraft continued from 1936 virtually up to the end of the war, totaling more than 7,300 in numerous variants. These were operational on all fronts in a variety of roles, proving the initial project's great qualities even in the presence of more modern and battle-hardened models.

The first prototype of the He.111 took to the air on February 24, 1935. The aircraft was clearly inspired by the single-engine He.70, although it was notably larger. It was followed by another two prototypes, with a shorter wingspan, and the fourth prototype became the progenitor of the civilian version, capable of carrying 10 passengers and a postal load. The aircraft was presented on January 10, 1936, and 10 planes were built, designated He.111 C. These went into regular service with Lufthansa by the end of the year.

Following the disappointing performance of the third prototype (designed for military use), at the beginning of 1936, a fifth experimental aircraft appeared and led to the creation of the first bomber variant, the He.111 B. Characterized by the use of two Daimler Benz DB 600 engines, these aircraft went into service at the end of the year, and, in February 1937, 30 or so were assigned to the Condor Legion in Spain, where they formed the nucleus of what was to become a large force. On the assembly lines, the military versions soon followed one after another. After only a few D series aircraft had been completed, a shortage of Daimler Benz engines led to the development of the successive He.111 E variant of 1938, in which Junkers Jumo 211 engines were used. The He.111 G was characterized by substantial modifications to the wing structure, but it was in 1938, with the appearance of the prototypes of the P and H series, that the bomber assumed its definitive configuration. In these aircraft, the front part of the fuselage was redesigned. It was completely glazed and blended into the rest of the structure, assuming the characteristic asymmetrical form in order to allow the pilot maximum visibility.

The He.111 Hs (in which the Jumo engine was used definitively, in increasingly powerful versions) became the major production variant: these aircraft went into service in May 1939, and more than 800 were operational by September; approximately 5,000 were to come off the production lines, in many versions. After the H-2 and the H-3, one of the most widely used was the He.111 H-6, which appeared in 1941, specially designed for naval warfare and used with great success in the role of torpedo launcher. The 1943 H-10 and H-12 variants were characterized by the increase in their bomb loads (the Heinkel He.111 H-12 could launch two radio-controlled Henschel Hs.293 missiles), while the bomb load in the H-16 series reached 7,174 lb (3,250 kg). The final H-23 version appeared in 1944 and was destined for the launching of parachutists. Lastly, mention of 10 He.111 Zs should be made. In reality, these consisted of two H-6 airframes joined by means of a new central wing trunk in which a fifth engine was installed. These aircraft were designed to tow the massive Messerschmitt Me.321 transport glider.

The Heinkel's career lasted well beyond World War II. In Spain, 263 of the H-16 variant were built on license by CASA, and they remained in service throughout the 1960s.

---

color plate
Heinkel He.111 H II/KG 53 Condor Legion - USSR 1941

Aircraft:	Heinkel He.111 H-2
Nation:	Germany
Manufacturer:	Ernst Heinkel AG
Type:	Bomber
Year:	1939
Engine:	2 Junkers Jumo 211A-3, 12-cylinder V, liquid-cooled, 1,100 hp each
Wingspan:	74 ft 1 in (22.60 m)
Length:	53 ft 9 in (16.39 m)
Height:	13 ft 1 in (4.00 m)
Weight:	30,865 lb (14,000 kg) loaded
Maximum speed:	252 mph (405 km/h)
Ceiling:	27,900 ft (8,500 m)
Range:	1,280 miles (2,060 km)
Armament:	6 machine guns; 5,501 lb (2,495 kg) of bombs
Crew:	5

Heinkel He.111 in service on the Russian front with additional external bomb load.

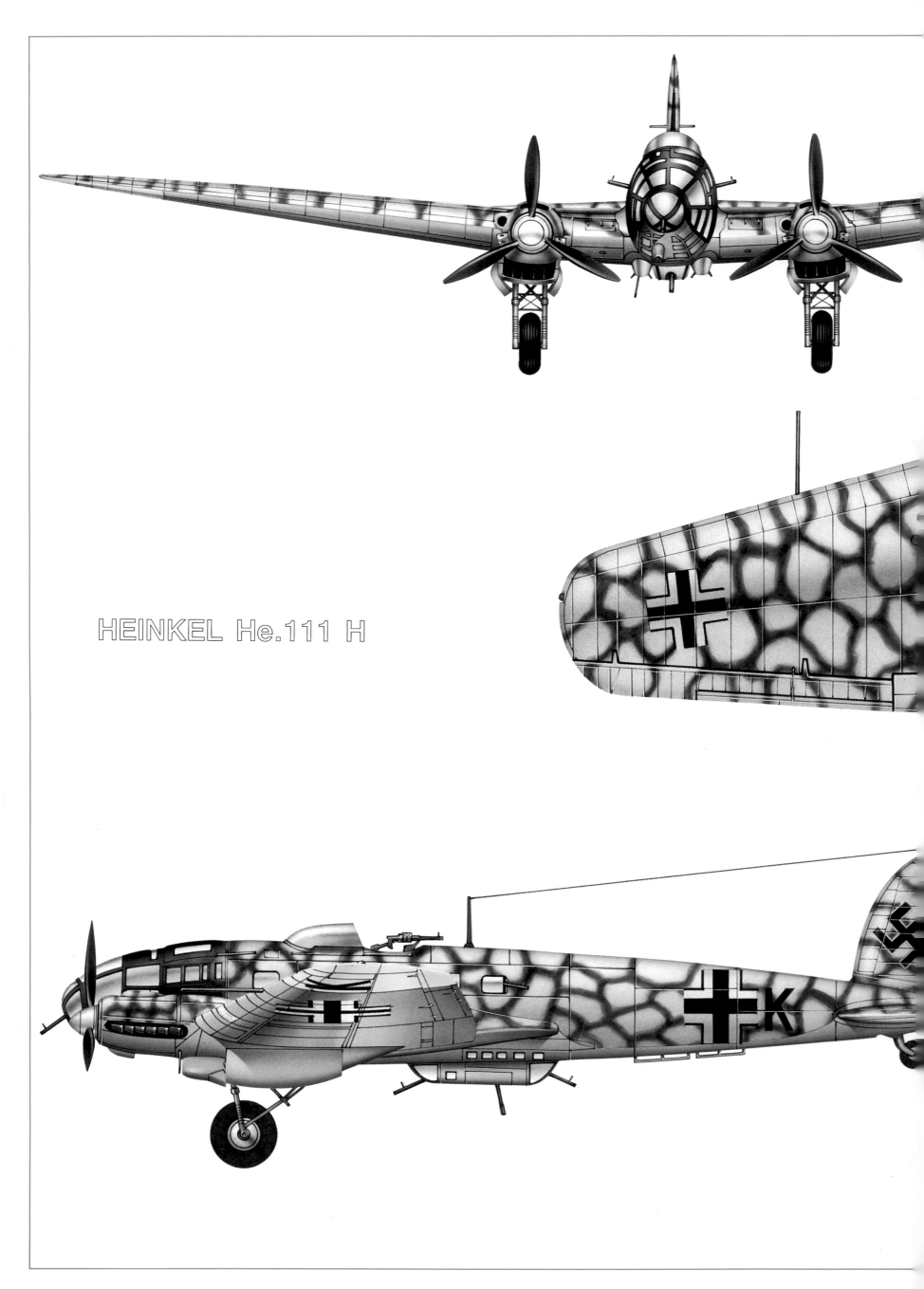

HEINKEL He.111 H

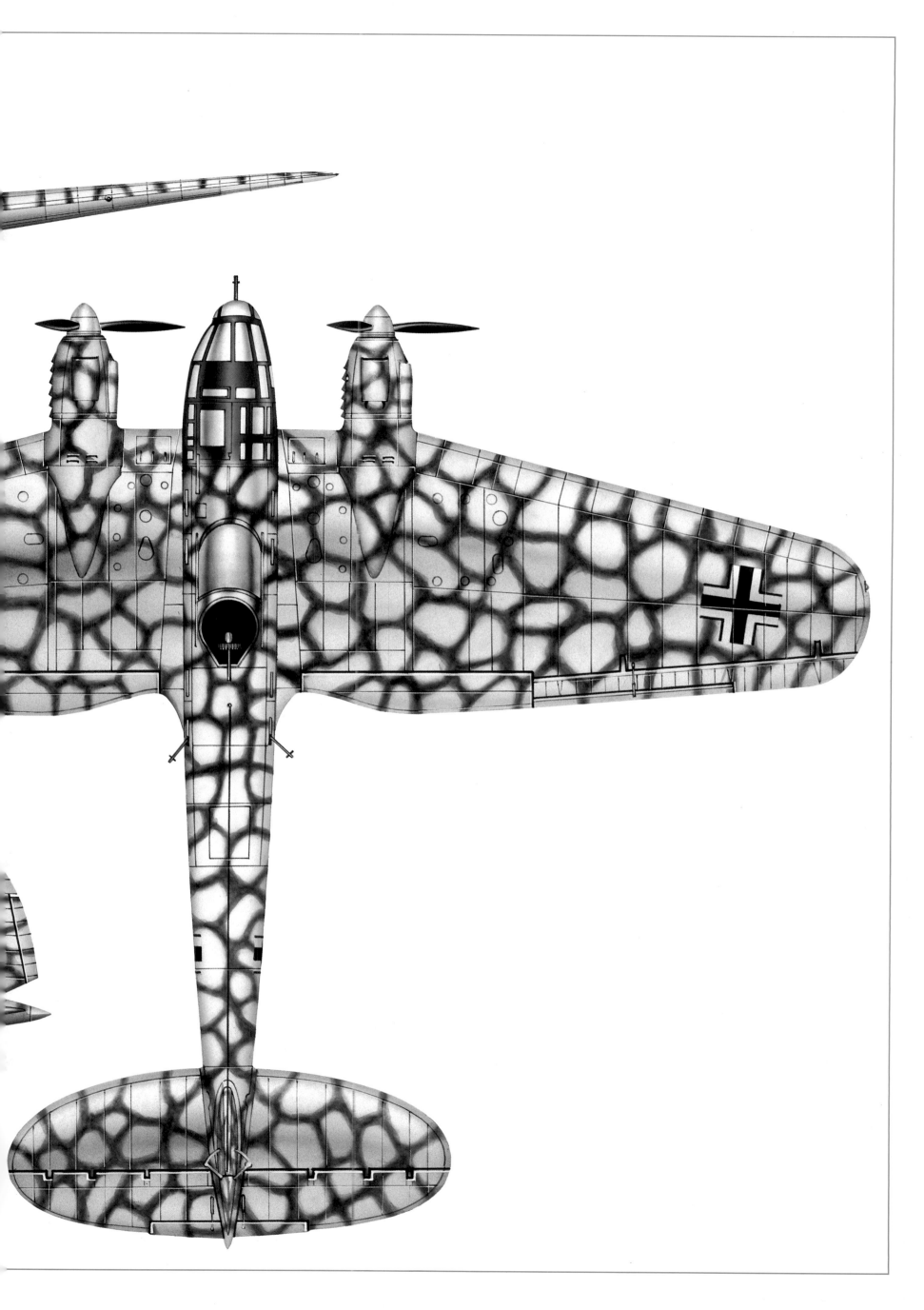

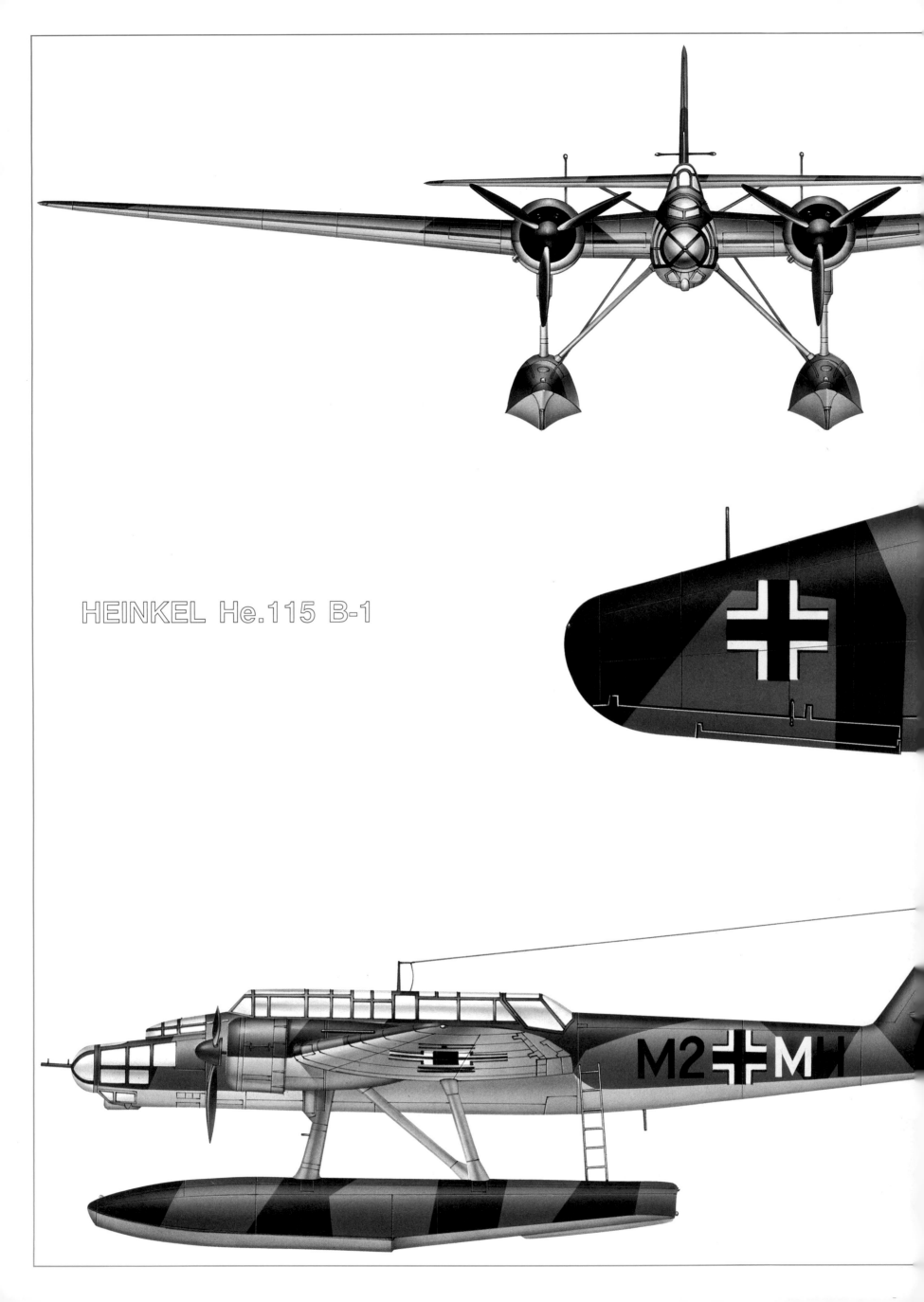

HEINKEL He.115 B-1

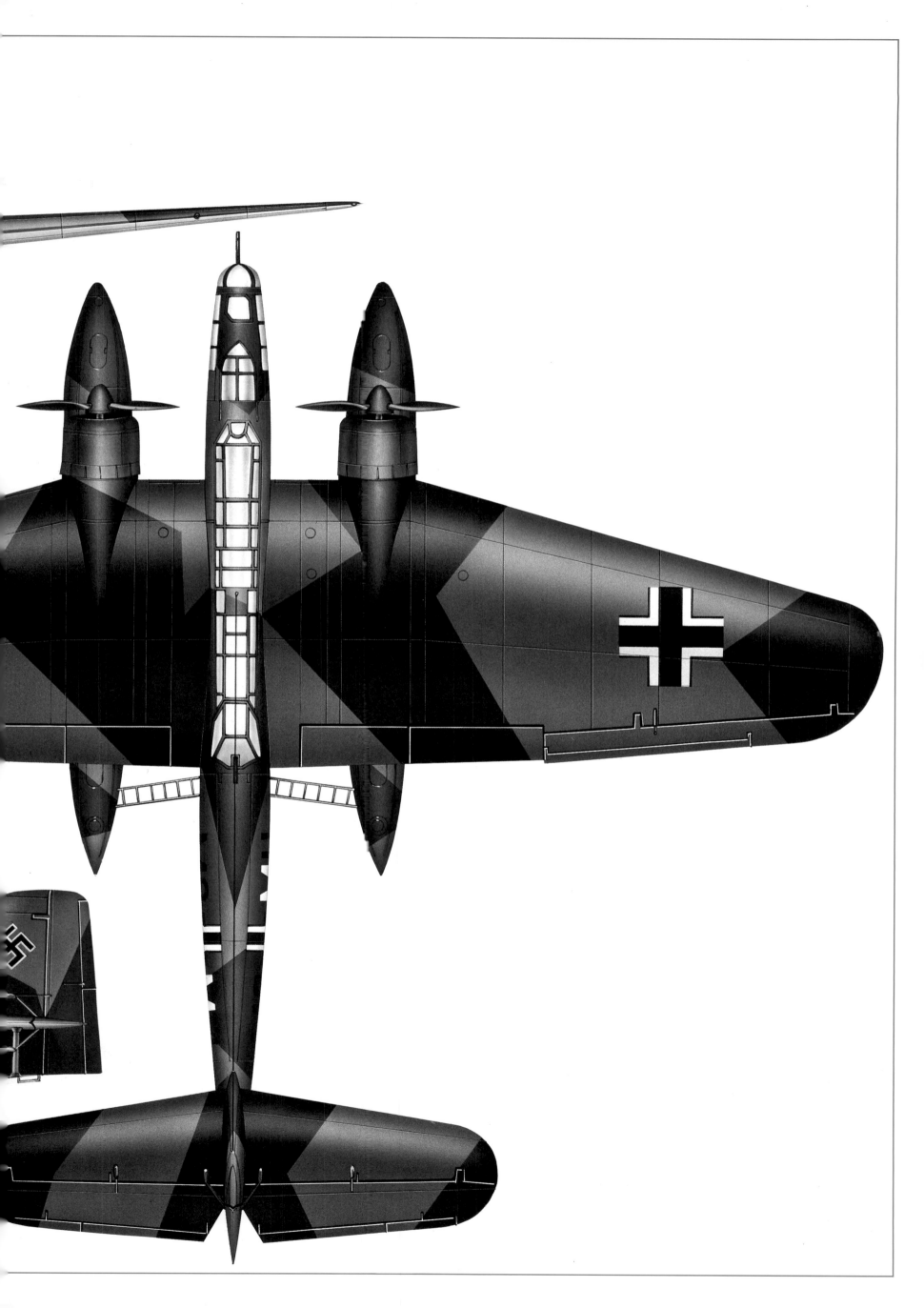

Considered one of the best seaplanes of the war, the Heinkel He.115 was used by the Luftwaffe in a multitude of roles, and although it had originally been conceived as a torpedo bomber, it eventually proved to be irreplaceable as a reconnaissance aircraft and in the role of mine-layer, roles it played until late in the summer of 1944. The He.115s served almost everywhere, from the Atlantic to the Baltic Sea and from the Mediterranean to the Black Sea.

The first prototype took to the air in 1936: it was a large, mid-wing two-engine monoplane, provided with two floats, powered by a pair of BMW 132K radial engines generating 960 hp at takeoff and armed with two machine guns. After the initial series of tests, the aircraft was prepared in order to break the speed record for its category. The modifications basically consisted of the elimination of military equipment and in carefully studied fairing of the nose, with the original structure being replaced by a wooden cone. The attempt was carried out on May 20, 1938, and was successful: the He.115 V1 broke no fewer than eight class records, flying over distances of 620 miles (1,000 km) and 1,240 miles (2,000 km) with loads of 1,103 lb (500 kg), 2,207 lb (1,000 kg), and 4,415 lb (2,000 kg) at an average speed of 200 mph (325 km/h).

Another three prototypes followed. Production was based on the last of these and began in 1937, with 10 preseries aircraft designated He.115 A-0 and with an initial order for 34 of the A-1 version. Norway showed great interest in these aircraft, and six were ordered in August 1938, being delivered in the second half of the following year.

Production continued with the aircraft of the A-3 subseries (with modified bomb compartment and improved radio equipment), but a request for greater range led to the development of the second B version (characterized mainly by larger fuel tanks and an overall increase in weight), and 52 of these were delivered during 1939. However, in the course of operative service, the He.115 soon began to reveal its limitations as an attack aircraft and it was gradually relegated to observation and mine-laying duties.

During 1940, 66 He.115s were delivered, and in 1941 the C version appeared, characterized by an increase in the defensive armament. The evolution of the project was considered interesting, but it came to a sudden standstill in 1941 when, due to urgent requests for land-type aircraft, the military authorities decided to suspend production. However, it resumed toward the end of 1943, with the final E variant. The preseries E-0 aircraft and those of the E-1 series were similar overall to the previous B and C models, although their defensive armament was strengthened still further, to the point of including four 7.9 mm MG 81-type machine guns. In all, a total of 141 were built during 1944.

In the course of production, an interesting version of the He.115

was developed in an attempt to improve the aircraft's performance. This was the D, characterized by the substitution of the original power plants with two 1,600 hp BMW 810C engines. This remained at the prototype stage, due to the lack of availability of this engine, and the only example to be completed took part in operations in 1941. The He.115 D had a four-man crew and defensive armament consisting of three 7.9 mm machine guns and a 20 mm cannon. As for its performance, it reached a maximum speed of 248 mph (399 km/h) and had a ceiling of 23,355 ft (7,100 m).

A captured Heinkel He.115 B used in combat by the British.

Aircraft:	Heinkel He.115 B-1
Nation:	Germany
Manufacturer:	Ernst Heinkel AG
Type:	Torpedo-bomber
Year:	1939
Engine:	2 BMW 132K, 9-cylinder radial, air-cooled, 960 hp each
Wingspan:	72 ft 2 in (22.00 m)
Length:	56 ft 9 in (17.30 m)
Height:	21 ft 8 in (6.60 m)
Weight:	20,065 lb (9,100 kg) loaded
Maximum speed:	220 mph (305 km/h) at 11,150 ft (3,400 m)
Ceiling:	18,040 ft (5,500 m)
Range:	2,080 miles (3,350 km)
Armament:	2 machine guns; 3,300 lb (1,500 kg) of bombs
Crew:	3

color plate

Heinkel He.115 B-1 1/Kü. Fl. Gr. 106 Luftwaffe - Baltic Sea 1941

A Heinkel He.115 during takeoff.

Germany's only attempt to put a heavy bomber into action resulted in a virtual failure. This aircraft was the Heinkel He.177 *Greif*, a large, powerful, and sophisticated plane created to carry out a multitude of tasks including that of dive-bomber, an unusual role for an aircraft weighing 30 tons. Moreover, although it was designed in 1936, the *Greif* did not go into production until six years later, following a long laborious and tormented preparation phase that never succeeded in solving all the problems that plagued the aircraft: structural weaknesses and unreliability of the power plants. Of the approximately 1,000 aircraft that were built, only a few hundred actually went into service, during the final years of the conflict, and even then on an irregular basis.

The specifications that gave rise to Heinkel's P 1041 project, issued in 1936, called for the construction of a long-range strategic bomber, capable of carrying two tons of bombs for 993 miles (1,600 km) and of flying at a maximum speed of 335 mph (540 km/h). These characteristics were undoubtedly exceptional for the time and greatly influenced the project, which was entrusted to Siegfried Günther.

The greatest problem was caused by the engines. In order to reduce the aircraft's air resistance, the designer decided to install only two engines instead of four. Since no 2,000 hp engines were available, the problem was solved by pairing two Daimler Benz DB 601 engines on a single axis, creating the DB 606, which could generate 2,700 hp. This power plant eventually proved to be very complicated and difficult to tune, and it was subject to overheating, which often even caused fires to break out. Things were further complicated by a fresh request from the official authorities, specifying that the He.177 also be capable of carrying out dive-bombing attacks. This meant a series of structural reinforcements, which led to an increase in weight and a subsequent decline in performance.

The first of the five prototypes took to the air on November 19, 1939. The He.177 was a large all-metal two-engine aircraft with cantilever shoulder wing and retractable rear tricycle landing gear. The main landing gear was unusual, with two independent legs on each side, one retracting into the inside of the engine nacelles and the other into their exterior. However, the series of flight tests was not simple. The *Greif* immediately revealed problems in stability and overheating in its power plants, and, subsequently, serious

structural weaknesses. Three of the prototypes crashed, and tests continued with 35 preseries aircraft (He.117 A-0) that were built later.

The first production variant was the A-1, of which 130 were built, and deliveries commenced in July 1942. They were followed toward the end of the year by the He.177 A-3 (170 completed), and gradually by the other series, the last of which was the A-5, characterized by numerous modifications to its structure, landing gear, and power plants; 565 were built in all.

In the course of its operative career (which came to a conclusion toward the end of 1944), the He.177 was employed with a great variety of offensive armament. These included the Henschel Hs.293 radio-controlled missiles, which were extremely effective in an antishipping role; the bomber could carry a maximum of three.

color plate

Heinkel He.177 A-5/R6 Kampfgeschwader 40 Luftwaffe - Bordeaux-Mérignac, France 1944

Aircraft:	Heinkel He.177 A-1
Nation:	Germany
Manufacturer:	Ernst Heinkel AG
Type:	Bomber
Year:	1942
Engine:	2 Daimler Benz DB 606, 24-cylinder, liquid-cooled, 2,700 hp each
Wingspan:	103 ft 2 in (31.44 m)
Length:	66 ft 11 in (20.40 m)
Height:	21 ft (6.40 m)
Weight:	66,139 lb (29,960 kg) loaded
Maximum speed:	317 mph (510 km/h) at 19,030 ft (5,800 m)
Ceiling:	22,966 ft (7,000 m)
Range:	745 miles (1,200 km)
Armament:	1 × 20 mm cannon; 5 machine guns; 5,290 lb (2,400 kg) of bombs
Crew:	5

A Heinkel He.177 *Greif* in flight during evaluations carried out by the Allies following Germany's surrender. The aircraft bears British insignia.

HEINKEL He.177 A-5/R6

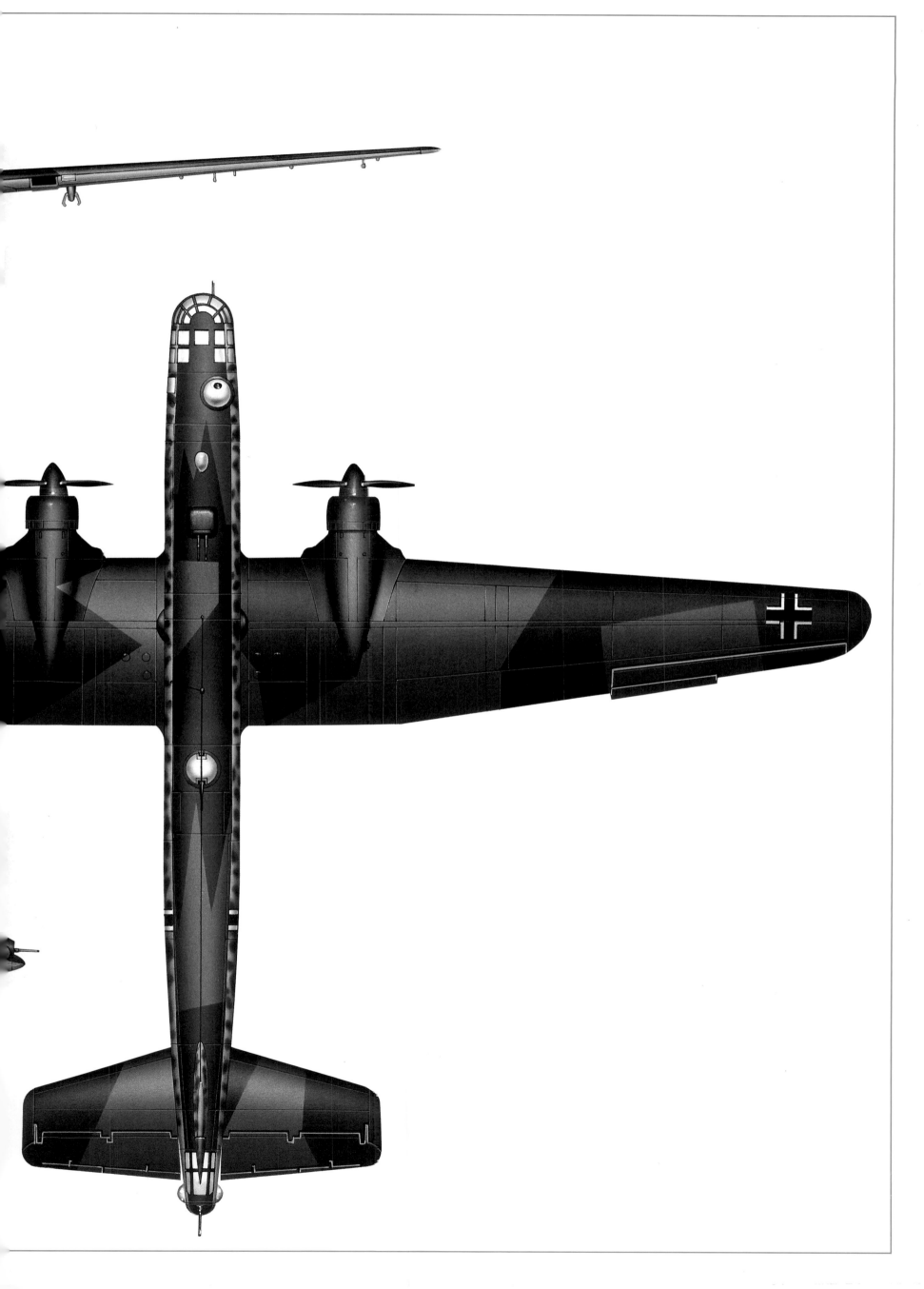

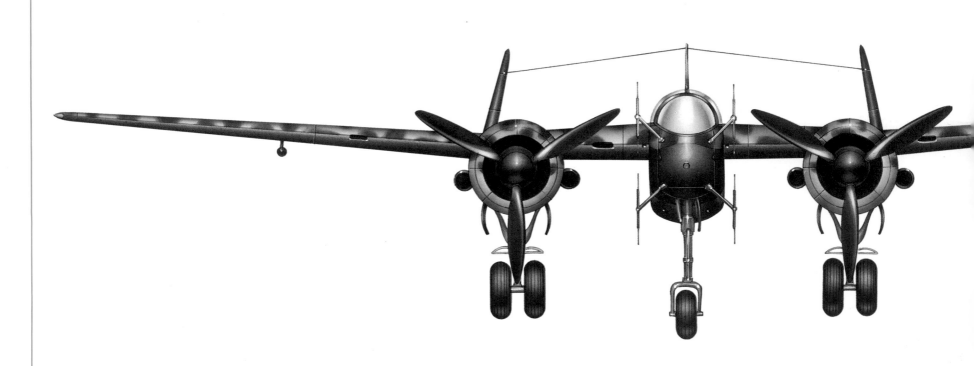

HEINKEL He.219 A-7/R4

Still judged today as the best night fighter sent into combat by Germany during World War II, the Heinkel He.219 *Uhu* (Owl) never succeeded in arousing the complete approval of the Luftwaffe high command, too obsessed with the idea of avoiding waste in production and developing radically new models. It was thus that very few (fewer than 300) of this fast, powerful, and effective combat plane, which could perhaps have influenced the course of the war had it been available in sufficient numbers, equipped the units. Moreover, production was suspended in May 1944, and all the promising plans for the development of the aircraft were dropped.

The great potential of the He.219 in the role of night fighter was demonstrated in an uncontestable way in the course of its first operative mission, carried out in the Netherlands on the night of June 11-12, 1943, by a preseries aircraft still in the evaluation stage: in just under half an hour, its pilot, Werner Streib, managed to shoot down five British Avro Lancaster bombers. During the next five missions, 20 enemy aircraft suffered the same fate, among them six de Havilland Mosquitos, aircraft considered practically invincible in combat due to their remarkable speed.

The highly innovative characteristics of the project had emerged right from the moment its drafting began, in the summer of 1940, and it was continued privately by Heinkel. It was conceived as a multirole aircraft and was fitted with a pressurized cockpit, forward tricycle landing gear, and defensive armament installed in a remote-controlled turret. About a year and a half was to pass before the German Air Ministry began to show an interest in the new two-engine plane, although it did ask Heinkel to transform it into a night fighter.

The first prototype took to the air on November 15, 1942, and was followed by a second experimental aircraft in December. It was a slender high-wing monoplane, which retained the innovative (at least for the Luftwaffe) forward tricycle landing gear, and was powered by a pair of Daimler Benz DB 603 A engines generating a maximum of 1,750 hp, provided with the characteristic circular radiators; the pilot's cockpit was completely glazed, and the two crew members (who sat back to back and, for the first time ever, on ejectable seats) had a remarkable field of vision. The armament was composed entirely of 20 mm and 30 mm cannons installed in a belly fairing, in the wings, and later even on the back of the fuselage, slanting upward.

From January to March 1943, the Heinkel He.219 carried out a long series of comparative tests with a Dornier Do.217 and a Junkers Ju.188 and eventually proved superior to both. The initial order for 100 aircraft was therefore increased to 300.

However, the prototypes that preceded the preseries aircraft

An He.219 *Uhu* equipped with FVG 27 radar.

were numerous in order to experiment various types and combinations of offensive armament and different radar equipment for night time tracking. After the A-1 variant for use in reconnaissance had been abandoned, the first definitive version of the fighter was the A-2/R1, which was followed by the He.219 A-5/R1, R2, R3, R4, in which more powerful engines and different armament combinations were adopted. However, the major production variant was the He.219 A-7, which had formidable firing power, guaranteed by six 30 mm MK 108 and two 20 mm MG 151 cannons. The aircraft of the A-7/R6 subseries were provided with two Junkers Jumo 222 A/B engines, and these power plants increased the fighter's performance, which reached 434 mph (700 km/h).

color plate
Heinkel He.219 A-7/R4 1st Staffel Nachtjagdgeschwader 1 - Munster, Germany 1944

Aircraft:	Heinkel He.219 A-2/R1
Nation:	Germany
Manufacturer:	Ernst Heinkel A.G
Type:	Night Fighter
Year:	1943
Engine:	2 Daimler Benz DB 603 A, 12-cylinder V, liquid cooled, 1,750 hp each
Wingspan:	60 ft 10 in (18.50 m)
Length:	51 ft 1 in (15.54 m)
Height:	13 ft 6 in (4.11 m)
Weight:	27,697 lb (12,547 kg)
Maximum speed:	416 mph (670 km/h) at 23,026 ft (7,000 m)
Ceiling:	41,776 ft (12,700 m)
Range:	1,242 miles (2,000 km)
Armament:	2 × 20 mm cannons, 4 × 30 mm cannons
Crew:	2

A Heinkel He.219 A-7 bearing British insignia. All the German aircraft that were captured undamaged were then tested in flight by the Allies.

HEINKEL He.162 A-2

One of the last aircraft to bear the insignia of the Luftwaffe before the final defeat was the Heinkel He.162 Salamander, once again a jet combat plane, it was built in the record breaking time of only three months. The program was launched officially on September 8, 1944, and the first prototype took to the air on December 6. All this haste was caused by the simple need to send into combat an interceptor which had a performance equal to that of the Messerschmitt Me.262, but which cost less, and which could be constructed using the same engine and non-strategic materials. Moreover, its construction needed to be simple enough overall to mean that it could be entrusted to a not particularly skilled workforce. The difficult terms of this complex equation were entirely solved by Heinkel, although the disastrous conditions that existed in Germany during the final months of the war actually prevented the ambitious production program from being carried out. The intended program foresaw the construction of no fewer than 4,000 aircraft per month, involving three different manufacturers. In the end, only 116 Salamanders came off the assembly lines (after the war, another 800 were found at various stages of construction in German factories below ground), and very few of them went into service.

Almost all of the major German aeronautical manufacturers participated in the specifications for the construction of the Volksjäger (people's fighter, as the project was christened officially): Arado, Blohm und Voss, Fieseler, Focke Wulf, Junkers, Messerschmitt and Heinkel. In the end, on September 30, 1944, the project submitted by Heinkel was chosen. The company's technicians had not been especially daunted by the particularly severe requests as far as development time was concerned (the prototype was to have been ready for December 1 and production was to begin exactly a month later) and they prepared the first experimental aircraft in great haste.

Objectively, the aircraft was an unusual one. It was a high wing monoplane with inclined twin tail planes. It had a small metal and wood fuselage in which the retractable forward tricycle landing gear, and the pilot's position (provided with ejectable seat and canopy) were installed, as well as the armament consisting of two 30 mm caliber cannons (later replaced by two 20 mm weapons for structural reasons) and the engine, the latter being housed in fairing on the aircraft's back. As for the wings, their frame and covering were entirely made of wood.

However, the initial series of tests was not successful. When the first prototype took to the air from Heinkel's field at Vienna-Schwechat, a structural failure was revealed (due to the breakage of one of the covers of the landing gear housing) probably caused by a welding error. On December 10 during a demonstration before the military authorities, a wing gave away and the aircraft fell while flying at high speed at low altitude, crashing to the ground. Once again, the cause of the failure was attributed to a welding error, and the program went ahead all the same, encouraged by the excellent overall performance demonstrated prior to the accident: good overall flying characteristics and high speed, in the region of 521 mph (840 km/h) at 19,736 ft (6,000 m).

The series of tests was completed by another two prototypes and 31 pre-series aircraft, which were evaluated between January and February, 1945. These were followed by the first production series aircraft, designated He.162 A-2, which were fitted with a more powerful engine and standardized armament consisting of two 20 mm cannons. The Salamander's combat career was virtually non-existent.

color plate
Heinkel He.162 A-2 I/JG 1 - Leck Airfield, Germany, 1945

Aircraft: Heinkel He.162 A-2
Nation: Germany
Manufacturer: Ernst Heinkel AG
Type: Fighter
Year: 1945
Engine: BMW 003 E-1, Turbojet with 1,766 lb (800 kg) thrust
Wingspan: 25 ft 3 in (7.70 m)
Length: 29 ft 9 in (9.05 m)
Height: 8 ft 4 in (2.55 m)
Takeoff weight: 5,949 lb (2,695 kg)
Maximum speed: 521 mph (840 km/h) at 19,736 ft (6,000 m)
Ceiling: 39,473 ft (12,000 m)
Range: 605 miles (975 km)
Armament: 2×2 mm cannons
Crew: 1

A Heinkel He.162 captured by the Allies. The aircraft appears to be slightly damaged.

Together with the Junkers Ju.86 and the Heinkel He.111, the Dornier Do.17 was one of the products of the deceptive policy of rearmament carried out by Germany. This fast and elegant two-engine aircraft originated in the first half of the 1930s, in response to a request by Deutsche Lufthansa for the construction of a fast postal plane capable of carrying six passengers, but it found its true dimension in the role of bomber. It was, in fact, as a combat plane that the Do.17 went down in aviation history, one of the Luftwaffe's best known and most widely used in battle. It was an aircraft that, in a continuous evolution composed of numerous series, versions, and derivatives, remained in production for the entire duration of the war and operated on practically all fronts.

The project was begun in 1933, and three prototypes were completed in the course of the following year. However, after evaluations, these aircraft were not considered suitable for commercial use (one of the reasons being that the fuselage was too narrow, preventing the passengers from being housed comfortably), and they were sent back to the manufacturer. Nevertheless, the potential of the aircraft remained great, and it was immediately transformed for military use. The fourth prototype, which appeared in the summer of 1935, became the founder of a long series of bombers, whose initial production series (the E-1 and the F-1, the latter being for reconnaissance) received their baptism of fire in Spain, as part of the Condor Legion, in 1937.

Apart from the advanced nature of its layout (all-metal, mid-wing monoplane with retractable landing gear and carefully designed from the point of view of aerodynamics), the most modern feature of the Dornier Do.17 lay in its performance, and more especially in its speed. A sensational demonstration of this was provided by the victory gained by one of the prototypes in the 1937 Alps Circuit, a race held in Zurich for military aircraft, during which it proved to be the fastest of all the fighters then in production.

After a series of minor variations in which attempts were made to improve and to optimize the features on the project, the most widely produced variant was the Z, which went into service in 1939 and of which just over 500 were built up to the summer of 1940. This series, as well as being the last model before the switch to the 217 type (larger and more powerful), incorporated substantial modifications as compared to the previous ones, particularly in the structure and in the configuration of the front part of the fuselage. This was deepened (in order to increase the efficiency of the rear ventral defensive position) and was almost completely glazed, with the aim of improving the bombardier's position. In particular, in the Do.17 Z-2 series, the use of more powerful power plants (two 1,000 hp BMW Bramo radial engines) made it possible to increase the defensive armament to eight machine guns and the offensive armament to a ton of bombs.

Other variants of particular interest were the Z-6 and Z-10, con-

ceived as night bombers and fitted with heavy armament concentrated entirely in the nose (three machine guns and a 20 mm cannon in the Do.17 Z-6 and four machine guns and two cannons in the Do.17 Z-10). Although the few aircraft built did not have an extensive operational career, they made a valuable contribution to the development of techniques for this particular type of combat.

At the outbreak of the conflict, 370 Do.17s were in service in the Luftwaffe, of which two-thirds belonged to the Z series, and these aircraft took part in all operations during the first two years of the war. Although they were good aircraft overall, they were not particularly outstanding, lacking the bomb-load capacity of the Heinkel He.111 and the speed of the Junkers Ju.88. The Do.17s were withdrawn from front-line service toward the end of 1942, replaced by the more powerful and efficient Do.217s, and were gradually relegated to secondary roles.

color plate

Dornier Do.17 Z-2 3/KG 2 Holzhammer - Balkans 1941

A Dornier Do.17 with blacked-out insignia during the Battle of Britain.

Do.17s of the 3rd Kampf Geschwader flying toward targets in French territory in 1940.

Aircraft:	Dornier Do.17 Z-2
Nation:	Germany
Manufacturer:	Dornier Werke GmbH
Type:	Bomber
Year:	1939
Engine:	2 BMW Bramo 323P, 9-cylinder radial, air-cooled, 1,000 hp each
Wingspan:	59 ft (18.00 m)
Length:	51 ft 10 in (15.79 m)
Height:	14 ft 11 $^1/_2$ in (4.55 m)
Weight:	18,930 lb (8,590 kg) loaded
Maximum speed:	255 mph (410 km/h) at 13,120 ft (4,000 m)
Ceiling:	26,900 ft (8,200 m)
Range:	721 miles (1,160 km)
Armament:	6/8 machine guns; 2,200 lb (1,000 kg) of bombs
Crew:	4

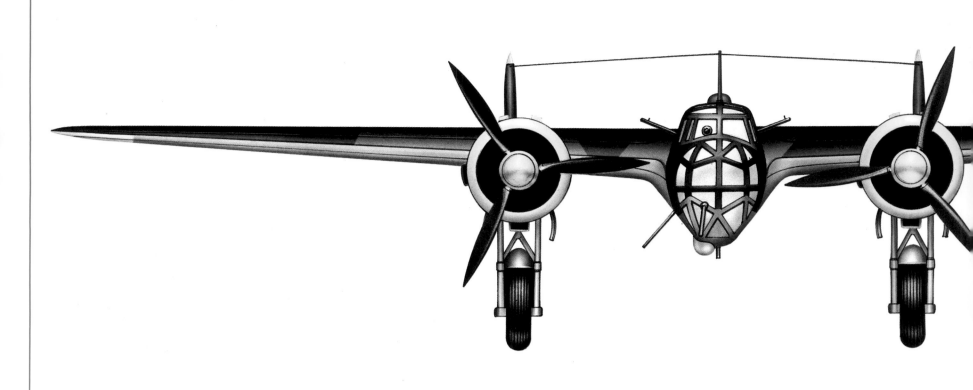

DORNIER Do.17 Z-2

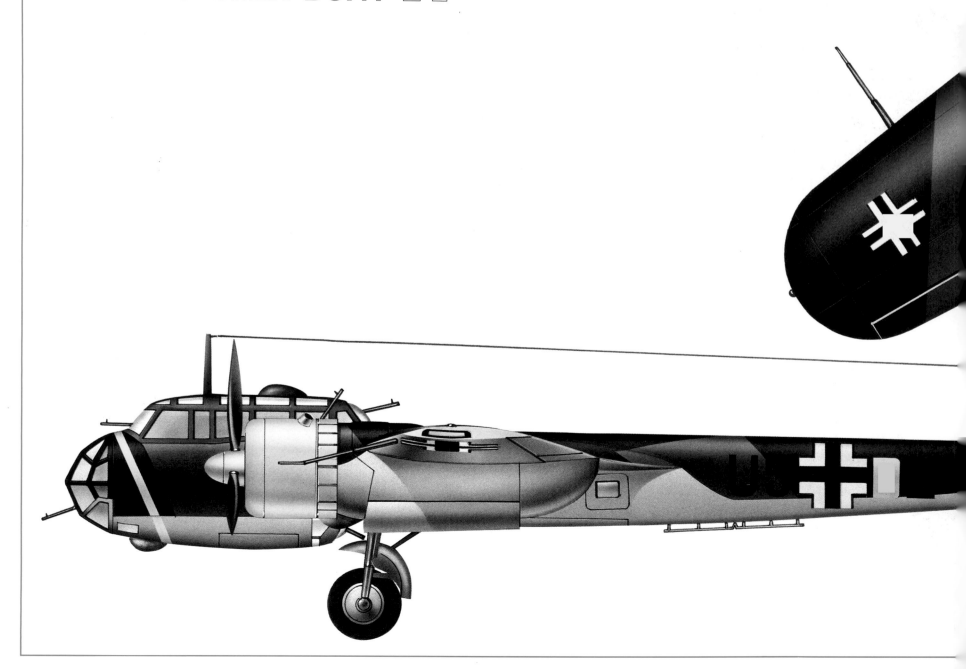

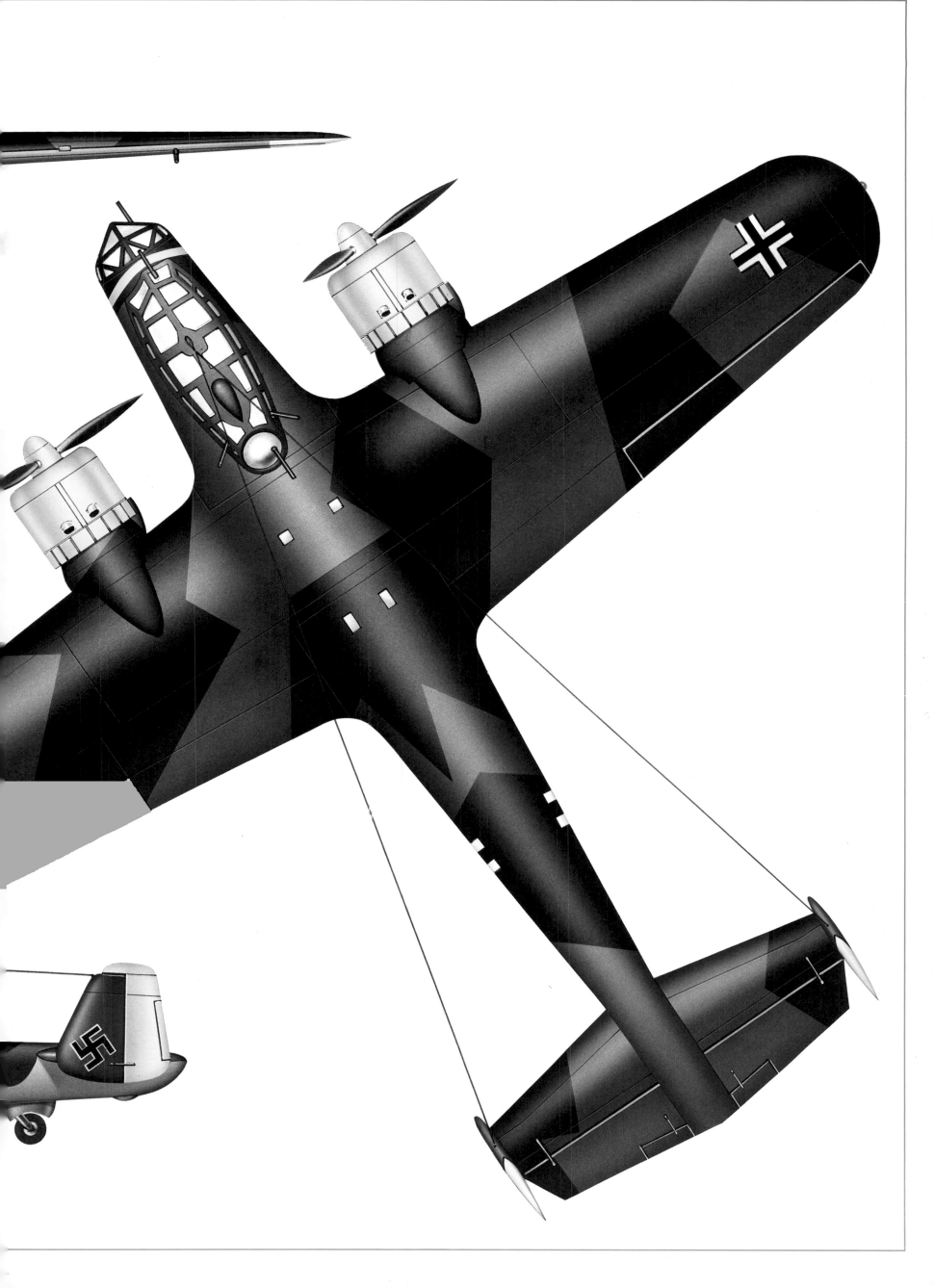

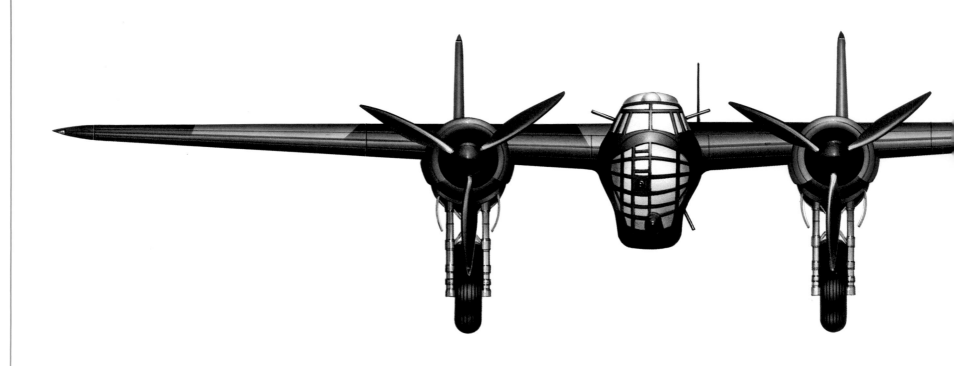

DORNIER Do.217 E-2

U5+HN

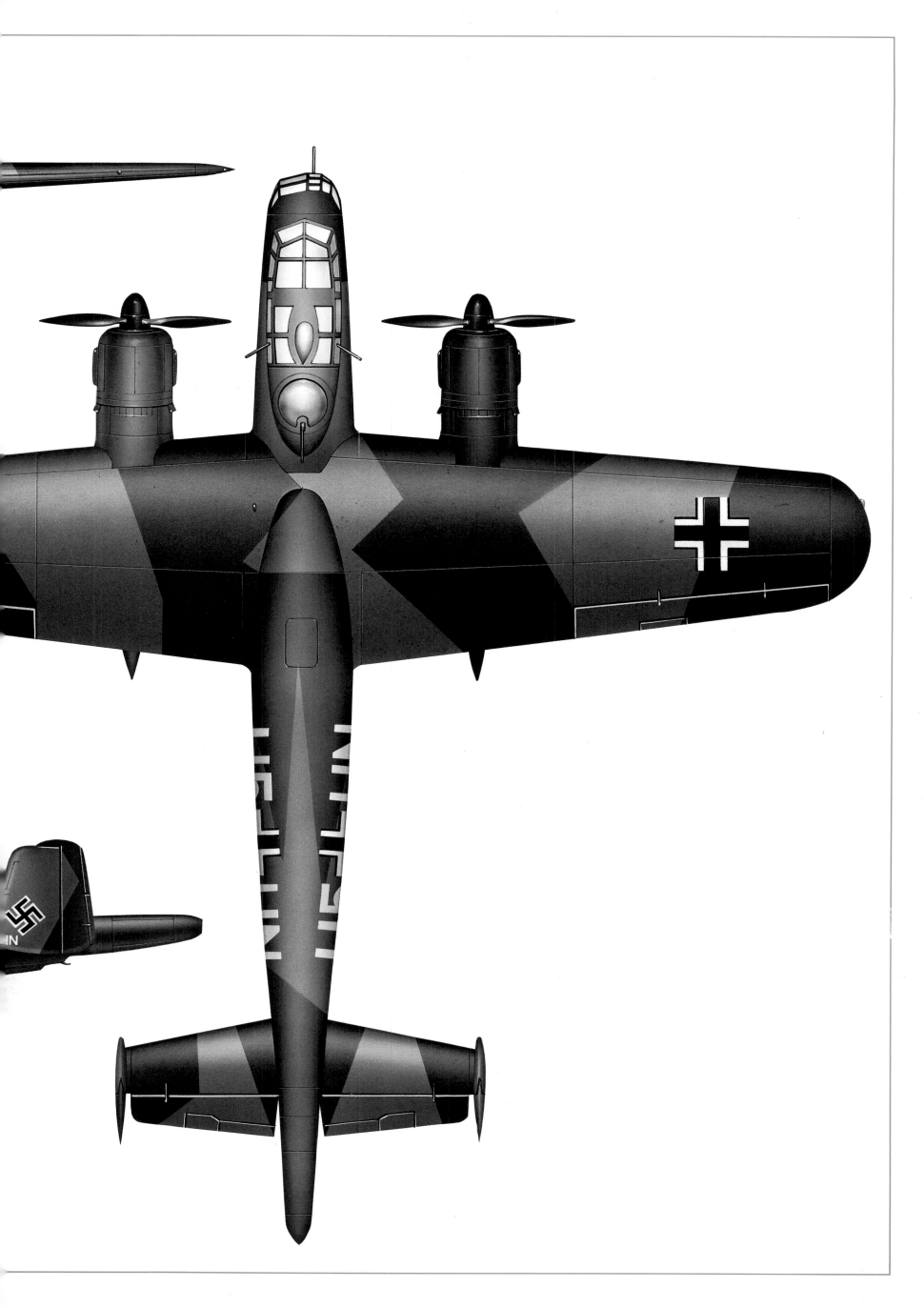

The family of two-engine Dorniers, which originated with the Do.17 in the early 1930s, holds a place in the history of aviation as one of the Luftwaffe's best known and most widely used aircraft. This series of combat planes was developed continuously in numerous versions and derivatives and remained in production for the duration of the conflict, operating on practically all fronts and in a great variety of roles. The success of the original Do.17 model led Dornier to develop a larger and more powerful version of the aircraft. This was the Do.217, an aircraft that embodied the potential of the original project to the full and that was to make its mark due to its great versatility. The approximately 1,900 aircraft built in various versions from 1940 until June 1944 were in fact used with great success as bombers, reconnaissance planes, torpedo planes, and night fighters.

The project went ahead while production of the Do.17 was in full swing, and the prototype took to the air for the first time in August 1938. Although its overall layout was the same as that of its predecessor (it resembled the Do.17s of the final production series in particular), the aircraft was characterized by a longer and wider fuselage that terminated beyond the empennage in an "umbrella-type" aerodynamic brake (with four sections that opened up, braking and stabilizing the aircraft during dive-bombing, although this solution did not prove to be very effective, and this method was eventually eliminated). It was powered initially by a pair of Daimler Benz DB 601 A engines, generating 1,075 hp each.

During flight testing of the first prototype a series of problems emerged, especially as far as the aircraft's stability was concerned, and it crashed after barely a month of trials. Preparation of the other prototypes went ahead, with special study being dedicated to the installation of the various types of engine foreseen in the project, but proved to be long and laborious. In fact, the definitive configuration was reached only in the Do.217 V9 prototype, during the first weeks of 1940. The main change was represented by a notable deepening of the entire fuselage, necessary to rationalize and increase to the maximum the installation of the bomb load, the fuel tanks, and other equipment. In addition, in place of the two in-line Daimler Benz engines, powerful BMW 801 series radial engines, capable of generating more than 1,500 hp at takeoff, were installed.

The first production series, the Do.217 A reconnaissance plane (of which only eight were built), was derived from this prototype and went into service in 1940. The principal variant, the Do.217 E, appeared in the same year and went into service as a bomber in the spring of 1941. In the aircraft of the initial E-1 series, the defensive armament consisted of a small 15 mm MG 151 cannon and five 7.9 mm MG 15 machine guns, all of which were installed in the front part of the aircraft, and a 4,415 lb (2,000 kg) bomb load inside the fuselage. This was followed by the E-2 and E-3 series, in which the defensive armament was modified, with the addition of a turret on the back provided with a 13 mm machine gun. Among the numerous versions that followed were the Do.217 E-2/A-4 torpedo plane; the Do.217 E-2/A10, used for naval patrol and able to carry 4,415 lb (2,000 kg) of bombs under its wings; and the Do.217 E-5, capable of launching two Hs.293 type radio-guided bombs.

The development of the bomber versions proceeded alongside that of the night fighter variants. Toward the middle of 1942, the Do.217 K appeared, characterized by a redesigned nose and more powerful armament: eight machine guns for defense and a maximum of 8,830 lb (4,000 kg) of bombs, including two radio-guided ones (Do.217 K-2). The Do.217 M series was prepared in the same year, marking a return to the use of in-line engines, with two 1,650 hp Daimler Benz DB 603s. In all, a total of 1,541 aircraft were built in the bomber version, and 364 in the night fighter version.

color plate

Dornier Do.217 E-2 5th Staffel 2nd Kampfgeschwader (5th Squadron 2nd Bomber Group) Luftwaffe - France 1941

Aircraft:	Dornier Do.217 E-1
Nation:	Germany
Manufacturer:	Dornier Werke GmbH
Type:	Bomber
Year:	1940
Engine:	2 BMW 801 MA, 14-cylinder radial, air-cooled, 1,580 hp each
Wingspan:	62 ft 4 in (19.00 m)
Length:	59 ft 8 1/2 in (18.19 m)
Height:	16 ft 6 in (5.03 m)
Weight:	33,070 lb (14,980 kg) loaded
Maximum speed:	320 mph (515 km/h) at 17,060 ft (5,200 m)
Ceiling:	24,600 ft (7,500 m)
Range:	1,430 miles (2,300 km)
Armament:	1 × 15 mm cannon; 5 machine guns; 4,415 lb (2,000 kg) of bombs
Crew:	4

A Dornier Do.217 bomber with its under surfaces blacked out for use at night.

In 1938, the prolific family of two-engine Dorniers that had originated with the Dornier Do.17 in the early 1930s was enriched by the addition of a new variant (the Do.217), which embodied the potential of the original project to the full and which eventually made its mark mainly due to its great versatility. In fact, the approximately 1,900 aircraft built in the period between June 1940 and June 1944 were successfully employed as bombers, reconnaissance planes, torpedo planes, and night fighters.

Following the initial production series, the Do.217 A, which was for reconnaissance (only eight were built, and they went into service in 1940), and the subsequent series, the Do.217 E (which went into service as a bomber in the spring of 1941), the development of the bomber versions went ahead at the same time as that of the night fighter variants. The former included the Do.217 K, which appeared during 1942 and was characterized by a modified nose and heavier armament consisting of eight machine guns for defense and a bomb load of up to 8,830 lb (4,000 kg). In the same year, the Do.217 M also appeared and was provided with 1,650 hp in-line Daimler Benz DB 603 engines.

Although the Do.217 bombers eventually absorbed most of the overall production (a total of 1,541 was built in several variants), the growing importance of defense against the continuous heavy bombing raids carried out by the Allies on German territory gave a powerful impetus to the construction of the night fighter versions.

The first of these was the Do.217 J, which appeared toward the end of 1941 in the initial J-1 series. The aircraft was derived directly from the E-2 variant, maintaining its overall configuration except for the nose, in which the glazed position for a bombardier was replaced by a "solid" housing for the offensive armament. This consisted of four 7.9 mm MG 17 machine guns and four 20 mm MG FF cannons. In addition, there were another two 13 mm MG 131 machine guns, while the bomb hold was retained in order to carry up to 883 lb (400 kg) of bombs. The J-1 series was followed by the J-2 (which was produced in the second half of 1942), similar to the previous version but provided with Liechtenstein radar apparatus in the nose and lacking the central bomb hold.

The second version of the night fighter, the Do.217 N, was derived from the M variant bombers. The prototype of the initial N-1 series appeared halfway through 1942, and although it was similar to its predecessor, the J-2, it was fitted with a pair of Daimler Benz DB 603 A engines, generating 1,750 hp each in place of the BMW 801 radial engines. Its armament consisted of four 7.9 mm MG 17 machine guns, four 20 mm MG 151 cannons, and of four two 13 mm MG 131 weapons for rear defense. Moreover, the bomb hold was once again retained and had a capacity of 883 lb (400 kg) of bombs. In the next series, the N-2 (which went into service in 1943), the radar apparatus was improved, and the two rear MG 131 machine guns were eliminated. In these aircraft it was also possible to mount four 20 mm MG 151 cannons on the back, installed in such a way as to shoot upward at a 70 degree angle. Known as Schräge Musik, these weapons were employed flying below the formations of enemy bombers. In all, about 200 Do.217 N-2s were built, out of a total of 364 night fighters in several variants. However, these two-engine aircraft were not popular with their crews. They remained in service until the early months of 1944.

---

color plate

Dornier Do.217 J-2 Nachtjagd Luftwaffe - Germany 1943

A Dornier Do.217 J-2 night fighter, fitted with radar.

A Dornier Do.217 M bomber with in-line engines during the evaluations carried out in Great Britain after the war.

Aircraft:	Dornier Do.217 J-2
Nation:	Germany
Manufacturer:	Dornier Werke GmbH
Type:	Night fighter
Year:	1942
Engine:	2 BMW 801D, 14-cylinder radial, air-cooled, 1,580 hp each
Wingspan:	62 ft 4 in (19.00 m)
Length:	62 ft 1 in (18.89 m)
Height:	16 ft 4 in (4.98 m)
Weight:	29,094 lb (13,180 kg)
Maximum speed:	323 mph (520 km/h) at 13,125 ft (4,000 m)
Ceiling:	29,065 ft (9,000 m)
Range:	1,428 miles (2,300 km)
Armament:	4 × 20 mm cannon; 6 machine guns
Crew:	3

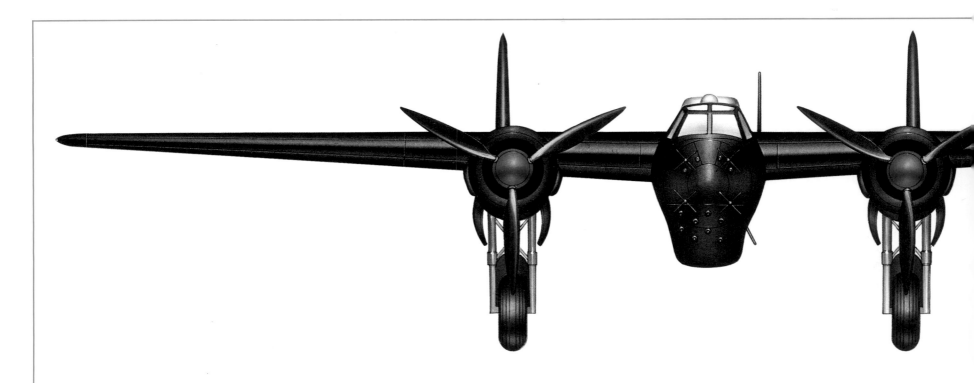

DORNIER Do.217 J-2

ARADO Ar.234 B

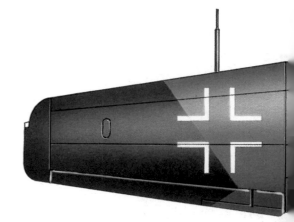

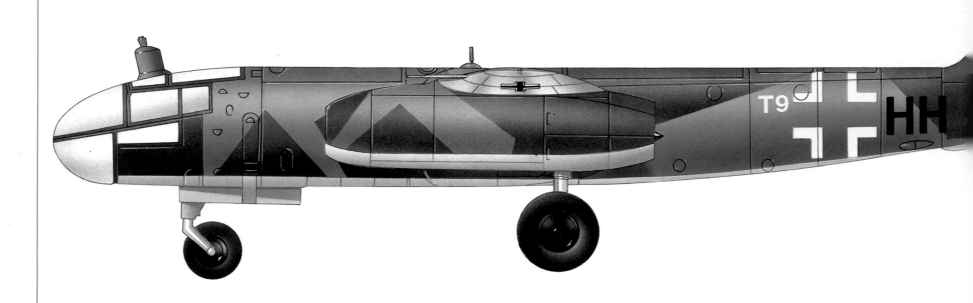

Although the Messerschmitt Me.262 was the world's first jet fighter, the Arado Ar.234 was the first combat bomber in history to be provided with the revolutionary form of propulsion. Together, these two remarkable combat planes represented the best weapons to be sent into action by the Luftwaffe during the last year of the war, although their careers were able to influence the course of the conflict very little. A couple of hundred Arado Ar.234s (christened Blitz) were built and had a very limited career.

The project, initially designated E 370, was launched by Walter Brume and Hans Rebeski (directors of Arado Flugzeugwerke AG's technical department) at the beginning of 1941. The aircraft which they designed utilized a pair of new jet engines which were in the final phase of development at the time. It was a slender high wing monoplane, whose fuselage was carefully studied from the point of view of its aerodynamics, and with the engines installed in nacelles suspended below the semi-wings. The pilot's cockpit was located right in the front of the aircraft and was completely glazed. Due to the narrowness of the fuselage and the wing position, it was decided initially not to adopt traditional type landing gear, but to provide the aircraft with three skids (one on the belly and the other two beneath the engine nacelles) for landing. As far as takeoff was concerned, the aircraft possessed a three-wheel support, which could be detached after leaving the ground.

Between 1941 and 1942 two prototypes were built, although in this case too (as in that of the Me.262), delays in the delivery of the Junkers Jumo 004 engine meant that the first experimental aircraft was not ready until February, 1943. The Arado Ar.234 V-1 made its maiden flight on June 15, and immediately proved to have remarkable flight characteristics and lack any serious faults. This was joined in the months that followed by other prototypes. Those worthy of mention included the V-3 (which took to the air on August 23, 1943) fitted with auxiliary rockets for takeoff and a pressurized cockpit with ejectable seat; and the V-6 and V-8, both fitted with four engines instead of two, installed in separate nacelles and in pairs respectively. It was from the V-9 prototype (which took to the air on March 10, 1944) that the main production variant, the Ar.234 B was derived. It was characterized by the elimination of the rather unpractical skids, which were replaced by retractable forward tricycle landing gear.

The first pre-production B-0s were delivered in June 1944 and were followed on the assembly lines by several subseries: B-1 (photo reconnaissance), B-2 (bomber), B-2/1 (target search and signalling), B-2/b (reconnaissance), and B-2/r (provided with supplementary fuel tanks). The Arado bombers had their bomb loads installed in racks below the engine nacelles, while the offensive armament consisted of a pair of MG 151 cannons.

The first to go into service were the Ar.234s used for reconnaissance. In July 1944, two preseries aircraft assigned to an experimental unit carried out several photo reconnaissance missions, showing that they were capable of eluding the Allied fighters without any difficulty. In September, a special unit was formed (the Sonderkommando Götz) charged with reconnaissance to prevent eventual Allied invasions from the Netherlands. Two months later, another two units followed (Sonderkommando Hecht and Sonderkommando Sperling) entrusted with the task of evaluating the bomber version. The latter entered service for the first time with the 76th KG's Stabstaffel: among the missions in which the Ar.234 B-2s participated, the best known is that which had as its target the Remagen bridge on the Rheine in March 1945.

The numerous experimental version which were evaluated by the Luftwaffe should also be remembered. These included the Ar.234 C, fitted with four BMW 003 A-1 engines, each with a 1,766 lb (800 kg) thrust, which appeared as a prototype on September 30, 1944. Numerous pre-series aircraft were built in several forms and for several roles, including that of night fighter. However, the end of the conflict prevented any further development.

---

color plate

Arado Ar.234 B Sonderkommando Sperling Luftwaffe - Rheine, Germany, 1944

Aircraft:	Arado Ar.234 B-2
Nation:	Germany
Manufacturer:	Arado Flugzeugwerke GmbH
Type:	Bomber
Year:	1944
Engine:	2 Junkers Jumo 004, with 1,964 lb (890 kg) thrust each
Wingspan:	46 ft 4 in (14.10 m)
Length:	41 ft 6 in (12.64 m)
Height:	14 ft 1 in (4.30 m)
Weight:	21;734 lb (9,850 kg)
Maximum speed:	460 mph (742 km/h) at 19,736 ft (6,000 m)
Ceiling:	32,894 ft (10,000 m)
Range:	1,012 miles (1,630 km)
Armament:	2 × 20 mm cannons; 4,415 lb (2,000 kg) of bombs
Crew:	1

An Arado Ar.234 B captured by the British, during technical evaluations carried out after the war.

The Fiat C.R.42 *Falco*, the *Regia Aeronautica*'s last biplane fighter, was paradoxically the combat aircraft built in the greatest number by the Italian aeronautical industry during the conflict. In fact, no fewer than 1,781 of these agile and robust aircraft came off the assembly lines in the course of production, which — despite the presence of (and obvious need for) more modern and competitive planes, such as the Fiat G.50 and the Macchi M.C.200 and 202 — continued uninterruptedly from February 1939 to June 1943.

Created in a period when the monoplane had already gained predominance over the biplane (especially with the excellent aircraft produced by the British and German aeronautical industries), the C.R.42 was the most obvious result of an error of judgment made by the military high command based on combat experiences in the Spanish Civil War. Among the various aircraft that Italy had sent to flank the German Condor Legion was another biplane fighter, the Fiat C.R.32, an extremely agile aircraft that was fast and well armed. Its excellent qualities aroused great enthusiasm both in the technicians and the strategists, and these very experiences gave rise to the conviction that a combat plane should be endowed with such qualities as lightness and maneuverability, considered ideal in close-range confrontations, to the detriment of other characteristics, such as speed, sturdiness, and firepower.

The C.R.42, christened *Falco* (Hawk), was developed following these criteria, with the aim of improving still further the characteristics of its predecessor. Its designer was once again Celestino Rosatelli, the technician who had created the Model 32 in 1933. Rosatelli maintained the overall layout of the earlier aircraft, especially as far as the sesquiplane type wing was concerned, and modified its structure in order to make it more suited to carry a radial engine (considered safer and more reliable) instead of an in-line one. This step was achieved through the production of two experimental models, designated the C.R.40 and the C.R.41 respectively, and the new prototype made its maiden flight on May 23, 1938.

From the beginning, the C.R.42 produced reasonably satisfactory results, and it went into production immediately on the basis of an initial order for 200 aircraft, the first of which came off the assembly lines in February 1939. The plane had an all-metal airframe and a mixed canvas and aluminum covering, as well as fixed, completely faired landing gear. The cockpit was open, and the pilot had good visibility, thanks to the "clean" lines of the wing struts. It was powered by an 840 hp Fiat A.74 RC.38 radial engine, while the armament consisted of two 12.7 mm fixed machine guns mounted in the nose and synchronized to fire through the propeller, which was three-bladed, variable pitch and metal.

In May 1939, the 53rd air regiment based at Caselle became the first Italian unit to be equipped with the new fighter, and when Italy entered the war 272 C.R.42s were in service. June 1940 marked the beginning of a long active career, that continued without interruption on all fronts up to the end of the conflict. By September 1943, only 113 C.R.42s remained, of which 64 were operational. The aircraft was used most of all in the Mediterranean area and, more particularly, in Africa. With the arrival of a new generation of aircraft, the *Falco* was relegated to less demanding roles, such as escort, reconnaissance, ground attack, and night fighter.

The C.R.42 was a successful export aircraft and was ordered by Belgium (40 aircraft), Hungary (68), and Sweden (72).

color plate

Fiat C.R.42 18° Gruppo Caccia Terrestre, 85ª Squadriglia Regia Aeronautica (18th Fighters Group, 85th Squadron *Regia Aeronautica*) - Battle of Britain Belgium 1941

Aircraft:	Fiat C.R.42
Nation:	Italy
Manufacturer:	Fiat SA
Type:	Fighter
Year:	1939
Engine:	Fiat A.74 RC.38, 14-cylinder radial, air-cooled, 840 hp
Wingspan:	31 ft 10 in (9.70 m)
Length:	27 ft 3 in (8.30 m)
Height:	11 ft 9 in (3.58 m)
Weight:	5,060 lb (2,295 kg) loaded
Maximum speed:	272 mph (439 km/h) at 19,700 ft (6,000 m)
Ceiling:	33,550 ft (10,200 m)
Range:	480 miles (775 km)
Armament:	2 machine guns
Crew:	1

Formation of Fiat C.R.42 fighters flying over the Libyan desert in the summer of 1940.

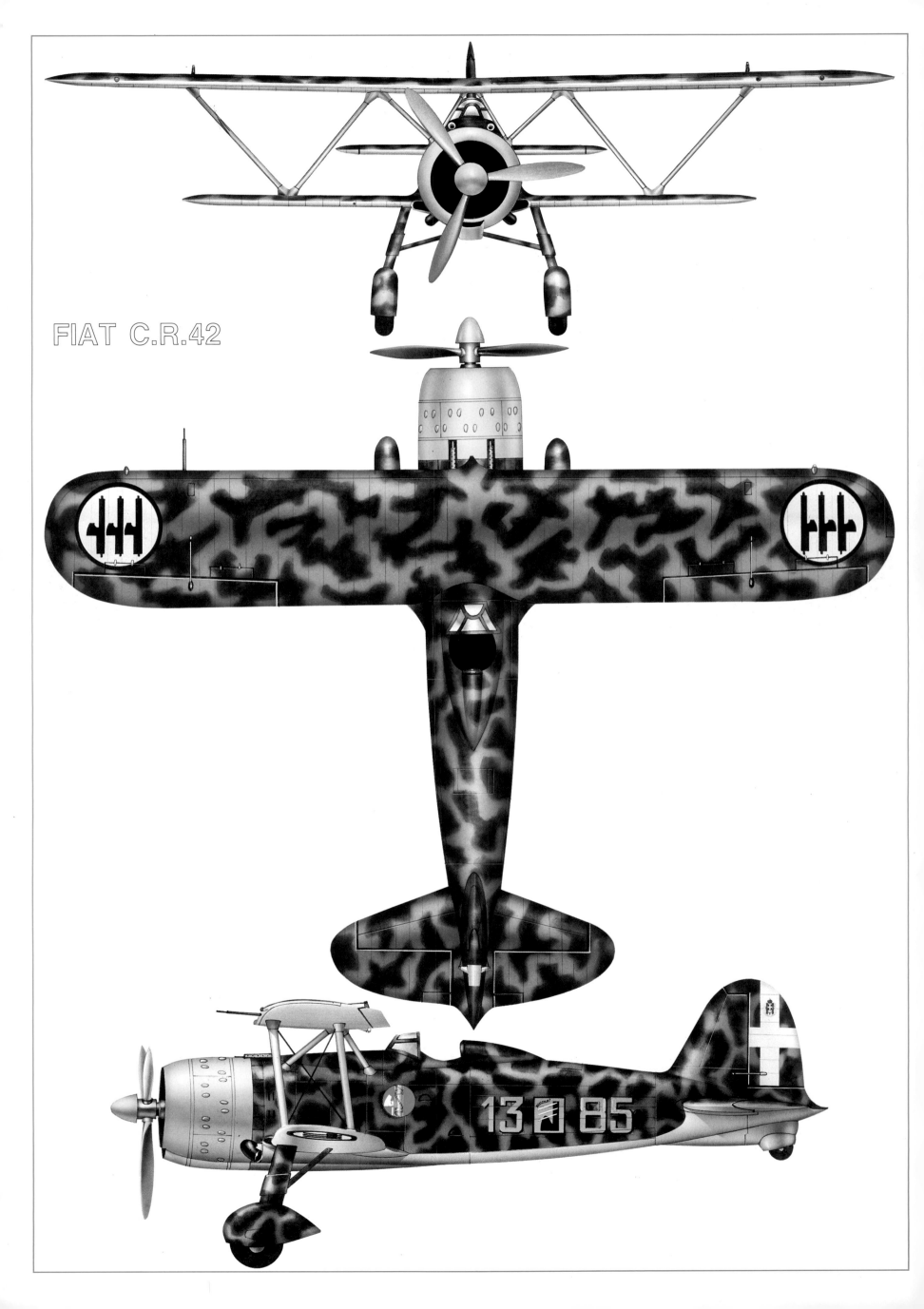

FIAT C.R.42

FIAT G.50 bis

An initial production series Fiat G.50 with completely glazed cockpit, bearing prewar colors.

The Fiat G.50 was the first representative of the *Regia Aeronautica's* initial generation of "modern" fighters. A contemporary of both the C.R.42 biplane and the Macchi M.C.200 monoplane, this project was designed by Giuseppe Gabrielli and had all the merits and defects of a transitional aircraft. Although it featured technical and technological solutions that were advanced for the time (such as the all-metal airframe, the cantilever monoplane wing, and retractable landing gear), it proved to be difficult to tune and, above all, to have a disappointing overall performance, as well as a lack of armament. Up to the spring of 1942, a total of 782 of these fighters was built, including the four prototypes. It was used in all the main theaters of war, from Greece and the Mediterranean area to Africa.

The project was launched by Giuseppe Gabrielli in April 1935 and was presented in a competition, announced by the Aeronautical Ministry in 1936, to choose a new interceptor. The aircraft was a low-wing monoplane with retractable landing gear, powered by an 840 hp Fiat A.74 RC.38 radial engine that drove a three-bladed, variable pitch, metal propeller. Initially, the armament was to consist of two Breda-SAFAT 12.7 mm machine guns (one to be installed in the engine cowling and synchronized to fire through the propeller arc, and the other to be fitted on the left wing) and a 20 mm cannon on the right wing.

In the official contest, the G.50 found itself competing with the Macchi M.C.200, the Caproni F.5, and the Imam Ro.51, and following evaluation tests it remained in direct competition with the first. In the end it was chosen for production, despite the overall superiority of the Macchi fighter. A series of modifications was requested for the definitive aircraft: the elimination of the closed canopy, with a cockpit that could be either open or closed being planned (even if, in most cases, the operational units preferred to adopt the latter solution); a landing gear blocking system; an independent ignition system; oxygen apparatus for the pilot; standard armament, with the elimination of the cannon and the concentration of the two machine guns in the nose.

In January 1939, the first 12 preseries aircraft were grouped together in an experimental fighter unit and sent to Spain for a series of operational tests. This experience led to further improvements (modified flaps and redesigned vertical empennages) that were put into production and it was only toward the end of the year that the G.50 was definitively approved and sent to the units. At the same time, 35 aircraft were sold to Finland, where they remained in service until the end of the conflict.

When the war broke out, two front line *Stormi* were equipped with a total of 118 G.50s (officially christened *Freccia,* or Arrow). The aircraft's first missions took place during the early days of the campaign in France, and then with the Italian Air Corps in Belgium. However, operations on the fierce English Channel front showed the Fiat fighter in its true colors: the adverse weather conditions and its clear inferiority compared to the enemy aircraft fully demonstrated the project's limitations.

Production went ahead nevertheless, as did the aircraft's use in combat. In 1940, in an attempt to improve the aircraft's performance (particularly its range), a second version (the G.50 *bis*) appeared, with modifications to the tail planes and the installation of the fuel tanks. This became the major production version, with 421 being built in all. However, the modifications did not rejuvenate the aircraft, nor did they make it more competitive. The G.50 was gradually withdrawn from the role of front line fighter and used for ground attack. After September 8, only four were still operative and were used for training the air force of the Repubblica Sociale Italiana. From 1940 to 1943, 100 G.50B trainers were built, featuring a two-seater cockpit and dual controls.

Among the experimental versions, mention should be made of a G.50 *ter* prototype (June 1941) fitted with a 1,000 hp Fiat A.76 engine; one G.50 A/N (October 1942) planned for use on board the aircraft carrier *Aquila,* which was designed but never built; and a prototype (August 1941) fitted with an in-line Daimler-Benz DB 601 engine.

---

color plate

Fiat G.50 bis A.S. 352ª Squadriglia 20° Gruppo 51° Stormo Regia Aeronautica (352nd Squadron 20th Group 51st *Stormo Regia Aeronautica*) - Libya 1942

Aircraft:	Fiat G.50
Nation:	Italy
Manufacturer:	Fiat S.A.
Type:	Fighter
Year:	1939
Engine:	Fiat A.74 RC.38, 14-cylinder radial, air-cooled, 840 hp
Wingspan:	36 ft (10.98 m)
Length:	25 ft 7 in (7.80 m)
Height:	9 ft 8$\frac{1}{2}$in (2.95 m)
Weight:	5,280 lb (2,395 kg) loaded
Maximum speed:	294 mph (437 km/h) at 19,685 ft (6,000 m)
Ceiling:	35,200 ft (10,700 m)
Range:	420 miles (675 km)
Armament:	2 machine guns
Crew:	1

A tropical-version G.50 *bis* in service with the 352nd Squadron in flight over the Libyan desert.

Formation of B.R.20 M bombers flying toward French targets in June 1940.

Together with the SIAI Marchetti SM.79 and the CANT Z.1007 *bis*, the Fiat B.R.20 was the standard bomber of the *Regia Aeronautica* during World War II. Although it was the only two-engine aircraft of the three, as opposed to the three-engine formula that characterized the production of large aircraft in Italy for years, it proved to be equally competitive in terms of overall performance, and more than 500 planes were produced from 1936 to July 1943, and these served on practically all fronts until the armistice.

The prototype of the B.R.20, designed by Celestino Rosatelli and christened *Cicogna* (Stork), took to the air for the first time on February 10, 1936, and immediately made a favorable impression. The aircraft was a cantilever low-wing monoplane with an all-metal airframe and mixed aluminum and canvas covering, a completely retractable landing gear, and it was powered by a pair of 1,000 hp Fiat A.80 RC.41 radial engines that drove three-bladed metal propellers. Defensive armament consisted of three machine guns installed in the front, the belly, and the rear, while the bomb

load reached 3,527 lb (1,600 kg). As for its performance, this more than fulfilled the official specifications, which called for a maximum speed of 240 mph (385 km/h) and the possibility of carrying 2,640 lb (1,200 kg) of bombs for a range of 600 miles (1,000 km).

Following a series of operational evaluations, the B.R.20 went into production. In the meantime, in the wake of propagandistic encouragement by the Fascist regime, two special versions of the aircraft (B.R.20 A) were prepared, largely modified, to participate in long distance races. They were entered in the prestigious Istres-Damascus-Paris race of 1937, and although they arrived in only sixth and seventh place, they provided ample proof of their speed and long-range accomplishments. Success arrived in 1937, however, in the form of a world record for its category gained by another modified aircraft (the B.R.20 L, christened *Santo Francesco*), piloted by Maner Lualdi, which carried out a non-stop flight from Rome to Addis Abeba on March 6, covering about 2,800 miles (4,500 km) at an average speed of over 250 mph (404 km/h).

However, the civilian achievements of the B.R.20 were few when compared to its military ones. The two-engine aircraft had its baptism of fire in Spain in 1937, part of an operational service that lasted for a year and a half. At the outbreak of World War II, it took part in the earliest campaigns, starting with the one in France. In June 1940, the *Regia Aeronautica* had a total of 216 B.R.20s in service and the initial production series (233 aircraft built up to February, 85 of which had been sold to Japan, where they were renamed Type 1) had already been replaced by a second variant, the B.R.20 M (modifications being mainly of a structural nature), 264 of which would be completed by the spring of 1942. These aircraft took part in the *Regia Aeronautica*'s only combat experience in the Battle of Britain: 80 B.R.20 Ms were incorporated into the Italian Air Corps and sent to Belgium, from where they carried out raids on England from October to December 1940. The experience was not a positive one: in the course of missions totalling fewer than 300 hours in all, 20 or so aircraft were shot down, proving their overall inferiority compared to the British fighters. The remaining aircraft were withdrawn.

The final variant of the *Cicogna* was the 1942 B.R.20 *bis*, of which only 15 were produced in the early months of the following year. The front part of the fuselage was redesigned, and the aircraft was fitted with 1,250 hp Fiat A.82 RC.32 engines. The increase in power improved the plane's performance noticeably and allowed for better armament, although these aircraft never went into service.

A Fiat B.R.20 bomber with prewar markings.

color plate

Fiat B.R.20 M 43° Gruppo B.T. Regia Aeronautica (43rd Bombers Group *Regia Aeronautica*) - Battle of Britain Belgium 1941

Aircraft:	Fiat B.R.20
Nation:	Italy
Manufacturer:	Fiat SA
Type:	Bomber
Year:	1937
Engine:	2 Fiat A.80 RC.41,18-cylinder radial, air-cooled, 1,000 hp each
Wingspan:	70 ft 8 in (21.53 m)
Length:	52 ft 10 in (16.10 m)
Height:	14 ft 1 in (4.30 m)
Weight:	21,850 lb (9,900 kg) loaded
Maximum speed:	286 mph (460 km/h) at 16,400 ft (5,000 m)
Ceiling:	29,500 ft (9,000 m)
Range:	1,860 miles (3,000 km)
Armament:	3 machine guns; 3,527 lb (1,600 kg) of bombs
Crew:	5

Close up detail of nose of a B.R.20. The subsequent variants were modified with more glazing.

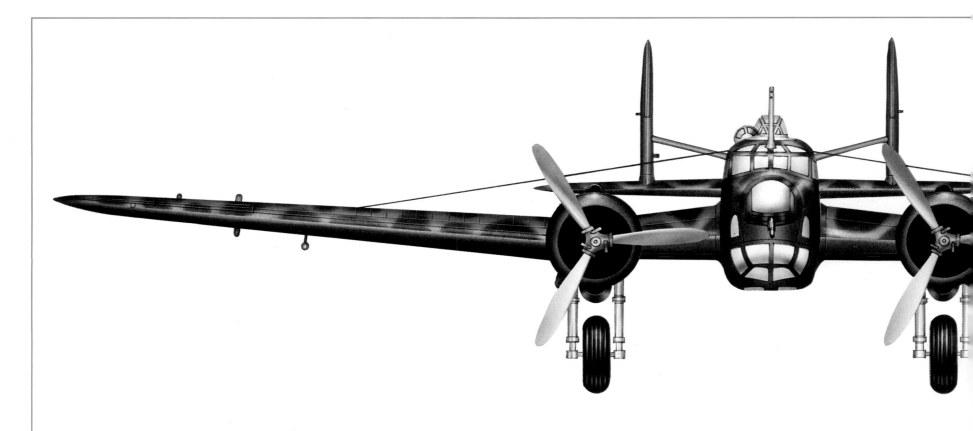

FIAT B.R.20 M

At a qualitative level, the final generation of Italian fighters represented a dramatic evolution compared to the standards of the aircraft that equipped the *Regia Aeronautica*. Powerful, well armed, and with performances equal to if not better than those of the most sophisticated aircraft in production at the time (both Allied and Axis), the only limitation of the Macchi M.C. 205, the Fiat G.55, and the Reggiane Re.2005 (the three models of the so-called Series 5) was that they arrived on the scene of the conflict too late. Their construction was made possible by the availability of a more powerful version of the German Daimler Benz engine, which already equipped the Macchi M.C. 202 *Folgore* in the DB 601 version.

Of the Series 5 fighters, the Fiat G.55 *Centauro* emerged as the best overall, and in the course of its brief but intense operative career, carried out almost exclusively bearing the insignia of the aviation of the *Repubblica Sociale Italiana* after September 8, 1943, this fast and robust combat plane proved to be an unbeatable interceptor at altitude. In the air battles that took place in northern Italy during the last year of the war, the *Centauro* cashed with formidable adversaries (such as the British Spitfires and the American Mustangs, Thunderbolts, and Lightnings) and proved to be a fearsome antagonist on all occasions.

The G.55 project was developed by Giuseppe Gabrielli, on the basis of a study made by the construction directors of the Defense and Aeronautical Ministry that called for the building of a high-altitude, highly efficient fighter interceptor provided with remarkable wing surface area. The prototype, which was built in the early months of 1942, took to the air on April 30 and was soon followed by another two experimental planes. The aircraft was an all metal low-wing single-seater monoplane with retractable landing gear. It was powered by a Daimler Benz DB 605A engine generating a maximum of 1,475 hp, which drove a three-bladed variable-pitch metal propeller. The armament included two 12.7 mm machine guns in the nose, synchronized to fire through the propeller; two 20 mm Mauser cannons on the wings; a third cannon that fired through the propeller hub.

Evaluation tests took place at the same time as those of the other two Series 5 aircraft and went on for a long time, due to the difficulty in choosing between similar, equally effective aircraft. However, the Fiat project proved to be more advanced, better armed, and faster at altitudes over 23,026 ft (7,000 m) than the

Macchi M.C. 205 and stronger than the Reggiane Re.2005. In the end no choice was made. The orders were subdivided among all three models: 250 M.C. 205s, 600 G.55s, and 750 Re.2005s. Although this decision rewarded the quality of the projects, it also led to a loss of time and a dispersal of production effort.

The G.55's operative career began in June 1943, with the 353rd Squadron based at Rome's Ciampino airport, but the unit never took part in any significant combat in all; the *Regia Aeronautica* received 16 preseries aircraft and 15 of the initial production lot before September. However, following the armistice, the assembly lines continued to complete aircraft, which all went to the fighter units of the Republican aviation, which used approximately 150 until the final phase of the conflict.

After the war, Fiat recommenced production in two versions, the single-seater G.55A and the two-seater G.55B trainer: both were used by the Italian air force (19 and 10 aircraft respectively) and by the Argentinian air force (30 and 15). It is worth mentioning a version developed in 1944, destined for the role of torpedo plane: the G.55S, which remained in the prototype phase.

color plate

Fiat G.55 2nd Fighter Group *Aeronautica Nazionale Repubblicana* — Northern Italy 1944-45

Aircraft:	Fiat G.55
Nation:	Italy
Manufacturer:	Fiat SA
Type:	Fighter
Year:	1943
Engine:	Daimler Benz DB 605A, 12-cylinder V, liquid-cooled, 1,475 hp
Wingspan:	38 ft 11 in (11.85 m)
Length:	30 ft 9 in (9.37 m)
Height:	12 ft 4 in (3.77 m)
Weight:	8,211 lb (3,720 kg)
Maximum speed:	385 mph (620 km/h) at 23,026 ft (7,000 m)
Ceiling:	42,763 ft (13,000 m)
Range:	1,025 miles (1,650 km)
Armament:	3 × 20 mm cannons, 2 machine guns
Crew:	1

The prototype of the Fiat G.55. The weapons on the wings have not yet been installed.

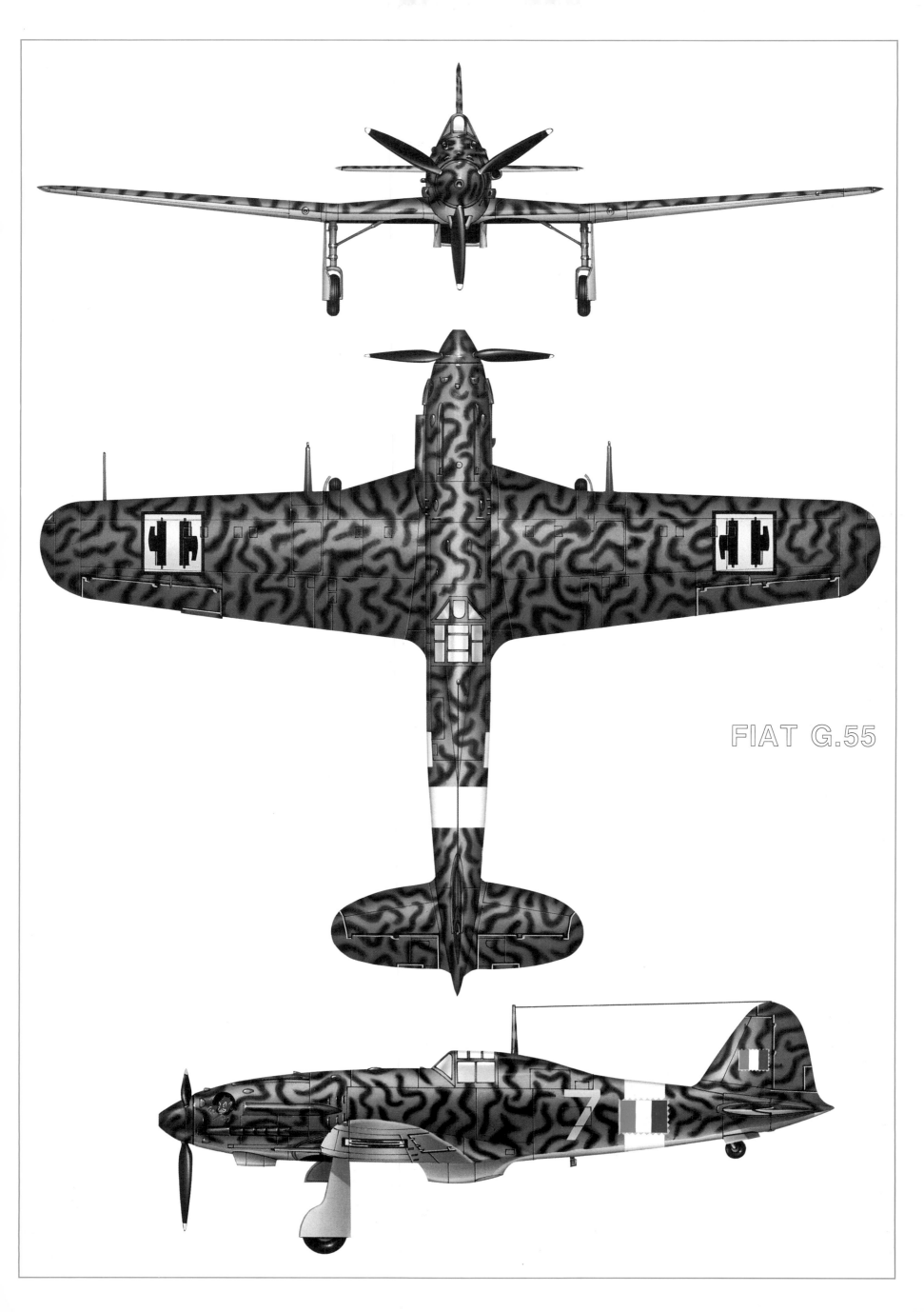

FIAT G.55

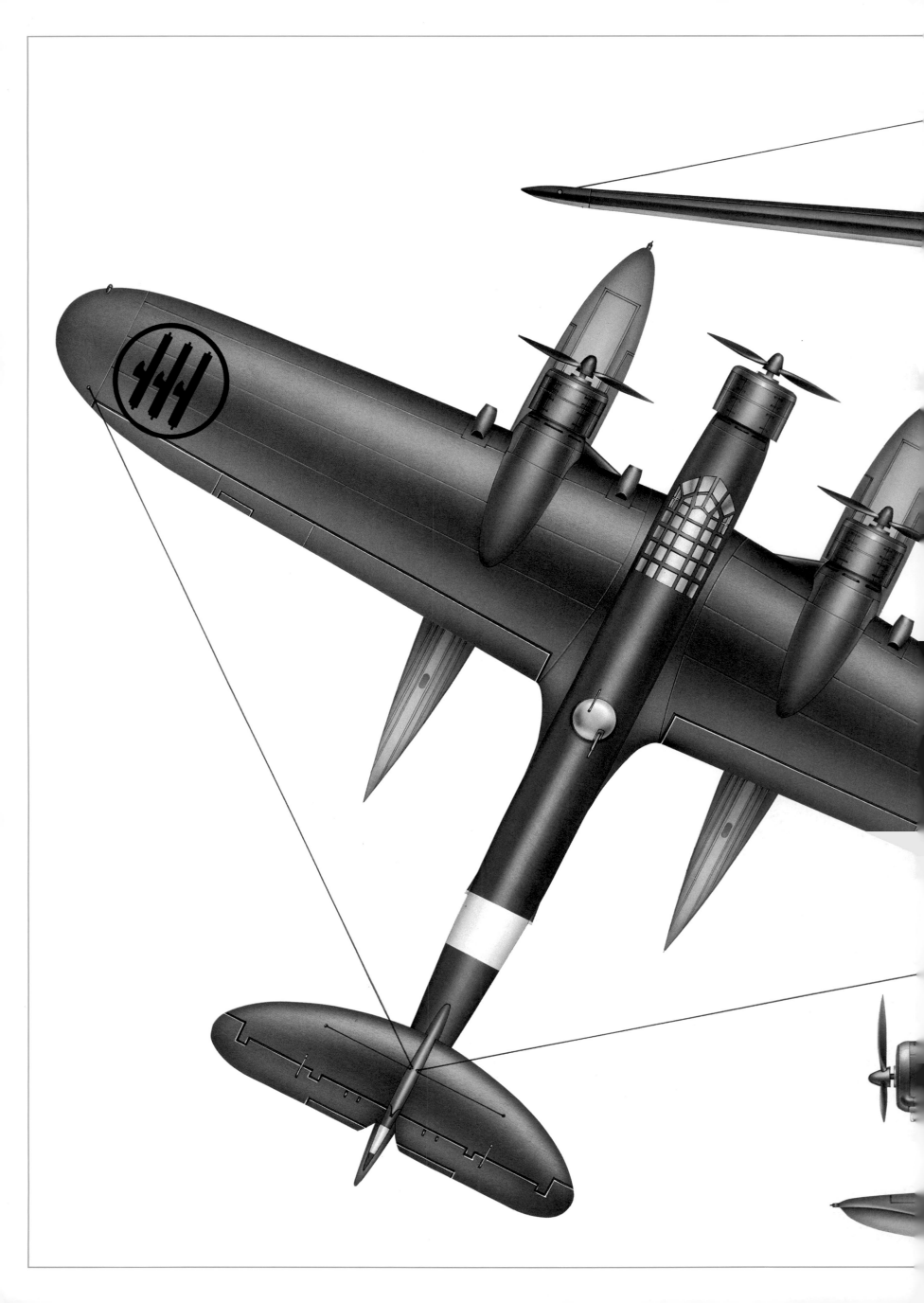

CANT Z.506B

287·6

The CANT Z.506, like many planes used in the war, originated as a civilian transport plane and, in an era in which aeronautical prestige was still measured by the performance of commercial aircraft, this large three-engine seaplane with lateral floats provided remarkable proof of the value of its features, breaking a considerable number of records. In 1936, alone, the first prototype, piloted by the chief test pilot Mario Stoppani, established eight world speed records in its category over distances of 625 miles (1,000 km) and 1,250 miles (2,000 km) carrying loads of up to 2 tons (2,000 kg), and two altitude records with a payload of 2 tons and 5 tons (2,000 and 5,000 kg). The same records were improved the following year and included speed records over distances of 3,100 miles, 1,250 miles, and 625 miles (5,000, 2,000, and 1,000 km respectively) at 191.56 mph (308.25 km/h), 198.70 mph (319.78 km/h), and 200.18 mph (322.06 km/h) respectively. Subsequently, the Z.506 also established a distance record in a closed circuit, covering 3,345.2 miles (5,383.6 km).

The project was begun in 1935, and the prototype of the commercial version, designated Z.506A, made its first flight on August 19, powered by three 610 hp Piaggio P.IX radial engines. Production began immediately, and the first 38 aircraft to be completed went into service in 1936, bearing the insignia of the Ala Littoria line, which used them on Mediterranean routes. The military version, the Z.506B, designed as a bomber and naval reconnaissance plane and christened *Airone* (Heron), appeared in October 1937. Structurally, it was very similar to its civil counterpart in that it was a three-engine, low-wing monoplane seaplane, and its structure was entirely in wood with a mixed wood-and-canvas covering (with the exception of the floats, which were all-metal). The only external differences were the raised pilot's cockpit and the deepening of the fuselage by means of a long pod in the belly, for use as bomb storage and as an observation post. The engines were three 750 hp Alfa Romeo 126 RC 34s, which powered three-bladed, variable-pitch metal propellers. Defensive armament consisted of four machine guns, while offensive armament was composed of 2,650 lb (1,200 kg) of bombs.

Even bearing military insignia, the *Airone* continued to break records. In October 1937, a new ceiling record was established of 33,645 ft (10,255 m) with a payload of 2,200 lb (1,000 kg), followed by a successful non-stop Atlantic crossing of 4,362 miles (7,020 km) from Cadiz (Spain) to Caravelas (Brazil).

The first units to receive the new aircraft were the 35th and the 31st naval bomber groups, and the need to reequip the reconnaissance units, too, led to a stepping up in production, which was entrusted to Piaggio. The last CANT Z.506B came off the production line at the Piaggio factory in Finale Ligure in January 1943: 324 aircraft had been completed, up to this date, including the two prototypes.

The *Airone*'s operational debut took place in the Spanish Civil War (although it was limited to very few missions), and when Italy entered World War II, 97 of these aircraft were in service, equipping two naval bomber units and several reconnaissance squadrons. However, as the war proceeded, the plane's limitations soon became apparent, and it was relegated to naval reconnaissance, to escorting convoys, and to sea rescue duty.

The CANT Z.506B's career, however, continued well beyond World War II. In fact, 30 or so of these aircraft remained in service in a rescue role after the war, the *Airone* forming part of the Italian air force's units up to 1960, when the final examples were withdrawn. For the specific task of sea rescue, a special version was produced, designated Z.506S.

color plate

Cant Z.506B 287ª Squadriglia Ricognizione Marittima Regia Aeronautica (287th Naval Reconnaissance Squadron *Regia Aeronautica*) - Mediterranean 1942/43

Aircraft:	CANT Z.506B
Nation:	Italy
Manufacturer:	Cantieri Riuniti dell'Adriatico
Type:	Bomber
Year:	1937
Engine:	3 Alfa Romeo 126 RC 34, 9-cylinder radial, air-cooled, 750 hp each
Wingspan:	86 ft 11 in (26.50 m)
Length:	63 ft 1 1/2 in (19.24 m)
Height:	24 ft 3 in (7.39 m)
Weight:	27,115 lb (12,299 kg) loaded
Maximum speed:	226 mph (364 km/h) at 13,120 ft (4,000 m)
Ceiling:	26,240 ft (7,997 m)
Range:	1,700 miles (2,745 km)
Armament:	4 machine guns; 2,650 lb (1,200 kg) of bombs
Crew:	5

Cant Z.506B ashore on its launching cradle.

The three-engine formula, much developed by Italian manufacturers, had another noteworthy representative in the CANT Z.1007, the bomber that, together with the SM.79 and the B.R.20 constituted the *Regia Aeronautica's* standard equipment during the conflict. A total of 560 aircraft was built in three production series from 1939 to 1943, and the *Alcione* (Kingfisher, the official name given to the plane) was widely used on all fronts, proving to be an effective aircraft, despite the emergence of problems of structural weakness in extreme climates (such as those in Africa or Russia) due to its being built entirely of wood.

The project was launched by Filippo Zappata in 1935, and the first prototype took to the air on March 11, 1937. However, flight tests did not produce the expected results. This was due, above all, to the engines (three Isotta-Fraschini Asso XI RC.15s, liquid-cooled and driving two-bladed, variable pitch, metal propellers) that proved to be incapable of generating the rated power of 840 hp. With the aim of improving the aircraft's performance, a series of modifications was carried out (including the introduction of a three-bladed propeller), and the first production series (consisting of 34 aircraft) was characterized by the installation of anular-type frontal radiators. Nevertheless, the problems concerning the lack of reliability of the power plants remained virtually unsolved in these aircraft (built between February and October 1939), so much so that the evaluation tests, carried out mainly by the units of the 16th *Stormo* based in Vicenza, advised against its being used operationally.

In the meantime, Filippo Zappata had completely reworked the initial project, basing it on the installation of three powerful Piaggio P.XI RC.40 14-cylinder radial engines, capable of generating 1,000 hp each. The new prototype (rechristened CANT Z.1007 *bis*) appeared in 1938 and was substantially modified as compared to its predecessor: apart from the engines, the cross-section of the aircraft had been enlarged and completely reworked, while its overall dimensions had been increased; other changes regarded the defensive positions on the back and belly and the tail planes, characterized by lower horizontal empennages (in the course of production, two subvariants of the CANT Z.1007 *bis* were built, one with a single rudder and fin and the other with twin rudders and fins). The effectiveness of these modifications became apparent during flight tests and official evaluations, carried out at Guidonia on eight preseries aircraft: the *Alcione* proved to have a maximum speed of 283 mph (456 km/h) at an altitude of 15,100 ft (4,600m), a range of 1,242 miles (2,000 km), and a maximum ceiling of 27,630 ft (8,400 m); as for its bomb load, this reached 2,430 lb (1,100 kg) in various combinations. These features were developed further in the final production version (the

Z.1007 *ter*, which appeared early in 1943, a total of 50 aircraft being built), in which the maximum speed increased to 304 mph (490 km/h) and the ceiling to 32,890 ft (10,000 m), thanks to the installation of three Piaggio P.XIX radial engines.

Deliveries of the CANT Z.1007 *bis* to the units commenced in the spring of 1940 (106th and 107th Groups of the 47th *Stormo*), although none could yet be considered operative when Italy entered the war. The aircraft's first mission took place in September, when several of the single-rudder and fin type were incorporated into an experimental unit and sent to Belgium as part of the Italian Air Corps. It was not an outstanding debut: the three-engine CANTs carried out only a few missions on the tough English Channel front and with little success.

However, immediately after, in October, the large-scale use of the *Alcione* began in Greece. Later, the bomber operated mainly in the Mediterranean area and in North and East Africa, where it took part in all operations until 1942. On the Russian front, however, use of the three-engine plane was only sporadic and intermittent. At the time of the armistice in Italy, 30 or so of these aircraft were requisitioned by the Germans and were taken north, although they were not used operationally. A similar number served in the cobelligerent air force, as part of a bomber group that operated for a long period on the Balkan front.

Aircraft:	CANT Z.1007 *bis*
Nation:	Italy
Manufacturer:	Cantieri Riuniti dell'Adriatico
Type:	Bomber
Year:	1940
Engine:	3 Piaggio P.XI RC.40, 14-cylinder radial, air-cooled, 1,000 hp each
Wingspan:	81 ft 4 in (24.80 m)
Length:	61 ft (18.59 m)
Height:	17 ft 1 in (5.22 m)
Weight:	38,200 lb (17,327 kg) loaded
Maximum speed:	283 mph (456 km/h) at 15,100 ft (4,600 m)
Ceiling:	26,500 ft (8,100 m)
Range:	1,242 miles (2,000 km)
Armament:	4 machine guns; 2,430 lb (1,100 kg) of bombs
Crew:	5

color plate

CANT Z.1007 bis 210ª Squadriglia 50° Gruppo 16° Stormo Regia Aeronautica (210th Squadron 50th Group 16th *Stormo Regia Aeronautica*) - Italy 1942

A CANT Z.1007 *bis* in service with the 60th Squadron during takeoff. Its fuselage and tail markings are hidden.

CANT Z.1007 bis

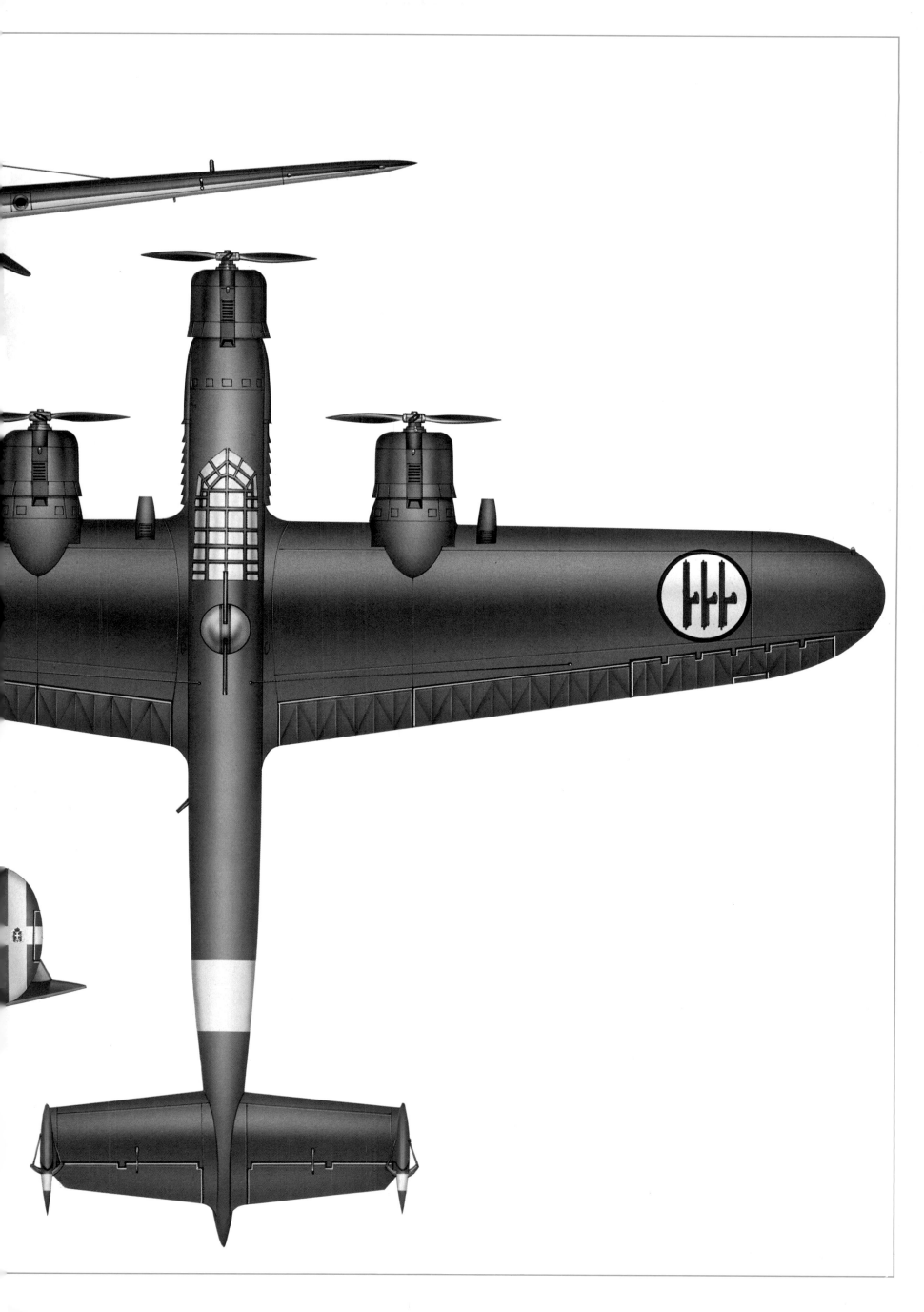

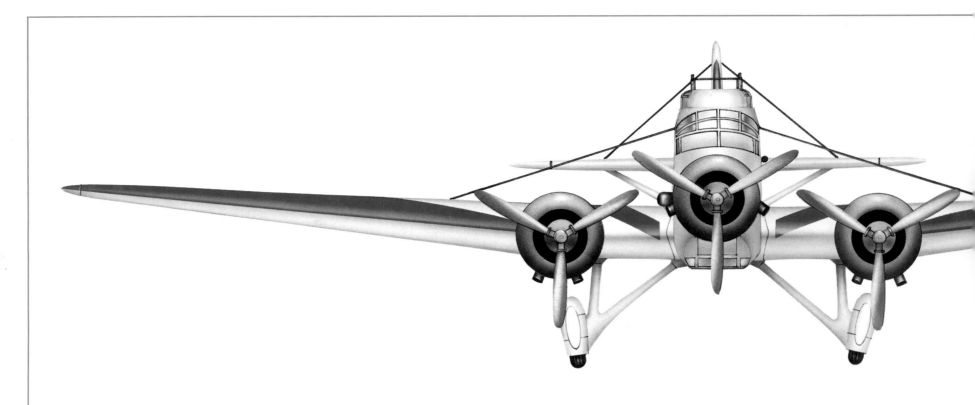

SIAI MARCHETTI SM.81

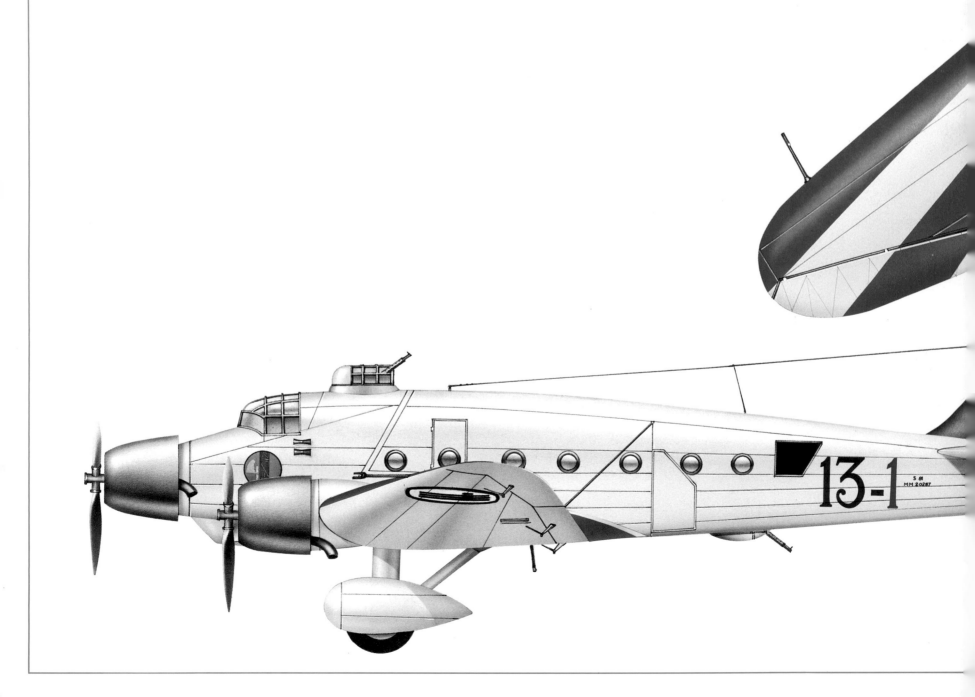

13-1

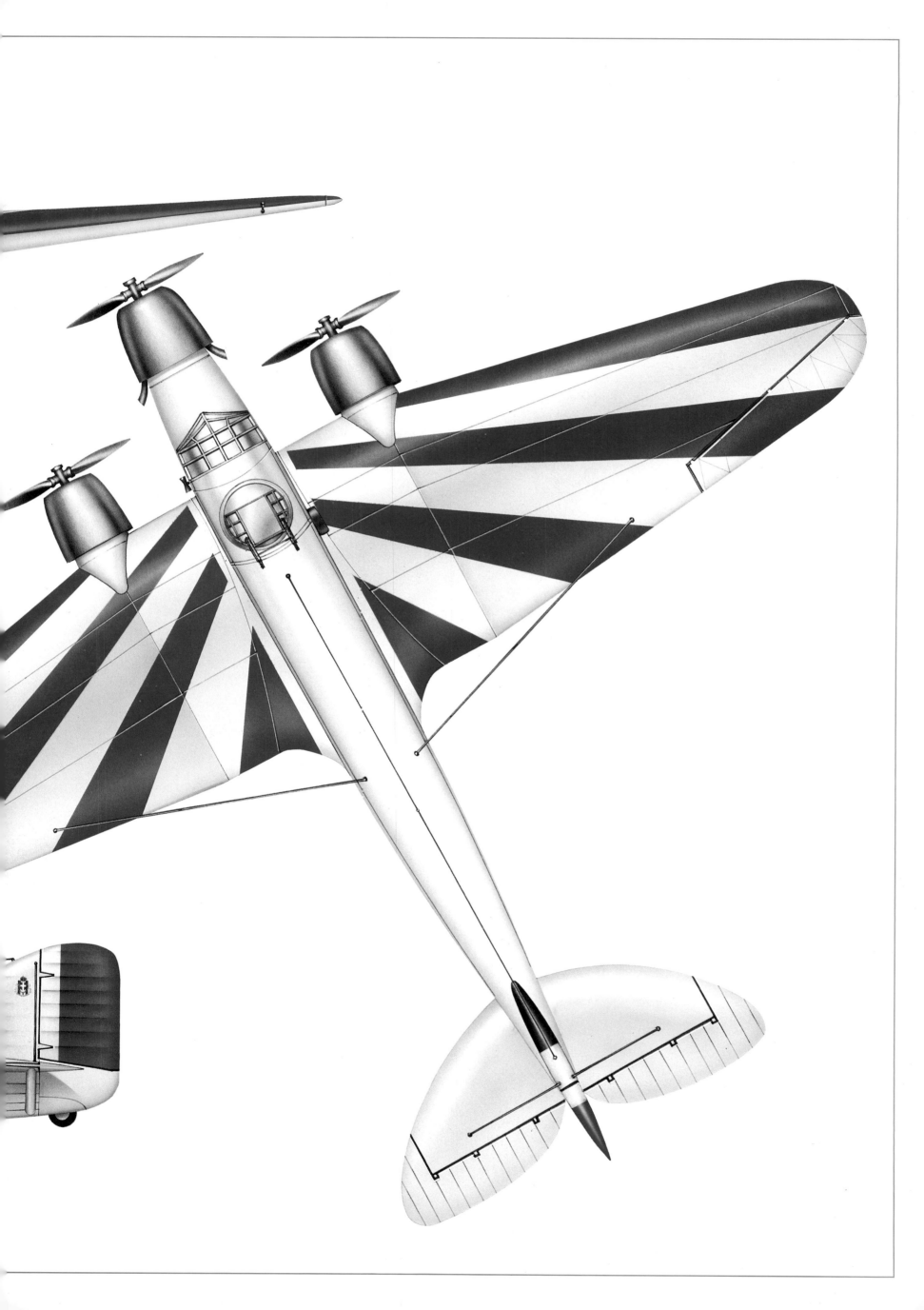

The three-engine formula met with particular success in Italian aeronautical production, and the manufacturer SIAI Marchetti made it world famous, with its civilian and military aircraft produced during the 1930s. The SM.81, one of the *Regia Aeronautica*'s most characteristic bombers, inaugurated this formula in 1935, and at the time of its appearance marked a definite step forward in the development of military aviation. The excellent overall qualities of this aircraft were first tested in the Ethiopian campaign and then in the Spanish Civil War, and its success in combat was directly transformed into a series of orders that eventually led to 534 of these aircraft being produced.

However, as in the case of other combat planes produced in the same period, the Spanish Civil War did not provide very reliable proof of what subsequent needs were to be, and the SM.81, although clearly out-of-date by the outbreak of World War II, remained in service for the duration of the hostilities, operating on almost all fronts, although it was gradually phased out to play a secondary role in transport.

The SM.81's direct predecessor was a commercial aircraft, the SM.73, whose prototype appeared on June 4, 1934, and which was an immediate commercial success. It was this aircraft that actually provided the basis for the construction formula that was to remain virtually unchanged in SIAI Marchetti's later production: a three-engine, low-wing monoplane with a wood and metal structure and wood-and-fabric covering. The military version was presented toward the end of the year and was subjected to a whole series of operational tests by the *Regia Aeronautica* before going into mass production.

As in the case of the civilian version, the fitting of several types of engine was also planned for the SM.81, and each of the engines characterized a particular version of the aircraft: these included the Piaggio P.IX and P.X (680 hp and 700 hp respectively); the Alfa Romeo 125 and 126 (680 hp and 900 hp respectively) and the 1,000 hp Gnome-Rhône 14K. Defense armament consisted of six machine guns, four of which were disposed in pairs in two turrets (a retractable ventral one and another on the back) with the remaining two in lateral positions on the fuselage. Its payload was normally composed of 1 ton of bombs (1,000 kg), but it could carry a maximum of 2 tons, although in this case its range was reduced considerably. The prototype of an experimental version, known as the SM.81 *bis*, was also produced, with only two engines

(in-line Isotta-Fraschini Asso, liquid-cooled and generating 840 hp each) and with a substantial modification to the nose, by which the position of the third propeller was occupied by a place for a bombardier. This variant, however, was not followed up.

The SM.81, christened *Pipistrello* (Bat), went into service early in 1935, and made its military debut in Africa in the same year. After the experiences of the Spanish Civil War, the appearance of the stronger and more reliable SM.79 consigned the older bomber to a secondary role, and at the beginning of World War II the SM.81 was gradually withdrawn from front-line service in national territory and was used mainly on the African front and as transport on the Russian one. After the armistice, only four *Pipistrello*s were left in the south of Italy. The others that remained went in the north to form part of two groups of transport planes in the air force of the *Repubblica Sociale Italiana*. Only two of these planes survived the war.

---

color plate

SIAI Marchetti SM.81 13ª Squadriglia Bombardamento Terrestre Regia Aeronautica (13th Ground Bomber Squadron *Regia Aeronautica*) - Abyssinia 1936

Aircraft:	SIAI Marchetti SM.81
Nation:	Italy
Manufacturer:	SIAI Marchetti
Type:	Bomber
Year:	1935
Engine:	3 Alfa Romeo 125 RC35, 9-cylinder radial, air-cooled, 680 hp each
Wingspan:	78 ft 9 in (24.00 m)
Length:	60 ft 1 in (18.31 m)
Height:	14 ft 4 in (4.47 m)
Weight:	23,190 lb (10,505 kg) loaded
Maximum speed:	211 mph (340 km/h) at 13,120 ft (4,000 m)
Ceiling:	23,000 ft (7,000 m)
Range:	1,200 miles (1,931 km)
Armament:	6 machine guns; 4,415 lb (2,000 kg) of bombs
Crew:	6

Formation of SM.81s on the battlefield at Addis Abeba following the end of the Abyssinian War. In the foreground, aircraft with Piaggio PX engines and four-bladed propellers.

The series of three-engine aircraft launched by SIAI Marchetti with the SM.73 saw its most famous and effective version in the SM.79 model. Better known under its official name of *Sparviero* (Sparrow Hawk), although affectionately rechristened *Gobbo* (Hunchback) due to the characteristic fairings on its back, this aircraft played an extremely important role in World War II, rightly finding a place in the ranks of the immortal protagonists of aviation history. The SM.79 was adopted by Italy on all fronts for the duration of the war, and although it had been created as a bomber, its true role became the more aggressive one of torpedo launcher, in which it proved to be insuperable. From October 1936 to June 1943, a good 1,217 of these planes came off the production lines, a quantity that was clearly superior to the production standards of the Italian aeronautical industry at the time.

The SM.79's origins went back to 1934, when Alessandro Marchetti decided to develop a more modern derivative of the SM.73 transport model and the SM.91 bomber. The design formula remained essentially unchanged (three-engine, low-wing monoplane with wood-and-metal structure and mixed covering), although remarkable improvements and innovations were made. These included more powerful power plants (with a consequent increase in overall performance); improved aerodynamics; and retractable landing gear.

The prototype had been conceived as an eight-seater commercial aircraft with the aim of participating in the London-Melbourne race, and it made its maiden flight in October 1934, piloted by Adriano Bacula, from Cameri airport in the province of Novara. The aircraft's characteristics proved to be remarkable from the start, especially its velocity, which touched 220 mph (355 km/h) at sea level and over 248.5 mph (400 km/h) at altitude. The prototype was not ready in time to take part in the international race, but its preparation went ahead all the same. In the summer of 1935, the original 610 hp Piaggio P.IX engines were replaced by 750 hp Alfa Romeo engines, and the SM.79's performance improved still further. In September, the prototype broke no fewer than six world speed records: over 625 miles and 1,250 miles (1,000 and 2,000 km) respectively, with loads of 1,100 lb, 1 ton, and 2 tons (500, 1,000, and 2,000 kg), flying at 242.937 mph (390.971 km/h) and 236.711 mph (380.952 km/h). The military authorities showed an immediate interest and requested a second bomber version of the prototype.

The SM.79 made its debut in Spain in February 1937, but its racing activity continued despite its use in combat. On August 20/21, 1937, five SM.79Cs (racers) took the first five places in the Istres-Damascus-Paris race, with the winner covering the 3,846 miles (6,190 km) at an average speed of 219.212 mph (352.789

km/h), reaching 263 mph (424 km/h) at times. In January 1938, another three SM.79Ts (the transatlantic model) covered the 6,120 miles (9,850 km) from Guidonia (Italy) via Dakar to Rio de Janeiro at an average speed of 251 mph (404 km/h). On December 4, a plane powered by 1,000 hp Piaggio P.XI engines broke yet another speed record with an average of 293.798 mph (472.825 km/h) over 625 miles (1,000 km) carrying a load of 4,400 lb (2,000 kg).

One hundred and thirteen aircraft of the two-engine SM.79B version were also produced for export (they were sold to Yugoslavia, Iraq, Romania, and Brazil), while the three-engine variant known as the SM.79 III, with improvements and more powerful engines and armament, appeared in 1943.

At the outbreak of war, 594 SM.79s were in front-line service, and they soon added the role of torpedo launcher to their original one of bomber. In this role, the aircraft remained in service even after the armistice in the air force of the *Repubblica Sociale Italiana*, while after the war the surviving planes served for several years as transport planes and for target towing. The last were scrapped in 1952.

---

color plate

SIAI Marchetti SM.79 278ª Squadriglia Aerosiluranti Regia Aeronautica (278th Torpedo Squadron *Regia Aeronautica*) - Mediterranean 1942/43

Aircraft:	SIAI Marchetti SM.79
Nation:	Italy
Manufacturer:	SIAI Marchetti
Type:	Torpedo-bomber
Year:	1937
Engine:	3 Alfa Romeo A.R. 126 RC 34, 9-cylinder radial, air-cooled, 750 hp each
Wingspan:	69 ft 7 in (21.20 m)
Length:	53 ft 2 in (16.20 m)
Height:	13 ft 5 1/2 in (4.10 m)
Weight:	23,180 lb (10,500 kg) loaded
Maximum speed:	267 mph (430 km/h) at 13,120 ft (4,000 m)
Ceiling:	23,000 ft (7,000 m)
Range:	1,180 miles (1,900 km)
Armament:	4/5 machine guns; 2,756 lb (1,250 kg) of bombs
Crew:	6

Detail of the torpedo housing on a SIAI Marchetti SM.79.

SM.79 bombers of the *Aviacion del Tercio*.

SIAI MARCHETTI SM.79

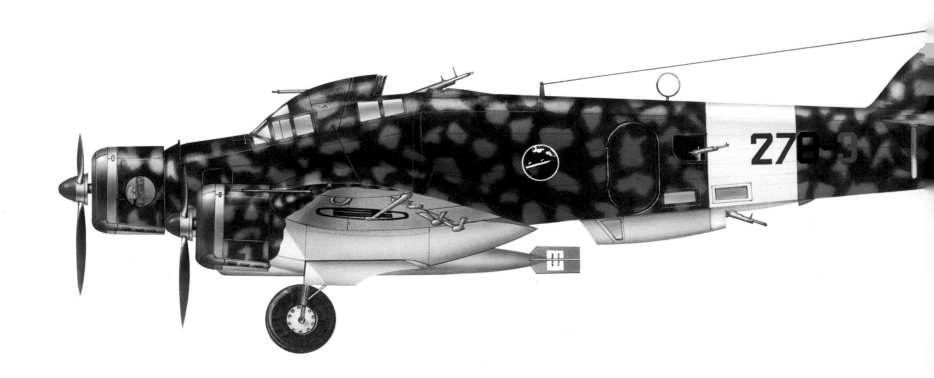

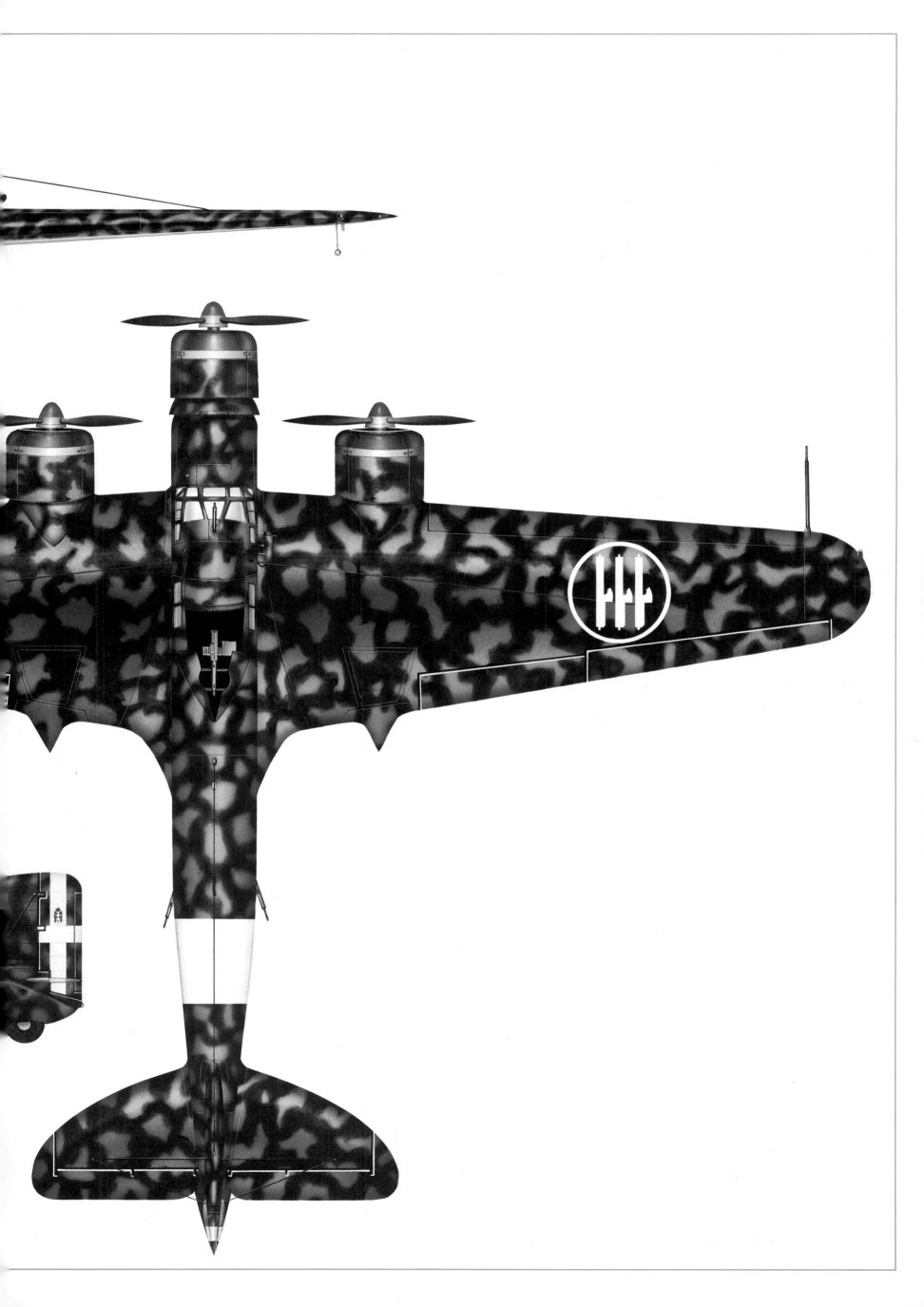

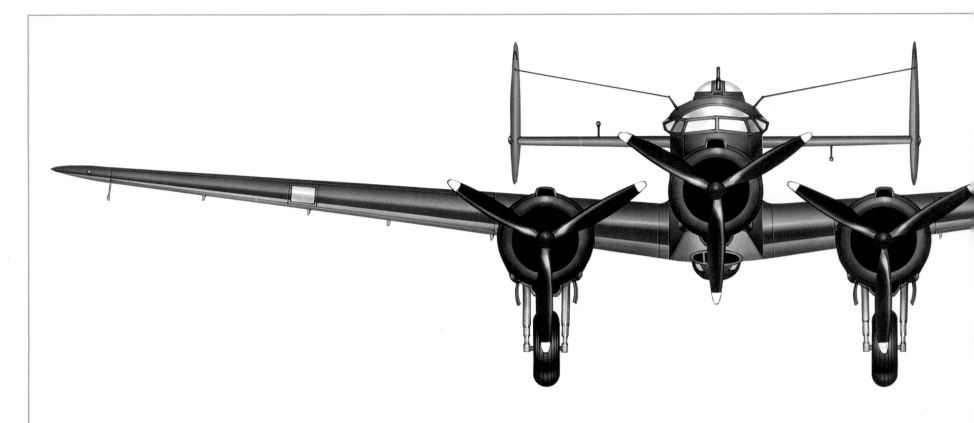

SIAI MARCHETTI SM.84 bis

In 1940, the three-engine formula, typical of Italian aeronautical production during the war, was enriched by the addition of a new bomber, the SIAI Marchetti SM.84. This aircraft was designed to replace the SM.79 *Sparviero* (Sparrowhawk), but it never succeeded in equalling its more illustrious predecessor. This was principally due to its lack of maneuverability, making it anything but ideal in the role of torpedo-bomber, and to the general lack of reliability of the Piaggio P.XI engines.

The project was launched by Alessandro Marchetti in 1939, and the prototype made its maiden flight on June 5 of the following year. Marchetti based his proposal for the aircraft on the airframe of the SM.79, retaining the same wings and substantially modifying the fuselage and empennage. The former, with its more advanced and innovative lines, lacked the characteristic hump on its back, while the latter was doubled. As far as the rest of the aircraft was concerned, it was characterized by its low wings, airframe of wood and steel tubing, and it had a covering of fabric, plywood and duraluminum. The aircraft was powered by three Piaggio P.XI radial engines, generating 1,000 hp each and driving three-bladed variable-pitch metal propellers. The defensive armament consisted of four 12.7 mm machine guns, installed in a turret on the aircraft's back and in three defensive positions, two on the sides of the fuselage and the third in the belly. The bomb load could be housed either under the wings or inside the belly. In the first instance, four rockets or two torpedos or bombs weighing up to 3,532 lb (1,600 kg) could be carried, while in the fuselage the maximum bomb load was 2,207 lb (1,000 kg).

performance had led to the realization of a *bis* version, with modifications mainly to the wing (now provided with a positive dihedral) and the cockpit, as well as to the ventilation of the engine and the torpedo-launching controls. However, these aircraft also went into service with bomber units, where they were to be operative until the armistice. In July 1943, the 43rd *Stormo* was the only unit to be equipped with the SM.84, and by September 8, it had 30 of these aircraft at its disposal. A further 130 bombers, of which only a hundred or so were effective, were distributed among several of the *Regia Aeronautica*'s supply centers.

Following the armistice, a certain number of SM.84s were requisitioned by the Germans which incorporated a dozen or so aircraft into the 132nd Transport Group, where they served until the end of the war.

Original model of the SIAI Marchetti SM.84 with horizontal wing.

An S.M.84 *bis* with positive dihedral wing in original factory finish before assignation to its unit.

Prior to the prototype's maiden flight, several tests had been carried out with a specially modified SM.79, provided with double empennage and 860 hp Alfa Romeo engines, and the aircraft's performance and potential had proved to be generally satisfactory. This was not so when the prototype of the SM.84 began its evaluation tests: it immediately proved to have a series of problems, especially during takeoff and landing, principally caused by the great weight of the wings and by the inadequacy of the vertical empennage. Moreover, the Piaggio engines proved to be unreliable and difficult to build.

Despite these problems, a large number of the new bombers were immediately ordered by the *Regia Aeronautica*, with an initial request for 246 aircraft placed almost at the same time that the prototype appeared and evaluation tests began. Eventually, orders were to amount to 309 aircraft.

The SM.84 began its operational career with the 41st Bomber Group in February 1941, and several months later it was also to serve with the 36th *Stormo Aerosiluranti* (Torpedo Flight Wing). The three-engine aircraft served in the role of torpedo plane for almost a year, until the autumn of 1942, when it was reassigned to bomber units. In the meantime, attempts to improve the SM.84's

color plate

SIAI Marchetti SM.84 bis 8ª Squadriglia 25° Gruppo Bombardamento 7° Stormo (8th Squadron 25th Group 7th Flight Wing) *Regia Aeronautica* - Sicily (Italy) 1942

Aircraft:	SIAI Marchetti SM.84
Nation:	Italy
Manufacturer:	SIAI Marchetti
Type:	Bomber
Year:	1941
Engine:	3 Piaggio P.XI RC40, 14-cylinder radial, air-cooled, 1,000 hp each
Wingspan:	69 ft 7 in (21.20 m)
Length:	58 ft 10 in (17.93 m)
Height:	15 ft 1 in (4.59 m)
Weight:	29,330 lb (13,288 kg) loaded
Maximum speed:	268 mph (432 km/h) at 15,000 ft (4,600 m)
Ceiling:	25,900 ft (7,900 m)
Range:	1,137 miles (1,830 km)
Armament:	4 machine guns; 3,532 lb (1,600 kg) of bombs
Crew:	5

Of the several attack aircraft produced by Breda during World War II, the Ba.65 was the only one to have a concrete operational role. Although advanced when it appeared, this sturdy monoplane nevertheless proved to be outdated when the war broke out, and its limitations (especially as far as handling and overall performance were concerned) soon became apparent, even in North Africa, the field of operations where it was used most.

The project was first produced in 1935. The specifications that gave rise to it were very ambitious, considering that they provided for a plane capable of carrying out many roles, ranging from interception to reconnaissance and ground attack, and Breda's technicians drew directly on the preceding model, the Ba.64. The latter, which appeared in 1934, had been conceived as an assault plane, and although its performance had been somewhat lacking, the *Regia Aeronautica* had requested that it go into production.

The new prototype made its maiden flight in September 1935, piloted by Ambrogio Colombo. It was a cantilever low-wing monoplane with all-metal structure and covering, except for the trailing edge of the wings which were fabric covered. It was powered by a 700 hp Gnome-Rhône K-14 radial engine, which drove a three-bladed, variable-pitch metal propeller. The defense armament consisted of two 12.7 mm and two 7.7 mm machine guns installed on the wing, and its maximum payload was 2,200 lb (1,000 kg) of bombs, some of which were carried in a section of the fuselage and others in bomb racks on the wings.

The Ba.65 was immediately accepted by the *Regia Aeronautica,* and production started at the beginning of 1936, with an order for 81 planes. By 1939, another 137 were to be built, featuring a 1,000 hp Fiat A.80 RC41 engine. Many planes of the latter type were completed in a two-seater version in which the second cockpit, situated to the rear, housed an observer who could make use of the 7.7 mm flexible machine gun, which was, in some cases, installed in a Breda-type revolving turret.

The Ba.65 made its operational debut in Spain, where 13 planes of the first series were sent initially, followed by 10 or so of the second. Experience in combat quickly led to a reassessment of the aircraft's supposed versatility, and it proved to be suited only to the role of an assault plane. It was, in fact, in this role that the Ba.65 took part in World War II, and after Italy entered the war the 154 planes in service were used mainly on the African front. Generally outclassed by the more modern British fighters, the Bredas fought valiantly, and the last plane in service was lost in February 1941.

The Ba.65 also enjoyed notable success as far as export was concerned. In 1938, 25 of the two-seater version with Fiat A.80 engines were sold to Iraq (two of which had dual controls for training and the rest with Breda-type turrets). Again in 1938, another 20 planes with Piaggio P.XI C.40 power plants were sent to Chile (17 single-seaters and three trainers); in 1939, 12 two-seater planes with Fiat engines and turrets were exported to Portugal. Finally, an interesting modification tested in June 1937 on a Ba.65 series model should be mentioned: the plane was deprived of its original Fiat engine, and the power plant was replaced with an American Pratt & Whitney R-1830 radial engine. This modification was carried out in preparation for an order (never placed) from Nationalist China.

color plate

Breda Ba.65 K14 65th Attack Squadron Aviaciòn del Tercio (Spanish Nationalist Air Force) - Puig Moreno 1938

Aircraft:	Breda Ba.65
Nation:	Italy
Manufacturer:	Società Italiana Ernesto Breda
Type:	Fighter-bomber
Year:	1936
Engine:	Fiat A.80 RC41, 18-cylinder radial, air-cooled, 1,000 hp
Wingspan:	39 ft 8 in (12.10 m)
Length:	31 ft 6 in (9.60 m)
Height:	10 ft 6 in (3.20 m)
Weight:	7,695 lb (3,490 kg) loaded
Maximum speed:	267 mph (430 km/h)
Ceiling:	27,230 ft (8,300 m)
Range:	342 miles (550 km)
Armament:	4 machine guns; 2,200 lb (1,000 kg) of bombs
Crew:	1

Formation of Breda Ba.65s in training flight bearing prewar insignia.

Maintenance and refuelling of a Breda Ba.65 at an Italian airport.

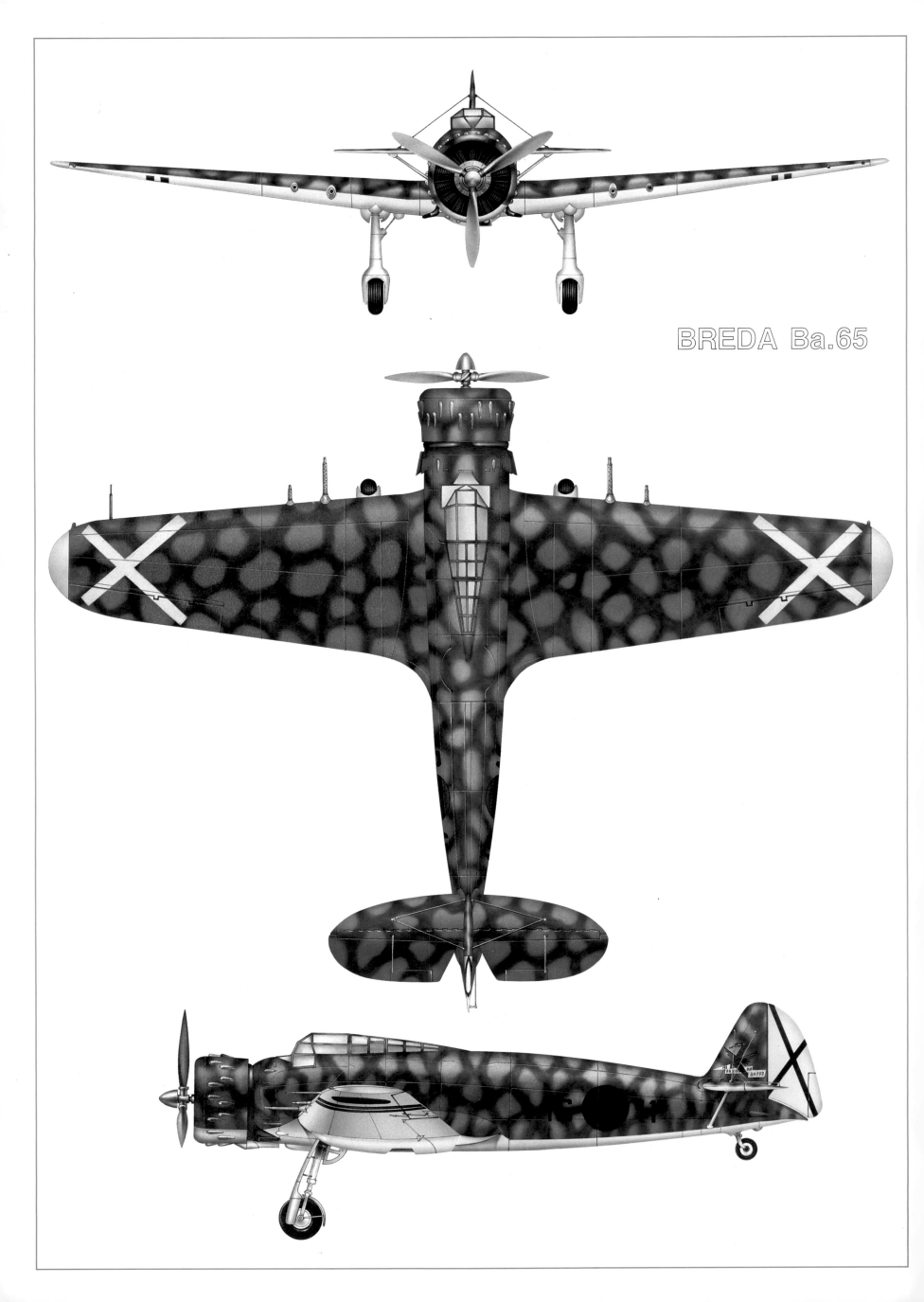

BREDA Ba.65

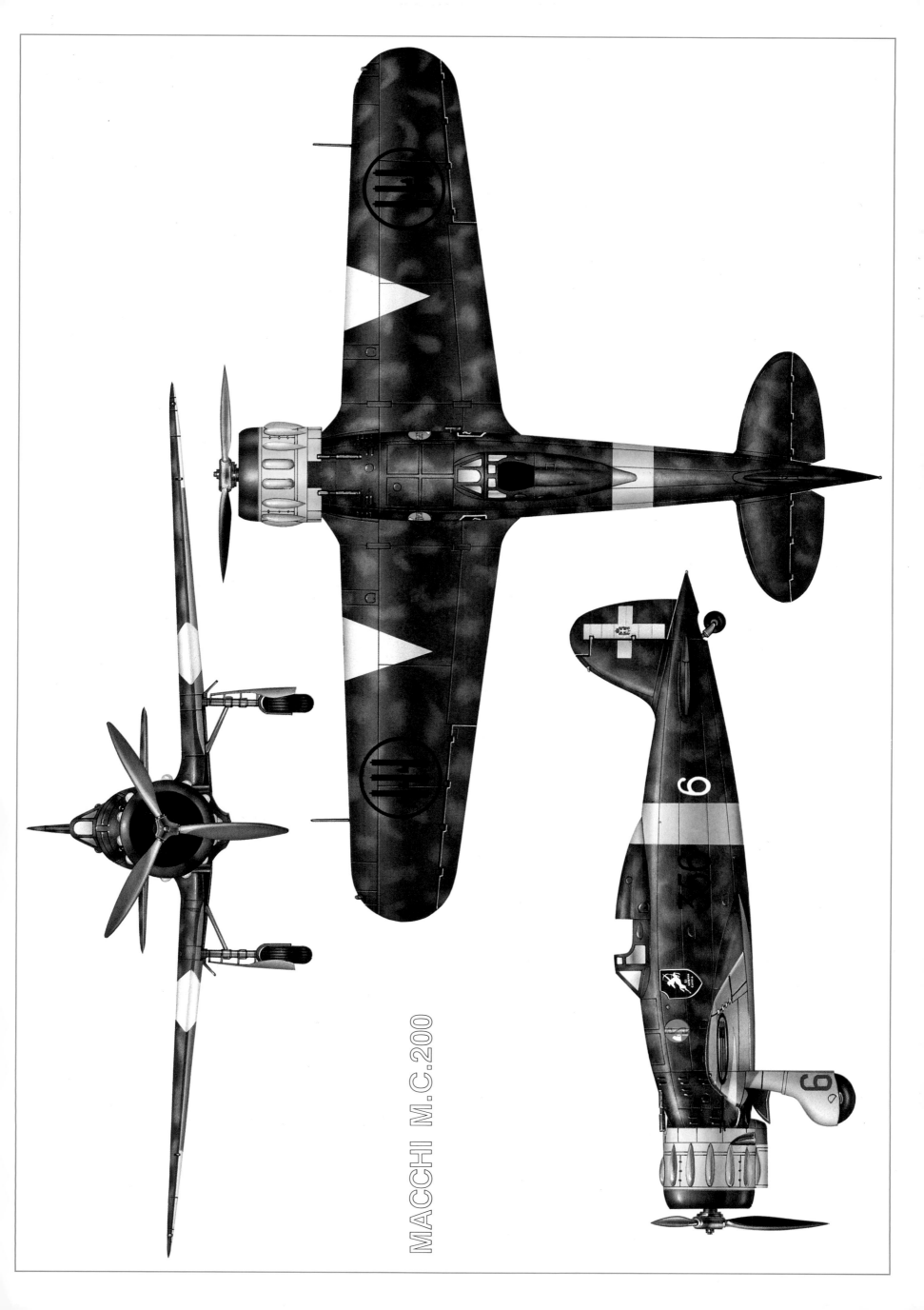

MACCHI M.C.200

The Macchi M.C.200 *Saetta* (Arrow) was the best representative of the first generation of fighters to be used in combat by the *Regia Aeronautica* during the conflict. However, the importance of this agile and robust aircraft was not merely confined to its merits as a combat plane. Designed by Mario Castoldi, the technician who created a successful series of seaplane racers during the era of the Schneider Cup, including the prestigious M.C.72, holder of the world speed record for its category, the *Saetta* was also the ancestor of what could be considered the most important family of Italian fighters of World War II. In fact, the 200 was followed by the model 202 *Folgore* (Thunderbolt) and the 205 *Veltro* (Greyhound), aircraft that ranked among the best of the entire conflict and that allowed (albeit with some delay) Italian aeronautical production to compete at the level of those of other nations.

The project was launched in 1935, although almost two years were to pass before it assumed its final configuration. In fact, the definitive prototype of the *Saetta* took to the air on December 24, 1937, and in the following months it underwent a laborious preparation phase that was indispensable for the correction of stability problems that had emerged during flight testing. In his design, Mario Castoldi had drawn widely on the experience he had acquired during the construction of the seaplane racers, especially as far as aerodynamic solutions were concerned. In fact, in the model 200 the designer succeded in combining the massive front section of the radial engine (a Fiat A.74 RC.38 generating 870 hp at takeoff and 840 hp at altitude) with an agile fuselage of reduced dimensions. As for the wings and tail planes, proof of their structural and aerodynamic qualities was provided by the fact that these components were to remain virtually unchanged throughout the course of the evolution that led to the 202 and 205 types, aircraft characterized by a much better performance and more powerful engines than those of the *Saetta*.

During evaluation tests, the Macchi M.C.200 proved to be strong, extremely maneuverable, and fast in ascent. The only black spots were its maximum speed, which was not particularly high, and its armament, which was limited (in accordance with the standards of the time) to two 12.7 mm machine guns synchronized to fire through the propeller. The fighter proved to be the winner in the competition announced by the *Regia Aeronautica* in 1938, and large series were ordered: production continued from June 1939 until July 1942 and amounted to a total of 1,151 aircraft, of which 345 were built by Macchi and the rest by Breda and SAI Ambrosini.

The first production series aircraft came off the assembly lines in the summer of 1939, and 144 were in service in the fighter units when the war broke out. However, the Macchi M.C.200 did not reach full operational efficiency until the end of 1940, following modifications to the wing profile carried out with the aim of definitively eliminating the autorotation problems that still persisted,

and the removal of the sliding canopy, which had made it difficult for the pilot to bail out in emergency situations.

The *Saetta* remained the *Regia Aeronautica*'s front line fighter throughout 1941, being replaced only by the appearance of its more advanced successor, the M.C.202, and it was used on practically all fronts, the only exception being the English Channel. Later, it was gradually withdrawn from the most advanced sectors and continued to serve as a fighter-bomber (in this role it was capable of carrying 660 lb — 300 kg — of bombs in fittings under the wings), as an escort fighter, and as an interceptor based on national territory. In September 1943, at the time of the armistice, 52 aircraft remained in service, the greater part (23) of which were used by the cobelligerent air force, while another eight passed to the air force of the Repubblica Sociale Italiana. In both cases, these aircraft were used as trainers. Some *Saettas* survived the war and were withdrawn in 1947.

color plate
Macchi M.C.200 Saetta 356ª Squadriglia 21º Gruppo Caccia Regia Aeronautica (356th Squadron 21st Fighter Group *Regia Aeronautica*) - Russian front 1942

Factory fresh M.C.200 before delivery to its unit.

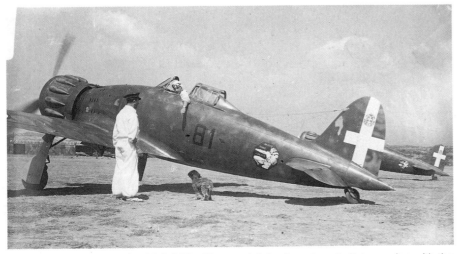

An initial production series M.C.200 with completely glazed cockpit, in service with the 1st *Stormo*.

Aircraft:	Macchi M.C.200
Nation:	Italy
Manufacturer:	Aeronautica Macchi
Type:	Fighter
Year:	1,939
Engine:	Fiat A.74 RC.38, 14-cylinder radial, air-cooled, 870 hp
Wingspan:	34 ft 8 1/2 in (10.57 m)
Length:	26 ft 11 in (8.19 m)
Height:	11 ft 6 in (3.51 m)
Takeoff weight:	5,590 lb (2,533 kg) loaded
Maximum speed:	312 mph (503 km/h) at 14,800 ft (4,500 m)
Ceiling:	29,275 ft (8,900 m)
Range:	540 miles (870 km)
Armament:	2 machine guns
Crew:	1

A Macchi M.C.202 in service with the 91st Squadron bearing the insignia of the rearing horse.

A Macchi M.C.202 is started manually at an airport in Libya.

color plate

Macchi M.C.202 personal aircraft of the Commander of the 153rd Gruppo Caccia 53rd Stormo (153rd Fighter Group 53rd Flight Wing) *Regia Aeronautica* · Libya 1942

Aircraft:	Macchi M.C.202
Nation:	Italy
Manufacturer:	Aeronautica Macchi S.p.A.
Type:	Fighter
Year:	1941
Engine:	Daimler Benz DB 601A-1, 12-cylinder V, liquid-cooled, 1,175 hp
Wingspan:	34 ft 8 1/2 in (10.58 m)
Length:	29 ft 1 in (8.85 m)
Height:	9 ft 11 1/2 in (3.02 m)
Weight:	6,480 lb (2,937 kg) loaded
Maximum speed:	372 mph (600 km/h) at 18,050 ft (5,500 m)
Ceiling:	37,700 ft (11,500 m)
Range:	475 miles (765 km)
Armament:	2 machine guns
Crew:	1

A factory fresh Macchi M.C.202 bearing national insignia and without operational markings.

Following the M.C.200 *Saetta* (Arrow), the family of combat planes presented by Macchi during the second half of the 1930s was enriched by a new, more effective model in 1940. This was the M.C.202 *Folgore* (Thunderbolt), an aircraft that is generally remembered as the best Italian fighter to go into service with the *Regia Aeronautica* during World War II, due to its characteristics, the number that were built, and the extent to which it was used. The *Folgore* went into service in November 1941 and was operational on practically all fronts. From May 1941 to August 1943, more than 1,100 aircraft came off the assembly lines, production being divided between Macchi itself, Breda, and SAI Ambrosini.

The factor that allowed the effective airframe of the model 202 to be exploited to the full was the availability of the German Daimler Benz DB 601 engine and, from this point of view, the construction of the new Macchi fighter marked a fundamental turning point in the design philosophy that the Italian aeronautical industry had followed up till then. This foresaw the adoption of radial engines, whose development had been preferred over that of liquid-cooled in-line engines. This was in spite of the excellent results achieved in the latter sector during the various aeronautical contests held in the period between the two world wars, and in the Schneider Cup in particular.

However, the limitations of this choice had been apparent right from the earliest combat experiences: the fighters of the so-called first generation (Fiat G.50 and Macchi M.C.200) had proved to be totally inadequate and uncompetitive, not only as far as their immediate adversaries, the British, were concerned but also compared to the products of Germany, Italy's principal ally. The most obvious disadvantages derived not only from the clear aerodynamic limitations imposed by the installation of a massive radial engine, but also, and above all, from the relatively limited amount of power available. Thus, in the search for an effective in-line engine which was indispensable to keep up with the evolution of the most advanced combat planes, Italy turned to Germany for help, first through the importation of the Daimler Benz DB 601s, and second, through Fiat and Alfa Romeo building them on license. This choice, albeit delayed, proved to be the right one: in fact the various variants of the Daimler Benz engines made the creation of the *Regia Aeronautica*'s most prestigious fighters possible, that is to say, the excellent Macchi M.C.205, the Fiat G.55 and the Reggiane Re.2005s belonging to the "5 series," all of which, despite their late arrival and the fact that only few were built, soon figured among the best of the entire conflict. They also placed the Italian aeronautical industry on a competitive level with other nations.

In 1940, on its own initiative, Macchi acquired a German engine and began studies for a new version of the *Saetta*. Its designer was Mario Castaldi, and the prototype, which made its maiden flight on August 10, retained the wings and empennage of its direct predecessor. On the other hand, its fuselage was entirely different and was characterized by carefully studied aerodynamic lines and a closed cockpit. As soon as flight testing began, the performance of the new aircraft proved to be clearly superior: its maximum horizontal speed touched 372 mph (600 km/h), while in ascent it could reach 19,735 ft (6,000 m) in five minutes 55 seconds. Its only defect lay in its armament, which was limited to two 12.7 mm machine guns synchronized to fire through the propeller. However, attempts were made to improve this in the later production series, adding another two weapons of smaller caliber under the wings.

A large number of *Folgore* were ordered immediately, and the aircraft made its operational debut in Libya, although it was soon to be used on all fronts in Africa, as well as the Balkan and Russian fronts and in the Mediterranean. It continued to be used after the armistice, both in the units of the cobelligerent air force and those of the *Repubblica Sociale Italiana*. The surviving aircraft were used for training by the *Aeronautica Militare Italiana* until 1948.

MACCHI M.C.202

MACCHI M.C.205

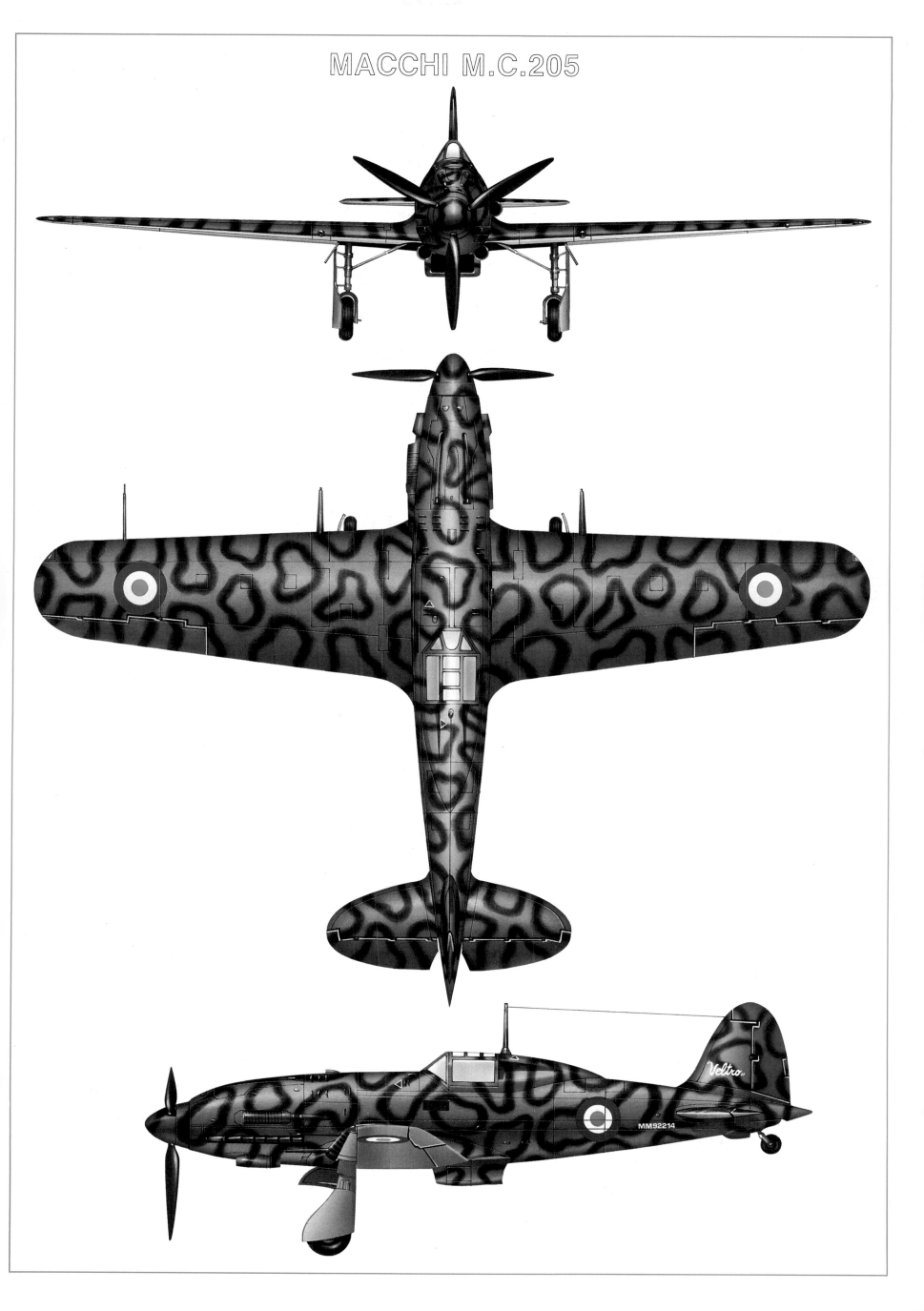

Of the final generation of Italian fighters, the Macchi M.C. 205 *Veltro* (Greyhound) was the first to exploit the potential provided by the new version of the German Daimler Benz engine (which, moreover, was built on license by Fiat under the name of RA.1050 RC 58 *Tifone*, Typhoon), and was the only Series 5 combat plane to have a consistent operative career in the units of the *Regia Aeronautica* prior to September 8, 1943.

The project, developed by Mario Castoldi, was laid out at more or less the same time as those of the Fiat G.55 and the Reggiane Re.2005, and Macchi was initially favored by the fact that it already had an excellent airframe on which to develop the new model at its disposal, that of the M.C. 202 *Folgore*. In fact, when the first M.C. 205 prototype took to the air on April 19, 1942 (with test pilot Guido Carestiato at the controls), it bore a strong resemblance to its direct precedessor. The *Veltro* was an all metal low-wing monoplane with retractable landing gear, with elegant and aerodynamic lines. The only external differences compared to the *Folgore* lay in the engine housing and the presence of two oil radiators on the side of the fuselage. However, its performance differed greatly: thanks to an extra 400 hp of power, the prototype proved capable of reaching 404 mph (65 km/h) in horizontal flight and of climbing to 19,735 ft (6,000 m) in four minutes 52 seconds. Moreover, the excellent qualities of maneuverability characteristic of the *Folgore* were improved upon still further. As for the defensive armament, the *Veltro* was the first Italian fighter have two 20 mm cannons and thus to have firing power equal to the standards of the time.

After evaluation tests, the M.C. 205 went into production immediately, on the basis of an order for 250 aircraft, and the first of these came off the assembly lines in September 1942. However, the production rate was extremely slow, affected by the increasing difficulties in providing strategic materials and power plants: barely ten aircraft were delivered in the course of the year, with the monthly production rate reaching 18 aircraft in February 1943. It was not until June that Macchi succeeded in completing the initial series of 100 aircraft. These were not yet fitted with 20 mm cannons (the two positions on the wings housed a pair of 7.7 mm Breda-Safat machine guns) and this armament was installed subsequently in the aircraft of the definitive series III. In all, up to September, production amounted to a total of 177 aircraft, 146 of which were assigned to the units of the *Regia Aeronautica*.

The *Veltro* went into service in April 1943 and was used mainly in the Mediterranean and Sicily, at the time of the Allied landings. However, its career became more intensive following the Italian armistice. After September 8, 1943, 37 aircraft were incorporated into the cobelligerent air force (firstly in the 4th and then in the 51st Flight Group), and they remained in active service until the

A Macchi M.C. 205, with cannons on the wings, in service with the Italian Co-Belligerent Air Force.

A Macchi M.C. 205 in service with the air force of the R.S.I.

end of the conflict. In the north of Italy the Macchi M.C. 205s costituted the initial backbone of the fighter units of the *Repubblica Sociale Italiana*, which were equipped with 28 recovered aircraft at first and then with a further 112 built up to May 1944.

During the war Macchi continued to develop the project and built two prototypes designated M.C. 205N-1 and M.C. 205N-2 *Orione* (Orion), which made their maiden flights on November 1, 1942 and May 19, 1943, respectively. Although they were provided with the same engine as their predecessor, they were larger and more heavily armed. These aircraft never went into production, while two subsequent experimental models in which Mario Castoldi intended to improve the aircraft's performance still further, the M.C. 206 and M.C. 207, remained at various stages of construction.

At the end of World War II a small number of M.C. 205s served with the 5th Flight Group of the Italian air force, where they remained in service until May 1947, being replaced by Spitfire Mk.IXs left over from the war.

---

color plate

Macchi M.C. 205 Italian Co-Belligerent Air Force - Southern Italy 1943-44. On October 6, 1943, this aircraft dropped pamphlets on Rome, occupied by the Germans at the time

A Macchi M.C. 205 *Veltro* in service with the *Regia Aeronautica*. This aircraft was one of the first to be built and lacks cannons on the wings.

Aircraft:	Macchi M.C. 205
Nation:	Italy
Manufacturer:	Aeronautica Macchi S.p.A.
Type:	Fighter
Year:	1943
Engine:	Daimler Benz DB 605A, 12-cylinder V, liquid-cooled, 1,475 hp
Wingspan:	34 ft 8 in (10.50 m)
Length:	29 ft 1 in (8.85 m)
Height:	10 ft (3.05 m)
Weight:	7,523 lb (3,408 kg)
Maximum speed:	400 mph (644 km/h) at 24,670 ft (7,500 m)
Ceiling:	39,310 ft (11,950 m)
Range:	590 miles (950 km)
Armament:	2 × 20 mm cannons, 2 machine guns
Crew:	1

The most famous and widely used of the first generation Italian fighters during the war were the Fiat G.50 and the Macchi M.C.200. However, in addition to these two aircraft, a third contemporary combat plane deserves to be remembered, not so much for its extremely limited operative career in the *Regia Aeronautica*, as for the excellent qualities of its design, which were truly innovative for the time. This aircraft was the Reggiane Re.2000, designed by Roberto Longhi and Antonio Alessio in 1938. Paradoxically, the aircraft was rejected by the authorities and was produced for export, serving brilliantly bearing the insignia of Hungary and Sweden.

The Re.2000's lack of success led the Reggiane company to develop a new version of its fighter, which was designated Re.2001. The determining factor behind this decision was the availability of German Daimler Benz DB 601 engines. Longhi and Alessio had adapted these to the airframe of the original project, in place of the Piaggio P.XI radial engine. The result, which appeared as a prototype in June 1940, was a notably improved aircraft with a good overall performance. However, this was to be as unlucky as its predecessor had been. In fact, delays in completing the aircraft (in order to carry out a long series of modifications requested by the *Regia Aeronautica*) and a relative shortage of engines (priority was given to the Macchi M.C.202 fighter as far as these were concerned) limited the Re.2001's operative career. Only 237 aircraft were built, and they were never used in the role of interceptor, but relegated to the role of fighter-bomber initially, and then to that of night fighter.

The initial delays meant that the first production series aircraft were not delivered until June 1941, almost a year after the prototype's maiden flight. In fact, Reggiane's technicians were forced to substantially redesign the wing in order to adapt the structure and conformation of the internal fuel tanks to the requests of the authorities. Production also went ahead slowly: approximately 40 aircraft were completed in 1941, a further 100 or so in 1942, and the rest in the first half of 1943. As well as the original fighter version, there were two variants: the CB (fighter-bomber) and the CN (night fighter), both with more powerful armament. The first could carry a 220 lb (100 kg) or 550 lb (250 kg) bomb externally. In exceptional circumstances it could also carry a 1,412 lb (640 kg) bomb. In the second variant, the machine guns on the wings were replaced by the two 20 mm cannons housed in external nacelles.

The Re.2001 started its operational career at the beginning of December 1941, and it was assigned to three *Squadriglias* of the 2nd Fighter Group of the 6th *Stormo*, being used mainly in the Mediterranean and in Italy itself as a night fighter. Following the armistice, several of the surviving aircraft served in the cobelligerent air force and, to a lesser extent, in that of the *Repubblica Sociale Italiana*. Five aircraft served for several years in the *Aeronautica Militare Italiana* after the war had ended.

Mention should be made of several prototypes that Reggiane developed from the Re.2001 in an attempt to improve the original project still further. The first of these was the Re.2001 *bis*, on which modifications, mainly of an aerodynamic nature, were carried out. It began flight testing in April 1941, piloted by Francesco Agello, who held the world speed record for seaplanes. Its performance proved to be excellent, and it reached speeds of over 38 mph (60 km/h) faster than the original version of the aircraft. The second prototype was the Re.2001 *Delta*, in which an attempt was made to overcome the problems caused by the shortage of available Daimler Benz engines by installing the 840 hp Isotta-Fraschini Delta V-12 air-cooled engine as an alternative. The fighter, successfully tested toward the end of 1942, crashed in January of the following year and an order for 100 aircraft was cancelled.

color plate

Reggiane Re.2001 22nd C.T. Group *Regia Aeronautica*. One of the two aircraft that attacked the aircraft carrier H.M.S. *Victorious* in the Mediterranean on August 12, 1942, hitting it with 1,412 lb (640 kg) bombs that failed to explode.

Aircraft:	Reggiane Re.2001
Nation:	Italy
Manufacturer:	Officine Meccaniche Reggiane SpA (Caproni)
Type:	Fighter
Year:	1941
Engine:	Daimler Benz DB 601 A-1, 12-cylinder V, liquid cooled, 1,175 hp
Wingspan:	36 ft 1 in (11.00 m)
Length:	27 ft 5 in (8.36 m)
Height:	10 ft 4 in (3.15 m)
Weight:	6,700 lb (3,040 kg) loaded
Maximum speed:	349 mph (563 km/h) at 17,700 ft (5,400 m)
Ceiling:	36,000 ft (11,000 m)
Range:	684 miles (1,100 km)
Armament:	4 machine guns
Crew:	1

One of the two Reggiane Re.2001s that attacked H.M.S. *Victorious* in the Mediterranean on August 12, 1942.

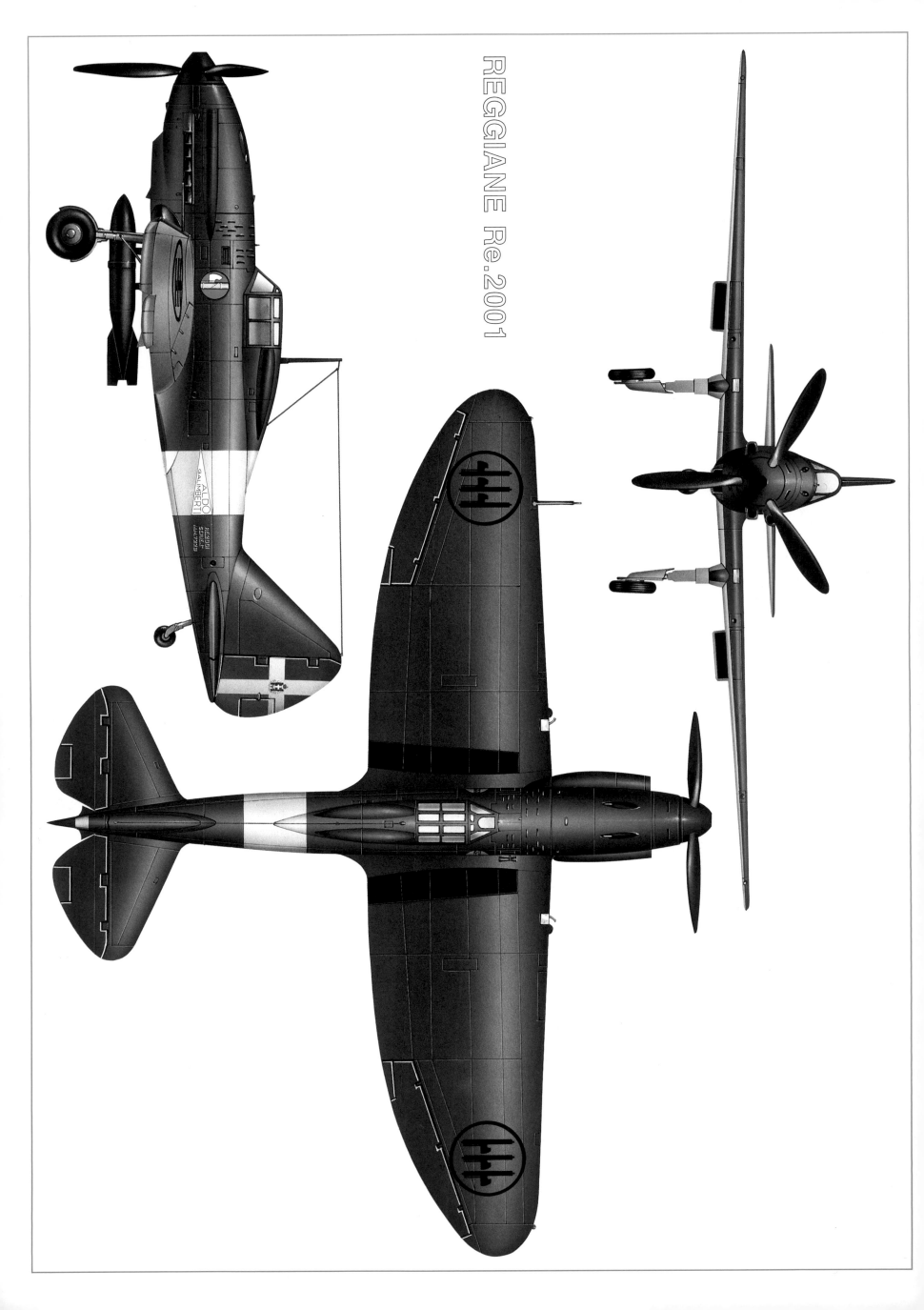

REGGIANE Re.2001

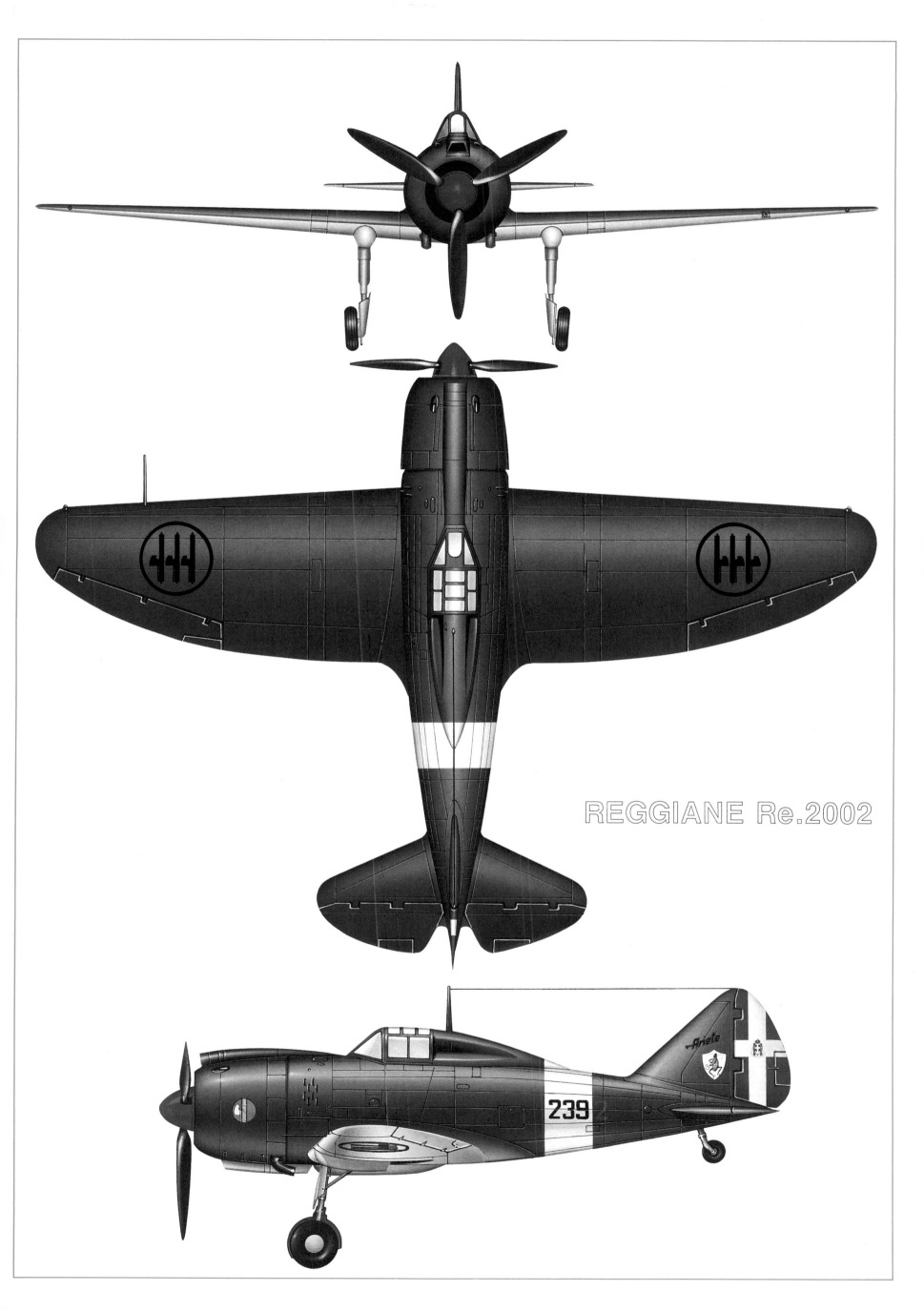

REGGIANE Re.2002

In 1941, the series of fighters built by Reggiane during the conflict was enriched by the addition of a new model, the Re.2002 *Ariete* (Aries). The aircraft's designers, Roberto Longhi and Antonio Alessio, further improved the basic project, which had originated in 1938 with the unsuccessful Re.2000 and had subsequently been developed in the Re.2001, creating an effective combat plane which, in its category (fighter-bomber/attack), proved to be the best the *Regia Aeronautica* had. The *Ariete*'s excellent qualities were also recognized by Germany, which planned to build a variant powered by a 1,600 hp BMW radial engine in 1943. However, the program did not go ahead, and the Luftwaffe merely used sixty or so Re.2002s, which served in its attack units between the end of 1943 and 1944. Total production of the *Ariete* amounted to 225 aircraft, 149 of which went into service in the *Regia Aeronautica*.

The project was created in the summer of 1940, on the basis of experiences gained from the construction of the Re.2001 model. With an airframe that had already been amply tested at their disposal, Longhi and Alessio decided to use it with and engine other than the in-line Daimler Benz, which, moreover, was in short supply. The choice fell on the Piaggio P.XIX RC 45 radial, capable of generating a maximum of 1,175 hp, and, from this point of view, the new aircraft was directly related to the progenitor of the entire family, the Re.2000, which had paradoxically been rejected by the *Regia Aeronautica* a year earlier.

The Re.2002 prototype took to the air for the first time in October 1940, and right from the time of the first tests, it proved to have remarkable characteristics and overall performance, in some ways superior to those of the Reggiane Re.2001. The new fighter retained the wings and empennage of its direct predecessor, although it had a substantially modified fuselage. The defensive armament consisted of a pair of 12.7 mm machine guns installed in the nose and synchronized to fire through the propeller, and two 7.7 mm weapons on the wings; the offensive armament consisted of a 927 lb (420 kg) or 1,103 lb (500 kg) bomb installed in the belly, while another two bombs could be attached to two racks below the wings.

However, preparation of the prototype proved lengthy, due mainly to persistent problems with the power plants, and it was not until eleven months after the aircraft's maiden flight (in September 1941) that the *Regia Aeronautica* placed a production order for an initial 200. The first of these was delivered in March of the following year, although the aircraft's operational debut was also marked by notable delays: the 5th *Stormo Tuffatori* did not become operative until March 1943, at a time when an intensive series of missions began to contest the Allied landings in Sicily.

The aircraft's service bearing the insignia of the *Regia Aeronautica* therefore lasted only a few months until the armistice, although this did not mean the end of the *Ariete*'s career. After

A Reggiane Re.2002 in service with the 239th Squadron of the *Regia Aeronautica*.

September 8, 1943, forty or so Reggiane Re.2002s continued to serve in the cobelligerent air force, and served until the summer of the following year. In the opposing camp, although the aircraft was hardly used at all by the units of the *Repubblica Sociale Italiana*, it was widely employed by the Luftwaffe, which succeeded in taking approximately 40 factory-fresh planes and a further 20 requisitioned immediately following the armistice to Germany. These aircraft, bearing German insignia, were used mainly in France, to counter the action of the partisans.

color plate

Reggiane Re.2002 239th Squadron 102nd *Gruppo Tuffatori Regia Aeronautica* - Manduria, Italy July 1943

Aircraft:	Reggiane Re.2002
Nation:	Italy
Manufacturer:	Officine Meccaniche Reggiane S.p.A.
Type:	Attack
Year:	1943
Engine:	Piaggio P.XIX RC 45, 14-cylinder radial, air-cooled, 1,175 hp
Wingspan:	36 ft 2 in (11.00 m)
Length:	26 ft 10 in (8.16 m)
Height:	10 ft 4 in (3.15 m)
Weight:	7,152 lb (3,240 kg)
Maximum speed:	329 mph (530 km/h) at 18,092 ft (5,500 m)
Ceiling:	34,539 ft (10,500 m)
Range:	683 miles (1,100 km)
Armament:	4 machine guns, 1,412 lb (640 kg) of bombs
Crew:	1

An Re.2002 in service with the Luftwaffe.

The Piaggio P.108 was the only four-engine heavy bomber employed by the *Regia Aeronautica* during World War II. Although it arrived on the scene too late to play an effective role in the course of operations, from many points of view this aircraft was remarkable compared to the rest of Italian aeronautical production of the period. Its overall performance was excellent, and its combat potential was great, but above all was the advanced nature of its design, which made it competitive with the best aircraft in the world at the time. Only 24 P.108B (bombers) were completed, between November 1939 and August 1943: their operative career started at the beginning of June 1942 and took place mainly in the Mediterranean, although on an irregular basis.

The project was launched in March 1937 by Giovanni Casiraghi, a young engineer called in by Piaggio to replace Giovanni Pegna, the chief designer who had left the company early in 1936. Casiraghi had acquired valuable experience (from November 1927 to February 1936) working in the American aeronautical industry, and this training lay at the basis of his design for a four-engine bomber, already developed by Pegna with the P-50 model. The P.108 slowly took shape, revealing the originality behind its layout and characteristics. It was an all-metal low-wing monoplane with retractable landing gear and was powered by four Piaggio P.XII radial engines generating 1,350 hp each. The defensive armament was particularly effective and consisted of four 12.7 mm machine guns installed in pairs in two radio-controlled turrets in the external engine nacelles, two 7.7 mm weapons situated to the sides of the central part of the fuselage, a 12.7 mm machine gun in a turret in the belly, and a similar weapon in the nose; the offensive armament could reach a maximum of 7,725 lb (3,500 kg) of bombs, all contained inside the fuselage.

The project was presented in the ministerial competition that took place in 1939, in which it came up against a strong rival in the CANT Z.1014, presented by Filippo Zappata. This model was initially judged the winner, although Piaggio eventually succeeded in winning the competition by drastically lowering its prices (by 50 percent). The P.108 prototype was completed by October 1939 and took to the air on November 24. A long phase of official evaluations followed, during which the new bomber was prepared definitively. The only unit to be equipped with the P.108B was the 274th Long-Range Bomber Squadron, which was formed at the end of May 1941 with the first production series aircraft. However, operative training proved to be longer than expected, and it was not until June 9, 1942, that the aircraft carried out its first mission, research and bombing of shipping near the Balearic islands. The 274th Squadron was subsequently used in attacks on Gibraltar and Algeria. The P.108B's career came to an end in September 1943, when most of the surviving aircraft fell into the hands of the Germans who, however, did not use them in missions.

Several versions were derived from the basic model. An interesting one was the P.108A (Artillery) for antishipping attack. It began flight testing in March 1943 and was derived from the B but provided with a 102 mm cannon in the nose. In 1942 the prototypes of the P.108C version appeared (this was a civilian version with pressurized cabin for 32 passengers and was destined for service on routes to South America) as well as that of the P.108T (for military transport); both were characterized by a new and larger fuselage. The P.108Ts were the only ones to go into production, with an order for nine aircraft. Almost all of these were captured by the Germans and were used by the transport units of the Luftwaffe, together with the Junkers Ju.290 and the Arado Ar.232. They were widely adopted during the evacuation of Sevastopol and the Crimea from April to May 1944.

---

color plate

Piaggio P.108B 274th Bomber Squadron *Regia Aeronautica* - Pisa 1941. The aircraft which crashed during landing at Pisa on August 7th, 1941, killing Captain Bruno Mussolini

---

Aircraft:	Piaggio P.108B
Nation:	Italy
Manufacturer:	S.A. Piaggio & Co.
Type:	Bomber
Year:	1942
Engine:	4 Piaggio P.XII RC 35, 18-cylinder radial, air-cooled, 1,350 hp each
Wingspan:	105 ft 3 in (32.00 m)
Length:	75 ft 4 in (22.92 m)
Height:	25 ft 3 in (7.70 m)
Weight:	59,205 lb (26,820 kg)
Maximum speed:	267 mph (430 km/h) at 13,815 ft (4,200 m)
Ceiling:	19,736 ft (6,000 m)
Range:	2,173 miles (3,500 km)
Armament:	8 machine guns; 7,725 lb (3,500 kg) of bombs
Crew:	6

The Piaggio P.108 *Artigliere*, a bomber transformed for an antishipping role by the installation of a 102 mm cannon in the fuselage.

The first production aircraft of the Piaggio P.108 bomber. The remote-controlled armament is installed on the external engines.

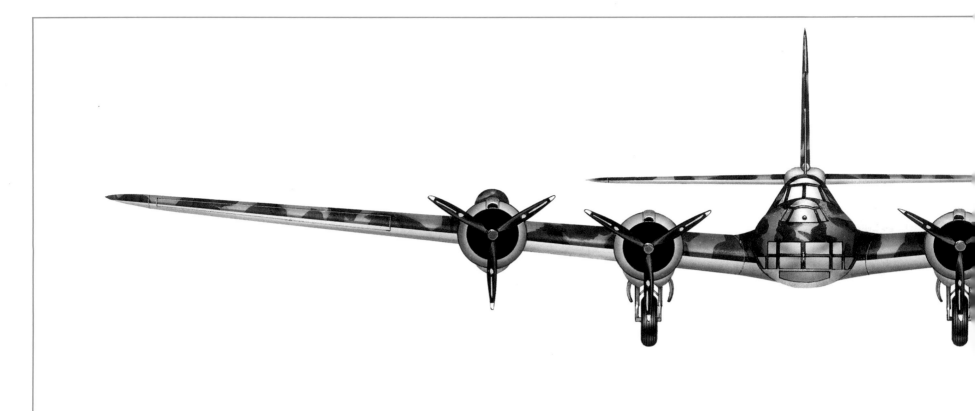

PIAGGIO P.108 B

274-1

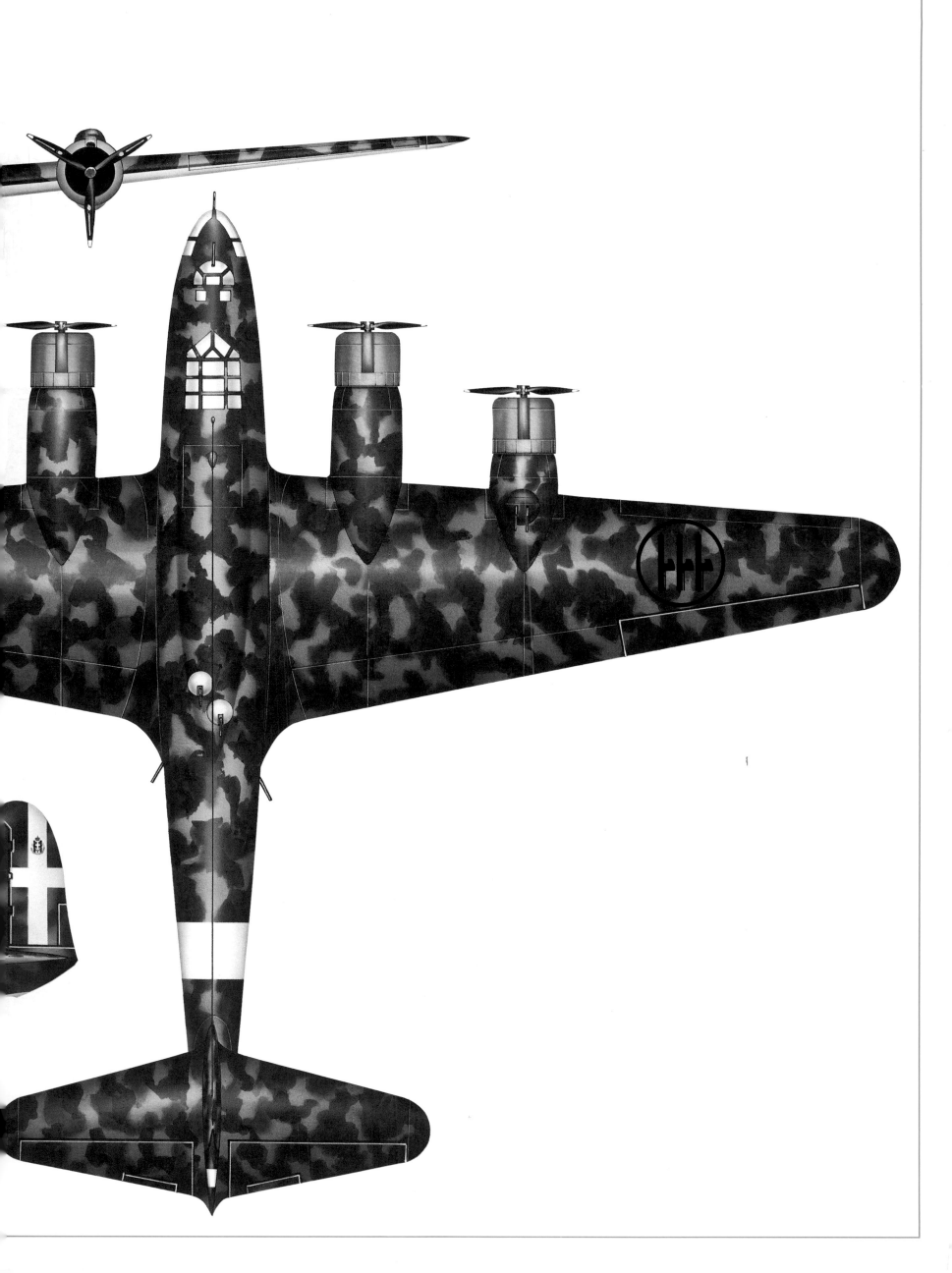

The Re.2005 *Sagittario* (Sagittarius), defined by many as «the most beautiful aircraft of World War II,» was the final development in the line of fighters built by Reggiane during the conflict. This elegant and powerful combat plane was also the third exponent of the so-called Series 5 and, together with the Fiat G.55 and the Macchi M.C. 205, it worthily represented the third generation of the *Regia Aeronautica*'s fighters. However, like its two rivals, the *Sagittario* arrived on the scene too late, and its operative career was virtually non existent: only 30 or so came off the assembly lines before production was halted by the armistice.

The project was launched in 1941, and the first of the two prototypes was completed in December of the same year. Compared to its predecessors, the Re.2001 and Re.2002, the new model was in many respects an entirely different aircraft. Although the wings were very similar in plan, their structure and profile were very different and improved. The main landing gear, which retracted outward, marked a total break with Reggiane's building traditions; moreover, the fuselage, onto which a 1,475 hp German Daimler Benz DB 605 engine was fitted, was characterized by carefully studied aerodynamic lines and was very stable. As for the armament, it was intended to install three 20 mm cannons (two in the wings and a third to fire through the propeller hub) and two 12.7 mm machine guns in the engine housing and synchronized.

However, preparation of the aircraft went ahead slowly, due mainly to delays in the supply of the power plants, which had to be sent directly from Germany. It was not until April 1942 that the new fighter was ready for tests, and its first «official» flight took place on May 9. In practice, the aircraft had already made its maiden flight a week before, although the test had ended with an accident: during landing, due to the collapse of one of the landing gear legs, the prototype had been slightly damaged following a long slide down the runway.

In the meantime, the new Fiat and Macchi fighters had already taken to the air, and the Re.2005 was soon submitted to a long series of comparative tests. These brought to light the excellent overall characteristics of the *Sagittario*, above all its qualities as far as speed and handling were concerned: the prototype reached 421 mph (678 km/h) at 6,578 ft (2,000 m), a performance worthy of all respect. The only complaint was a certain structural weakness in the rear part of the fuselage, which led the judging committee to classify the Reggiane fighter in third place. However, production was not authorized immediately. Initially 16 «zero series» aircraft were ordered, then a further 18 preseries aircraft, and it was not until February 1943 that the final request for 750

definitive aircraft was made. However, these were to remain on paper.

The first deliveries of the Re.2005 occurred in March 1943, and its operative career began in May with the 362nd Squadron of the 22nd Land Fighter Group, based at Naples-Capodichino. The unit was sent to Sicily at the time of the Allied landings and at the end of June was based at Capua, from where it defended the area against Allied bombings. In this period, the pilots complained of structural weaknesses once again, and on August 26 it was decided to suspend the use of the aircraft in combat.

At the time of the armistice, the seven *Sagittario* that remained in the 22nd Group were destroyed by *Regia Aeronautica* personnel. Not one aircraft was employed by the cobelligerent aviation, while six Re.2005s were used in training by the aviation of the *Repubblica Sociale Italiana* during the first six months of 1944. However, the Germans (who had shown an interest in the fighter) captured a certain number of aircraft (probably 13) and took them to Germany. The reports concerning their use in the Luftwaffe are somewhat confused: according to some sources these aircraft were used toward the end of 1943 in the defense of Berlin against Allied raids; according to others, these Re.2005s were transferred to Rumania and used as interceptors.

---

color plate

Reggiane Re.2005 362nd Squadron 22nd Fighter Group *Regia Aeronautica* - Sigonella, Sicily - Italy July, 1943

Aircraft:	Reggiane Re.2005
Nation:	Italy
Manufacturer:	Officine Meccaniche Reggiane S.p.A.
Type:	Fighter
Year:	1943
Engine:	Daimler Benz DB 605A, 12-cylinder V, liquid-cooled, 1,475 hp
Wingspan:	36 ft 2 in (11.00 m)
Length:	28 ft 8 in (8.73 m)
Height:	10 ft 4 in (3.15 m)
Weight:	7,969 lb (3,610 kg)
Maximum speed:	390 mph (628 km/h) at 22,861 ft (6,950 m)
Ceiling:	39,473 ft (12,000 m)
Range:	776 miles (1,250 m)
Armament:	3×20 mm cannons, 2 machine guns
Crew:	1

A Reggiane Re.2005 in service with the *Regia Aeronautica*.

A Reggiane Re.2005 that was damaged and captured at the airport of Sigonella (Sicily) in July, 1943.

REGGIANE Re.2005

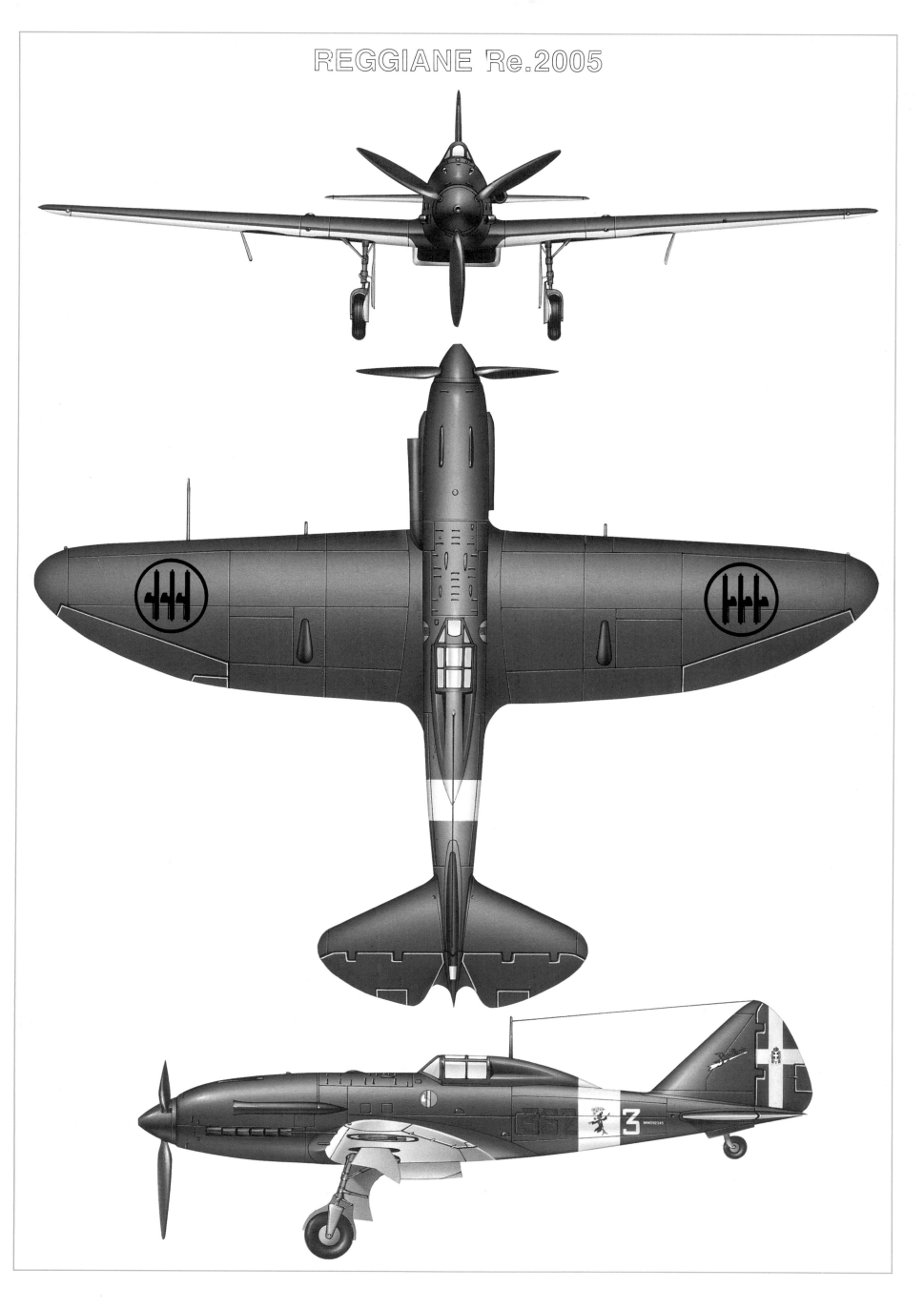

Even a small nation like Finland entirely designed and built its own combat plane during World War II. This was the Myrsky (Tempest), a fighter which did not possess outstanding characteristics. Fifty were built in two production variants by Valtion Lentokonetehdas, the state aeronautical industry founded back in 1928.

The project, entrusted to E. Wageluis, the technical director, was launched in 1941, and appeared in the form of a prototype the following year. It was a low wing monoplane with retractable rear tricycle landing gear, a wood and metal airframe and covering and a Swedish version of the Pratt & Whitney SCG-3 Twin Wasp built on license and capable of generating 1,650 hp. The armament planned consisted of four machine guns installed in the fuselage, synchronized to fire through the propeller disc.

The first prototype was followed by three pre-series aircraft, designated Myrsky I, and together these were submitted to tests and initial evaluations which lasted for a lengthy period. In fact, there were many structural problems which the technicians had to solve before creating the definitive production version, the Myrsky II. The wings' composite covering tended to become detached under strong pressure. In addition the main landing gear proved to be dangerously weak and the joinings of the halfwings showed signs of giving way, making it necessary to redesign them completely, as well as to reinforce the whole wing structure. In fact, due to these problems (to which was added a pronounced lateral instability during flight testing), all four initial aircraft were destroyed during flying accidents, and consequently, the timing of the entire production program was subject to serious delays.

All the modifications which originated from the test flights were incorporated into the production version, 46 of which were built during 1944. However, the Myrsky II went into service too late to contest the Soviet offensive against Finland. The rapid evolution of the conflict and the peace treaty stipulated in September 1944, led to a drastic change in the scenario and the Finnish fighters were employed against their ex-allies, the Germans, above all in the role of tactical support. In combat the Myrsky was not particularly successful, and moreover did not meet with the full approval of its pilots.

Prior to September 1944, a new version of the fighter had been prepared, with the aim of improving the aircraft's mediocre performance. It was designated Myrsky III and 10 were put into production. However, they were never completed.

color plate
Myrsky II 26 HLeLv (Fighter Group) Finnish Air Force - Kemi Finland, 1944

Aircraft:	VL Myrsky II
Nation:	Finland
Manufacturer:	Valtion Lentokonetehdas
Type:	Fighter
Year:	1944
Engine:	SFA-Pratt & Whitney Twin Wasp SCG-3, 14-cylinder radial, air-cooled, 1,650 hp
Wingspan:	36 ft 4 in (11.00 m)
Length:	27 ft 5 in (8.35 m)
Height:	9 ft 10 in (3.00 m)
Weight:	7,088 lb (3,211 kg)
Maximum speed:	328 mph (529 km/h) at 10,690 ft (3,250 m)
Ceiling:	29.572 ft (8,990 m)
Range:	579 miles (933 km)
Armament:	4 machine guns
Crew:	1

The first Myrsky I, bearing Finnish insignia during the period of the alliance with the Germans.

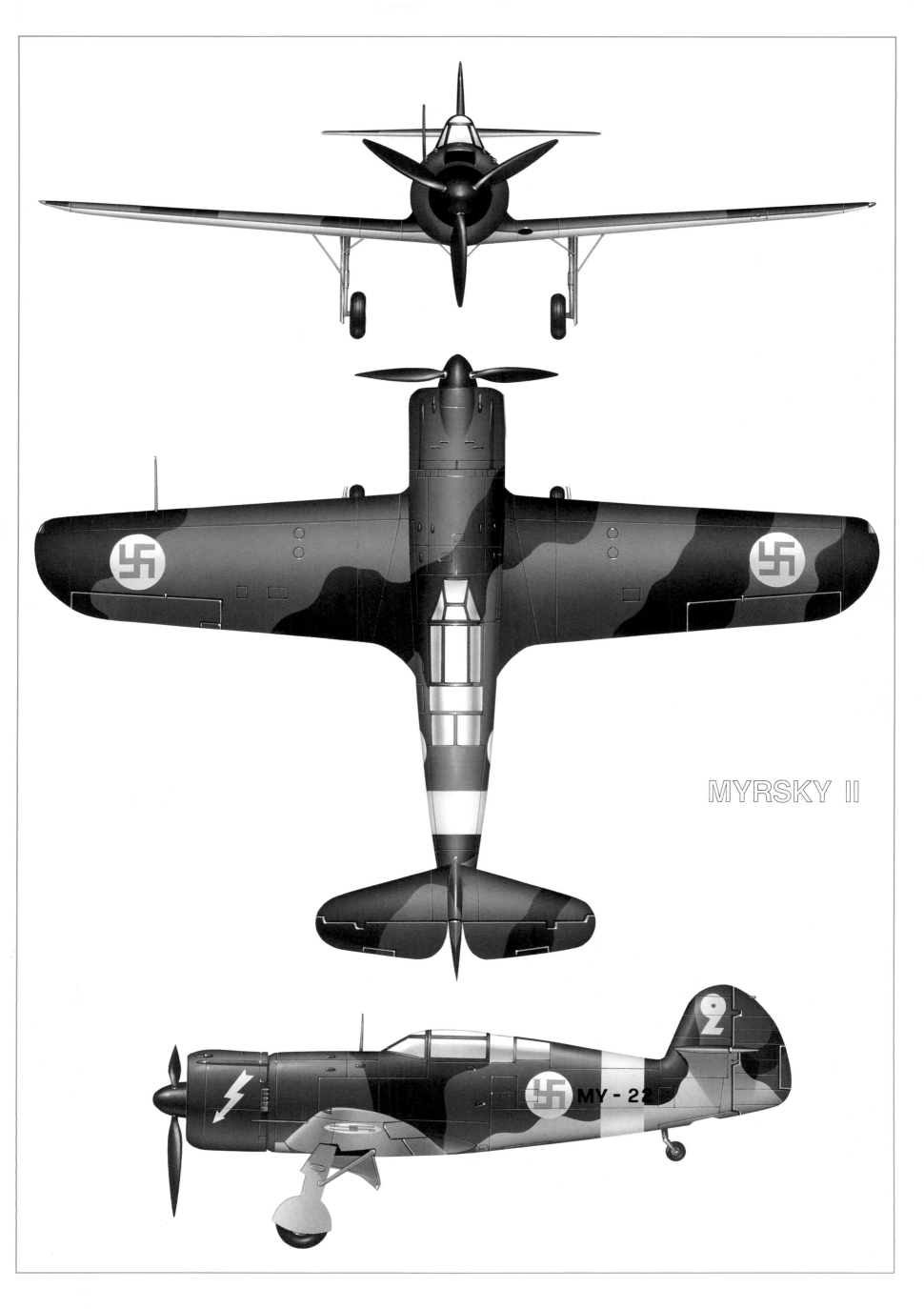

MYRSKY II

An IAR 80B taxiing a frozen runway.

The IAR 80 was the only Rumanian-designed fighter plane of World War II. This slender and fast monoplane marked the crowning point in a series of projects, designed by the Rumanian Aeronautical Industry (based in Brasov), that had evolved during the 1930s through a family of fighters, all of which were derived from the Model IAR 11. From this all-metal low cantilever wing monoplane with fixed landing gear were derived the IAR 12 (1932), the IAR 13, the IAR 14, and the IAR 15, all dating to 1933.

The IAR 80, which appeared in the form of a prototype in April 1939, was developed by a group of designers led by Ion Grossu on the basis of experience acquired during the building on license of the Polish fighter, the PZL P-24. The new fighter retained the front section of the fuselage, the tail fins, and the engine with relative housing and supports of this aircraft. However, the central and rear sections of the fuselage and the wing were entirely new. The IAR 80 was an all-metal low-wing monoplane with retractable landing gear and open cockpit. As for the armament, the installation of four 7.92 mm Browning FN machine guns in the wings was planned. The fighter was powered by a Gnome-Rhone 14K radial engine built on license by IAR and generating 940 hp.

After evaluation tests, the IAR 80 was judged favorably and went into production. The first production series aircraft came off the assembly lines in 1941 and were slightly modified with regard to the prototype. A sliding canopy was adopted, providing an excellent field of vision, while the defensive armament was also reinforced and a more powerful engine was fitted. The aircraft of the first series (50 built in all) retained the four 7.92 mm weapons. The 90 IAR 80As that came off the assembly lines had six machine guns, while in the 30 IAR 80Bs two weapons were replaced by others of greater caliber (13.2 mm Brownings). Deliveries to the units of the Rumanian air force began early in 1942.

A later variant (designated IAR 81) was also derived from the IAR 80 and was intended mainly for the role of dive-bomber. The first series (50 built in all) was armed with six machine guns installed in the wings and could carry one 550 lb (250 kg) bomb, thanks to a support on the belly, and a further four weighing 110 lb (50 kg) in racks beneath the wings. Although the second variant (the IAR 81A, of which 29 were built) was provided with the same offensive load as its predecessor, the weapons on the wings consisted of four 7.92 mm machine guns and two 20 mm caliber cannons. The third version (IAR 81B, of which 50 were built) was intended as a long-range fighter: it retained the same armament as the previous model and was built to carry two extra fuel tanks beneath the wings. The last variant (IAR 81C) was conceived as a multirole aircraft, considering that it could operate both as a dive-bomber and a fighter. A total of 137 were built before the Brasov factory began to produce the German Messerschmitt Bf.109 G fighter on license.

The IAR fighter's operative career was intensive, especially during the last two years of the war, when it was used to defend national territory against the attacks of American bombers. However, many survived the war and were modified for training, not being withdrawn until the end of 1952.

color plate
IAR 80A Rumanian Air Force - Rumania 1943

Aircraft:	IAR 80A
Nation:	Rumania
Manufacturer:	Rumanian Aeronautical Industry (I.A.R.)
Type:	Fighter
Year:	1942
Engine:	IAR14K - 1000A, 14-cylinder radial, air-cooled, 1,025 hp
Wingspan:	32 ft 10 in (10.00 m)
Length:	26 ft 10 in (8.16 m)
Height:	11 ft 10 in (3.60 m)
Weight:	5,485 lb (2,485 kg)
Maximum speed:	316 mph (510 km/h) at 13,059 ft (3,970 m)
Ceiling:	34,539 ft (10,500 m)
Range:	583 miles (940 km)
Armament:	6 machine guns
Crew:	1

An IAR 80 before take-off for a combat mission.

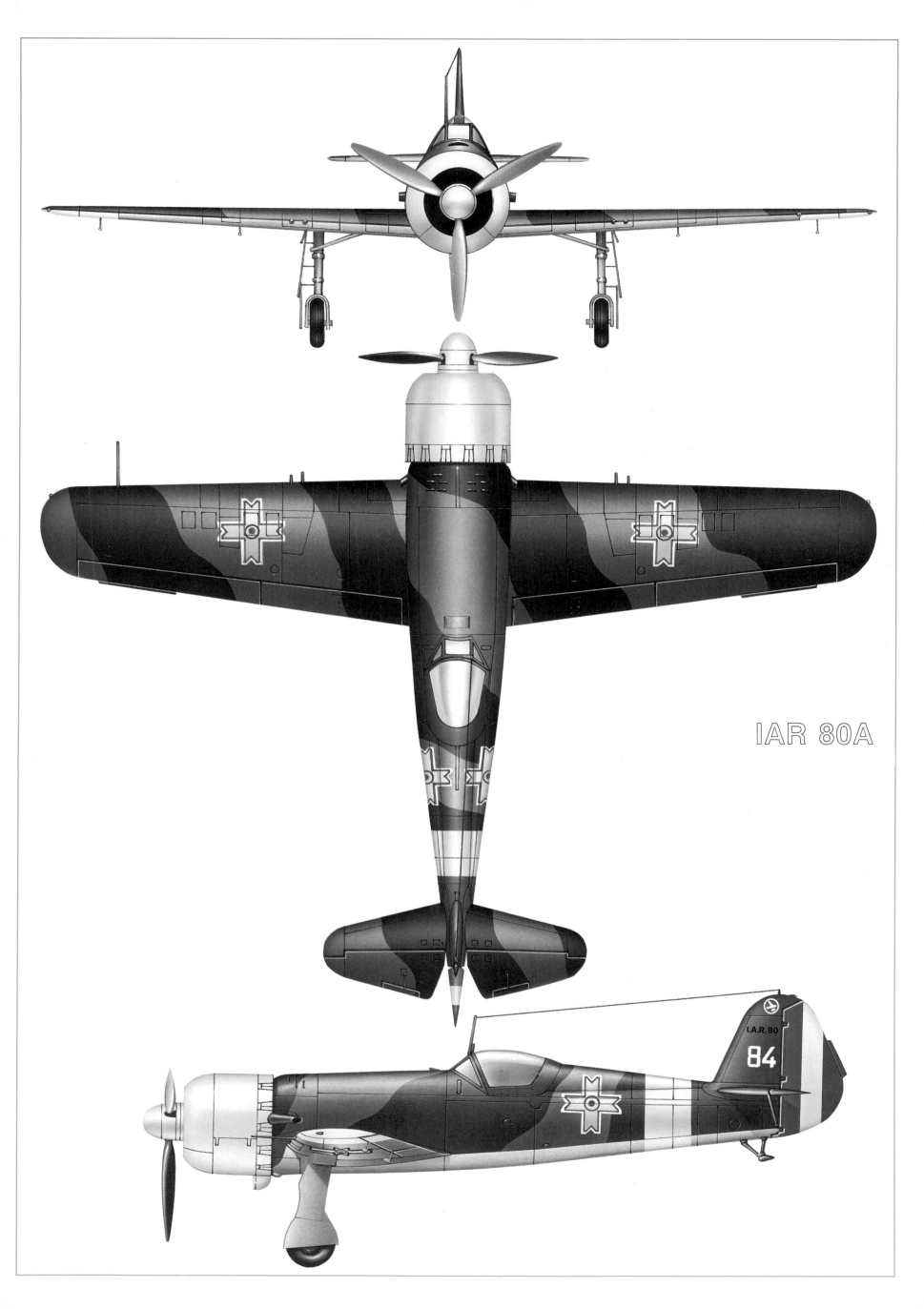

IAR 80A

I.A.R. 80

84

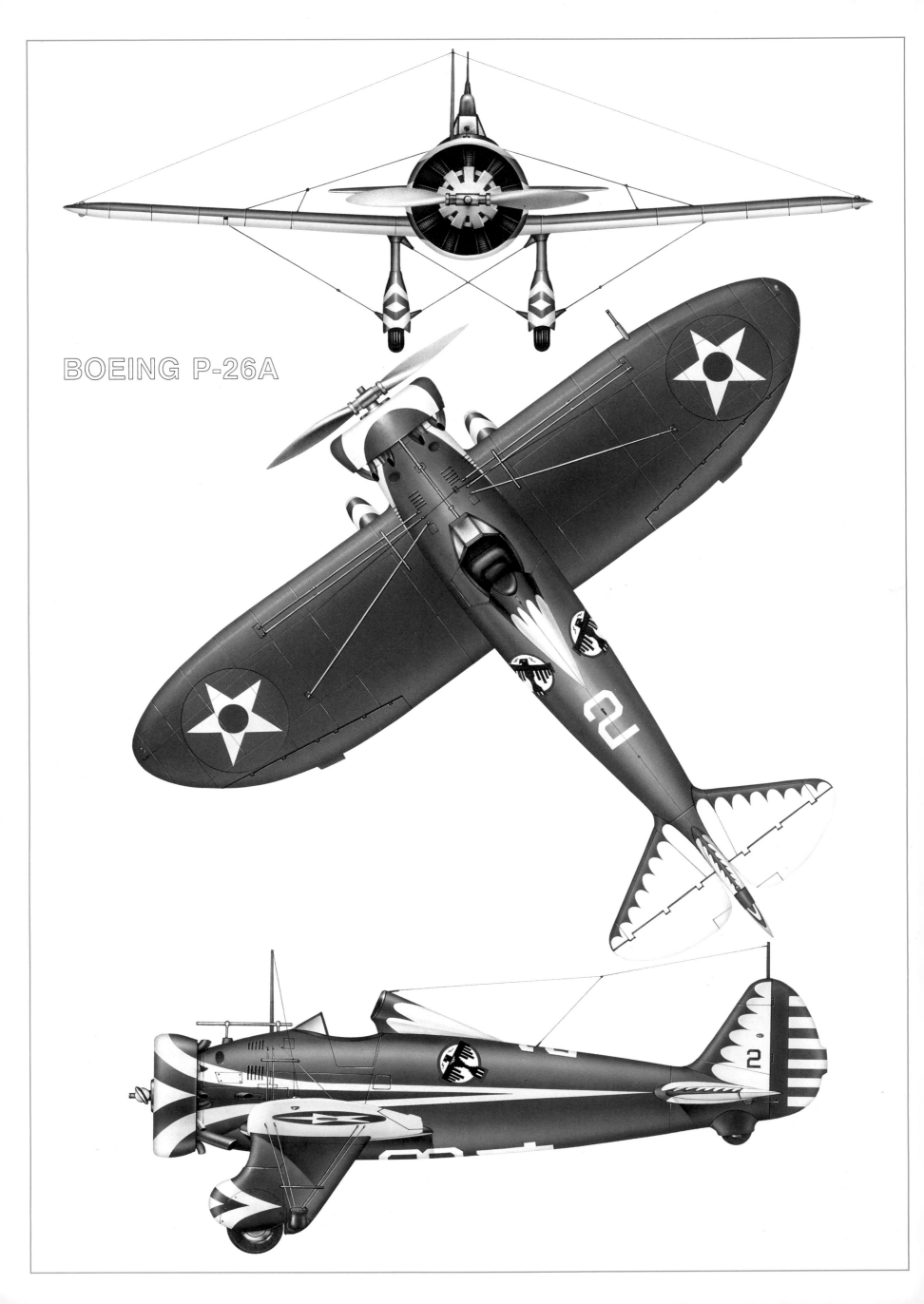

BOEING P-26A

The Boeing P-26 was the first all-metal monoplane fighter to be adopted by the U.S. Army Air Corps. It was produced in 1934, and although clearly a transitional plane, for over five years this small, agile combat aircraft equipped the front-line units based in national territory, in the Panama Canal Zone, and in Hawaii.

It was withdrawn only on the eve of the United States entering the war. Despite this, the P-26 took part in military action, even if bearing the insignia of other nations. In 1936, 11 planes were sold to China, where they were used in the brave struggle against Japanese aggression, while other planes sold to the Philippines took part in the defense of the archipelago at the time of the earliest military operations in the Pacific.

The program that led to the creation of the P-26 was launched by Boeing in September 1931, in collaboration with the U.S. Army Air Corps. The intention of producing a modern airplane, however, was fulfilled only in part. In fact, although the project had some innovative features, such as the all-metal structure and the low-wing configuration, from many points of view it also included some by-then outdated ones, such as the fixed landing gear and the noncantilever wings. All this was surprising, seeing that Boeing had already anticipated extremely advanced technical constructions in other projects (such as the 1930 postal plane, the Monomail).

The definitive P-26 prototype, designated XP-936, made its first flight on March 20 the following year. Immediately after, it began testing with the front-line units, and an order was subsequently placed for 111 production models. These had the builder's designation of Model 266 and the official designation of P-26A, although they were immediately nicknamed Peashooter. Compared to the prototype, they featured many improvements, including modifications to the wing structure and the fitting of radio equipment and emergency floats. The armament consisted of two forward fixed 12.7 mm machine guns (or one 12.7 mm and one 7.7 mm) plus a bomb load of up to 200 lb (91 kg). The first production model took to the air on January 10, 1934, and delivery to the units began immediately after, the last aircraft ordered coming off the production line at the end of June.

A second order followed for a further 25 planes, featuring the use of a more powerful engine; two of these were completed as P-26Bs (Pratt & Whitney R-1340-33 injection engine) and 23 as P-26Cs (minor alterations to the power plant). Many of the latter type were subsequently brought up to the standards of the previous version. During production, the design underwent an important change, dictated by the need to reduce landing speed, in the form of landing flaps fitted on the trailing edge of the wing. This technical solution was consequently introduced into planes already in service, as well as those still in production.

Production was completed by 12 planes destined for export (the Model 281), 11 of which went to China and one to Spain.

color plate
Boeing P-26A 34th Pursuit Squadron U.S. Army Air Corps - 1934

Aircraft:	Boeing P-26A
Nation:	USA
Manufacturer:	Boeing Airplane Co.
Type:	Fighter
Year:	1934
Engine:	Pratt & Whitney R-1340-27 Wasp, 9-cylinder radial, air-cooled, 507 hp
Wingspan:	27 ft 11 in (8.52 m)
Length:	23 ft 7 in (7.19 m)
Height:	10 ft (3.06 m)
Weight:	2,995 lb (1,340 kg)
Maximum speed:	234 mph at 7,500 ft (377 km/h at 2,286 m)
Ceiling:	27,400 ft (8,352 m)
Range:	934 miles (580 km)
Armament:	2 machine guns; 200 lb (91 kg) of bombs
Crew:	1

A Boeing P-26A of the 73rd Attack Group with its brightly colored livery.

BOEING B-17G

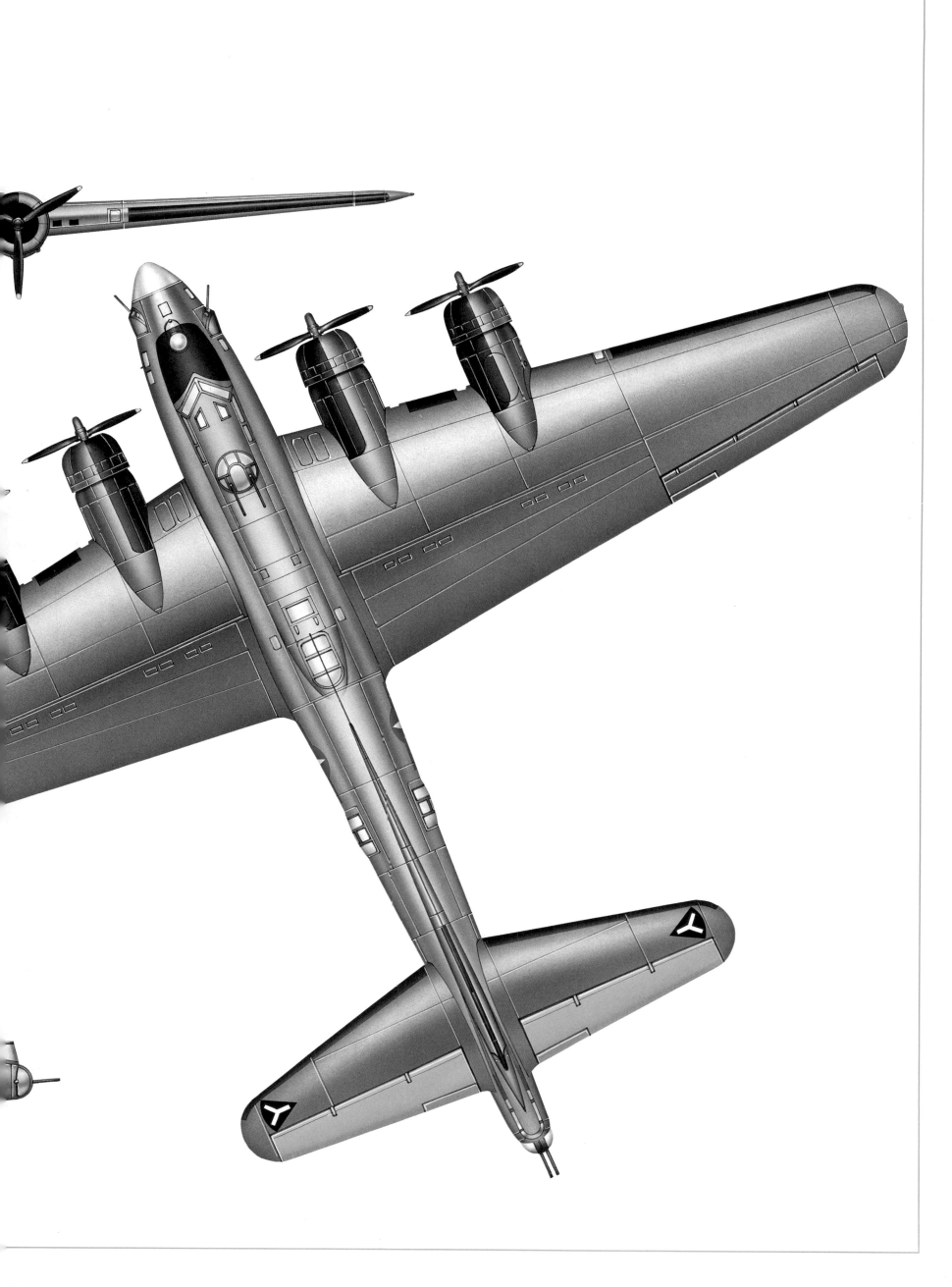

Rarely in the history of aviation has an aircraft become both a true symbol of military power and a myth for pilots and crew. This aircraft was the Boeing B-17 Flying Fortress, the first strategic bomber used in combat by the United States during World War II and the aircraft that contributed perhaps more than any other to the annihilation of the Third Reich and the conclusion of the war in Europe. In all, a total of 12,731 B-17s were built (without interruption) in the course of the war, and their most fierce and intensive use is marked by two dates in particular: August 17, 1942, when daylight bombing raids on Europe commenced; and January 27, 1943, when similar bombing raids on Germany began.

Project 299, as Boeing called it, was launched in the summer of 1934, on the basis of specifications issued by the Army requesting a multiengine bomber to be used in the defense of American territory against a hypothetical invader. In particular, the aircraft was to be capable of carrying a bomb load of 2,002 lb (907 kg) for a distance ranging from 1,025 miles (1,650 km) to 2,175 miles (3,500 km) at speeds between 200 mph (320 km/h) and 250 mph (400 km/h). Boeing's designers interpreted the concept of multiengine in its ''widest'' sense and, instead of concentrating on proposals for an aircraft powered by two engines, following conventional practice at the time, made use of the experience acquired in building the Model 247 civilian transport plane, as well as the solutions studied for a bomber that was still in the process of development, the Model 294. Thus, the prototype assumed the form of a large low-wing four-engine aircraft, with a circular-section fuselage and partially retractable main landing gear. It made its maiden flight on July 28, 1935, and slightly less than a month later, the aircraft revealed its capabilities when it covered a distance of 2,110 miles (3,400 km) nonstop in nine hours. Following official evaluations, the Douglas B-18 emerged as the winner of the contest, although the Boeing project's great potential was also recognized when, on January 17, 1936, an order was placed for 13 preseries aircraft, to be used for flight tests and operational evaluation. The first of these aircraft (designated Y1B-17) took to the air on December 2, 1936, while the others were delivered between March 1 and August 5 the following year.

Following a series of evaluation tests, the results (especially after the installation of Wright engines with superchargers) were so promising that the USAAC requested that it go into production immediately. The first order was placed in 1938, with a request for 39 B-17Bs; in 1939, these were followed by 38 B-17Cs (provided with more powerful engines, armor and better defensive armament), and by 42 B-17Ds, which were basically identical to their predecessors, in 1940. The last two versions were the first to see

combat duty: from May 1941, with the British, and immediately after Pearl Harbor with the Americans. On December 10, 1941, the aircraft that survived the Japanese attack had the honor of carrying out the first American offensive attack of the conflict, against Japanese shipping.

In 1941, a turning point occurred, as far as production was concerned, with the appearance of the B-17E. The entire rear section of the aircraft was radically altered in order to provide greater stability and to allow for the installation of a defensive gun position in the tail. The armament was then increased, with the addition of two turrets, one on the back and the other in the belly, provided with 12,7 mm machine guns. The B-17E was the first to be built in any great number, 512 being produced in all, and it was followed on the assembly lines by 3,400 B-17Fs (the aircraft made its maiden flight on May 20, 1942), with even heavier armament. The total production of the final variant, the B-17G, was much greater and, from 1943 onward, it was sent in increasing numbers to the European front: in all, no fewer than 8,685 aircraft came off the assembly lines. Thanks to experiences in combat, the defensive armament of these Fortresses was increased still further, with the installation of a ''chin'' turret below the nose.

color plate

Boeing B-17G 463rd Bomber Group 15th Air Corps U.S. Army Air Force - Italy 1945

Aircraft:	Boeing B-17G
Nation:	USA
Manufacturer:	Boeing Aircraft Co.
Type:	Bomber
Year:	1943
Engine:	4 Wright R-1820-97 Cyclone, 9-cylinder radial, air-cooled, 1,200 hp each
Wingspan:	103 ft 9 in (31.62 m)
Length:	74 ft 9 in (22.70 m)
Height:	19 ft 1 in (5.82 m)
Weight:	65,500 lb (29,710 kg) loaded
Maximum speed:	287 mph (462 km/h) at 25,000 ft (7,620 m)
Ceiling:	35,600 ft (10,850 m)
Range:	3,400 miles (5,200 km)
Armament:	13 machine guns; 17,600 lb (7,985 kg) of bombs
Crew:	10

A formation of preseries YB-17s during operative tests in 1937.

A factory fresh B-17G with all metal finish and its formidable defensive armament.

With the release of the two atomic bombs on Hiroshima and Nagasaki, the dates August 6 and 9, 1945 marked both the end of the war and the beginning of the atomic age. The aircraft which will always remain associated with these two dates in history was the Boeing B-29 Superfortress, the largest and most powerful bomber of the conflict and the first strategic weapon at a worldwide level. The construction of this aircraft occupied the American aeronautical industry in the largest and most complex program of the war from a technical and technological point of view. It embodied the synthesis of the enormous contribution that the bomber aircraft's development gave to the conflict with thousands of companies involved in the production of components and systems destined to feed the assembly lines. In all, 3,970 B-29s were built, 2,000 of these being delivered between 1943 and 1945. In addition to the basic version, there were two principal variants of the B-29: the A, with a slightly larger wing and modifications to the fuel capacity and armament (1,222 built) and the B (311), in which the defensive armament (apart from the machine guns in the tail) was removed.

The specifications which led to the creation of the B-29 were issued on January 29, 1940, and Boeing, Consolidated, Douglas, and Lockheed all took part in the contest. The latter two companies later withdrew from the competition, and on September 6, the first contracts were drawn up with Boeing and Consolidated for the construction and development of the prototypes, designated XB-29 and XB-32, respectively. Boeing found itself at a great advantage compared to its rival. Since 1937, the Seattle-based company had been preparing a strategic bomber prototype and although this aircraft (Model 294, designated XB-15, was developed on the basis of a USAAC request issued four years earlier) had remained at an experimental stage, it allowed the technicians to prepare further studies and to update the basic project continuously. Thus, considering the excessive amount of time taken to develop the XB-32, the Boeing Model 345 (the internal designation of the XB-29 prototype) proved to be the winner.

The course of the war in Europe led to the program being sped up in a remarkable way. In the summer of 1941, a request was made for 14 pre-series YB-29s, and immediately after the first orders were placed for 500 production series aircraft to which a further 1,000 were added in September 1942. On the 21st of that month, the first prototype made its maiden flight in Seattle, with test pilot Eddie Allen at the controls, followed by the second prototype on December 28 (Allen and the 11 technicians lost their lives on board this very aircraft, which crashed on February 18, 1943). The first YB-29 took to the air on June 26, and at the same time as the appearance of the first pre-series aircraft, the vast production program was prepared. In addition to the two Boeing assembly lines at Renton and Wichita, this also included the participation of Bell in Marietta and of Martin in Omaha.

The great bomber's preparation was not simple, and during the initial tests, it was the engines and propellers which caused the most problems. In the first 175 production series aircraft no fewer than 9,900 faults of various kinds had to be eliminated. The B-29 was a complex aircraft: it was an extremely long middle wing monoplane with forward tricycle landing gear, and with an entirely pressurized circular section fuselage (apart from the bomb hold). It was powered by four large Wright R-3350 Cyclone radial engines fed by two turbocompressors. The defensive armament consisted of 10-12 12.7 mm machine guns in four turrets that were remote-controlled from centralized positions and in the tail turret, which also housed a 20 mm cannon.

In 1943, the first unit meant to receive the new bombers, the 58th Very Heavy Bombardment Wing, was organized and rendered operative. Toward the year's end it was decided to employ the B-29 in the Pacific, where the 20th Bomber Command was ready to fight against the Japanese from bases in India and China. The first units reached these countries in the spring of 1944, and the first mission was carried out on June 5, on Bangkok. Ten days later, the first raid on Japan occurred, with an attack on the steel works at Kyushu. This marked the beginning of an increasingly intense and devastating series of raids which, beginning on November 24, were carried out from the Mariana Islands bases. On that very same day, the first mission on Tokyo was completed, and until August 6, 1945, the B-29s specialized in attacks using incendiary bombs, initially by day, and then by night at low altitude.

---

color plate

Boeing F-13A (photoreconnaissance version of the B-29) 3rd Photoreconnaissance Squadron 20th Air Force U.S. Army Air Force - Mariana Islands, 1944-45. Another F-13 was christened with the same nick-name of Double Exposure

---

The assembly lines of the Flying Superfortress in the Boeing factory.

A picture following the beginning of an era. The B-29 christened Enola Gay lands on the island of Tinian on its return from the mission on Hiroshima, during which it released the first atomic bomb.

Aircraft:	Boeing B-29
Nation:	USA
Manufacturer:	Boeing
Type:	Bomber
Year:	1944
Engine:	4 Wright R-3350-23 Cyclone, 18-cylinder radial, air-cooled, 2,231 hp each
Wingspan:	141 ft 7 in (43.05 m)
Length:	99 ft 3 in (30.18 m)
Height:	29 ft 8 in (9.02 m)
Takeoff weight:	124,161 lb (56,245 kg)
Maximum speed:	357 mph (576 km/h) at 25,065 ft (7,620 m)
Ceiling:	31,907 ft (9,700 m)
Range:	3,247 miles (5,230 km)
Armament:	1 × 20 mm cannon; 10 machine guns; 19,867 lb (9,000 kg) of bombs
Crew:	10

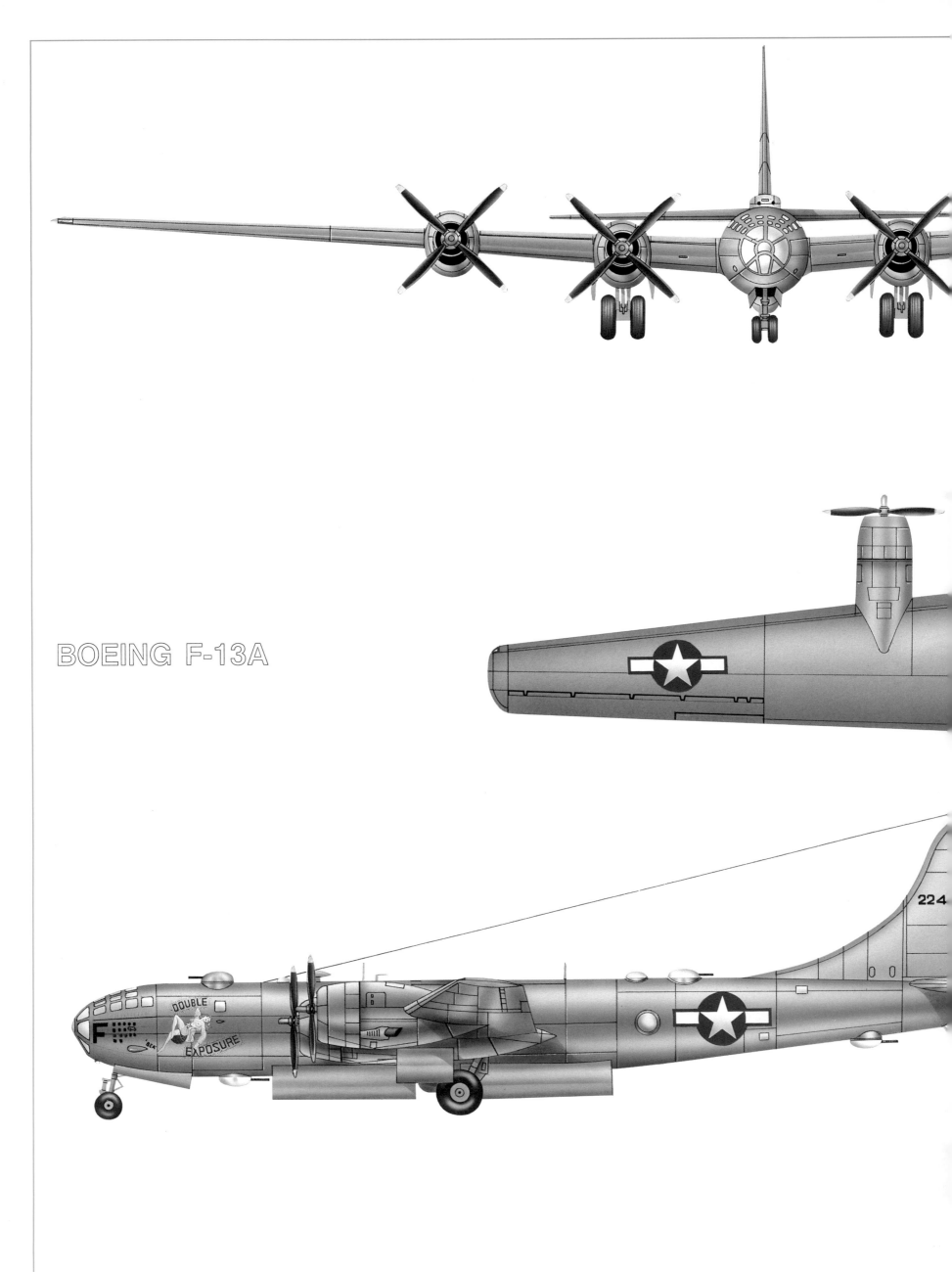

BOEING F-13A

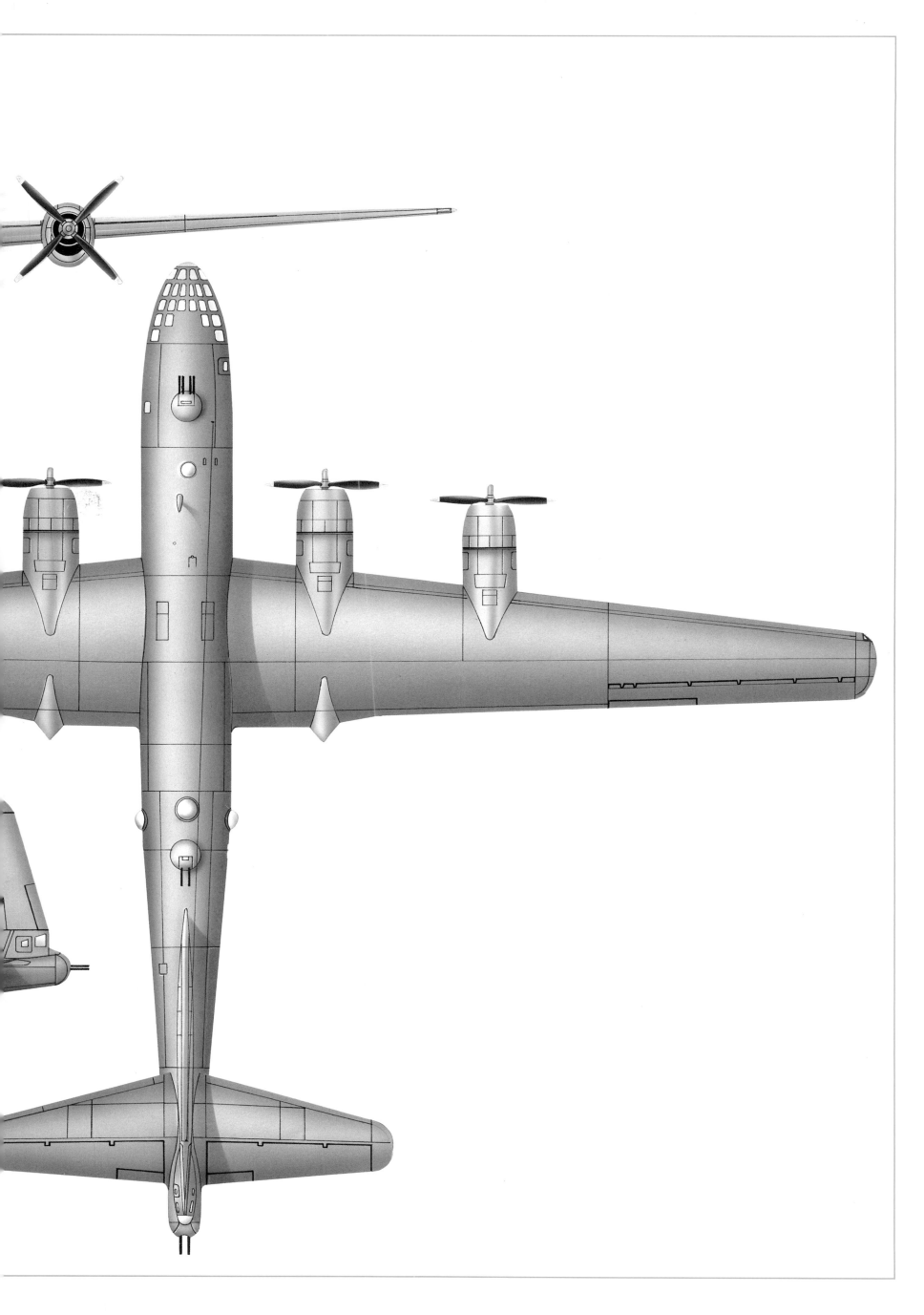

MARTIN BALTIMORE Mk.V

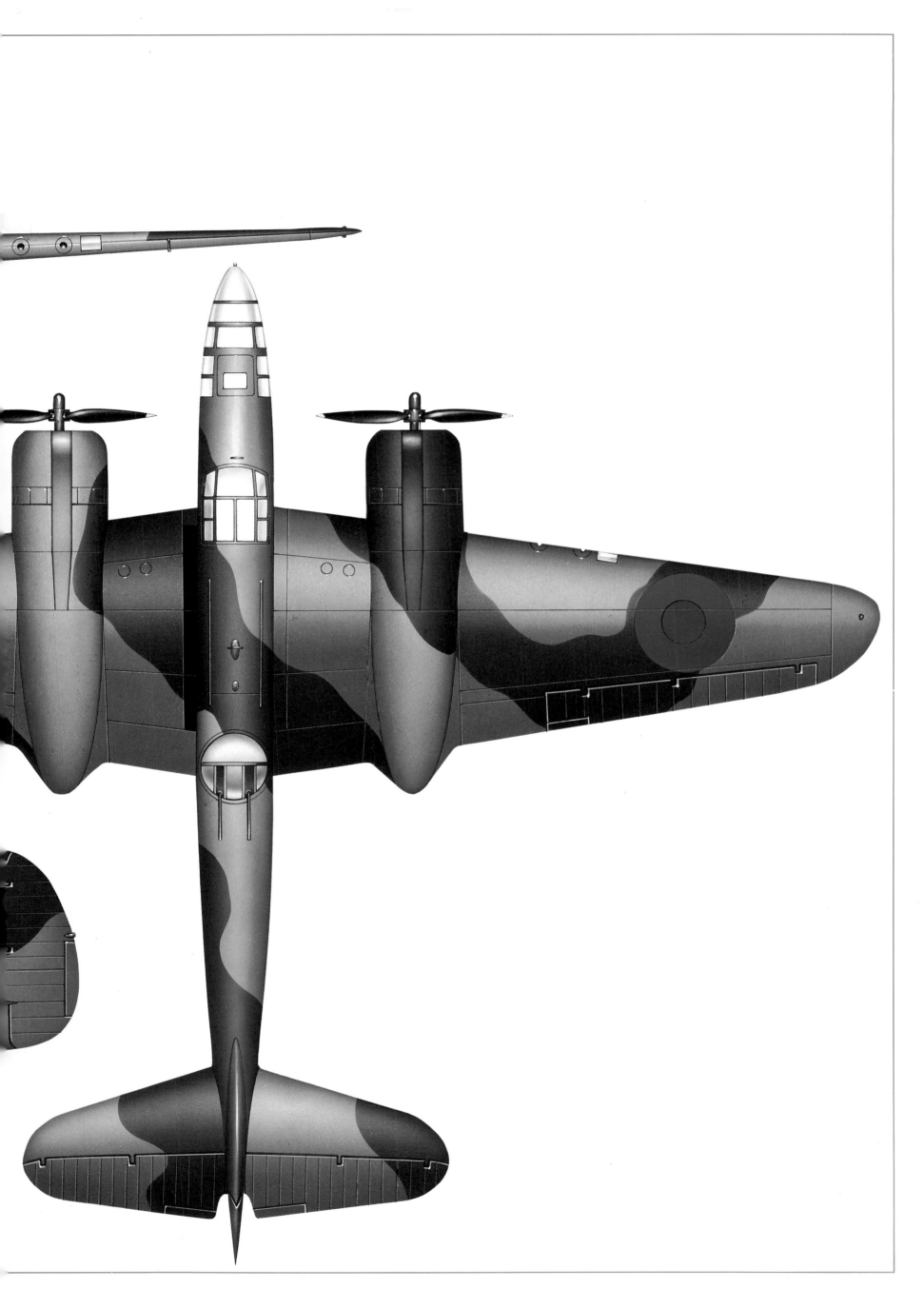

The family of Martin Maryland and Baltimore light bombers originated back in 1937, on the basis of a request by the U.S.Army Air Corps, although paradoxically these aircraft never served bearing American insignia, but those of the French and British air forces, which received all those produced.

The Maryland prototype (Model 167) made its maiden flight on March 14, 1939: it was a two-engine middle to low-wing aircraft with retractable rear tricycle landing gear and a three-man crew. However, following evaluation tests, the USAAC rejected the aircraft. Production went ahead nevertheless, on the basis of an order for 115 placed by France. Deliveries did not begin until October 1939, when orders had been increased by a further 100 aircraft, although only 140 (designated Martin 167 A-3) reached the *Armée de l'Air*. Following the fall of France, it was the British RAF that received and sent into service the remaining 75 aircraft, to which another 225 were subsequently added. The two-engined planes were designated Maryland Mk.I and Mk.II, and they went into operative service in September 1940.

It was in that year that the RAF requested a development of the basic model, characterized by more powerful engines and modifications to the fuselage, in order to make it larger and deeper. The defensive armament was also improved: in addition to those on the aircraft's back, it had four fixed machine guns on the wings and two in the belly, while the installation of a further four fixed weapons that fired backward was also foreseen in May 1940. British authorities signed an initial order for 400 aircraft, and the first prototype of the new bomber (designated Model 187 in the factory and christened Baltimore by the RAF) took to the air on June 14 of the following year. At the same time, an order was placed for another 575 aircraft, and the final order, for a further 600, was placed in July.

The first Baltimore Mk.Is (50 were built) reached Britain in October 1941 and were assigned initially to the conversion units. They began their operative career early the following year, with the aircraft of the Mk.II series (100 built), which differed from the previous one solely in the installation of two machine guns (instead of only one) on the back. The remaining production versions were characterized by the adoption of a hydraulically controlled turret in place of the manual one. These came off the assembly lines until May 1944: the Baltimore Mk.III (250 built, in service from July 1942) was fitted with more powerful Wright engines, as well as a Boulton Paul type turret with four machine guns, while a coupl-

ed system built by Martin was adopted in the subsequent 281 Mk.IIIAs (these aircraft also received the American A-30 designation). Production continued with 294 Baltimore Mk.IVs (A-30A in the USAAF), similar to the previous versions but with modifications to details, and 600 Mk.Vs, provided with Wright R-2600-29 engines capable of generating a maximum of 1,724 hp. The final two series became operative in the last months of 1943 and 1944 respectively.

The Baltimores were used mainly in the Mediterranean and North Africa, where they had a long and intensive career, especially during the Italian campaign. These aircraft did not fight bearing the insignia only of the RAF, but also those of other Allied Forces: the Australian, South African, Greek, Turkish air forces as well as the Free French and Italian Co-Belligerent air forces. In fact, it was in a Baltimore serving in the Balkan air force that Major Carlo Emanuele Buscaglia, the italian torpedo-plane ace, lost his life on August 7, 1944. After being held prisoner in the United States for a year, he succeeded in returning to his own country to fight in the aviation of the forces in the south.

---

color plate

Martin Baltimore Mk.V 454th Squadron Royal Air Force - Pescara, Italy 1944

Aircraft:	Martin Baltimore Mk.III
Nation:	USA
Manufacturer:	Glenn L. Martin Co.
Type:	Bomber
Year:	1942
Engine:	2 Wright R-2699-19, 14-cylinder radial, air-cooled, 1,683 hp each
Wingspan:	61 ft 5 in (18.69 m)
Length:	48 ft 7 in (14.78 m)
Height:	17 ft 11 in (5.41 m)
Weight:	21,278 lb (9,639 kg)
Maximum speed:	308 mph (496 km/h) at 13,032 ft (3,962 m)
Ceiling:	22,358 ft (6,797 m)
Range:	1,081 miles (1,741 km)
Armament:	8-10 machine guns (+4), 2,002 lb (907 kg) of bombs
Crew:	4

A Martin Baltimore in service with the Middle East Air Force in flight.

The first Allied bomber to carry out 200 combat missions was a 9th Air Force B-26B christened Flak Bait. This record is even more enviable if one considers that it was achieved by an aircraft that in the initial phase of its career, was not liked by the crews, because its excellent performance made it difficult to fly. However, once it was better known, the B-26 Marauder proved to be an extremely effective aircraft, and one of the most efficient in its category during World War II. In all, 5,157 came off the assembly lines between February 1941 and March 1945, serving on all fronts and in all theaters of operations. In particular, 522 of them served in the units of the British Royal Air Force and in those of the South African Air Force, in the Mediterranean.

The project was launched in 1939, in response to specifications issued by the USAAC on January 25, calling for a fast medium bomber with particular qualities as far as its range and ceiling were concerned. In September, the Glenn L. Martin company presented its Model 179, and the proposal was considered so superior to its rivals that it was accepted «on the drawing board» with an initial order being placed for 201 aircraft. The new plane was designed by Peyton M. Magruder, and was two-engined with high wings, a rounded fuselage, and aerodynamic lines. It had retractable forward tricycle landing gear and was powered by a pair of large Pratt & Whitney Double Wasp 18-cylinder engines.

The first B-26 made its maiden flight on November 25, 1940, and in the course of its initial flight tests confirmed the expectations of its technicians, achieving a maximum speed of 305 mph (508 km/h). However, in order to guarantee the high performance requested, the aircraft was characterized by a high wing load, greater than that of any other military aircraft. It was not, therefore, an easy plane to fly (especially during landing), and this did not facilitate training or the launching of its operative career. There were many accidents, and although the A version aircraft (139 built in all) were delivered in 1941, they did not see combat until April of the following year, in the Pacific. Production was even halted, and a specific inquiry launched to investigate the actual danger of the aircraft. Nevertheless, the commission decided to continue to build the B-26, introducing a series of modifications to improve its performance at low altitude and to perfect its maneuvering techniques.

In May 1942, production of the B-26B was launched. This was the version of which the most aircraft were built (1,883) and in which, apart from improvements to the armament, equipment, and the active and passive protection, a substantial modification was adopted, beginning with the B-10 subseries: the wingspan was lengthened by six feet (183 cm), with a subsequent increase in surface area and relative lowering of the wing load. The surface area of the tail fins and rudder were also increased.

However, as well as having more defensive armament, the next variant, the B-26C, was characterized by a further increase in weight. 1,235 of these aircraft were built and went into service in the USAAF toward the end of 1942, in North Africa. The final versions were the B-26F and the B-26G, which differed only slightly in their equipment. An attempt was made in both aircraft to further improve the takeoff and landing characteristics by increasing the angle of attack of the wing by 3.5 degrees. The last Marauder was delivered on March 30, 1945, and the aircraft that survived the conflict remained in service for another three years.

color plate

Martin B-26 598th Squadron 397th Bombardment Group 9th Air Force U.S. Army Air Force - England, June 1944

Marauder carrying out a raid on Germany.

A B-26 bomber returning to a base in Great Britain with only one engine working. The other was damaged during a raid on occupied France.

A Martin B-26 Marauder in flight. Note the machine guns on the sides of the fuselage.

Aircraft:	Martin B-26B-10
Nation:	USA
Manufacturer:	Glenn L. Martin Co.
Type:	Bomber
Year:	1942
Engine:	2 Pratt & Whitney R-2800-43 Double Wasp, 18-cylinder radial, air-cooled, 2,000 hp each
Wingspan:	71 ft 2 in (21.64 m)
Length:	58 ft 4 in (17.75 m)
Height:	21 ft 6 in (6.55 m)
Weight:	37,048 lb (16,783 kg)
Maximum speed:	281 mph (454 km/h) at 15,032 ft (4,570 m)
Ceiling:	21,052 ft (6,400 m)
Range:	1,149 miles (1,851 km)
Armament:	12 machine guns, 5,207 lb (2,359 kg) of bombs
Crew:	7

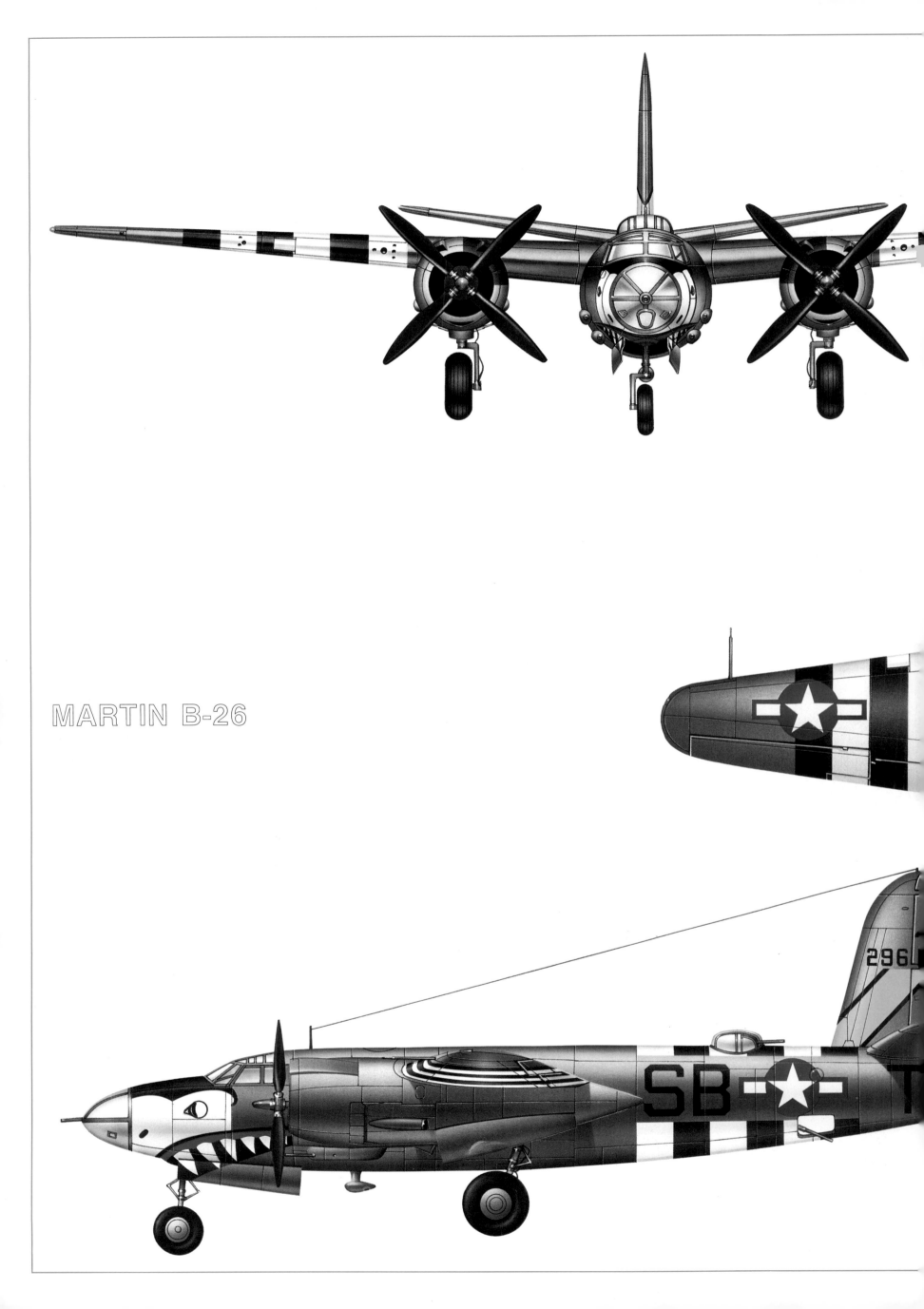

MARTIN B-26

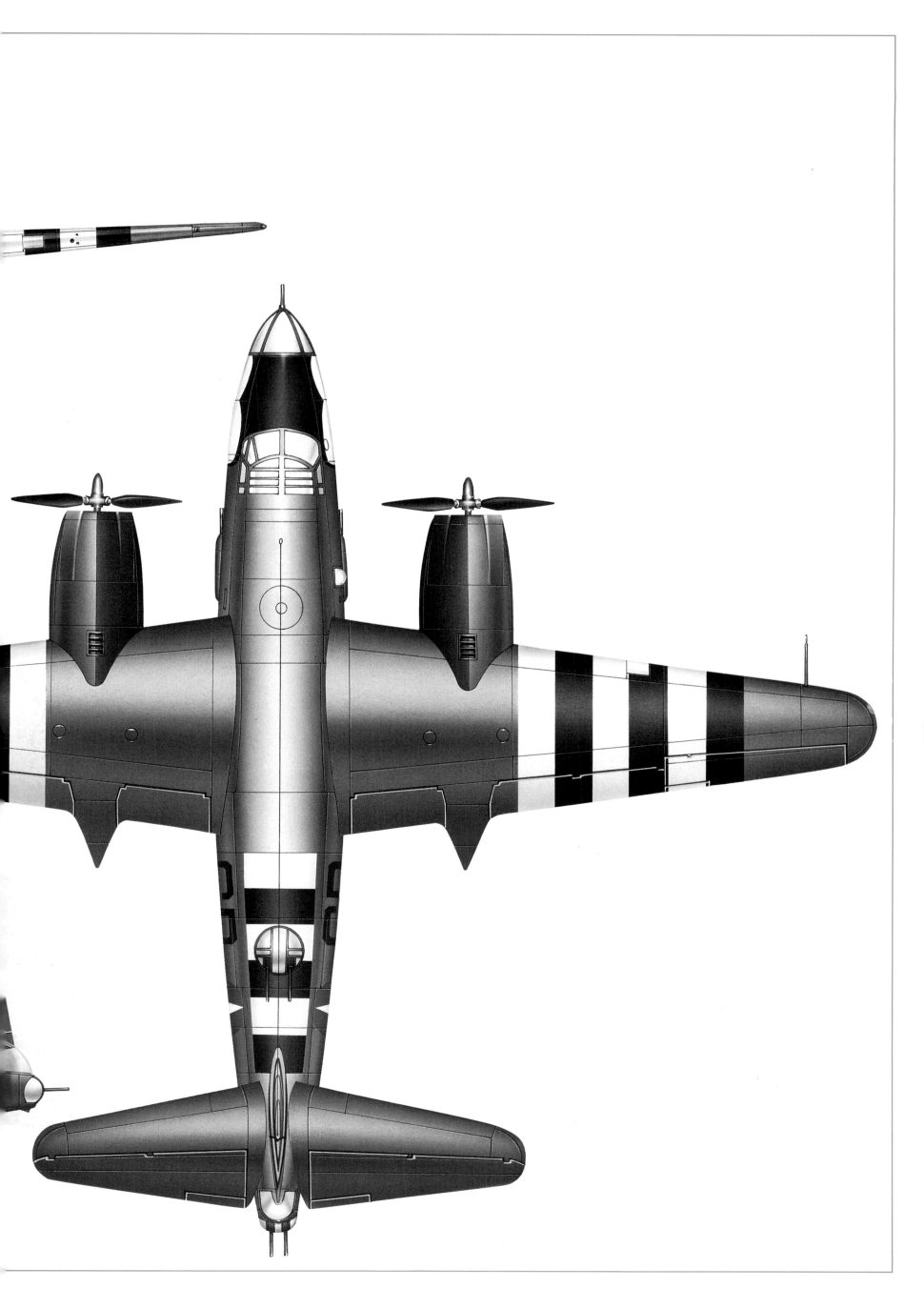

22

Douglas TBD-1

The Douglas TBD Devastator was the first all-metal low-wing monoplane with retractable landing gear to go into service in the U.S. Navy. However, although advanced at the time that occurred, this sturdy and reliable torpedo plane was virtually out-of-date when the war broke out and it found itself fighting with a clear disadvantage compared to the fierce fighters of the enemy. Proof of its being obsolete was dramatically provided on June 4, 1942, during the Battle of Midway: 15 TBD-1s that had taken off from the aircraft carrier *Hornet* to attack the Japanese naval force were literally wiped out (only one managed to return to the carrier) by antiaircraft fire and by the violent counterattack of the Mitsubishi A6M Zeros, against which they were practically defenseless. During the next two days of battle, the fate of the entire torpedo plane force on the carriers *Yorktown*, *Enterprise,* and *Hornet* was sealed, and it was reduced from a total of 41 aircraft to five. This episode in the air-sea battle in the Pacific also marked the end of the Devastator's operative career, which had commenced in November 1937 on board the aircraft carrier *Saratoga*. The total number of aircraft produced was not very high: 129 planes of a single production series version, designated TBD-1.

The project originated in 1934, on the basis of specifications issued by the U.S. Navy calling on manufacturers to design a new carrier-based torpedo plane to operate from the aircraft carriers then being built. As well as Douglas, several other companies participated: prototypes were also prepared by the Great Lakes Aircraft Corporation of Cleveland (XTBG-1, a biplane) and by the Hall Aluminum Aircraft Corporation of Bristol, Pennsylvania (XPTBH-2, a high-wing seaplane). Among the competitors, the XTBD-1 submitted by Douglas clearly appeared the most potent and technologically advanced. It was a low-wing monoplane (the cantilever wings could be folded back by means of hydraulic controls), with all-metal airframe and covering (apart from the rudder and the elevator, which were fabric covered). The main landing gear was partially retractable (the wheels protruding half-way, to facilitate emergency landing). The prototype was powered by an 811 hp Pratt & Whitney XR-1830-60 radial engine, and the three-man crew was housed in a single enclosed cockpit. The aircraft's defensive armament was to consist of two machine guns, one fixed forward one, and another flexible one for the defense of the side and rear sections, and of a 1,000 lb (454 kg) bomb load or a torpedo.

The prototype took to the air for the first time on April 15, 1935, and it began a series of flight tests and operative evaluations at the Anacostia naval base immediately after. This phase proved to be particularly long, and several modifications were carried out, the principal ones being the substitution of the engine, the installation of a better and more aerodynamic engine cowling, and the redesigning of the crew's cockpit. The latter was provided with a different hood, carefully studied to improve the pilot's visibility during landing on deck. The first contract was signed in February 1936, and production commenced immediately after. Deliveries began on June 25, the following year.

When the United States entered the war, 100 TBD-1s were in service, although only 69 could be considered operative. In addition to the Battle of Midway, this torpedo plane took part in all the air-sea operations involving the United States during the first six months of the war and, in spite of everything, generally produced satisfactory results in the role of a traditional bomber.

color plate
Douglas TBD-1 V.T.6 *USS Enterprise* - United States 1940

Aircraft:	Douglas TBD-1
Nation:	USA
Manufacturer:	Douglas Aircraft Co.
Type:	Torpedo-bomber
Year:	1937
Engine:	Pratt & Whitney R-1830-64 Twin Wasp, 14-cylinder radial, air cooled, 900 hp
Wingspan:	50 ft 4 in (15.24 m)
Length:	35 ft (10.67 m)
Height:	15 ft 1 in (4.60 m)
Weight:	10,194 lb (4,624 kg) loaded
Maximum speed:	206 mph (332 km/h) at 8,000 ft (2,440 m)
Ceiling:	19,500 ft (6,000 m)
Range:	716 miles (1,150 km)
Armament:	2 machine guns; 1,000 lb (454 kg) of bombs
Crew:	3

A Devastator TBD-1 of the V.T.6 Squadron, based on the *USS Enterprise*.

6-T-1

TBD-1
0322
US NAVY

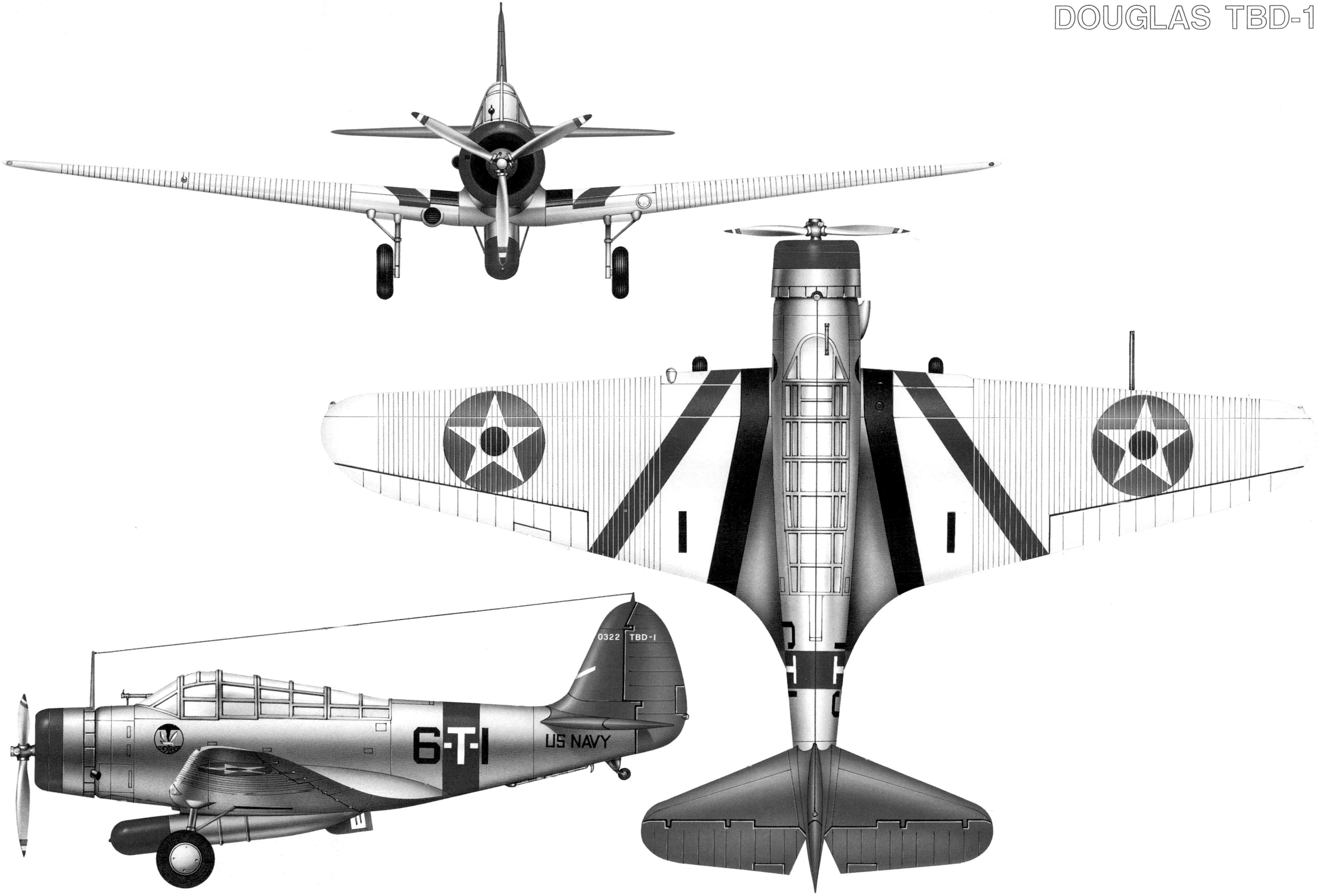

Although conceived in 1938, the Douglas SBD Dauntless has gone down in history as the best dive-bomber built by the American aeronautical industry during World War II. A total of 5,936 was built in all, and this tough monoplane remained in front-line service in the units of the U.S.Navy and the U.S.Marine Corps until the end of 1944, when it was relegated to secondary roles. However, many SBDs survived the conflict and remained in service for several years after the war had ended. In the course of its long and extensive career, the Dauntless' greatest moment of glory occurred during the air-sea battles that took place in 1942, marking the turning point in the war in the Pacific. On May 7, during the Battle of the Coral Sea, SBDs based on the aircraft carriers *Yorktown* and *Lexington* sank the Japanese carrier *Shoho*. At Midway a month later, on June 4, the *Akagi*, the *Kaga*, and the *Soryu* were also sunk, while the *Hiryu* was seriously damaged.

The project for the Dauntless was directly derived from that of the Northrop BT-1, which had started to go into service in the U.S.Navy in the spring of 1938. In fact, at that time, the Northrop Corporation was about to become a subsidiary of the Douglas Company, and the new aircraft was given the designation characteristic of the latter company. Although the prototype was very similar to its direct predecessor, it was much more advanced, and flight tests immediately revealed its excellent qualities. The aircraft was a low-wing two-seater monoplane with retractable landing gear. It was all-metal, with the exception of the steering areas, which were fabric-covered, and was provided with an arrester hook. It was powered initially by a 1,000 hp Wright XR-1820-32 Cyclone radial engine.

In April 1939 the first orders were placed for 57 SBD-1s and 87 SBD-2s (the latter had a greater fuel capacity and modified armament) by the U.S.Marine Corps and the U.S.Navy respectively. These Dauntlesses went into service beginning at the end of 1940. However, in March of the following year, they were replaced by the first aircraft of the SBD-3 version, which had strengthened and improved armament as well as more protection.

When the war against Japan broke out, these aircraft were sent to equip the bomber units based on the aircraft carriers *Lexington*, *Enterprise*, *Yorktown* and *Saratoga*. Beginning in 1942 production was heavily increased, and following the construction of 584 SBD-3s and 780 SBD-4s (which differed only in that their electrical system was 24 volts instead of 12), the SBD-5 appeared. This was the major variant and was characterized by the adoption of a 1,217 hp Wright engine, and by improvements to the

armament and systems on board. After the assembly lines had completed 2,409 SBD-5s, the final SBD-6 version appeared. This was fitted with a 1,350 hp engine and had a greater fuel capacity. Production came to an end in July 1944.

However, the Dauntless' career was not limited solely to its service in the units of the U.S. Navy and the U.S.Marine Corps. In 1940, impressed by the great successes scored in Europe by the German Junkers Ju.87 Stuka dive-bomber, the U.S.Army Air Corps realized that it did not have a similar weapon at its disposal and hurriedly ordered 78 SBD-3s without equipment for naval use from Douglas. This initial order was followed by another for 90 aircraft, which were redesignated A-24. In November 1941, 52 of these aircraft were sent to the Philippines. However, following the surprise attack on Pearl Harbor, they were transferred to Australia and subsequently to the Dutch Indies. It was in this theater of operations that the A-24s first saw combat, but strangely their performance was not considered satisfactory. Nevertheless, orders were placed for a further 170 A-24As (the equivalent of the SBD-4) and 615 A-24Bs (similar to the SBD-5). Most of these aircraft were used for training duty.

color plate
Douglas SBD-5 V.C.40 U.S.Navy Air Force - Torokina, Bougainville, New Guinea, April 1944

Aircraft:	Douglas SBD-3
Nation:	USA
Manufacturer:	Douglas Aircraft Co.
Type:	Bomber
Year:	1941
Engine:	Wright R-1820-52 Cyclone, 9-cylinder radial, air-cooled, 1,000 hp
Wingspan:	41 ft 6 in (12.65 m)
Length:	32 ft 8 in (9.96 m)
Height:	13 ft 7 in (4.14 m)
Weight:	10,400 lb (4,717 kg) loaded
Maximum speed:	250 mph (402 km/h)
Ceiling:	27,100 ft (8,260 m)
Range:	1,345 miles (2,164 km)
Armament:	4 machine guns; 1,200 lb (544 kg) of bombs
Crew:	2

An example of the Douglas SBD-3, redesignated A-24 in flight with the defensive position on the back open.

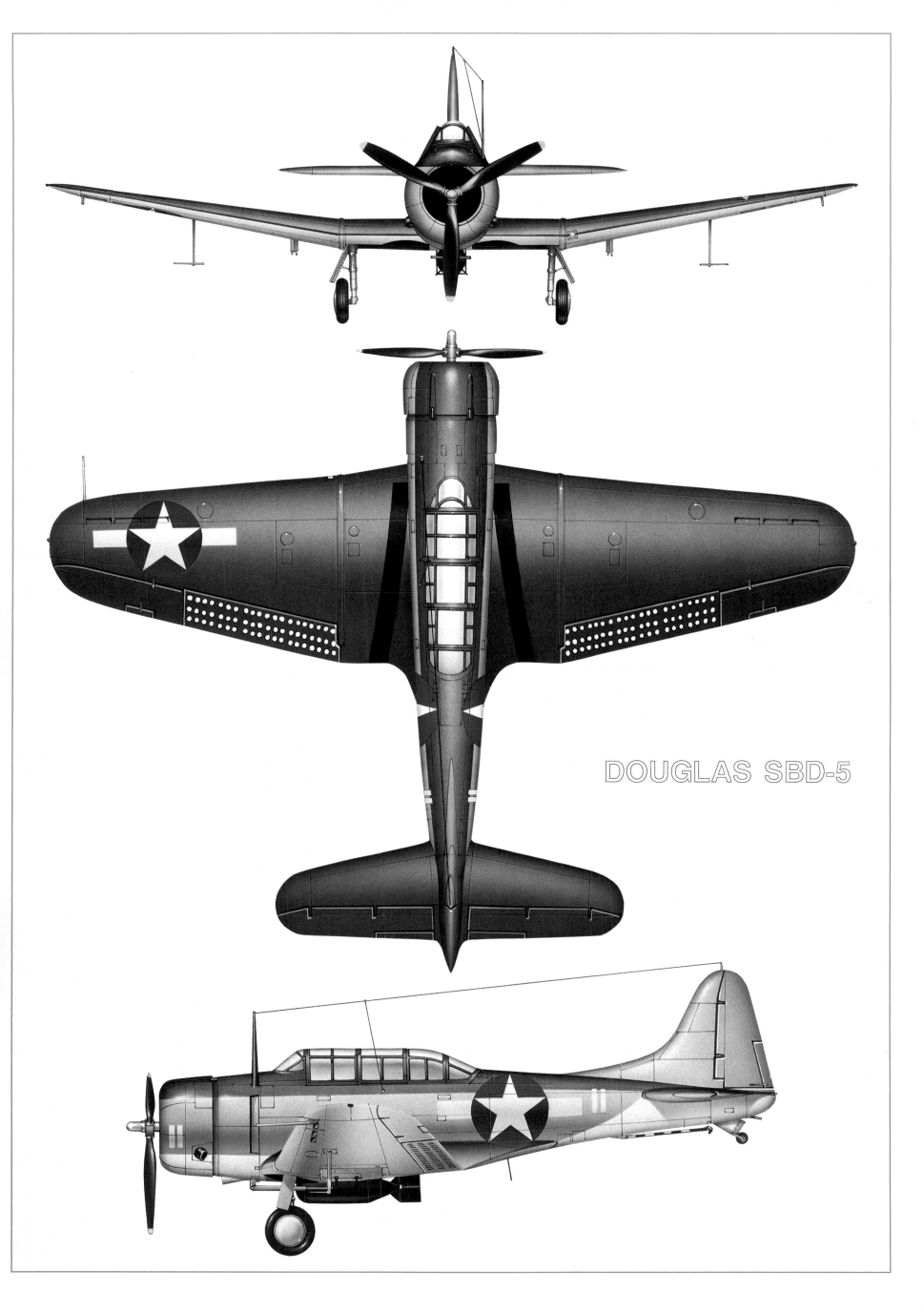

DOUGLAS SBD-5

DOUGLAS A-20G

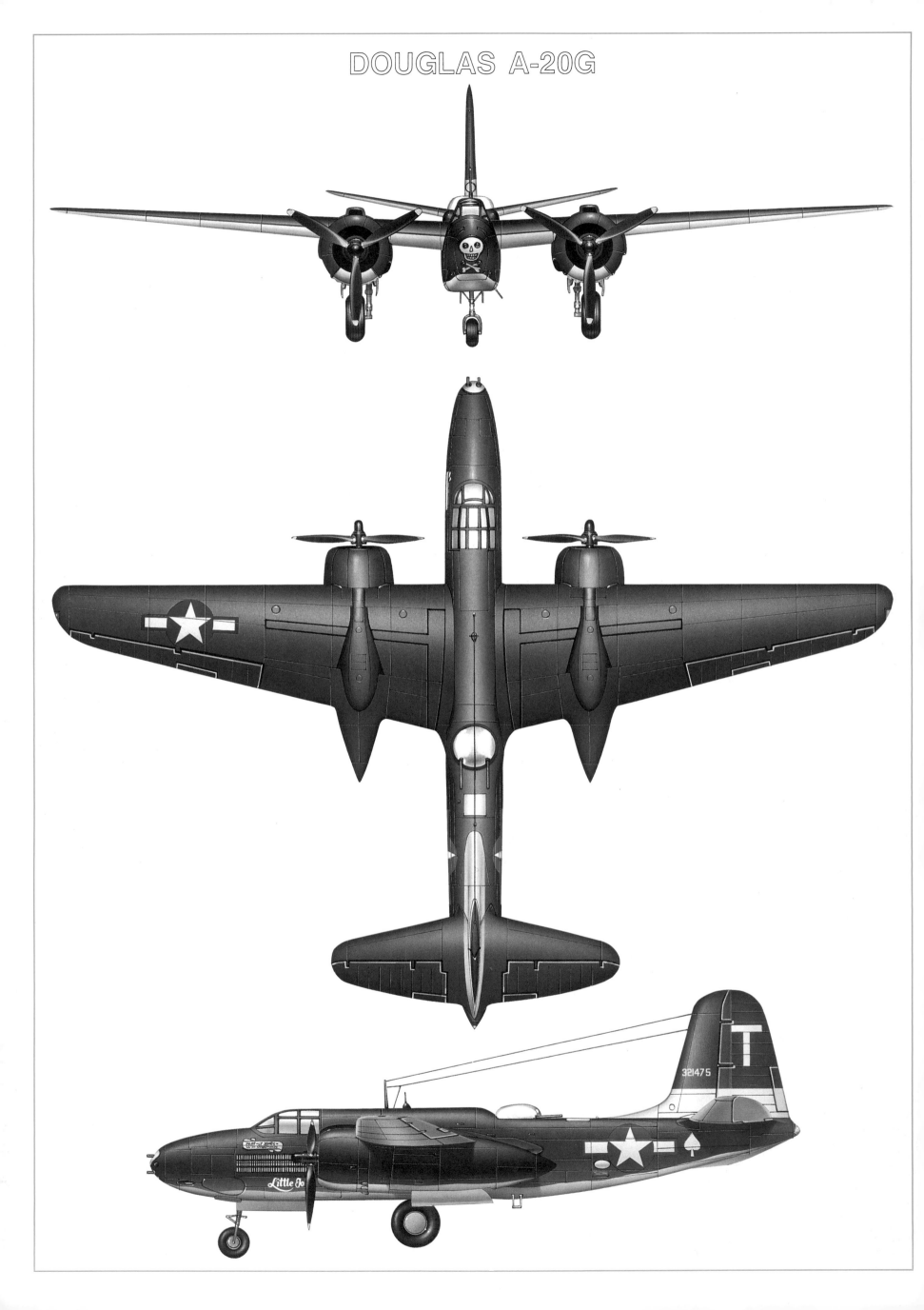

In production from 1939 to 1944, a total of 7,385 of the light, two-engine Douglas was built in numerous versions, and they constituted one of the most prolific and versatile families of fighting aircraft built by the American aeronautical industry during the war. These aircraft were known by various names and designations in the course of their long and extensive operative career. The best known of these were DB-7 in France (the first nation to place an order for them, in 1938, in the wake of the *Armée de l'Air*'s urgent need for rearmament); Boston and Havoc in Great Britain; and A-20, P-70, A-3 in the United States. Bomber, fighter, ground attack, night fighter, reconnaissance: the two-engine Douglas operated in all of these roles and on all fronts from the first day of the conflict to the last. Among the countries that adopted the aircraft, prime position was held by the Soviet Union, which received almost half of the entire production, a total of 3,215 aircraft.

The project originated in 1936. At that time, although no official specifications had been issued, Douglas was considering the development of a high-performance modern tactical bomber to offer to the USAAC. The project, initially designated Model 7A and entrusted to the chief designer, Ed Heinemann, assumed its definitive form in 1938, and its maiden flight took place on October 26. It was an elegant, all-metal middle high-wind two-engine aircraft with retractable tricycle forward landing gear and was powered by a pair of 1,115 hp Pratt & Whitney R-1830 Twin Wasp radial engines. An unusual feature was the interchangeable formula foreseen for the tip of the nose in order to facilitate the production of the bomber and ground-attack versions.

Despite the plane's promising performance, the U.S.Army Air Corps did not show an immediate interest in the new aircraft, and Douglas began to search for a foreign buyer. The first order, placed by France, was not long in coming and was for an initial lot of 105 aircraft. Redesignated DB-7 and substantially modified in order to make it more suited to the operative needs of the war in Europe, the first production series aircraft took to the air on August 17, 1939. The *Armée de l'Air* subsequently placed orders for a total of 260 DB-7s and almost 700 DB-7As (with improvements to the equipment and armament and provided with more powerful engines). To these was added a small order from Belgium for 16 aircraft. However, the course of the war drastically reduced the deliveries to the *Armée de l'Air* and most of the aircraft ordered were subsequently sent to Great Britain. These planes (which the RAF designated Boston and Havoc, the former

A night fighter variant of the Havoc, equipped with radar and designated P-70.

being the bomber version and the latter the night-fighter version) became operative toward the end of 1940.

In the meantime, the USAAC had begun to show an interest. An initial contract had been signed in May 1939, immediately after the French one, and concerned 63 aircraft designated A-20. Provided with R-2600 series Wright engines, three of them were transformed into prototypes for photographic reconnaissance (XF-3) and one into the prototype of a night fighter (XP-70). The remaining 59 (P-70A-1) were the first production series with this specialization. Later, the first bomber variants, the A-20A and A-20B, also appeared (with 143 and 999 being built respectively) with improvements above all to the engines. Production was standardized with the next version, the A-20C (known as the Boston Mk.III in the RAF). In May 1942, these aircraft were the first to see combat bearing American insignia in Europe.

In the same year the major production variant appeared. This was the A-20G and was destined exclusively for the USAAF and the Soviet air force, a total of 2,850 being built in all. Characterized by the adoption of a solid nose with heavy offensive armament, this aircraft proved to be particularly effective in ground attack and scored some great successes, especially on the Pacific front. The next version, the A-20H, was very similar but was provided with more powerful engines; 412 were built. The final variants, the J and K, were derived from this and the previous variant, but they marked a return to the glazed-in nose and the role of traditional bomber. These series (of which 450 and 413 were built respectively) served in the RAF as Boston Mk.IVs and Mk.Vs.

A Douglas A-20G in flight; the aircraft's armament is concentrated in the nose.

color plate

Douglas A-20G Havoc 389th Bomber Squadron 312th Bomber Group 5th Air Force U.S.Army Air Force-Florida Blanca Airfield, Luzon, the Philippines, January 1945

Aircraft:	Douglas A-20G
Nation:	USA
Manufacturer:	Douglas Aircraft Co.
Type:	Bomber
Year:	1942
Engine:	2 Wright R-2600-23 Cyclone, 14-cylinder radial, air-cooled, 1,622 hp each
Wingspan:	61 ft 4 in (18.69 m)
Length:	48 ft (14.63 m)
Height:	17.17 ft 7 in (5.63 m)
Weight:	27,200 lb (12,338 kg) loaded
Maximum speed:	339 mph (545 km/h) at 12,400 ft (3,780 m)
Ceiling:	25,065 ft (7,620 m)
Range:	1,090 miles (1,750 km)
Armament:	9 machine guns; 4,004 lb (1,814 kg) of bombs
Crew:	3

DOUGLAS A-26C

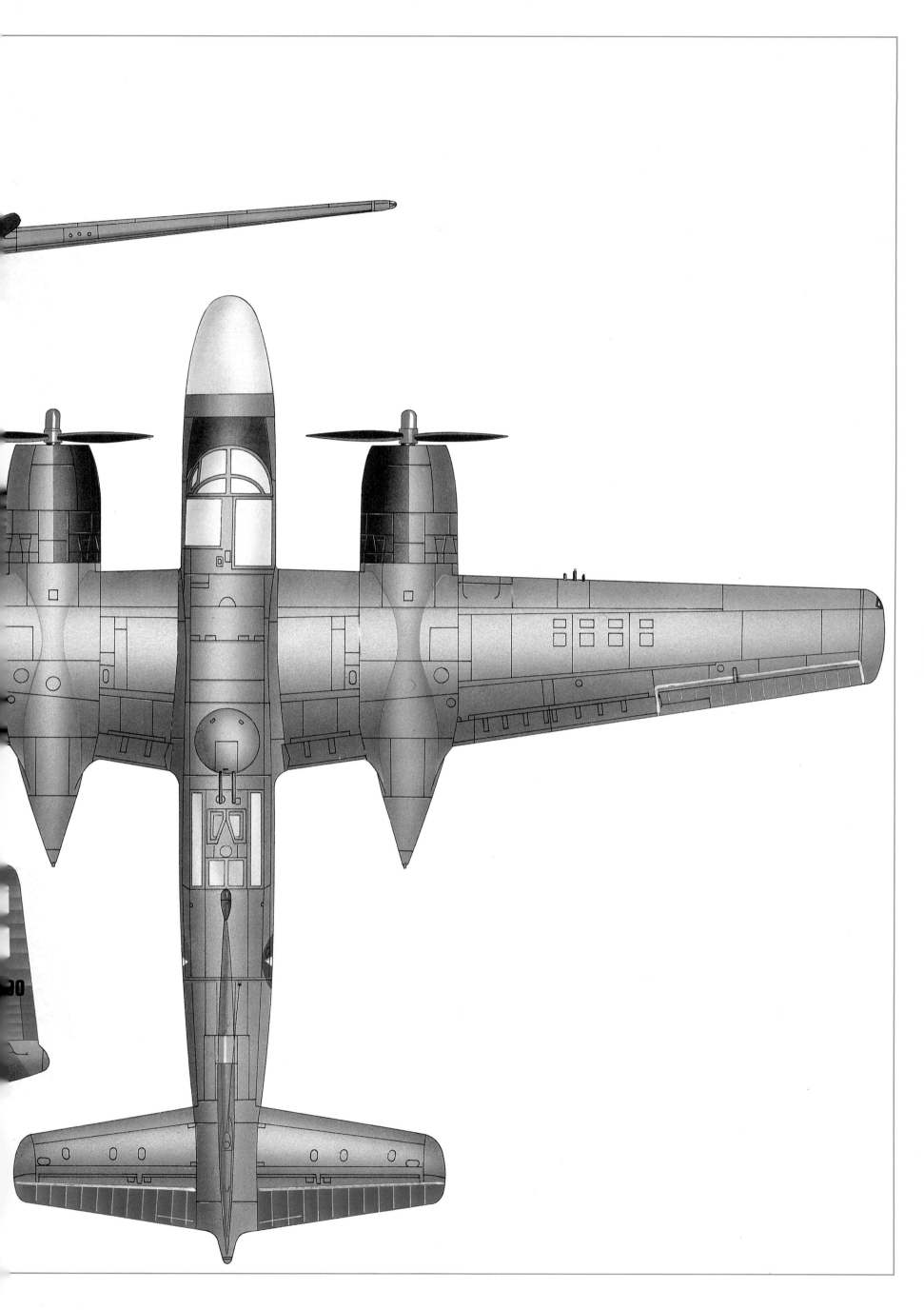

Considered the best ground attack plane and tactical bomber sent into combat by the American aviation, the Douglas A-26 Invader represented the high point in the development of a family of high performance two-engined light aircraft that Douglas had started to build back in 1936, with the DB-7 and the later Boston-Havocs. 2,446 Invaders were built in two main versions. The end of the war led to the cancellation of a further 5,254 aircraft in still more powerful and improved variants. The great effectiveness of this combat plane is illustrated by the fact that, after the war, several hundred remained in active service in the units of the USAAF (with the designation B-26). They also continued their active career both in the Korean and the Vietnamese war.

The specifications for a new high performance well-armed ground attack plane were issued in 1940, and in June of the following year, Douglas signed an initial contract for the construction of three prototypes. These aircraft fulfilled various operative needs. The first (XA-26, maiden flight on July 10, 1942) was a traditional bomber with firing apparatus installed in the glazed nose. The second (XA-26A) was prepared as a night fighter, with four machine guns in a remote-controlled turret on the back of the fuselage and four 20 mm cannons in a fixed position in the belly. The third assumed the configuration of an attack plane and was armed with a 75 mm cannon installed in the nose.

The cycle of evaluations and comparative tests continued for a long time, and in the end, the third prototype was chosen as the first production variant (A-26B). The heavy cannon was eliminated, and in its place, six 12.7 mm machine guns were installed. This offensive armament was accompanied by four more weapons installed in pairs in two remote-controlled turrets on the back and belly of the aircraft respectively. Moreover, for special missions, it was possible to add another 10 machine guns: eight on the wings, in four containers, and two in external installations on the sides of the fuselage. Lastly, to complete this powerful armament, the bomb hold was capable of carrying up to 4,004 lb (1,814 kg) of bombs. Furthermore, in the case of an emergency, rockets, supplementary fuel tanks, or a further 2,002 lb (907 kg) of bombs could be installed in wing supports.

This veritable flying arsenal were first used in November 1944 on the European front, in the units of the 9th Air Force. The A-26Bs had their baptism of fire on November 19, and they proved to be the fastest bombers to be used by the USAAF in the conflict. Some months later, they also began their career on the Pacific front, with equally successful results.

Douglas completed 1,355 A-26Bs before production of the second version began (the A-26C, of which 1,091 were built). This marked a return to the configuration of a horizontal bomber with glazed nose and a reduction in the heavy armament on board. These Invaders went into service in 1945, and they took part in the last phase of the conflict.

color plate

Douglas A-26C 319th Bomber Group U.S.Army Air Force - Okinawa July 1945

Aircraft:	Douglas A-26B
Nation:	USA
Manufacturer:	Douglas Aircraft Co.
Type:	Bomber
Year:	1944
Engine:	2 Pratt & Whitney R-2800-27 Double Wasp, 18-cylinder radial, air-cooled, 2,000 hp each
Wingspan:	70 ft 1in (21.33 m)
Length:	50 ft 1 in (15.24 m)
Height:	18 ft 6 in (5.64 m)
Weight:	35,046 lb (15,876 kg)
Maximum speed:	353 mph (570 km/h) at 15,032 ft (4,570 m)
Ceiling:	22,154 ft (6,735 m)
Range:	1,399 miles (2,253 km)
Armament:	10 machine guns; 4,004 lb (1,814 kg) of bombs
Crew:	3

One of the earliest A-26As, still armed with a 75 mm cannon in the nose.

The Buffalo, the first monoplane fighter to go into service in the U.S. Navy, proved in practice to be totally unsuitable for the important role for which it had been conceived. After operative duty lasting only a few months in the units of the U.S. Navy and the U.S. Marine Corps, the small and squat Brewster fighters began to be replaced by the more effective Grumman F4F Wildcat. The only American unit to use the Buffaloes in combat was the VMF-221 Marine Corps Squadron, at Midway on June 5, 1942, with disastrous results: during the battle, only seven out of a total of 25 aircraft managed to return to base, the other 18 were destroyed by Japanese Mitsubishi Zeros. Nevertheless, 507 Brewster F2As were built up to March 1942, in three major production series, and most of them went into service bearing the insignia of Great Britain, Finland, and the Netherland.

The XF2A-1 project was launched in 1936, almost contemporaneously with that of Grumman, on the basis of a request by the U.S. Navy for a carrier-based fighter capable of reaching a speed of 300 mph (483 km/h). The prototype took to the air at the end of 1937, and following flight tests, production of an initial series of 54 aircraft was ordered on June 11, 1938. The aircraft was an all-metal, mid-wing monoplane powered by the first version of a 940 hp Wright R-1820-34 radial engine and armed with one 7.9 mm and three 12.7 mm machine guns.

Deliveries (to the VF-3 Fighter Squadron based on the aircraft carrier *Saratoga*) commenced exactly a year later, but the U.S. Navy put only 11 of the aircraft ordered into service. The remaining 43 were sent to Finland, which was in open conflict with the Soviet Union at the time. Meanwhile, another 43 aircraft of a second version, the F2A-2, had been requested and were delivered beginning in August 1940 provided with more powerful engines. These were also destined mainly for export: in addition to the aircraft ordered by the U.S. Navy, Belgium ordered 40, Great Britain 170, and the Dutch Indies air force 72. The developments of the war in Europe subsequently led to 28 of the Buffaloes ordered by Belgium being delivered to Great Britain.

In the meantime, service in the U.S. Navy had underlined the aircraft's limitations and, in particular, weaknesses in the landing gear and insufficient armor-plating. On January 21, 1941, 108 aircraft of the third version, the F2A-3, were ordered, but even in this version the problems remained unresolved. In fact, the increase in weight led to a further deterioration in the fighter's already disappointing overall performance. Consequently, in January 1942, the F2A-3s were assigned to ground-based Marine Corps units. The Battle of Midway led to their definitive withdrawal.

Apart from its experiences bearing American insignia, the Brewster fighter saw combat for the first time in Finland, where it fought brilliantly against the Soviets. Subsequently (after the British Royal Air Force had declared that the aircraft was totally unsuitable for duty on the European front and had sent most of those in its possession to the Far East), the Buffaloes were used against the Japanese, although bearing British and Dutch insignia. The defense of Singapore, Burma, Java, and Manila were the main episodes in a desperate struggle against an enemy that was infinitely superior, both at a quantitative and a qualitative level. Resistance continued until the end of March 1942, when most of the aircraft having been destroyed, the rest were subsequently abandoned.

Mention should be made of a final lot of 20 aircraft ordered by the Dutch Indies that were assigned to the Royal Australian Air Force in July 1942.

Aircraft:	Brewster F2A-2
Nation:	USA
Manufacturer:	Brewster Aeronautical Corp.
Type:	Fighter
Year:	1940
Engine:	Wright R-1820-40 Cyclone, 9-cylinder radial, air-cooled, 1,200 hp
Wingspan:	35 ft (10.67 m)
Length:	25 ft 7 in (7.80 m)
Height:	12 ft 1 in (3.68 m)
Takeoff weight:	7,755 lb (3,125 kg) loaded
Maximum speed:	323 mph (520 km/h) at 16 542 ft (5,029 m)
Ceiling:	34,000 ft (10,363 m)
Range:	1,015 miles (1,633 km)
Armament:	4 machine guns; 220 lb (91 kg) of bombs
Crew:	1

color plate

Brewster F2A-2 Buffalo VF-2 Fighter Squadron U.S. Navy *USS Lexington* - USA 1941

A Brewster Buffalo in service with the Finnish air force.

A Brewster F2A-3, an improved version of the Buffalo.

A taxiing Buffalo F2A-2 bearing prewar markings.

BREWSTER F2A-2

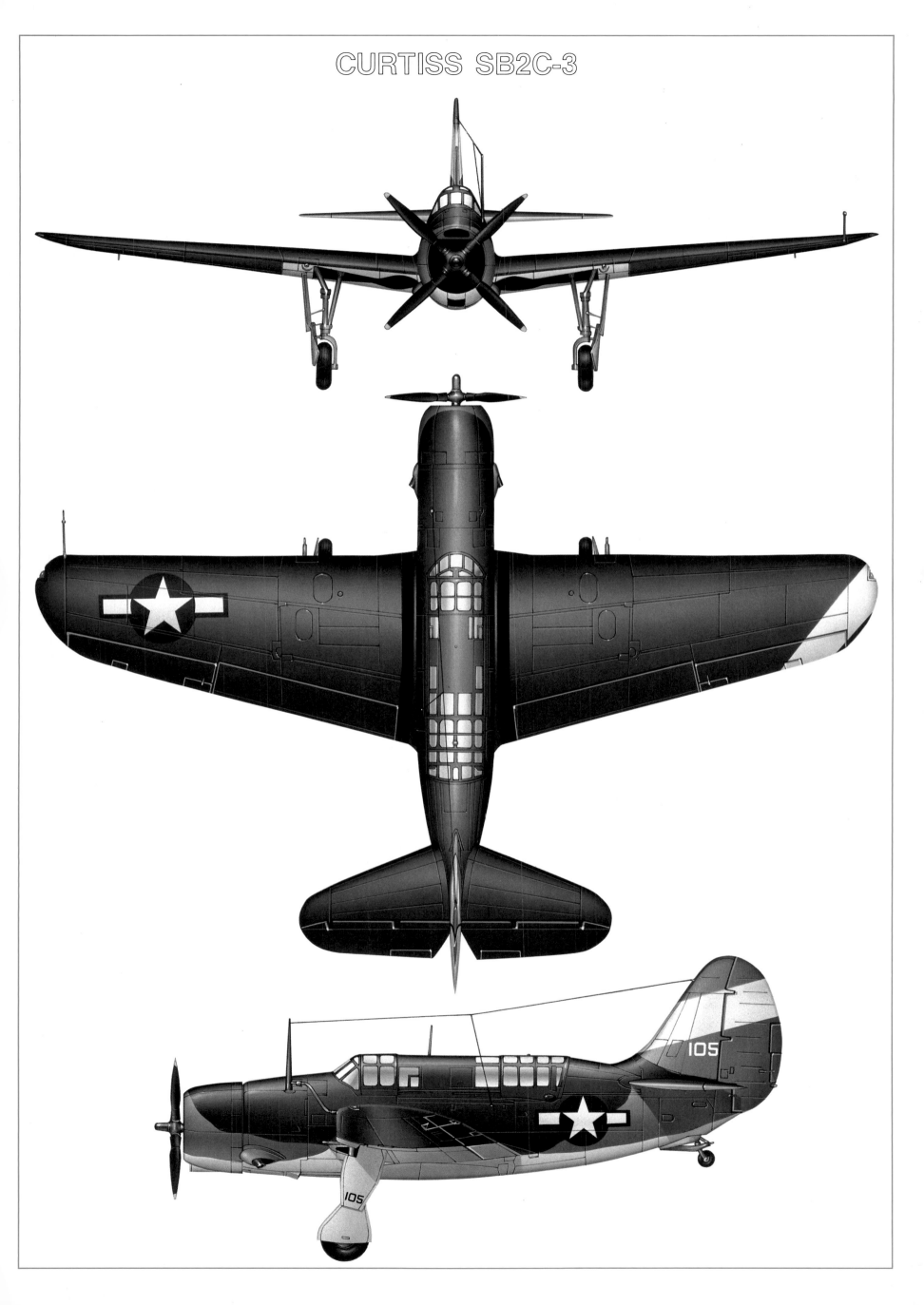

CURTISS SB2C-3

The SB2C Helldiver was the last combat plane that Curtiss built for the U.S.Navy and the Marines. Approximately 7,200 of these large and powerful single-engine carrier-based bombers were built in several versions. Beginning in November 1943, it backed the old SBD Dauntless as a dive-bomber, taking part in all air-sea operations until the end of the conflict. Many of the final production variants survived World War II and remained in service until the 1950s.

The Helldiver originated in 1938, when the U.S.Navy established a competition for a new carrier-based bomber-reconnaissance plane. Curtiss-Wright received an order for the construction of a prototype on May 15 of the following year and the aircraft, designated XSB2C-1 took to the air for the first time on December 18, 1940. It was not initially a success, in that it was destroyed in an accident at the beginning of January 1941, but the program went ahead nevertheless, sustained by orders for mass production which the Navy had already placed (November 29, 1940). However, the delays began to accumulate, not only due to the need to build another prototype, but also to carry out a whole series of modifications to the structure and equipment requested by the military technicians. These included an increase in fuel capacity and armament, the installation of self-sealing fuel tanks, and the enlarging of the surface area of the fins and rudder.

The first of the initial SB2C-1 series did not leave the factory until June 1942, and although deliveries to the units began in December, the aircraft did not become fully operative until the second half of the following year. The Helldiver made its debut in combat on November 11, 1943, with a bombing raid on Rabaul.

The SB2C was a large low-wing two-seater monoplane with retractable landing gear, and it was powered by a 1,700 hp Wright R-2600 radial engine. The defensive armament consisted of four machine guns on the wings (or two 20 mm cannons) and one or two similar weapons installed in a rear defensive position, at the observer's disposal. In addition, the bomb load could maintain a maximum of 2,002 lb (907 kg) of bombs installed in the hold and in supports below the wings.

In 1944, the second principal production version (SB2C-3, 1,112 built in all) appeared. It possessed a more powerful engine that drove a four-bladed propeller characterized by further detailed improvements. However, the major variant was the subsequent SB2C-4, in which the armament's flexibility was increased by the installation of four racks beneath the wings to hold a similar number

of 127 mm rockets or 501 lb (227 kg) of bombs. Curtiss alone built almost 2,000 of this version of the Helldiver. In fact, to sustain the increasing demands of the U.S.Navy, the production program was widened to include the participation of the Canadian companies Fairchild Aircraft Ltd. in Longueil, and the Canadian Car & Foundry in Montreal. These two firms built on license 300 and 894 aircraft respectively in several variants, designated with the characteristic abbreviation of SBF and SBW. The final version was the SB2C-5, which appeared in the early month of 1945, and was characterized mainly by an increase in fuel capacity. 970 were built in all.

In the course of the conflict the Helldivers were employed almost exclusively by the U.S.Navy.

Only 26 (that were never used) were sent to Great Britain, while the Marines took most of the 900 aircraft specially built for the Army aviation, that had ordered them in April 1941. They were designated A-25A and then SB2C-1A.

color plate
Curtiss SB2C-3 VB-9 aircraft carrier *Lexington* U.S.Navy Air Force - Pacific sea, February 1945

Aircraft:	Curtiss SB2C-1
Nation:	USA
Manufacturer:	Curtiss-Wright Corp.
Type:	Bomber
Year:	1943
Engine:	Wright R-2600-8 Cyclone, 14-cylinder radial, air-cooled, 1,700 hp
Wingspan:	49 ft 10 in (15.16 m)
Length:	36 ft 9 in (11.18 m)
Height:	13 ft 2 in (4.01 m)
Weight:	16,637 lb (7,537 kg)
Maximum speed:	280 mph (452 km/h) at 16,743 ft (5,090 m)
Ceiling:	25,164 ft (7,650 m)
Range:	1,108 miles (1,785 km)
Armament:	2 x 20 mm cannons; 2 machine guns; 2,002 lb (907 kg) of bombs
Crew:	2

An SB2C-1 taking off from an aircraft-carrier during operations in the Pacific.

An SBC2-4 employed as a torpedo plane. This was the Helldiver's major variant.

The definitive passage from biplane to monoplane in the American military aviation was marked toward the mid-1930s by two fighters: the Curtiss P-36 and the Seversky P-35. However, they were both transitional aircraft that met with only limited success in the United States, eventually being produced mainly for export. In particular, only 210 Curtiss P-36s were delivered to the units, although it remained the USAAC's standard fighter from 1938 until the United States entered the war, and the aircraft concluded its brief operative career at Pearl Harbor on December 7, 1941. During the Japanese attack, most of the 39 P-36As in the base were destroyed on the ground, although four of them managed to take to the air and to shoot down two enemy aircraft.

The project for the Model 75 (the designation given by Curtiss to its new model) was launched in the summer of 1934 by Donovan A. Berlin, an ex-Northrop technician who had just started to work for the old established Buffalo-based manufacturer. The aim was to participate in the competition announced by the USAAC for the construction of a new monoplane fighter with a speed of around 300 mph (483 km/h) to replace the Boeing P-26s that were in their final production phase at the time. Construction work on the prototype commenced on November 1, 1934, and its maiden flight took place on May 15 the following year.

The aircraft was an all-metal, low cantilever wing monoplane, with enclosed cockpit and retractable landing gear, originally powered by a 900 hp Wright XR-1760 radial engine. In the meantime, however, the date of the competition was postponed and it was not until April 10, 1939, that a second Curtiss prototype (with modified power plant) could be evaluated. The results were not exceptional, although the aircraft's potential was recognized in the form of an order for three experimental planes, placed on August 5. In 1937, the USAAC made its choice, with a request for 210 P-36As. The first of the 178 aircraft actually completed was delivered on April 20, 1938, and from December production was concentrated on 32 of the second version, the P-36C, with more powerful engine and armament.

The Curtiss fighter met with greater success on the foreign market. The first sales took place in 1938 and involved a simplified version with fixed landing gear (Model 75H) ordered by Nationalist China (30 aircraft, plus 82 on license), by Thailand (12), and by Argentina (29, plus 200 on license). In 1939, export of the major variant was authorized, and this was built in nine versions (designated H75A-1 to H75A-9), of which the first four were for France and the remaining five, respectively, for China (a single prototype), Norway (24 H75A-6s and 36 H75A-8s ordered), the Netherlands (20 H75A-7s ordered), and Iran (10 H75A-9s ordered, subsequently sent to Great Britain).

However, the greatest user of all was France, which in the effort of rearming just before the war, eventually ordered around 1,000 of these fighters from May 13, 1938, up to October 1939. In practice, however, by June 1940, the *Armée de l'Air* had succeeded in putting only 291 H75As into service, and these fought valiantly to oppose the German invasion. In particular, the Curtiss fighter had the honor of gaining the first French air victory of the conflict. This occurred on September 8, 1939, during combat between five H75A-1s and a squadron of Messerschmitt Bf.109Es, in the course of which two German aircraft were shot down.

The aircraft that had not been delivered to France following the armistice and those that had managed to escape to Britain in the meantime, a total of 227 in all, were incorporated into the Royal Air Force and redesignated Mohawk. However, they were not used on the European front.

color plate
Curtiss P-36C Fighting Training Units - United States 1941

Curtiss P-36 Hawk during evaluation tests by the U.S. Army Air Corps.

Prototype of the Curtiss P-36.

Curtiss P-36 of the 51st Pursuit Group

Aircraft:	Curtiss P-36C
Nation:	USA
Manufacturer:	Curtiss Wright Corp.
Type:	Fighter
Year:	1939
Engine:	Pratt & Whitney R-1830-17 Twin Wasp, 14-cylinder radial, air-cooled, 1,200 hp
Wingspan:	37 ft 4 in (11.35 m)
Length:	28 ft 6 in (8.68 m)
Height:	9 ft 4 in (2.84 m)
Weight:	6,150 lb (2,790 kg) loaded
Maximum speed:	311 mph (501 km/h) at 10,000 ft (3,048 m)
Ceiling:	33,700 ft (10,272 m)
Range:	820 miles (1,320 km)
Armament:	2 machine guns
Crew:	1

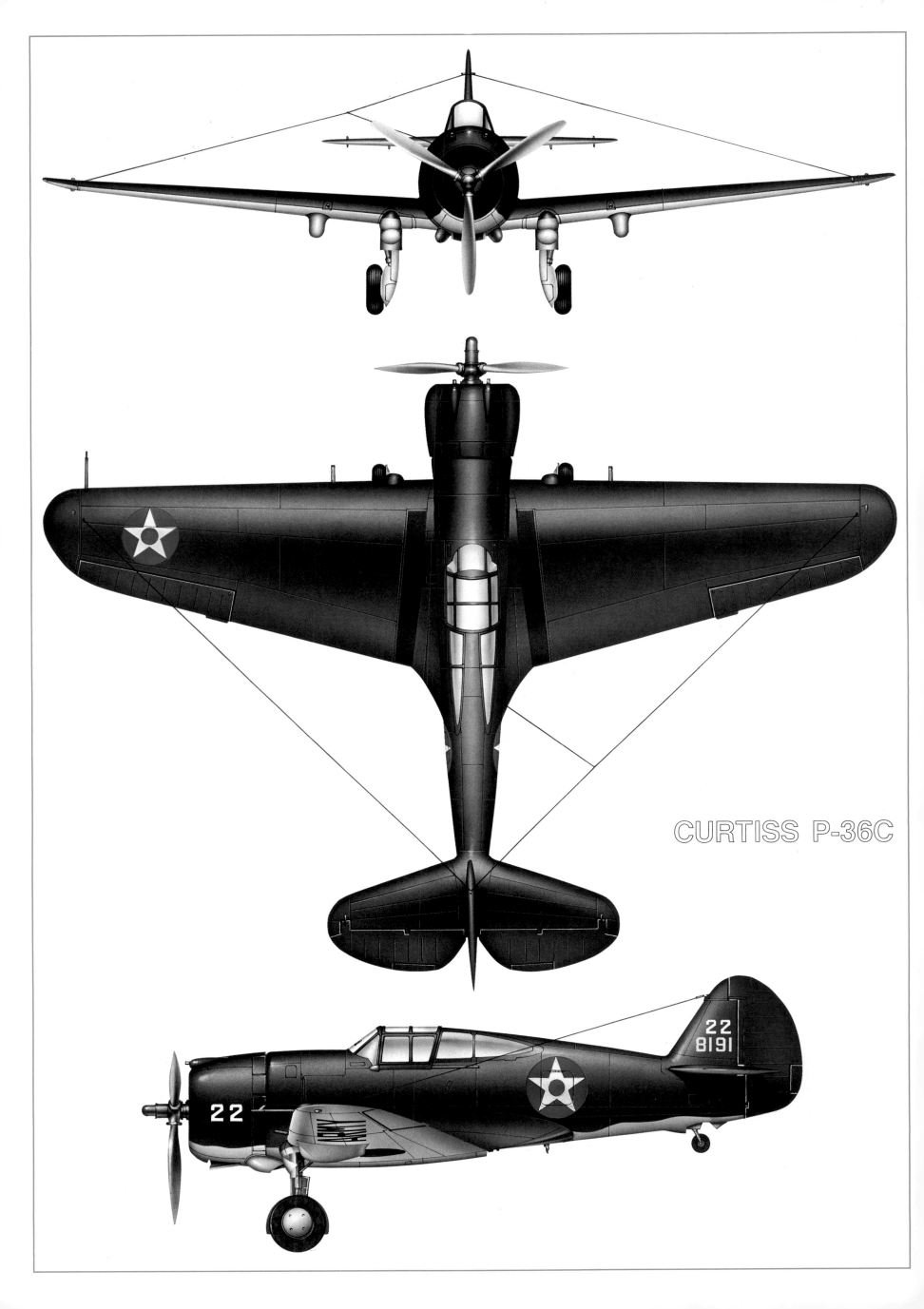

CURTISS P-36C

CURTISS P-40C

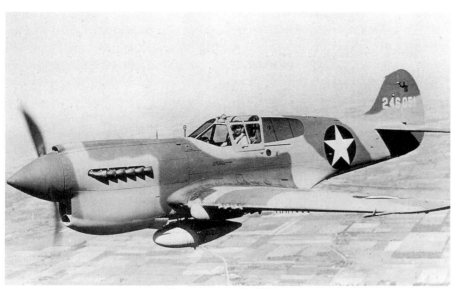
A P-40K with more powerful Allison engine, in flight.

The Curtiss P-40 was not an exceptional aircraft, although paradoxically it was the most important American fighter during the first two years of the war. Its strength, rather than lying in its quality, was to be found in two factors that were fundamental at a time in which all available resources had to be exploited by the Allies in order to fight off attacks in Europe and the Far East: it was immediately available and in a large quantity. In fact, from 1939, no fewer than 13,738 P-40s came off the Curtiss assembly lines, a number that was eventually to place the fighter in third place as far as its total production was concerned, behind rather more effective aircraft such as the Republic P-47 and the North American P-51. Its operational service was also extensive, and it was used on all fronts, in Europe, Africa, the Pacific, and Russia, bearing the insignia of almost all the Allied countries.

The P-40 project was not new at the time it was prepared, in March 1937. In fact, it was based on the airframe of the Curtiss P-36A, and it was planned to replace the original radial engine with an Allison V-1710 12-cylinder liquid-cooled engine. This had been tried out on the tenth P-36A to be built and, modified in this way, the aircraft had taken to the air for the first time on October 14, 1938, with good overall results: carrying a total weight of 6.270 lb (2,840 kg), the aircraft had reached a maximum speed of 340 mph (550 km/h) at 12,230 ft (3,718 m), faster than that of the British Hawker Hurricane, although inferior to the performance of the

Supermarine Spitfire and the German Messerschmitt Bf.109. In 1939, when the USAAC invited bids for the manufacture of a new fighter, the project submitted by Curtiss thus found itself with an overall advantage, due not so much to the inherent potential of the aircraft as to the relative simplicity of launching mass production immediately. On April 27, 1939, the War Department issued an order for the construction of an initial lot of 524 P-40s, although this decision caused a lot of fuss, not so much due to the aircraft being chosen instead of the viable prototypes presented by Bell, Lockheed, and Republic, as to the financial significance of the contract ($12,872,898), the most important of its kind to be approved since 1918.

The first production series P-40 took to the air on April 4, 1940, and almost 200 aircraft had been delivered to the units of the U.S. Air Force by October. At the same time, 140 export models, originally ordered by France, were acquired by Great Britain, where they were known as Tomahawk I and assigned to training duty. The second variant was the P-40B (Tomahawk II in the RAF), which appeared in 1941. It had heavier armament and was provided with armor and self-sealing fuel tanks. This aircraft was the first to see combat duty, bearing British insignia in Africa and American insignia at Pearl Harbor and in China, where it also served in the famous American Volunteer Group, the Flying Tigers.

After a few P-40Bs and P-40Cs had been built, the first important alterations appeared in the P-40D (which made its maiden flight on May 22, 1941, and almost all of the 582 that were built went to the RAF where they were designated Kittyhawk I) and in the subsequent P-40E, delivered in August 1941. These were characterized by different engines and armament, and modified and shortened fuselage and landing gear. The P-40E (2,320 of which were built) was the first to serve in American units based in Europe, in the Mediterranean. Despite the evident limitations of the aircraft, which increasingly proved to be unsuited to the role of interceptor and suited to that of attack, Curtiss continued in its attempts to improve it. In 1942, the P-40F version appeared (1,311 built in all), provided with 1,300 hp Rolls-Royce/Packard Merlin V-1650-1 engines. This was followed in the same year by the P-40K, and by the L, M, and N variants in 1943. In these versions an attempt was made to lighten the airframe in various ways and to increase the power of the engine. The P-40Ns (deliveries began in March 1943) were also the last to serve in the USAAF, and after their production (5,220 aircraft) the assembly lines closed on November 30, 1944.

color plate

Curtiss P-40C 3rd Squadron American Volunteer Group Chinese Nationalist Air Force - Kunming, China 1942

Aircraft:	Curtiss P-40C
Nation:	USA
Manufacturer:	Curtiss-Wright Corp.
Type:	Fighter
Year:	1942
Engine:	Allison V-1710 39,12-cylinder V, liquid-cooled, 1,150 hp
Wingspan:	37 ft 4 in (11.38 m)
Length:	31 ft 2 in (9.50 m)
Height:	11 ft 10 in (3.61 m)
Weight:	9,200 lb (3,900 kg) loaded
Maximum speed:	367 mph (592 km/h) at 12,120 ft (3,685 m)
Ceiling:	29,000 ft (8,840 m)
Range:	850 miles (1,360 km)
Armament:	6 machine guns; 700 lb (317 kg) of bombs
Crew:	1

A Royal Air Force Kittyhawk in service in North Africa.

Although modern in conception and with good overall qualities, when it first appeared, the Seversky P-35 did not receive in the United States the consent it deserved, and production was destined mainly for export. After building 77 aircraft for the USAAC, production lines worked on the completion of a further 120 ordered by Sweden. The imminence of war, however, induced the American military authorities to requisition half of this order and to send the P-35s to equip fighter units. These planes went into service with the designation P-35A and were the only ones to go into combat bearing the American insignia when the war broke out in the Pacific. However, when actually put to the test, the plane's inferiority compared to its more modern and stronger adversaries was evident: after the first two days of Japanese attacks in the Philippines, only eight P-35s out of a total of 48 were still operative.

The small Seversky fighter was designed by Alexander Kartveli, the technician who was to become famous with the P-47 Thunderbolt. The program's origins went back to 1935, the year in which the designer had built the prototype of a two-seater fighter, known as the SEV-2XP. Completion of the aircraft was not easy, because in June it had been seriously damaged in an accident. This incident and the consequent halting of tests led Kartveli to reconsider the project: the aircraft was updated, the most substantial changes consisting in the fitting of retractable landing gear and a single-seat cockpit. The new prototype, known as the SEV-1XP, began tests immediately, powered by an 850 hp Wright R-1820-G5 Cyclone radial engine. However, the engine caused further problems and slowed down completion of the aircraft. In the end these problems were solved with the fitting of a 950 hp Pratt & Whitney R-1830-9 Twin Wasp engine. In this form and rechristened the AP-1, the fighter was finally accepted by the USAAC, and an order for 77 planes, designated P-35, was placed on June 16, 1936. The first of these came off the production line in July 1937, and the last in August of the following year. However, production never really reached maximum potential, and deliveries to the units began only in the spring of 1938.

The low rate of construction (due mainly to Seversky's financial difficulties, which were only really overcome in April 1939, by a radical reorganization of the company and by its changing its name to Republic Aircraft Corporation) and the appearance of other fighter prototypes that were more effective (such as the Curtiss P-36, which came second in the competition in 1936), led the military authorities to show a declining interest in the development of the P-35. Seversky consequently proposed its model for export and found an enthusiastic client in Sweden. After an initial lot of 15 planes belonging to a second series known as the EP-106, fitted with a more powerful engine (1,050 hp Pratt & Whitney R-1830-45) and almost twice the original armament consisting of two 7.7 mm and two 12.7 mm machine guns, the Swedish *Flygvapnet* requested a total of 120. Delivery of these began in February 1940, and they went into service under the designation of J9.

However, the outbreak of war in Europe and the consequent embargo on armament not destined for Great Britain, that was brought into force by the United States in June 1940, led to the requisition of 60 EP-106s, which had been built but not yet delivered. They were absorbed into the newly created USAAF, redesignated P-35A, and assigned for the most part to units based in the Philippines. However, the Seversky fighters lasted only 48 hours on the scene of battle.

color plate

Seversky P-35 94th Pursuit Squadron U.S. Army Air Corps - 1938

Formation of Swedish air force Seversky P-35s.

The Seversky P-35 version adopted by the United States air force.

Aircraft:	Seversky P-35
Nation:	USA
Manufacturer:	Seversky Aircraft Corp.
Type:	Fighter
Year:	1937
Engine:	Pratt & Whitney R-1830-9 Twin Wasp, 14-cylinder radial, air-cooled 950 hp
Wingspan:	36 ft (10.97 m)
Length:	25 ft 1 in (7.67 m)
Height:	9 ft 9 in (2.76 m)
Weight:	6 294 lb (2,855 kg)
Maximum speed:	282 mph (454 km/h) at 10,000 ft (3,050 m)
Ceiling:	30,600 ft (9,330 m)
Range:	1,150 miles (1,850 km)
Armament:	2 machine guns; 300 lb (136 kg) of bombs
Crew:	1

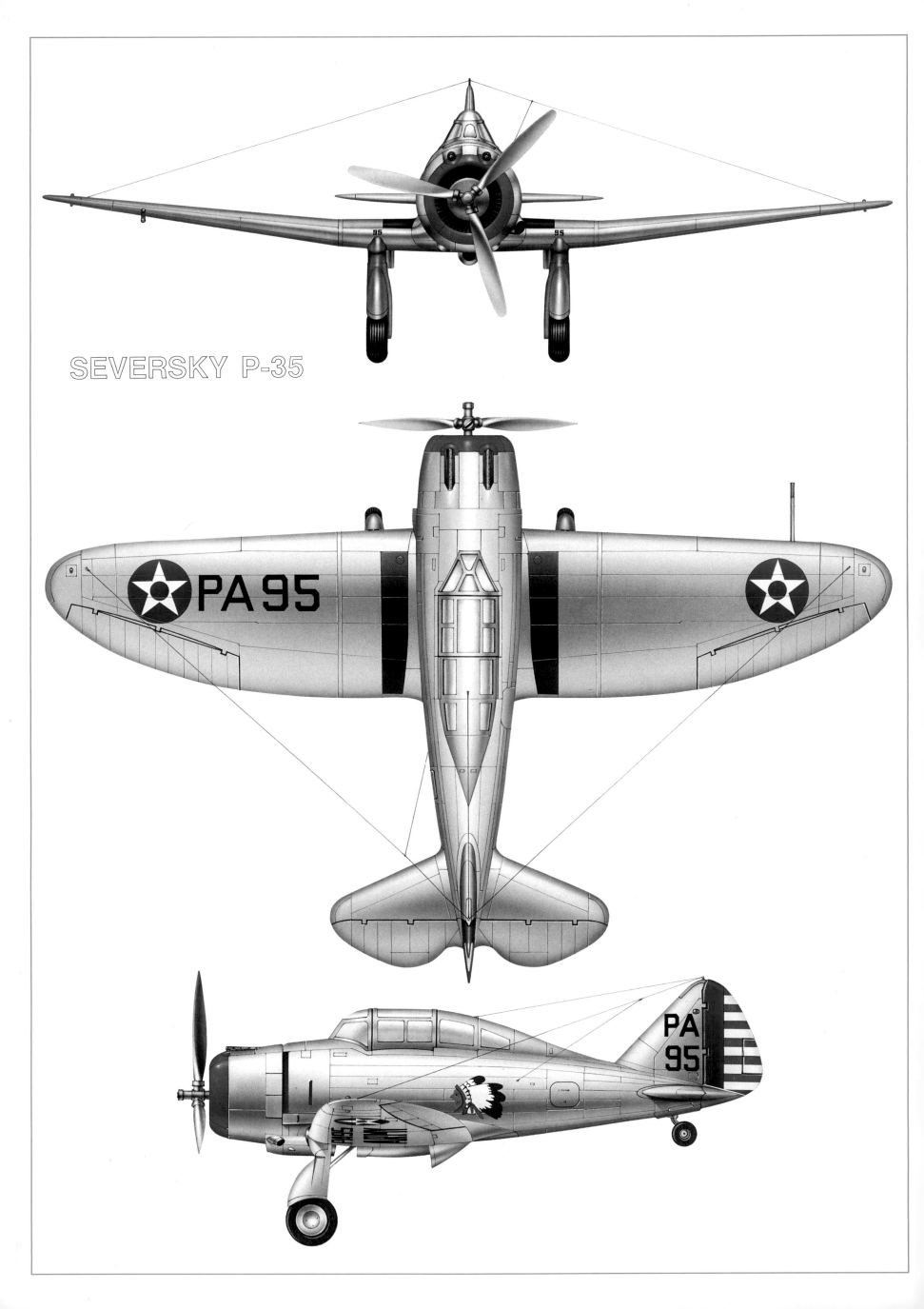

SEVERSKY P-35

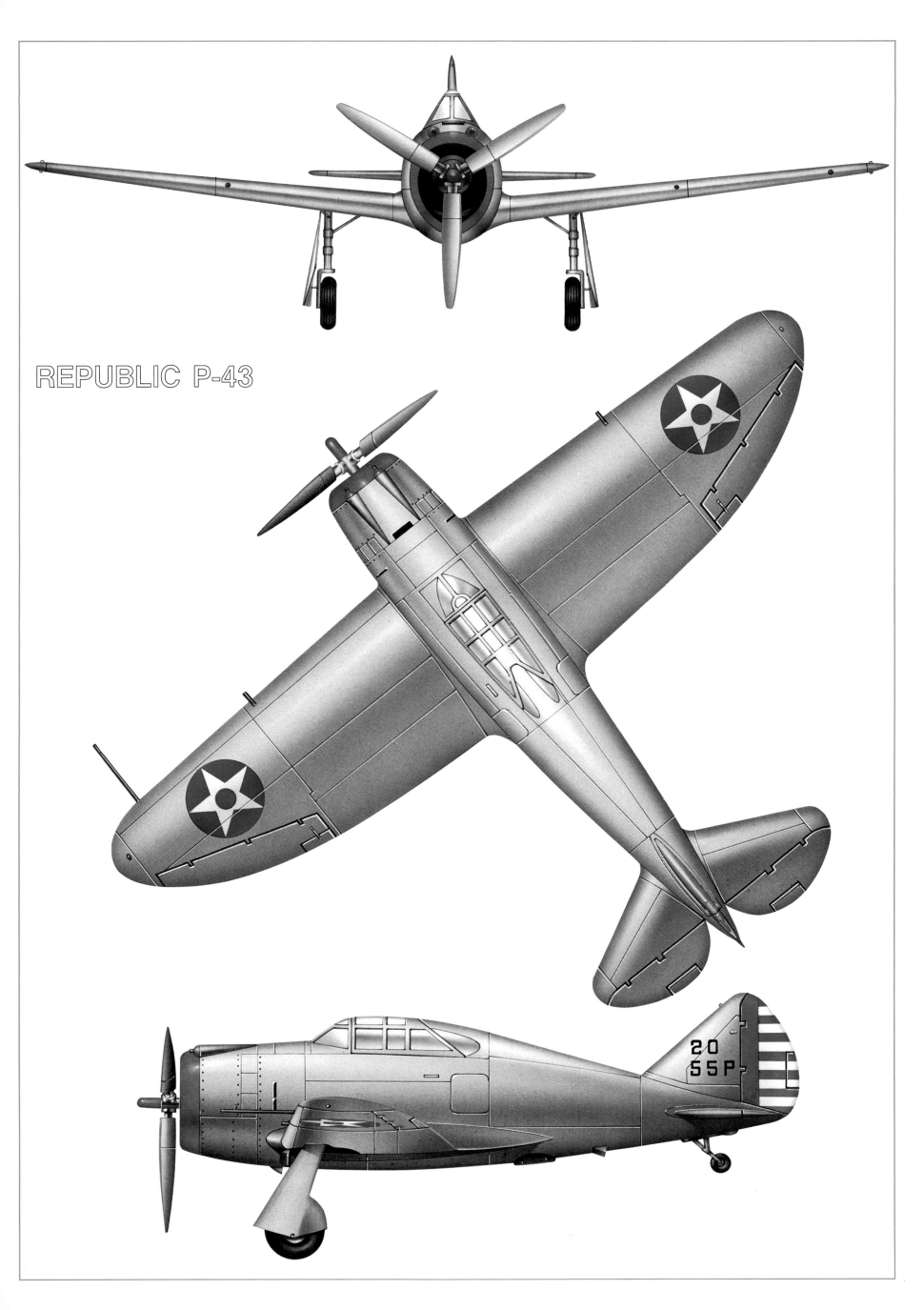

REPUBLIC P-43

One of the 13 preseries YP-43s.

Designed to participate in the competition announced by the USAAC on January 25, 1939, the Republic P-43 Lancer was derived directly from the P-35 model created by Alexander Kartveli three years earlier. However, like its predecessor, this fighter was not successful, due above all to its inadequate overall performance, and its production was authorized only to keep the assembly lines occupied while awaiting the development of the P-47 Thunderbolt. A total of 272 Lancers were built (including prototypes and preseries aircraft) in two versions that were basically similar, except for the type of engine adopted and the consequent slight differences in general performance and weight. The only Lancers to see combat duty were 103 of the P-43A type that were given to the Chinese air force, which used them against the Japanese, although with little success. The others were used for photo reconnaissance, after photographic equipment had been installed in the rear part of the fuselage.

The prototype, designated AP-4, was constructed by modifying a P-35 airframe and providing it with a 1,200 hp Pratt & Whitney R-1830-35 engine with turbo-supercharger. In the competition, the aircraft found itself competing with hardened rivals: the Lockheed XP-38, the Curtiss XP-40, and the Bell XP-39, all provided with in-line Allison V-1710 engines. After comparative tests, 13 AP-4s were ordered, and the aircraft was redesignated YP-43. In 1940, mass production was launched with an initial order for 54 planes.

Although the first P-43s were notably improved as compared to their direct predecessor, especially in terms of speed, they were not up to the level of the potential adversaries that were already fighting in the skies of Europe. This situation was so apparent that a new version of the aircraft had already been requested on October 12, 1939, powered by a 1,400 hp Pratt & Whitney R-2180-1 type engine or by a 1,750 hp R-2800-7 type. Although the aircraft was designated P-44 Rocket, and 80 were ordered, the project nevertheless remained incomplete: at that time Alexander Kartveli had already shown the plans for the future P-47 Thunderbolt to the military authorities, and considering the enormous potential of this entirely new aircraft, it was decided to continue with the construction of the P-43 Lancer in order to keep the assembly lines busy until the new production cycle was launched. The order for 80 P-44s was therefore transformed into a commission for a similar number of P-43As, the second Lancer variant powered by a Pratt & Whitney R-1830 engine, again generating 1,200 hp.

In all, 205 P-43As were completed, the first of which took to the air during 1941. The Lancers of the two versions that were modified for photo reconnaissance were redesignated RP-43-RE and RP-43A-RE respectively.

color plate
Republic P-43 Lancer 55th Pursuit Group U.S.Army Air Force - USA 1940

Aircraft:	Republic P-43
Nation:	USA
Manufacturer:	Republic Aviation Corp.
Type:	Fighter-bomber
Year:	1941
Engine:	Pratt & Whitney R-1830-47 Twin Wasp, 14-cylinder radial, air-cooled, 1,200 hp
Wingspan:	36 ft (10.97 m)
Length:	28 ft 6 in (8.68 m)
Height:	14 ft (4.26 m)
Weight:	7,935 lb (3,600 kg) loaded
Maximum speed:	349 mph (562 km/h) at 25,000 ft (7,620 m)
Ceiling:	38,000 ft (11,582 m)
Range:	800 miles (1,290 km)
Armament:	4 machine guns
Crew:	1

A Lancer P-43A fighting colored.

The XP-47H, an experimental version fitted with a 2,500 hp Chrysler in-line engine.

The Republic P-47 Thunderbolt was not only the largest and heaviest single-engine single-seater built during World War II, but also an outstanding combat plane, which demonstrated its qualities to the full in the roles of bomber escort and ground attack. Between 1942 and the end of 1945, no less than 15,683 P-47s came off the assembly lines (the highest number of any American fighter in the course of the war), and a large proportion of them remained in service once the war was over in the air forces of approximately 15 countries.

Created by Alexander Kartveli, Republic's chief designer, the P-47 represented the crowning point in a series of projects that had originated back in 1936, with the Seversky P-35, and which had evolved through the unsuccessful P-43 of 1940. It was after he had launched the latter project that Kartveli began to study another two fighter models derived from it, which he had designated AP-4 and AP-10. These aircraft were very different, the former being powered by a large radial engine, and the latter being designed around the slim V-12 liquid-cooled engine built by Allison. Paradoxically, the origins of the large and heavy Thunderbolt lay in this project for a light fighter. In fact, on August 1, 1939, the USAAC technical authorities rejected the offer of the AP-10 proposed by Kartveli and asked Republic to study a larger and more powerful version. In November two prototypes were commissioned (XP-47 and XP-47A), again powered by the same power plant, although Kartveli, who had realized the enormous limitations of the Allison engine, elaborated an alternative project based on the most powerful engine available at the time, the 2,000 hp Pratt & Whitney R-2800 Double Wasp.

The new aircraft was literally designed around this huge power plant and its complex exhaust gas powered feeding system, and the project was presented to the USAAC in June 1940. This time it was favorably received, and an order for the prototype (designated XP-47B) was placed on June 6, followed a week later by an initial order for 773 production series aircraft.

The prototype took to the air for the first time on May 6, 1941, and following a particularly laborious preparation, brilliantly tackled the series of flight tests. During evaluation, the Thunderbolt revealed its power to the full, flying at 393 mph (633 km/h) and climbing to 15,039 ft (4,572 m) in five minutes, despite its great takeoff weight. In March 1942, the aircraft of the initial P-47A series (170 in all) began to leave the assembly lines and were followed in August by the first of the 602 P-47Bs. The new fighter went into service at the beginning of 1943, in the units of the 8th Air Force based in Great Britain.

However, the major production variant (12,602 built in all) was the P-47D, which went into front-line service in 1943. This version of the Thunderbolt was fitted with a more powerful engine at altitude and in case of emergency and was capable of carrying a heavier bomb load. Beginning with the P-47D-25 production lot, it also had a transparent canopy providing 360-degree visibility, and the fuselage was consequently modified. The P-47Ds were the first to serve in the Pacific in the units of the USAAF and, in addition, they were also supplied to Allies: the Soviet Union, Great

Britain, Brazil, Mexico, and the Free French units.

Following an order for 130 P-47Ms (with more powerful engines), the final production was concentrated on the N variant, of which 1,816 were built, and which was suited to the needs of the war in the Pacific. These last Thunderbolts were fitted with a new wing and had a maximum range of 2,173 miles (3,500 km). After their completion, production ceased in December 1945.

color plate
Republic P-47D 514 F.S. 406th F.G. 9th Air Force U.S. Army Air Force - Italy 1944

Aircraft:	Republic P-47D
Nation:	USA
Manufacturer:	Republic Aviation Corp.
Type:	Fighter-bomber
Year:	1943
Engine:	Pratt & Whitney R-2800-63 Double Wasp, 18-cylinder radial, air-cooled, 2,000 hp
Wingspan:	40 ft 11 in (12.44 m)
Length:	36 ft 3 in (11.02 m)
Height:	14 ft 7 in (4.44 m)
Weight:	19,426 lb (8,800 kg)
Maximum speed:	427 mph (689 km/h) at 30,078 ft (9,144 m)
Ceiling:	42,105 ft (12,800 m)
Range:	474 miles (764 km)
Armament:	6-8 machine guns, 2,501 lb (1,133 kg) of bombs
Crew:	1

A formation of P-47Ns, the final version of the Thunderbolt with larger wings and increased range.

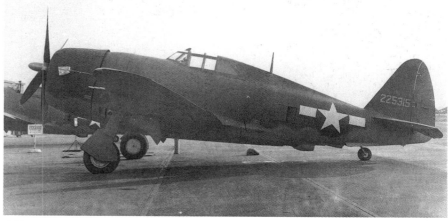

A P-47D Thunderbolt with the faired canopy typical of the initial versions.

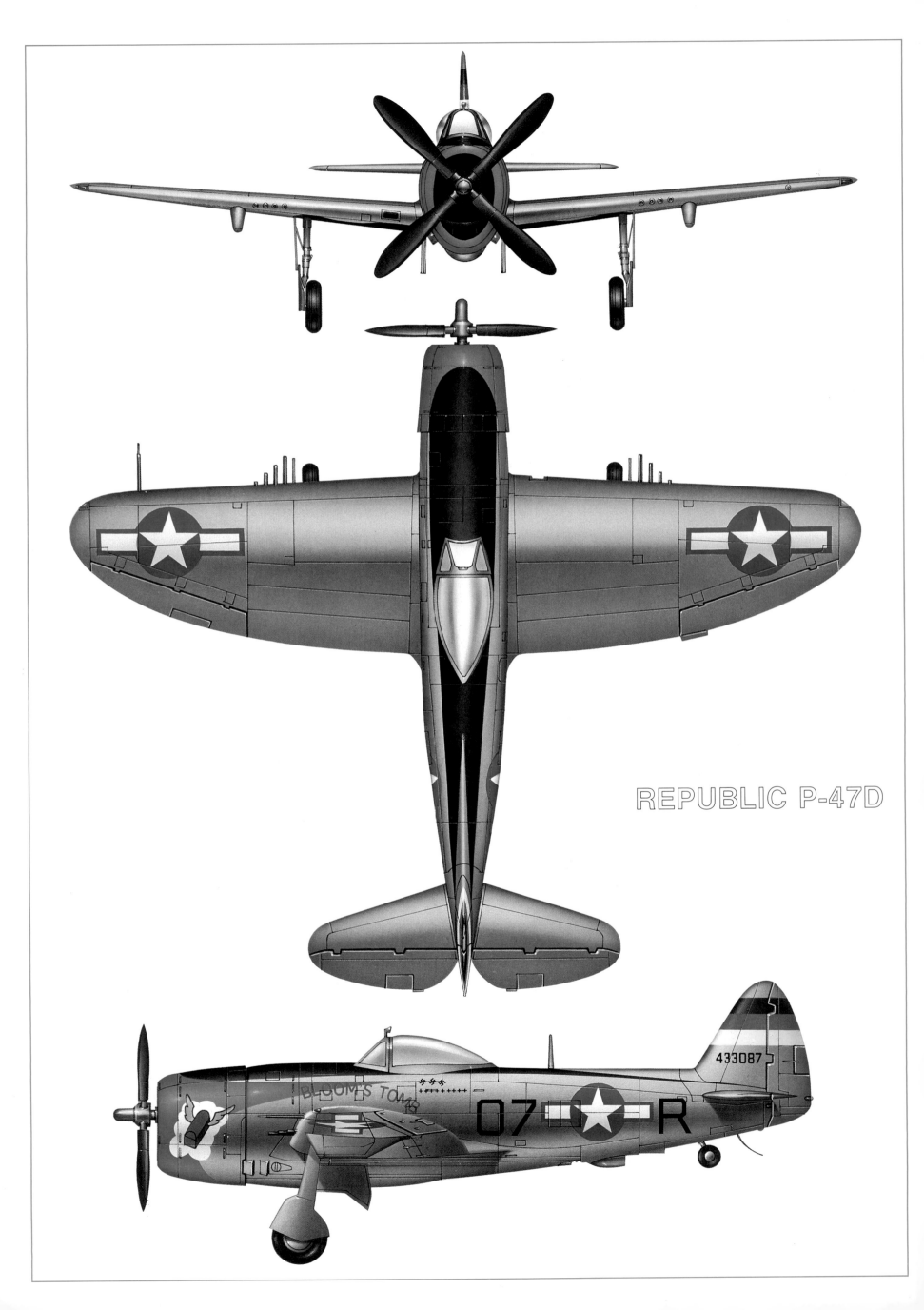

REPUBLIC P-47D

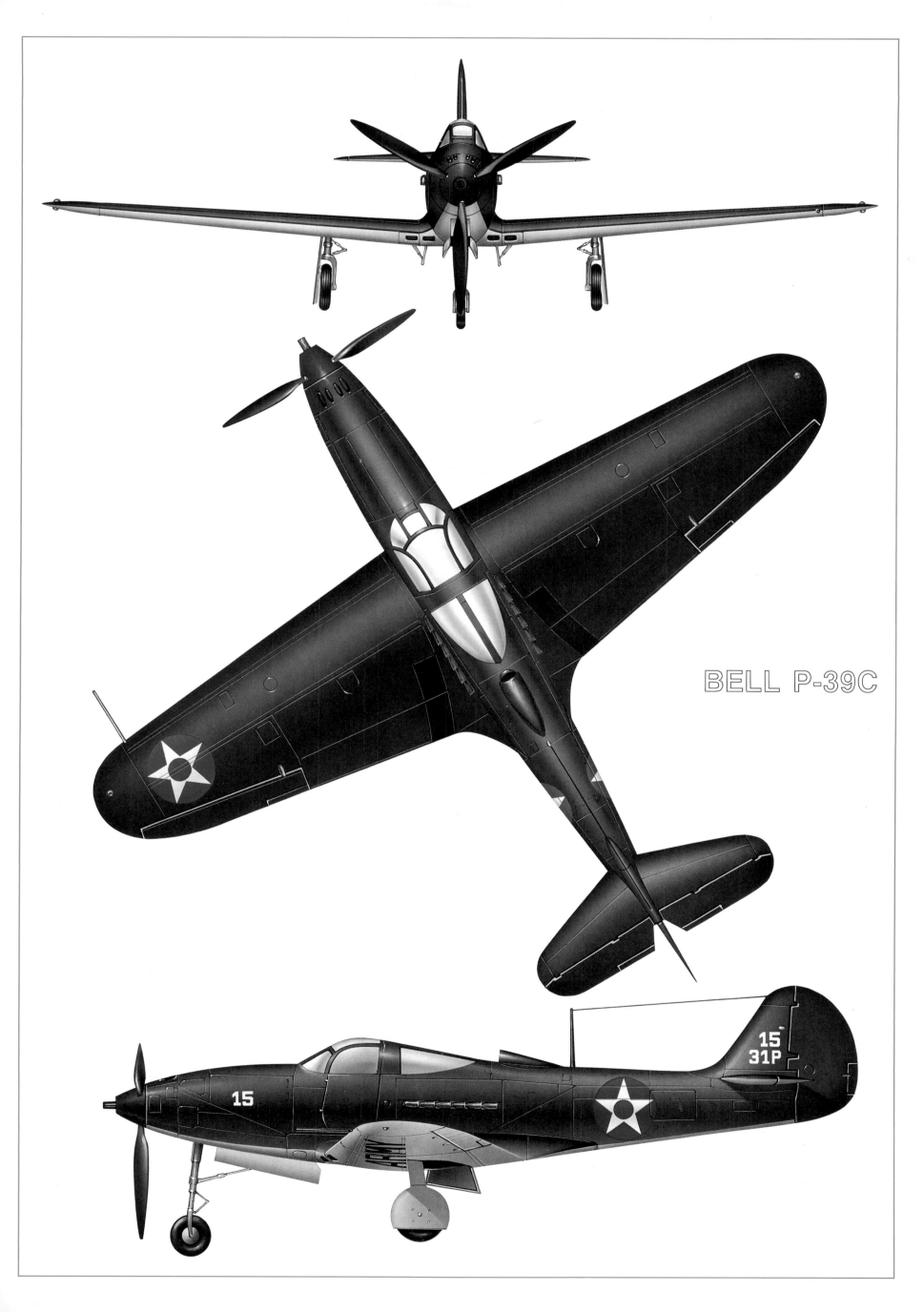

BELL P-39C

Designed as an interceptor, when the Bell P-39 Airacobra appeared it was acclaimed as one of the most advanced combat planes of the time, although ultimately it proved to be rather controversial due to the inadequacy of its engine. This led to it eventually being relegated to the less prestigious role of ground attack. Apart from this, this elegant aircraft still remains one of the most original built by the American aeronautical industry during the war. It was the first fighter in the world to be provided with three-wheel forward landing gear and also the first to have its engine installed centrally (behind the pilot). The latter drove the propeller by means of a transmission shaft that was more than 9 ft (3 m) long and that passed between the pilot's legs.

A total of 9,588 aircraft in several versions was built in all, and almost half of them (4,773) went to the Soviet Union. Despite everything, once the United States entered the war the P-39, together with the Curtiss P-40, was entirely responsible for supporting the front line until its more modern successors, the Lockheed P-38, Republic P-47, and North American P-51, appeared.

In March 1937, Bell presented the project for its revolutionary interceptor to the USAAC. It was literally built around one of the most original and powerful weapons in existence at the time: the American Armament Corporation's 37 mm cannon, which had been tested two years earlier with great success. The design was supervised by Robert Woods, and the result was decidedly original: the aircraft was an all-metal low-wing monoplane in which careful attention had been paid to aerodynamics. The fact that the engine (originally a 1,150 hp Allison V-1710 with supercharger) was installed in a central position was due to the need to install the cannon in the best position, that is to say the nose, together with the two 7.62 mm machine guns. The same need also led to the adoption of the three-wheel forward landing gear, which

had never been used in a single-seater fighter before. However, the central engine, installed in the proximity of the barycenter, also served to improve the aircraft's maneuverability. The prototype, designated XP-39, was ordered in October 1937, and it took to the air for the first time on April 6, 1938. Its performance proved remarkable from the start: without armament and armor, it reached a maximum speed of 390 mph (628 km/h) at 20,050 ft (6,096 m), having taken barely five minutes to reach this altitude. Its characteristics were clearly those of an interceptor, although numerous modifications were imposed on the Bell project by the USAAC authorities. The most important of these included the installation of an Allison engine without a supercharger, and therefore unsuitable at high altitudes. The prototype modified in this way was redesignated XP-39B, and its performance was marked by a notable decline, although it was followed by 12 similar preseries aircraft (YP-39). On October 8, 1939, an order was placed for an initial lot of 80 aircraft in a military version, designated P-39C. Delivery of these aircraft commenced in January 1941.

The next variant, the P-39D, was the first to be produced in any great number and the first to be built for export, although it was also the version that most disappointed the designers. The 675 aircraft ordered by Great Britain were rejected by the RAF after only a few days' service on the English Channel front, in September 1941. The judgment of the pilots was unfavorable: in practice, confronting the German fighters with the P-39 was equal to suicide. Consequently, approximately 200 aircraft were sent to the Soviet Union and a further 250 returned to the United States.

However, the fighter's lack of success did not slow down production. The P-39 continued to come off the assembly lines, not only to satisfy the demands of the U.S. Air Force, but also to satisfy those of the Soviet Union. The final series, the P-39N and P-39Q totaled 2,095 and 4,905 aircraft respectively.

A Bell P-39D with attachments for bombs on the belly and enlarged tail fin.

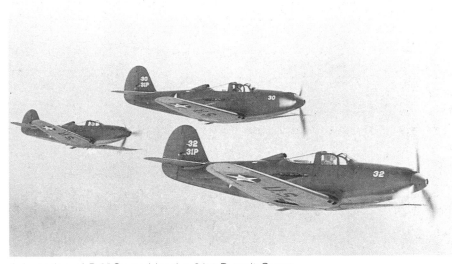

A formation of P-39C used by the 31st Pursuit Group.

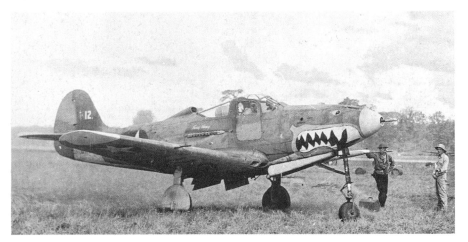

An Airacobra P-400 of the version originally built for Great Britain in service with the 67th Fighter Squadron in New Guinea. Note the characteristic shark mouth.

color plate
Bell P-39C 31st Pursuit Group U.S. Army Air Corps - Selfridge Field 1941

Aircraft:	Bell P-39C
Nation:	USA
Manufacturer:	Bell Aircraft Corp.
Type:	Fighter
Year:	1941
Engine:	Allison V-1710-35, 12-cylinder V, liquid-cooled, 1,150 hp
Wingspan:	34 ft (10.36 m)
Length:	30 ft 2 in (9.19 m)
Height:	11 ft 10 in (3.60 m)
Weight:	7,845 lb (3,520 kg) loaded
Maximum speed:	335 mph (536 km/h) at 13,800 ft (4,200 m)
Ceiling:	29,000 ft (8,900 m)
Range:	600 miles (960 km)
Armament:	1 × 37 mm cannon; 4 machine guns; 500 lb (226 kg) of bombs
Crew:	1

The final exponent of the family of P-39 Airacobras, the P-63 Kingcobra, differed from its predecessors not only in its more carefully studied aerodynamics, its greater size, and its more powerful Allison engine, but above all to the fact that it had been conceived initially as a fighter-bomber for tactical support. The P-63 carried out this role excellently, although the USAAF never used it in combat. In fact, of the 3,303 aircraft that were built, the majority (2,421) were sent to the Soviet Union. Another 300 were delivered to the Free French units. These aircraft were used by American military aviation only as trainers or targets. A special variant (RP-63) was built expressly for this purpose. This model possessed no armament and had been provided with reinforced covering in order to withstand the impact of the special shattering bullets used during training. Every hit made a red light on the wing tips blink.

The Kingcobra project was launched in the same period as the initial development of the P-39. The aim was to introduce the P-39's aerodynamic improvements to the other aircraft. Three experimental aircraft were built (XP-39E). They possessed the P-39D's fuselage and a wing provided with a laminar profile and squared tips; the tail planes were also modified. The tests went ahead successfully, stimulating the request for series production, with the designation P-76.

However, this program was cancelled after a few months. Instead, it was decided to build a larger and more powerful version of the aircraft, to be used as a fighter-bomber and tactical support fighter. In June 1941, two XP-63 prototypes were ordered, and they took to the air on December 7 and February 5, 1943, respectively. They were fitted with a 1,325 hp Allison V-1710-47 engine that drove a four-bladed metal variable-pitch propeller. During tests, the two aircraft crashed and a third prototype (XP-63A) had to be built. It made its maiden flight on April 26, 1943. In the meantime, the first production order had been placed for 1,725 aircraft (on September 29, 1942) and the first deliveries of the initial P-63A version commenced in October.

These Kingcobras were followed by 1,227 of the second principal variant, the P-63C (first delivered in January 1945), in which, as well as aerodynamic modifications an Allison V-1710-117 engine was fitted. This could generate 1,825 hp in an emergency, thanks to a water injection system. Besides these basic models, numerous subseries were built, differing from each other in their equipment (carrying supplementary fuel tanks) and offensive armament. Lastly, mention should be made of the only P-63D, characterized by

An XP-63D with modified canopy and cannon in the propeller hub.

a greater wingspan, drop canopy and 1,425 hp Allison V-1710-109 engine, and thirteen P-63Es, similar to the previous models, but with a traditional canopy. No fewer than 2,930 of these aircraft delivered in May 1945, were ordered before the course of the war led to their cancellation.

color plate
Bell P-63A Soviet Air Force - 1944

Aircraft:	Bell P-63A Kingcobra
Nation:	USA
Manufacturer:	Bell Aircraft Corp.
Type:	Fighter
Year:	1943
Engine:	Allison V-1710-95, 12-cylinder V, liquid-cooled, 1,325 hp
Wingspan:	38 ft 5 in (11.68 m)
Length:	32 ft 11 in (9.96 m)
Height:	12 ft 5 in (3.84 m)
Weight:	10,514 lb (4,763 kg)
Maximum speed:	409 mph (660 km/h) at 25,065 ft (7,620 m)
Ceiling:	43,111 ft (13,106 m)
Range:	449 miles (724 km)
Armament:	1 x 37 mm cannon; 4 machine guns; 523 lb (237 kg) of bombs
Crew:	1

A Kingcobra that was modified as an experiment, with skis being adopted instead of wheels.

An E series Kingcobra characterized by substantial modifications to the rear end of the fuselage.

BELL P-63A

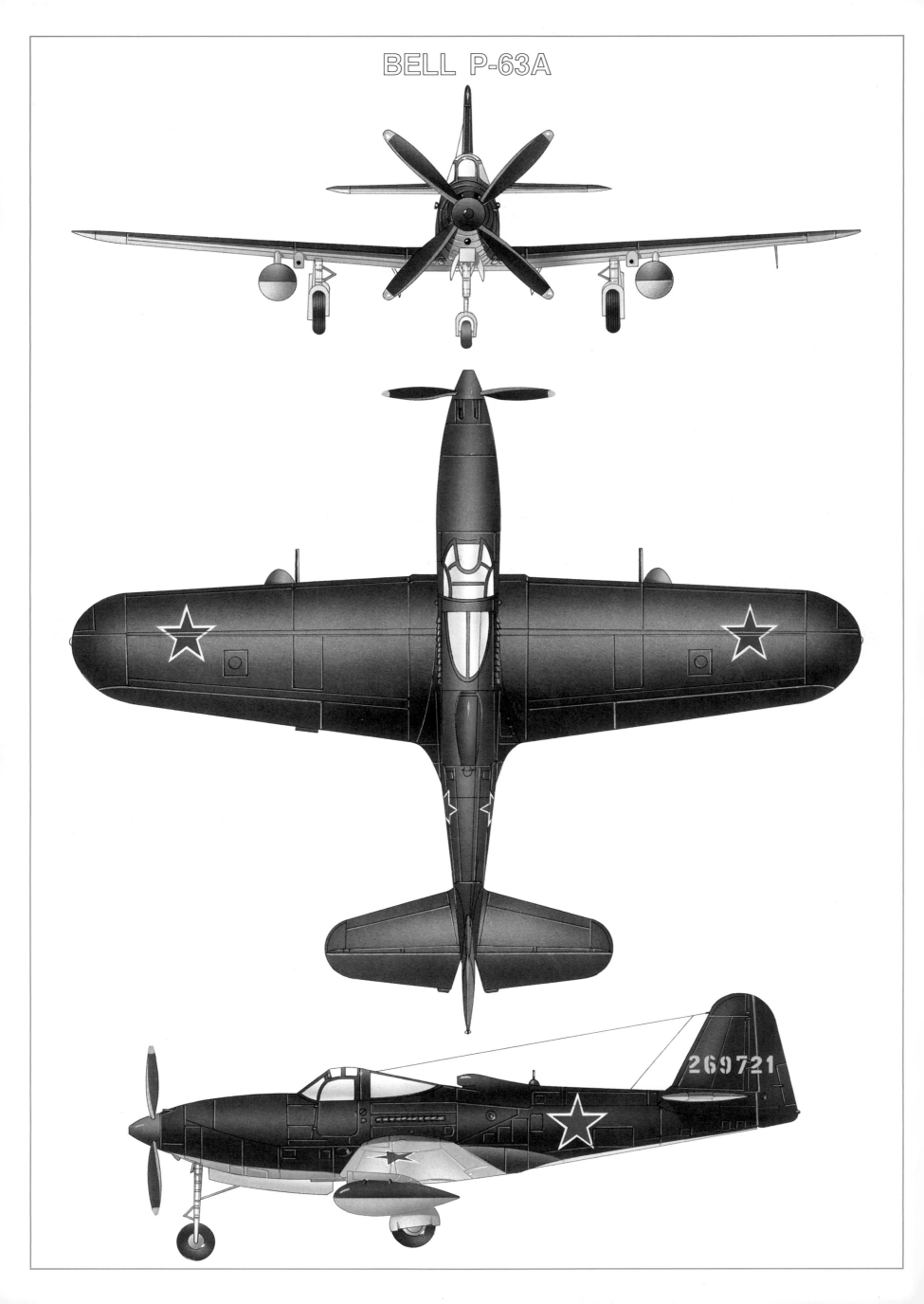

269721

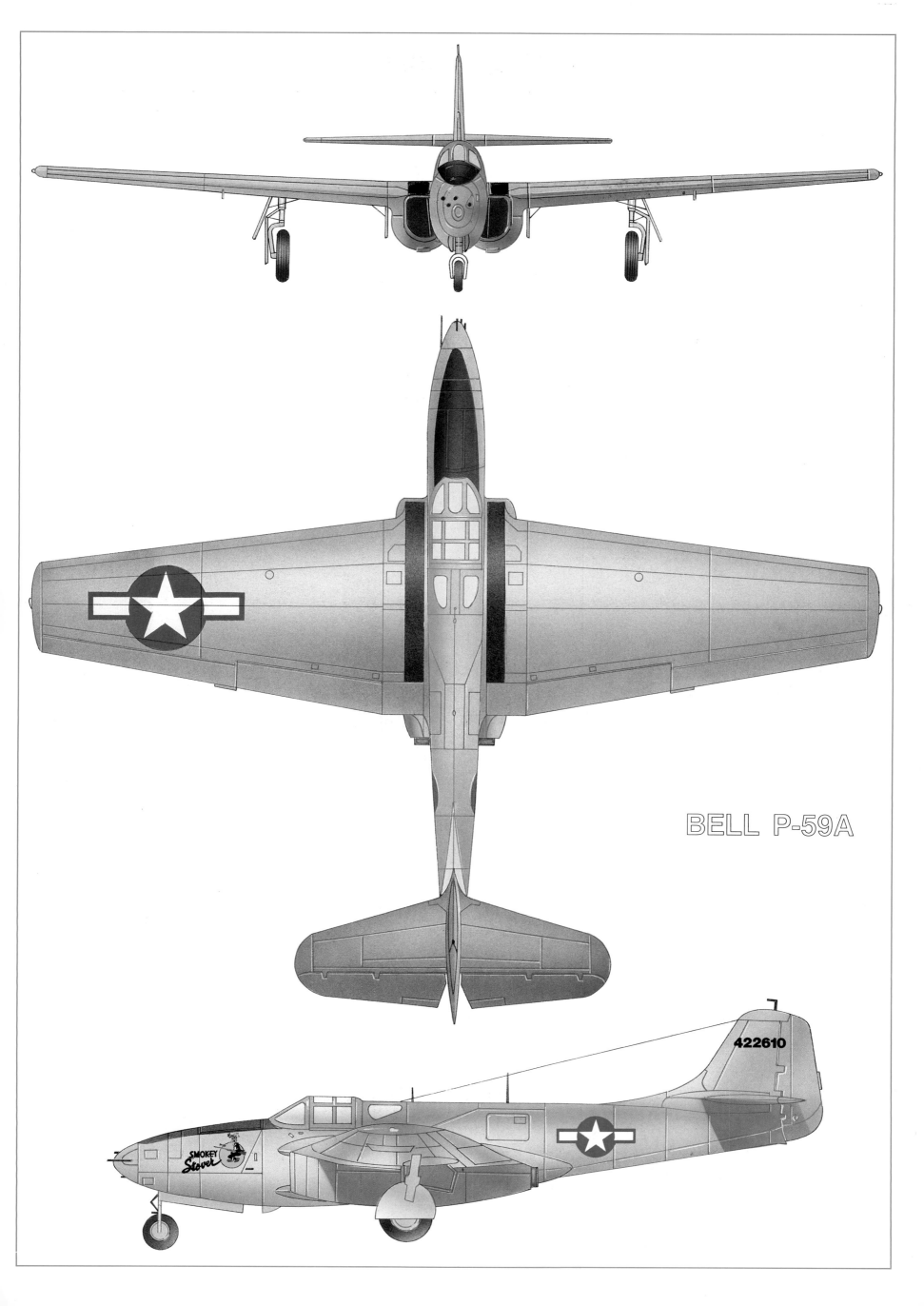

BELL P-59A

422610

SMOKEY Stover

The jet age began late in the United States compared to its British ally and German adversary. The aircraft that characterized the beginning of this veritable revolution was the P-59 Airacomet, a transitional plane produced by Bell which never saw combat and which, used for training and operative evaluations, prepared the ground for the American air force's first "true" jet fighter, the Lockheed P-80 Shooting Star. In all, just under 80 P-59s (prototypes included) came off the assembly lines in two versions between 1944 and 1945.

The project for the Airacomet (designated Model 27 by Bell) was launched during 1941. In April of that year, General Henry H. Arnold, head of the USAAF's General Staff, had happened to see the prototype of the Gloster E-28/39 in England (this was the first experimental jet aircraft to take to the air in Great Britain) and had obtained from the British the drawings of the Whittle W.2B turbojet, the new engine which was being built by Rolls-Royce at the time. The task of creating an initial series of jet engines was entrusted to General Electric, while on September 4, 1941, the Bell Aircraft Corporation was chosen to develop a combat plane provided with the revolutionary engine.

The program went forward in great secrecy, and in order to speed up the initiative, the new aircraft was assigned the designation XP-59A, a code that had already been given to a project for a two-seater fighter with piston engines and co-axial thrusting propellers that Bell was busy preparing. Construction of the first of the three XP-59A prototypes was launched in the spring of 1942, and the aircraft was flown on October 1, by the chief test pilot Robert M. Stanley. It was a single-seater middle wing monoplane with forward tricycle landing gear, characterized by the raising of the horizontal empennages (in order to place them out of the way of the turbojet's exhaust) and powered by a pair of General Electric I-A engines, each with a thrust of 1,250 lb (567 kg). During the initial evaluation tests, the airframe did not appear to have any particular weakness, although the engines proved to have several "teething problems," the main one being their lack of power. The 13 pre-series YP-59As were in fact intended to test the engines, and the first of these made its maiden flight on August 18, 1943. General Electric I-16 engines (later designated J-31) with 1,650 lb (748 kg) nominal thrust were installed on these aircraft.

The Airacomet never proved to be an outstanding aircraft, being hampered by a scarcity of power and a lack of maneuverability at low speeds. Nevertheless, in March 1944 the USAAF issued an order for 100 of the initial P-59A series, the first of which was delivered in August of the same year. The course of the conflict (but above all, the development of the more effective Lockheed model) led to drastic cuts being made in the orders: the assembly lines completed 20 P-59As and 30 P-59Bs, which differed from each other in the type of engines adopted and in their fuel capacity. The turbojets installed on the two models were, respectively, the General Electric J31-GE-3 with a thrust of 1,650 lb (748 kg) and the J31-GE-5 with a thrust of 2,976 lb (907 kg).

Most of the P-59s were assigned to the 412th Fighter Group, a special experimental unit formed within the 4th Air Force which became a veritable training center for the pilots and ground staff destined for future jet aircraft. Moreover, several Airacomets were modified for target towing, with a second cockpit being installed.

---

color plate

Bell P-59A 412th Fighter Group 4th Air Force U.S. Army Air Force - Land Field, Alaska, December 9, 1944. This was the first jet plane to land in Alaska

---

Aircraft:	Bell P-59A
Nation:	USA
Manufacturer:	Bell Aircraft Corp.
Type:	Fighter
Year:	1944
Engine:	2 General Electric J-31-GE-3, each with 1,650 lb (748 kg) thrust
Wingspan:	45 ft 7 in (13.87 m)
Length:	38 ft 11 in (11.84 m)
Height:	12 ft (3.66 m)
Takeoff weight:	19,398 lb (5,897 kg)
Maximum speed:	412 mph (665 km/h) at 30,078 ft (9,144 m)
Ceiling:	46,322 ft (14,082 m)
Range:	375 miles (604 km)
Armament:	1 × 37 mm cannon; 3 machine guns; 2,002 lb (907 kg) of bombs
Crew:	1

A production series P-59 with square wing tips. In this war-time photograph, the last two figures of the series number have been canceled.

Lockheed's first military aircraft to go into production was also one of the most famous and effective fighters of World War II. Between 1940 and 1945 almost 10,000 P-38 Lightnings were built. The aircraft was powerful and versatile, as well as being very unusual: it was the first two-engine interceptor to go into service in the USAAC; the first American fighter to surpass 400 mph (644 km/h); and the first production series aircraft to have double tail fins. The Lightning had a long and extensive career, during which it was used on practically all fronts in a great variety of roles, thus revealing the great potential of the original project. In fact, as well as serving as an interceptor, it was also used for photographic reconnaissance missions, as a fighter-bomber and as a night fighter. Christened *Der Gabelschwanz Teufel* ("The Devil with the Cleft Tail") by the Germans and "Two fighters, one pilot" by the Japanese, the P-38 was also the first USAAF fighter to shoot down one of the Luftwaffe's planes as well as being that which destroyed more Japanese aircraft than any other. The Lightning was also the aircraft used by the leading American aces in the conflict: Major Richard I. Bong (40 aircraft shot down), Major Thomas B. McGuire (38) and Colonel H. McDonald (27). Bong in fact shot down all his adversaries while flying a P-38, between December 12, 1942, and December 17, 1944. Among the numerous war missions in which the Lockheed fighter played a major role, one of the most memorable occurred on April 18, 1943, when a Lightning intercepted and shot down the two-engine G4M carrying Admiral Isoroku Yamamoto, commander-in-chief of the Japanese fleet, and the man who had planned the attack on Pearl Harbor.

The specifications that gave rise to the P-38 were issued by the technical authorities of the U.S.Army Air Corps in 1937. They called for a high-altitude interceptor capable of reaching 360 mph (580

km/h) at 20,000 feet (6,100 m) and 290 mph (467 km/h) at sea level. It was also to be capable of reaching its optimum ceiling in six minutes. These characteristics were far to be easy to satisfy in a monoplane of traditional configuration, but Lockheed's chief designers, Hall L. Hibbard and Clarence L. "Kelly" Johnson, were not to be discouraged, and they examined six possible solutions before presenting their Model 22. This was a middle wing two-engine aircraft with double tail beams (this solution was necessary in order to house the engines and their superchargers), central pod for the pilot and armament, double vertical tail units linked by a single horizontal plane, and a completely retractable tricycle forward landing gear. The project proved to be a success, and on June 23, 1937, a prototype was ordered. This took to the air on January 27, 1939, and before official evaluations, the USAAC decided to use it in an attempt at breaking the speed record for crossing the United States from coast to coast. The flight took place on February 11: from March Field in California to Mitchell Field, New York, in seven hours 43 minutes, including two stops for refueling. The aircraft crashed when landing due to a fault in one of the engines, but its effectiveness as a combat plane had been proved sensationally. On April 27, an order was placed for 13 preseries YP-38s, followed immediately after by the first contracts for production-series aircraft.

Following the construction of the first 29 P-38s, which were substantially the same as the prototype, 36 P-38Ds (with modifications to the systems on board) came off the assembly lines, together with 210 P-38Es (the first major production version, with heavier armament and in service from November 1941). At the same time a variant destined for export to Great Britain was prepared. In fact the British, who were in desperate need of fighters, had ordered no fewer than 667 P-38s in March 1940. However, the engines of these aircraft were not provided with superchargers, and their performance was decidedly inferior. They were therefore rejected by the RAF: 147 of the 150 ordered initially were completed in the United States as the P-38F. This variant (which went into production early in 1942 and was operative by March) was the first to see combat, initially in Europe toward the middle of the year and then in North Africa in November. It had more powerful engines and wing racks for bombs or supplementary fuel tanks. A total of 527 was built in all. These were followed by 1082 P-38Gs.

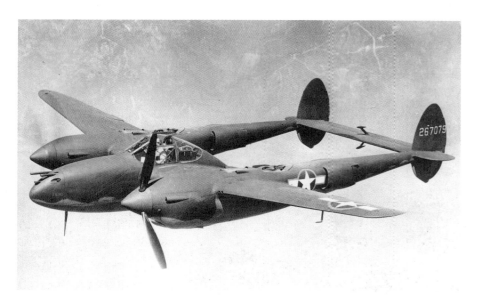

A P-38 in flight with one engine immobile.

A Lockheed F-5, the photo reconnaissance version of the P-38G in which the armament was replaced by photographic equipment. This aircraft (2364) was one of the first American planes to operate from the airports on the island of Malta, piloted by Lt. Berry.

color plate

Lockheed P-38G piloted by Captain Thomas G. Lanphier Jr. 339th Fighter Squadron U.S. Air Force. This aircraft took part in the shooting down of the plane carrying Admiral Yamamoto, the commander-in-chief of the Japanese Imperial Navy Combined Fleet on April 18, 1943

Aircraft:	Lockheed P-38F
Nation:	USA
Manufacturer:	Lockheed Aircraft Corp.
Type:	Fighter
Year:	1942
Engine:	2 Allison V-1710-49, 12-cylinder V, liquid-cooled, 1,385 hp each
Wingspan:	52 ft 1 in (15.84 m)
Length:	37 ft 10 in (11.53 m)
Height:	12 ft 10 in (3.91 m)
Weight:	20,000 lb (9,065 kg) loaded
Maximum speed:	395 mph (636 km/h) at 25,000 ft (7,620 m)
Ceiling:	39,000 ft (11,880 m)
Range:	425 miles (684 km)
Armament:	1 × 20 mm cannon; 4 machine guns; 2,002 lb (907 kg) of bombs
Crew:	1

LOCKHEED P-38G

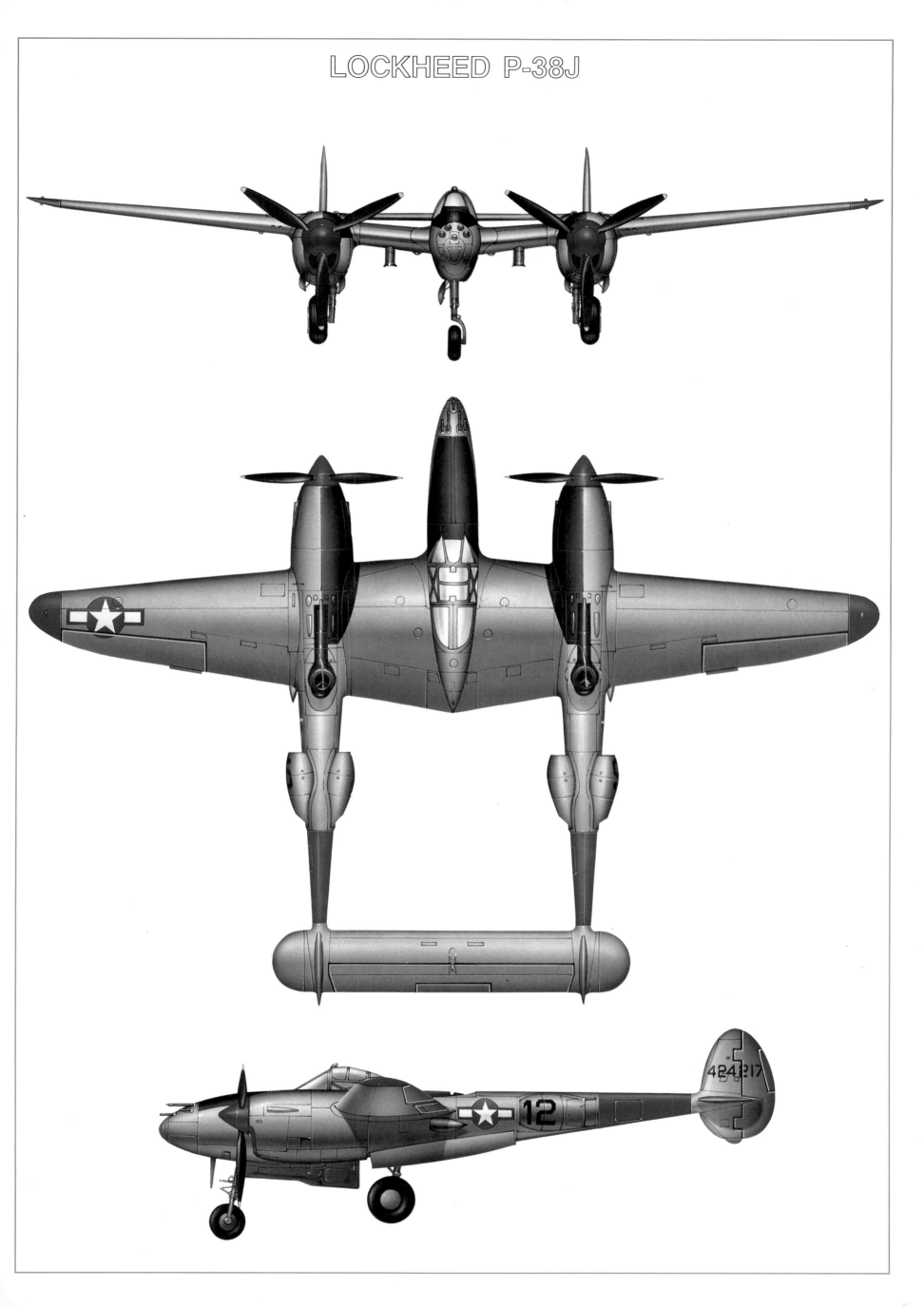

LOCKHEED P-38J

A pair of P-38J. The aircraft in the foreground is a photographic reconnaissance version.

Following the initial D, E, and F versions, production of the Lockheed P-38 Lightning assumed a steady pace with the subsequent G variant, of which 1,082 were built in all. 381 of these were transformed into photo reconnaissance planes: 181 with the code F-5A, and 200 with the code F-5B. These aircraft differed very little from their direct predecessors. The main modifications introduced in the various series concerned primarily the engine and equipment details. The P-38Gs went into service in the Pacific in the early months of 1943, and in fact several of these aircraft (belonging to the 347th and 18th Fighter Groups based at Guadalcanal) managed to intercept and shoot down the twin-engine Mitsubishi G4M that was carrying Admiral Isoroku Yamamoto, Commander-in-chief of the Japanese fleet and the arteficer of the attack on Pearl Harbor, on April 18 of the same year.

Approximately a month later the P-38H, the nex variant, went into service. Its engines were further modified and the aircraft itself was characterized by overall structural reinforcements, with the aim of increasing the bomb load, which weighed 3,203 lb (1,451 kg) compared to the 2,002 lb (907 kg) weight of the previous versions. Production of these aircraft amounted to 601, before the assembly lines were used for the building of a new variant, the P-38J. The latter became one of the most effective and widely used of the entire family. It went into service in August 1943, and no fewer than 2,970 were built in six production series, which differed from each other in modifications to details. Features they shared were the further strengthening of the engines and, above all, the remarkable increase in fuel capacity. This passed to 433 US gals (1,552 liters) in the internal tanks. A further 721 US gals (2,726 liters) contained in supplementary external tanks could be added. This capacity was an advantage to the aircraft's overall range, which reached a maximum of 2,598 miles (4,184 km). Moreover, the external appearance of the P-38Js was slightly different: modifications to the position of the radiators led to a more prominent shape of the front of the engine nacelles.

However, the development of the Lockheed fighter (which had by then become a constant presence in the skies of Europe and Asia) proceeded. In 1944, production passed to the P-38L variant, which was built in the greatest number. In all, 3,810 were constructed (as a further 113 were built by Consolidated Vultee) on an order for no fewer than 2,000 aircraft issued by the USAAF in June 1944, which was later cancelled due to the course of the conflict. Strengthening of the engine and heavier armament (among other things, these Lightnings were the first to carry rockets) enhanced the role in which the P-38s had proved to be especially suited since the appearance of the J version: that of

tactical bomber. A special technique was prepared for this purpose. The formation's lead was entrusted to a two-seater aircraft. (The marks-man was installed in the tip of the nose, which lacked the usual machine guns and was provided with glazing). The bombs were thus released all at once, following an order given by the leader of the formation. These Lightnings were remarkably successful, so much so that they earned themselves another nickname: Droop Snouts.

In the context of the extensive production of the P-38, it is worth mentioning the last variant to be used during the conflit. This was the P-38M night fighter, characterized by the adoption of radar apparatus in a pod in the nose and beneath the wings, as well as by the fact that it was a two-seater. The second crew member was housed behind the pilot, in a raised cockpit. Production of these aircraft, obtained by transforming the P-38L, amounted to approximately 80 planes. Only very few succeeded in taking part in the operations of the final weeks of the war against Japan.

The Lightning, which is remembered as one of the most famous and efficient American fighters of the war, began to be withdrawn from the units of the USAAF in 1946 and was officially declared surplus three years later.

---

color plate

Lockheed P-38J 27th Fighter Squadron 1st Fighter Group 15th Air Force U.S. Army Air Force - Salsola Italy, 1944

Aircraft:	Lockheed P-38L
Nation:	USA
Manufacturer:	Lockheed Aircraft Corp.
Type:	Fighter
Year:	1944
Engine:	2 Allison V-1710-111/113, 12-cylinder V, liquid-cooled, 1,475 hp each
Wingspan:	52 ft 1 in (15.84 m)
Length:	37 ft 11 in (11.53 m)
Height:	12 ft 10 in (3.91 m)
Weight:	21,629 lb (9,798 kg)
Maximum speed:	415 mph (666 km/h) at 25,065 ft (7,620 m)
Ceiling:	44,115 ft (13,411 m)
Range:	450 miles (724 m)
Armament:	1 × 20 mm cannon; 4 machine guns; 3,203 lb (1,451 kg) of bombs
Crew:	1

The P-38M, the night fighter version with radar equipment and a second seat for its operator.

NORTH AMERICAN P-51B

The North American P-51 Mustang, destined to go down in history as the best fighter of World War II, was the remarkable product of two advanced technologies: that of the American aeronautical industry, which managed to create an airframe that was extremely advanced both structurally and aerodynamically in only 117 days; and that of the British motor industry, which provided the ideal complement in the form of its prestigious Rolls-Royce Merlin engine. The result is still an «immortal» aircraft nowadays, its fame having survived the events of the war in which it played the leading role to remain as indisputable testimony of an entire era of aviation that has now gone for ever. Many of the 15,367 aircraft that were built survived World War II and remained in service until the Korean War, well into the jet age.

The P-51 project originated in April 1940. In the weeks before this, the British purchasing commission, which had gone to the United States in the desperate search for effective aircraft, had asked James H. «Dutch» Kindelberger, the president of North American, to build the Curtiss P-40 fighters on license for the RAF. Kindelberger, who had directed the company for only a few years, had replied with the claim that his designers were capable of building a combat plane fitted with the same power plant as the P-40 (the Allison V-1710) but with characteristics that were far superior. On April 10 the proposal was accepted by the British, who ordered a prototype, but on the condition that the project be completed within 120 days and that the aircraft's performance really be superior to that of its rival. The work, entrusted to a group of young technicians led by Raymond H. Rice and Edgar Schmued, went ahead at an alarming rate. The prototype (designated NA-73X) was ready three days before the deadline, although it lacked an engine and the wheels were borrowed from an AT-6 trainer. Its maiden flight took place on October 26, 1940, and the aircraft's characteristics were more than remarkable, since it proved to be faster than the P-40 by about 25 mph (40 km/h). The British purchasing commission confirmed the initial production order for 320 planes: the first production series aircraft took to the air on May 1, 1941, and remained at North American for technical evaluations; in November the second arrived in Great Britain, where it was given the official designation of Mustang Mk.I. These aircraft, judged to be far superior to any other American fighter, went into service in the spring of 1942 as tactical reconnaissance planes. At more or less the same time, the British ordered a further 300, which differed only in minor details.

In the meantime, two aircraft have been tested in the United States with the designation XP-51, although despite the excellent results, no production order had followed. After Pearl Harbor, 53 aircraft meant for Great Britain were retained and used as reconnaissance planes, and in 1942 alone the USAAF ordered 310 P-51As and 500 others modified for use as dive-bombers and designated A-36A.

However, the Mustang had still not achieved perfection, being penalized as it was by the inadequate performance of the Allison engine. Thus, in October 1942, the British RAF entrusted five fighter versions of the aircraft to Rolls-Royce, designating them Mustang X, so that experiments could be carried out with the installation of a Merlin 65 engine. At the same time, a similar experiment was conducted in the United States using the same engine built on license by Packard (V-1650-3) on two aircraft designated XP-51B. The results exceeded all expectations: the first XP-51B prototype, tested on November 30, 1942, proved capable of reaching 440 mph (710 km/h) at 29,605 ft (9,000 m), compared to the 390 mph (628 km/h) at 20,012 ft (6,100 m) achieved by the P-51A. Moreover, it could climb to 20,065 ft (6,100 m) in five minutes and 54 seconds (compared to the nine minutes taken by the previous model).

The aircraft went into production in the late spring of 1943, and was built as the P-51B (1,988 aircraft) in the Inglewood factory and as the P-51C in the new Dallas factory (1,750 aircraft). Great Britain received a total of 300, which it designated Mustang Mk.III. The USAAF's first P-51Bs went to Britain, as part of the 8th Air Force, in November 1943 and carried out their first mission on December 1.

color plate

North American P-51B 336th Fighter Squadron 4th Fighter Group 8th Air Force U.S. Army Air Force - England 1943

Aircraft:	North American P-51B
Nation:	USA
Manufacturer:	North American Aviation Inc.
Type:	Fighter
Year:	1943
Engine:	Packard V-1650-3, 12-cylinder V, liquid-cooled, 1,400 hp
Wingspan:	37 ft (11.27 m)
Length:	32 ft 3 in (9.82 m)
Height:	13 ft 8 in (4.16 m)
Weight:	11,814 lb (5,352 kg)
Maximum speed:	439 mph (708 km/h) at 30,082 ft (9,145 m)
Ceiling:	42,111 ft (12,802 m)
Range:	1,299 miles (2,092 m)
Armament:	4 machine guns, 2,002 lb (907 kg) of bombs
Crew:	9

A P-51C with fuel tanks on the wings and rocket launchers.

A P-51B Mustang characterized by remarkable aerodynamic refinements.

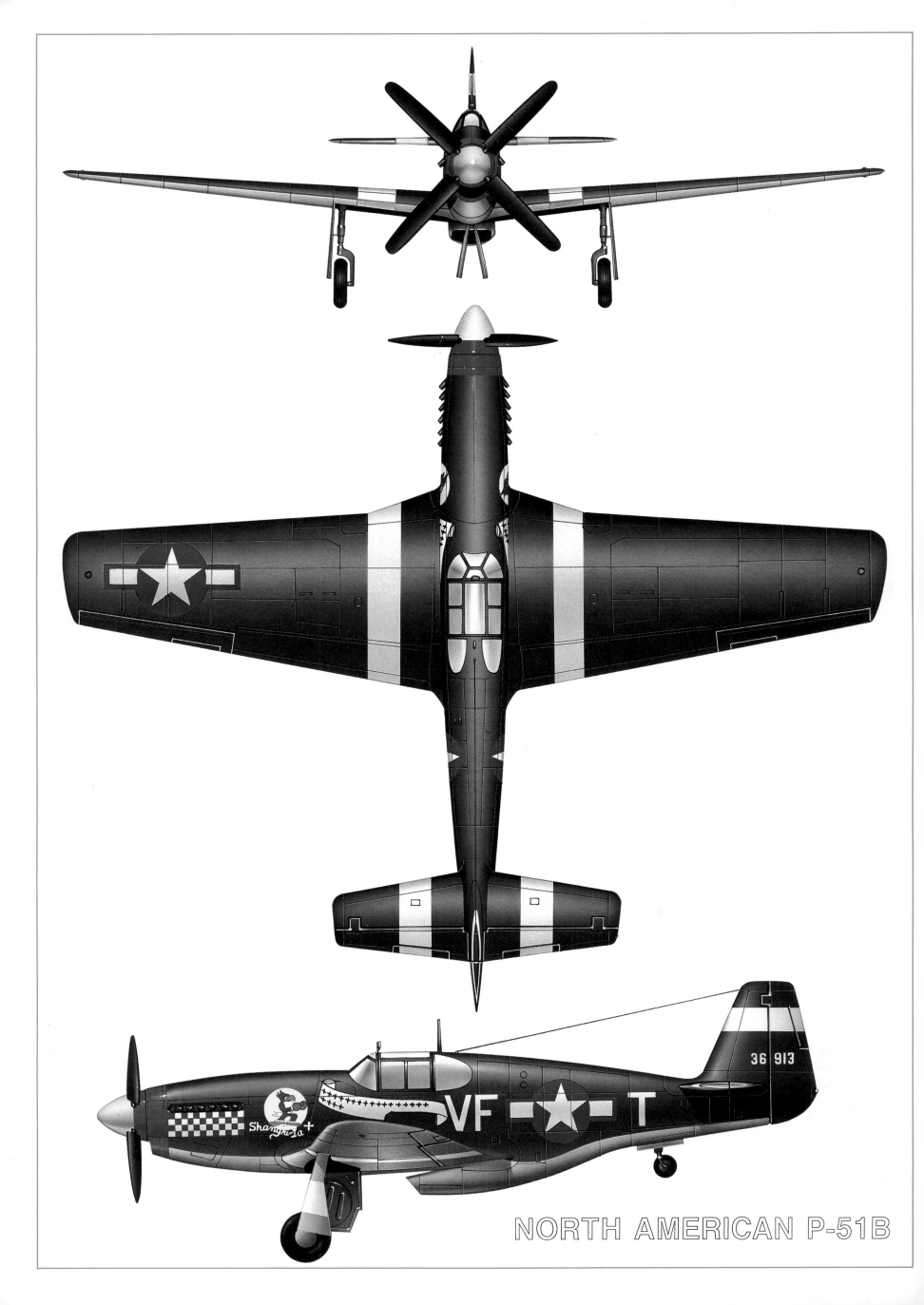

NORTH AMERICAN P-51B

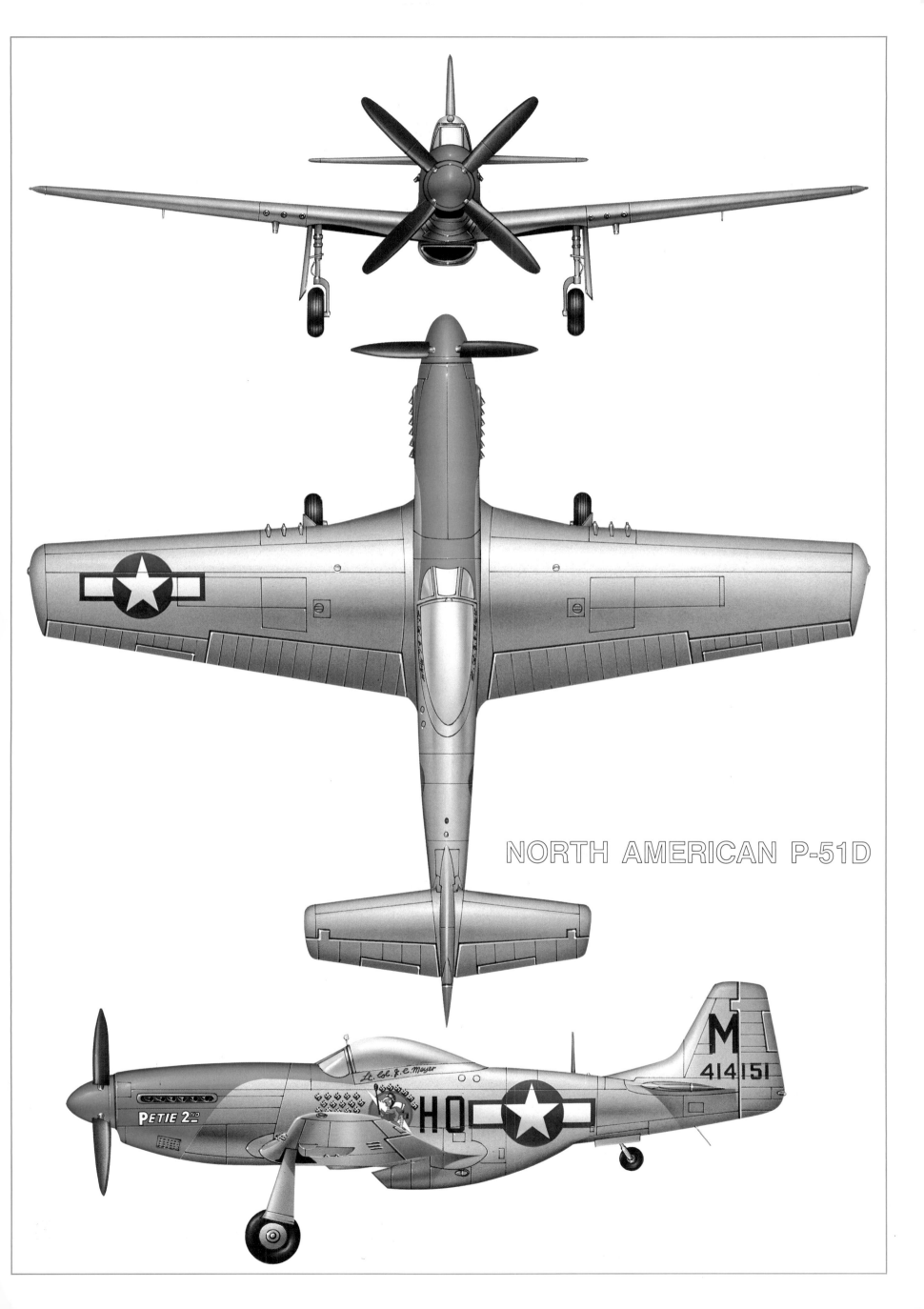

NORTH AMERICAN P-51D

In 1944, the development of the North American P-51 Mustangs destined to go down in history as the best fighter of World War II, led to the appearance of a new version, the D, which became the major production version. The main characteristic of this aircraft (7,956 were built in all) was the fuselage's drastic revision. This change was made necessary to overcome problems concerning the pilot's field of vision which had been complained of in the previous variants. These problems had been only partly solved in the Royal Air Force's Mustang Mk.III with the adoption of a round structureless canopy (known as the Malcolm hood, after its inventor), although this solution was a compromise. In the P-51Ds, the fairing's front part of the pilot's seat was eliminated and the cockpit was covered by a completely transparent drop canopy which was able to guaranteed total visibility. Moreover, in order to compensate for the decreased lateral surface area, a fin was added to the rudder.

These structural modifications, together with the adoption of a more powerful engine and an increased offensive armament, brought the Mustang to its optimum form, that remained basically unaltered throughout the rest of its long production. Alongside the production of the P-51Ds, 1,500 P-51Ks were built. These were almost identical to the previous variant apart from a different kind of propeller. A number of these two Mustang's versions were also given to the British RAF: 280 P-51Ds and 594 P-51Ks, which were redesignated Mustang Mk.IV and Mk.IVA, respectively.

In Europe above all (thanks to its excellent performance as far as range and speed were concerned) the Mustang imposed itself as the dominator of the skies. It became a constant presence, especially escorting the massive bombers formations sent to targets in Germany. Nevertheless, the project's development went ahead still further, the intention being to build an even more prestigious combat plane. The last variant to go into series production emerged from tests carried out on several lightened prototypes (designated XP-51F, XP-51G and XP-51J). This was the P-51H which, at 486 mph (784 km/h), proved to be the fastest of the entire family. However, only 555 of these Mustangs were built before the end of the conflict and only very few participated in the war's last operations against Japan. Victory led to the original

order for 1,700 aircraft being cancelled, and at the same time, orders for another 700 P-51Ls and 1,628 P-51Ms, similar to the H version (apart from their engines), were also cancelled.

The Mustang played an extremely important role in World War II. Some idea of its activity can be gained from figures relative to the theater of war in Europe. The P-51s in service with the USAAF alone carried out no fewer than 213,873 missions, flying for more than 1,120,000 hours. They destroyed 4,950 enemy aircraft, 4,131 of which were on the ground, a number amounting to 48.9% of the total losses suffered by the enemy. The last mission of the conflict was carried out on August 14, 1945 on Osaka. This, however, did not bring the long active career of the P-51 to an end, as it was soon employed in Korea.

The years following World War II marked a new phase in the Mustang's career. Apart from its employment in the U.S. Air Force, it served in those of more than 50 other countries.

color plate

North American P-51D 352nd Fighter Group 487th Squadron U.S. Army Air Force. This was the personal aircraft of Colonel Meyer

Aircraft:	North American P-51D
Nation:	USA
Manufacturer:	North American Aviation Inc.
Type:	Fighter
Year:	1944
Engine:	Packard V-1650-7, 12-cylinder V, liquid-cooled, 1,612 hp
Wingspan:	37 ft (11.27 m)
Length:	32 ft 3 in (9.82 m)
Height:	13 ft 8 in (4.16 m)
Takeoff weight:	11,615 lb (5,262 kg)
Maximum speed:	436 mph (703 km/h) at 25,065 ft (7,620 m)
Ceiling:	42,009 ft (12,771 m)
Range:	949 miles (1,529 km)
Armament:	6 machine guns; 2,002 lb (907 kg) of bombs
Crew:	1

A North American P-51D with dorsal fin in flight.

One of the best medium bombers of the entire conflict, the North American B-25 Mitchell was one of the great protagonists of air warfare. More than 11,000 came off the assembly lines in numerous versions between 1940 and 1945, and production was characterized by continuous improvements to the aircraft, as well as an increase in its power, allowing the remarkable features of the original project to be fully exploited. This versatile and efficient two-engine aircraft's intense career lasted well beyond World War II: after having served on all fronts, not only bearing the insignia of the U.S. Army and Navy air forces, but also those of Great Britain, the Commonwealth countries, and the Soviet Union, once the war ended the B-25 was to remain in service until the 1960s, especially in some of the less important air forces.

The original project, designated NA-40, had been launched by the North American company's technicians in 1938 on the basis of specifications issued by the U.S. Army Air Corps requesting a two-engine attack plane and bomber. The prototype made its first flight in January 1939. It was a medium-high wing monoplane that featured three-wheel forward landing gear and was powered by two Pratt & Whitney R1830-56C3-G radial engines generating 1,115 hp each. These engines were replaced with a pair of 1,369 hp Wright GR-2600-A71 Cyclones, and with this modification the prototype (designated NA-40B) was handed over to the military authorities in March. After only two weeks of flight testing, the aircraft crashed, but there were no longer any doubts concerning its potential: North American was authorized to proceed with the development of the prototype, incorporating a series of modifications into it. The definitive project (NA-62) was completed six months later and immediately went into production (an initial order was placed for 184 aircraft) with the official designation of B-25. The name Mitchell was chosen in memory of General William "Billy" Mitchell, the man who, since 1920, had prophesied the future role of the air force, and whose outspokenness had led to his being court-martialed for insubordination in 1925.

The principal modifications consisted in the widening of the fuselage and the lowering of the wing, from a medium-high to a medium position, in order to improve housing for the crew and the bomb load capacity. The engines were also replaced by two 1,700 hp Wright R-2600 Cyclones. The first B-25 took to the air on August 19, 1940, but showed signs of instability, making further structural modifications necessary. After 24 aircraft had been built, the designation was altered to B-25A, and these 40 aircraft incorporated armor protection for the pilots and fuel tanks. The remaining 120 aircraft ordered in the initial contract were completed as the B version, in which the defensive armament was strengthened through the addition of servo-controlled turrets on the back and in the belly. The production rate then increased with the next two variants, the B-25C and B-25D, delivered at the end of 1941, and of which 1,619 and 2,290 were built respectively. As well as being fitted with a new version of the R-2600 engine, these aircraft were also provided with an autopilot and bomb racks under the wings. The increase in the bomb load also provided the possibility of carrying a torpedo in the case of antishipping attacks. Deliveries to the United States' major allies, Great Britain and the Soviet Union, began with these two versions, and they received a total of 595 and 870 aircraft.

The first operative unit to be equipped with the B-25 was the 17th Bombardment Group, which received the B-25As in the spring of 1941. On April 18, 1942, it was from this unit that the 16 aircraft were chosen to carry out one of the Mitchell's most daring missions: the first air raid on Tokyo. The mission, thought up and commanded by James A. Doolittle, the famous racing pilot of the 1920s, was carried out by B-25Bs that had been specially modified so as to hold the greatest amount of fuel possible. They took off from the aircraft carrier *Hornet*, situated at a distance of 715 miles (1,150 km) from the Japanese coast, and the mission was successfully concluded, although its effects were above all psychological.

---

color plate

North American B-25B U.S. Army Air Force. Personal aircraft of Lt. Col. James Doolittle with fake machine guns on the tail, during the air raid on Tokyo that took place on April 18, 1942.

Aircraft:	North American B-25C
Nation:	USA
Manufacturer:	North American Aviation Inc.
Type:	Bomber
Year:	1941
Engine:	2 Wright R-2600-13 Cyclone, 14-cylinder radial, air-cooled, 1,724 hp each
Wingspan:	67 ft 9 in (20.60 m)
Length:	53 ft (16.13 m)
Height:	15 ft 10 in (4.82 m)
Takeoff weight:	34,044 lb (15,422 kg)
Maximum speed:	284 mph (457 km/h) at 15,040 ft (4,572 m)
Ceiling:	21,256 ft (6,462 m)
Range:	1,500 miles (2,414 km)
Armament:	5-6 machine guns; 5,207 lb (2,359 kg) of bombs
Crew:	3-6

A formation of B-25 of the 83rd Bomber Squadron in flight over Tunisia in 1943. In order to facilitate identification, a British type "fin flash" has been painted on the tail fin.

NORTH AMERICAN B-25B

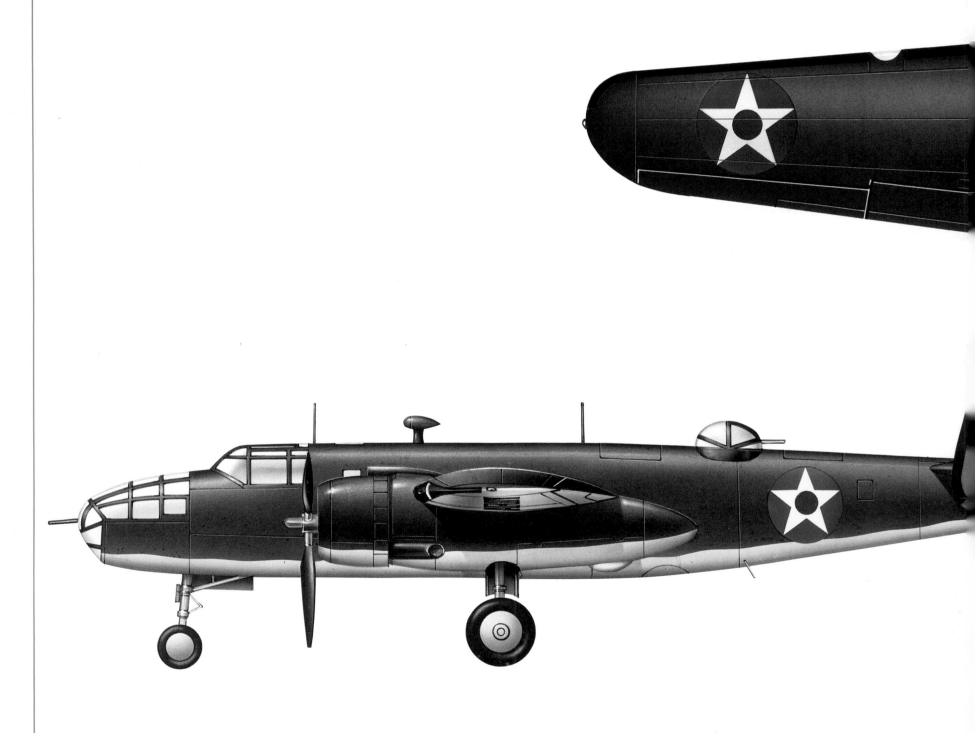

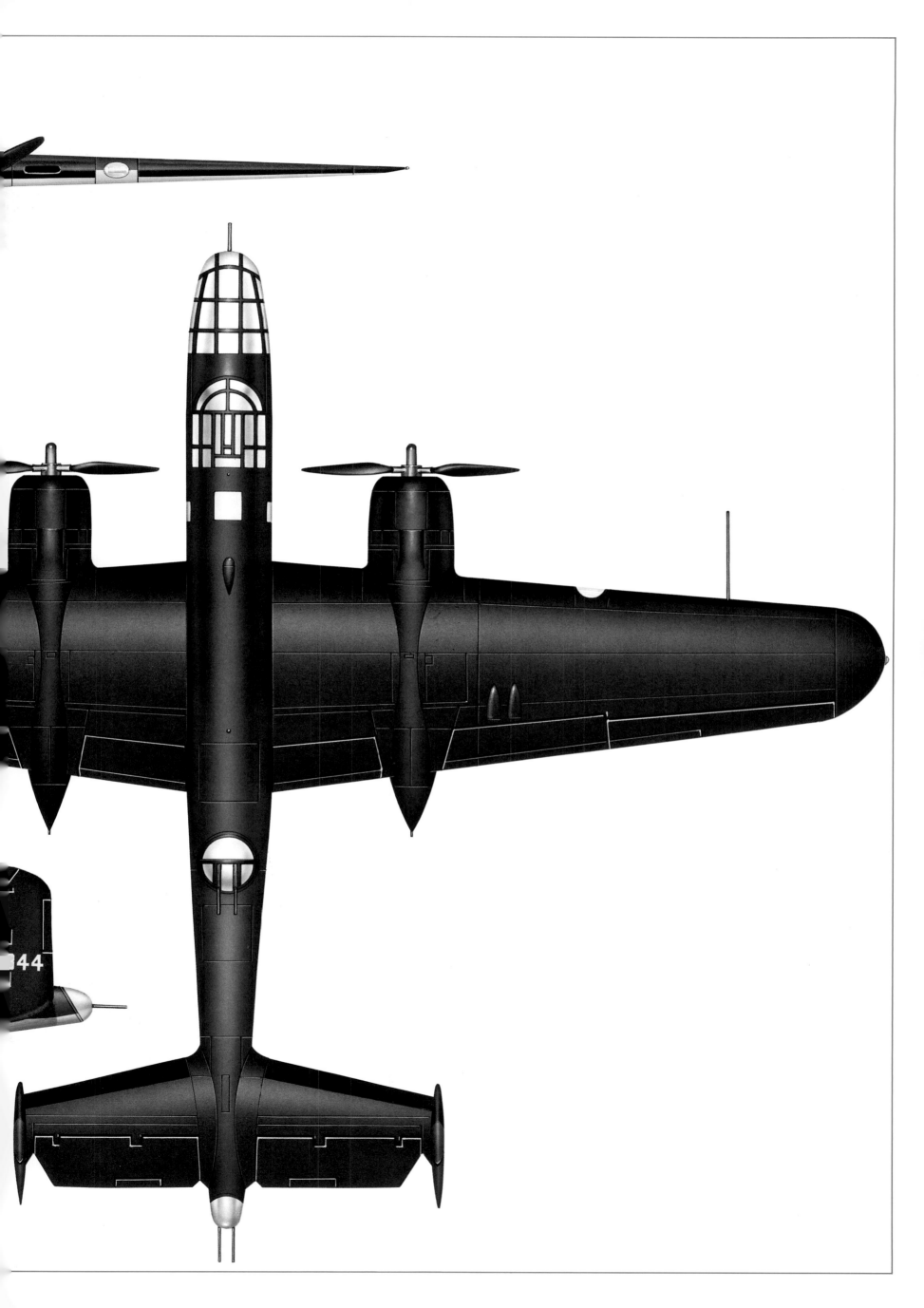

NORTH AMERICAN B-25H

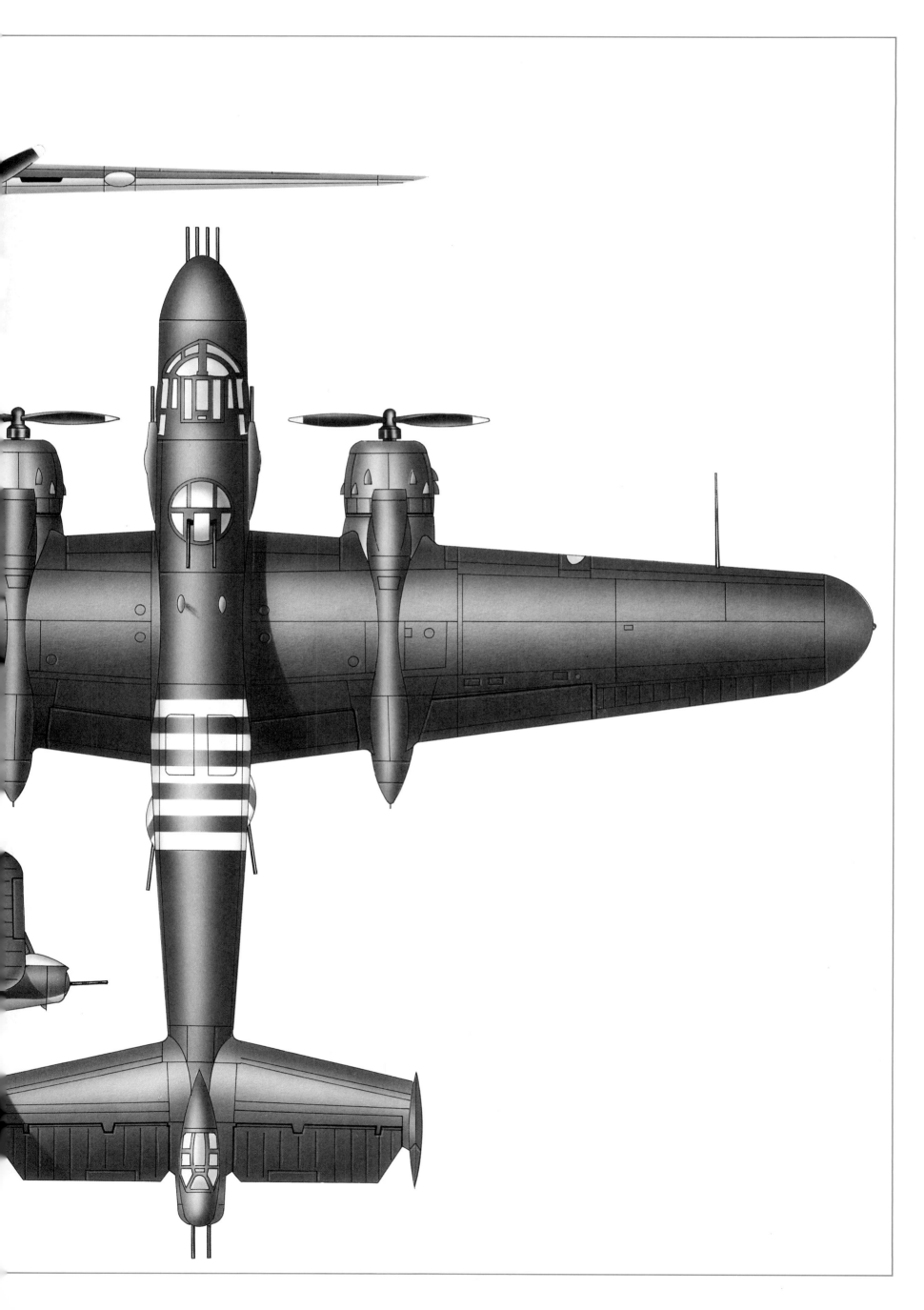

Created back in 1938, more than 11,000 North American B-25 Mitchells were built between 1940 and 1945. The aircraft had a long and intensive career that lasted well beyond World War II. This occurred due to continuous modernization and strengthening which exploited to the full this two-engine aircraft's great potential. The Mitchell went down in history as one of the best bombers of the war.

The first versions to be produced in any number were the B-25C and B-25D, which were delivered at the end of 1941, and of which 1,619 and 2,290 were built respectively. In 1942, it was in fact as a result of modifications carried out on three experimental prototypes of the B-25C that the subsequent G variant came into being. This was subjected to a radical change in armament, the first step towards the subsequent developments that were to transform the Mitchell into a veritable flying cruiser: the installation in the nose of a 75 mm caliber M4 cannon. This weapon could fire 21 bullets — each of which weighed 15 lb (6.81 kg) — and its intended use was to be in anti-shipping attacks, especially in operations in the Pacific.

405 B-25Gs were built in all, but due to practical problems in loading and firing the cannon, production was altered in favor of the subsequent H version (1,000 built in all). This was a remarkable improvement. In this aircraft, the M4 cannon was replaced by a lighter, more modern weapon (the T-13E1), the crew was reduced to five members, and the offensive armament was reinforced still further by the installation of eight heavy machine guns in the fuselage's front section, in addition to the six for the defense of the side, back and rear sections. This impressive firing power (which could be integrated with a maximum of eight rockets installed in racks beneath the wings), together with the ''normal'' bomb load contained in the hold, made the Mitchell a formidable weapon. The first B-25Hs arrived on the Pacific front in February 1944, and following a few months of acclimatization, they went into action with great success against Japanese land and sea traffic. The heavy armament installed in the nose proved to be particularly effective especially in anti-shipping attacks.

The next major production version, the B-25J (this was built in the greatest number: 4,390 out of total 4,805 ordered of which 295 were sent to Great Britain) embodied the final evolution of the airframe. This variant initially marked a return to the classic structure of a horizontal bomber equipped with glazed nose, and

then to that of ground attack plane with basic armament consisting of 12 machine guns and an enlarged crew of six men.

During the conflict, the two-engine North American operated on all fronts and without interruption until the final day of the war, although the principal theater of war, as far as the aircraft of the USAAF and the U.S. Navy were concerned, was that of the Pacific. In this sector, the B-25s carried out an invaluable role, guaranteeing support to the land forces in the slow and difficult advance until the battle for Okinawa. In Europe, the USAAF's Mitchells were flanked by those of the British RAF and the aircraft of a Free French bombing group. Starting with the Allied landings in Morocco and Algeria, the B-25s carried out a total of 63,177 missions, releasing 84,980 tons of bombs and shooting down 193 enemy aircraft.

The third great consumer of the B-25, after the USAAF and the RAF, was the U.S. Navy which, from January 1943 onward, received 50 PBJ-1Cs (equivalent to the B-25C), 152 PBJ-1Ds (B-25D), one PBJ-1G (B-25G), 248 PBJ-1Hs (B-25H) and 225 PBJ-1Js (B-25J).

---

color plate

North American B-25H 1st Air Command Group 10th Air Force USAAF - Hailakandi, India, 1944

Aircraft:	North American B-25H
Nation:	USA
Manufacturer:	North American Aviation Inc.
Type:	Bomber
Year:	1944
Engine:	2 Wright R-2600-13 Cyclone, 14-cylinder radial, air-cooled, 1,724 hp each
Wingspan:	67 ft 11 in (20.60 m)
Length:	51 ft 1 in (15.54 m)
Height:	15 ft 9 in (4.80 m)
Weight:	37,198 lb (16,351 kg)
Maximum speed:	274 mph (442 km/h) at 13,026 ft (3,960 m)
Ceiling:	23,865 ft (7,255 m)
Range:	1,350 miles (2,173 km)
Armament:	1 x 75 mm cannon; 14 machine guns; 3,004 lb (1,361 kg) of bombs
Crew:	5

A formation of North American B-25 in flight.

The widespread use of dive-bombers also influenced Great Britain and, in 1940, it explicitly requested the American manufacturer Vultee to create an aircraft of this kind. The result was the Vultee V-72, a large and heavy monoplane that was to assume several designations in the course of its career: A-31 and A-35 in the United States and Vengeance in Great Britain. It never proved to be an exceptional aircraft, and its general inferiority was demonstrated by the fact that even the Royal Air Force (the only one to use it in combat) eventually used it in a theater of war that was less demanding than the European one. In fact, the Vengeance was to remain in service in Burma until the end of the conflict.

The V-72 project was developed by Vultee on the basis of the experience it had acquired during the construction of the V-11 and V-12 bombers, in 1935 and 1939 respectively. The formula chosen was that of an all-metal mid-wing monoplane with retractable landing gear. It was powered by a radial engine, and the two crew members were housed in a long, completely glazed cockpit. The defensive armament consisted of four machine guns on the wings and a mobile position provided with one or two similar weapons for the observer; the aircraft could carry a maximum bomb load of 2,002 lb (907 kg).

In the summer of 1940, an initial order for 700 aircraft was placed by the British Purchasing Commission and was to consist of 400 Vengeance Mk.Is and 300 Mk.IIs. This number was clearly excessive considering Vultee's capabilities and therefore Northrop was also called to participate in the production program. The first prototype took to the air in July 1941, but the need for a series of structural modifications (to the empennage and the aerodynamic brakes) delayed the completion of the aircraft: the first production series Vengeances did not take to the air until June of the following year.

The aircraft of the initial production series, designated A-31 in the United States, were also ordered by the U.S. Army Air Force and subsequently rechristened A-35. Production continued with the appearance of two versions with heavier armament and equipment, and they were designated A-35A and A-35B. A total of 562 of the second variant were assigned to Great Britain (where they were known as Vengeance Mk.IV) and 29 to Brazil. In all, the Royal Air Force received 1,205 aircraft in several versions, out of a total production that, up to September 1944, amounted to 1,528 aircraft.

Once it had been decided not to use the Vengeance in combat in Europe, the career of the Vultee dive-bombers bearing British insignia was generally satisfactory. This decision was made in 1942, when the first aircraft became operational. Experiences in combat had clearly demonstrated that the dive-bombers were extremely vulnerable and that they could carry out their role only if heavily protected by fighters, and even then only against particular targets. In Burma, the Vengeances replaced the two-engine Bristol Blenheims, and they carried out their first mission in July 1943. Later, the RAF ceded some aircraft to Australia and transformed others (Vengeance TT Mk.IV) for use in target-towing.

However, in the United States, the fate of the Vultee bombers was to be less fortunate. They were all used in the secondary role of target-towing and the fact that they were used at all was severely criticized. A high-ranking officer in the U.S. Army described the aircraft as "an evident waste of time, material, and man-power."

color plate

Vultee V-72 built for the RAF and requisitioned by the U.S. Army Air Corps, in service at the Gunnery Training Center at Patterson Field in 1941

Aircraft:	Vultee A-35A
Nation:	USA
Manufacturer:	Vultee Aircraft Inc.
Type:	Dive-bomber
Year:	1941
Engine:	Allison V-1710-39,12-cylinder radial, air-cooled, 1,150 hp
Wingspan:	37 ft 4 in (11.35 m)
Length:	31 ft 2 in (9.49 m)
Height:	10 ft 7 in (3.22 m)
Weight:	8,291 lb (3,756 kg) loaded
Maximum speed:	365 mph (589 km/h) at 15,040 ft (4,572 m)
Ceiling:	29,075 ft (8,839 m)
Range:	950 miles (1,529 km)
Armament:	6 machine guns; 501 lb (227 kg) of bombs
Crew:	2

A U.S. Army Air Corps Vultee A-35.

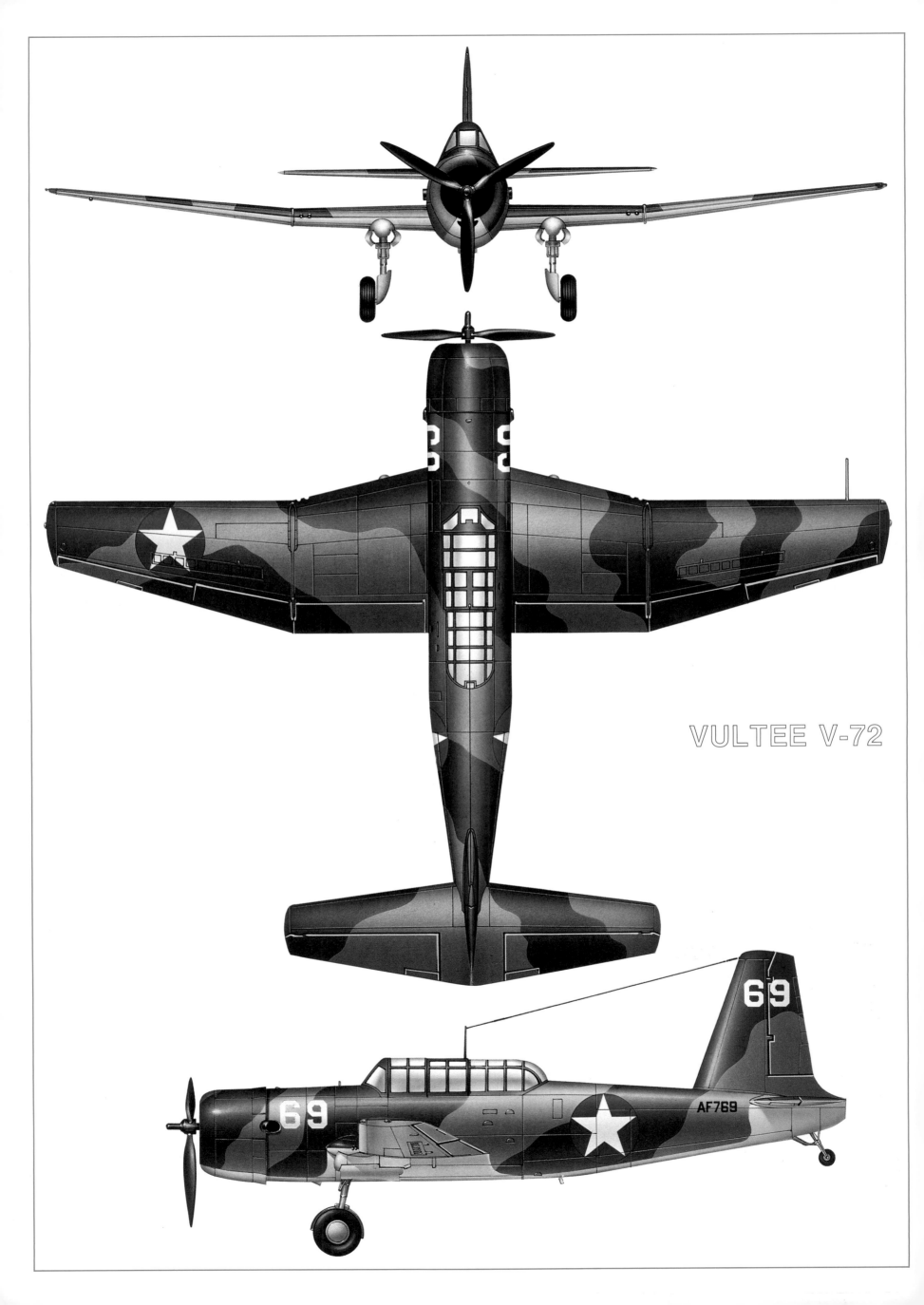

VULTEE V-72

NORTHROP A-17A

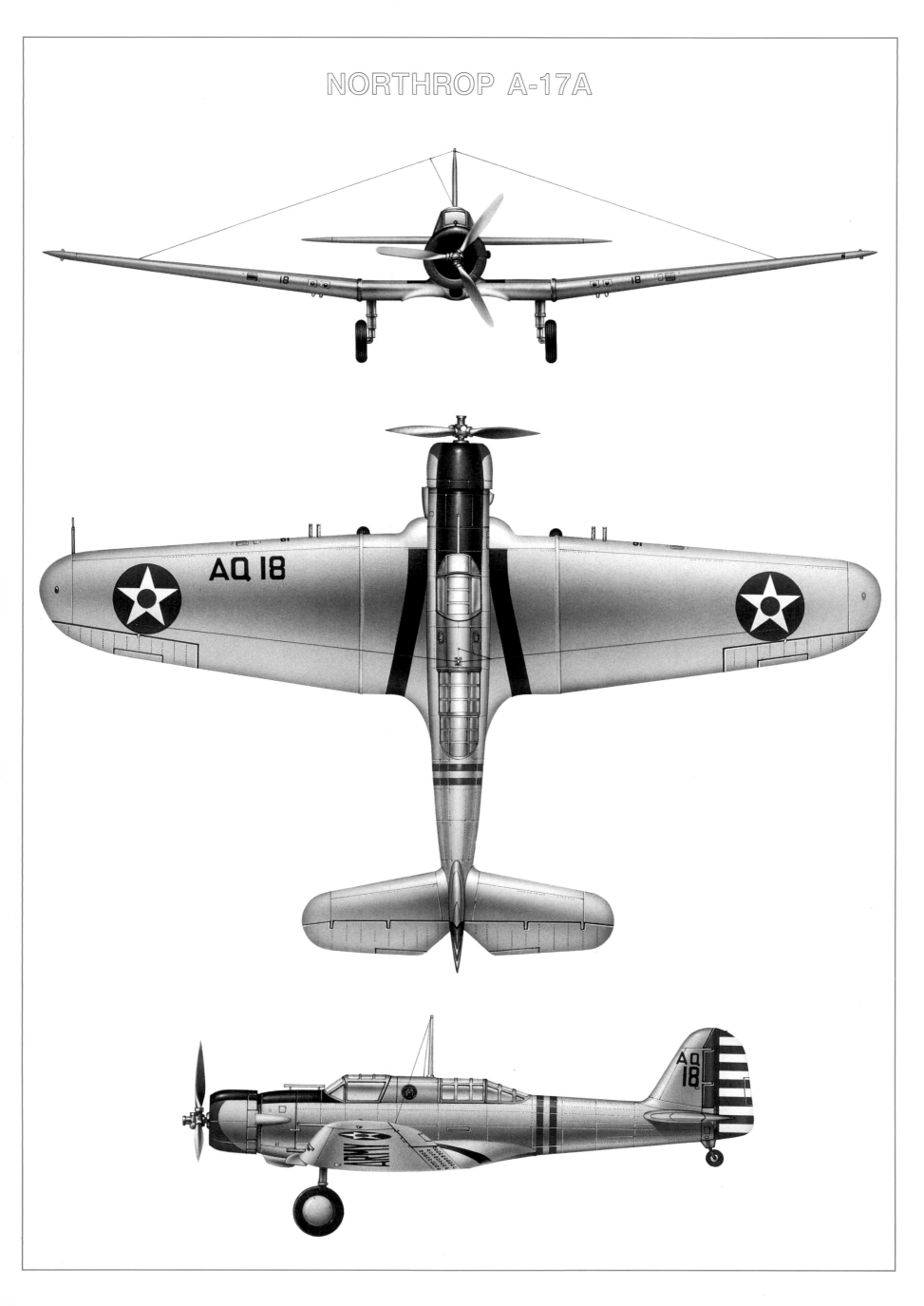

The series of brilliant commercial monoplanes that Northrop developed at the beginning of the 1930s — and that saw its best versions in the Gamma and Delta models — served the newly established California company as the basis for its entry into the military sector.

The model that marked this debut was the prototype of a light attack bomber, developed privately and directly derived from the Gamma. Powered by a 745 hp Wright SR-1820 F radial engine, the plane, designated YA-13, was acquired by the USAAC in June 1934 and underwent a series of tests. However, the tests were delayed by two successive engine replacements, and it was not until 1935 that Northrop was able to complete the definitive prototype. This was designated XA-16 and was fitted with a 761 hp Pratt & Whitney R-1535 Twin Wasp Junior engine, going into series production as the A-17 on the basis of an order for 109 aircraft. These differed from the prototype in a series of structural modifications carried out on the landing gear, the adoption of landing flaps, and the installation of a bomb load that could be partially housed inside the fuselage.

The first deliveries took place in December 1935, and during the same month the USAAC signed a second contract requesting that a more powerful and improved variant of the plane be produced. Apart from the fitting of an 825 hp Pratt & Whitney R-1535-13 Wasp power plant, the most obvious modification was to the landing gear, which now became completely retractable instead of being fixed as before. This new version was designated A-17A, and 129 were ordered.

Its service in the units of the army air force proved to be limited however: only 93 A-17As were accepted for delivery, and they remained in service for barely 18 months. The planes were subsequently sent back and then used for export: Great Britain received 60 in 1940, while the rest of the aircraft were sold to France. None of these aircraft ever went into combat, the French planes because they were not delivered in time, and the British ones because once they had been delivered to the RAF under the name of Nomad Mk.I they were then handed over to the South African air force, which used them for target towing.

In fact, the aircraft was a great success as far as export was concerned, especially particular versions of the A-17 produced from 1935 onward. In the same year, Northrop completed approximately 150 planes of a version destined for the Chinese air force featuring a 750 hp Wright Cyclone engine and armament reduced to two machine guns. In 1937, a special prototype (the 8A-1) was acquired by Sweden, which later built 100 or so on license, fitting them with Bristol Mercury XXIV engines, while 30 8A-2 models were sold to Argentina. Sales abroad continued even after the Douglas Aircraft Company merged with Northrop in August 1937. The plane was renamed the Douglas DB-8A and had constant success due to the regular updating of the aircraft, especially its power unit. Among the buyers were Peru, which first ordered 10 and then 34 planes, the Netherlands (18), Iraq (15), and Norway (36). With the German invasion, delivery of Norway's aircraft (of the DB-8A-5 type, fitted with 1,200 hp engine) was blocked, and the planes were sent to Canada, where they were used for training. A similar fate awaited the 31 planes built for Peru: during 1942, they were requisitioned by the USAAF and went into service with the designation A-33. Although they bore the military insignia of an attack plane, the aircraft basically served as trainers.

Formation of U.S. Army Air Corps Northrop A-17s.

Aircraft:	Northrop A-17A
Nation:	USA
Manufacturer:	Northrop Co.
Type:	Attack
Year:	1936
Engine:	Pratt & Whitney R-1535-13 Wasp, 9-cylinder radial, air-cooled, 825 hp
Wingspan:	47 ft 9 in (14.55 m)
Length:	31 ft 8 in (9.65 m)
Height:	12 ft (3.65 m)
Weight:	7,543 lb (3,421 kg) loaded
Maximum speed:	220 mph (354 km/h) at 2,500 ft (762 m)
Ceiling:	19,400 ft (5,900 m)
Range:	732 miles (1,180 km)
Armament:	5 machine guns; 400 lb (180 kg) of bombs
Crew:	2

color plate

Northrop A-17A 34th Attack Squadron U.S. Army Air Corps - 1938

Northrop A-17 with radio direction finder antenna mounted beneath the fuselage.

The P-61 Black Widow was not only the largest, heaviest and most powerful fighter of the entire war, but it was also the only night fighter designed as such by the American aeronautical industry. It proved to be one of the best aircraft in this category. Although designed in 1940, the P-61 did not go into action until the last year of the war, due to a long and complex preparation concerning its radar apparatus. Just over 700 were built in three principal versions. Some of them, in the photoreconnaissance version, survived the war and remained in active service until 1952.

It was in 1940, after the reports of a special commission, sent to Great Britain to evaluate the operative needs of the conflict, had been received that the USAAF strongly felt the need for a valid night fighter with radar apparatus that was being developed at the time. On October 2, highly secret specifications were issued for an aircraft of this type, and just over a month later, on November 5, Northrop, which was already working on a design of this kind, submitted its own project to the military authorities. The proposal was accepted and the program launched within a brief space of time. On January 11, 1941, two XP-61 prototypes were ordered, followed by 13 pre-series YP-61s on March 10, meant for operative evaluation tests. On September 1, the first order, for 150 series aircraft, was placed.

The project was developed bearing in mind these extremely short deadlines and the first prototype took to the air on May 21, 1942. The Black Widow (named after the deadly spider found in the American desert) was a large high-wing two-engine aircraft with forward tricycle landing gear. It was powered by a pair of Pratt & Whitney Double Wasp radial engines, each generating 2,000 hp and driving four-blade metal variable-pitch propellers. In addition it was characterized by double tail beams, which lengthened the engine fairings and supported the horizontal and vertical fins. The aircraft was provided with a specific system of control surfaces which notably increased its maneuverability. The radar apparatus (based upon British projects and developed by the Massachusetts Institute of Technology) was installed in the nose. The armament consisted of four 20 mm cannons fixed in the belly pod and a similar number of 12.7 mm machine guns installed in a remote-controlled turret on the aircraft's back.

Deliveries of the initial production series aircraft (P-61A) began in October 1943, and these became operative the following year, going into action in the spring and summer, both on the European and Pacific fronts. Beginning in August 1944, the first of the second variant (P-61B, 450 built in all) were delivered. In this aircraft, the Black Widow's already powerful armament was further increased with the installation of wing supports capable of carrying four 1,602 lb (726 kg) bombs or supplementary fuel tanks containing 340 gallons (1,363 liters). The last major production variant was the P-61C, strengthened above all in the engines. The Pratt & Whitney R-2800-73s with supercharger, capable of generating 2,839 hp in an emergency was installed. Only 41 of the latter were built, out of an order for 517, and they were delivered in July 1945.

In the immediate post-war years another variant appeared, intended for use as a photoreconnaissance, and only 36 were built in all. Designated F-15A Reporter, the aircraft had a modified fuselage and was characterized by its lack of radar equipment and armament. Moreover, it had remarkable qualities: a maximum speed of 440 mph (708 km/h), a 41,101 ft (12,495 m) tangent, and a range of 3,997 miles (6,437 km). This variant was the last to withdrawn from service.

A long nose P-61B with its characteristic black paint.

---

color plate

Northrop P-61B 548th Night Fighter Squadron 7th Air Force U.S.Army Air Force - Ryukyu Island August 1945. This aircraft shot down the last plane in World War II

A P-61A with short nose. On the back of the fuselage there are four fixed 12.7 mm weapons.

Aircraft:	Northrop P-61B
Nation:	USA
Manufacturer:	Northrop Aircraft Inc.
Type:	Night fighter
Year:	1944
Engine:	2 Pratt & Whitney R-2800-65 Double Wasp, 18-cylinder radial, air-cooled, 2,000 hp each
Wingspan:	66 ft 1 in (20.11 m)
Length:	49 ft 7 in (15.11 m)
Height:	14 ft 8 in (4.47 m)
Weight:	29,739 lb (13,472 kg)
Maximum speed:	365 mph (589 km/h) at 20,052 ft (6,096 m)
Ceiling:	33,187 ft (10,089 m)
Range:	2,998 miles (4,828 km)
Armament:	4 x 20 mm cannons; 4 machine guns; 6,410 lb (2,904 kg) of bombs
Crew:	3

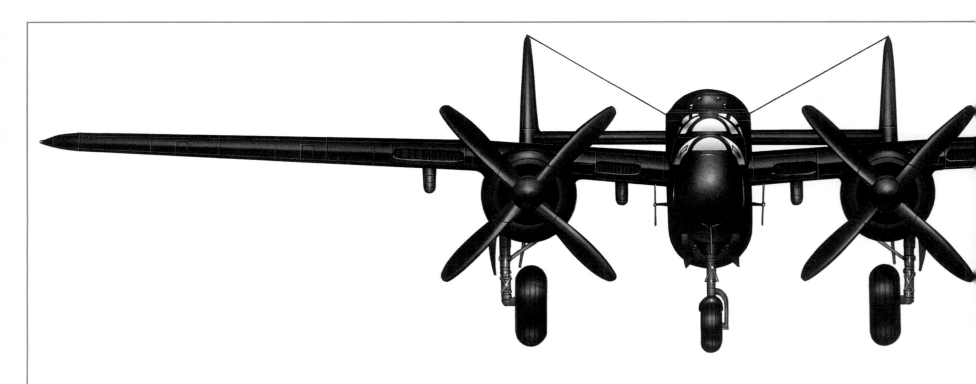

NORTHROP P-61B

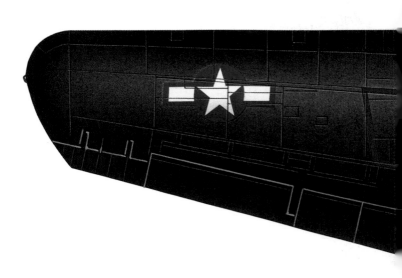

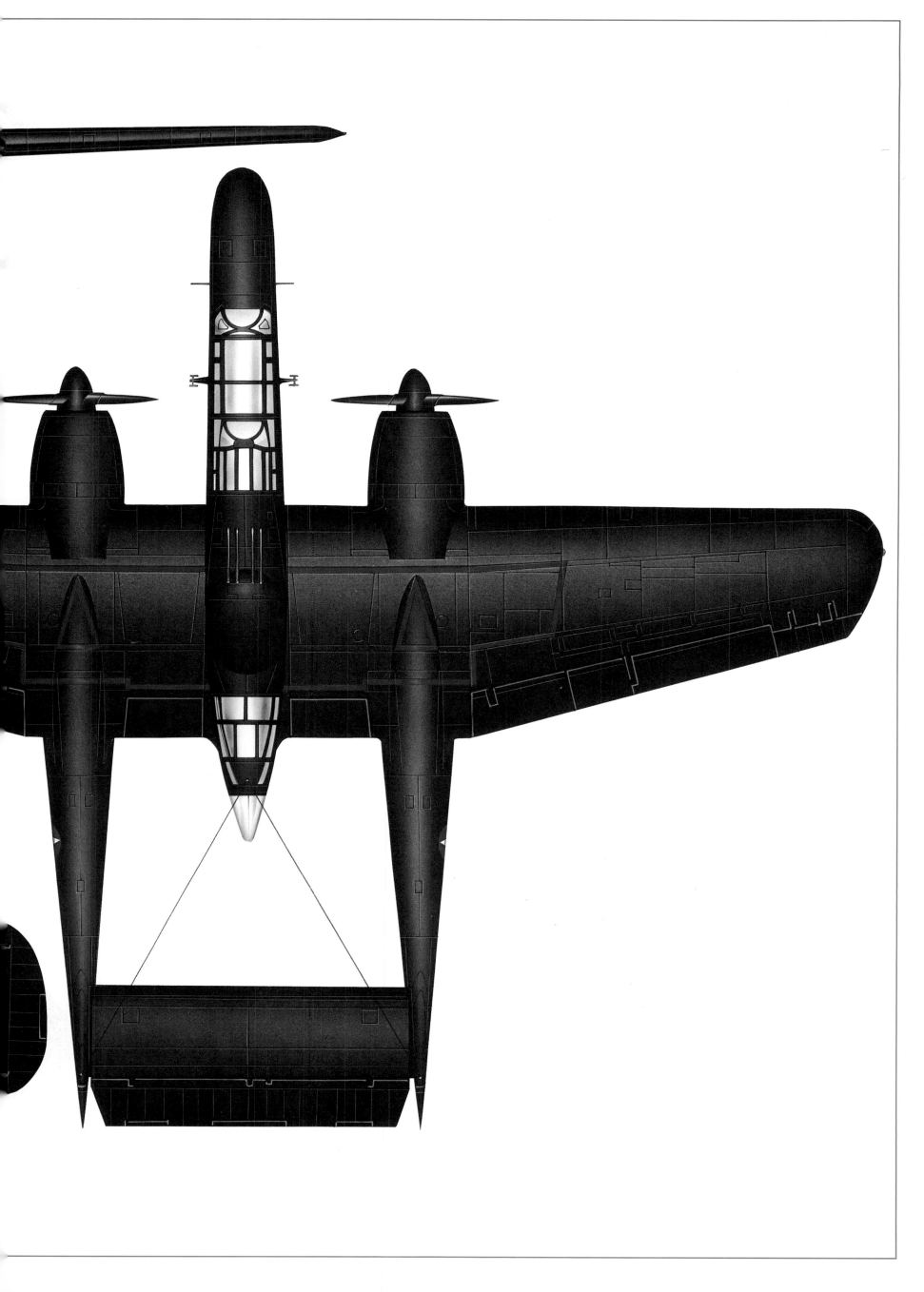

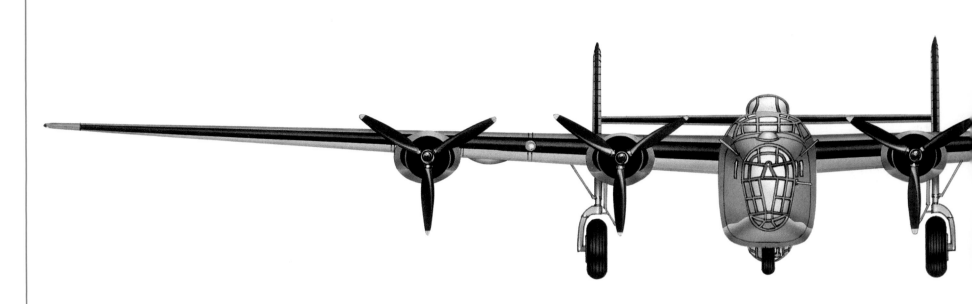

CONSOLIDATED B-24D

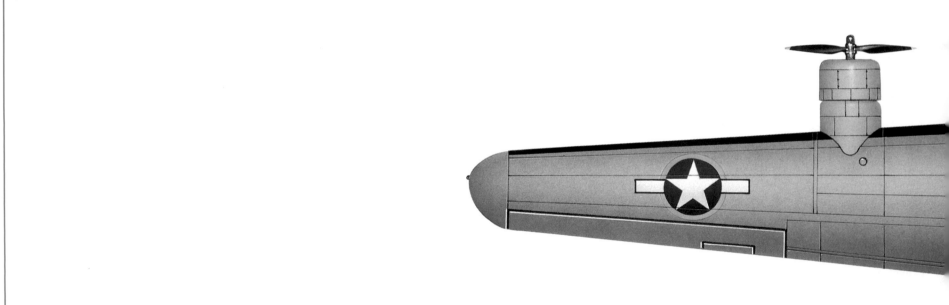

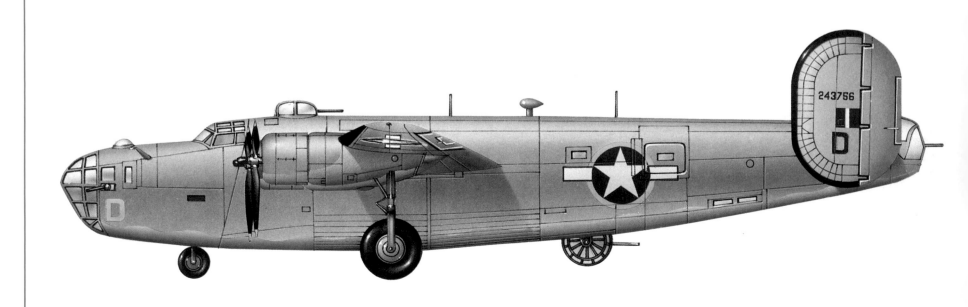

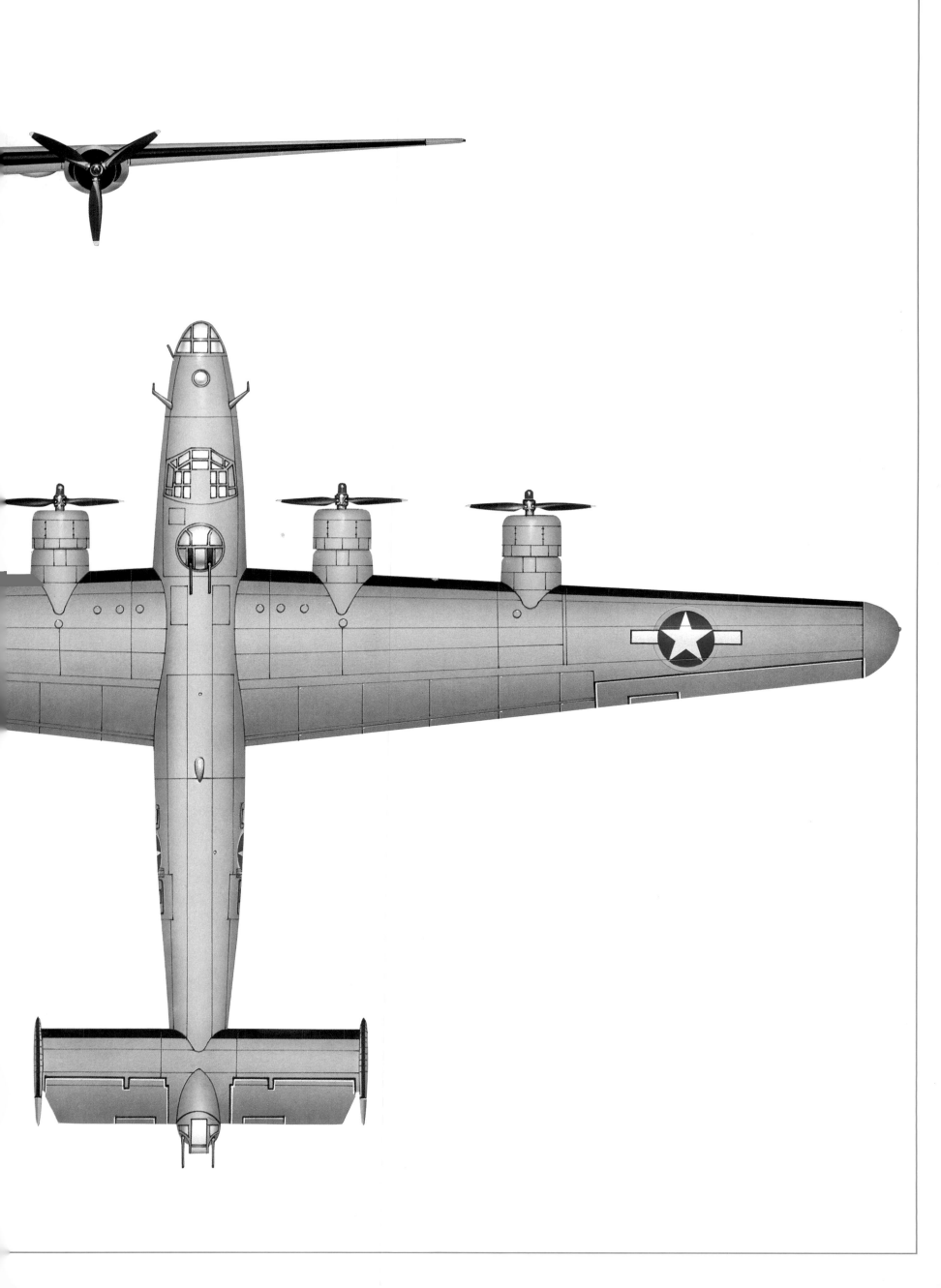

CONSOLIDATED B-24J

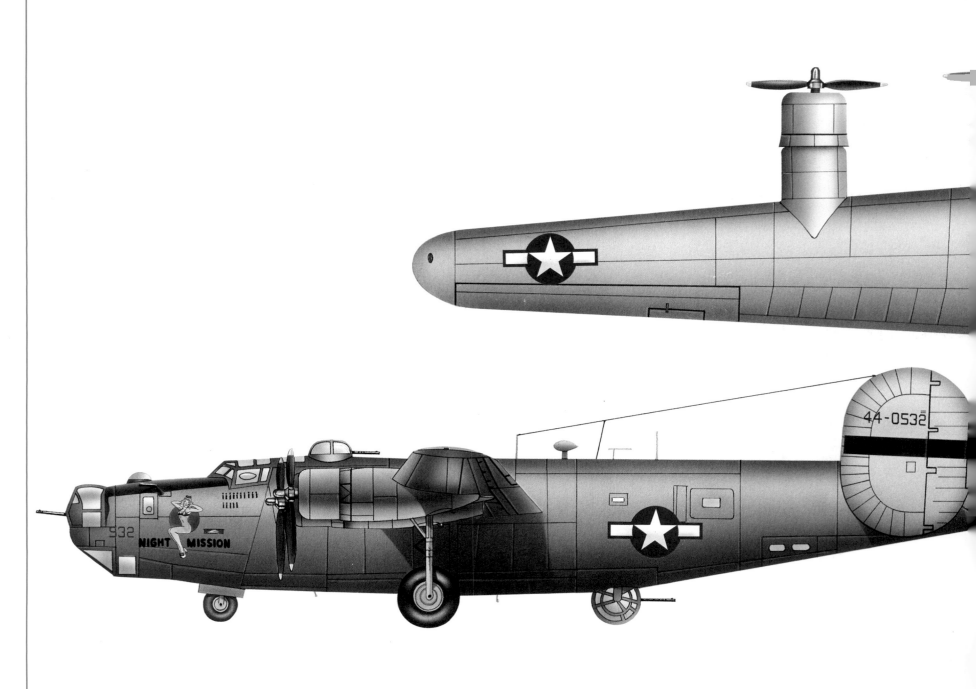

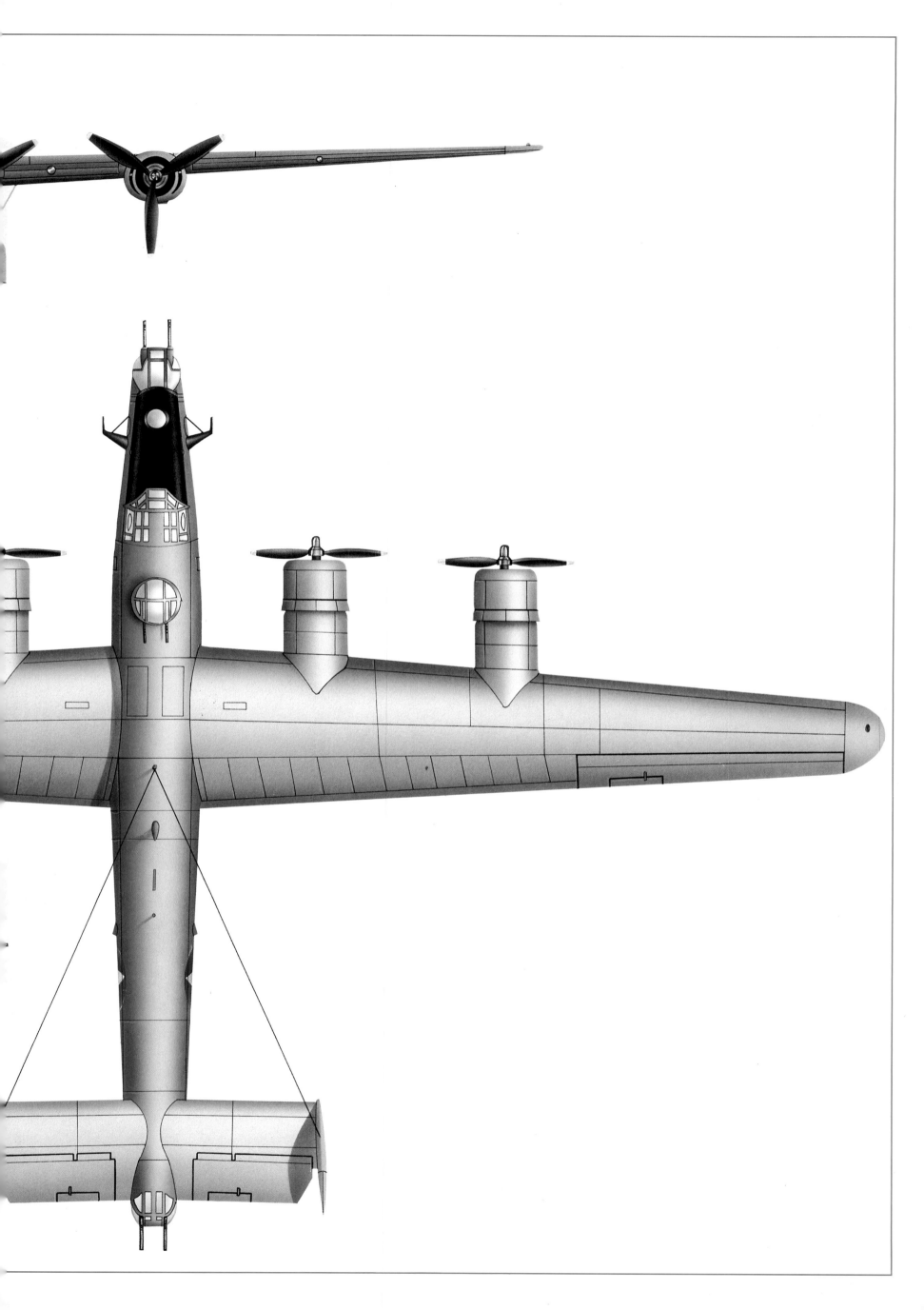

The second strategic bomber to be used in action by the United States, the B-24 Liberator never achieved the popularity of its companion and rival, the B-17. Nevertheless, the contribution that this large four-engine aircraft made to the course of the war was considerable, as was the quantity of aircraft produced greater than that of any other American combat plane in World War II. In all, a total of 18,188 came off the assembly lines prior to May 31, 1945. The quantitative ''importance'' of the Liberator can best be appreciated when compared with the production of the B-17 (12,731 built) and with that of the best British bomber, the Avro Lancaster (7,366). Used extensively on all fronts, the B-24 proved over all to be a versatile aircraft and, thanks to its excellent range, it was able to operate brilliantly in roles that were very different from its basic one, including transport, naval reconnaissance, and antisubmarine attack. The Liberator did not only serve bearing American insignia: the second major user was the British RAF, which received 1,694 in various versions, while other aircraft went to equip the Australian, Canadian, and South African air forces.

The project was launched by Consolidated in January 1939, on the basis of a request by the USAAC for a new heavy bomber with a performance that was generally superior to that of the Boeing B-17 in production at the time. Its main quality, however, was to be its range, and in order to satisfy this request to the full, the chief designer, Isaac M. Laddon, created a wing with advanced characteristics, which was greatly lengthened and provided with Davis laminar contours, around which the rest of the plane was literally constructed. The aircraft was a high wing monoplane with twin tail fins and rudders, tricycle forward landing gear, and was initially powered by four Pratt & Whitney R-1830-33 engines with two-stage mechanical superchargers, enclosed in a housing that was carefully studied from an aerodynamic point of view. The fuselage, which was very high, had sliding hatches that notably reduced the aircraft's drag.

On March 30 a contract was signed for the development of a full-scale model and a prototype, and nine months later, on December 29, 1939, the XB-24 made its maiden flight. In the meantime, seven YB-24 preseries aircraft had been ordered, as well as 36 B-24As of the initial production series. A further 175 aircraft had been ordered by France. However, the course of the war in Europe led to the French order being cancelled, and the aircraft were sent to Great Britain which, in the meantime, had also ordered 165 of the new bombers giving them the name that was also adopted in the United States: Liberator. The first of these took to the air on January 17, 1941, and deliveries began in March. Some of these aircraft were used for transport duty, but their use was subsequently extended to the RAF's Coastal Command.

In the meantime, the XB-24 prototype had been transformed into the XB-24B. The most substantial changes, excluding the strengthening of the defensive armament, consisted of more armor protection and, above all, in the adoption of engines provided with superchargers driven by exhaust gas. The latter change led to modifications in the structure of the engine nacelles, which assumed their characteristic oval shape. Nine aircraft of this type were completed with the designation B-24C, and from these was derived the most important production series version, the B-24D, for which a huge number of orders was issued during 1940 for a total of 2,738 aircraft. New assembly lines were opened in order to satisfy production requirements, and other manufacturers became involved in the program as well as Consolidated (these included Douglas, Ford, and North American). The B-24Ds (designated Liberator Mk.III by the RAF and PB4Y-1 by the U.S.Navy) were used as bombers by the USAAF from June 1942, and most of their initial service took place in the Middle East and the Pacific. The next version, the B-24E, was basically similar (with the exception of the propellers and other small details) and was the first to be built by Ford.

color plate
Consolidated B-24D 98th Bomb Group U.S.Army Air Force - North Africa 1943

Aircraft:	Consolidated B-24D
Nation:	USA
Manufacturer:	Consolidated Aircraft Corp.
Type:	Bomber
Year:	1942
Engine:	4 Pratt & Whitney R-1830-43 Twin Wasp, 14-cylinder radial, air-cooled, 1,200 hp
Wingspan:	110 ft (33.52 m)
Length:	66 ft 4 in (20.22 m)
Height:	17 ft 11 in (5.46 m)
Weight:	60,000 lb (27,216 kg) loaded
Maximum speed:	303 mph (488 km/h) at 25,000 ft (7,620 m)
Ceiling:	32,000 ft (9,750 m)
Range:	2,850 miles (4,585 km)
Armament:	10 machine guns; 8,830 lb (4,000 kg) of bombs
Crew:	8-10

A Consolidated B-24D in service on the Pacific front during a mission in New Guinea.

The growth in demands led to a continuous development of the B-24 Liberator, the second strategic bomber to be sent into combat by the United States. Following the first mass produced B-24D series and the subsequent B-24E (the first was built by Ford at Willow Run, and it was similar to the previous one apart from the propellers, the engine type and modifications to details), the new North American factory in Dallas was entrusted with the construction of the subsequent G variant. Beginning with the 26th of these Liberators, a substantial modification was introduced on the assembly lines: a mechanically controlled turret in the nose's tip in order to increase the chances of defense in the case of frontal attacks, during which the bomber had proved to be particularly vulnerable. This alteration led to the fuselage being slightly lengthened (by about eight inches or 25 cm) in order to relocated the marksman's position and to allow the ammunition for the two machine guns to be stored.

In practice, these modifications were the last of any importance to be introduced on the assembly lines, and from mid-1943, the huge industrial machine which produced the B-24s built aircraft that were practically identical as far as external appearance was concerned. In fact, the subsequent B-24Hs were similar to the B-24Gs (although they were provided with a different front turret) and 3,100 were completed by Consolidated (in Fort Worth), Douglas, and Ford. In 1943, the major production series, the B-24J, was derived from this variant. A total of 6,678 were built in all. These Liberators differed from the previous aircraft solely in equipment details, including new engine controls, a new firing system, modifications to the engine feeding system and to the fuel tanks. The B-24Hs and Js delivered to the British Royal Air Force under the Rent and Loan laws were designated Liberator Mk.VI.

The final versions of the Liberator, the B-24L and B-24M, were characterized by further improvements to the on board systems, and up till May 31, 1945, 1,677 and 2,593 aircraft were completed, respectively. The first variant was identical to the B-24D, except for the tail turret which was replaced by two manually controlled 12.7 mm machine guns; the second was directly derived from the B-24J version, although it was provided with a different tail turret.

Production of the Liberator was characterized by numerous experimental variants and derivatives. Amongst the latter, mention should be made of the F-7 for photo reconnaissance (obtained by transforming B-24Hs and Js); the C-87 for transport (derived from the B-24D); the C-109 air cistern (derived from the B-24D and B-24E); the AT-22 for training navigators (C-87s specially modified). The prototypes that never went into production included the XB-24K and the XB-41. The former was obtained by providing a B-24D with a single vertical tail fin. This aircraft subsequently gave rise to another prototype (XB-24N, first flight November, 1944) from which the final version of the Liberator was to have been created. However, the end of the war led to the cancellation of orders for no fewer than 5,168 production series aircraft, and only seven preseries YB-24Ns were completed before production was suspended on May 31, 1945. The XB-41 was also adopted from a B-24D, modified to serve as a heavy escort fighter for the bomber formations. It was armed with fourteen 12.7 mm machine guns. However, it was to remain the only model.

Lastly, it should be recalled that total production of the Liberators amounted to 18,188 aircraft. Despite this enormous number (the highest for any American combat plane in World War II), at the conflict's end most of the B-24s serving in the USAAF were declared surplus, and only a very small number remained in service until 1953.

---

color plate

Consolidated B-24J 819th Bomber Squadron 30th Bomber Group 7th Air Force U.S. Army Air Force - Saipan October 1944

Aircraft:	Consolidated B-24M
Nation:	USA
Manufacturer:	Consolidated Aircraft Corp.
Type:	Bomber
Year:	1944
Engine:	4 Pratt & Whitney R-1830-65 Twin Wasp, 14-cylinder radial, air-cooled, 1,217 hp each
Wingspan:	110 ft (33.52 m)
Length:	67 ft 4 in (20.47 m)
Height:	18 ft (5.49 m)
Weight:	71,293 lb (32,296 kg)
Maximum speed:	290 mph (467 km/h) at 25,000 ft (7,620 m)
Ceiling:	28,098 ft (8,535 m)
Range:	2,098 miles (3,380 km)
Armament:	10 machine guns; 12,803 lb (5,800 kg) of bombs
Crew:	8-10

Two Consolidated B-24s during a raid on Augsburg.

A B-24 damaged during a raid on Germany, in flight.

An F4F-4, version with folding wings.

An F4F-3, of the "Red Rippers" Squadron (USS *Ranger*), with fixed wings.

If the Brewster F2A Buffalo went down in aviation history as the U.S. Navy's first carrier-based monoplane fighter, the Grumman F4F Wildcat which followed it a few months later acquired a bame of a much different sort. This small, squat combat plane became the navy's standard fighter during the first half of the conflict, and although it was inferior to its direct adversary (the Japanese Mitsubishi A6M Reisen), it played this difficult role until 1943, when more powerful aircraft, such as the Grumman F6F Hellcat and the Vought F4U Corsair, entered front line service. However, this did not put an end to the Wildcat's operative career: the assembly lines remained active from 1939 until August 1945, with the final variant (of which 4,777 were built by General Motors as the FM-2 beginning in September 1943) being used on small British and American escort aircraft carriers. In all, a total of approximately 7,800 aircraft were built.

The F4F project originated as a biplane, on the basis of the same specifications, issued in November 1935, that had led to the creation of the F2A by Brewster. The monoplane formula still met with much skepticism within the U.S. Navy and encouraged by the success of its F3F, which had recently gone into service, Grumman felt that it was its duty to propose a new biplane fighter. In practice, however, the differences between the two types were not particularly apparent, and following the assigning of an order for a prototype to Brewster, Grumman requested and obtained authorization to modify its project radically in July 1936. Thus

originated the XF4F-2, the first Wildcat prototype, which made its maiden flight on September 2, 1937. The aircraft was a mid-wing monoplane with a characteristic barrel-shaped fuselage and retractable landing gear with manual controls. It was powered by a 900 hp Pratt & Whitney R-1830-66 Twin Wasp radial engine with supercharger, driving a three-bladed, variable pitch metal propeller.

Flight tests did not initially provide favorable results. The Grumman fighter proved to be inferior both in speed and handling to its direct rival, and in June 1938, the Buffalo was declared the winner and went into production. Nevertheless, the XF4F-2 had great potential, and three months later, the designers received authorization to proceed with its development. On February 12, 1939, the second prototype (XF4F-3) made its maiden flight. It was much improved and modified, especially as regards the engine, a 1,200 hp Pratt & Whitney XR-1830-76 with two-stage supercharger, which was the main key to its success: at 21,380 ft (6,500 m) it guaranteed a speed of about 330 mph (530 km/h), while allowing equally good performance at low and medium altitudes, generally exceeding that of the F2A by about 35 mph (56 km/h). In August, after evaluation tests, the Navy ordered a lot of 78 F4F-3s to evaluate them from an operative point of view. Only three months earlier, another 81 aircraft had been ordered by France.

These aircraft (designated Model G-36A) were, in fact, the first to see combat. Once France's fate was sealed, they were taken over by Great Britain and went into service in the units of the Fleet Air Arm in the fall of 1940, under the name of Martlet I. Their first mission took place on Christmas Day, over Scapa Flow, when a German Junkers Ju.88 was shot down. A year later, it was the turn of the American Wildcats at Pearl Harbor. At that time, the U.S. Navy had received 183 F4F-3s and 65 F4F-3As (out of totals of 285 and 95), but in the meantime the F4F-4, the second major version (provided with heavier armament, greater protection and folding wings), had appeared. Its prototype had taken to the air on April 14, and the first production series aircraft on November 25. Production of this variant amounted to 1,169 aircraft built by Grumman and 1,060 built by General Motors (which designated them FM-1). General Motors also built the final FM-2 version, provided with a 1,350 hp Wright R-1820-56 engine.

The Fleet Air Arm received 370 FM-2s (designated Wildcat VI), bringing the total number of F4Fs and FMs used by Great Britain during the war to approximately 1,100.

color plate
Grumman F4F-3 Wildcat VF-3 Squadron U.S. Navy *USS Saratoga* - South East Pacific 1942

Aircraft:	Grumman F4F-3
Nation:	USA
Manufacturer:	Grumman Aircraft Engineering Corp.
Type:	Fighter
Year:	1940
Engine:	Pratt & Whitney R-1830-76 Twin Wasp, 14-cylinder radial, air-cooled, 1,200 hp
Wingspan:	38 ft (11.58 m)
Length:	28 ft 10 in (8.78 m)
Height:	11 ft 9 in (3.58 m)
Takeoff weight:	8,163 lb (3,698 kg) loaded
Maximum speed:	330 mph (530 km/h) at 21,154 ft (6,431 m)
Ceiling:	37,500 ft (11,430 m)
Range:	845 miles (1,360 km)
Armament:	6 machine guns; 200 lb (91 kg) of bombs
Crew:	1

The F4F-3, an experimental transformation of the Wildcat into a seaplane.

GRUMMAN F4F-3

During 1943, superiority in the air, firmly in the hands of the Japanese since Pearl Harbor, began to weigh decisively in favor of the Americans. The Grumman F6F Hellcat, together with the Vought F4U Corsair, was the aircraft that most contributed to this decisive redressing of the balance. Fast, powerful, well-armed and protected, this outstanding combat plane represented the high point of the American carrier-based aviation in the last two years of the war. The importance of the Hellcat in the conflict in the Pacific is clearly shown by the production figures and by those of its combat activity. In all, 12,275 came off the assembly lines. The aircraft began its career on August 31, 1943. It succeeded in shooting down a remarkable number of aircraft. Out of a total of 6,477 enemy planes destroyed by the carrier-based pilots, no fewer than 4,947 fell under the Hellcats' fire. This figure increases to 5,156 if one adds the victories scored by the F6Fs based on land and those serving in the U.S. Marine Corps.

The project was developed by Grumman in order to build a successor to the F4F Wildcat, and the contract for the construction of two prototypes was signed on June 30, 1941. The program went forward very quickly and the first experimental version (designated XF6F-1) took to the air a year later on June 26, 1942. The aircraft was a large all-metal low-wing monoplane with retractable landing gear and arrester hook. It was fitted with a 1,700 hp Wright R-2600-10 engine and it was joined a month later, by the second prototype, in which the more powerful Pratt & Whitney R-2800-10 engine had been installed. From this aircraft, designated XF6F-3, the first series version was derived. This began to leave the assembly lines at the beginning of October, on the basis of the first, massive orders placed by the U.S. Navy back

in May. The installation of a more powerful engine proved decisive for the future success of the Hellcat, in that it allowed it to absorb the notable weight increase suffered in the course of production without a substantial reduction in performance. Their first assignments took place on January 16, 1943, when they were delivered to the aircraft carrier *Essex*, and on August 31, to the aircraft carriers *Essex*, *Yorktown* and *Independence*. The F6F-3s had their baptism of fire during an attack on the island of Marcus.

In the meantime, production was going ahead at a substantial pace: during 1943, 2,545 F6F-3s were delivered, 252 of which went to the British Fleet Air Arm that christened them Hellcat Mk.I and put them into service in July. In all, 4,403 of the first version left the assembly lines and of these, 205 were equipped as night fighters and designated F6F-3E and F6F-3N.

On April 4, 1944, the first F6F-5 variant of the Hellcat took to the air. This was the major production variant, with 7,870 being built, of which 932 were given to the British Navy. It differed from the previous version above all in its engine (a Pratt & Whitney R-2800-10W with water injection to increase power in the case of emergency) and in its heavier armament, which eventually included a maximum bomb load of 2,002 lb (907 kg). A series of night fighters (F6F-5N) were derived from this version too, with 1,434 being built in all. Production ceased on November 16, 1945.

color plate
Grumman F6F-5 VF-17 aircraft carrier *Hornet* U.S. Navy Air Force - Pacific area 1945

Aircraft:	Grumman F6F-3
Nation:	USA
Manufacturer:	Grumman Aircraft Engineering Corp.
Type:	Fighter
Year:	1943
Engine:	Pratt & Whitney R-2800-10 Double Wasp, 18-cylinder radial, air-cooled, 2,000 hp
Wingspan:	42 ft 11 in (13.05 m)
Length:	33 ft 10 in (10.31 m)
Height:	12 ft 7 in (3.9 m)
Weight:	15,507 lb (7,025 kg)
Maximum speed:	375 mph (605 km/h) at 20,052 ft (6,096 m)
Ceiling:	37,398 ft (11,369 m)
Range:	1,089 miles (1,754 km)
Armament:	6 machine guns
Crew:	1

An F6F-3 equipped with a radar on its wings and used as a night fighter.

A F6F-5 bearing post-war insignia.

GRUMMAN F6F-5

Intended to replace the TBD Devastator in the role of carrier-based torpedo plane, the Grumman TBF Avenger made its debut in combat during the same event in which the old Douglas monoplane dramatically left the scene: in June 1942, during the battle of Midway. It was not a successful debut: of the six Avengers that took part in the action, five did not return to the aircraft carrier *Hornet*, and, in addition, the attacks on the Japanese naval squadron did not produce one hit. Nevertheless, this initial failure was fully redeemed by the aircraft's subsequent career: the large and heavy Grumman torpedo plane eventually proved to be one of the navy's strong points during the last three years of the war: in all, 9,836 came off the assembly lines in numerous versions until June 1945, and after having distinguished themselves in both the Atlantic and the Pacific, many of them remained in front-line service until 1954. During World War II, not only did the Avengers fight bearing American insignia, but also those of the British Fleet Air Arm (which used 958) and New Zealand. After the war, they served in Canada, France, the Netherlands, and Japan itself.

The project was launched on April 8, 1940, when the U.S. Navy ordered both from Grumman and Chance Vought two prototypes for a new carrier-based torpedo plane, designated XTBF-1 and XTBU-1 respectively. Although they had no previous experience of this particular type of combat plane, the Grumman technicians fully exploited the company's long tradition of building naval fighters and succeeded in creating a prototype that was far superior to its rival. Its maiden flight took place on August 1, 1941, and it was a large all-metal mid-wing monoplane with retractable landing gear. A crew of three was foreseen, and the aircraft could house a torpedo or the equivalent weight in bombs in its hold. As for the defensive armament, it was planned to install a 12.7 mm fixed machine gun in the front of the fuselage, another similar weapon in a dorsal turret, and a 7.62 mm flexible machine gun. The aircraft was powered by a 1,700 hp Wright radial engine, driving a three-bladed variable-pitch metal propeller.

The Grumman's flight tests were followed by a series of evaluations conducted by the U.S. Navy, which ended in December. On January 3, 1942, the first TBF-1, which formed part of the initial order for 286, came off the assembly lines, and by the end of May a total of 85 aircraft had been delivered. Despite its rather unsuccessful debut, there was soon a growing demand for the aircraft, and consequently production at the Grumman factory (which built 2,293 TBF-1s) was supported by that entrusted to

Eastern Aircraft (a division of General Motors), which built the aircraft on license, with the designation TBM.

In the meantime, the original project had been developed further. Following the construction of an XTBF-2 prototype (in the spring of 1942) fitted with a more powerful engine, the TBF-3 variant was built. It was fitted with a 2,000 hp Wright Cyclone engine and was characterized by notable improvements, especially in its bomb capacity. This version was produced exclusively by Eastern, which completed 4,664, and went into service from April 1944. The British Royal Navy received 222, which went to equip the units based on the aircraft carriers *Formidable, Illustrious, Indefatigable*, and *Victorious*. The last Avenger was the XTBM-4, in which the wings and fuselage were reinforced, although it never went beyond the prototype stage.

The two major production variants were developed in numerous subseries, transformed in various configurations: for photo-reconnaissance, for night tracking with infrared equipment, for passenger transport, for target towing and for antisubmarine tracking and attack.

---

color plate

Grumman TBF-3 17th Air Group aircraft carrier USS *Bunker Hill* U.S.Navy Air Force - Pacific Ocean 1944-45

Aircraft:	Grumman TBF-1
Nation:	USA
Manufacturer:	Grumman Aircraft Engineering Corp.
Type:	Torpedo
Year:	1942
Engine:	Wright R-2600-8 Cyclone, 14-cylinder radial, air-cooled, 1,723 hp
Wingspan:	54 ft 3 in (16.51 m)
Length:	40 ft 1 in (12.19 m)
Height:	16 ft 5 in (5.00 m)
Weight:	15,927 lb (7,215 kg)
Maximum speed:	270 mph (436 km/h) at 12,039 ft (3,660 m)
Ceiling:	22,368 ft (6,800 m)
Range:	1,214 miles (1,955 m)
Armament:	3 machine guns, 1,600 lb (725 kg) of bombs
Crew:	3

An Avenger in service with the U.S.Navy was the first aircraft to land at the airport on the island of Guam, which was occupied on July 30, 1944.

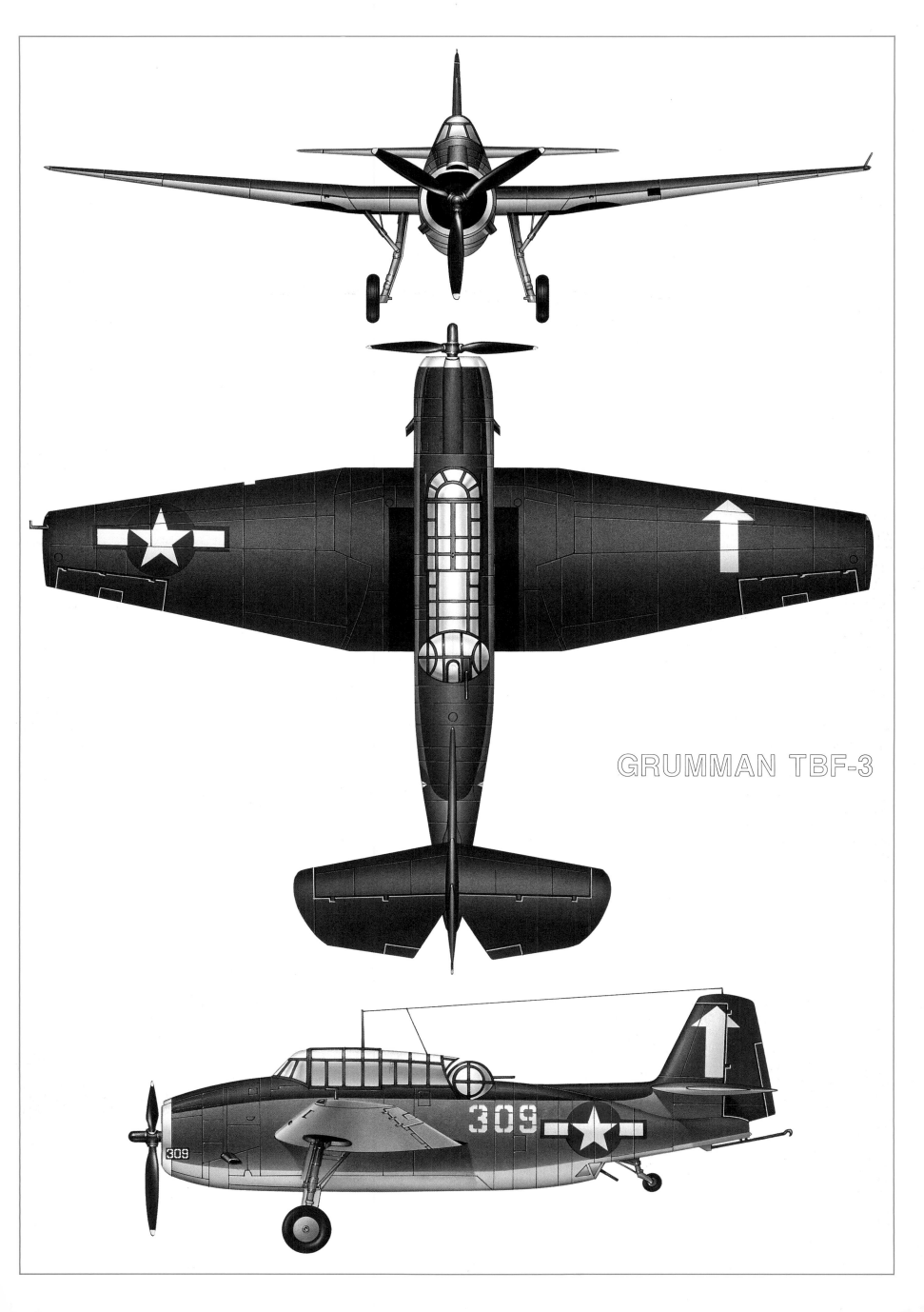

GRUMMAN TBF-3

A formation of F4U-1As in service with the British Navy.

visibility problems which were subsequently to create difficulties in the aircraft's qualification for carrier-based use.

On June 30, 1941, an initial contract for 584 F4U-1s was signed and the first production series aircraft appeared on October 30 of the following year. However, operations on board the aircraft carriers did not commence until April 1944, and the Corsair first went into service in the units of the Marines and then in the land based units of the U.S.Navy. In the course of the year, the Fleet Air Arm's F4Us went into frontline service on board the British aircraft carriers. The Fleet Air Arm received 2,012 aircraft (a further 370 going to the Royal New Zealand Air Force).

The aircraft of the initial version numbered 688 and they were followed on the assembly lines by 2,066 F4U-1As, with modifications to the engine, the landing gear and the cockpit canopy. The final change was carried out in order to improve the pilot's visibility. Subsequently, the principal variants were the F4U-1C (armed with four 20 mm cannons, 300 being built in all), and in 1944 the F4U-1D, with a more powerful engine and armament, of which Vought built 1,375. Vought's production was backed by that of Goodyear and Brewster. The former built 2,302 F4U-1Ds (designated FG-1D) and 1,704 F4U-1As (designated FG-1A), while the latter completed 735 F4U-1s with the designation F3A-1.

The Vought F4U Corsair went down in history as one of the best fighters of the entire Second World War. With the Grumman F6F Hellcat, it shared the honor and the burden of the last two years of battle against Japan. In the course of the 64,051 missions (54,470 carried out from land bases and 9,581 from aircraft carriers) completed by the pilots of the U.S.Navy and the U.S.Marine Corps, the F4Us destroyed 2,140 enemy aircraft in combat, compared to only 189 losses, marking an incredible ratio of more than 11:1. Nevertheless, as these figures show, the Corsair passed about half of its career in the Pacific confined to land bases, despite its indisputable skills. This was due to the fact that for almost a year the U.S.Navy did not consider it suitable for use on board ship. However, the great potential of this powerful combat plane was eventually recognized. In fact, production continued without interruption for more than 10 years (until December 1952), and amounted to 12,571 aircraft in all. It continued to serve in the frontline of the units of the U.S.Navy until December 1954. Its career in the French Navy was even longer. The F4Us were used for another 10 years (until October 1964).

The Corsair was developed at the beginning of 1938, at the request of the U.S.Navy, which ordered the construction of the prototype of a new single-seater carrier-based fighter with advanced characteristics on June 30. Rex B. Beisel, Vought's chief designer, wanted to build the smallest possible airframe compatible with the most powerful engine available at the time, the Pratt & Whitney XR-2800 Double Wasp (a large 18-cylinder radial, generating 2,000 hp). The characteristic ''inverted gull wing'' shape was chosen, which also allowed for the adoption of a propeller with a large diameter. Such a propeller was capable of absorbing the remarkable engine power and shortening the legs of the forward landing gear to a maximum.

The XF4U-1 prototype took to the air for the first time on May 29, 1940, and right from the start its remarkable characteristics became apparent. During a transfer flight on October 1, the aircraft reached 403 mph (650 km/h), thus becoming the first American-produced fighter to go beyond the 400 mph (643,6 km/h) ''limit.'' However, despite this brilliant performance, the preparation of the prototype proved to be long and laborious. An initial request was made for the strengthening of its armament. This modification made it necessary to move the fuel tanks on the wings and to add another in the fuselage. The pilot's seat was thus moved back by about three feet (90 cm), posing serious

An F4U-1A of the VMF 127 with 16 kill's markings.

color plate

Vought F4U-1D VMF 124 U.S.Marine squadron - New Guinea 1943. Personal aircraft of Major Greg Boyington (28 confirmed victories)

Aircraft:	Vought F4U-1D
Nation:	USA
Manufacturer:	United Aircraft Corp.
Type:	Fighter
Year:	1944
Engine:	Pratt & Whitney R-2800-8W Double Wasp, 18-cylinder radial, air-cooled, 2,250 hp
Wingspan:	41 ft (12.47 m)
Length:	33 ft 5 in (10.16 m)
Height:	16 ft 1 in (4.90 m)
Weight:	13,136 lb (5,951 kg)
Maximum speed:	424 mph (684 km/h) at 20,052 lb (6,096 m)
Ceiling:	33,990 lb (10,333 m)
Range:	1,014 miles (1,633 km)
Armament:	6 machine guns; 2,002 lb (907 kg) of bombs
Crew:	1

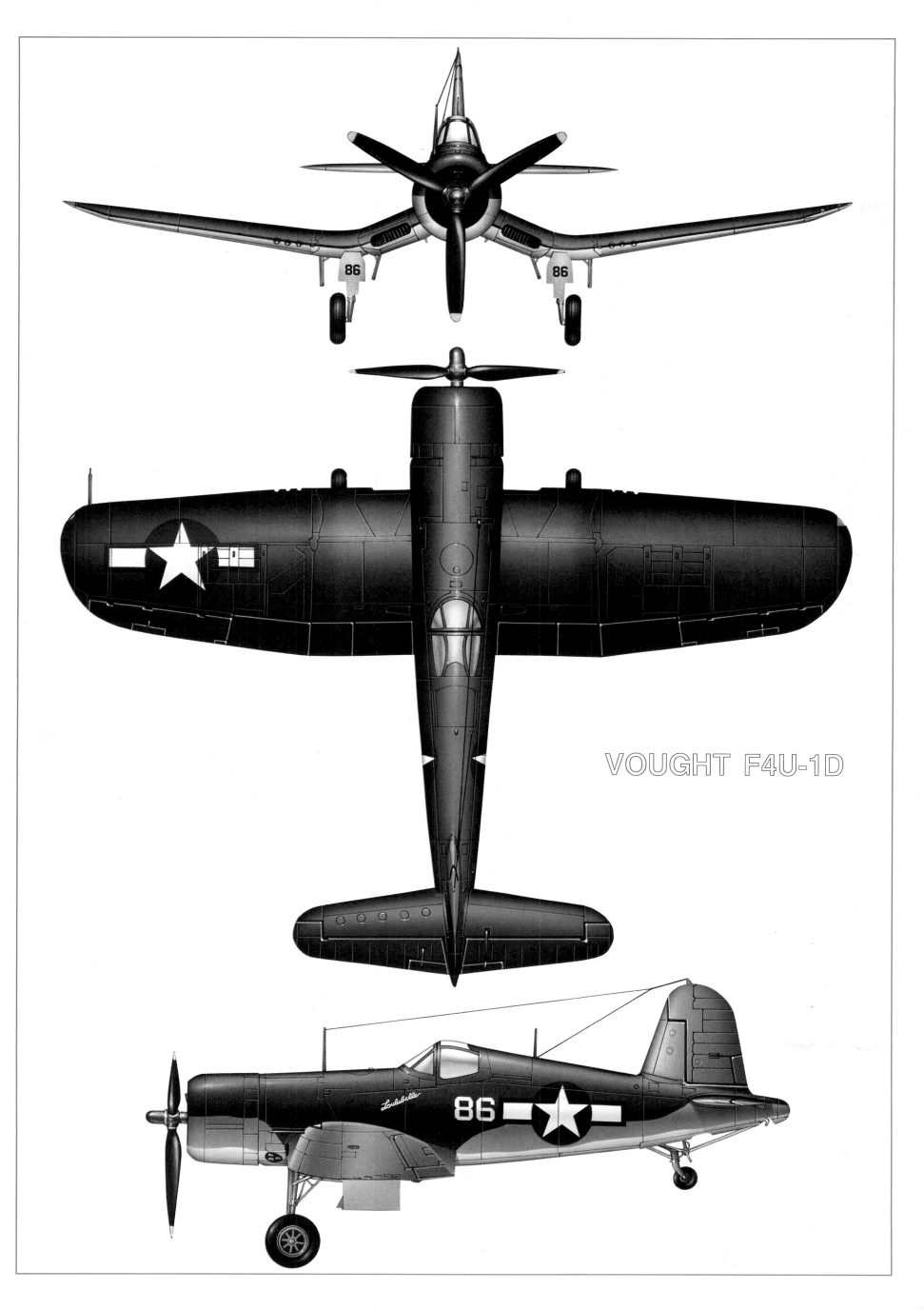

VOUGHT F4U-1D

The development of the F4U Corsair was marked by a new phase toward the end of 1944, with the appearance of the first of a new variant, the F4U-4, the last of the war. This aircraft was fitted with Pratt & Whitney R-2800 engines, capable of generating 2,100 hp in normal conditions and no less than 2,485 hp with water injection. With the aim of absorbing the notable increase in power, the propeller became a four-bladed one, with a diameter of almost 13 ft (4 m). Consequently, the already excellent performance of Rex B. Beisel's fighter was improved still further, although the new Corsairs were ready in time only to take part in the last battles of the war against Japan.

However, another conflict, the Korean war, was imminent and the final versions of the F4U proved their great effectiveness as combat planes all the same. The F4U-4 (of which a total of 2,357 were built until August 1947) was followed by a new variant (the F4U-5), the prototype of which had taken to the air on April 4, 1945. These aircraft had even more powerful engines, as well as modifications to the airframe, its covering, and the armament. In all, 568 were completed, of which 101 were F4U-5NLs (night fighters suited to particularly severe climates), 214 were F4U-5Ns (standard night fighters) and 30 were F4U-5Ps (for photo reconnaissance). The final development of the Corsair was prepared in the course of 1951, with the designation F4U-6, although it appeared as the AU-1, in January of the following year. It was intended for ground attack and tactical support. For this purpose, it was fitted with a Pratt & Whitney R-2800-83WA engine with single stage compressor which provided maximum power at low altitude. It was capable of carrying a bomb load of over 4,415 lb (2,000 kg) below its wings and fuselage, as well as detachable fuel tanks.

The final version of the Corsair, the F4U-7, was derived from the AU-1, and 94 were built for the French Aéronavale, which wanted a multi-role tactical aircraft for operations in Indochina. Production ceased definitively in December 1952, and the French order was completed in January of the following year. The last aircraft to be delivered brought the total to 12,571. The aircraft's front-line service in the U.S.Navy continued until December 1954. Its career in the French Navy was longer still, lasting until October 1964.

The Corsair has gone down in history as one of the best fighters of World War II, and in particular, as the aircraft which, together with the Grumman F6F Hellcat, shared the honor and the burden of the final two years of struggle against Japan. During the 64,051 missions (54,470 carried out from land bases and 9,581 from aircraft carriers) completed by the pilots of the U.S.Navy and the U.S. Marine Corps, the F4Us destroyed 2,140 enemy aircraft in combat, compared to only 189 losses, marking an exceptional ratio of 11:1. In the Korean war, well into the jet age, the Corsairs carried out an invaluable role in tactical support and ground attack, but they managed to show great courage in air combat too. In August 1952, one of them succeeded in shooting down an enemy MiG 15.

The prototype of the F4U-4 Corsair in flight.

An F4U-4 in postwar service. The F4U-4s went into service during the final days of the war and, together with the later versions, they participated actively in the Korean War.

This photograph shows the bombs and munitions for the weapons installed on board that the F4U-5 was capable of carrying.

color plate

Vought F4U-4 CV39 *Lake Champlain* aircraft carrier U.S.Navy Air Force · Pacific Sea June 1945

Aircraft:	Vought F4U-4
Nation:	USA
Manufacturer:	United Aircraft Corp.
Type:	Fighter
Year:	1944
Engine:	Pratt & Whitney R-2800-18W Double Wasp, 18-cylinder radial, air-cooled, 2,100 hp
Wingspan:	41 ft 1 in (12.49 m)
Length:	33 ft 9 in (10.26 m)
Height:	14 ft 9 in (4.49 m)
Weight:	14,037 lb (6,359 kg)
Maximum speed:	445 mph (718 km/h) at 26,269 ft (7,986 m)
Ceiling:	41,710 ft (12,680 m)
Range:	1,618 miles (2,607 km)
Armament:	6 machine guns; 2,002 lb (907 kg) of bombs
Crew:	1

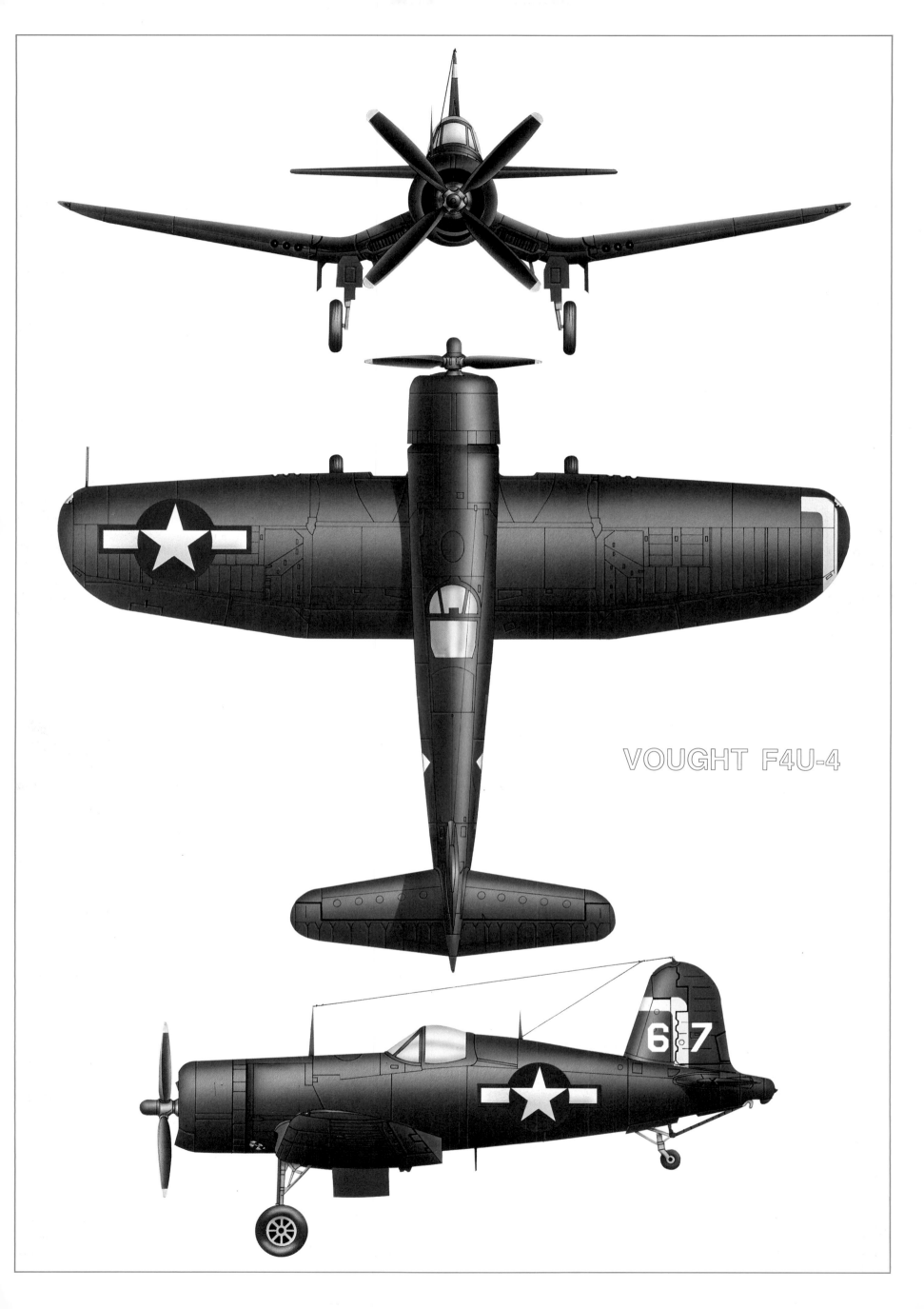

VOUGHT F4U-4

The Mitsubishi A5M, the Japanese Imperial Navy's first metal monoplane fighter, was the creation of a technician who was to become world famous: Jiro Horikoshi, "father" of the celebrated A6M Reisen (better-known as the Zero), one of the best-known combat planes in the entire war. A total of 1,094 of these aircraft were produced in several versions (they were christened "CLAUDE" in the Allies' code), but the A5M was clearly a transitional fighter. However, its delivery to the units marked a significant step in the development of the Imperial Navy's air force, which underwent a period of strengthening and reorganization in the first half of the 1930s. The advanced nature of the plane's design and its excellent overall qualities were demonstrated to the full during the Second Sino-Japanese War, and at the outbreak of hostilities in the Pacific, the A5M was still in service on several aircraft carriers. These aircraft were subsequently relegated to secondary roles, including training.

The project got under way at the beginning of 1934, on the basis of somewhat ambitious specifications requesting a small monoplane fighter with particularly advanced characteristics. These included a maximum speed of 220 mph (350 km/h) at 10,000 ft (3,000 m), the ability to climb to 16,000 ft (5,000 m) in six and a half minutes, plus armament consisting of two 7 mm machine guns. These requirements were more than fulfilled from the moment testing of the first prototype began. It made its maiden flight on February 4, 1935, arousing great interest. However, some serious aerodynamic problems emerged during tests and led to a complete redesigning of the wing, which had been of the "inverted-gull" type. The second prototype featured the definitive form and, in addition, four others were built with the aim of experimenting with the installation of various power plants.

In 1936, after evaluation, the aircraft (designated the A5M1) was accepted and immediately went into production. Delivery commenced the following year, but after 36 planes had been built, production was concentrated on a second variant, the A5M2a, powered by a 610 hp Nakajima Kotobuki 2 Kai 3 engine, and later on the A5M2b, powered by a 640 hp Kotobuki 3 engine and featuring an enclosed cockpit (the latter version did not enjoy much success with the pilots, however, and was withdrawn after only a brief period in service). Beginning in September 1937, the Mitsubishi fighter was employed in the Second Sino-Japanese War and stood out for its overall superiority as compared to the faster Polikarpov I-16s used by the adversaries.

It was, in fact, these combat experiences (and in particular the need for greater range) that led to the production of a subsequent version of the aircraft. This was the A5M4, which featured a 710 hp Kotobuki 41 engine and had a 35.2 US gal. (160 liter) external tank installed under the belly. The new fighter went into production in 1938, and was immediately sent to units in China, where it undoubtedly contributed to confirming the supremacy of the Japanese air force. The A5M4 was the variant built in the greatest numbers, and it remained in production until 1940.

Among the other versions produced were the experimental A5M3, provided with a 610 hp in-line Hispano-Suiza 12Xcrs engine and with a 20 mm cannon in the propeller axis; and the A5M4-K two-seater trainer of 1940. In 1935, the A5M attracted the attention of the Japanese army, for which Mitsubishi produced two prototypes, designated Ki-18 and Ki-33. However, both were judged inadequate, particularly from the point of view of handling, and were therefore rejected.

color plate
Mitsubishi A5M2 13th Flying Group - China 1938

Aircraft:	Mitsubishi A5M2a
Nation:	Japan
Manufacturer:	Mitsubishi Jukogyo K.K.
Type:	Fighter
Year:	1937
Engine:	Nakajima Kotobuki 2 Kai 3, 9-cylinder radial, air-cooled 6,610 hp
Wingspan:	36 ft (11.00 m)
Length:	25 ft 2 in (7.71 m)
Height:	10ft 9in((3.27 m)
Weight:	3,307 lb (1,500 kg)
Maximum speed:	280 mph at 6,900 ft (405 km/h at 2,100 m)
Ceiling:	—
Range:	—
Armament:	2 machine guns
Crew:	1

Formation of A5M2 Claudes at the time of the Sino-Japanese conflict.

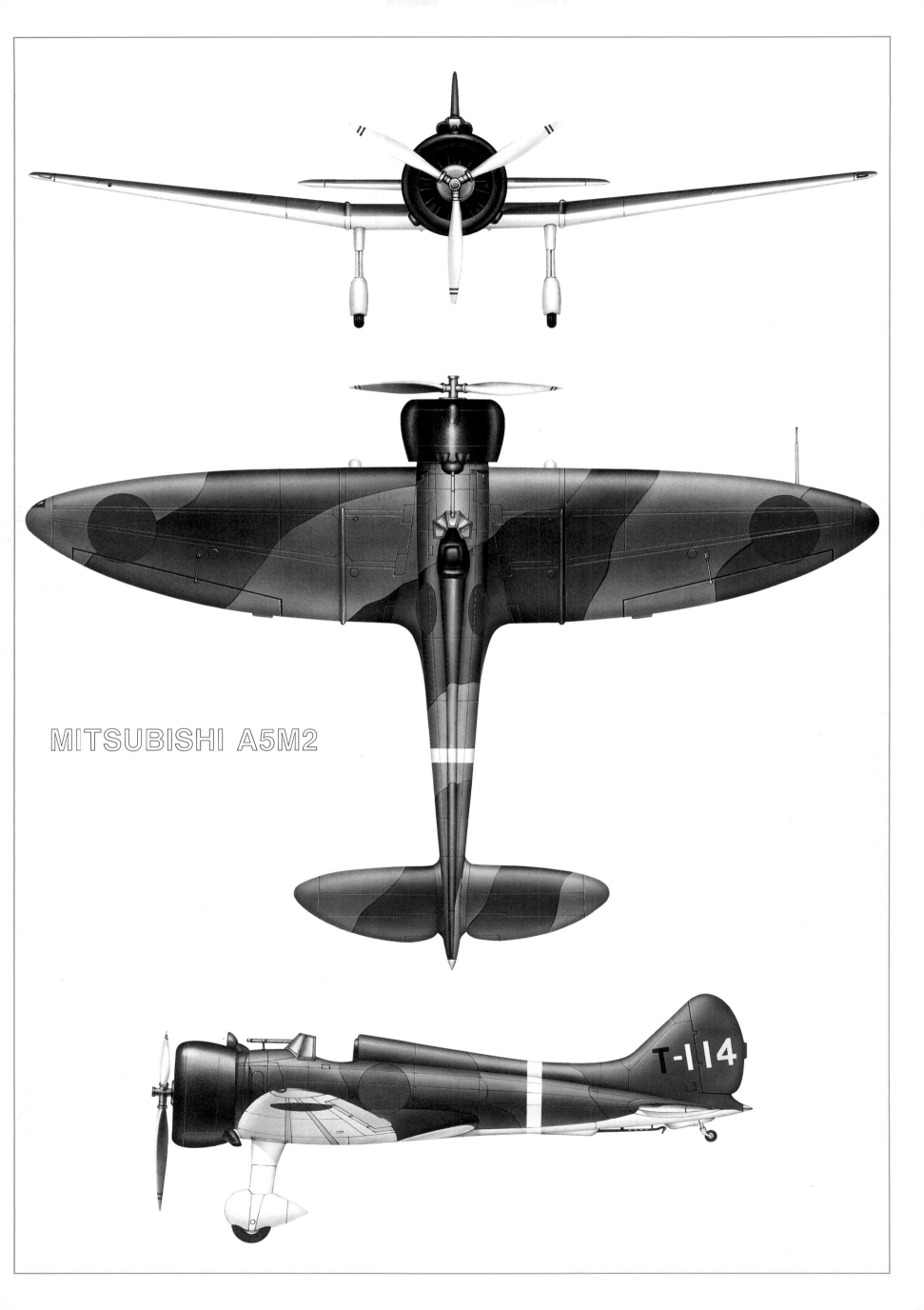

MITSUBISHI A5M2

MITSUBISHI A6M2

EI-111

An immortal fighter whose fame was equal to that of the British Supermarine Spitfire, the German Messerschmitt Bf.109, and the U.S. North American Mustang, the Mitsubishi A6M still calls to mind the symbol of power in the air achieved by the Japanese during World War II. Better known as Zero (from the Japanese navy's official designation), this remarkable aircraft was a protagonist of the war in the Pacific from Pearl Harbor up to the time of the last suicide missions. The reputation of invincibility earned by the A6M from its very first missions gradually diminished with the appearance of increasingly powerful Allied aircraft, created expressly to contest its supremacy. Despite this, the Mitsubishi fighter remained a tough adversary, thanks to a continual updating in its production which lasted from March 1939 until August 1945. In this period of more than six years, a total of 10,449 came off the assembly lines, the highest number of any aircraft to be built by the Japanese aeronautical industry in the course of the war.

The Zero was designed by Jiro Horikoshi, Mitsubishi's chief designer in 1937. He started work on the new fighter on the basis of specifications issued by the Imperial navy on May 19, 1937, requesting manufacturers to build an aircraft carrier-based combat plane to replace the Mitsubishi A5M which was beginning to go into service at the time. The original request was modified in October, on the basis of operative experiences in the conflict with China, and the specifications became more rigid. The new fighter was to have a maximum speed of 310 mph (500 km/h) at 13,150 ft (4,000 m); ascent to 9,870 ft (3,000 m) in nine and a half minutes; a range of one and a half to two hours at normal power and eight hours at cruising speed and with extra fuel tanks; maneuverability at least equal to that of the A5M; takeoff distance of no more than 230 ft (70 m) in a head wind of 27 knots; complete radio apparatus. The armament was to include two 20 mm cannons, two 7.7 mm machine guns and two 132 lb (60 kg) bombs. It was not easy to satisfy these demands, and Nakajima, which was also preparing a project, abandoned the competition.

This was not so for Mitsubishi's technicians, who went ahead with the A6M1 project, a slender, all-metal monoplane powered by a 780 hp Mitsubishi Zuisei 13 radial engine. The first prototype took to the air on April 1, 1939, and its remarkable qualities immediately became apparent, fulfilling or exceeding all the official specifications during flight tests. Its performance improved still further with the installation (on the third prototype) of a 950 hp Nakajima NK1C Sakae 12 engine. The first aircraft of the initial A6M2 version completed evaluation tests in July 1940, and immediately after, the navy decided to send an initial lot of 15 aircraft to China for operative tests. The Zero had its baptism of fire on September 13, and it was on this occasion that the myth of its invincibility was

born. In the meantime (at the end of July), the new fighter had gone into mass production.

When the war broke out in the Pacific, the A6M2s constituted the strong point in the Japanese carrier-based fighter force, 328 being operative in a front line totalling 521 aircraft. It played an increasingly important role as operations proceeded, and until the Battle of Midway, in June 1942, these aircraft maintained uncontested supremacy in the air due to their overall superiority (especially in speed and handling) compared to the Allied fighters of the period. In fact, it was at the time of the Battle of Midway that the A6M3, the second major version, appeared, with more powerful engine and armament, while in the fall of 1943 the A6M5 was delivered to the units. This was perhaps the best variant of all, with further improvements to the power plant, armament, and the protection of the pilot and fuel tanks, as well as being strengthened at a structural level.

However, the war in the Pacific had already reached its turning point. Even this version of the Zero did not manage to redress the balance in the struggle for supremacy in the air, faced with adversaries that were by now superior in terms both of quality and quantity. Mitsubishi made a final effort with the development of the A6M8 variant, which appeared as a prototype in April 1945 and was provided with a 1,560 hp engine. However, the massive production program (6,300 aircraft) never got under way.

Aircraft:	Mitsubishi A6M2
Nation:	Japan
Manufacturer:	Mitsubishi Jukogyo KK
Type:	Fighter
Year:	1940
Engine:	Nakajima NK1C Sakae 12, 14-cylinder radial, air-cooled, 950 hp
Wingspan:	39 ft 4½ in (12.10 m)
Length:	29 ft 9 in (9.15 m)
Height:	10 ft (3.05 m)
Weight:	6,164 lb (2,800 kg) loaded
Maximum speed:	332 mph (534 km/h) at 14,930 ft (4,550 m)
Ceiling:	32,810 ft (10,000 m)
Range:	1,930 miles (3,105 km)
Armament:	2 × 20 mm cannons; 2 machine guns; 264 lb (120 kg) of bombs
Crew:	1

color plate

Mitsubishi A6M2 Zero 5th Koku-Sentai of *Shokaku* aircraft carrier Japanese Imperial Navy Air Force - Pacific Sea 1942

Two different versions of the Zero during testing trials carried out by the Allies after their capture.

Formation of A6M5 Zeros in a Japanese base.

MITSUBISHI G3M2

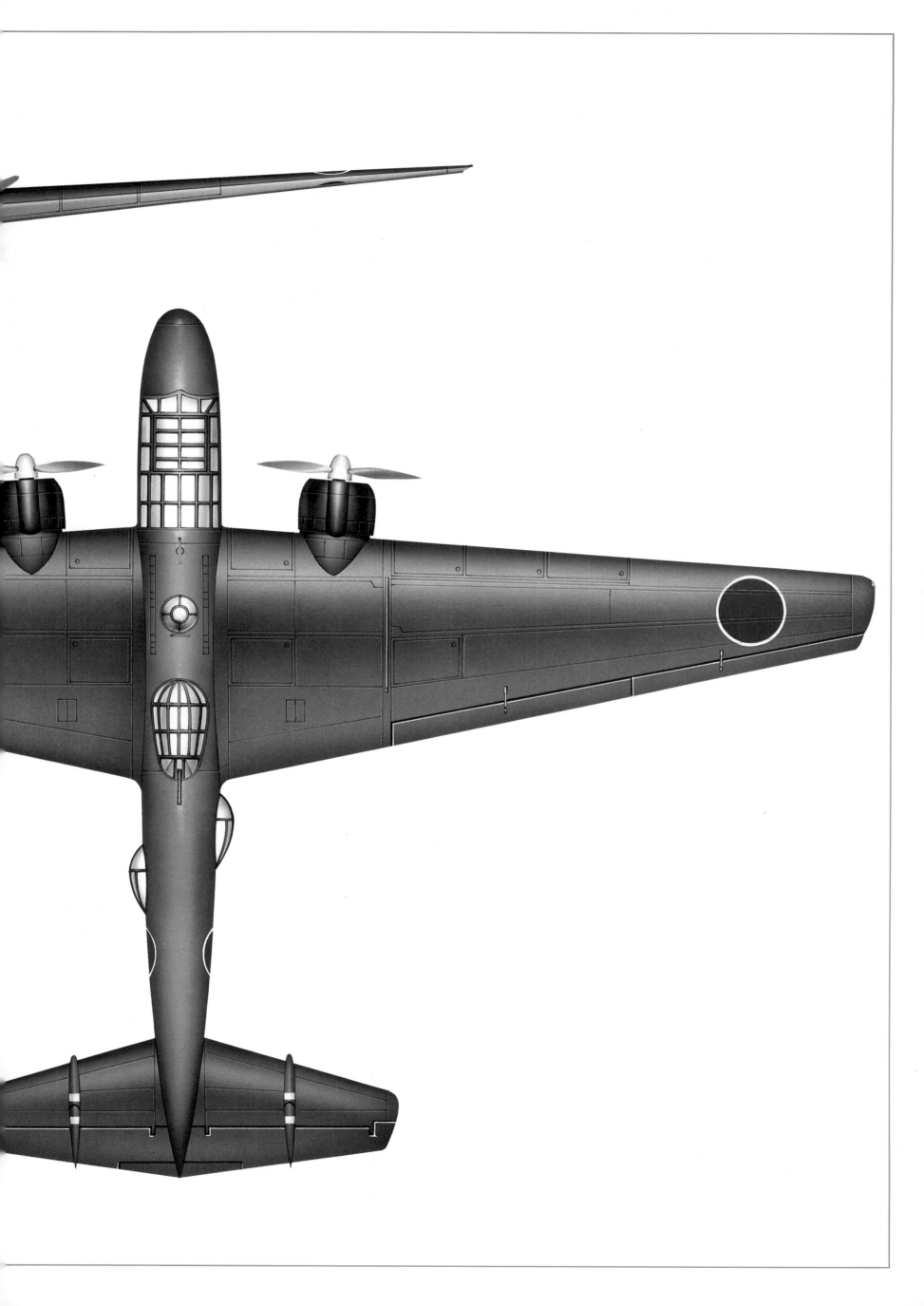

G3M2 of the Kisarazu Kokutai. The horizontal band on the rudder indicates the aircraft of a section leader.

In Japan, as in Germany, during the years of peace, ocean crossings or sporting events represented the most suitable and effective means of revealing to the world the enormous potential, achieved almost by surprise, of its aeronautical industry. In the years immediately prior to World War II, a series of intercontinental flights carried out by a modern twin-engine aircraft built by Mitsubishi caused a sensation. These included a round-the-world flight, sponsored by the daily newspaper *Mainichi Shimbun,* and carried out between August 26, and October 20, 1939, by an aircraft christened *Nippon* and registered J-BAC I: a total of more than 32,820 miles (52,850 km) were covered in 194 hours of flying time. This aircraft was a G3M2 model modified for civilian use and was the same as that which, little more than a year later, was to become famous for a feat of a very different kind: the sinking of the British battleships *Prince of Wales* and *Repulse* off Malaysia on December 10, 1941. During this operation (representing a second setback for the Allies after Pearl Harbor), the Mitsubishi bombers played a determining role, thanks mainly to their great range which made action possible in areas considered by the British and American high commands to be outside the range of the Japanese air force.

The G3M2 (designated NELL in the Allies' code, while the military transport model derived from it was known as TINA) constituted the main force in the Japanese navy's bomber units during the first year of the war, and a total of 1,048 were built up to 1943. The project had been launched in great secrecy in 1933, on the instigation of Admiral Isoroku Yamamoto, who was director of the technical division of the Aeronautical Office of the Imperial Navy at the time. Yamamoto, convinced of the need to build a long-range land plane capable of supporting the carrier-based aircraft in naval operations, succeeded in gaining approval for the program and for the immediate construction of a prototype.

This prototype (designed by Sueo Honjo, Tomio Kubo, and Nobuhiko Kusabake and designated Ka-9) made its maiden flight in April 1934 and immediately produced excellent results. The aircraft had been completed without taking military specifications into account, and, in June 1935, following a long series of evaluations, it was joined by the first of 21 prototypes built with a future military function in mind.

The initial G3M1 version went into production a year later. The bomber was an all-metal mid-wing monoplane, with retractable landing gear, characterized by double tail fins and powered by a pair of Mitsubishi Kinsei radial engines. Only 34 of this variant were built, and on their completion production continued with the principal G3M2 version. The latter (fitted with more powerful engines) was divided into two subseries (G3M2 Model 21 and G3M2 Model 22), of which 343 and approximately 400 aircraft were built respectively. The final variant (built exclusively by Nakajima from 1941), the G3M2 Model 23, was provided with 1,300 hp engines and larger fuel tanks, making it the fastest aircraft and the one with the greatest range.

The G3M made its operative debut in August 1937, during the second Sino-Japanese conflict. Following Japan's entry into the war, the Mitsubishi bombers took part in all operations in the Pacific islands, although they were gradually joined by the more modern G4Ms. The G3Ms were also used both as military and civilian transport planes. In the latter sector, the converting of 20 or so G3M2s in 1939 for commercial use should be mentioned. They were used mainly by the Nippon Koku K.K. and the Dai Nippon Koku K.K. airlines.

---

color plate
Mitsubishi G3M2 707th Naval Air Corps - Java 1942

Aircraft:	Mitsubishi G3M2
Nation:	Japan
Manufacturer:	Mitsubishi Jukogyo KK
Type:	Bomber
Year:	1937
Engine:	2 Mitsubishi Kinsei 41,14-cylinder radial, air-cooled, 1,075 hp each
Wingspan:	82 ft (25 m)
Length:	53 ft 11 in (16.45 m)
Height:	12 ft 1 in (3.68 m)
Weight:	17,637 lb (8,000 kg) loaded
Maximum speed:	232 mph (373 km/h) at 13,715 ft (4,180 m)
Ceiling:	29,950 ft (9,130 m)
Range:	2,722 miles (4,380 m)
Armament:	1 × 20 mm cannon; 4 machine guns; 1,764 lb (800 kg) of bombs
Crew:	7

Two Mitsubishi G3M s of the Mihoro Kokutai. The aircraft in the foreground is a G3M2, the other a G3M1. The differences in the dorsal defensive armament are clearly visible.

Perhaps the bomber most widely used by the Japanese Imperial army air force during the war, the Mitsubishi Ki-21 was in service from the first day of the conflict to the last, and some 2,064 were built in five major series from March 1938 to September 1944. This achievement was not due so much to the intrinsic characteristics of the aircraft (which actually soon demonstrated the limitations of its layout, despite being continuously updated), as to the lack of a valid successor. However, at least during the first year of war in the Pacific, the Ki-21 succeeded in bringing the army's bomber units up to the same qualitative level as those of the navy, which used the excellent Mitsubishi G3M and G4M series. In the Allies' identification code, the Ki-21 was known as "Sally."

The project was launched by Mitsubishi on the basis of specifications issued on February 15, 1936, requesting a two-engine heavy bomber to replace the older ones in service at the time, such as the Ki-20 and the Ki-1. The requirements were particularly advanced for the period: operational altitude between 6,500 ft (2,000 m) and 13,000 ft (4,000 m); range of more than five hours at a cruising speed of 186 mph (300 km/h); maximum speed of 250 mph (400 km/h) at 9,850 ft (3,000 m); ascent to 9,850 ft (3,000 m) in eight minutes; takeoff distance of fewer than 985 ft (300 m). As for the engines, two 850 hp Nakajima Ha-5s or two 825 hp Mitsubishi Ha-6s were requested, while the defensive armament was to consist of a minimum of three machine guns and the offensive armament was to vary between 1,650 lb (750 kg) and 2,205 lb (1,000 kg) of bombs.

Lastly, the standard crew was to consist of four men, with the possibility of housing another two machine gunners in additional positions.

Two prototypes were prepared in the course of the year, and the first of these took to the air on December 18, 1936. However,

evaluation tests lasted almost six months and also involved two aircraft prepared by Nakajima with the designation Ki-19. Following the construction of a further two prototypes for each model, the Mitsubishi project was chosen, and in November 1937 the aircraft went into production with the designation Ki-21-Ia.

Following the construction of 143 aircraft, Mitsubishi's assembly lines completed another 120 and 160 aircraft of the Ki-21-Ib and Ki-21-Ic variants, strengthened above all in their defensive armament and in the quantity and disposition of the fuel tanks. From November 1938, these aircraft were all used in combat in the conflict with China.

It was "in fact" this operational experience that led to the building of the next variant, the Ki-21-II, which appeared in December 1940 and was characterized by the use of more powerful engines that guaranteed an increase in performance, especially as far as speed and operational altitude were concerned. This version of the bomber was built in two subseries (the Ki-21-IIa and the Ki-21-IIb, of which 590 and 688 aircraft were built respectively), which differed mainly in their defensive armament, leading to structural modifications to the fuselage, due to the fitting of a turret on the back of the Ki-21-IIb model in place of the characteristic long glazed cockpit of the previous series.

The bombers of this second version equipped many of the Imperial army units when Japan entered the war. They remained in front-line service until 1944 and were then relegated to secondary roles. Some aircraft also took part in suicide missions during the final months of the war in the Pacific.

---

color plate

Mitsubishi Ki-21-IIb 98th Group, 2nd Squadron Japanese Imperial Army Air Force - India 1943

A Ki-21 which took part in a suicide mission at Okinawa airport on May 24, 1945.

Aircraft:	Mitsubishi Ki-21-IIb
Nation:	Japan
Manufacturer:	Mitsubishi Jukogyo KK
Type:	Bomber
Year:	1941
Engine:	2 Mitsubishi Ha-101, 14-cylinder radial, 1,530 hp each
Wingspan:	73 ft 10 in (22.50 m)
Length:	52 ft 6 in (16 m)
Height:	15 ft 11 in (4.85 m)
Weight:	23,392 lb (10,632 kg) loaded
Maximum speed:	302 mph (486 km/h) at 15,485 ft (4,720 m)
Ceiling:	32,810 ft (10,000 m)
Range:	1,680 miles (2,700 m)
Armament:	6 machine guns; 2,205 lb (1,000 kg) of bombs
Crew:	5-7

A Mitsubishi Sally flying low over the jungle in the Philippines.

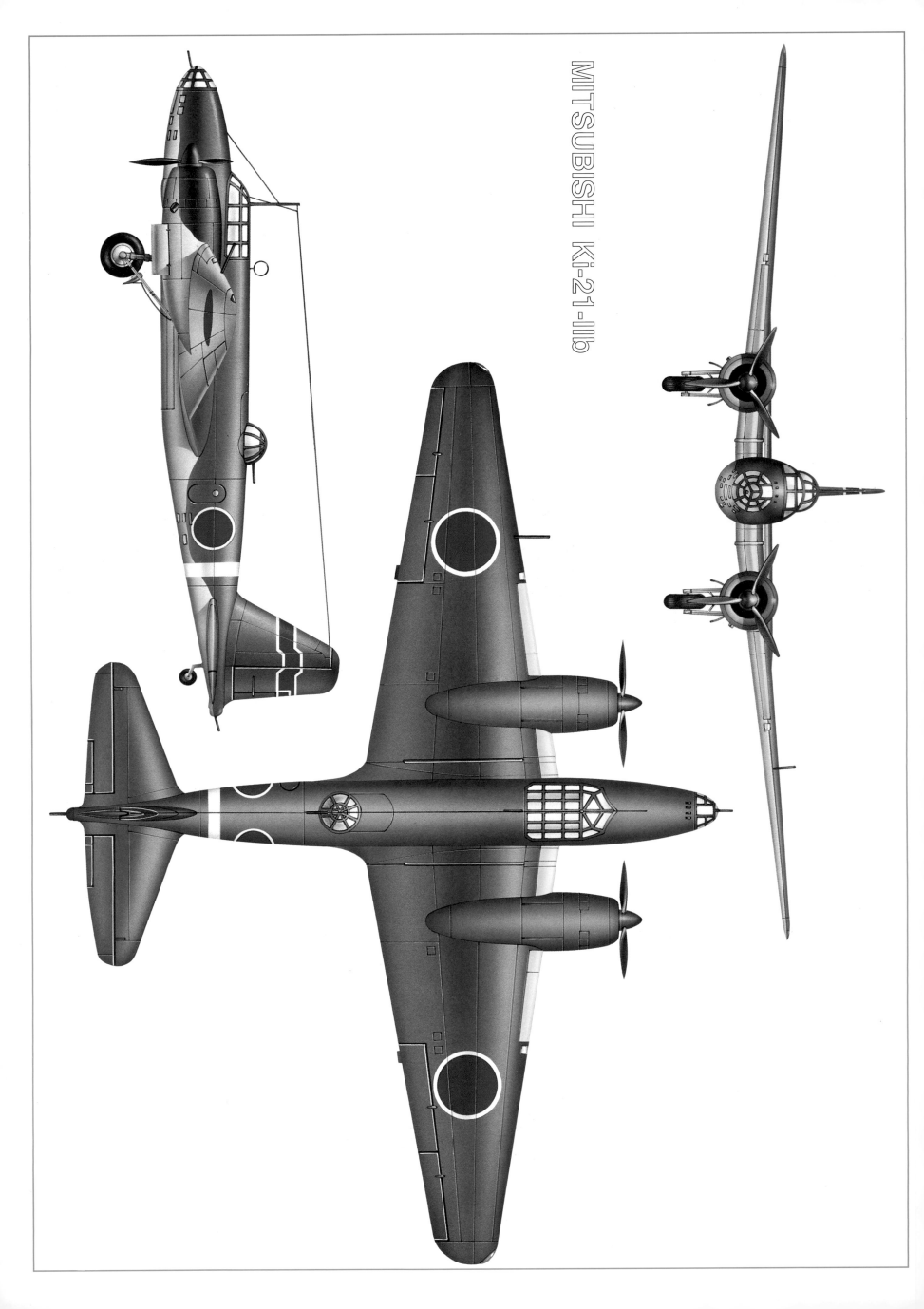

MITSUBISHI Ki-21-IIb

MITSUBISHI Ki-51

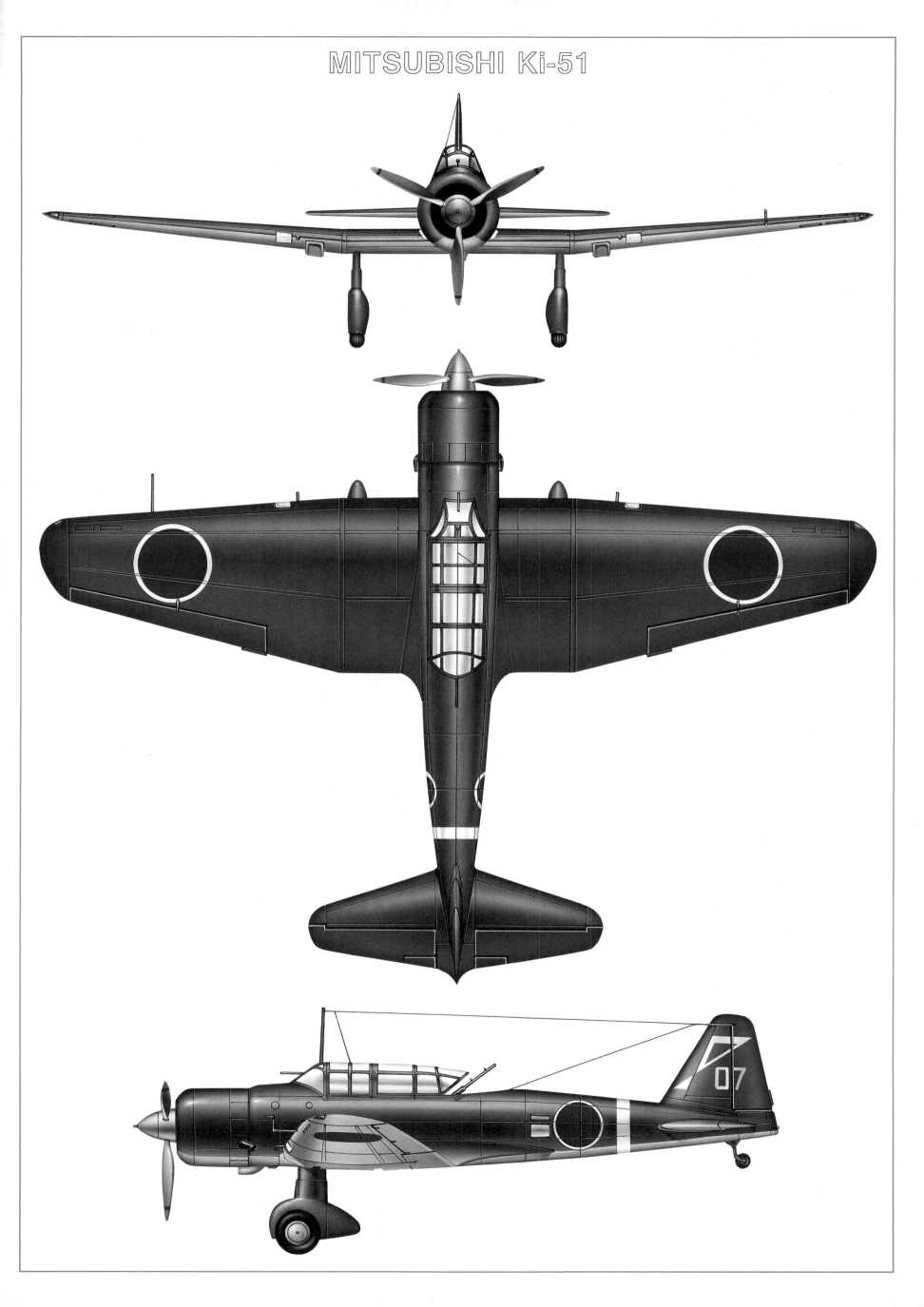

The Mitsubishi Ki-51 was the Imperial Army air force's true "all-rounder." Conceived in 1938 as a ground-attack plane and overtaken by more modern aircraft in the course of the conflict, it was never withdrawn from front-line duty, thanks to excellent features, including sturdiness, reliability, and maneuverability, that made it practically irreplaceable in tactical roles. The overall effectiveness of the project is demonstrated by the fact that the Ki-51 (christened SONIA in the Allies' identification code) remained virtually unaltered throughout the long period in which it was produced. In fact production commenced in 1940 and ceased in July 1945 and amounted to no fewer than 2,385 aircraft.

In 1937 Imperial Army authorities issued the specifications that were to lead to the creation of the Ki-51. These requested a ground-attack plane derived from the earlier Ki-30 light bomber, but more agile and compact. Great emphasis was placed on maneuverability, on protection for the crew, and on the possibility of operating from emergency airstrips located near the combat area. As for the aircraft's performance, its maximum speed was to be no less than 260 mph (420 km/h) at 6,578 ft (2,000 m), takeoff weight was to be 5,960 lb (2,700 kg), it was to have a bomb load of 440 lb (200 kg) and defensive armament consisting of three machine guns, one of which was to be movable.

The Mitsubishi project was entrusted to the same team that had designed the Ki-30, Kawano, Ohki, and Mizuno, and the first two prototypes were completed in the summer of 1939. These were followed by 11 preseries aircraft that were used for evaluation tests, during which their already remarkable characteristics were further improved through modifications of an aerodynamic nature.

The Ki-51 was an all-metal low-wing monoplane with fixed and faired landing gear, and it was characterized by the long glazed cockpit that housed the pilot and the observer-gunner. The latter had a 7.7 mm machine gun fitted onto a movable mounting at his disposal for the defense of the rear, while the rest of the defensive armament consisted of two similar weapons (subsequently replaced by two 12.7 mm machine guns) which were fixed and installed on the wings. The power plant was a 940 hp Mitsubishi Ha-26 II radial engine.

The aircraft made its operational debut in China, and when Japan entered World War II, it was widely used in the Pacific, equipping almost all the operative units. In 1944, the continually growing demand, and the need to satisfy it, led to the opening of a new assembly line at the Tachikawa Dai-Ichi Rikugun Kokusho (Tachikawa Army Air Force Arsenal), which built no fewer than 913 aircraft. Thus, the Ki-51's career continued until the end of the war, when the final role assigned it was that of suicide plane.

Attempts to develop a more powerful version of the SONIA were not lacking. In 1941 Mitsubishi prepared three prototypes for use in tactical reconnaissance and designated Ki-71. These aircraft were provided with more powerful engines and with retractable landing gear. However, the improvements were not satisfactory enough to justify their going into production.

---

color plate
Mitsubishi Ki-51 44th Sentai Japanese Imperial Army Air Force - China 1942

Above, final control before takeoff; note the bombs under the wings. Below, a formation of Ki-51s employed by the 44th Sentai. Above right, a Ki-51 with landing gear lacking fairing and with the modified spinner characteristic of the last models to be built.

Aircraft:	Mitsubishi Ki-51
Nation:	Japan
Manufacturer:	Mitsubishi Jukogyo KK
Type:	Attack
Year:	1940
Engine:	Mitsubishi Ha-26 II, 14-cylinder radial, air-cooled, 940 hp
Wingspan:	39 ft 8 1/2 in (12.10 m)
Length:	30 ft 2 1/2 in (9.21 m)
Height:	8 ft 11 1/2 in (2.73 m)
Weight:	6,415 lb (2,915 kg) loaded
Maximum speed:	263 mph (424 km/h) at 9,840 ft (3,000 m)
Ceiling:	27,130 ft (8,270 m)
Range:	660 miles (1,060 km)
Armament:	3 machine guns; 440 lb (200 kg) of bombs
Crew:	2

Although it was designed in October 1938, almost five years passed before the Mitsubishi J2M Raiden (Lightning) was used in combat. In fact, the preparation of this interceptor took an extremely long time, due above all to numerous technical problems connected with the functioning of the engines, which were never entirely resolved. Only 476, including the various prototypes, came off the assembly lines and most of these were used to defend Japan during the last months of the war.

The Imperial Navy had issued a request for a land-based interceptor some months after the program for the Mitsubishi A6M Reisen (the famous Zero) had been launched, and this coincidental timing was the primary cause for the delays. In fact, since all of Mitsubishi's technical staff was occupied with the development of the new fighter, eleven months were to pass before the exact specifications were defined. The requests included a maximum speed of 372 mph (600 km/h) at 19,736 ft (6,000 m), the ability to climb to the same altitude in less than five and a half minutes, and the ability to operate at combat speed for 45 minutes. These characteristics, which for the first time called for qualities of horizontal speed and ascent (in an interceptor), rather than those concerning range and maneuverability, indicated a change in mentality in the general staff of the navy, as well as great foresight.

However, this foresight was not compensated by practical results. The first of three prototypes took to the air on March 20, 1942, and a whole series of problems immediately emerged. A further eight months were necessary to solve them. The initial problems concerned the retracting mechanism of the main landing gear as well as that which regulated the pitch of the propeller. Later on, problems occurred with the engine, a large 1,430 hp Kasei 13 radial, which drove the propeller by means of a transmission shaft. A decision to pull back the propeller consequently improved the aerodynamics of the aircraft. In addition, the Imperial Navy's pilots complained of highly limited visibility through the windscreen.

It was thus necessary to carry out many modifications and as a result, even the original engine was replaced by the more powerful Kasei 23, which generated 1,800 hp at takeoff. However this change was the cause of fresh problems. The engine, that possessed a water and gas injection system to increase its power in the case of an emergency, was the first of its kind to be developed by the Japanese aeronautical industry, and it proved to be the source of complex tuning problems. In addition,

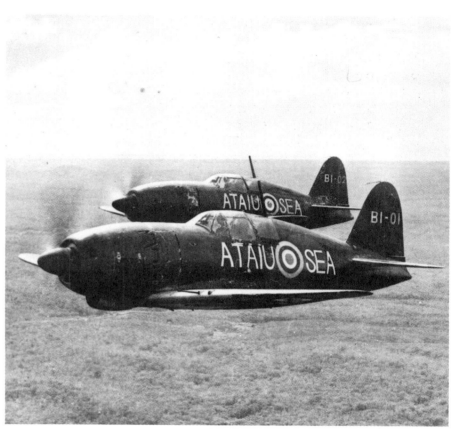

Two Mitsubishi Raidens tested in flight by the Allies following their capture.

dangerous vibrations within the engine at certain speeds also had to be eliminated.

The fighter went into production in December 1942, with the designation J2M2, but after only a few months the assembly lines came to a halt. Soon after, the cause of two inexplicable accidents was discovered: the mistaken position of the tail wheel's retracting mechanism which, set in motion immediately after takeoff, blocked the controls in a diving position. It was not until December 1943, that the Raiden was ready and by that time a new version (J2M3) with heavier armament was already prepared. Production completed 155 J2M2s and 281 J2M3s, plus 34 J2M5s, fitted with a Kasei 26 engine generating 1,820 hp at takeoff. However, the fighter retained its initial faults, even in the new versions. Nevertheless, the Raiden remained active right up till the end of the conflict, and scored several successes in the struggle against the enemy bombers.

color plate

Mitsubishi J2M3 1st Hilotai 302nd Kokutai Imperial Japanese Navy Air Force - Atsugi Airfield, Tokyo 1944-1945

A Mitsubishi J2M3 during takeoff.

Aircraft:	Mitsubishi J2M3
Nation:	Japan
Manufacturer:	Mitsubishi Jukogyo KK
Type:	Fighter
Year:	1943
Engine:	Mitsubishi MK4R-A Kasei 23, 14-cylinder radial, air-cooled, 1,800 hp
Wingspan:	35 ft 7 in (10.82 m)
Length:	32 ft 8 in (9.95 m)
Height:	12 ft 11 in (3.95 m)
Weight:	7,560 lb (3,435 kg)
Maximum speed:	369 mph (595 km/h) at 19,407 ft (5,900 m)
Ceiling:	38,486 ft (11,700 m)
Range:	1,179 miles (1,900 km)
Armament:	4 x 20 mm cannons; 264 lb (120 kg) of bombs
Crew:	1

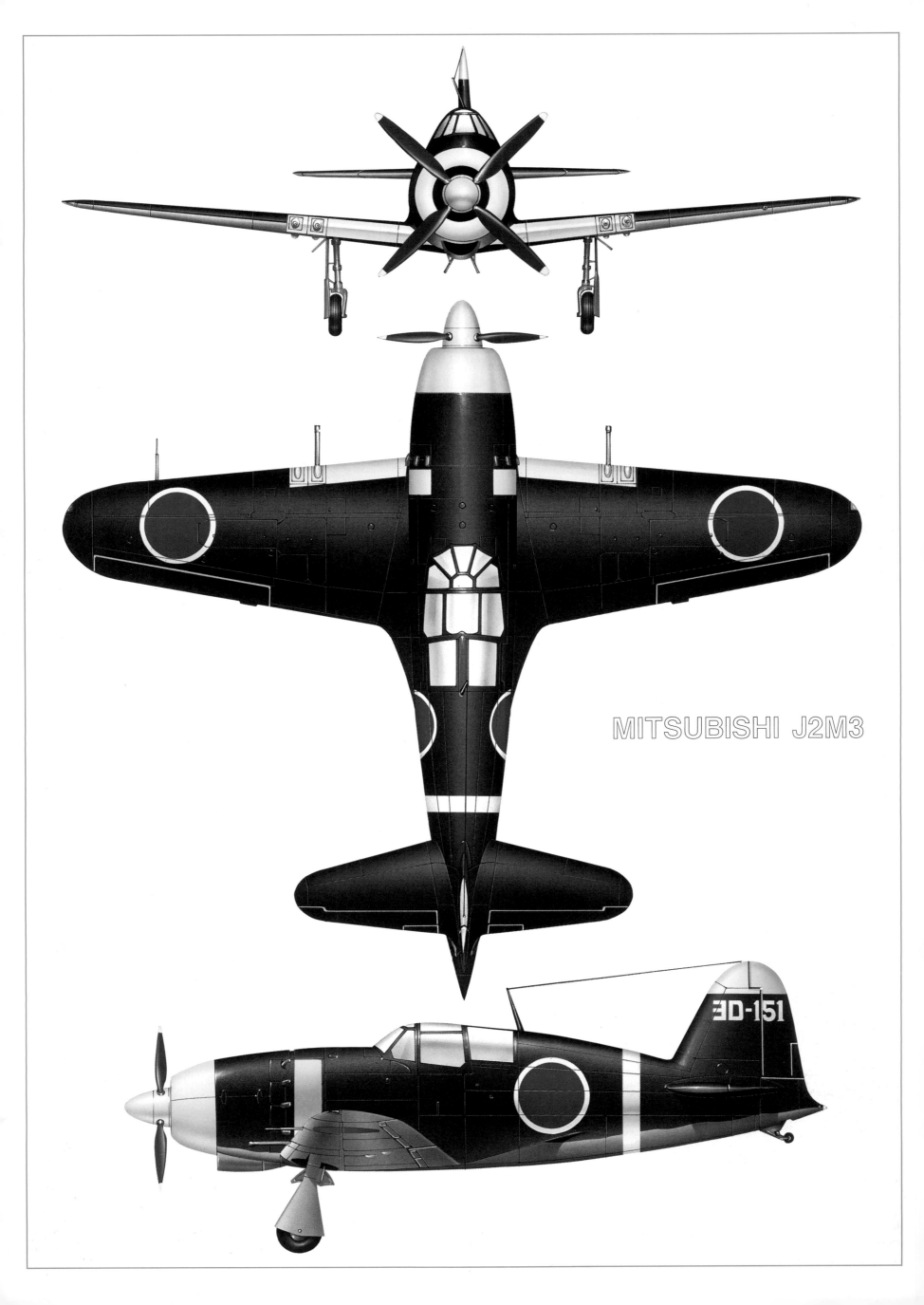

MITSUBISHI J2M3

Considered the best Japanese bomber of the war in the Pacific, the Mitsubishi Ki-67 Hiryu (Flying Dragon) was also the last aircraft in this category to be used in any number by the Imperial Army. Fast, agile, and well-armed, this elegant two-engine aircraft was officially classified as a heavy bomber, although in practice, according to the standards of the Allies, it could have been included in the category of medium bombers (such as the B-25 or the B-26). Nevertheless, the Ki-67 proved to be an outstanding combat plane, and its only limitations were that it arrived too late on the scene of the conflict, and was employed in too small a number. The startling potential of these bombers was revealed during the desperate Japanese counteroffensive on Iwo Jima and the Mariana Islands, and during the American landings at Okinawa. In all, 698 came off the assembly lines and production was given maximum priority right until the last day of the war.

The specifications for a successor to the Nakajima Ki-49 Donryu were defined in February 1941, when Mitsubishi was asked to build three prototypes of a new bomber with modern characteristics. The specifications called for a maximum speed of 341 mph (550 km/h), a bomb load of 1,766 lb (800 kg), and an operative ceiling between 13,157 ft (4,000 m) and 23,026 ft (7,000 m). Moreover, the defensive armament was to consist of five machine guns, while the crew was to range from a standard of 6-8 members, to a maximum of 10 in certain situations.

Mitsubishi's technicians developed the project bearing in mind easy assembly and maintenance, paying very close attention to its protection, both of the crew and the fuel tanks. The aircraft took on the form of a slender all-metal middle-wing two-engine plane with retractable landing gear. It was powered by a pair of 1,900 hp Ha-104 radial engines that drove four-bladed metal variable-pitch propellers. The three prototypes were completed respectively in December 1942, and February and March of the following year. The first of them took to the air on December 27, 1942. The initial series of tests did not bring to light any particular defects; in fact, they fully confirmed the excellent characteristics of the project. So much so that it was also decided to employ the aircraft in the role of torpedo plane.

Series production was launched on December 3, 1943, under the official designation of Ki-67-I, and starting with the 160th, the aircraft were also fitted with an external support for a torpedo.

The Hiryu made its debut in an anti-shipping attack, in October 1944, during the violent air-sea battles off Formosa. From then onward, the two-engined Mitsubishis were employed both by the army and the navy, in all the principal theaters of operations.

In the course of production very few modifications were made to original, although several experimental variants were designed during the last year of the war. Of these, the only one that went into production (22 built in all) was the Ki-67 that was transformed into a heavy fighter. Designated Ki-109, the aircraft was characterized by the installation of a 75 mm cannon in the nose. This weapon, provided with 15 bullets, was meant for use against the B-29s that flew at great altitude. The tests produced good results; however in practice the effectiveness of this type of operation was cancelled due to the low altitude night bombing raids carried out by the American bombers.

color plate

Mitsubishi Ki-67 98th Bomber Sentai 3rd Chutai Japanese Imperial Air Force - Okinawa, 1945

Aircraft:	Mitsubishi Ki-67-I
Nation:	Japan
Manufacturer:	Mitsubishi Jukogyo KK
Type:	Bomber
Year:	1944
Engine:	2 Mitsubishi Ha-104, 14-cylinder radial, air-cooled, 1,900 hp each
Wingspan:	74 ft 0 in (22.50 m)
Length:	61 ft 6 in (18.70 m)
Height:	25 ft 3 in (7.70 m)
Weight:	30,386 lb (13,765 kg)
Maximum speed:	333 mph (537 km/h) at 20,032 ft (6,090 m)
Ceiling:	31,151 ft (9,470 m)
Range:	2,360 miles (3,800 km)
Armament:	1 x 20 mm cannon; 4 machine guns; 1,766 lb (800 kg) of bombs
Crew:	6-8

A Mitsubishi Ki-67 Hiryu bearing American insignia during tests carried out after its capture.

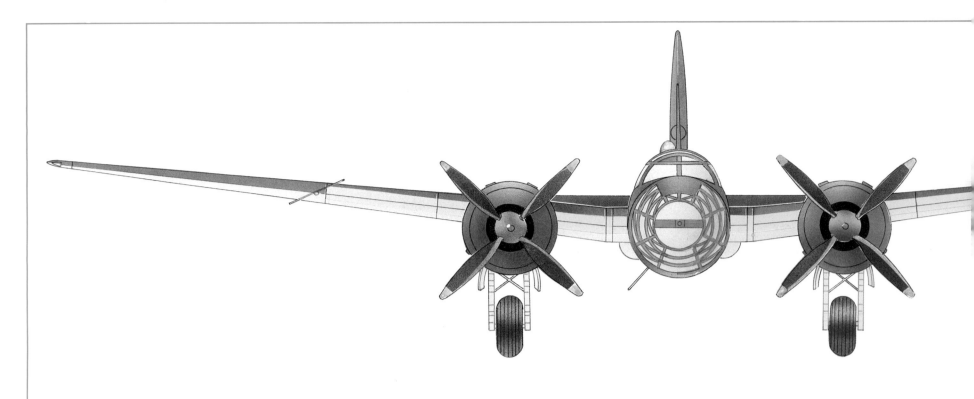

MITSUBISHI Ki-67

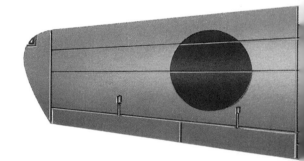

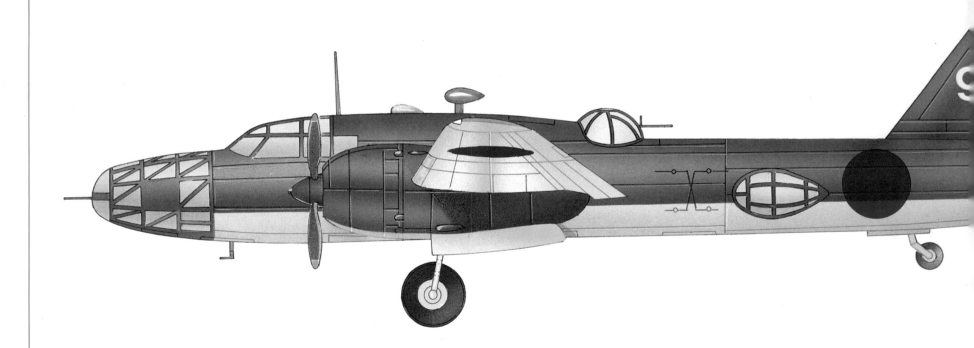

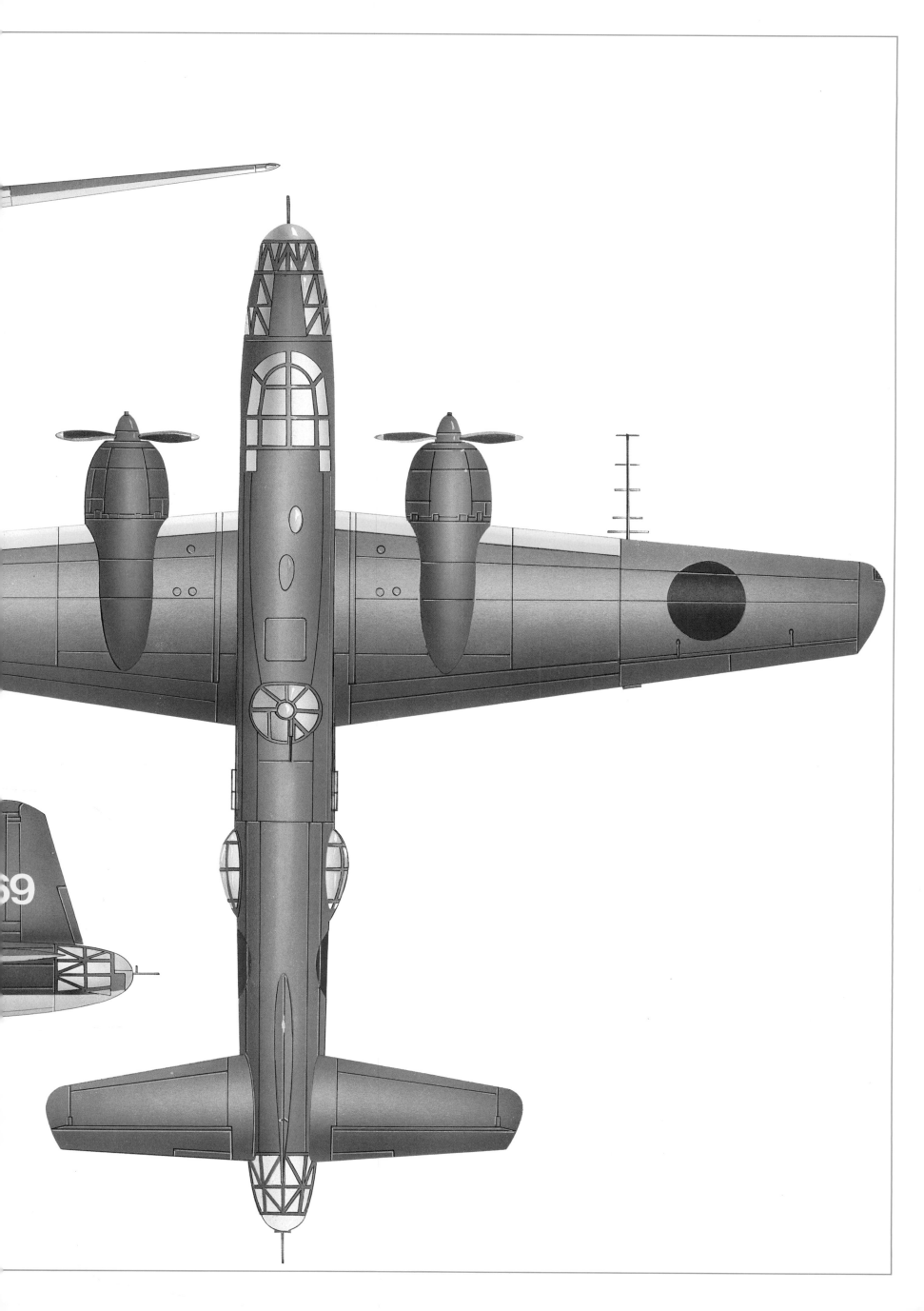

MITSUBISHI G4M3

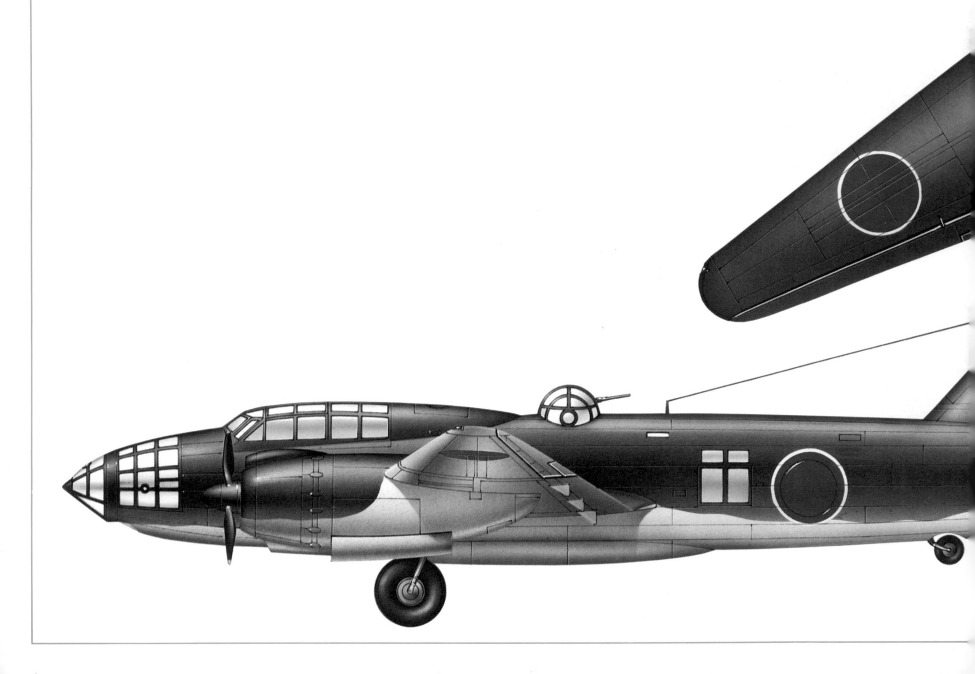

303

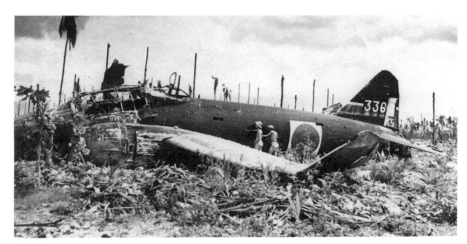

A wrecked Betty at Munda airport in the Solomon Islands.

Undoubtedly the most famous Japanese bomber of the war, the Mitsubishi G4M was one of the protagonists of the conflict in the Pacific. Between October 1939 and August 1945, no fewer than 2,445 of these large two-engine aircraft came off the assembly lines, the largest quantity for a plane in this category, and their operative career lasted from the first day of the conflict to the last. In fact, on August 19, 1945, two G4M1s painted white and bearing green crosses surrender in place of the Rising Sun insignia carried the Japanese surrender committee to Ie-Shima.

In 1937 the Imperial Navy issued the specifications that gave rise to the G4M. They called for the construction of a land-based bomber with characteristics superior to those of the G3M, which was then about to go into service. These included a maximum speed of 248 mph (400 km/h) at an altitude of 9,868 ft (3,000 m) and a range of no less than 2,980 miles (4,800 km) without bombload and 2,297 miles (3,700 km) with a torpedo weighing 1,766 lb (800 kg). Mitsubishi started work on the project immediately, and the first of two prototypes took to the air on October 23, 1939. The initial series of tests proved that the designer, Kiro Honjo, had succeeded in satisfying the rigid specifications brilliantly: the aircraft lacked any intrinsic faults, and above all it had no difficulty in surpassing the speed and range that had been requested. In fact, the second prototype reached a maximum speed of 276 mph (445 km/h) and a range of over 3,415 miles (5,500 km). The aircraft was a large all-metal middle-wing monoplane with retractable rear tricycle landing gear. It was powered initially by a pair of 1,530 hp Mitsubishi Kasei 11 radial engines.

However, mass production did not commence immediately. Operative experiences during the war in China had revealed the lack of a long-range combat plane capable of escorting the bombers during their missions in enemy territory. Considering the G4M's excellent qualities, a proposal was made to develop a heavy fighter escort aircraft from it. Redesignated G6M1 and armed with four 20 mm cannons (two of which were situated in the

hold) plus a 7.7 mm machine gun, 30 of these aircraft were built in 1940. However, once they went into service their performance proved to be disappointing, due to the great disadvantages caused by an increase in weight and by the consequent reduction in fuel capacity. These aircraft were thus modified for use as trainers, and subsequently for transport.

In the same year, authorization for the production of the aircraft as a bomber was finally granted, and the first of the initial variant came off the assembly lines in April 1941. The aircraft made its operative debut in China a few weeks later, providing combat experience for the crews that was to prove extremely useful at the beginning of the subsequent conflict.

During the early months of the war in the Pacific, and throughout the first year, the Mitsubishi bombers scored some great successes, due above all to their remarkable range. These included a role in the mission that led to the sinking of the British battleships *Prince of Wales* and *Repulse* on December 10, 1941. However, their operative career also revealed what was to prove to be the G4M's greatest fault: the absence of protective armor and the lack of self-sealing fuel tanks. The latter, together with the fact that the aircraft caught fire easily, earned the ''Betty'' (as the bomber was known in the Allies' code) the unfortunate nickname of ''Flying Cigar.'' These defects were also present in the second version, the G4M2, of which 1,154 were built beginning in November 1942. The main differences between the two versions lay in their armament and engines. In fact, the problems were solved only in the final variant, the G4M3, although only 60 were built in all, starting in late 1943.

color plate
Mitsubishi G4M3 Yokosuka Chutai - Japan 1945

Aircraft:	Mitsubishi G4M1
Nation:	Japan
Manufacturer:	Mitsubishi Jukogyo KK
Type:	Bomber
Year:	1941
Engine:	2 Mitsubishi Mk4A Kasei 11, 14-cylinder radial, 1,530 hp each
Wingspan:	82 ft (25 m)
Length:	65 ft 7 1/2 in (20 m)
Height:	19 ft 8 in (6 m)
Weight:	20,944 lb (9,500 kg) loaded
Maximum speed:	266 mph (428 km/h) at 13,780 ft (4,200 m)
Ceiling:	29,000 ft (8,840 m)
Range:	3,748 miles (6,030 km)
Armament:	1 × 20 mm cannon; 4 machine guns; 1,766 lb (800 kg) of bombs
Crew:	7

A Mitsubishi G4M2 Betty during evaluations by Allied technicians after the end of the war.

Christened Donryu (Dragon of the Storms), the Nakajima Ki-49 was developed in 1938 to replace the Mitsubishi Ki-21, which was just going into service at the time. However, this aim was not fulfilled, in that the new bomber proved to be generally inferior: it lacked power, and its performance was not exceptional. Above all, it was provided with insufficient defensive armament, which made it easy prey for enemy fighters. Nevertheless, production went ahead for four years, from December 1940 until December 1944, with a total of 819 aircraft being built in two major variants.

The specifications that gave rise to the Ki-49 were issued at the beginning of 1938. The Imperial Army wanted a two-engine heavy bomber capable of carrying out its missions without a fighter escort. The aircraft was therefore to be especially fast and well armed. Moreover, a maximum speed of 310 mph (500 km/h) and a range of 1,863 miles (3,000 km) were requested, while the offensive armament was to amount to 2,205 lb (1,000 kg) of bombs and the defensive armament foresaw the installation of a 20 mm cannon in a turret on the aircraft's back.

The project was launched by Nakajima's technicians toward the summer, and the first of the three prototypes was ready within a year and made its maiden flight in August 1939. It was a large monoplane with middle cantilever wing and retractable rear tricycle landing gear, powered initially by two 950 hp Nakajima Ha-5 KAI radial engines. The other two prototypes and seven preseries aircraft, built between January and December 1940, were fitted with two 1,450 hp Nakajima Ha-41 engines, which remarkably improved their performance.

However, evaluations and operative tests lasted much longer than expected. The war in China had revealed the need for a fighter escort plane with a sufficient range to accompany bombers throughout their long missions, and as in the case of the Mitsubishi G4M, the general staff of the Imperial Army requested that a version of the heavy fighter be built. This was designated Ki-58, and between December 1940 and March 1941 Nakajima built three prototypes. These aircraft were characterized by the elimination of the bomb hold, an increase in armour, and heavier armament, which included five 20 mm cannons and three 12.7 mm machine guns. However, the program was abandoned, and not until March 1941 was production of the Ki-49 as a bomber launched. The first aircraft of the initial Ki-49-I series came off the assembly lines in August, and their operative career began in the autumn on the Chinese front.

However, the imminence of the new conflict led to the construction of a new variant with more powerful engines and better armament. This was the Ki-49-II, which did not appear until 1942, when the war was already at an advanced stage. Production began in September (following the construction of the last of the 129 Ki-49-Is in August, and after two new prototypes had been

built), and a total of 667 aircraft was built in all (50 of which were constructed by Tachikawa) in two subseries, the IIa and the IIb, which differed only in their defensive armament. These aircraft were employed extensively, although in the course of their career their original faults were never eliminated, and these faults became even more apparent when the aircraft were faced with the more advanced Allied fighters. In 1943 an attempt at improvement was made with a third version, the Ki-49-III, fitted with new 2,420 hp Nakajima Ha-117 engines. However, between March and December of the same year only six prototypes were built, and they never went beyond the experimental phase due to problems caused by the new engines. Of the experimental versions, the Ki-80 (two prototypes were completed in October 1941) should be mentioned. In theory it was to carry out the role of guide in indicating targets for bombers.

A preproduction Nakajima aircraft in flight.

color plate

Nakajima Ki-49 Hamamatsu Army Flying School, Japanese Imperial Army Air Force - Japan 1944

Aircraft:	Nakajima Ki-49-IIb
Nation:	Japan
Manufacturer:	Nakajima Hikoki KK
Type:	Bomber
Year:	1942
Engine:	2 Nakajima Ha-109, 14-cylinder radial. air-cooled, 1,450 hp each
Wingspan:	67 ft (20.42 m)
Length:	54 ft 1 1/2 in (16.50 m)
Height:	13 ft 11 in (4.25 m)
Weight:	25,133 lb (11,424 kg) loaded
Maximum speed:	306 mph (492 km/h) at 16,447 ft (5,000 m)
Ceiling:	30,510 ft (9,300 m)
Range:	1,833 miles (2,950 km)
Armament:	1 × 20 mm cannon; 5 machine guns; 2,205 lb (1,000 kg) of bombs
Crew:	8

A Nakajima Ki-49 of the Hamamatsu Flying School.

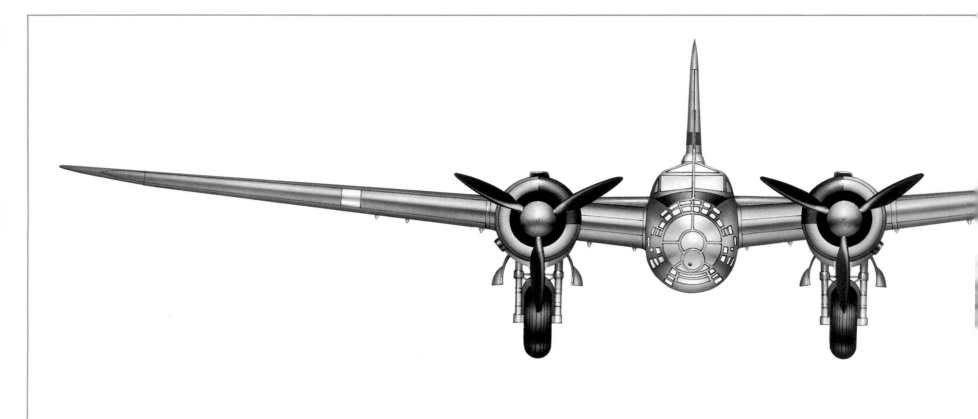

NAKAJIMA Ki-49

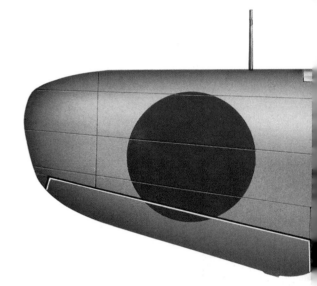

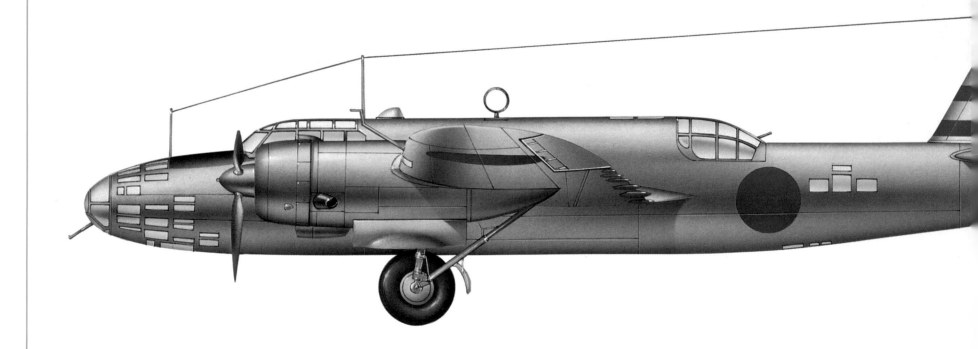

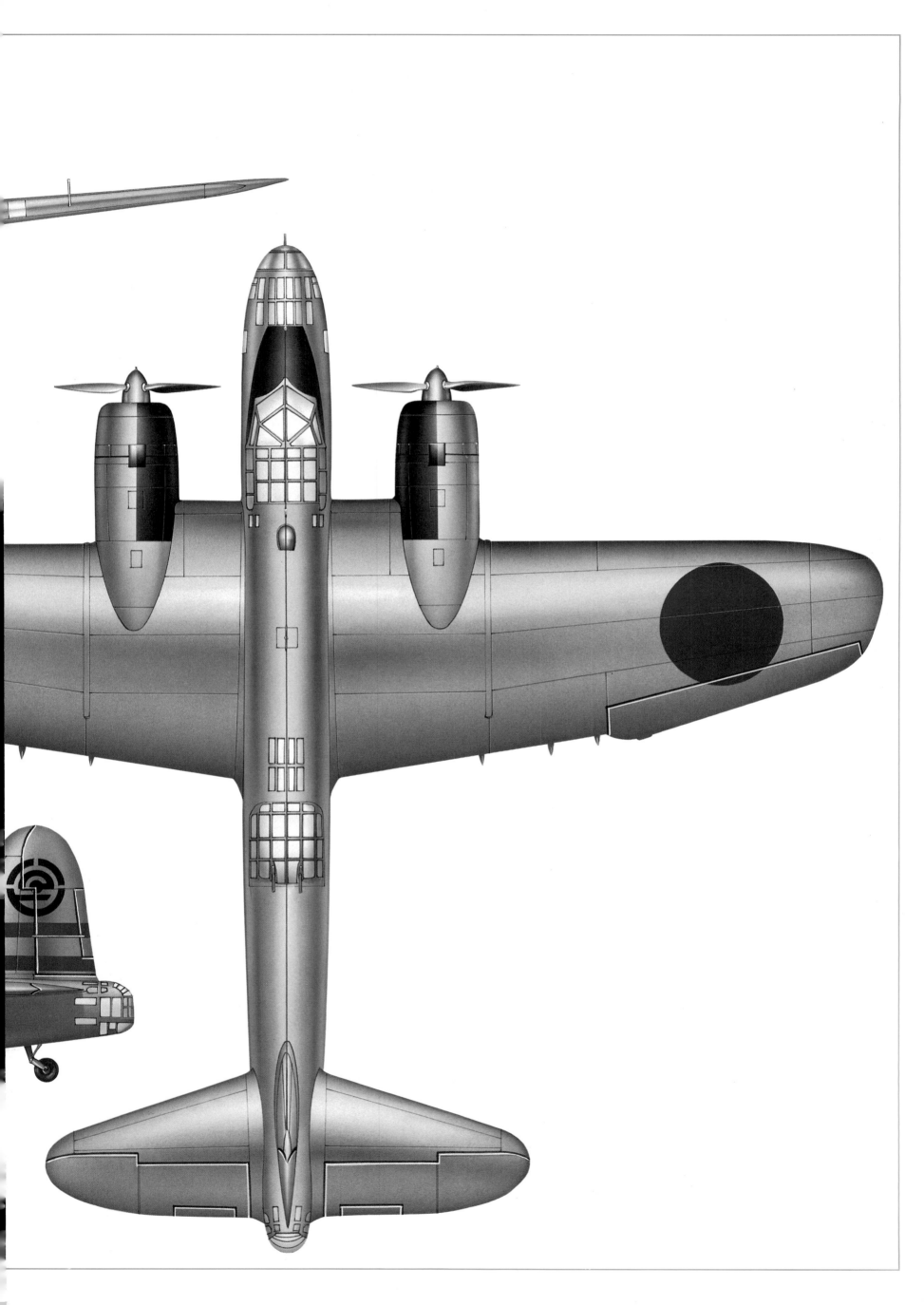

In 1940, the need for a single-seater fighter seaplane was strongly felt by the Japanese Imperial Navy. In fact, an aircraft of this type was to prove fundamental not only in supporting the amphibious operations that the general staff was already planning but also for use at military bases on small islands where the building of runways was impossible. The first manufacturer to respond to the navy's request was Kawanishi, which began to study the project that was to give rise to the powerful N1K Kyofu. However, the advanced nature of the technical solutions adopted in this aircraft (especially the use of a pair of contrarotating propellers) and the problems in preparing the aircraft that soon became evident led to great delays in the program, and therefore the technical authorities of the Imperial Navy asked Nakajima to develop a seaplane version of the most famous fighter in service at the time: the Mitsubishi A6M Reisen, the famous Zero. In fact, the A6M2-N (known as ''Rufe'' in the Allies' code) derived from this aircraft, and although it did not prove to be exceptional it served a useful role, especially during the initial phases of the war in the Pacific.

The construction of the aircraft did not pose any particular problems, considering the remarkable qualities of the airframe from which it was derived. Nakajima's technicians, who had already helped Mitsubishi with the construction of the Zero, used an A6M2 Model II as their base and work began in February 1941. In practice, the prototype maintained almost the entire structure and configuration of the original fighter, apart from the obvious differences due to the fitting of a large central float and of two smaller side floats: the landing gear was removed and the wheel housing covered, while a small ventral fin was added to the tail to increase stability. To compensate for the lack of supplementary external fuel tanks (which could no longer be installed in the belly of the fuselage) an auxiliary fuel tank was installed inside the largest float. The aircraft's engine was identical to that of the original model, as was its armament.

The prototype of the A6M2-N made its maiden flight on December 7, 1941, the very same day that Japan entered the war, and a series of flight tests and evaluations did not reveal any particular problems: despite an increase in overall weight and the high aerodynamic drag of the floats, the fighter proved to be very fast and, above all, extremely maneuverable. From December 1941 to September 1943, a total of 327 A6M2s came off the assembly lines.

The aircraft began its operative career the following year in the Solomon Islands, and it proved to be reasonably successful. However, the appearance of the more powerful and modern Allied fighters revealed the aircraft's inferiority and its inability to sustain front-line roles. During the final months of the war, many A6M2-Ns were used as trainers for the more powerful Kawanishi N1K1.

color plate

Nakajima A6M2-N 802 Kokutai Japanese Imperial Navy Air Force - Solomon Islands 1943

Aircraft:	Nakajima A6M2-N
Nation:	Japan
Manufacturer:	Nakajima Hikoki KK
Type:	Fighter
Year:	1942
Engine:	Nakajima NK1C Sakae 12, 14-cylinder radial, air-cooled, 950 hp
Wingspan:	39 ft 4 1/2 in (12 m)
Length:	33 ft 2 in (10.10 m)
Height:	14 ft 1 in (4.30 m)
Weight:	6,349 lb (2,895 kg)
Maximum speed:	270 mph (434 km/h) at 16,447 ft (5,000 m)
Ceiling:	32,810 ft (10,000 m)
Range:	1,107 miles (1,780 km)
Armament:	2 × 20 mm cannon; 2 machine guns; 264 lb (120 kg) of bombs
Crew:	1

A Nakajima A6M2-N of the Sasebo Kokutai in flight over Sasebo Harbor.

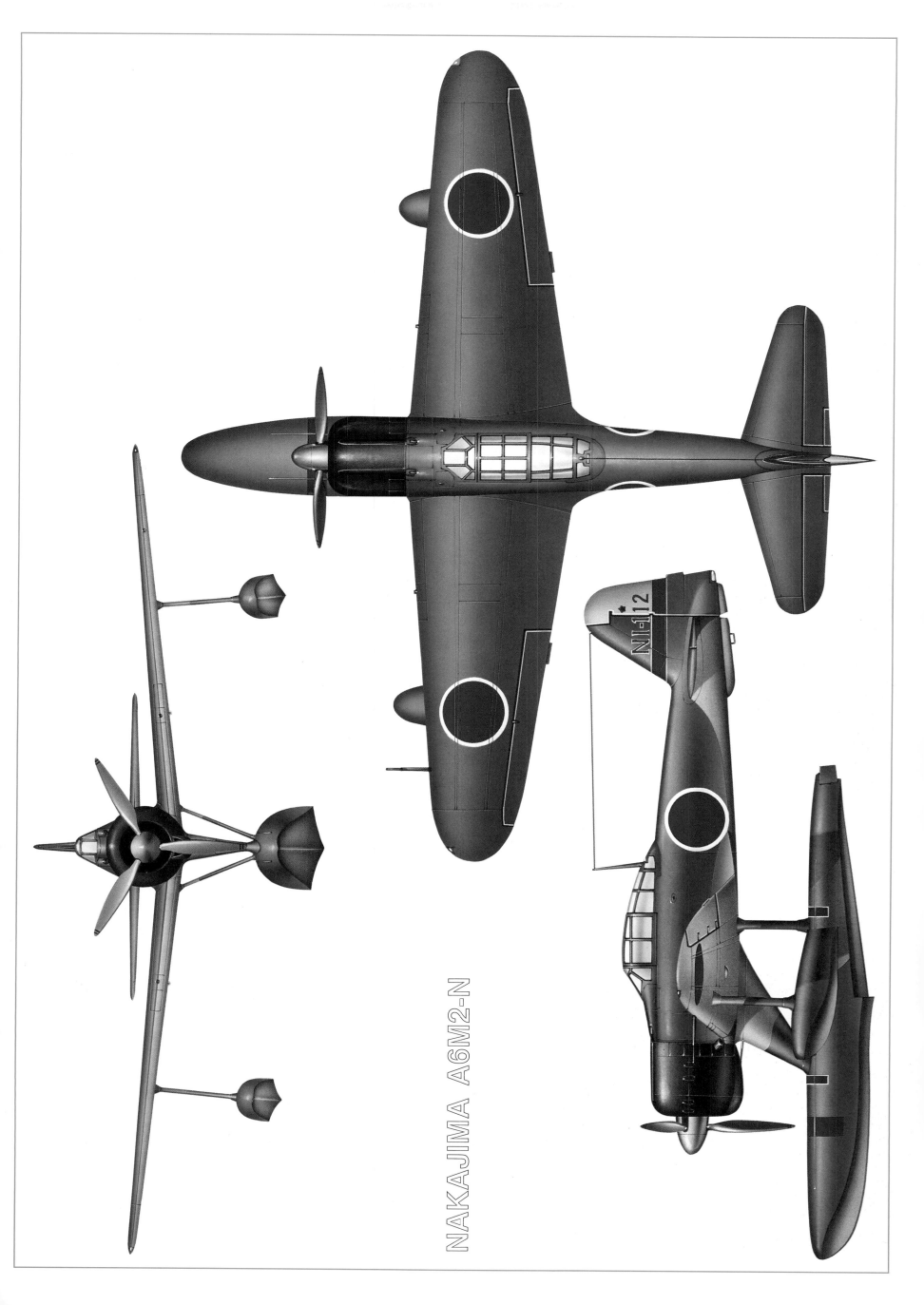

NAKAJIMA A6M2-N

NAKAJIMA KIKKA

The Nakajima Kikka was Japan's first jet plane.

The Kikka was very similar to the Messerschmitt Me.262.

Due to influence of its major ally, Germany, and encouraged by the great success of the Messerschmitt Me.262 in Europe in the desperate war effort of the final months of the war, Japan also decided to build a jet combat plane. This was the Nakajima Kikka (Orange Blossom) which was an entirely original project, although it greatly resembled its German counterpart.

Only two prototypes were built between June and August 1945, before the entire program was halted due to the end of the war, and only one of them succeeded in taking to the air, on two occasions.

The project was launched in September 1944 when the General Staff of the Imperial Navy decided to entrust Nakajima with the development of a single-seater two-engine jet plane based on the German Me.262. It was used as a fast bomber and attack plane. The aircraft's characteristics were particularly ambitious: a maximum speed of 431 mph (695 km/h); a range of 125 miles (200 km) with a bomb load of 550 lb (250 kg); a landing speed of under 93 mph (150 km/h); and takeoff distance of 1,150 ft (350 m), with the use of two auxiliary external rockets each with a 993 lb (450 kg) thrust. In addition, the aircraft was to have folding wings (similar to those of carrier-based aircraft) so that they could be hidden

in caves and tunnels. As for the engines, initially the use of two Tsu-11 type motor reactors with 440 lb (200 kg) thrust each was foreseen, then that of two 750 lb (340 kg) Ne-12 turbojets. In practice, considering these engines' lack of power, the prototypes were driven by Ne-20 turbojets each with 1,048 lb (475 kg) thrust, built in great haste on the basis of the data and characteristics of the German BMW 003.

Nakajima's group of technicians, headed by Kazuo Ohno and Kenichi Matsumara, went ahead with the work rapidly, developing an aircraft that was similar to the Messerschmitt Me.262 A as far as layout and form were concerned, although it was smaller overall. The first prototype was completed at the beginning of August 1945 and on Tuesday, August 7, it made its maiden flight at the Naval Aviation Base of Kisarazu, with Susumu Tanaoka at the controls. However, four days later, during an assisted takeoff, the aircraft had a serious accident, caused by an error in the installation of the two auxiliary rockets. The testing program was consequently suspended, while awaiting completion of the second prototype. At the same time, the assembly lines were occupied by 18 pre-series aircraft in various stages of construction.

The program established by the Imperial Navy was not limited to a single version of the Kikka. The Allies discovered that Nakajima had various other projects derived from it in a preparation phase. These included a two-seater version without armament meant for training, a similar reconnaissance variant; and a third, single-seater interceptor version. The last was to have been armed with two 30 mm cannons and fitted with Ne-130 or Ne-330 type engines with 1,986 lb (900 kg) and 1,953 lb (885 kg) thrust respectively, and was also at a design stage.

It should be remembered that the construction of the Kikka was not the only one that Japan carried out in the field of rocket or jet planes. In 1944, Mitsubishi also began to design an interceptor derived from the German Messerschmitt Me.163 B and was occupied, together with technicians from the navy and the army, in the construction of a rocket engine intended to power it. Seven prototypes of this aircraft, designated J8M Shusui (Swinging Sword), were built, only one of which succeeded in taking to the air (July 7, 1945), but with disastrous results. The program had been launched between 1943 and 1944, when Japan had acquired the rights to build the Me.163 B and its Walter HWK rocket engine on license. However, it had received a serious blow following the sinking of the submarine that was carrying a disassembled example of the aircraft and the construction drawings from Germany.

color plate

Nakajima Kikka Japanese Imperial Navy Air Force - Kisarazu, Japan 1945

Aircraft:	Nakajima Kikka
Nation:	Japan
Manufacturer:	Nakajima Hikoki KK
Type:	Bomber
Year:	1945
Engine:	2 Ne-20 turbojets, with 1,048 lb (475 kg) thrust each
Wingspan:	32 ft 10 in (10.00 m)
Length:	26 ft (8.12 m)
Height:	9 ft 8 in (2.95 m)
Weight:	7,726 lb (3,500 kg)
Maximum speed:	442 mph (712 km/h) at 39,894 ft (10,000 m)
Ceiling:	39,473 ft (12,000 m)
Range:	590 miles (950 km)
Armament:	1,766 lb (800 kg) of bombs
Crew:	1

The first prototype of the Nakajima Kikka before tests.

In 1937, the passage from the biplane to the monoplane in the Imperial army air force was marked by the appearance of a small and agile fighter, the Nakajima Ki-27, of which no fewer than 3,399 were built up to 1942. From many points of view, the role of this combat plane was similar to that carried out by the Mitsubishi A5M in the Japanese navy: both fighters (curiously alike not only in overall layout and dimensions, but also in performance) were transitional aircraft, built to try out advanced technical and operative solutions and thus to prepare the ground for the Japanese aeronautical industry's first truly "modern" projects. Although the A5M was replaced by the remarkable Mitsubishi A6M Zero, the Ki-27's successor was an equally effective aircraft, the Ki-43 Hayabusa, which immediately made its mark, because of its overall superiority as compared to contemporary Western products.

The Ki-27 originated in 1934. That year, the Imperial army announced a competition to find a successor to the outdated Kawasaki KDA-5 (Army Type 92 fighter). The competitors included Kawasaki itself, with the Ki-10 biplane, and Nakajima, with the Ki-11 model, a braced low-wing monoplane. Although it had a performance that was generally superior to that of its rival, the latter project was rejected, and the Ki-10 was chosen for mass production, the last biplane to go into service in the army air force. Nakajima continued to work independently on studies for a monoplane fighter and was thus ready to satisfy the request for a modern fighter made in June of the following year.

In October 1936, Nakajima's project appeared in its definitive form, and the first prototype took to the air on the fifteenth. During subsequent evaluation tests, the aircraft was compared with another two competitors (the Mitsubishi Ki-33 and the Kawasaki Ki-28), and although its maximum speed was inferior, it was chosen for production thanks to its remarkable maneuverability. In an era in which pilots were still conditioned by the flight characteristics of biplanes and especially by their great agility, this factor proved to be the winning feature. The ten preseries aircraft ordered were

followed by those of the first production series, which appeared in December 1937. The Ki-27 was a low-wing monoplane with fixed landing gear powered by a Nakajima radial engine and armed with two 7.7 mm machine guns installed in the nose and synchronized to fire through the propeller arc. Production was carried out on two variants: the initial Ki-27a and the Ki-27b, the latter characterized by the adoption of a more powerful engine, by slight structural modifications, and by the capacity to carry a maximum of 220 lb (100 kg) of bombs in supports under the fuselage.

In March 1938, the Ki-27 made its operational debut in China, and in May of the following year the aircraft was used in Manchuria against the Soviets. Despite of the outcome of this confrontation which underlined the limitations of the aircraft (it was superior to the Polikarpov I-15 biplane, but generally inferior to the I-16 monoplane), production of the small Nakajima fighter continued even after the appearance of its more effective successor, the Ki-43. When Japan entered the war, the Ki-27 still equipped numerous front-line units, and it was widely used in the initial phase of operations.

However, these fighters were gradually withdrawn from frontline duty and relegated to training. Their career ended in the desperate defense efforts of the final months of the war: transformed into suicide planes and armed with a 1,250 lb (500 kg) bomb, the Ki-27s were used in missions of no return against the Allied fleet. In the Allies' code, the Ki-27s were known as "Nate" and "Abdul."

---

color plate

Nakajima Ki-27b Nate 246th Air Combat Regiment 3rd Company Japanese Imperial Army Air Force - Japan 1943

Aircraft:	Nakajima Ki-27b
Nation:	Japan
Manufacturer:	Nakajima Hikoki KK
Type:	Fighter
Year:	1939
Engine:	Nakajima Ha-1b, 9-cylinder radial air-cooled, 710 hp
Wingspan:	37 ft 1 in (11.31 m)
Length:	24 ft 8 1/2 in (7.53 m)
Height:	10 ft 8 in (3.25 m)
Weight:	3,946 lb (1,790 kg) loaded
Maximum speed:	292 mph (470 km/h) at 11,480 ft (3,500 m)
Ceiling:	40,190 ft (12,365 m)
Range:	1,060 miles (1,710 km)
Armament:	2 machine guns; 220 lb (100 kg) of bombs
Crew:	1

A Nakajima Ki-27 of the Akeno Fighter Training School.

A Nakajima warming up for takeoff at Kakogawa airfield.

A Nakajima Ki-27 during operational evaluations.

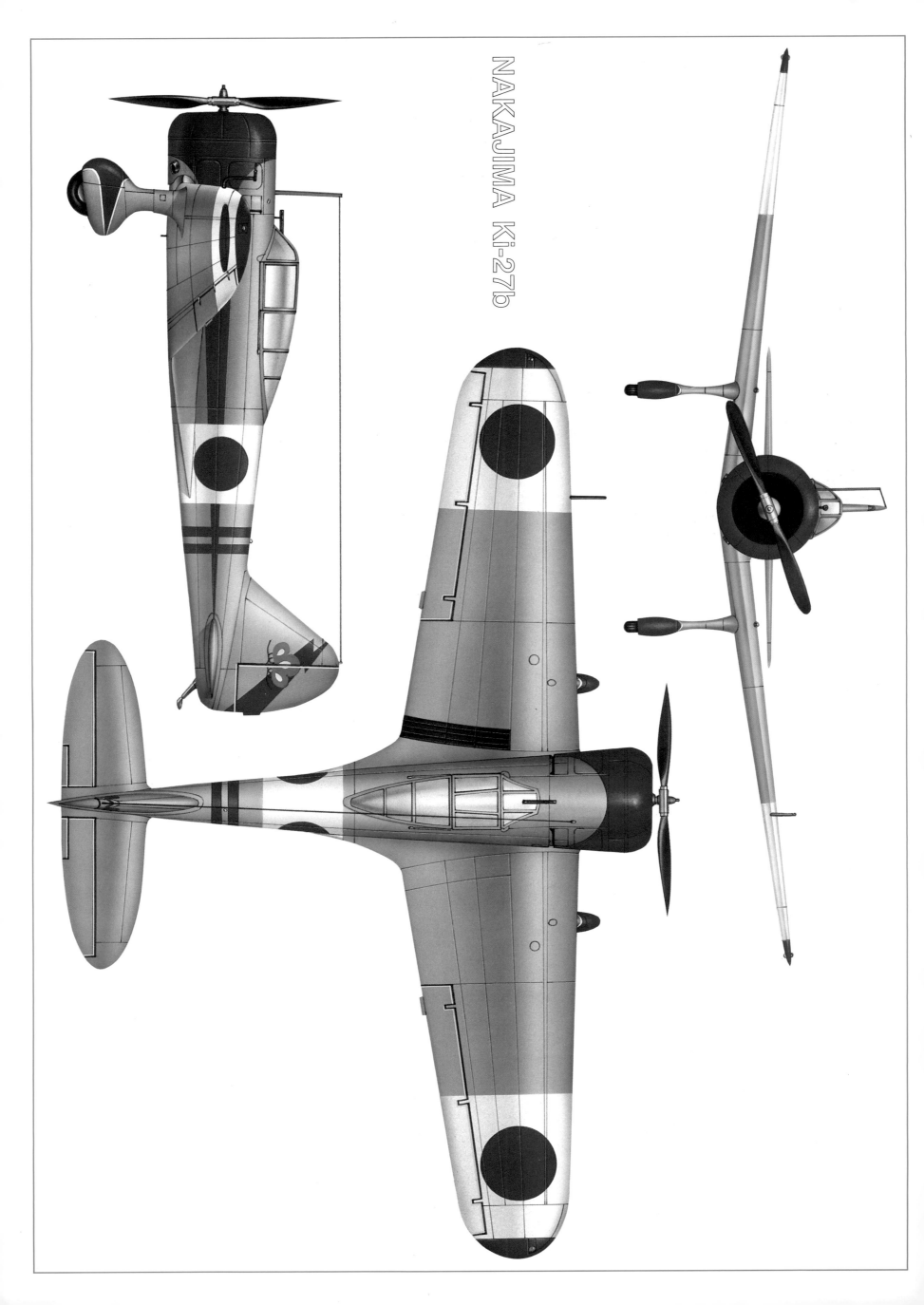

NAKAJIMA Ki-27b

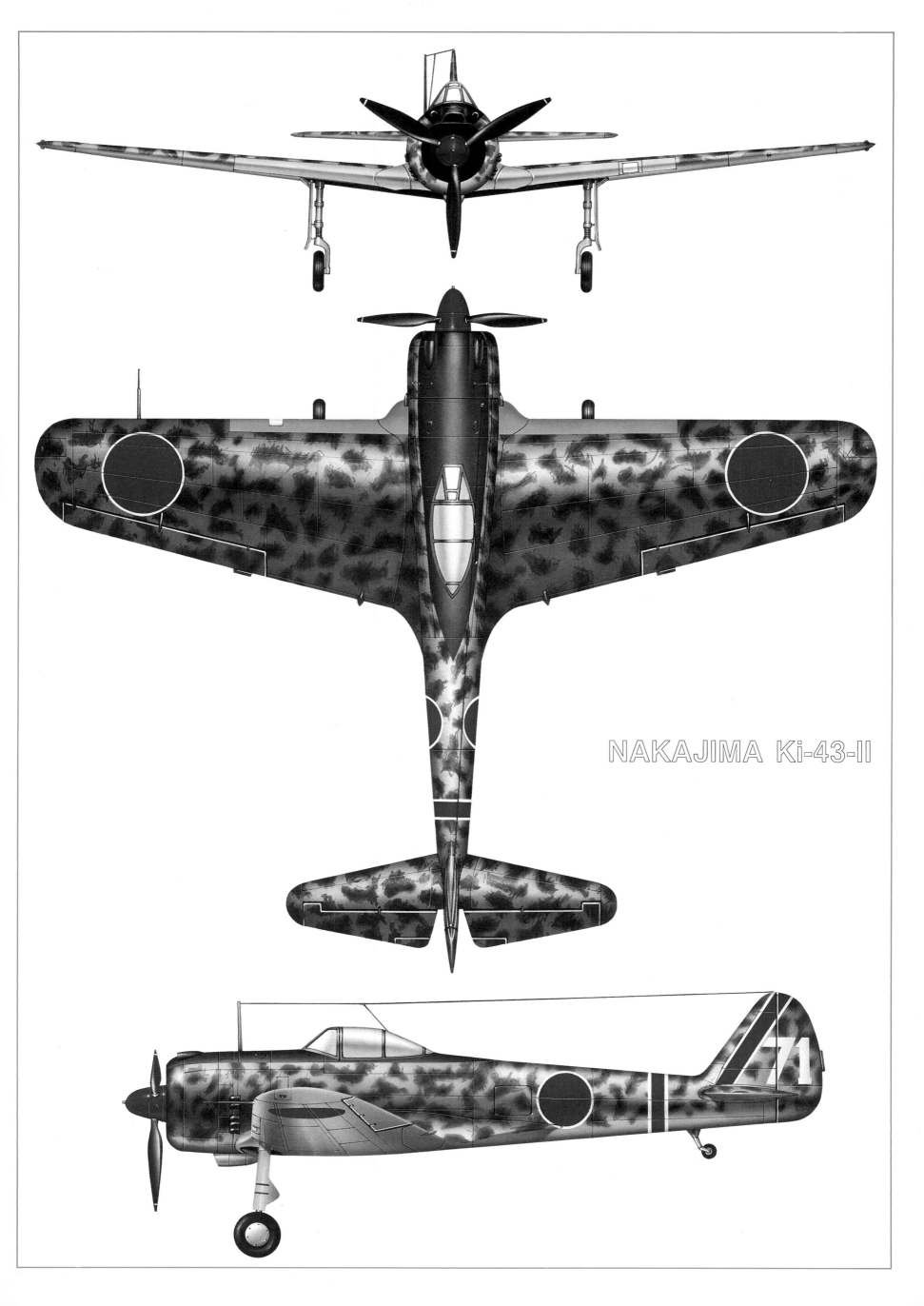

NAKAJIMA Ki-43-II

The Nakajima Ki-43 succeeded the Ki-27 as the Imperial Army's standard fighter and was created at more or less the same time as the Mitsubishi A6M Zero. Like its counterpart in the navy, it was the first advanced Japanese combat plane to be employed in the Pacific. Christened Hayabusa (Peregrine Falcon), the Ki-43 had a long and intensive operative career that lasted practically till the end of the war. Its moment of glory occurred during the first year of the conflict when, faced with less effective adversaries, the Nakajima Ki-43 fighter earned the reputation of being invincible.

The project was launched in December 1937 on the basis of specifications issued by the army requesting the construction of a modern fighter to replace the Ki-27. This fighter was to have a maximum speed of 310 mph (500 km/h); to be capable of reaching 16,447 ft (5,000 m) in five minutes; to have a range of 496 miles (800 km); and armament consisting of two 7.7 mm machine guns. Moreover, the new aircraft was to be provided with great maneuverability, equal to if not greater than that of the model it was to replace.

The project was entrusted to a team headed by Hideo Itokawa, and studies for the construction of a prototype lasted for exactly one year. In January 1939 the first of three experimental aircraft made its maiden flight, followed by the other two within the next couple of months. The aircraft was a low cantilever wing monoplane with retractable rear tricycle landing gear and was powered initially by a 975 hp Nakajima Ha-25 radial engine. Although no great problems emerged from the series of tests, the fighter's maneuverability was severely criticized by Imperial Army technicians during operational evaluations. The pilots complained in particular about the uselessness of the retractable landing gear, whose presence did not justify the increase in the aircraft's weight. Consequently, by September 1940, Nakajima had built a further 10 preseries aircraft that employed various solutions to resolve these complaints. An overall reduction in weight and the adoption of a wing with a greater surface area fitted with special "combat" high-lift devices (used in particular circumstances, these allowed the aircraft to carry out tight turns, thus increasing its maneuverability in a remarkable way) proved to be decisive modifications. The Nakajima fighter was finally accepted and went into mass production.

The initial variants (the Ki-43-Ia and Ki-43-Ib) differed only in armament and went into service in June 1941, a total of 716 being built in all. However, after a series of initial successes, the strengthening of the Allied forces revealed an overall inadequacy in performance during the aircraft's operative service, and in 1942 Nakajima developed an improved version (the Ki-43-II), which became the major production series. The main differences lay in the adoption of a more powerful engine and a three-blade variable pitch metal propeller that, together with aerodynamic refinements and structural modifications, made the aircraft more competitive compared to the more advanced Allied fighters. The Ki-43-II variant was built in three series (IIa, IIb, and KAI) that incorporated the various modifications developed in the course of production. In 1944, the final version, the Ki-43-III, appeared and was provided with a 1,230 hp Nakajima Ha-115-II engine (or a 1,250 hp Mitsubishi Ha-112), proving to be the most successful of all, although only 10 prototypes were built. Out of a total of 5,919 aircraft that came off the assembly lines, 3,239 were completed by Nakajima, 2,631 by Tachikawa, and 49 by the arsenal of the Japanese army. The aircraft's career came to an end in the desperate suicide missions that occurred during the final months of the war.

---

color plate
Nakajima Ki-43-II 2nd Chutai 25th Fighter Sentai Imperial Japanese Army Air Force - China 1943-45

Aircraft:	Nakajima Ki-43-IIb
Nation:	Japan
Manufacturer:	Nakajima Hikoki KK
Type:	Fighter
Year:	1942
Engine:	Nakajima Ha-115, 14-cylinder radial, air-cooled, 1,150 hp
Wingspan:	35 ft 7 in (10.50 m)
Length:	29 ft 3 in (8.92 m)
Height:	10 ft 9 in (3.29 m)
Weight:	6,450 lb (2,932 kg) loaded
Maximum speed:	329 mph (530 km/h) at 13,125 ft (4,000 m)
Ceiling:	36,750 ft (11,200 m)
Range:	1,095 miles (1,760 km)
Armament:	2 machine guns; 1,103 lb (500 kg) of bombs
Crew:	1

A Hayabusa belonging to the 25th Sentai stationed in China.

A Hayabusa with the typical markings of home defense.

Used above all during the final year of the war, to challenge the increasing threat that the American B-29 bombers posed on Japan, the Nakajima Ki-44 proved to be the Imperial Army's best pure interceptor. Well armed and remarkably fast in ascent — climbing to 16,500 ft (5,000 m) in four minutes 17 seconds — this small and powerful fighter was a formidable weapon in the hands of the Japanese pilots who were by then fighting to defend their country and well deserved the name Shoki (Demon) with which it had been christened four years earlier. From January 1942 to December 1944, a total of 1,225 aircraft came off the assembly lines in three basic versions.

The project was launched by Nakajima almost at the same time as that of the Ki-43 model, on the basis of specifications issued by the army that called for a combat plane whose main strongpoints were to be horizontal speed and (above all) speed in ascent, rather than maneuverability and range. In particular, a speed of 372 mph (600 km/h) at 13,125 ft (4,000 m) was requested, as well as the ability to reach the same ceiling in less than five minutes, while the armament was to include two 12.7 mm machine guns and another two weapons of lesser caliber.

The first prototype appeared in August 1940. It was a small, compact all-metal low-wing monoplane with retractable landing gear, literally constructed around the large Nakajima Ha-41 radial engine, which generated a maximum of 1,250 hp. According to the designer, T. Koyama, this was the only available engine capable of guaranteeing the remarkable performances that were requested.

Although the flight tests were generally satisfactory, they did not initially provide the results that had been hoped for, especially as far as speed in horizontal flight and in ascent was concerned. Therefore a long and careful preparation, including aerodynamic improvements, was necessary, especially as far as the engine housing was concerned. The aircraft's characteristics eventually improved greatly, and the series of evaluations continued with another two prototypes and seven preseries aircraft, the latter being built in 1941.

In September 1942, the Shoki was officially accepted by the Imperial Army aviation, and units began to receive the first aircraft of the initial version, the Ki-44-I, of which 40 were completed between January and October. However, the pilots did not welcome the Shoki with much enthusiasm: the aircraft was characterized by a heavy wing load, high landing speed, and was, above all, much less maneuverable than the fighters already in service. A long operative period was necessary before this unpopularity changed to respect, especially in the case of the less experienced pilots.

The aircraft's already excellent performance at speed and in ascent improved still further in the Ki-44-II, the second variant, of which five prototypes and three preseries aircraft were built in

1942, and which went into production in November of the same year. These results were obtained by using a more powerful engine, the Nakajima Ha-109, which could generate no less than 1,520 hp at takeoff and in emergency. In addition, the armament was increased, passing from two 12.7 mm machine guns and a similar number of 7.7 mm weapons in the Ki-44-IIa subseries, to four 12.7 mm weapons in the IIb subseries and four 20 mm cannons (or two 37 mm or 40 mm cannons plus two 12.7 mm machine guns) in the IIc subseries. The latter proved to be particularly effective in the pursuit of bombers.

The third and final variant of the Shoki (Ki-44-III), which appeared as a prototype in June 1943, was characterized by an increase in offensive armament and the adoption of a 2,000 hp Nakajima Ha-145 engine. Very few were built before production was suspended in favor of the Nakajima Ki-84 Hayate and two subseries that differed in their armament: the IIIa, which had four 20 mm cannons; and the IIIb, armed with two 20 mm and two 37 mm cannons.

color plate

Nakajima Ki-44-II 2nd Chutai 47th Sentai Imperial Japanese Army Air Force - Home defense - Japan 1945

Ki-44 bearing the characteristic national insignia adopted by the units for the defense of the Japanese islands.

A Ki-44-II, version with more powerful engine and heavier wing armament.

Aircraft:	Nakajima Ki-44-IIb
Nation:	Japan
Manufacturer:	Nakajima Hikoki KK
Type:	Fighter
Year:	1943
Engine:	Nakajima Ha-109, 14-cylinder radial, air-cooled, 1,520 hp
Wingspan:	31 ft 1 in (9.45 m)
Length:	28 ft 10 in (8.78 m)
Height:	10 ft 8 in (3.25 m)
Weight:	6,607 lb (2,993 kg)
Maximum speed:	375 mph (605 km/h) at 17,105 ft (5,200 m)
Ceiling:	36,842 ft (11,200 m)
Range:	1,055 miles (1,700 km)
Armament:	4 machine guns
Crew:	1

NAKAJIMA Ki-44-II

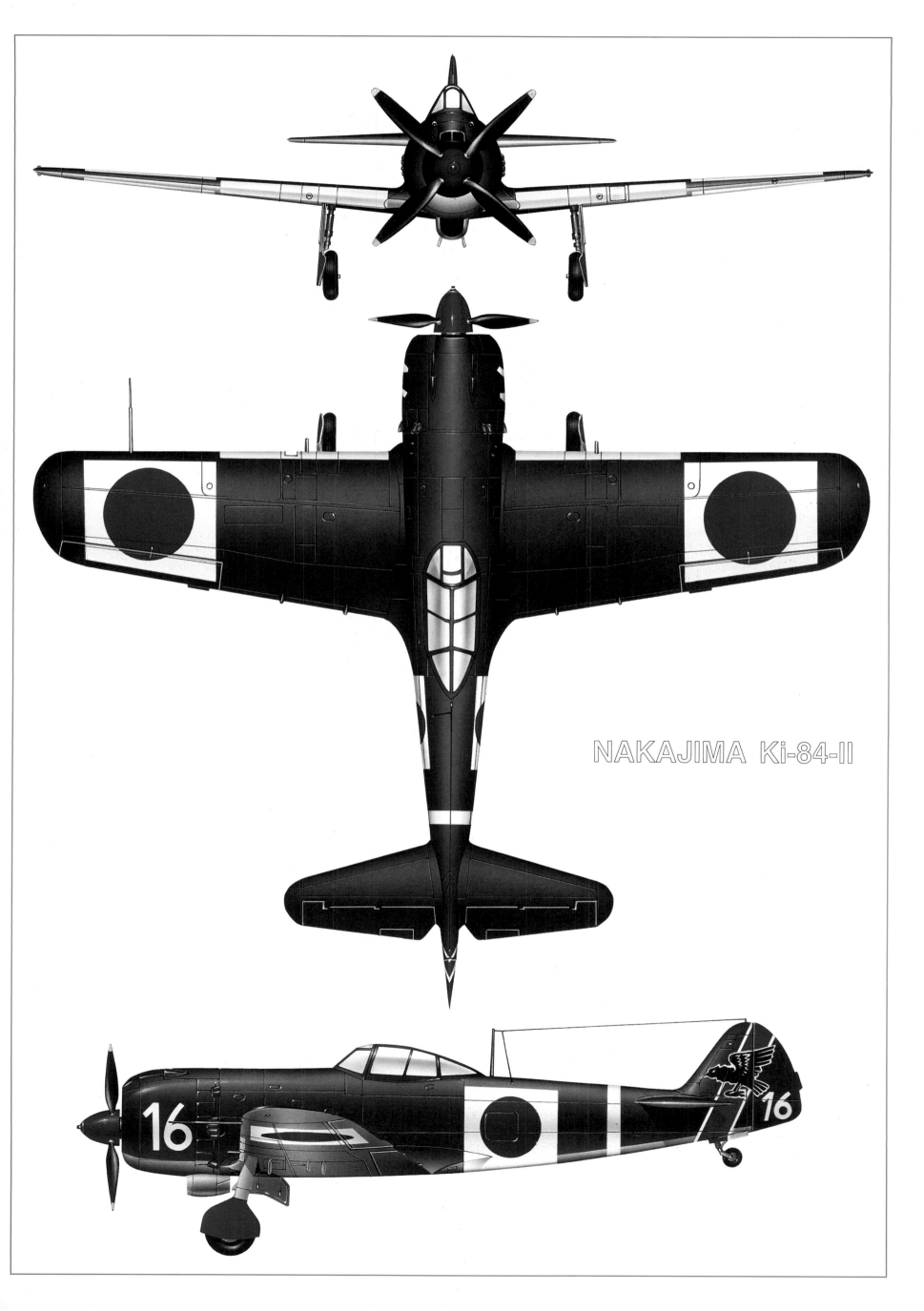

NAKAJIMA Ki-84-II

Considered the best Japanese fighter of the last two years of the war in the Pacific, the Nakajima Ki-84 Hayate (Storm) brilliantly bears witness to the great war effort carried out by the Japanese aeronautical industry in an attempt to oppose the growing American offensive. Powerful, fast, well-protected and armed, this agile interceptor proved to be completely competitive with the fiercest adversaries. A precise idea of its performance was gained after the war, in the spring of 1946, when an aircraft taken to the United States underwent a lengthy series of tests and evaluations. With a fully loaded weight of 7,505 lb (3,400 kg) the aircraft reached 426 mph (687 km/h) at an altitude of 20,050 ft (6,096 m), about 3 mph (5 km/h) faster and over 21 mph (35 km/h) more than those registered in identical conditions by a North American P-51D Mustang and a Republic P-47D Thunderbolt, respectively. These were two of the best American fighters. From March 1943 until June 1945, a total of 3,514 Nakajima Ki-84s were built, a remarkable number considering the critical conditions in which the Japanese aeronautical industry found itself: plagued and reduced to chaos by the American bombings. In the final months of the war, factories were even built underground, yet still capable of turning out 200 aircraft per month.

The project was launched at the beginning of 1942, and a year later, in April 1943, the first of the two prototypes took to the air. The aircraft was a compact all-metal low-wing monoplane with retractable landing gear, and originally powered by a 1,800 hp Nakajima Ha-45 radial engine. Its armament consisted of a pair of 12.7 mm Ho-103 machine guns installed in the engine housing and two 20 mm Ho-5 cannons installed on the wings. The initial series of tests took place without any particular problems and in the summer of 1943, the first of the initial lot of 83 pre-series aircraft were consigned to the technical units of the Imperial Army for evaluation tests. Furthermore, in October, an experimental unit was equipped with the Ki-84s, with the aim of testing them in operative conditions. The promising results led to the decision to launch series production immediately on a vast scale. The aircraft was officially designated Ki-84-Ia.

The model was developed in two subseries, with substantial modifications made to the armament and with a more powerful engine adopted. In the final production series, it reached 1,990 hp at takeoff. The Ki-84-Ib was fitted with four 20 mm cannons, while the Ki-84-Ic had two 20 mm cannons and two 30 mm Ho-105 weapons. The latter aircraft were specialized in the interception of bombers.

The increasing difficulties in supplying strategic materials led Nakajima to develop a second version (Ki-84-II) in which many components, including the rear section of the fuselage and the wing tips, were built of wood. In addition, during the last months of the war, the Tachikawa Hikoki KK built a new variant entirely of wood. Designated Ki-106, this aircraft proved to be a complete success, although the production program was initially slowed down and then suspended due to the dramatic situation of the conflict. Other projects suffered the same fate. They had been started with the aim of exploiting the already excellent characteristics of this aircraft as an interceptor. These included the high altitude Ki-84N, driven by a 2,500 hp engine, and the Ki-116, which was lighter and fitted with a 1,500 hp Mitsubishi Ha-33 radial engine.

---

color plate

Nakajima Ki-84-II 520th Temporary Interception Regiment for Home Island Defense, Japanese Imperial Army Air Force - Nakatsu Air Base, Japan, 1945

Aircraft:	Nakajima Ki-84-Ia
Nation:	Japan
Manufacturer:	Nakajima Hikoki KK
Type:	Fighter
Year:	1943
Engine:	Nakajima Ha-45, 18-cylinder radial, air-cooled, 1,900 hp
Wingspan:	36 ft 11 in (11.24 m)
Length:	32 ft 7 in (9.92 m)
Height:	11 ft 1 in (3.39 m)
Weight:	8,587 lb (3,890 kg)
Maximum speed:	390 mph (631 km/h) at 20,131 ft (6,120 m)
Ceiling:	34,540 ft (10,500 m)
Range:	1,052 miles (1,695 km)
Armament:	2 x 20 mm cannons; 2 machine guns; 1,001 lb (500 kg) of bombs
Crew:	1

A Nakajima Ki-84 that was captured, repaired and then kept in the United States.

When war broke out in the Pacific, the Imperial Navy possessed one of the most modern carrier-based torpedo planes in the world at the time, the Nakajima B5N. Known as KATE in the Allies' identification code, this large single-engine aircraft made its debut in combat on the day of Pearl Harbor. Its extensive operational career came to an end in 1944. Between 1937 and 1943, a total of 1,149 of these torpedo planes were built in two principal series.

Nakajima prepared the prototype on the basis of specifications issued by the Imperial Navy in 1935, requesting a carrier-based bomber to replace the Yokosuka B4Y1. The project was executed by a team headed by Katsuji Nakamura. The specifications called for a monoplane with a wingspan no greater than 52 ft (16 m) — to be reduced to a maximum of 25 ft (7.50 m) when the wings were folded — and capable of carrying a 1,764 lb (800 kg) torpedo or equivalent bomb load. Moreover, it was to be able to fly at 206 mph (333 km/h) at 6,580 ft (2,000 m) and to be provided with a range of four to seven hours at cruising speed.

The prototype, powered by a 770 hp Nakajima Hikari 3 engine, made its maiden flight in January 1937, and, during flight tests and evaluations, it more than fulfilled the requirements. After a series of minor modifications (including the replacement of the hydraulic system for folding back the half-wings by a manual one), the aircraft was preferred to its rival, designed by Mitsubishi, and it immediately went into production.

The first variant was the B5N1, which made its operational debut in China (it was used in the role of conventional bomber, among others), where it achieved notable success. These combat experiences, together with the appearance of more modern Soviet fighters in the same theater of war, led to a second variant being developed in 1939. This was much improved and provided with a more powerful engine. In fact, the major differences consisted in the fitting of the 1,000 hp Nakajima Sakae engine and in a series of modifications to the aerodynamics of the aircraft. This version, designated B5N2, went into production in 1940 and began to reach the units at the end of the year. By the time of the attack on Pearl Harbor, the new Nakajima torpedo plane had entirely replaced its predecessor in the front-line units. On December 7, 1941, the day of the attack on the American naval base, 144 B5N2s took part in the operation and contributed to its success in a decisive way. For almost three years, these aircraft were among the best in their category and took part in all air-sea operations. One of their most notable successes was the mission carried out against the aircraft carriers USS *Yorktown*, *Lexington*, and *Hornet*, which sank as a consequence of the precise and deadly attacks of the B5N2s.

It was not until 1944, when they were faced with new and more effective Allied aircraft, that the Nakajima torpedo planes were

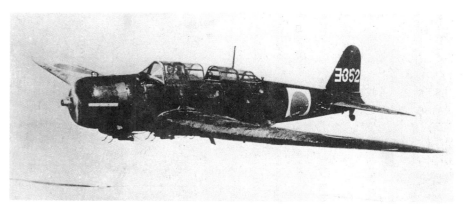

Nakajima B5N in flight. The racks for the bombs are visible beneath the fuselage.

withdrawn from front-line service and assigned to land-based units. This did not mean that they became any less effective, and they performed admirably in the role of antisubmarine convoy escort. Initially reconnaissance was entirely visual, but later some KATEs were fitted with radar equipment (the antenna being installed on the sides of the fuselage and along the leading edges of the wings) and magnetic detectors. In the last months of the war, many B5N2s were relegated to training duty (flanking the special B5N1-K aircraft derived from the first production version for this purpose), and target and glider-towing.

color plate

Nakajima B5N2 Imperial Japanese Navy Air Force. Commander Mitsuo Fuchida's personal aircraft, from which he led the attack on Pearl Harbor on December 7, 1941

Aircraft:	Nakajima B5N2
Nation:	Japan
Manufacturer:	Nakajima Hikoki KK
Type:	Torpedo-bomber
Year:	1940
Engine:	Nakajima NK1B Sakae 11, 14-cylinder radial, air-cooled, 1,000 hp
Wingspan:	50 ft 11 in (15.51 m)
Length:	33 ft 9 1/2 in (10.30 m)
Height:	12 ft (3.70 m)
Weight:	9,039 lb (4,108 kg) loaded
Maximum speed:	235 mph (378 km/h) at 11,810 ft (3,600 m)
Ceiling:	27,100 ft (8,260 m)
Range:	1,237 miles (2,000 km)
Armament:	1 machine gun; 1 × 1,764 lb (800 kg) torpedo
Crew:	3

The first wave of Japanese bombers during the dramatic moment of takeoff from the aircraft carrier *Akagi* at dawn on December 7, 1941 for the attack on Pearl Harbor. Fifteen Nakajima KATE bombers and 12 KATE torpedo bombers took off from the *Akagi*.

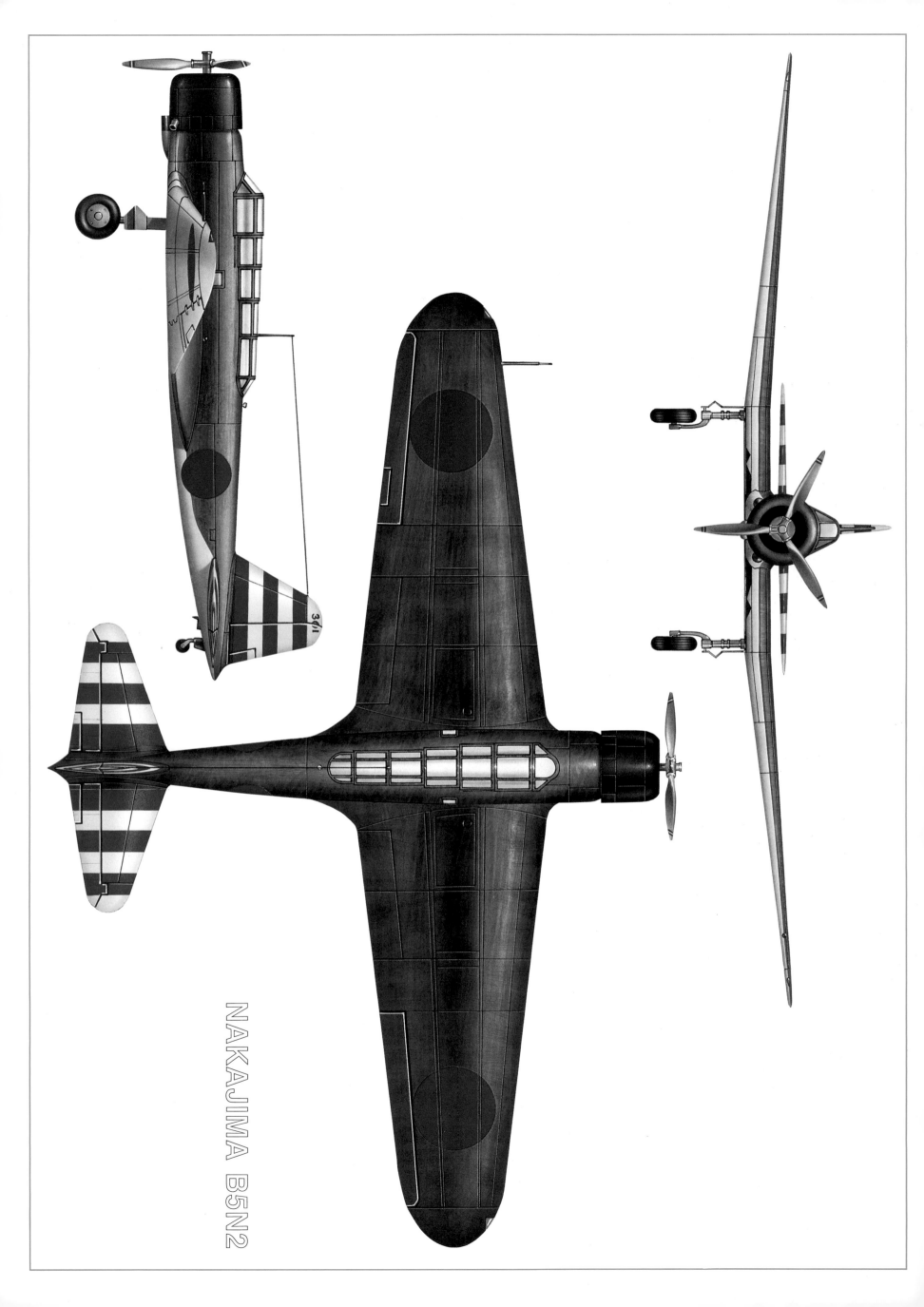

NAKAJIMA B5N2

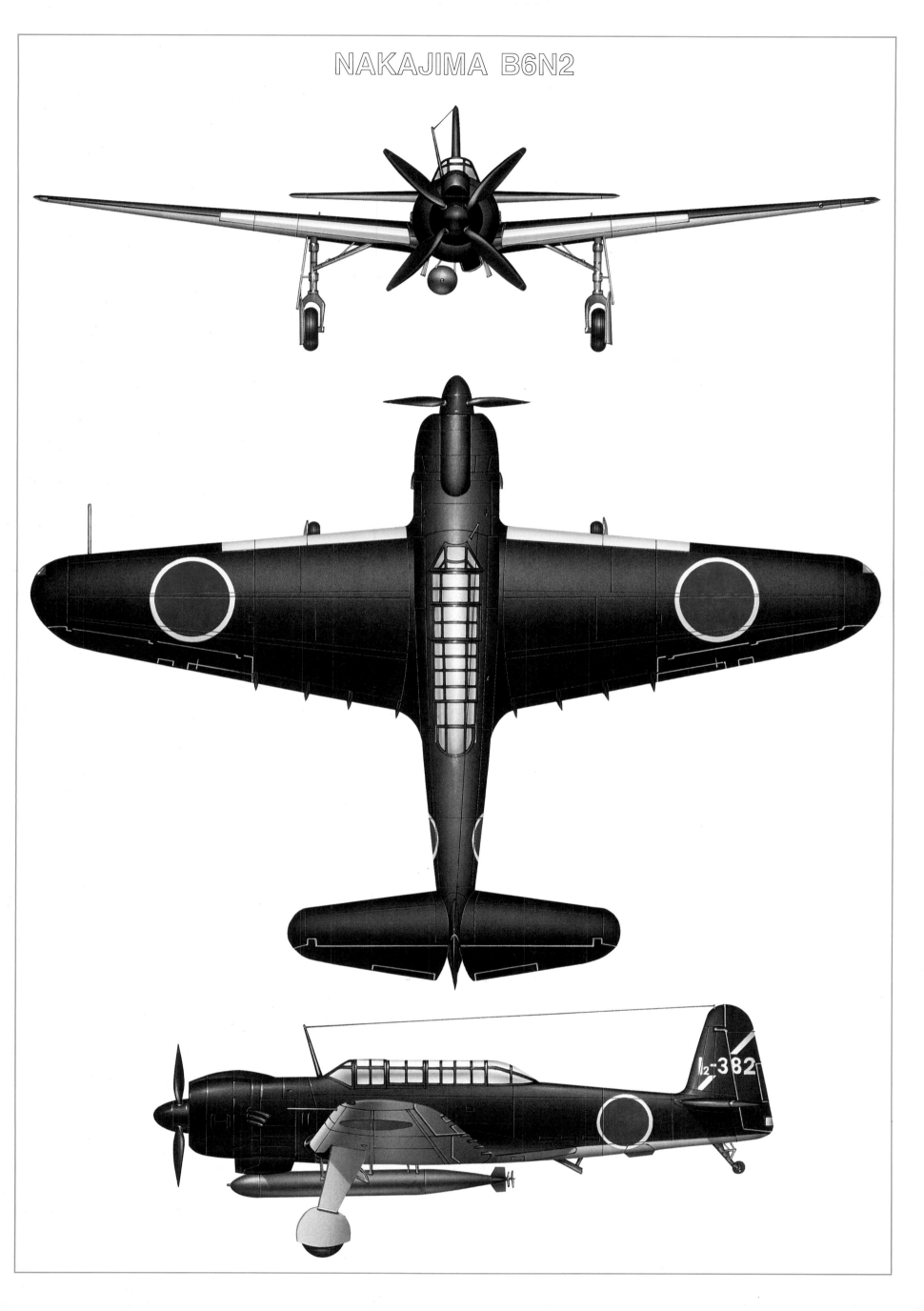

NAKAJIMA B6N2

Intended to replace the Nakajima B5N in the role of carrier-based torpedo plane, the B6N Tenzan (Mountain of the Sky) was designed toward the end of 1939, although it went into service much later, after more than two years of evaluations. In all, 1,268 were built, in two principal variants. Their careers were particularly intensive during the last two years of the war.

The specifications issued by the navy called for very modern characteristics: a maximum speed of 288 mph (463 km/h), a cruising speed of 230 mph (370 km/h) and a range of 1,000 nautical miles (1,853 km) with a 1,766 lb (800 kg) torpedo and of 1,800 nautical miles (3,335 km) without a bomb load. The project was carried out under the direction of Kenichi Matsamura, who basically took his inspiration from the airframe of the plane's direct predecessor. The new torpedo plane retained the general configuration of the B5N; however, the structure of the tail planes was substantially modified. Despite the fact that the navy insisted that the aircraft be provided with a Mitsubishi Kasei radial engine, the designer chose the new 1,870 hp Nakajima Mamoru engine, characterized by relatively low specific consumption. The first of the two prototypes was completed in the early months of 1941, and was ready for its first tests in the spring.

However, evaluations brought to light a number of problems, the most serious of which concerned the aircraft's directional stability. Subsequently, the preparation phase of the aircraft was further delayed by difficulties in the tuning of the engine and the need to reinforce the landing gear and arrester hook. This particular weakness had emerged during the final tests carried out toward the end of 1942, on board the aircraft carriers Ryuho and Zuikaku.

Production finally got under way in February 1943, although further problems emerged. After 135 of the initial B6N1 version had been completed, Nakajima received an order to suspend production of the Mamoru engine and to install the more reliable Mitsubishi Kasei 25 on the Tenzan. Thus, the second and major variant of the aircraft (the B6N2) was prepared and it began to come off the assembly lines in June. In all, up till August 1945, 1,133 aircraft were completed in this version.

In combat, the Tenzan behaved satisfactorily, although it was never an outstanding aircraft. Its employment on board ship was limited to the larger aircraft carriers due to its high landing speed and heavy wing load.

Very few modifications were introduced in the course of production. The aircraft of the final series (designated B6N2a) had

A Nakajima B6N2 with folded wings.

heavier armament (a 13 mm machine gun, instead of the 7.7 mm weapon on the aircraft's back). Two of this subseries served as prototypes for a new variant (the B6N3) which was fitted with a Mitsubishi MK4T-C Kasei 25c engine generating 1,850 hp at takeoff, and with a reinforced landing gear, suitable also for operations on land and semi-prepared runways. However, this final version never went into production.

color plate
Nakajima B6N2 aircraft-carrier Zuikaku, Japanese Imperial Navy Air Force - Pacific area, 1944

Aircraft:	Nakajima B6N2
Nation:	Japan
Manufacturer:	Nakajima Hikoki KK
Type:	Torpedo plane
Year:	1943
Engine:	Mitsubishi MK4T Kasei 25, 14-cylinder radial, air-cooled, 1,850 hp
Wingspan:	49 ft 0 in (14.90 m)
Length:	35 ft 9 in (10.87 m)
Height:	12 ft 6 in (3.80 m)
Weight:	12,472 lb (5,650 kg)
Maximum speed:	298 mph (481 km/h) at 16,118 ft (4,900 m)
Ceiling:	29,736 ft (9,040 m)
Range:	1,890 miles (3,045 km)
Armament:	2 machine guns; 1,766 lb (800 kg) of bombs
Crew:	3

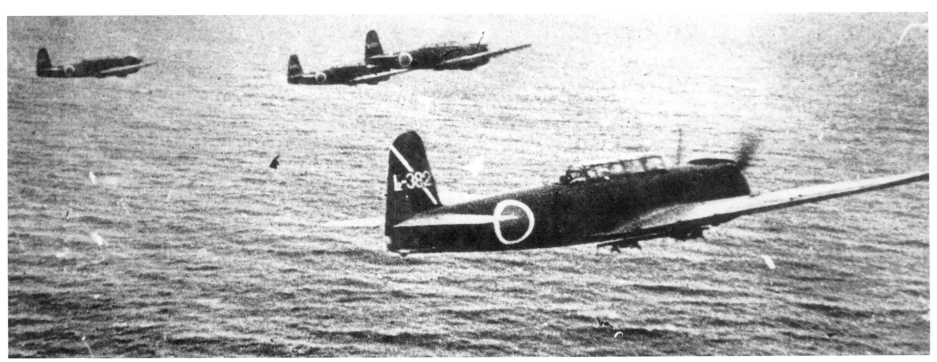

A formation of Nakajima Tenzan in flight at low altitude over the ocean.

The last carrier-based Japanese aircraft to have fixed landing gear, the Aichi D3A was also the first aircraft bearing the insignia of the Rising Sun to bomb American targets. This occurred on the morning of December 7, 1941, at Pearl Harbor, when 126 VALs (as the aircraft was known in the Allies' identification code) comprised the bulk of the Japanese bomber formations. Despite its apparently outdated lines and its rather modest overall performance, this large single-engine aircraft eventually proved to be one of the best dive-bombers of its time and was extremely successful in the Pacific during the first year of the war. In the course of its long and extensive operational career, the Aichi D3A was the aircraft that succeeded in sinking the greatest number of Allied warships, including the British aircraft carrier H.M.S. *Hermes* and the cruisers *Cornwall* and *Dorsetshire* in April 1942. In the course of these missions, the Japanese pilots succeded in dropping more than 80 percent of their bomb loads on target.

The D3A originated in the summer of 1936, when the Imperial Navy invited bids for the manufacture of a dive-bomber to replace the old D1A2 biplanes. Aichi, Nakajima, and Mitsubishi all responded with proposals, although only the first two companies remained in the competition. The Aichi prototype made its maiden flight in January 1938. It was an all-metal low-wing monoplane with fixed and faired main landing gear powered by a 710 hp Nakajima Hikari radial engine. The wing plan was elliptical and was similar to that of the German Heinkel He.70. The aircraft was also provided with aerodynamic brakes similar to those fitted on the Junkers Ju.87 Stuka. It had a traditional empennage and a circular section fuselage. The two crew members were housed in a long, completely glazed cockpit.

A series of problems emerged during the first flight tests: in particular, the aircraft was underpowered and proved to be unstable when carrying out tight turns, while the aerodynamic brakes were inadequate. Consequently, a second prototype had to be built with modifications to the wing and diving brakes, as well as a more powerful engine (an 840 hp Mitsubishi Kinsei 3). With these improvements, the Aichi D3A proved to be generally superior to its Nakajima rival and, in December 1939, it was chosen to go into production. This commenced at the beginning of the following year and continued for almost the entire duration of the conflict: up to August 1945, a total of 1,495 aircraft were completed in two principal versions.

Testing of the initial D3A1 variant (powered by a 1,000 hp Kinsei

43 engine) took place on board the aircraft carriers *Kaga* and *Akagi*, and during 1940 the aircraft was assigned to the remaining units of the Imperial Navy. The second version, the D3A2, replaced the first in the autumn of 1942, the principal modifications consisting of the fitting of a 1,300 hp Kinsei 54 engine and of much larger fuel tanks. A total of approximately 1,000 of these aircraft were completed, and the Showa Hikoki Kogyo was also called upon to build them, producing 201 aircraft between December 1942 and August 1945. However, with the appearance of the faster Yokosuka D4Y Suisei, the Aichi D3A was gradually relegated to the less important aircraft carriers and to land-based units and, from 1944, the surviving aircraft began to equip training units. As in the case of many Japanese aircraft, its final destination was that of the suicide missions, although in this desperate role the D3As proved to be particularly vulnerable when faced with the powerful and experienced American fighters: in fact, losses were very heavy, without producing particularly remarkable results.

color plate

Aichi D3A1 *Hiryu* aircraft carrier Imperial Japanese Navy Air Force Pearl Harbor strike - December 1941

Aircraft:	Aichi D3A1
Nation:	Japan
Manufacturer:	Aichi Kokuki KK
Type:	Bomber
Year:	1940
Engine:	Mitsubishi Kinsei 43, 14-cylinder radial, air-cooled, 1,000 hp
Wingspan:	47 ft 2 in (14.38 in)
Length:	33 ft 5 1/2 in (10.19 m)
Height:	12 ft 7 1/2 in (3.84 m)
Weight:	8,047 lb (3,650 kg) loaded
Maximum speed:	240 mph (386 km/h) at 9,840 ft (3,000 m)
Ceiling:	30,050 ft (9,300 m)
Range:	915 miles (1,472 km)
Armament:	3 machine guns; 813 lb (370 kg) of bombs
Crew:	2

A formation of Aichi D3As during a training flight. The aircraft belong to a training unit for carrier-based planes.

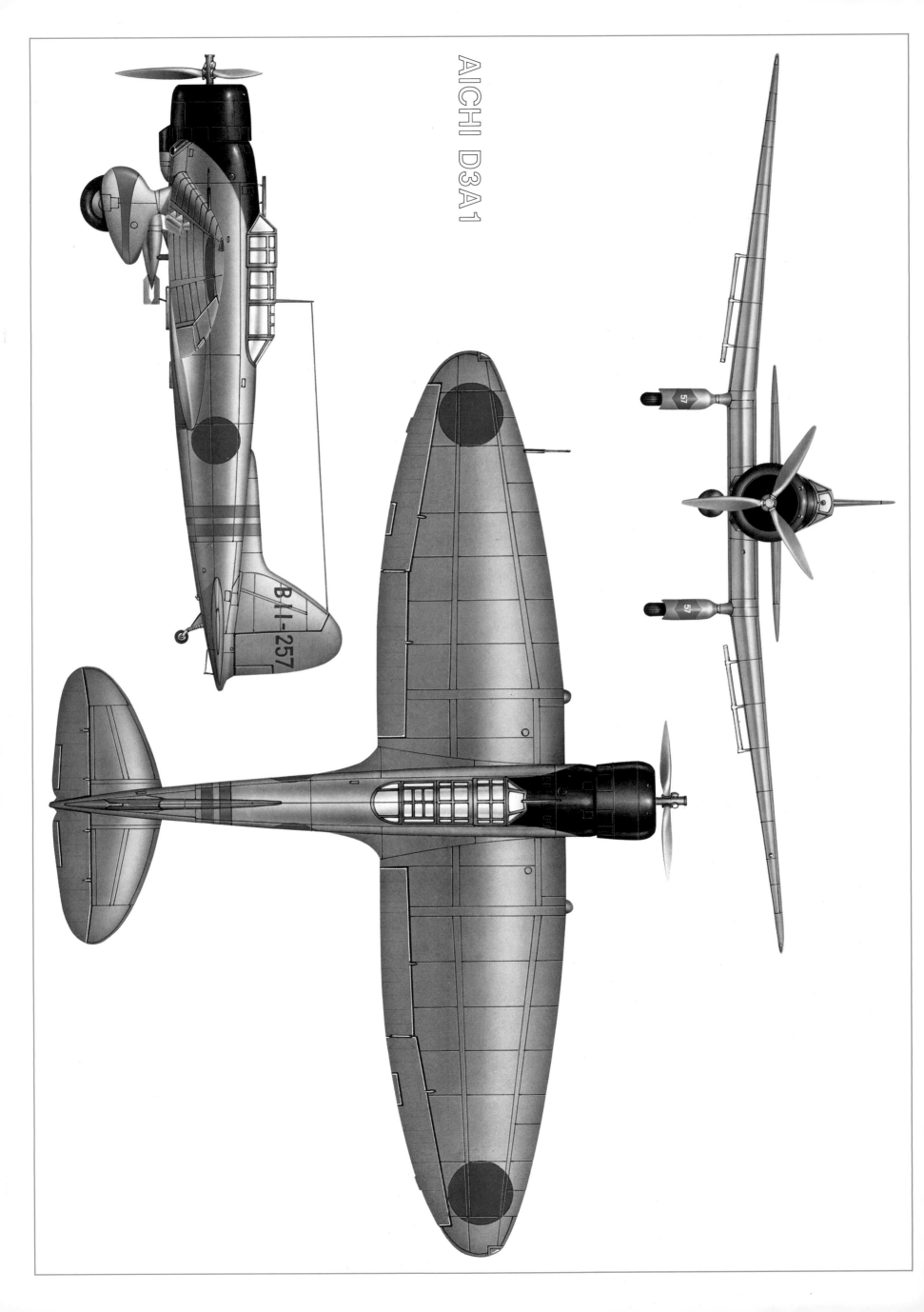

AICHI D3A1

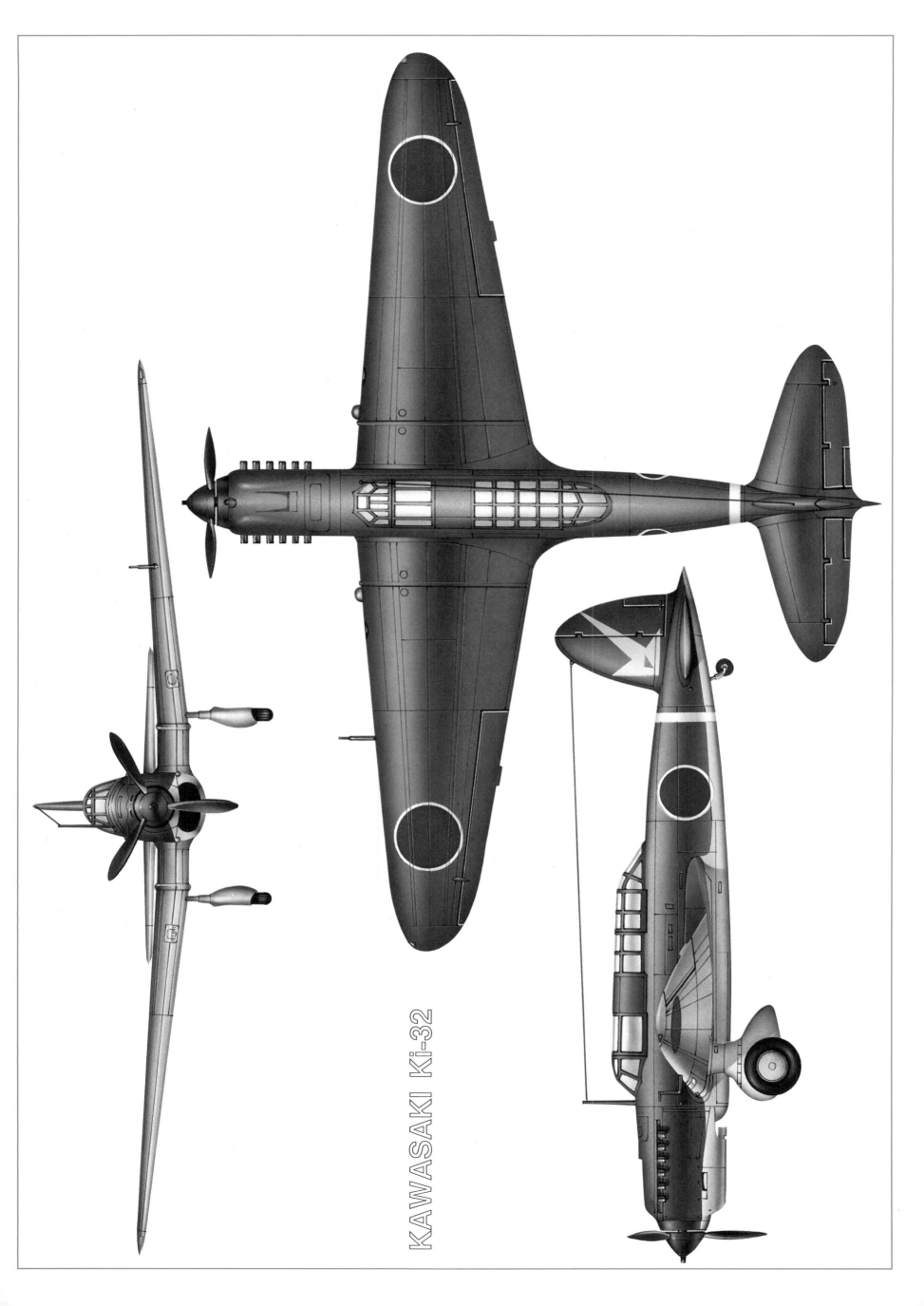

KAWASAKI Ki-32

Very few of the combat planes built in Japan during the war had in-line liquid-cooled engines. This was only partly due to the greater reliability of radial engines, which from many points of view were almost ideal for use in a theater of war characterized by vast expanses of ocean. In practice however, this situation resulted from the lack of a specific technological tradition, a lack that prevented the Empire of the Rising Sun's aeronautical industry from keeping up with the more aeronautically advanced nations. This is proved by the fact that the construction of the most famous Japanese aircraft provided with an "in-line" engine (the Kawasaki Ki-61 Hien fighter, an aircraft with a remarkable performance) was made possible only by the availability of German Daimler-Benz DB 601 engines (the same as those of the Messerschmitt Bf.109) built on license.

The only other exception worthy of mention is the Ki-32 light bomber, also manufactured by Kawasaki in the second half of the 1930s. This aircraft, inspired by the same operative concepts that led, more or less at the same time, to the development of the Fairey Battle in Great Britain, was the last bomber in the Imperial army to be powered by a liquid-cooled engine: in fact, its career was plagued by difficulties in engine tuning that, apart from making it generally unreliable, contributed to increasing the widespread diffidence toward this type of engine. From the second half of 1938 until May 1940, a total of 854 Kawasaki Ki-32s was built and, following their debut in combat during the second Sino-Japanese conflict, they remained in front-line service until the beginning of 1942, subsequently being relegated to training and secondary roles. In the Allies' code the Ki-32 was known as "Mary."

The project was launched in May 1936, when the Imperial army's technical authorities asked Kawasaki and Mitsubishi to develop a single-engine monoplane fighter capable of carrying a maximum of 992 lb (450 kg) of bombs at 186 mph (300 km/h) and at an altitude between 6,550 ft (2,000 m) and 13,150 ft (4,000 m); maximum speed was to be 250 mph (400 km/h) at 9,850 ft (3,000 m) and the defensive armament was to consist of two machine guns. The prototypes presented were quite similar: the formula chosen in both cases was that of an all-metal mid-wing monoplane with fixed landing gear and a bomb hold inside the fuselage. The only difference lay in the power plants: while the Mitsubishi Ki-30 was provided with a 950 hp Nakajima Ha-5 14-cylinder radial engine, the Kawasaki Ki-32 was powered by an 850 hp Ha-9-II "V-12" engine manufactured by the company itself.

The first of eight Ki-32 prototypes took to the air in March 1937, but right from the start of operative tests the aircraft revealed serious problems in tuning, caused by the unreliability of the engine, and these problems led to the project being suspended and set aside in favor of Mitsubishi's.

However, the threat of war led to a change of idea by the army's technical authorities. In 1938, it was decided to put the Kawasaki bomber into production, too, and the first aircraft came off the assembly lines later in the year. Paradoxically, the number of Ki-32s built was much higher than that of its Mitsubishi rival, of which 704 were built up to September 1941.

The Kawasaki Ki-32 Mary light bombers were quite advanced for their time.

Aircraft:	Kawasaki Ki-32
Nation:	Japan
Manufacturer:	Kawasaki Kokuki Kogyo KK
Type:	Bomber
Year:	1938
Engine:	Ha-9-IIb 12-cylinder, liquid-cooled, 850 hp
Wingspan:	49 ft 2 1/2 in (15 m)
Length:	38 ft 2 in (11.64 m)
Height:	9 ft 6 in (2.90 m)
Weight:	8,294 lb (3,770 kg) loaded
Maximum speed:	263 mph (423 km/h) at 12,925 ft (3,840 m)
Ceiling:	29,265 ft (8,920 m)
Range:	1,218 miles (1,965 km)
Armament:	2 machine guns, 992 lb (450 kg) of bombs
Crew:	2

color plate
Kawasaki Ki-32 Mary 6th Sentai (6th Attack Group) Japanese Imperial Army Air Force - Manchuria 1941

An early production Kawasaki Ki-32.

Ki-45 of the 53rd Sentai, a special ramming unit.

The tendency to build two-engine heavy fighters, present in the air forces of the major powers during the 1930s, was also to have a strong influence in Japan. In the spring of 1937, Imperial Army authorities issued specifications for a combat plane of this type, suitable for long-range missions. The result was the Kawasaki Ki-45, an aircraft that, like its Western counterparts, did not prove to be effective in the role for which it had originally been conceived, but, after having carried out a variety of duties, eventually found its true dimension as a night fighter. Between August 1941 and July 1945, a total of 1,701 Ki-45s were completed in several versions that remained in service for almost the entire duration of the conflict. In the last months of the war, during the Japaneses' desperate attempts to defend their country, the Ki-45s of the final production series fought extremely hard (and to great effect) to combat the massive night raids of the American Boeing B-29s.

The Imperial Navy's specifications for the new aircraft were remarkably precise. Some of the most notable requests included a maximum speed of 335 mph (540 km/h) at 11,515 ft (3,500 m), an operational ceiling between 6,580 ft (2,000 m) and 16,450 ft (5,000 m), a range of four hours and 40 minutes at 217 mph (350 km/h) plus a further half hour at full power. The three largest aeronautical manufacturers (Nakajima, Mitsubishi, and Kawasaki) all submitted projects but, toward the end of 1937, authorization to procede with the development of the project was granted to Kawasaki, and this task was carried out by Takeo Doi. Work on the prototype began in January 1938, and exactly one year later the first aircraft, designated Ki-38, took to the air for the first time.

This date marked the beginning of a long and tormented development phase that lasted almost two and a half years and led to the aircraft being substantially modified. The prototype was a cantilever mid-wing monoplane with retractable landing gear and was originally powered by two 820 hp Nakajima Ha-20B radial engines. The disappointing performance of the engines created the first set of problems, subsequently made worse by a series of difficulties of an aerodynamic nature caused mainly by the engine nacelles. Flight testing was suspended in the second half of 1939 in order to study solutions to these setbacks. The initial solutions involved fitting more powerful engines, but radical redesigning of the whole aircraft went ahead for a long time. The first of the three definitive prototypes did not appear until May 1941, and the optimum configuration was achieved in the subsequent 12 preseries aircraft. Following these modifications, the two-engine

Kawasaki was redesignated Ki-45 KAIa (KAI being the abbreviation for Kaizo, modified).

In Japan, the Ki-45 was ambitiously christened *Toryu* (Dragon-Killer), although in the Allies' code it was known by the more banal name of NICK, and it went into service in August 1942, initially being used as a ground-attack aircraft and in antishipping duty. Combat experiences (especially in the latter role) led to a second variant being developed. This was the Ki-45 KAIb, fitted with more powerful armament: one 20 mm and one 37 mm cannon were installed in the nose, replacing the two 12.7 mm machine guns and the 20 mm cannon in the belly of the first production series aircraft. However, the 7.92 mm flexible machine gun in the observer's position was retained. The armament was further improved in the next major production series (the Ki-45 KAIc of 1943, a total of 477 being built), with the installation of a pair of 20 mm cannons on the aircraft's back, so that they could fire upward at an angle in a similar way to those tested on German night fighters. These aircraft proved to be very efficient and, although they were not provided with radar, they proved to be an effective weapon against American air raids on Japan.

color plate

Kawasaki Ki-45 53rd Sentai Japanese Imperial Army Air Force - Japan 1944

Aircraft:	Kawasaki Ki-45 KAIa
Nation:	Japan
Manufacturer:	Kawasaki Kokuki Kogyo KK
Type:	Fighter
Year:	1941
Engine:	2 Nakajima Ha-25, 14-cylinder radial, air-cooled, 1,050 hp each
Wingspan:	49 ft 3 in (15.02 m)
Length:	34 ft 9 in (10.60 m)
Height:	12 ft 2 in (3.70 m)
Weight:	12,081 lb (5,491 kg) loaded
Maximum speed:	340 mph (547 km/h) at 22,965 ft (7,000 m)
Ceiling:	35,200 ft (10,730 m)
Range:	1,404 miles (2,260 km)
Armament:	1 × 20 mm cannon; 3 machine guns; 1,100 lb (500 kg) of bombs
Crew:	2

KAWASAKI Ki-45

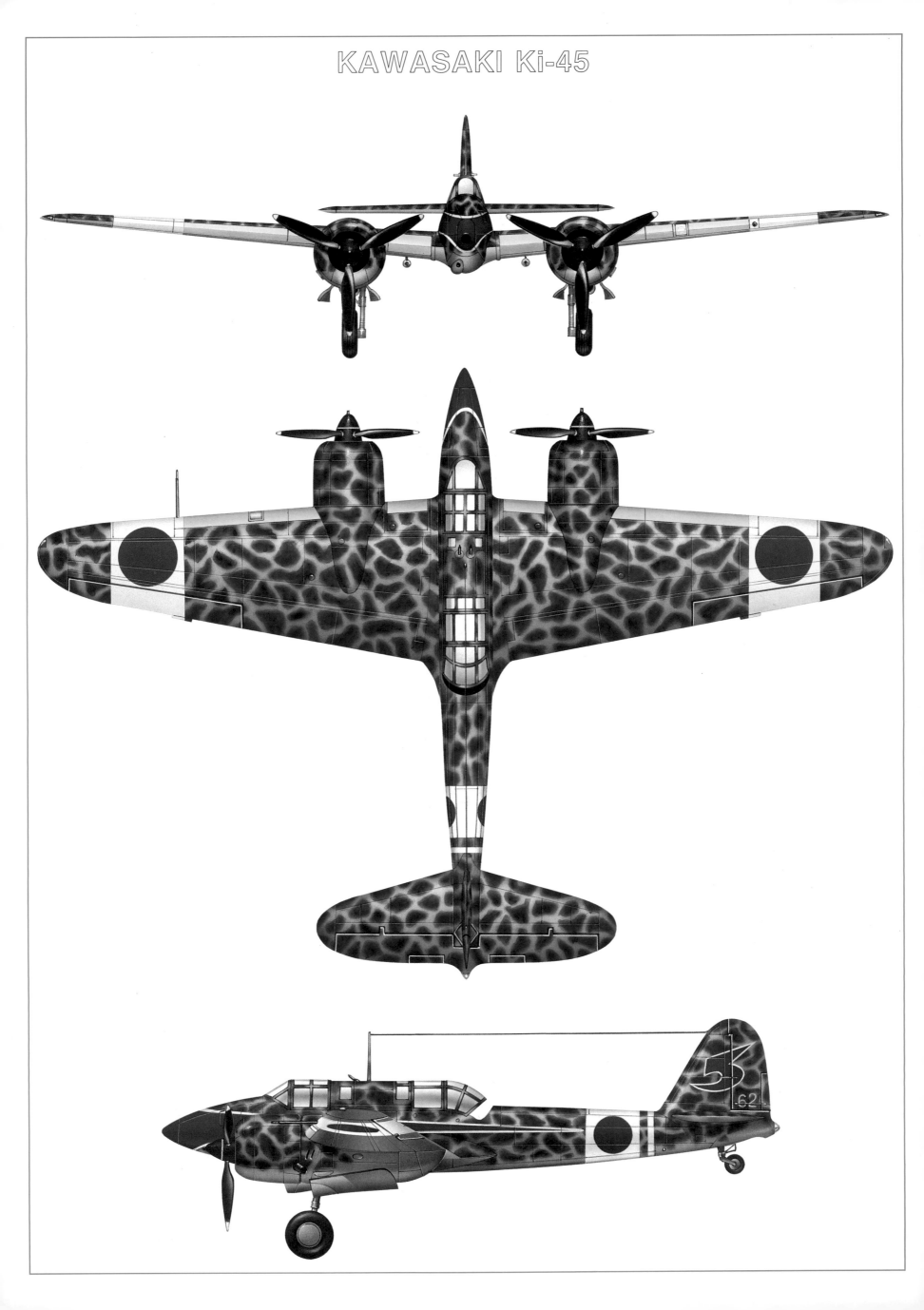

KAWASAKI Ki-48-IIb

The appearance of the Tupolev SB-2 in China led to the construction of the Kawasaki Ki-48 in Japan. In fact, the general staff of the Imperial Army was so impressed by the speed of the two-engine Soviet aircraft (which was equal to that of the Nakajima Ki-27, the latest fighter to go into service) that an immediate request was made to the aeronautical industry for the creation of a light bomber with a similar performance. From July 1940 to October 1944, no fewer than 1,977 Ki-48s came off the assembly lines, a remarkable number considering that in practice, with the changing situations presented by the world war, the aircraft actually proved to be extremely vulnerable and an easy prey for the enemy.

In December 1937 the Imperial Army issued the specifications. These were especially severe, calling for a maximum speed of 298 mph (480 km/h) at an altitude of 9,868 ft (3,000 m); a cruising speed of 217 mph (350 km/h) at the same altitude; ascent to 16,447 ft (5,000 m) in 10 minutes; a bomb load of 883 lb (400 kg); defensive armament consisting of three to four machine guns. Moreover, it was to be capable of operating in difficult weather conditions and at freezing temperatures. The project was entrusted to Takeo Doi, the technician who was also working on the construction of the Ki-45 heavy bomber, and preliminary studies began in January 1938. However, this phase was hampered by difficulties that emerged in the bomber program, and the first of the four Ki-48 prototypes did not take to the air until July of the following year. It was a middle cantilever wing monoplane with retractable rear tricycle landing gear. It was powered initially by a pair of 950 hp Nakajima Ha-25 radial engines. However, a series of problems emerged during the initial flight tests, the most worrying of which concerned strong tail vibrations. Several structural alterations were necessary to solve the problem. Production of

the Ki-48-I, the initial variant, was launched toward the end of 1939, although it was not until the summer of 1940 that the first aircraft came off the assembly lines (following the construction of five preseries planes). They were subsequently sent to China in the autumn. Kawasaki built a total of 557 aircraft, which were subdivided into two series, the Ia and the Ib, which differed only in small details.

At the beginning of 1942 (after the aircraft's relative inadequacy compared to the Allied fighters had become apparent), it was decided to build a second version (the Ki-48-II) with more powerful engines, provided with more effective defense and with the maximum bomb load increased to 1,766 lb (800 kg). In February 1942 three prototypes were completed and production commenced in April. This reached a total of 1,408 aircraft, divided into three subvariants: the IIa; the IIb (transformed into a dive-bomber); the IIc, similar to the first but with its defensive armament strengthened by the addition of an extra 7.7 mm machine gun in a forward position and the adoption of a 12.7 mm weapon on the aircraft's back. This series, which was the last, appeared in 1943, although even these improvements did not render the aircraft competitive. Production came to a definitive close in October of the following year, and the Ki-48 ended its career by being employed in the suicide attacks that occurred in the final months of the conflict. The Ki-48 was known as "Lily" in the Allies' code.

---

color plate

Kawasaki Ki-48-IIb 8th Sentai 2nd Chutai Japanese Imperial Army Air Force - Burma 1943

The Kawasaki Ki-48 twin-engine bomber was produced in many variants which differed only in small details.

A close-up of the canopy of a Ki-48.

Aircraft:	Kawasaki Ki-48-IIa
Nation:	Japan
Manufacturer:	Kawasaki Kokuki Kogyo KK
Type:	Bomber
Year:	1942
Engine:	2 Nakajima Ha-115, 14-cylinder radial, air-cooled, 1,150 hp each
Wingspan:	57 ft 3 in (17.45 m)
Length:	41 ft 10 in (12.75 m)
Height:	12 ft 6 in (3.80 m)
Weight:	14,880 lb (6,763 kg) loaded
Maximum speed:	314 mph (505 km/h) at 18,375 ft (5,600 m)
Ceiling:	33,135 ft (10,100 m)
Range:	1,491 miles (2,400 km)
Armament:	3 machine guns; 1,766 lb (800 kg) of bombs
Crew:	4

Italy was not the only member of the Axis alliance to use German aeronautical engines for its own aeronautical production. Japan also followed the same example, albeit to a much lesser extent. This occurred in April 1940, when Kawasaki acquired the rights to build the Daimler Benz DB 610A on license.

The result of this collaboration was another fighter, the Kawasaki Ki-61 Hien (Swallow), which, due to the fact that it was provided with an in-line liquid-cooled engine, completely stood out from the rest of the Japanese aircraft produced during the war, to the point that the Allies initially mistook it for a German or even an Italian aircraft. In fact, the Ki-61 was an entirely original project and was the only attempt made by the Japanese aeronautical industry to build an interceptor that was not fitted with a radial engine. The Hien remained in production for three years, beginning in August 1942, and the assembly lines completed 2,753 in several versions, including the prototypes. However, despite its excellent performance, the fighter was continuously plagued by problems in engine tuning that prevented its operative career from being entirely successful.

The project originated in 1941, at the time in which Kawasaki established the assembly lines for the production of the German engine. The technicians prepared two designs, the first (designated Ki-60) for a heavy fighter, and the second (Ki-61) for a multirole light fighter, submitting both to the Imperial Army authorities. At that time, reports of the war in Europe proved the superiority of combat planes powered by liquid-cooled engines, and approval was not long in coming. However, only the second of the two projects went ahead.

Created by Takeo Doi and Shin Owada, the first of the Ki-61's 12 prototypes took to the air in December 1941. It was an elegant aircraft, with lines very similar to those of the contemporary Macchi M.C. 202 and Messerschmitt Bf.109 F fighters, and right from the start it proved to have a remarkable overall performance, excellent armament, and good protection for the pilot and the principal mechanical components. A long and intensive series of evaluation test followed, during which the Ki-61 was compared with the best contemporary Axis and Allied fighters. In the summer of 1942, against a Messerschmitt Bf.109 E, a Nakajima Ki-43-II, a Nakajima Ki-44-I, and a captured Curtiss P-40E, the Hien emerged outright as the best aircraft. Production began in August, and the first aircraft of the initial Ki-61-I series reached the units in February 1943. The aircraft made its operative debut in New Guinea in May, and, during combat, the new aircraft proved to

be a difficult adversary for the American and Australian planes, thanks above all to its particularly heavy armament, its excellent protection, and the high speed reached during dives.

A total of 1,380 of the initial version of the Hien was completed (produced in two subseries that differed in their armament). In January 1944, the first Ki-61-I KAIs appeared (1,274 built in all), with further modifications to the armament and characterized by an overall structural strengthening. The last variant to go into production was the Ki-61-II KAI, which came off the assembly lines starting in September 1944. These aircraft, fitted with a more powerful version of the engine, capable of generating 1,500 hp, proved to be the best of all as far as performance was concerned.

However, the power plant was always to be the Hien's Achilles' heel: it was difficult to tune and subject to breakdowns. Kawasaki never succeeded in overcoming the congenital defects of its own production on license. The clearest proof of these difficulties was provided by the fact that, of the 374 Ki-61-II KAI structures built, only 99 were completed according to the original project. The remaining 275 were used in the initial production of the Ki-100, a new fighter derived from the Ki-61.

---

color plate

Kawasaki Ki-61-II 1st Chutai 18th Sentai Imperial Japanese Army Air Force - Home defense - Chiba, Japan 1945

Aircraft:	Kawasaki Ki-61-Ib
Nation:	Japan
Manufacturer:	Kawasaki Kokuki Kogyo KK
Type:	Fighter
Year:	1943
Engine:	Kawasaki Ha-40, 12 cylinder V, liquid-cooled, 1,175 hp
Wingspan:	39 ft 5 in (12.00 m)
Length:	28 ft 9 in (8.75 m)
Height:	12 ft 2 in (3.70 m)
Weight:	7,174 lb (3,250 kg)
Maximum speed:	367 mph (592 km/h) at 15,986 ft (4,860 m)
Ceiling:	38,157 ft (11,600 m)
Range:	683 miles (1,100 km)
Armament:	4 machine guns
Crew:	1

A Ki-61 with lengthened nose. The aircraft illustrated in the photo was used by the Chinese Air Force after the war.

KAWASAKI Ki-61-II

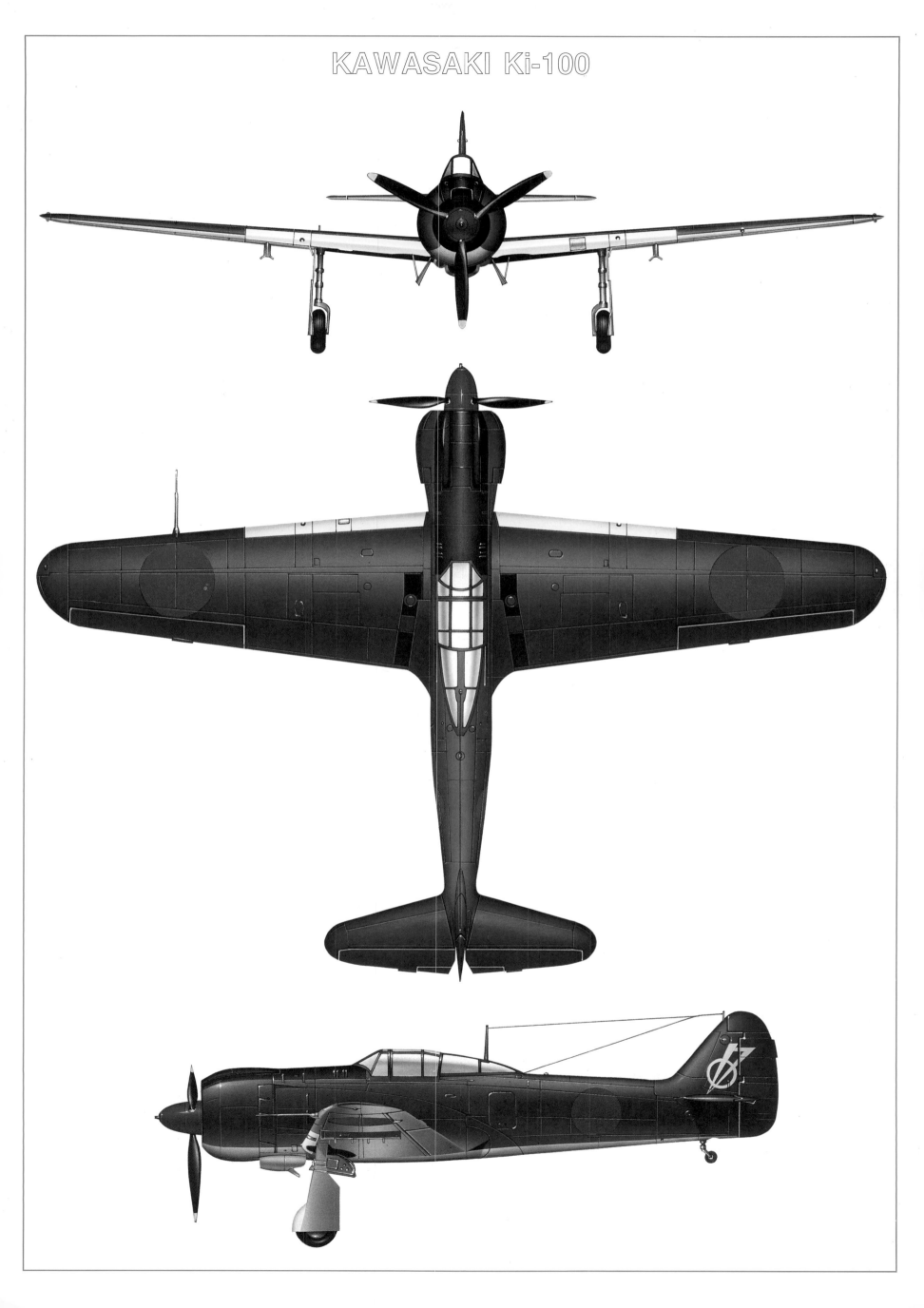

In the final months of the conflict, one of the most brilliant combat planes in the Imperial Army air force was derived from the Kawasaki Ki-61 Hien, the first and only interceptor powered by an in-line engine to be built by the Japanese aeronautical industry. It was the last to be sent into combat in the course of the conflict. Designated Ki-100, the new fighter was directly derived from its predecessor. The only difference lay in the engine, a large 1,500 hp Mitsubishi Ha-112-II radial which had replaced the unreliable liquid-cooled "V-12" (a copy of the German Daimler Benz DB 601A engine built on license). This adaptation, carried due to the impossibility of developing an entirely new aircraft in time, proved in practice to be much more than a mere compromise. In action, the Ki-100 was a superb interceptor, one of the few capable of effectively withstanding the formations of American B-29s which flew at extremely high altitude. In all, barely 396 of the two main series came off the Kawasaki assembly lines between February and August, 1945, while a subsequent version which remained at the prototype stage was much improved from the point of view of aerodynamics and had a more powerful engine.

The intensification of American bombing raids on Japan during the last year of the war and the consequent need for a particularly effective interceptor lay behind the creation of the Ki-100. In the second half of 1944, the production of a new variant of the Ki-61 Hien (which was to be provided with a 1,500 hp in-line Ha-140 engine, developed independently by Kawasaki from the previous Ha-40 built on license from Daimler Benz) was more difficult than had been foreseen. The delays were not only caused by serious problems which emerged in tuning the engine, but also by the fact that the factory where the Ha-140 was produced had been destroyed during a bombing raid. In order to overcome this stalemate, it was decided to use the Ki-61-II-KAI airframes already built and to fit them with a different engine.

The problems which emerged while adapting the slender fuselage of the Hien to the large Mitsubishi Ha-112-II radial engine which had a diameter of four feet (1.22 m) were many, and were not easily solved. However in the end, after having studied at length the engine mounting of a Focke Wulf Fw.190 A imported from Germany, the Kawasaki technicians managed to carry out the transformation brilliantly. Three prototypes were built by modifying a similar number of Ki-61-II-KAIs and the first of these took to the air on February 1, 1945. The cycle of tests and evaluations were done very quickly and the aircraft exceeded all expectations. Although it was slightly slower than its predecessor, the Ki-100 proved to be much more maneuverable and, above all, possessed a highly reliable engine. Production was launched immediately, using the remaining 272 Ki-61-II-KAI airframes that were available and these aircraft were designated Ki-100-Ia.

Between May and August, 1945, another series was added to this (the Ib, of which 118 were completed). This was characterized by a fuselage in which the rear section of the back was lowered and with a drop canopy allowing the pilot 360° visibility. However, the development of the fighter did not cease; in March 1945, with the aim of improving its altitude performance, Kawasaki began to construct the Ki-100-II version, with aerodynamic improvements, an Ha-112-II Ru supercharged engine and a water and alcohol injection device. The first prototype took to the air in May 1945, and within a few weeks, it was joined in flight tests by another two experimental aircraft. Series production was to have started in September, but this program was halted due to the end of the conflict.

color plate
Kawasaki Ki-100 17th Sentai 3rd Chutai Japanese Imperial Army Air Force - Japan, 1945

Aircraft:	Kawasaki Ki-100-II
Nation:	Japan
Manufacturer:	Kawasaki Kokuki Kogyo KK
Type:	Fighter
Year:	1943
Engine:	Mitsubishi Ha-112-II Ru, 14-cylinder radial, air-cooled, 1,500 hp
Wingspan:	39 ft 5 in (12.00 m)
Length:	29 ft (8.82 m)
Height:	12 ft 4 in (3.75 m)
Weight:	8,101 lb (3,670 kg)
Maximum speed:	366 mph (590 km/h) at 32,894 ft (10,000 m)
Ceiling:	36,184 ft (11,000 m)
Range:	1,117 miles (1,800 km)
Armament:	2 × 20 mm cannons; 2 machine guns; 1,103 lb (500 kg)
Crew:	1

A Kawasaki Ki-100-I, built by mounting radial engines onto the airframe of the Ki-61.

KAWASAKI Ki-102

Derived from the family of excellent two-engine Kawasaki Ki-45 Toryus (and in particular from the Ki-96 model, of which three prototypes were built in the course of 1943), the Ki-102 was built to replace its predecessor in all of its roles: heavy fighter, ground attack plane, and night fighter. In all, 238 were built between February 1944 and August 1945, although, despite their excellent performance, they had a very limited operative career.

The Ki-102's designer was Takeo Doi, the technician who had already created the successful Ki-45 series. The request for the new aircraft was issued by the Imperial Army in August 1943. At that time, the preparation of the first prototype of the Ki-96 heavy bomber was already at an advanced stage, and it was in fact from this aircraft that the new model was derived. It was an elegant all-metal middle cantilever wing monoplane with retractable rear tricycle landing gear, originally powered by a pair of 1,500 hp Mitsubishi Ha-112-II radial engines. The two crew members were housed in separate cockpits. Especially heavy armament was planned, consisting, in the case of the ground attack version, of two 57 mm caliber cannons in the nose, two 20 mm cannons in the belly, and a flexible 12.7 mm machine gun at the observer's disposal.

The first of the three prototypes took to the air in March 1944, and their construction was flanked by that of 20 preseries aircraft, initially intended for the development of the ground attack version. During flight tests and evaluations, the Ki-102 proved to have an excellent overall performance; however it was necessary to correct a strong lateral instability which was apparent during landing. Production of the ground attack variant was launched in October. Designated Ki-102b, 215 were ordered. Following limited use in the Okinawa campaign, almost all of these aircraft were kept in Japan as reserves.

In February 1944, the serious need for an effective interceptor led the Imperial Army to ask Kawasaki to develop a high altitude heavy fighter version of the Ki-102. This led to the creation of the Ki-102a. Six prototypes were obtained from a similar number of preseries aircraft of the basic model. The main differences lay in the use of two supercharged Mitsubishi Ha-112-II Ru engines and in armament modifications consisting of a 37 mm cannon and two 20 mm weapons in the fuselage. After evaluation tests, an additional series of 20 aircraft was built by modifying an equal number of Ki-102b airframes on the assembly lines, although it was possible to deliver only 15 to the units before the war ended.

The third versions, the Ki-102c night fighter, was developed towards the end of 1944. It remained at an experimental stage. It was characterized by a larger wingspan, longer fuselage, and modified empennages. It was armed with two 30 mm cannons

A Randy is prepared for takeoff. The ground crew have removed the camouflage nets which are still hanging from the propellers.

and a similar number of 20 mm caliber weapons. An interception radar was also installed in these aircraft in a fairing above the fuselage. The first of the two prototypes (both of which were obtained by modifying two Ki-102b airframes) was completed in July 1945, and the second a few weeks later. Flight tests and the entire program were interrupted by the end of the war.

color plate

Kawasaki Ki-102 45th Sentai 1st Chutai Imperial Japanese Army Air Force - Japan, 1945

Aircraft:	Kawasaki Ki-102a
Nation:	Japan
Manufacturer:	Kawasaki Kokuki Kogyo KK
Type:	Fighter
Year:	1944
Engine:	2 Mitsubishi Ha-112-II Ru, 14-cylinder radial, air-cooled, 1,500 hp each
Wingspan:	51 ft 2 in (15.57 m)
Length:	37 ft 7 in (11.45 m)
Height:	12 ft 2 in (3.70 m)
Weight:	16,114 lb (7,300 kg)
Maximum speed:	360 mph (580 km/h) at 19,736 ft (6,000 m)
Ceiling:	32,894 ft (10,000 m)
Range:	1,242 miles (2,000 km)
Armament:	1 × 37 mm cannon; 2 × 20 mm cannons
Crew:	2

A Kawasaki Ki-102 on the airfield. The aircraft was moved by means of the small wheels visible beneath the tail.

KAWASAKI Ki-102

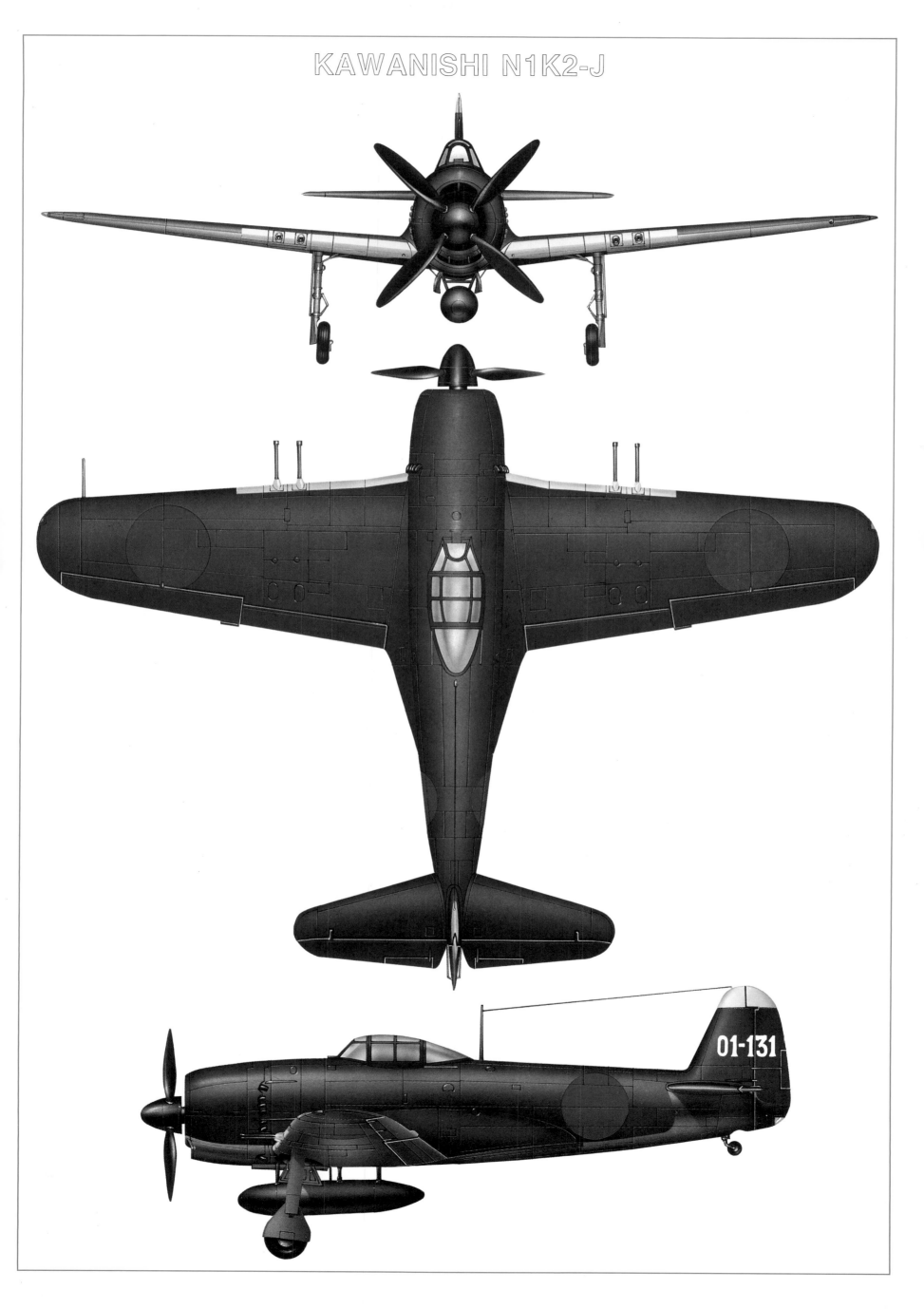

KAWANISHI N1K2-J

One of the best land fighters to be sent into action by Japan during the conflict was the Kawanishi Shiden (Violet Lightning). The origins of this powerful combat plane (of which 1,435 were produced in the last two years of the war) were unique in the history of military aviation: it was in fact derived from a seaplane fighter that Kawanishi was preparing in 1941, the N1K Kyofu model. Although valid on the drawing board, this aircraft never went into mass production due to the critical situation in the Japanese aeronautical industry (in fact, only 89 series aircraft came off the assembly lines between July 1943 and March 1944).

The project was launched privately by Kawanishi toward the end of 1941, and the first of the nine prototypes made its maiden flight on December 27 of the same year. Apart from the elimination of the large central float and the two on either side, which were replaced by conventional landing gear, and the adoption of a 2,000 hp Nakajima Homare engine instead of the original 1,530 hp Mitsubishi MK4E Kasei engine, the aircraft almost entirely retained the configuration and structure of its predecessor: it was an all-metal mid-wing single-seater monoplane, initially armed with a pair of 7.7 mm machine guns in the fuselage and two 20 mm cannons housed beneath the wings.

However, the initial series of tests did not produce entirely satisfactory results, due above all to difficulties in tuning the large engine and problems with the main landing gear. However, apart from these problems, the aircraft proved to possess excellent general characteristics in flight, great maneuverability, and a good maximum speed. One of the prototypes was offered to the navy for evaluation, but these tests lasted a long time, due to the reticence of the authorities about an aircraft developed without official specifications. Not until 1943, after the engine had been replaced and other problems eliminated, was the aircraft put into production with the designation N1K1-J Shiden, and sent to the units. Its entry into service was further delayed by a series of problems, but eventually, once it was fully operative, the Kawanishi fighter proved to be an outstanding aircraft.

In the meantime, while production of the first variant (built in several subseries that differed solely in their armament) went ahead, the Kawanishi technicians had set to work in order to eliminate the faults that were still present in their aircraft, starting with the landing gear, which was difficult to operate, and limited visibility on the ground. On December 31, 1943, the prototype of a new version, designated N1K2-J, took to the air for the first time. It was in fact substantially modified, retaining only the engine, the wing, and the armament of its predecessor. The fuselage and tail fins had been completely redesigned in order to allow the wing to be lowered from the middle of the fuselage farther down. This made it possible to shorten and simplify the landing gear and con-

A Kawanishi N1K2 with low wing and heavier armament.

sequently to improve overall visibility on the ground.

Eight prototypes were completed, and this time the tests were rapid and favorable. The aircraft was immediately accepted by the navy as a fighter and standard land fighter-bomber, and a huge production program was launched in June 1944, in which all Japan's major aeronautical manufacturers took part. However, this objective was never achieved, due to the critical situation in which the country found itself, devastated by the continuous raids carried out by American bombers. Only 423 N1K2-Js came off the assembly lines before the war ended. In the final phase of the conflict, many of them shared the fate of other excellent aircraft, being sacrificed in suicide attacks.

color plate

Kawanishi N1K2-J 1001st Naval Air Group Imperial Japanese Navy Air Force - Japan 1945

Aircraft:	Kawanishi N1K1-J
Nation:	Japan
Manufacturer:	Kawanishi Kokuki KK
Type:	Fighter
Year:	1943
Engine:	Nakajima NK9H Homare 21, 18-cylinder radial, liquid cooled, 1,990 hp
Wingspan:	39 ft 5 in (12.00 m)
Length:	29 ft 3 in (8.88 m)
Height:	13 ft 4 in (4.06 m)
Weight:	9,538 lb (4,321 kg)
Maximum speed:	362 mph (584 km/h) at 19,407 ft (5,900 m)
Ceiling:	41,118 ft (12,500 m)
Range:	1,577 miles (2,540 m)
Armament:	4x20 mm cannons, 2 machine guns, 264 lb (120 kg) of bombs
Crew:	1

A Kawanishi N1K1 Shiden, a single-seat monoplane with mid-wing.

The need for a fast medium bomber, recognized by all the major powers at war, was also observed by the Imperial Navy which sent into combat the Yokosuka P1Y Ginga (Milky Way). Although it was modern, well armed and provided with a good overall performance, the Ginga was nevertheless hampered by a particularly laborious preparation which eventually caused serious delays as far as its entry into service was concerned.

The development of this bomber was launched in 1940 by Yokosuka's First Technical Arsenal of Naval Aviation (Dai-Ichi Kaigun Koku Gijitsusho) on the basis of an official order which called for the construction of an aircraft in the same class as the German Junkers Ju.88 and the American North American B-25 and Martin B-26. In order to satisfy this request, the group of designers (headed by Tadanao Mitsuzi and Masao Yamana) studied an elegant two-engine aircraft, paying close attention to its aerodynamics. The group planned to install a pair of large Nakajima Homare radial engines which were being developed at the time and with which the aircraft should have achieved a maximum speed of 341 mph (550 km/h). In fact, in order to stress the aircraft's speed, the defensive armament was limited initially to a pair of 20 mm caliber cannons installed in the nose and the rear of the cockpit. The offensive armament consisted of a 1,766 lb (800 kg) torpedo or two bombs weighing 1,103 lb (500 kg) each.

The production program was launched in February 1943, before the prototype had made its maiden flight. The first of six experimental aircraft took to the air in August, and immediately proved to possess excellent qualities of speed and maneuverability. However, the enthusiasm expressed by the pilots was soon dispelled by heavy criticism on the part of the maintenance staff, who encountered serious problems with the on-board systems and the engines. These difficulties delayed acceptance of the aircraft by the Imperial Navy for many months, and made it necessary to carry out numerous modifications directly on the assembly lines which, despite everything, were already very busy. It was not until October 1944 that the P1Y was officially accepted by the Imperial Navy, and by that time, 453 aircraft had already been completed. However, their career continued to be plagued by an unreliable engine, and it was not until the early months of 1945, that the aircraft was able to begin operations. Nevertheless, in the brief period in which it took part in combat, the Yokosuka bomber proved to be a worthy adversary and a potentially valid aircraft.

Production of the first P1Y1 version amounted to 996 planes altogether. It was divided into several subseries following the basic one. The P1Y1a was provided with a different engine, the 1,825 hp NK9C Homare, and the rear armament was changed to a 13 mm caliber machine gun. In the P1Y1c a third machine gun was added in the nose. The P1Y1-S bomber was modified as a night fighter, with four fixed 20 mm cannons being installed to fire forwards and upwards at an angle and a 13 mm machine gun in the rear. Kawanishi was entrusted with the construction of the second variant, the P1Y2, characterized by more powerful engines. In all, 96 were built, and as the series of bombers similar to the previous version, they also came off the assembly lines as night fighters (P1Y2-S), armed with three 20 mm cannons.

Among the versions which remained at an experimental stage, mention should be made of the P1Y4 Model 12 and the P1Y5 Model 14. Lastly there was the P1Y3 Model 33, designed expressly for carrying the Ohka 21 and 22 suicide bombs.

A Yokosuka Frances taking off for a mission against American shipping in the Pacific.

The conclusion of a kamikaze attack carried out by a Ginga. Hit by anti-aircraft attack, it precipitates in flames without hitting its target.

color plate

Yokosuka P1Y1 Yokosuka Kokutai (Special Attack Unit), Japanese Imperial Navy Air Force - Japan, 1945

Aircraft:	Yokosuka P1Y1 Ginga
Nation:	Japan
Manufacturer:	Nakajima Hikoki KK
Type:	Bomber
Year:	1945
Engine:	2 Nakajima NK9B Homare 11, 18-cylinder radial, air-cooled, 1,820 hp each
Wingspan:	65 ft 9 in (20.00 m)
Length:	49 ft 4 in (15.00 m)
Height:	14 ft 1 in (4.30 m)
Weight:	29,801 lb (13,500 kg)
Maximum speed:	340 mph (547 km/h) at 19,407 ft (5,900 m)
Ceiling:	30,921 ft (9,400 m)
Range:	3,291 miles (5,300 km)
Armament:	2×20 mm cannons; 2,207 lb (1,000 kg) of bombs
Crew:	3

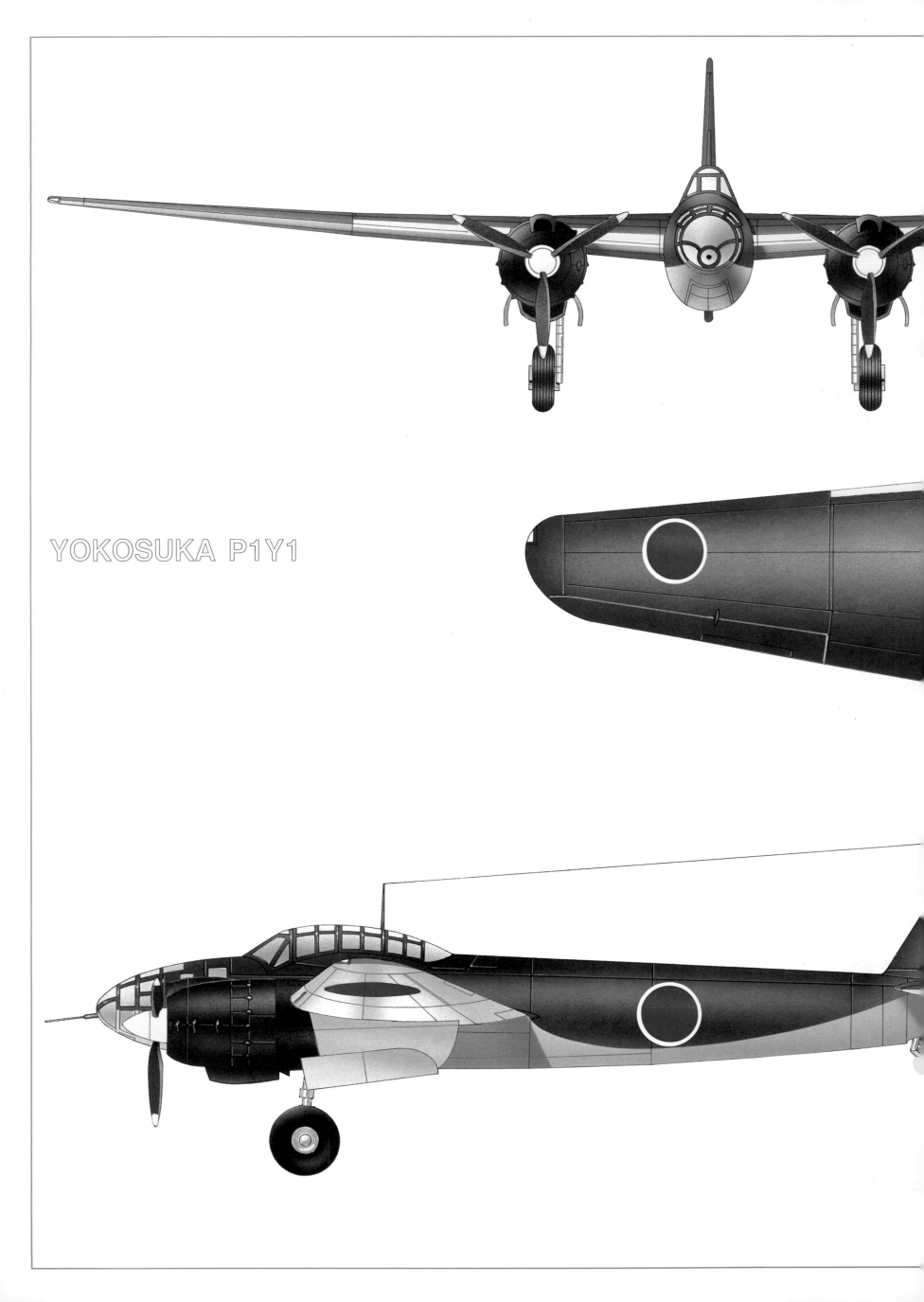

YOKOSUKA P1Y1

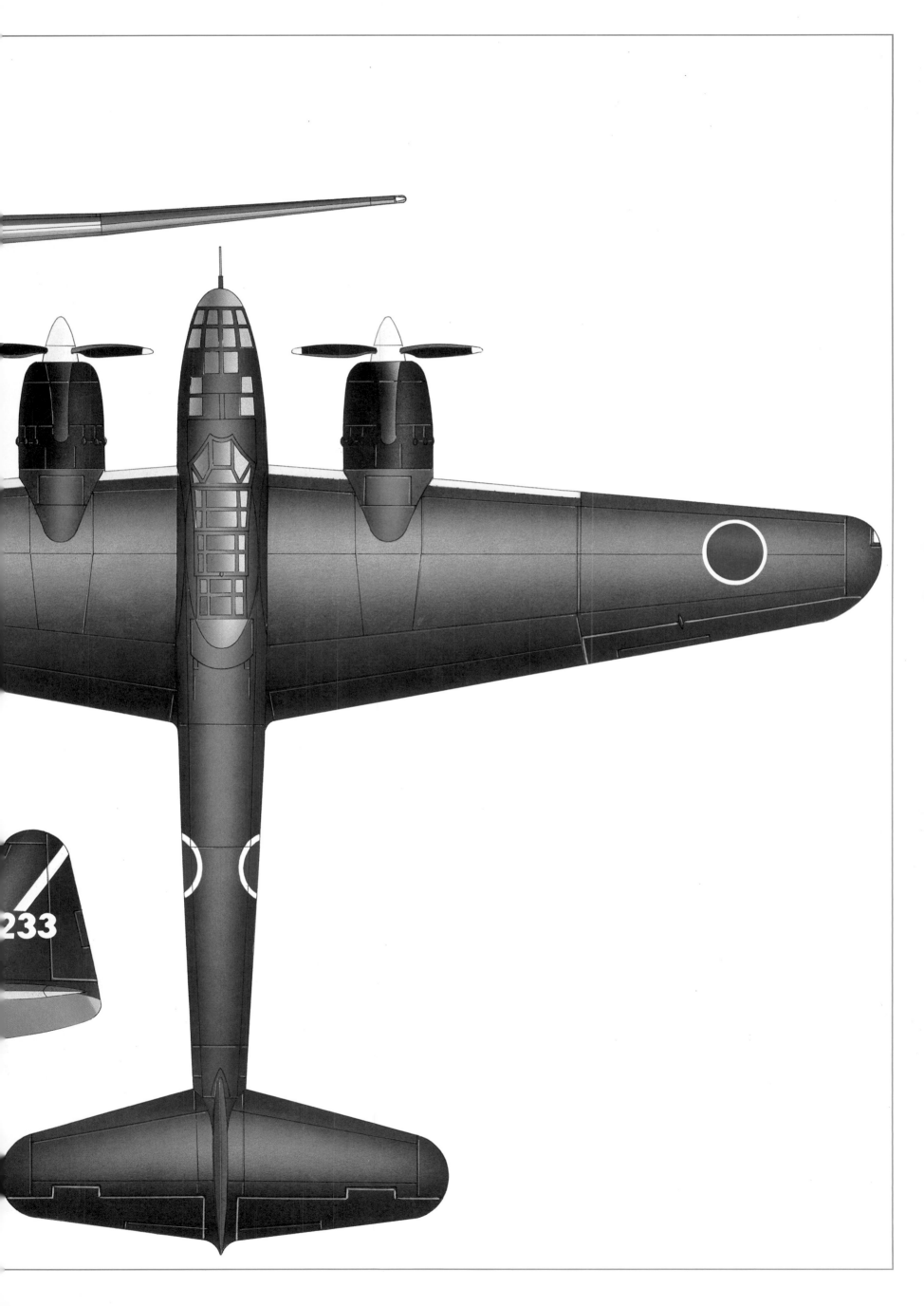

In the proliferation of projects prepared by the Japanese aeronautical industry toward the end of the conflict, the one which gave rise to the Kyushu J7W Shinden (Magnificent Lightning) remains unique in aviation history. In fact, this was the only "canard" type aircraft (that is to say with the horizontal empennage situated right at the front of the fuselage instead of on the tail) in the world for which mass production was ordered during World War II. However, despite its unquestionable potential, only two prototypes of this combat plane were built. The first took to the air on April 3, 1945.

The project was encouraged in 1943, by an official of the Imperial Navy's Technical General Staff, Captain Masaoki Tsurano, who foresaw right from the start the possibilities of installing a jet engine in order to exploit the advantages of the "canard" formula fully. He carried his idea forward with conviction, until the directors of Yokosuka's First Technical Arsenal of Naval Aviation (Dai-Ichi Kaigun Koku Gijitsusho) became interested. Therefore, the study of a glider was launched initially, in order to test the characteristics of the new aircraft in flight, and three prototypes, designated MXY6, were built. Flight tests began in the autumn of 1943, and in the course of a long series of tests carried out, one of the three aircraft was fitted with a small 22 hp engine, with the aim of studying its behaviour under power. The results of the experiments were judged promising, and in the early part of 1944, the navy ordered the Kyushu Hikoki KK company to begin the design of a fighter interceptor based on the form of the prototypes and on the original project's parameters. Despite its lack of experience in the construction of high performance aircraft, Kyushu was chosen because its technical staff and equipment were heavily involved in the war effort at the time. In any case, substantial support was guaranteed by a group from the First Technical Arsenal of Naval Aviation, headed by Captain Tsurano himself.

Work on the J7W1 began in June 1944, and the first of the two prototypes was completed in the brief space of 10 months. The aircraft retained the basic configuration already experimented on the MXY6 gliders and possessed some extremely interesting technical improvement. For example, the landing gear was of the forward tricycle type and was completely retractable and integrated by a pair of small auxiliary wheels in the rear, placed at the ends of the two tail fin-rudder units on the semi-wings, which were also retractable. The armament was concentrated in the nose's tip and was very powerful, with four 30 mm caliber cannons being planned. As for the engine, in the central part of the fuselage a large and powerful 18-cylinder Mitsubishi MK90 radial had been installed, provided with supercharger and driving a six-blade propeller by means of a camshaft. The cooling was guaranteed by large air inlets on the sides of the fuselage.

The navy, in its desperate search for a high performance interceptor, ordered mass production before the prototype had even taken to the air and charged Nakajima as well as Kyushu with organizing assembly lines that would produce no fewer than 150 aircraft per month. The course of the war led to the cancellation of this ambitious program which, even in normal conditions, would have taken a long time to set up. In fact, during the three brief test flights (lasting for a total of 45 minutes), the first J7W1 showed problems in stability during takeoff (caused by the high torque of the engine) as well as strong vibrations in the propeller shaft.

color plate

Kyushu J7W1 Japanese Imperial Navy Air Force - Japan, 1945

Aircraft: Kyushu J7W1
Nation: Japan
Manufacturer: Kyushu Hikoki KK
Type: Fighter
Year: 1945
Engine: Mitsubishi MK90, 18-cylinder radial, air-cooled, 2,130 hp
Wingspan: 36 ft 6 in (11.11 m)
Length: 31 ft 9 in (9.66 m)
Height: 12 ft 10 in (3.92 m)
Weight: 10,878 lb (4,928 kg)
Maximum speed: 465 mph (750 km/h) at 28,618 ft (8,700 m)
Ceiling: 39,473 ft (12,000 m)
Range: 527 miles (850 km)
Armament: 4×30 mm cannons; 264 lb (120 kg) of bombs
Crew: 1

The first prototype of the Kyushu J7W Shinden, which took to the air on April 3, 1945.

KYUSHU J7W1

The Imperial Army's Kawasaki Ki-61 and the Imperial Navy's Yokosuka D4Y Suisei were the only Japanese combat planes to be powered by a liquid-cooled in-line engine. Although they were totally different (the former was a single-seater interceptor, the latter, a two-seater dive-bomber), from many points of view these two aircraft shared a similar fate. They were both affected by continuous engine problems which prevented them from reaching their full potential. In addition, towards the end of their respective careers, they were both radically altered by the installation of the more reliable and more widely tested radial engines. However, in the case of the Yokosuka bomber, the results of this alteration were not particularly successful. From the spring of 1942 until August 1945, only 2,038 Suiseis (Comets) came off the assembly lines and their career came to an end in the final weeks of the war in the role of suicide planes.

The D4Y project was launched towards the end of 1938, and was strongly influenced by the acquisition of the license to build the German Heinkel He.118 aircraft in Japan. The characteristics of this elegant monoplane (powered by a Daimler Benz DB 601A engine) had so impressed the General Staff of the Imperial Navy that (following the destruction of the original German aircraft and the subsequent cancellation of the production program) the First Technical Arsenal of the Naval Aviation (Dai-Ichi Kaigun Koku Gijitsusho) of Yokosuka was commissioned to design a carrier-based dive-bomber directly based on the Heinkel He.118 prototype. The specifications included a maximum speed of 322 mph (518 km/h) and a cruising speed of 265 mph (426 km/h), a range of 800 nautical miles (1,482 km) with a 550 lb (250 kg) bomb load and 1,380 miles (2,223 km) without a bomb load. In addition, the ability to operate from smaller aircraft carriers was also required. Furthermore, the engine chosen was the Daimler Benz DB 601A, produced on license by Aichi.

However, due to delays in the construction of the German engine, the first D4Y1 was provided with a 960 hp DB 600, imported directly from Germany. Despite its inferior power, the prototype (completed in November 1940, and flown for the first time the following month) made an excellent impression thanks to its remarkable characteristics and its superior technical and aerodynamic qualities. Nevertheless, as flight tests proceeded, the aircraft developed serious structural problems when used as a dive-bomber, and the search for a solution proved to be slow. It was not until March 1943, that the Suisei was accepted by the Navy in this specific role. In the meantime, production had been launched and the first production series aircraft were used for reconnaissance. At the same time, its experiences as an attack plane were not successful. Intended to replace the by then obsolete Aichi D3A2s, the D4Y1s proved to be indefensible and, more importantly, plagued by unreliable engines. Their vulnerability was fully revealed in the summer of 1944, during the battles to prevent the Americans from landing in the Mariana Islands.

Not even the appearance in October 1944, of the subsequent variant (the D4Y2, with a more powerful engine and heavier defensive armament) changed the situation. Following the construction of 660 D4Y1s and 326 D4Y2s, production continued with 536 D4Y3s (in which a 1,560 hp Mitsubishi Kinsei 62 radial engine was adopted) and with 296 D4Y4s, specialized in suicide attacks. In fact, it was in one of these aircraft that, on August 15, 1945, Admiral Ugaki carried out the last kamikaze attack of the war, against the American fleet at Okinawa. At the time of the Japanese surrender, the D4Y5, final bomber's version, was at an advanced stage of development. It was better protected and powered by a 1,670 hp Nakajima Homare 12 radial engine.

---

color plate

Yokosuka D4Y2 2nd Section of Yokosuka Kokutai Japanese Imperial Navy Air Force - Japan 1945

Aircraft:	Yokosuka D4Y1
Nation:	Japan
Manufacturer:	Aichi Kokuki KK
Type:	Bomber
Year:	1943
Engine:	Aichi AE1A Atsuta, 12-cylinder V, liquid-cooled, 1,200 hp
Wingspan:	37 ft 9 in (11.50 m)
Length:	33 ft 7 in (10.22 m)
Height:	12 ft 1 in (3.68 m)
Weight:	9,381 lb (4,250 kg)
Maximum speed:	342 mph (552 km/h) at 15,625 ft (4,750 m)
Ceiling:	32,565 ft (9,900 m)
Range:	978 miles (1,575 km)
Armament:	3 x machine guns; 684 lb (310 kg) of bombs
Crew:	2

A Yokosuka D4Y2 taking-off from an airport in the South.

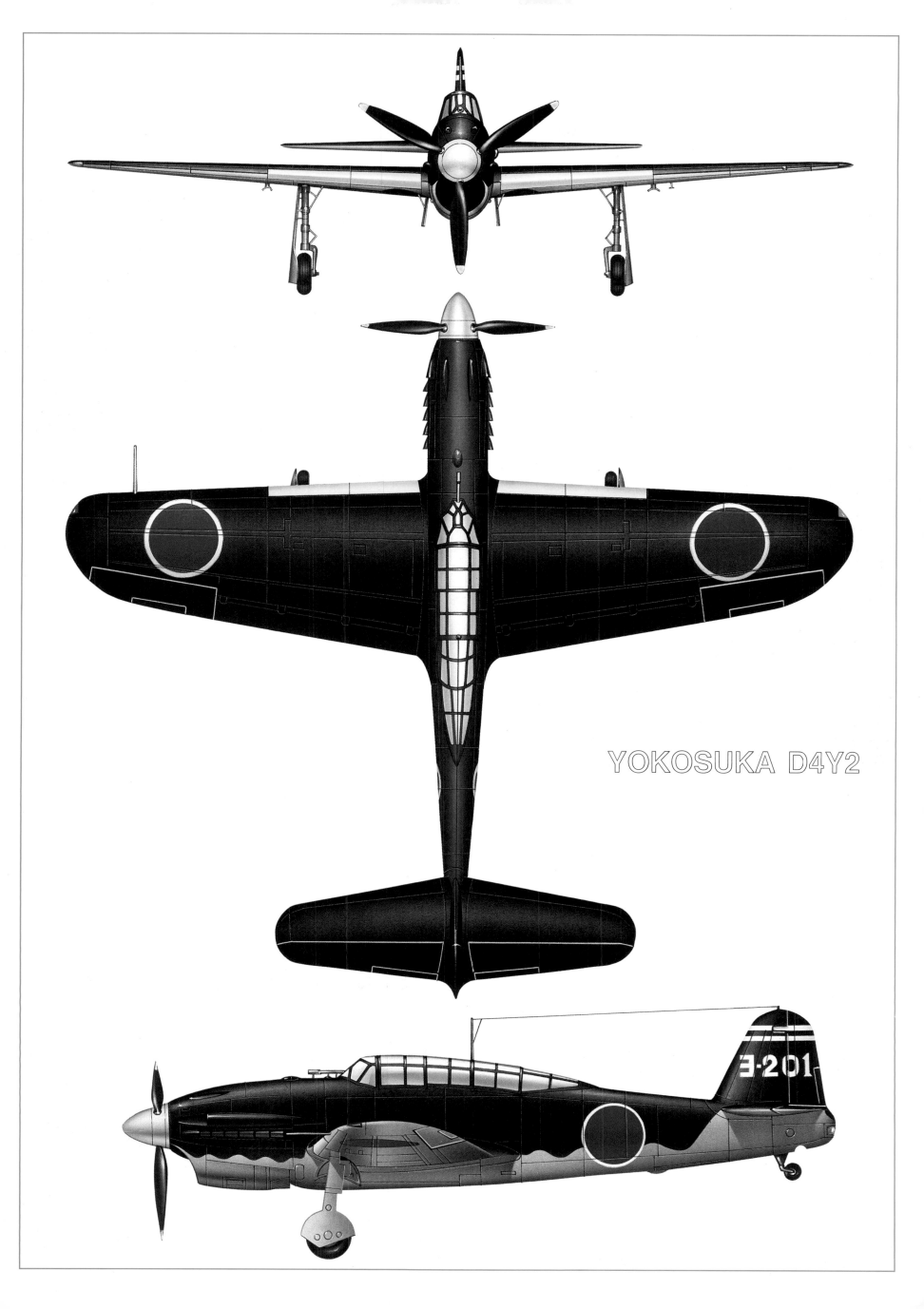

YOKOSUKA D4Y2

An Ohka flying bomb captured at Okinawa.

Inside the Yokosuka arsenal numerous aircraft similar to the Ohka flying bombs were captured. Lacking engines, they were meant to be used as gliders for training pilots.

In the context of Japan's last desperate defense, a special weapon intended for suicide missions was proposed by Mitsuo Ohta, a young official in the navy, in August, 1944. It was a veritable flying bomb, flown for a single one-way flight and powered by a rocket engine. The preliminary project, prepared by the staff of the Tokyo University's Aeronautical Research Institute, was submitted to Yokosuka's First Technical Arsenal of Naval Aviation (Dai-Ichi Kaigun Koku Gijitsusho) and received favorably by the Imperial Navy authorities, who decided to go ahead with the initiative. It was entrusted to a group of technicians led by Masao Yamana, Tadanao Mitsugi, and Rokuro Hattori. Thus the MXY7 Ohka (Cherry Blossom) suicide plane came into being, and no fewer than 852 were built in four versions during the final months of the war, many of them being successfully used against the ships of the Allied fleet. The American battleship *Virginia* was the first damaged on April 1, 1945. The first sinking took place eleven days later off Okinawa, the victim being the torpedo destroyer *Mannert L. Abele*.

The Ohka was designed initially for use in coastal defence. The Japanese intended that it be carried by a mother-aircraft. Once it was released, it would glide as far as possible toward its target. During the final phase of the approach, the speed increased to over 558 mph (900 km/h) (thanks to the thrust of the rocket engines) until the aircraft crashed into the chosen target. The project was relatively simple to produce at an industrial level and utilized non-strategic materials. The training of the candidates who were to act as pilots was also not particularly difficult.

The study and construction of a prototype without an engine went ahead rapidly and at the end of September 1944 ten aircraft of the initial MXY7 Ohka 11 version had already been completed. They were capable of carrying a 2,649 lb (1,200 kg) load

of explosives in the tip of the nose. The first test flight (without engine) was carried out in October, and the first powered flight, a month later. Without waiting for the complete test results the navy put the aircraft into production and a total of 775 Ohka 11s (the only ones to be used in combat) were completed between September 1944, and March of the following year.

The aircraft made its flight debut on March 21, 1945, although the mission was a total failure, as the 16 two-engine Mitsubishi G4M2e which were carrying the flying bombs were all intercepted by enemy fighters, and before being destroyed, were forced to release the explosives well in advance. The need to entrust the Ohkas to faster aircraft led to the construction of a subsequent version, designated MXY7-22, characterized by a smaller wingspan and lighter warhead, in consideration of the fact that it was planned to transport them on a two-engine Yokosuka P1Y1 Ginga. In addition, the new flying bomb was to have a Tsu-11 type motor reactor, fitted with a supercharger activated by a 100 hp Hitachi 4-cylinder in-line engine, instead of the rocket engines. In all, 50 of these aircraft were built, despite the fact that flight tests had shown the model to be generally unsatisfactory. A larger subsequent variant, the Ohka 43, remained at an experimental stage. In addition, production completed 45 training aircraft (designated Ohka K-1), characterized by the adoption of water ballast, instead of the warhead, and two Ohka 43 K-1 KAIs, once again for training. These were fitted with high-lift devices, extendable skids for landing, and a single rocket engine.

color plate

Yokosuka MXY7 Japanese Imperial Navy Air Force - Okinawa, Japan, 1945

Aircraft:	Yokosuka MXY7
Nation:	Japan
Manufacturer:	Dai-Ichi Kaigun Kokusho
Type:	Suicide plane
Year:	1945
Engine:	3 rockets type 4 Mk.1 Mod. 20 with solid propellants, with a total thrust of 1,766 lb (800 kg)
Wingspan:	16 ft 10 in (5.12 m)
Length:	19 ft 11 in (6.06 m)
Height:	3 ft 9 in (1.16 m)
Weight:	4,724 lb (2,140 kg)
Maximum speed:	402 mph (648 km/h) at 11,513 ft (3,500 m) (final speed: 575 mph or 926 km/h)
Ceiling:	—
Range:	—
Armament:	2,649 lb (1,200 kg) of explosives
Crew:	1

An Ohka captured at Singapore following the occupation of Seletar airport, another of the bases from which the kamikaze missions took place.

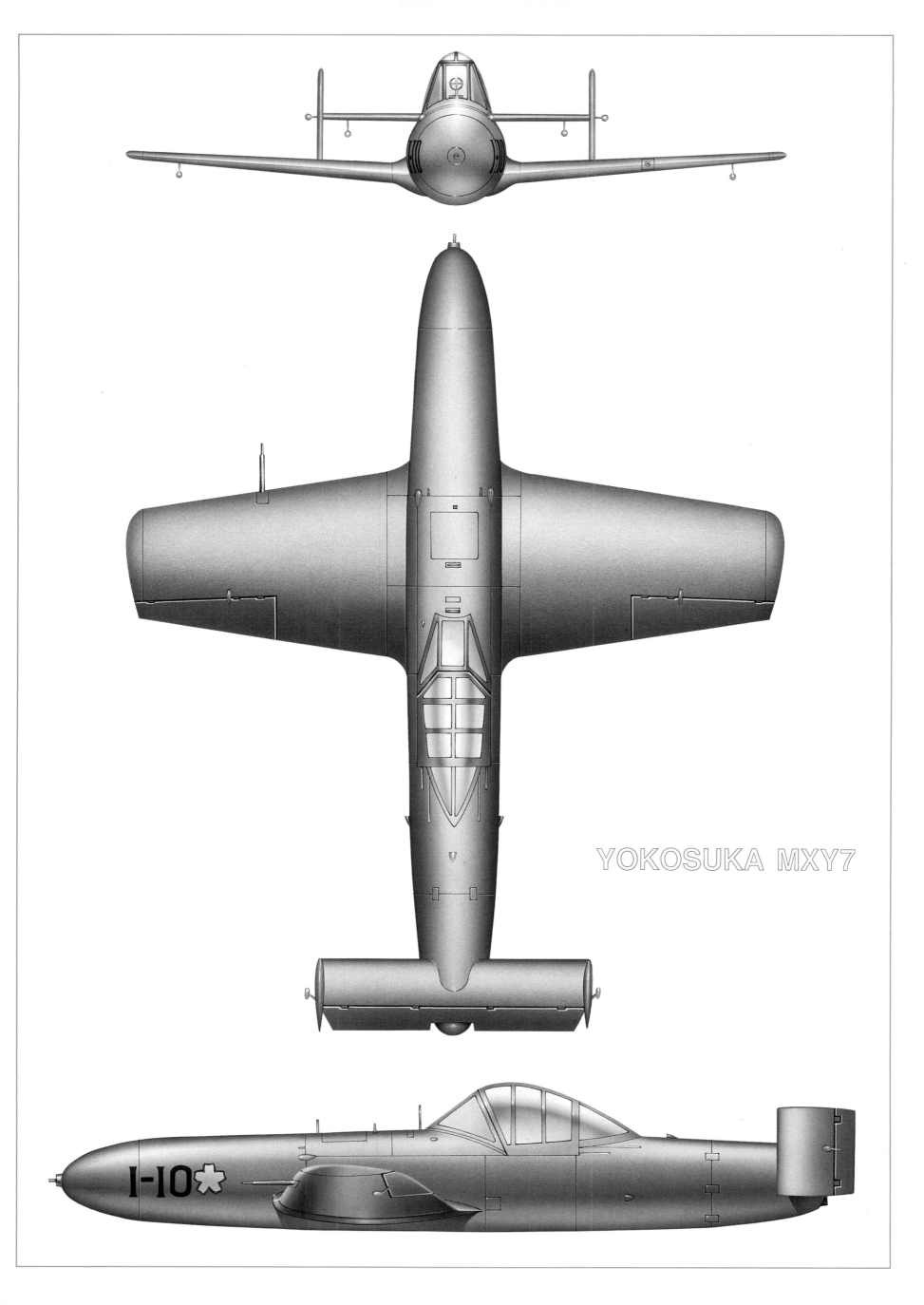

YOKOSUKA MXY7

I-10

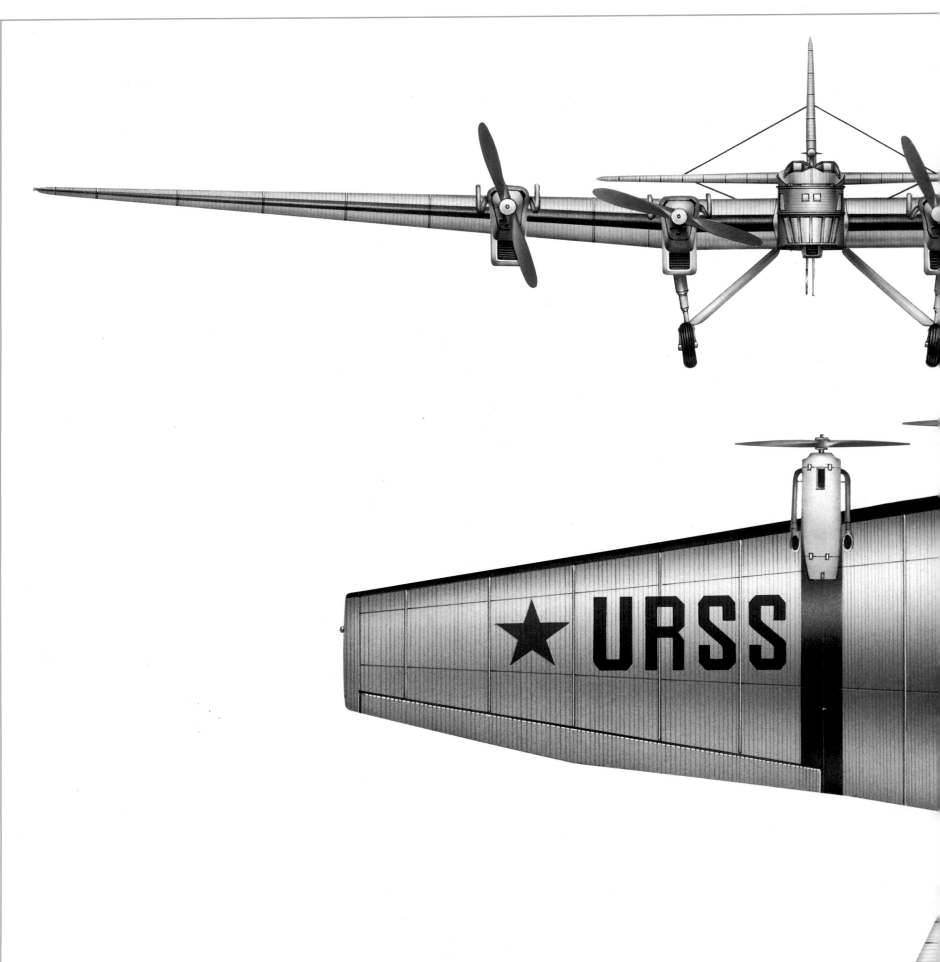
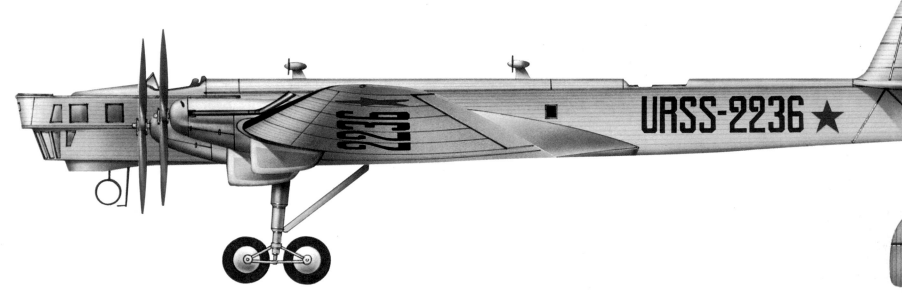

URSS

URSS-2236 ★

TUPOLEV TB-3

The tradition of "giant" planes — so dear to Soviet manufacturers and initiated with the 1914 Ilya Mourometz, the first four-engined bomber — was well represented by the Tupolev TB-3 (ANT-6), an enormous low-wing all-metal monoplane designed by Andrei Nikolaivich Tupolev in the late 1920s, which went into service in 1931. In all, eight hundred TB-3s were built and it proved to be a versatile combat plane. Despite its being outmoded, it was used during the early stages of World War II, although it was subsequently relegated to a secondary role as a transport plane, particularly for paratroops. It was first used in action in the summer of 1938, during the Russo-Japanese conflict. The last examples were withdrawn only in 1944.

Even after the war was over (and, in fact, right up to his death on December 23, 1972), Andrei Tupolev was famous particularly for the giant multiengined planes that he designed in the course of his long career. This began in 1920, when he was chief designer at the Central Institute of Aerodynamics (TsAGI), an organization founded in December 1918 with the aim of promoting studies of and research on the production of aeronautical projects in post-Revolution Russia. The ANT-6 was the first of these "monsters," and the experience acquired during its construction was to serve Tupolev in the following years for the planning of even bigger craft. These included the 1929 ANT-14, an all-metal high-wing monoplane, powered by five M.22 radial engines and capable of carrying 36 passengers and six crew members over a range of 745 miles (1,200 km) and the 1934 ANT-20, which, with its eight engines (900 hp each) and 206 ft 8 in (63 m) wingspan, was the world's largest plane.

The TB-3 project began in December 1925. The prototype's first flight took place on December 22, 1930, and almost turned into a disaster due to a malfunction in the throttle of the right-hand engines. After two months (in February 1931) and a series of modifications, including the introduction of 715 hp M.17F engines (BMW built on license) in place of the original American 600 hp Curtiss Conqueror, a positive verdict was passed on the aircraft, and it went into production. This got off to a slow start but soon picked up: in 1932, at the traditional May Day parade held in Moscow's Red Square, the nine aircraft already in service were on show; the following year 50 were exhibited, and by 1934 there were 250.

In the meantime, the TB-3 had undergone a series of altera-

tions aimed at improving its performance. The first (the prototype finished its tests in the fall of 1933) saw the introduction of 830 hp M.34 engines, but a real improvement was achieved only by installing M.34R engines provided with a reduction gear, which were used on the second version to go into production. In 1934, M.34RN engines were fitted, characterized also by a supercharger and able to generate 970 hp, while in 1935 for the final version 1,050 hp M.34RFNs were chosen. In its final series, the TB-3 showed that it was capable of carrying a larger payload than any other bomber then in production. During the same period, from 1937 to 1938 (the year in which production ceased), the assembly lines incorporated many other structural and aerodynamic modifications. Among these were the replacing of the corrugated wing-covering (Junkers type) with smooth metal sheet and the use of single wheel landing gear. The fixed tail fins were redesigned to allow for the installation of a new posterior defense position. The armament was reduced from the ten original machine guns to three in the final version. Lastly, the transport version (known as the G-2) could accommodate up to 30 paratroopers.

color plate
Tupolev TB-3 Soviet Air Force - 1934

Aircraft:	Tupolev TB-3
Nation:	USSR
Manufacturer:	State industries
Type:	Bomber
Year:	1931
Engine:	4 M.17F (BMW), 12-cylinder V, liquid-cooled, 715 hp each
Wingspan:	129 ft 6 in (39.50 m)
Length:	80 ft 3 in (24.50 m)
Height:	27 ft 7 in (8.45 m)
Take-off weight:	38,360 lb (17,400 kg)
Maximum speed:	134 mph (215 km/h)
Ceiling:	12,469 ft (3,800 m)
Range:	1,939 miles (3,225 km)
Armament:	3/10 machine guns; 4,800 lb (2,200 kg) of bombs
Crew:	6/10

TB-3 in a stopover at Rome's Ciampino airport during a propaganda flight in 1936.

The need to develop modern combat planes was considered to be particularly important in the Soviet Union during the 1930s. Thanks to the massive reorganization of its industrial resources, which took place in great secrecy between the two wars, the ceaseless effort of Soviet technicians often resulted in the production of technically advanced aircraft that captured the world's attention. The Tupolev SB-2 was one of these. Developed by a team headed by Andrei Nikolaevich Tupolev (and more especially by A.A. Arkhangelski, head of one of TsAGI's technical units), this elegant, mid-wing two-engine plane with all-metal structure and retractable landing gear was capable of a performance far beyond that of the other main fighters of the time.

In 1936, the SB-2's qualities were demonstrated to the full during the Spanish Civil War, in which the Soviets had decided to test the new bomber in action (it had first gone into service early in the same year). The results went beyond even the highest expectations. The Tupolev proved to be the fastest plane in existence, particularly when compared to other fighters, such as the Italian Fiat CR.32s and the German Heinkel He.51s. The first missions carried out by the Republican pilots (who received 210 SB-2s, which they christened "Katiusha") marked the beginning of a long career that continued throughout World War II and led to the production of over 6,600 planes in several versions.

The project got under way in 1933, under the builder designation of ANT-40. Military specifications called for a light bomber capable of improving by 50 percent on the performance of the four-engine TB-3. More specifically, its speed was to top 205 mph (330 km/h) and its ceiling was to be 26,315 ft (8,000 m). Arkhangelski reelaborated the design of a heavy fighter (the ANT-29) on which he was working, and these instructions were transformed into a careful study of aerodynamics and into the introduction of technical and technological solutions that were extremely advanced for the period, such as the monocoque structure and the fully retractable landing gear.

Two prototypes were prepared, each with a different power plant. The first adopted 700 hp M.25 radial engines (Wright Cyclone built on license), and the second a pair of 830 hp inline liquid-cooled M.100As (Hispano-Suiza 12Y). Both engines were fed by a supercharger. Even before the prototypes were completed, the Soviet government ordered that they go into mass production. The prototype with radial engines made its maiden flight on October 7, 1934; the second prototype followed on December 30. After flight testing, the second prototype was chosen, in the light of the remarkable overall benefits offered by its greater strength and its more accurate aerodynamics.

Production continued up to 1941. Among the principal versions were the 1938 SB-2bis with 960 hp M.103 engines housed in more aerodynamic fairings, and the 1940 SR-BK dive-bomber provided with M.105R engines that generated 1,100 hp at take-off. Transport versions (the PS-40 and the PS-41) also derived from the two earlier series.

After its debut in the Spanish Civil War, the Tupolev bomber was used against the Japanese on the Mongolian border in 1938 and 1939. At the outbreak of World War II, the SB-2s took part in the attack on Finland. Later, however, during the German attack, the planes began to show their limitations and were relegated to night missions and then to secondary roles. Among the major users of the airplane outside the USSR were Nationalist China (which received a substantial number of SB-2s in 1937), Bulgaria, and Finland.

color plate
Tupolev SB-2 Spanish Republican Air Force - Barajas 1939

SB-2 *bis*, equipped with M.103 engines, beside the wreckage of a Po-2.

An SB-2 *bis* after forced landing; note increased dorsal turret.

Aircraft:	Tupolev SB-2
Nation:	USSR
Manufacturer:	State industries
Type:	Bomber
Year:	1936
Engine:	2 Klimov M.100A, 12-cylinder V, liquid-cooled, 830 hp each
Wingspan:	66 ft 8 1/2 in (20.33 m)
Length:	40 ft 3 in (12.27 m)
Height:	10 ft 8 in (3.25 m)
Weight:	12,637 lb (5,725 kg) loaded
Maximum speed:	255 mph (411 km/h) at 13,120 ft (4,000 m)
Ceiling:	31,200 ft (9,500 m)
Range:	745 miles (1,200 km)
Armament:	4 machine guns; 1,320 lb (600 kg) of bombs
Crew:	3

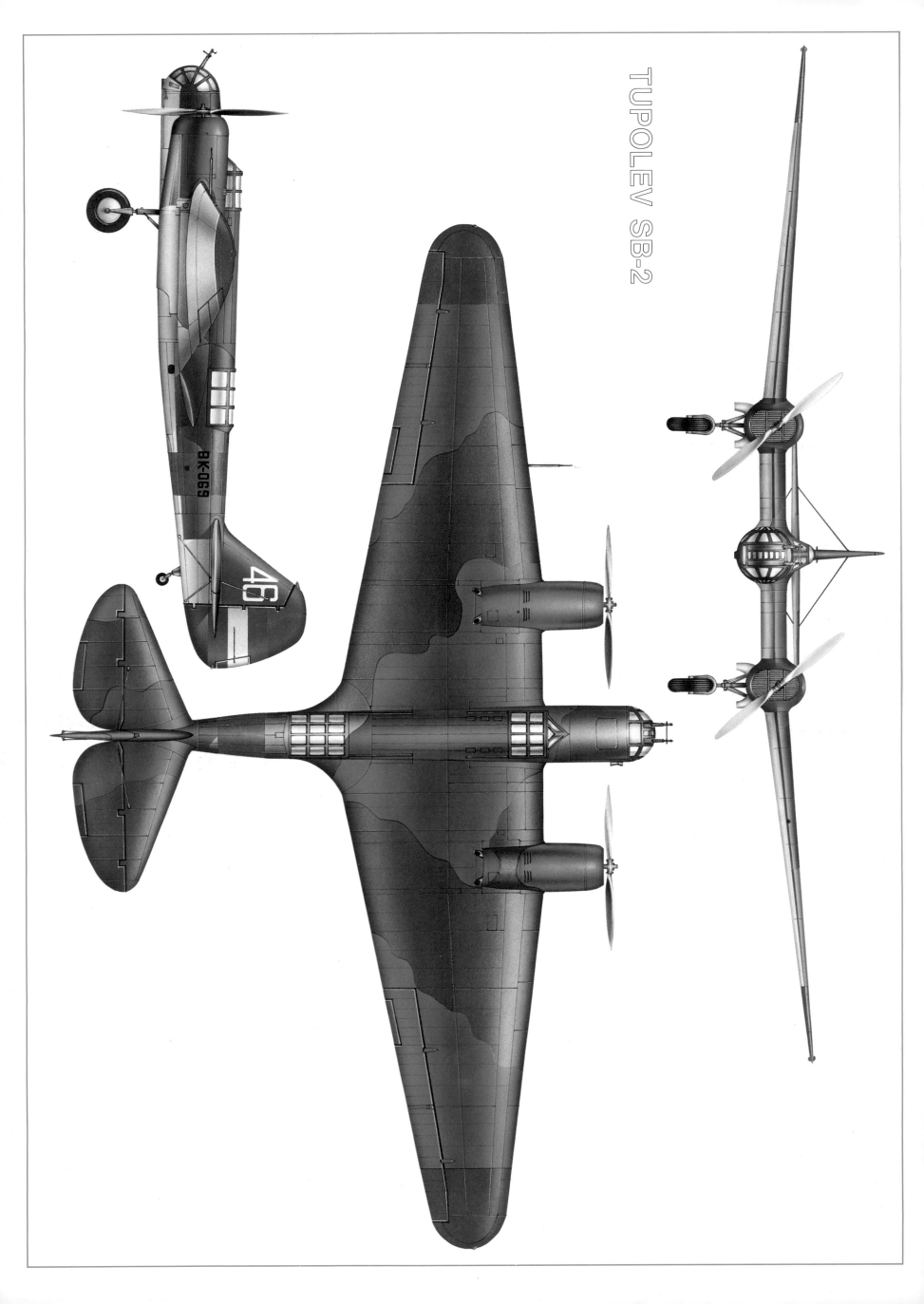

TUPOLEV SB-2

The Tupolev Tu-2 was the second most important medium bomber built in the Soviet Union during World War II. Modern in concept and well armed, it revealed the effectiveness of its design, remaining in service until the 1950s (in the Polish and Chinese air forces, as well as the VVS), and taking part in the Korean War in the North Korean forces. In all, production amounted to 2,527 aircraft in several variants, 1,111 of which were built during World War II.

The first prototype, initially designated Model 103 or ANT-58, was designed by Andrei N. Tupolev during the period of his imprisonment (the great Soviet technician was arrested in 1936 on charges of industrial espionage) and took to the air for the first time on January 29, 1941. The aircraft was then modified, and the new version (designated ANT-59) made its maiden flight on May 18. It was an all-metal mid-wing monoplane, with retractable forward tricycle landing gear and was powered by a pair of AM-37 12-cylinder liquid-cooled engines, generating 1,400 hp each. During tests, the power plants were replaced by more powerful ASh-82 radial engines and, in this configuration, the characteristics of the new bomber proved to be remarkable, especially as far as speed, range, and armament were concerned.

Nevertheless, a long period of time was to pass before production was authorized, due above all to the strong need to simplify the project. Tupolev had to prepare a new prototype (ANT-60), which began tests on December 15, 1941, concluding them on August 22 of the following year. Three preseries aircraft were evaluated in operative conditions in September, and the first aircraft of the final production series, designated ANT-61 or Tu-2S, started to come off the assembly lines in August 1943. Deliveries to the units began between the end of December and the first weeks of the following year. These aircraft had an intensive career and, together with the Petlyakov Pe-2, proved to be the most efficient in their category.

Production went ahead very slowly, due to the problems in which the Soviet factories were floundering, and, during the conflict, the Tu-2S remained the only variant. However, there were several experimental versions, built in small quantities and for specific tasks: they included the Tu-2R of 1944 for photo reconnaissance, and the Tu-2D, a long-range variant.

The development of the bomber continued in the years immediately after the war. Mention should be made of one of the models that were built: the Tu-8 (ANT-69) of 1947, the final long-range bomber variant, with more powerful engines and heavier armament, consisting of five 20 mm cannons.

color plate

Tupolev Tu-2 Soviet Air Force — USSR 1944

Aircraft:	Tupolev Tu-2S
Nation:	USSR
Manufacturer:	State Industries
Type:	Bomber
Year:	1943
Engine:	2 ASh-82 FNV, 14-cylinder radial, air-cooled, 1,850 hp each
Wingspan:	62 ft (18.86 m)
Length:	45 ft 4 in (13.80 m)
Height:	14 ft 11 in (4.55 m)
Weight:	25,077 lb (11,360 kg)
Maximum speed:	341 mph (550 km/h) at 17,763 ft (5,400 m)
Ceiling:	31,250 ft (9,500 m)
Range:	869 miles (1,400 km)
Armament:	2 × 20 mm cannons, 4 machine guns, 8,830 lb (4,000 kg) of bombs
Crew:	4

A postwar experimental Tu-2 with four-bladed propellers, carrying a jeep under the fuselage.

A Tupolev Tu-2 in service with a VVS regiment. It has the definitive tail fairings.

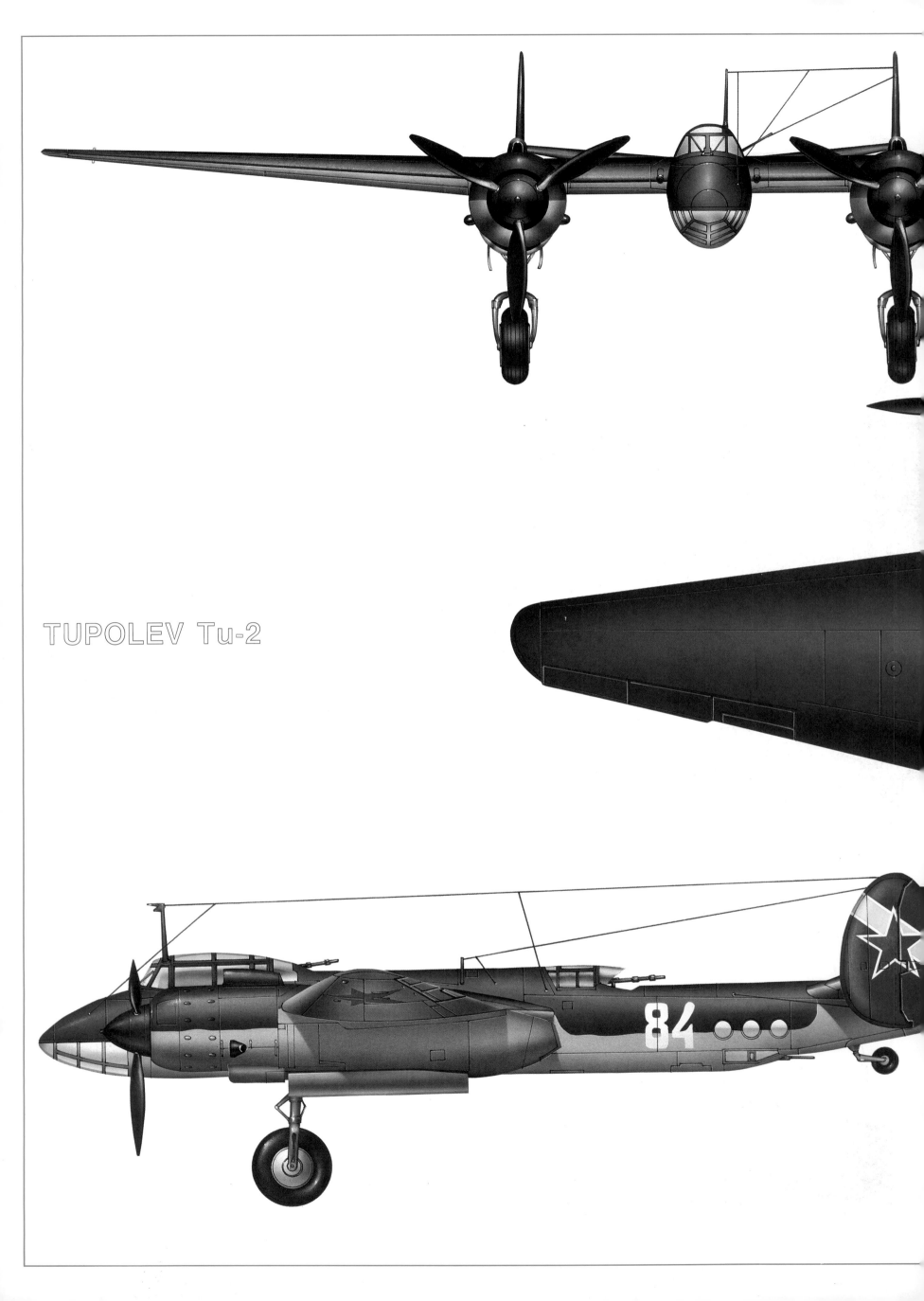

TUPOLEV Tu-2

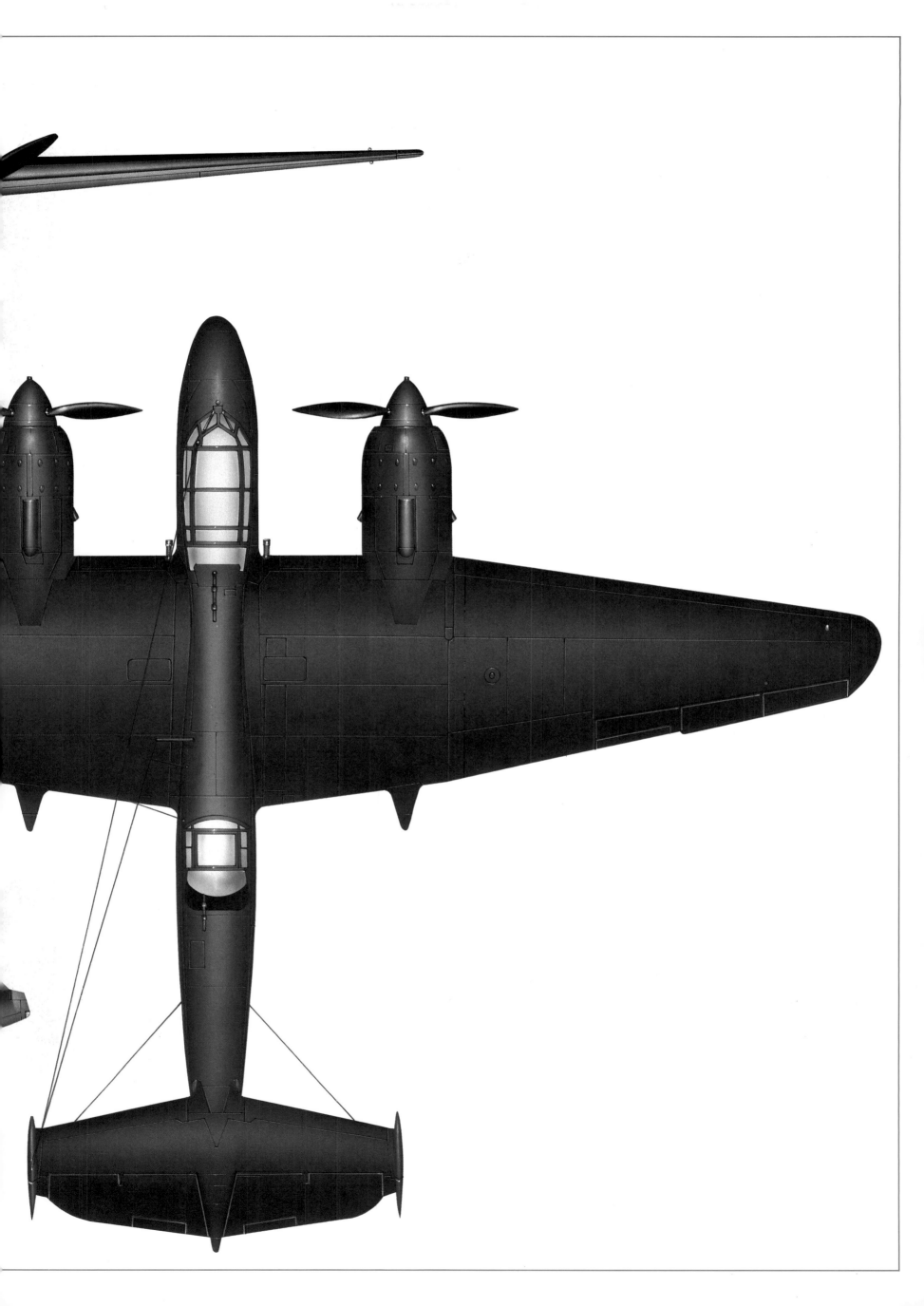

Polikarpov I-16 captured by the Germans during "Operation Barbarossa".

Finnish air force Polikarpov I-16 with the landing gear wheels replaced by skis.

Aircraft: Polikarpov I-16/10	
Nation: USSR	
Manufacturer: State Industries	
Type: Fighter	
Year: 1937	
Engine: M.25B, 9-cylinder radial, air-cooled, 775 hp	
Wingspan: 29 ft 6 in (9 m)	
Length: 19 ft 11 in (6.07 m)	
Height: 8 ft 5 in (2.56 m)	
Weight: 4,519 lb (2,054 kg) loaded	
Maximum speed: 288 mph (464 km/h) at 9,850 ft (3,000 m)	
Ceiling: 29,500 ft (9,000 m)	
Range: 497 miles (800 km)	
Armament: 4 machine guns	
Crew: 1	

A damaged I-16 abandoned by the Russians in retreat.

This was the first monoplane fighter with a cantilever wing and retractable landing gear. It was these characteristics, in particular, as well as the plane's overall performance and its strength and reliability that impressed the entire aeronautical world on December 31, 1933, when the prototype of the Polikarpov I-16 was flown for the first time. Nikolai Polikarpov's project had started at the beginning of 1932, in the context of a scheme aimed at developing a new fighter plane to reequip the divisions of the Soviet air force. The results proved to be beyond even the highest expectations. At a time when the biplane's limits were starting to become apparent, the production of an interceptor with such innovative characteristics carried the Soviet industry decisively to the fore. The success of the small, tough Polikarpov was clearly demonstrated by its production figures: about 20,000 were built in several versions in the course of almost a decade. After its debut in combat in the Spanish Civil War (500 planes were used in action), the I-16 took part in the early stages of World War II and was used in front-line duty until the summer of 1943, when it was replaced by more modern and competitive aircraft to confront those of the Luftwaffe.

The Polikarpov I-16 remained substantially unaltered throughout the long period in which it was produced. The features that characterize and differentiate the several variants built were to be found mainly in the engine unit and the armament. The prototype, powered by a 450 hp Bristol Jupiter radial engine, license built under the M.22 name, and armed with two 7.62 mm Shkas machine guns installed on the fuselage and synchronized to fire through the propeller hub, was followed by other versions, namely the I-16/1, I-16/4, and I-16/5, powered by a 750 hp M.25 engine with turbo-supercharger. The first aircraft were supplied to the Soviet air force in the fall of 1934, and the official debut of the new fighter (which passed virtually unnoticed by western observers) took place in Moscow's Red Square on May Day the following year.

The I-16/6 was the first version to be used operationally in combat, on November 5, 1936, in Spain. During this conflict the Polikarpov was to become better known by the nicknames given to it by the opposing sides: *Rata* (Mouse) by the Nationalists and *Mosca* (Fly) by the Republicans. In 1937, the I-16/10, the second major version to go into production, appeared and was characterized by a 775 hp M.25B engine and with twice the armament of the first. Moreover, in this version the installation of 82 mm air-to-ground rockets was experimented for the first time, dramatically increasing the plane's effectiveness in ground attack. The I-16/10s also were widely used in the Spanish Civil War.

In later versions, both the engine and armament were strengthened. For example, the I-16P series carried two 20 mm cannons in the fuselage, and two light machine guns were added to the I-16/17. In the I-16/18 model, the engine adopted was a 1,000 hp 9-cylinder M.62 with two-stage supercharger and all-metal wing structure and the plane's performance improved remarkably. Apart from the numerous training and experimental versions, those eventually built in the greatest number were the I-16/24 and the I-16/24B. These fighters, in fact, constituted the greater part of the Soviet front-line at the time of the German attack.

The I-16's operational career was not limited solely to Spain and to the Russian front. About 200 were supplied to Nationalist China and were used against the Japanese, especially between 1938 and 1939.

color plate

Polikarpov I-16/10 4ª Escuadrilla (4th Spanish Republican Air Force Squadron) - 1938

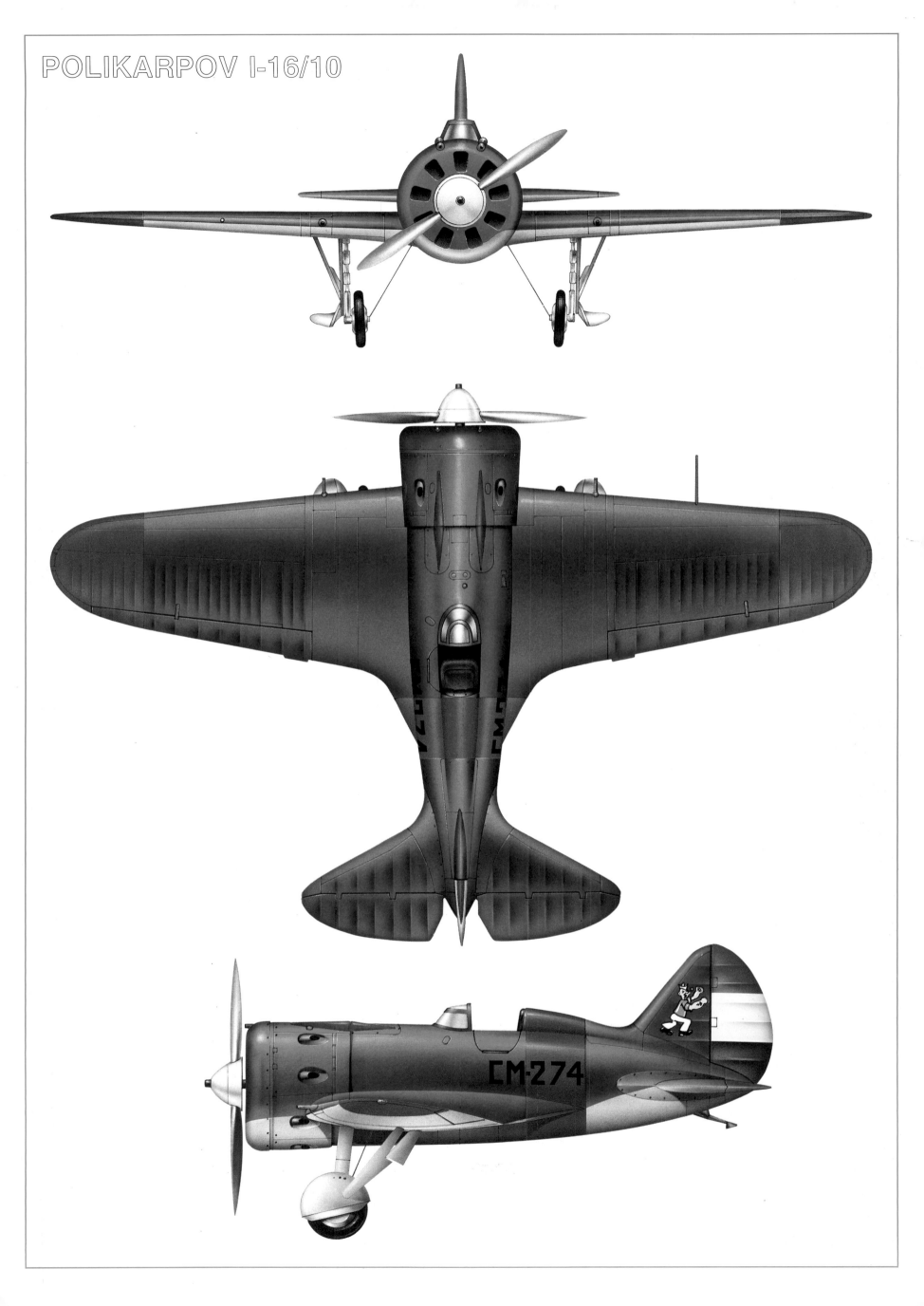

POLIKARPOV I-16/10

The MiG-1 was the first Soviet fighter of World War II and the first to bear the "signature" of Artem Ivanovich Mikoyan and Mikhail Iossipovich Gurevich, two designers who were to become world famous. Even today, despite the death of Mikoyan in 1970, and that of Gurevich in 1976, the designation MiG continues to be used to identify the most advanced Soviet combat aircraft, in remembrance of the partnership between the two great technicians, which originated in 1938, immediately prior to the outbreak of war.

In that year, Mikoyan and Gurevich began their long association with the intention of building a single-seater interceptor developed around the large and powerful Mikulin AM-35, a 12-cylinder V engine capable of generating 1,200 hp at 19,735 ft (6,000 m) and 1,350 hp at takeoff. Two projects were completed, although only work on the second went ahead: designated MiG-1, it was a small, slim low-wing monoplane, with retractable landing gear. Its airframe and covering were composite, wood and metal. In practice, it was the smallest and most compact airframe that could be created around the heavy engine, one of the most powerful in its category in the world at the time.

The prototype, redesignated I-200, was completed in only four months, and it made its maiden flight on April 5, 1940. During initial flight testing the aircraft proved to have an excellent performance as far as speed was concerned, touching 403 mph (648.5 km/h) at 22,640 ft (6,900 m) on May 24. Mass production was launched immediately, although the fighter was not without faults. The principal ones were its lack of maneuverability, its negative characteristics in flight (due to the excessive weight of the wings), its limited range, and a lack of protection and armament.

These problems caused production to be limited to 100 aircraft and led the designers to develop a new version. This was designated MiG-3 and began to reach the units at the beginning of 1941, proving to be greatly superior to the previous aircraft. In particular, its overall aerodynamic characteristics had been improved; larger fuel tanks were installed; in the cockpit the pilot's seat and the canopy were modified; the engine was rendered more powerful, due also to the installation of a new propeller.

In combat the MiG-3 displayed its potential to the full, proving capable of giving the best of its performance at altitudes over 16,450 ft (5,000 m), where it was able to compete on equal terms with the best adversaries. However, at lower altitudes there was a noticeable decrease in the fighter's overall performance and in its maneuverability that placed it in inferior conditions. The aircraft's armament constituted another weak point: the two 7.62 mm machine guns and the single 12.7 mm machine gun and the 440 lb (200 kg) of bombs were clearly not enough; various experiments were attempted to remedy this, but the use of heavier weapons seriously penalized the aircraft's qualities.

However, the MiG-3 always remained a transitional aircraft, while the Soviets were awaiting more modern and effective products (like the Yakovlev and Lavochkin fighters) with which they finally succeeded in gaining overall superiority compared to the Luftwaffe. Production of the MiG-3 was suspended in the spring of 1942, when building of the AM-35A engine ceased after it had made way for the more powerful AM-38, destined for the Ilyushin Il-2. A total of 3,322 were built, in addition to the 100 MiG-1s. However, Mikoyan and Gurevich's fighter remained in front-line service until the final months of 1943, and it was subsequently relegated to secondary roles.

---

color plate

MiG-3 34th IAP (Moscow Hawks) Soviet Air Force - Moscow-Vnukovo 1941

Aircraft:	Mikoyan-Gurevich MiG-3
Nation:	USSR
Manufacturer:	State Industries
Type:	Fighter
Year:	1941
Engine:	Mikulin AM-35A, 12-cylinder V, liquid-cooled, 1,350 hp
Wingspan:	33 ft 9 1/2 in (10.28 m)
Length:	26 ft 9 in (8.15 m)
Height:	11 ft 6 in (3.54 m)
Weight:	7,385 lb (3,356 kg) loaded
Maximum speed:	407 mph (655 km/h) at 22,960 ft (7,000 m)
Ceiling:	39,370 ft (12,000 m)
Range:	510 miles (820 km)
Armament:	3 machine guns; 440 lb (200 kg) of bombs
Crew:	1

MiG-3 in winter camouflage with red wings.

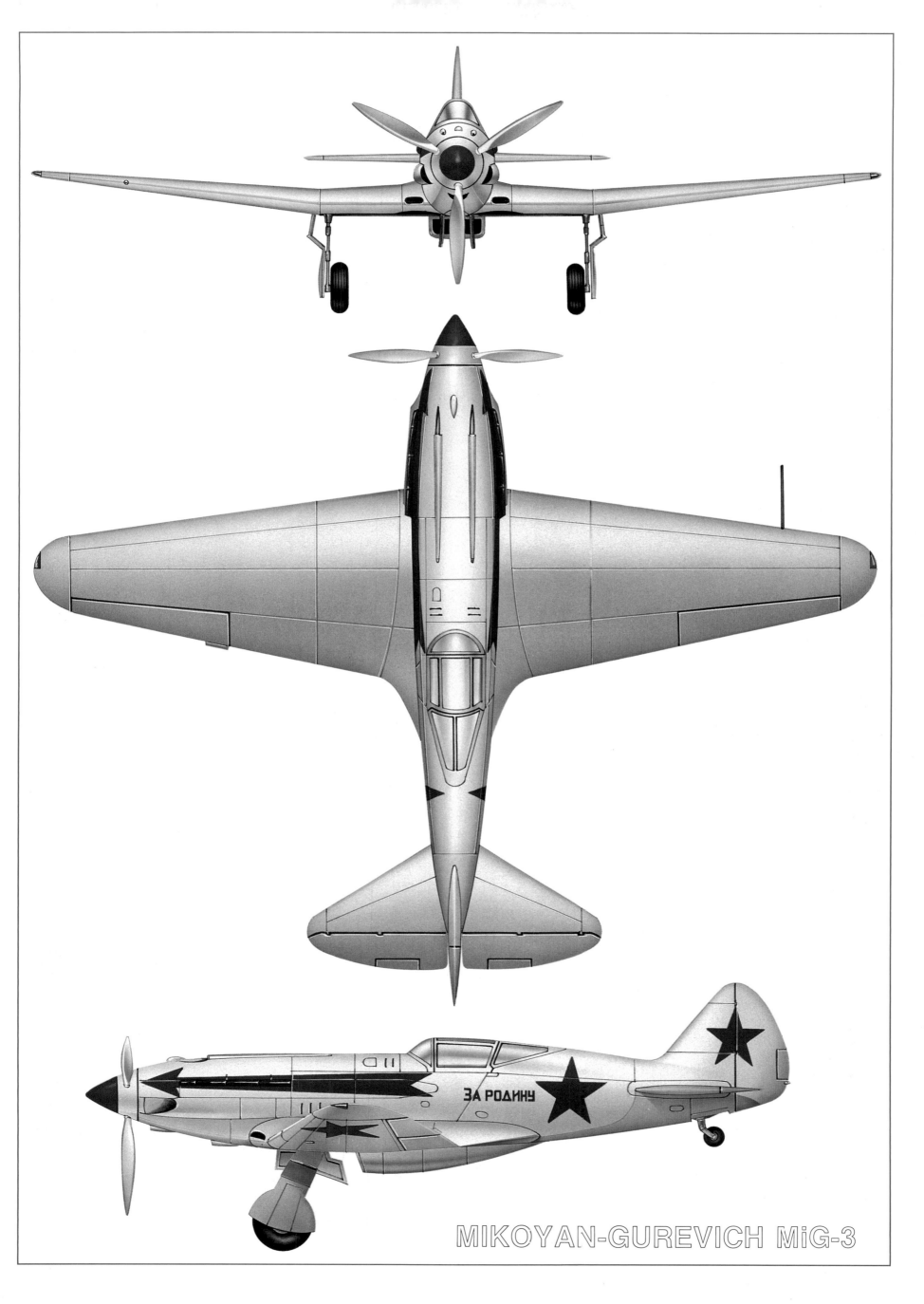

MIKOYAN-GUREVICH MiG-3

ЗА РОДИНУ

The Ilyushin Il-4 was perhaps the best medium bomber of the war, and was undoubtedly the most widely used: 5,256 were built between 1939 and 1944. The operative career of this sturdy and versatile two-engine aircraft continued uninterruptedly for the entire duration of the conflict, and many of the aircraft even remained in service in the years that followed (albeit in secondary roles), earning the designation "Bob" in the NATO code.

The basic project originated in 1935, the year in which the prototype of a long-range bomber appeared, designated TsKB-26 and designed by Sergei Vladimorovic Ilyushin and his team. From this aircraft, which went into production with the prefix DB-3 and of which 1,528 were built from 1937 to 1940, a substantially modified version was derived in 1938. While maintaining the basic structure of its predecessor, this aircraft (initially designated DB-3F and then Il-4) had undergone substantial improvements of a structural and aerodynamic nature, deriving from the complete redesigning of the front part of the fuselage. In their entirety, these modifications had improved the already excellent performance of the DB-3, especially as far as range and ceiling were concerned (in 1936, the prototype of this aircraft broke two world altitude records and in 1939 carried out a 4,968 mile — 8,000 km — crossing from Moscow to Canada; although this ended in a forced landing, it aroused the interest of the entire aeronautical world at the time). Following a series of flight tests and operative evaluations, the new two-engine aircraft immediately went into mass production. The Ilyushin Il-4 was an elegant, all-metal, low-wing monoplane powered by a pair of M.87A radial engines generating 950 hp each, well armed, and provided with excellent flying characteristics. The first were delivered to the units in 1940.

The events of the war led to an abrupt halt in the mass-production program ordered by the Soviet authorities. The German attack forced the evacuation of the factories that built the M.87A engines and caused serious shortages of aluminum and other strategic materials that were indispensable to the aeronautical industry. Because of this lack of supplies, the assembly lines of the Il-4 came to a virtual halt at the very time that the Soviet air force most needed modern and competitive aircraft. This standstill lasted for almost a year, the time necessary for the technicians to complete a frenetic revision of the project with the aim of substituting with wood, as far as possible, the structural components of the aircraft originally built of metal. After modifications to parts of the fuselage (such as the tail fairings and the floor of the cockpit), even the wing was redesigned, with wooden spars and external panels being adopted. These solutions were incorporated into many of the Il-4s built in 1942, although the final production series marked a return to the original structure. As for the engines, the problem was solved by the availability of the new

An Ilyushin Il-4 bomber in flight.

M.88B radial engine, provided with two-speed supercharger and capable of generating 1,100 hp, and it was chosen as standard equipment.

Apart from being used mainly as a long-range bomber, the Il-4 was also used for tactical duties, in which it was preferred to fully exploit the aircraft's bomb load capacity (maximum 5,520 lb, or 2,500 kg), to the detriment of its range. Soviet naval aviation also adopted the two-engine aircraft without substantial changes and widely used it for mine-laying and torpedo launching in units operating in the Baltic, the Black Sea and the North Sea. The naval version of the Il-4 was capable of carrying a 2,070 lb (940 kg) torpedo installed externally under the fuselage.

color plate
Ilyushin Il-4 Soviet Air Force - USSR 1943

Aircraft:	Ilyushin Il-4
Nation:	USSR
Manufacturer:	State Industries
Type:	Bomber
Year:	1940
Engine:	2 M.88B, 14-cylinder radial, air-cooled, 1,100 hp each
Wingspan:	70 ft 4 in (21.44 m)
Length:	48 ft 7 in (14.82 m)
Height:	13 ft 9 in (4.20 m)
Weight:	22,046 lb (10,000 kg) loaded
Maximum speed:	225 mph (410 km/h) at 21,000 ft (6,400 m)
Ceiling:	32,800 ft (10,000 m)
Range:	2,647 miles (4,260 km)
Armament:	3 machine guns; 5,512 lb (2,500 kg) of bombs
Crew:	3/4

Soviet navy air force Il-4 with auxiliary fuel tank and support for torpedo.

ILYUSHIN Il-4

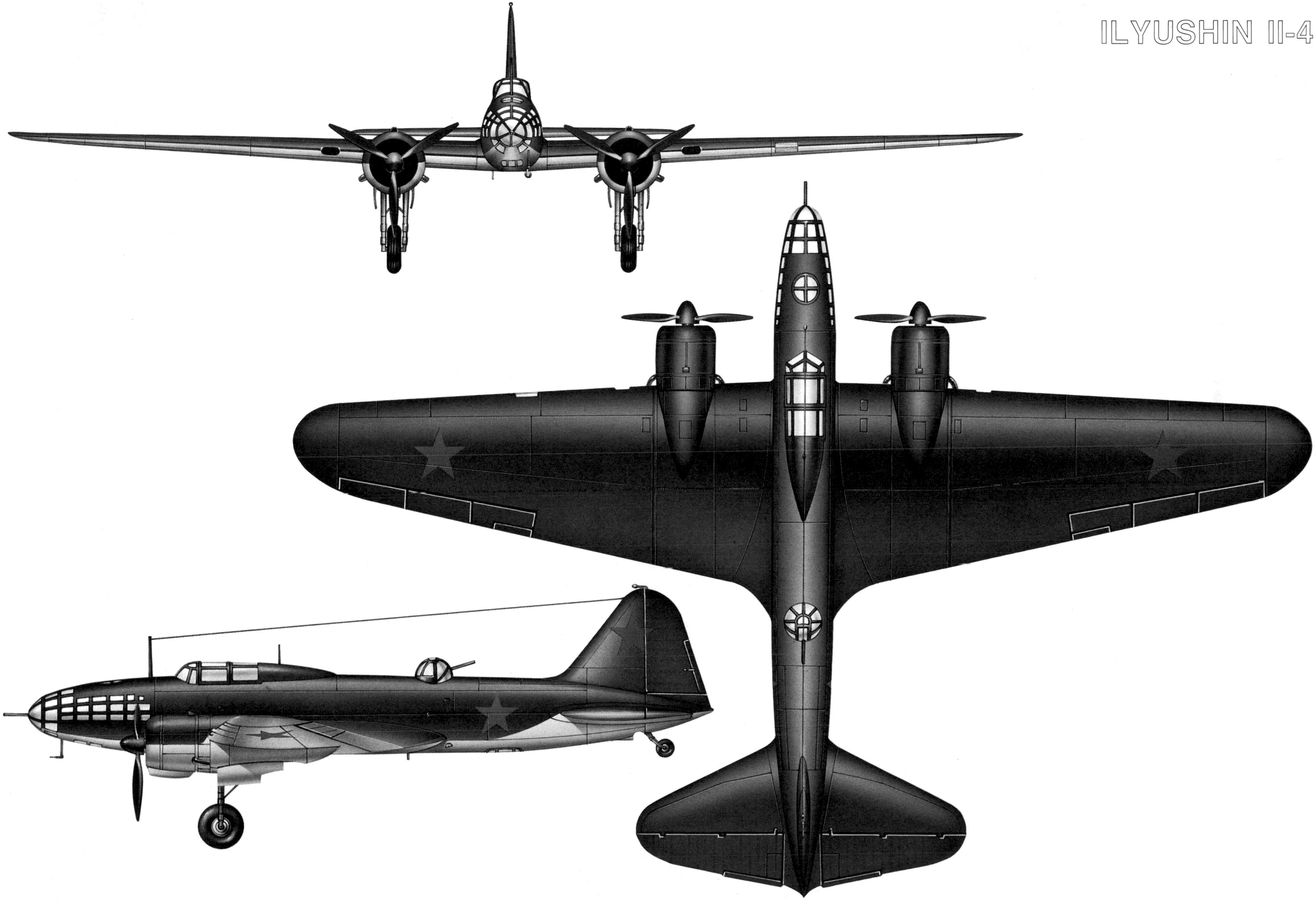

One of the most effective families of combat planes built in the Soviet Union during World War II was that which gave rise to the Ilyushin Sturmoviks. Starting with the initial Il-2 model of 1940, until the final Il-10 variant of 1944, these strong and capable single-engine ground attack planes proved to be a formidable weapon in the hands of the Soviet pilots. Their role in the conflict can be summed up by a phrase in which Stalin commented on the first production series aircraft in 1941: ''The Sturmovik is as essential to the Red Army as oxygen and bread''. In all, more than 35,000 (a record number for the production of combat planes) came off the assembly lines and the construction of the final variants continued until 1955. In fact, after the war, the Il-10 was delivered to the air forces of the satellite countries (Hungary, Rumania, North Korea, Albania, Czechoslovakia, Bulgaria and East Germany), Red China, and after serving in the Korean War, it was withdrawn from the Soviet VVS in 1956.

The origins of the Sturmovik (the Ilyushin fighters were known by this nick-name rather than by their official designations) went back to 1938, when a work team, led by Sergei Vladimorovic Ilyushin, prepared a prototype of a new single-engine ground attack plane and tactical bomber, developed on the basis of official specifications issued by the VVS technical authorities. The aircraft (designated ZKB-55 and characterized by its two-seater structure) appeared in the spring of 1939, and was evaluated immediately. However, the results of the flight tests and initial evaluations were not particularly promising, due above all to the engine's insufficient power and a marked longitudinal instability. It was not until the third prototype, which took to the air on October 12, 1940, that these problems were solved, with the adoption of a more powerful engine, various structural modifications, and the elimination of the observer-gunner position. Officially designated Il-2, the aircraft went into series production immediately, and deliveries to the units commenced at the beginning of April 1941. By the end of June, the VVS had received 249 aircraft which, from their first missions, proved to be formidable weapons against German armored cars and tanks.

The project originality basically lay in having built the aircraft's entire front section (from the engine support to the cockpit) in a single armored shell, which also served a structural function. As well as guaranteeing a maximum protection to the engines and the crew, this solution also allowed for a great weight reduction, compared to a traditional structure that was later fitted with ar-

mor. In addition, the entire fuselage was protected with 4 to 13 mm thick steel plating and 5 mm thick duraluminum. This turned the Il-2 into a veritable ''flying tank'', making it practically invulnerable to light weapons. This armor was complemented by heavy offensive weaponry which included two 20 mm cannons and up to 1,324 lb (600 kg) of bombs.

In July 1942, the second principal version, the better armed Il-2M3 (also fitted with a more powerful engine, and a second crew member) appeared. This version was produced in the largest quantity. In 1943, efforts to improve the aircraft still further led to the final Il-10 version. Although it retained the basic lay-out of its predecessor, from many points of view, this aircraft represented an entirely new project. It was characterized by an all-metal airframe, remarkable aerodynamic improvements and modifications to the power plant and principal landing gear. The 2,000 hp Mikulin AM-42 engine was adopted; the thickness and extension of its armoring was increase; and its armament received 20 mm and 23 mm cannons. Series production was launched in August 1944, and ceased more than ten years later, after almost 5,000 aircraft had been completed.

color plate
Ilyushin Il-2M3 Soviet Air Force - Oder front, 1945

Aircraft:	Ilyushin Il-10
Nation:	USSR
Manufacturer:	State Industries
Type:	Attack
Year:	1944
Engine:	Mikulin AM-42, 12-cylinder V, liquid-cooled, 2,000 hp
Wingspan:	44 ft 0 in (13.40 m)
Length:	36 ft 4 in (11.06 m)
Height:	11 ft 6 in (3.50 m)
Weight:	13,984 lb (6,335 kg)
Maximum speed:	329 mph (530 km/h) at 7,058 ft (2,400 m)
Ceiling:	13,157 ft (4,000 m)
Range:	496 miles (800 km)
Armament:	2 x 23 mm cannons; 1 x 20 mm cannons; 2 machine guns; 2,207 lb (1,000 kg) of bombs
Crew:	2

A formation of Il-2 assault plane in flight.

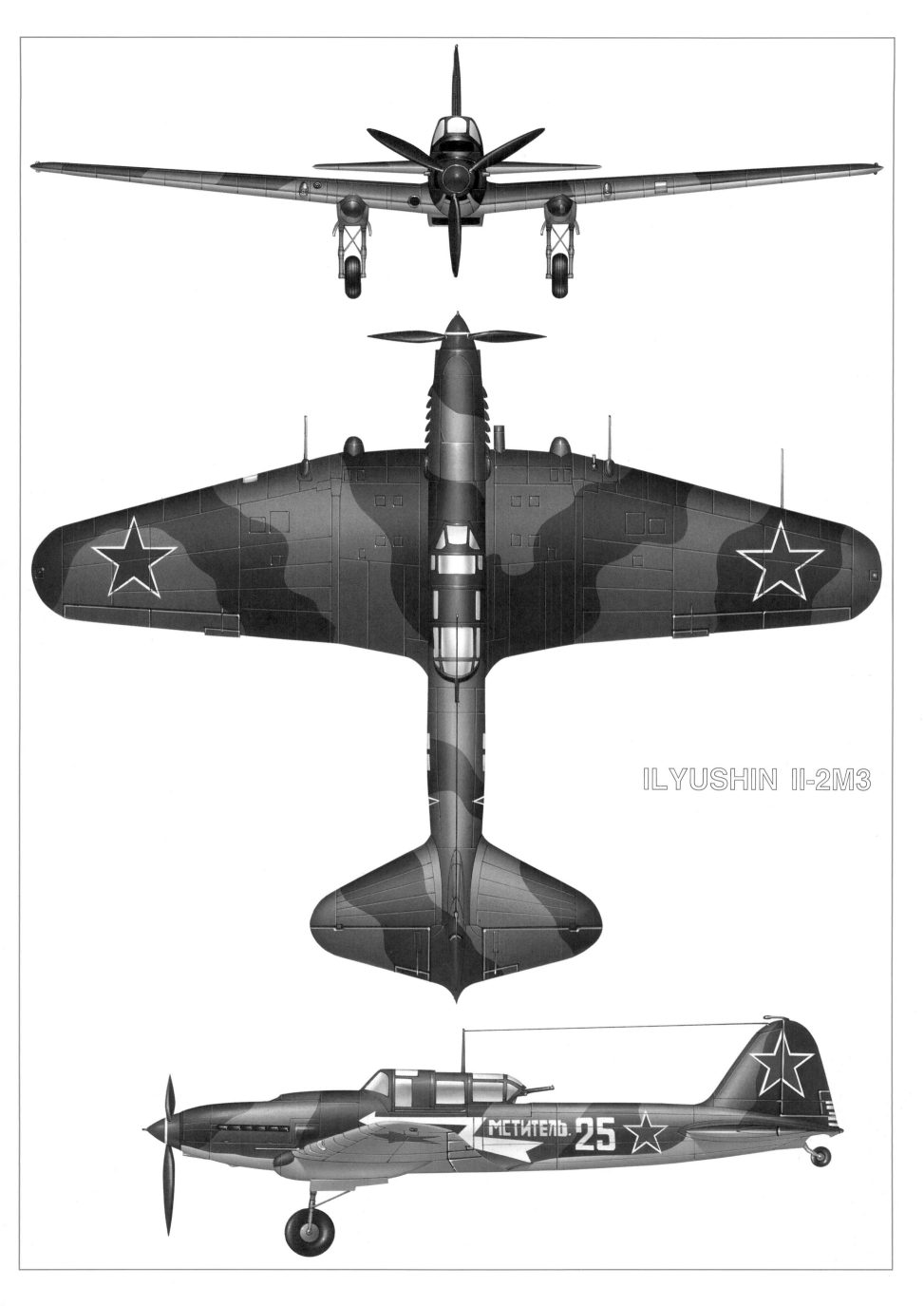

ILYUSHIN Il-2M3

МСТИТЕЛЬ. 25

Pavel Osipovich Sukhoi, still famous today for some of the most modern combat aircraft in service in the Soviet air force, began his career as a designer in 1924, as part of a team headed by Tupolev. Twelve years later, in 1936, he set to work on the study of a low-wing single-engine bomber-reconnaissance plane with retractable landing gear. This aircraft was designated ANT-51, and its prototype took to the air on August 25, 1937, but it did not prove reliable enough to go into production. Sukhoi stuck to his chosen formula and a year later, when he was made responsible for an independent team, he continued to develop the project and built a series of prototypes from which the Su-2 model of 1940 derived. This was an attack aircraft, and although it was clearly transitional it bore the brunt of much of the fighting during the early phases of the war until the reorganization of the Soviet aeronautical industry led to the creation of its more illustrious successor, the Ilyushin Il-2.

The Sukhoi Su-2 (originally designated BB-1, the letters indicating the role of medium-range bomber) was an all-metal low-wing monoplane of remarkable size, with retractable landing gear and a two-man crew housed in a long, completely glazed cockpit that had a turret to its rear. Originally the aircraft was powered by a 950 hp Shvetsov M-88 radial engine, while its defensive armament consisted of four 7.62 mm ShKas machine guns installed in the wings and a fifth machine gun mounted in the turret on the back for the observer-bombardier. The weight of the bomb load reached 1,325 lb (600 kg) and, if necessary, it could be carried entirely inside the fuselage.

In service from 1940, the Sukhoi nevertheless proved to have a series of faults and limitations, many of which were similar to those of aircraft in the same category produced by other nations. These included a lack of maneuverability, a rather disappointing overall performance, and inadequate defensive armament. Consequently, efforts were made to improve the aircraft during the entire period of production, which according to reliable estimates, exceeded 2,000 planes. The engine, in particular, was subject to the most radical changes: a 1,000 hp M-88B engine was used initially, then, in the final series, the choice fell on the more powerful 1,400 hp M-82. On the one hand, the increase in power improved the aircraft's performance, especially its maximum speed, but on the other, its overall flying characteristics were penalized.

Further modifications were carried out on the armament: some aircraft were provided with a second machine gun in the turret, while others had a weapon installed in a retractable housing in the belly. However, in the end, a compromise was reached by reducing the machine guns on the wings to two, and the bomb load to 880 lb (400 kg).

Even after the appearance of the more effective Ilyushin Il-2, Sukhoi proceeded with the development of his aircraft. At the end of 1941 he built a variant (designated Su-4) in which he installed the experimental Shvetsov M-90 engine generating no fewer than 2,100 hp. The aircraft was tested in December 1941, but it never went into production. A similar fate awaited the more effective and powerful Su-6 which was never produced in any great number, despite being superior in some ways to its Ilyushin rival. The fate of this aircraft, whose development had begun in 1939, was influenced by the length of time needed to tune the engine (a 2,000 hp Shvetsov M-71 18-cylinder radial); the developmental phase continued, amidst great difficulties, until December 1940. The development of the project proceeded with the Su-6-II model of 1942, built with the idea of developing it simultaneously with the Ilyushin Il-2, and the Su-6-III, powered by a 2,000 hp AM-42 liquid-cooled engine, which began flight testing early in 1944.

Once again, neither of these two aircraft reached the mass production stage.

---

color plate
Sukhoi Su-2 Soviet Air Force - USSR 1942

Aircraft:	Sukhoi Su-2
Nation:	USSR
Manufacturer:	State Industries
Type:	Bomber
Year:	1940
Engine:	Shvetsov M-82, 14-cylinder radial, air-cooled, 1,400 hp
Wingspan:	46 ft 11 in (14.30 m)
Length:	34 ft 4 in (10.46 m)
Height:	12 ft 3 in (3.75 m)
Takeoff weight:	10,362 lb (4,700 kg) loaded
Maximum speed:	302 mph (485 km/h) at 19,190 ft (5,850 m)
Ceiling:	29,605 ft (9,000 m)
Range:	683 miles (1,100 km)
Armament:	5 machine guns; 1,325 lb (600 kg) of bombs
Crew:	2

An early model of the Sukhoi Su-2.

SUKHOI Su-2

The Petlyakov Pe-2 was one of the most versatile combat planes to go into service with the Soviet air force in the course of World War II. Designed in 1938, this slim two-engine aircraft was not taken out of production until early in 1945, after the assembly lines had completed no fewer than 11,427. Its operative career was no less intense and continued for virtually the entire war in a great variety of roles: as well as being a standard tactical bomber (together with the equally effective Ilyushin II-2), the Pe-2 also served brilliantly as a heavy fighter, reconnaissance plane, and night fighter. It succeeded in carrying out these roles successfully thanks to a continuous series of modernizations and strengthening of the basic airframe. Moreover, in the years immediately following the war, some of the final series were also sent to Czechoslovakia, Yugoslavia, and Poland.

The Pe-2 originated in 1938, when Vladimir Mikhailovic Petlyakov (a technician who had gained great experience working on projects by Andrei N. Tupolev) was charged with developing a high-altitude heavy fighter. The prototype (initially designated VI-100) was a low-wing two-engine monoplane, with double tail fins and retractable landing gear. It was powered by a pair of Klimov M.105 engines with superchargers, generating 1,050 hp each. A pressurized cockpit was planned, but the initial series of flight tests (the aircraft made its maiden flight between the end of 1939 and the beginning of 1940) went ahead without this being installed. Despite several faults, flight tests revealed the new aircraft to have excellent overall qualities, and in May 1940 it was decided to transform the prototype into a dive-bomber, with the new designation PB-100. The modifications (overall structural restrengthening, redimensioning of the wing, the abolition of the pressurized cockpit, and the adoption of aerodynamic brakes in the lower part of the half-wings) were carried out on the second prototype, which took to the air in June. On the twenty-third of the same month it was decided to put the new aircraft into mass production with the official designation of Petlyakov Pe-2.

The first aircraft of the initial series took to the air on November 18, 1940, and the bomber became operative in the spring of the following year. The dive-bomber version was merely the first of many other variants that were built in the course of production. Of these, mention should be made of the following: the Pe-2M (which took to the air in October 1941), fitted with more powerful engines and capable of carrying four 1,103 lb (500 kg) bombs internally; the Pe-3, a version adapted for use as an interceptor, night fighter, and reconnaissance plane, characterized by heavier offensive armament, which was increased from the four or five initial machine guns to include eventually two 20 mm cannons, three 12.7 mm and two 7.92 mm weapons; the Pe-2FT, the standard version from 1942 onward, lacking the bomb hold and diving brakes and armed with two cannons, two heavy machine guns, and two light ones. The final bomber versions were the Pe-2B and

A Petlyakov Pe-2 of the initial production series identifiable by the antenna situated well to the rear.

the Pe-2M, both dating to 1944: as well as numerous structural and aerodynamic improvements, the former was characterized by armament consisting of four machine guns and by UK-105PF engines generating 1,260 hp each, while the latter was characterized by armament consisting of three 20 mm cannons, a 4,415 lb (2,000 kg) bomb load, and UK-107A engines capable of generating 1,650 hp each.

Paradoxically, this successful aircraft was not very generous to its designer. Petlyakov, who had been released from prison where he had been held since 1937 in order to create the aircraft, lost his life on January 12, 1942, while on board the second production series aircraft of the Pe-2. This aircraft, used as a transport plane by his department, caught fire in flight and crashed to the ground, where it was completely destroyed.

color plate
Petlyakov Pe-2 Soviet Air Force - USSR 1943

Aircraft:	Petlyakov Pe-2
Nation:	USSR
Manufacturer:	State Industries
Type:	Bomber
Year:	1941
Engine:	2 Klimov M.105R, 12-cylinder V, liquid-cooled, 1,100 hp each
Wingspan:	56 ft 5 in (17.16 m)
Length:	42 ft 2 in (12.78 m)
Height:	11 ft 3 in (3.42 m)
Weight:	16,635 lb (7,536 kg)
Maximum speed:	335 mph (540 km/h) at 16,447 ft (5,000 m)
Ceiling:	28,947 ft (8,800 m)
Range:	816 miles (1,315 km)
Armament:	4-5 machine guns; 2,205 lb (1,000 kg) of bombs
Crew:	3

A formation of Petlyakov Pe-2 bombers taxiing on a snow-covered airport runway.

PETLYAKOV Pe-2

PETLYAKOV Pe-8

The Petlyakov Pe-8 used by Soviet foreign minister Molotov photographed during a refueling stop in Scotland while on a flight to Washington in May 1942.

The Petlyakov Pe-8 was the only four-engine bomber put into service by the Soviet Union during World War II. Nevertheless, this large aircraft was never a particularly effective combat plane, and throughout the entire period of its production it was plagued by difficulties in engine-tuning. From 1939 until October 1941, only 79 aircraft came off the assembly lines: the Pe-8 went into service in May 1940 and remained there for almost the entire duration of the war, although it was gradually relegated to secondary roles. Apart from the numerous raids carried out on German territory, and on Berlin in particular, the Petlyakov bomber should be remembered especially for some of the remarkably long flights that it made, both during the war and after. These included a journey from Moscow to Washington and back on a diplomatic mission, with stops in Scotland, Iceland, and Canada on a flight totaling some 11,000 miles (17,700 km) that took place between May 19 and June 13, 1942.

The project was launched in 1934 by a team headed by Andrei Nicolaevich Tupolev that also included Vladimir Mikhailovich Petlyakov, in response to precise specifications requesting a modern four-engine strategic bomber, capable of reaching its maximum speed at an altitude of 26,315 ft (8,000 m). Originally designated ANT-42, the prototype took to the air for the first time on December 27, 1936. The solution chosen to guarantee supercharging to the four 1,100 hp Mikulin M-100 engines was unusual: by means of a supercharger installed in the fuselage that also drove a fifth M-100 engine. This arrangement was tested in 1937 and improved in the second prototype, which took to the air on July 26 the following year. This solution proved capable of guaranteeing the requested performance at high altitudes: the bomber's maximum speed was superior even to that of the German Messerschmitt Bf.109B and Heinkel He.112 fighters. The Pe-8 (it assumed this designation in 1941) was an all-metal aircraft, provided with a crew of 11 men and defensive armament consisting of four machine guns and two 20 mm cannons installed in turrets and in two positions in the rear part of the internal engine nacelles. As for its bomb load, it could carry a maximum of 8,830 lb (4,000 kg).

In 1939, the building of five preseries aircraft was authorized definitively and, in these aircraft, a radical change in the power plants (supercharged Mikulin AM-35As, generating 1,350 hp each)

rendered the complicated "centralized" supercharge system totally unnecessary. Deliveries to the units commenced in May 1940, but on the whole the aircraft's performance was disappointing. Thus a long search for more efficient engines began: first four ACh-30B diesel engines generating 1,500 hp each were installed, but they did not prove to be very reliable; then after production of the AM-35A engines ceased, M-82 and M-82FN Shvetsov radial engines were chosen (the latter were capable of generating no fewer than 1,700 hp), and they were fitted onto approximately fifty production series aircraft.

The final series also incorporated several aerodynamic improvements, devised by Iosif Formich Nyezval, who had succeeded Petlyakov, following his death in an aircraft accident in 1942. However, the Pe-8 never achieved an optimum configuration, due to a lack of interest on the part of the Soviet military authorities, who were more than satisfied with the performance of the two-engine Ilyushin Il-4. Nevertheless, approximately 30 Pe-8s survived the war and remained in service until the late 1950s.

color plate

Petlyakov Pe-8 Soviet Air Force - USSR. Personal aircraft of the foreign minister Molotov

Aircraft:	Petlyakov Pe-8
Nation:	USSR
Manufacturer:	State Industries
Type:	Bomber
Year:	1940
Engine:	4 Mikulin AM-35A, 12-cylinder V, liquid-cooled, 1,350 hp each
Wingspan:	128 ft 3 1/3 in (39.10 m)
Length:	77 ft 4 3/4 in (23.59 m)
Height:	20 ft 4 in (6.20 m)
Takeoff weight:	69,268 lb (31,420 kg)
Maximum speed:	265 mph (427 km/h) at 20,920 ft (6,360 m)
Ceiling:	27,560 ft (8,400 m)
Range:	2,920 miles (4,700 km)
Armament:	2 × 20 mm cannons; 4 machine guns; 8,830 lb (4,000 kg) of bombs
Crew:	11

The generation of combat aircraft built in the Soviet Union during the war witnessed the debut of designers who were to become world famous over the next few years. Following Mikoyan and Gurevich, another extremely talented technician was Semyon Alexseyevich Lavochkin, whose initials characterized a family of fighters that survived until the 1950s, ranging from the LaGG-1 of 1940, to the La-11 of 1947, the last aircraft powered by a piston engine to serve in the Soviet air force.

Lavochkin executed his first project together with another two talented technicians, Vladimir Petrovich Gorbunov and Mikhail Ivanovich Gudkov, with whom he had worked since 1938. This was a single-seater fighter, initially designated I-22 and then LaGG-1; the prototype made its maiden flight on March 30, 1940. The aircraft was a low-wing monoplane, carefully studied from an aerodynamic point of view and fitted with completely retractable landing gear. A predominant feature that made it unique among its kind, was its being built entirely in wood, with the exception of the moving parts, which were metal, and the fabric covering: the fuselage, empennage, and wings had a supporting structure in wood onto which a covering of diagonal strips of plywood was stuck using special resins. Its engine was a large Klimov M-105 liquid-cooled V-12 that generated 1,050 hp at takeoff.

However, flight tests proved to be unsatisfactory. Consequently, before production got under way, numerous modifications were carried out. These included the adoption of a more powerful and supercharged version of the M-105 engine and of a three-bladed variable-pitch metal propeller, increased fuel tank capacity, and the installation of slats on the leading edge of the wings. The prototype was redesignated I-301 and, once tests had been com-

A snow-covered Soviet Air Force LaGG-3.

color plate

Lavochkin LaGG-3 Soviet Air Force - USSR 1942

Aircraft:	Lavochkin LaGG-3
Nation:	USSR
Manufacturer:	State Industries
Type:	Fighter
Year:	1941
Engine:	Klimov M-105 P, 12-cylinder V, liquid-cooled, 1,050 hp
Wingspan:	32 ft 2 in (9.80 m)
Length:	29 ft 1 in (8.86 m)
Height:	8 ft 10 in (2.69 m)
Weight:	7,032 lb (3,190 kg)
Maximum speed:	348 mph (560 km/h) at 16,400 ft (5,000 m)
Ceiling:	31,500 ft (9,690 m)
Range:	404 miles (650 km)
Armament:	1 × 20 mm cannon; 2 machine guns; 440 lb (200 kg) of bombs
Crew:	1

Above, a captured LaGG-3 employed by the Finnish Air Force; below, German ground crewmen repair a captured LaGG-3.

pleted, the fighter went into production with the official designation LaGG-3. However, its initial operative service (from 1941) brought to light some negative flight characteristics, for example, a tendency to go into a spin following particularly tight turns, making further research and testing necessary.

Once in service with the units, the LaGG-3 was widely used in the early phases of the war against the Germans, especially on the Finnish front, and its performance proved to be satisfactory. However, the aircraft never possessed the characteristics of an interceptor that had been planned in the original project. Nevertheless, it was used with success in bomber escort duty, ground attack, and target attack against the least dangerous of the formidable German fighters, such as reconnaissance planes and bombers. Moreover, the LaGG-3 proved to be extremely versatile and reliable. Its typical armament included a 20 mm cannon that fired through the propeller hub and two 12.7 mm machine guns, while under the wings supports were planned for light bombs or rockets. Up to August 1942, a total of 6,528 LaGG-3s came off the assembly lines, a remarkable number considering the unexceptional performance of the aircraft.

In the course of production numerous other experimental prototypes were completed, built with the aim of improving the aircraft's characteristics. Lavochkin, in particular, dedicated himself to the task of perfecting it. Following a series of failed attempts, success was achieved when a radically new engine became available. This was the Shvetsov M.82 radial engine and, once it had been fitted on the LaGG-3, it transformed it into a first-class aircraft: the LaGG-5 of 1942, one of the best Soviet fighters of the entire war.

LAVOCHKIN LaGG-3

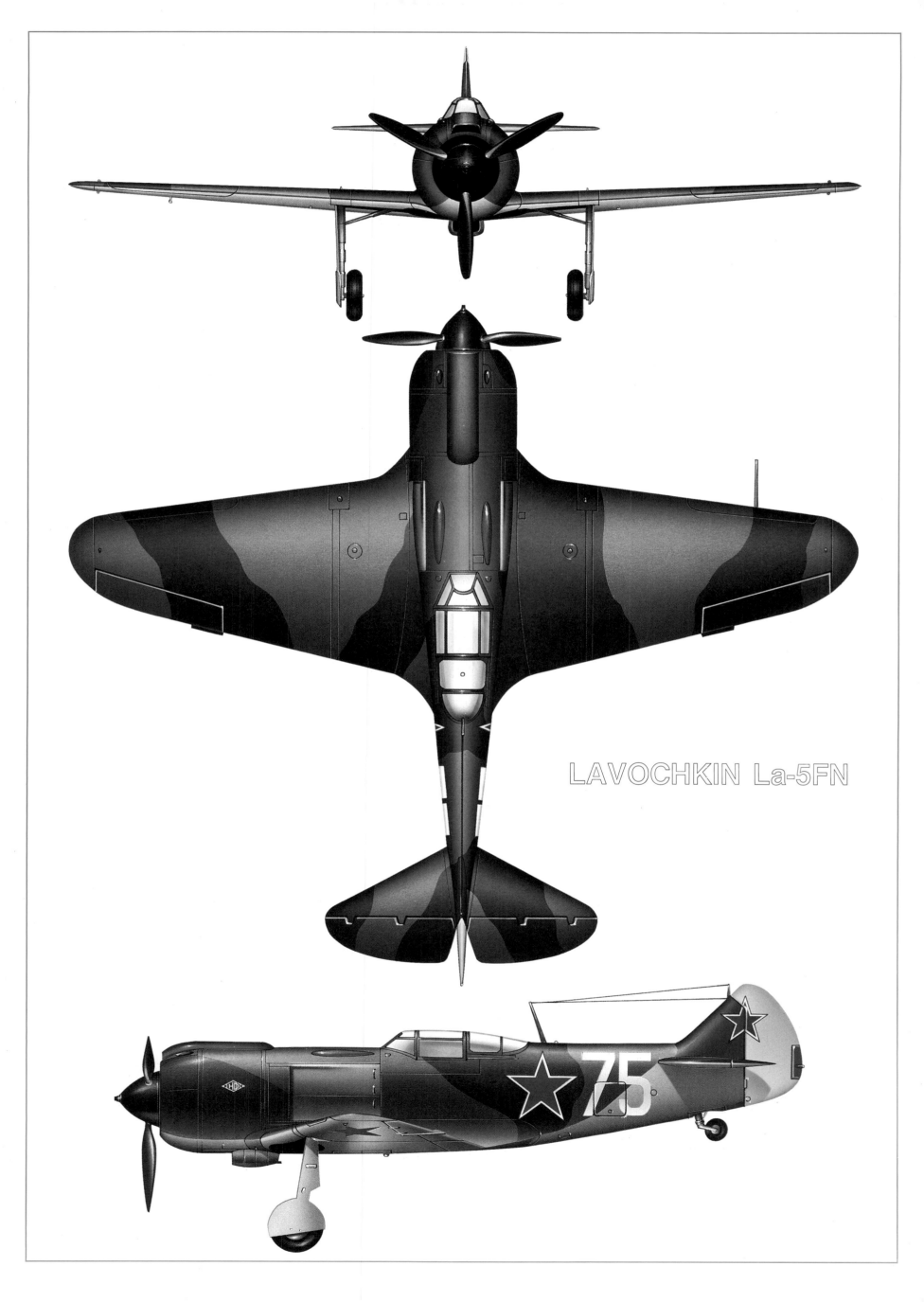

LAVOCHKIN La-5FN

The prolific family of combat planes built in the Soviet Union by Semyon Alexseyevich Lavochkin (its first notable exponents were the LaGG-1 and the LaGG-3) was enriched toward the end of 1941, by a new version, in which the Russian technician succeeded in expressing the full potential of his initial project. The factor which gave a new life to the mediocre LaGG-3 was the installation of a radically new engine, the 1,600 hp Shvetsov M.82 radial. When this engine was installed in place of the liquid-cooled Klimov M.105P, it transformed the aircraft into a first-class machine: the La-5, as it was designated, became one of the best Soviet fighters of the entire conflict.

Right from the first tests, which began toward the end of March 1942, it became clear that the new variant was a marked improvement over the basic model: the more powerful engine and lighter weight (obtained by eliminating the cooling systems) compensated for the increase in the front section (and the consequently greater aerodynamic resistance) due to the space occupied by the large double radial engine. The new variant also allowed for a remarkable increase in performance which, in horizontal speed alone, improved by almost 25 mph (40 km/h). The new power plant was installed in the LaGG-3 in May 1942. This modification gave rise to a transitional aircraft, designated LaGG-5, which was replaced a few weeks later by the definitive La-5 model. In this aircraft, the fuselage rear trunk was lowered in order to allow for the installation of a canopy providing 360° visibility.

The new fighters were sent immediately to the units, and production continued at a fast rate. By the time of the Battle of Stalingrad, the La-5 was being used on the whole front. Nevertheless, the aircraft still had to be perfected. Its performance could not be compared with that of its principal German rival, the Messerschmitt Bf.109 G. Consequently, Lavochkin carried out a series of studies to improve the aircraft's characteristics and his work led to the creation of a second variant (La-5FN), which became the principal production model. As well as the adoption of M.82FN direct injection engine (capable of generating 1,700 hp) and overall aerodynamic improvements, the designer changed from an entirely wood airframe to one that was mixed (metallic spars were used for the wings). In addition, he improved the control surfaces, thus decidedly increasing the fighter's maneuverability. The La-5FN was delivered to the units in 1943. By October 1944, about 10,000 had been completed. These remained in service for the rest of the war.

A two-seater training version was also built (designated La-5UTI, it appeared in August 1943), characterized by the installation of two cockpits (placed close together) with separate sliding canopies. These aircraft were distributed to the units and proved extremely useful in training pilots in what perhaps remained the Lavochkin fighter's only serious fault: its difficult handling during takeoff and landing. In the spring of 1944, the first aircraft of a new, improved, and more powerful variant began to leave the assembly lines. This was the La-7 which served in its turn for the subsequent developments that resulted in the La-11. The latter appeared immediately after the war. It was the only fighter in the Soviet Air Force to have a piston engine.

color plate

Lavochkin La-5FN Soviet Air Force - Poland and Berlin, 1944-45. Personal aircraft of Squadron Commander Vitali Ivanovich Popkov, "Double Hero of the Soviet Union"

Aircraft:	Lavochkin La-5FN
Nation:	USSR
Manufacturer:	State Industries
Type:	Fighter
Year:	1943
Engine:	Shvetsov M.82FN, 14-cylinder radial, air-cooled, 1,700 hp
Wingspan:	32 ft 2 in (9.80 m)
Length:	28 ft 3 in (8.60 m)
Height:	8 ft 4 in (2.54 m)
Weight:	7,417 lb (3,360 kg)
Maximum speed:	401 mph (647 km/h) at 16,447 ft (5,000 m)
Ceiling:	31,250 ft (9,500 m)
Range:	475 miles (765 km)
Armament:	2 x 20 mm cannons; 441 lb (200 kg) of bombs
Crew:	1

A Lavochkin La-7 in flight with its canopy open.

The Yak-3 holds an important place in the prolific series of Yakovlev fighters. These originated in 1941, with the Yak-1. More than 30,000 were built and their career continued well beyond the end of World War II, with the final Yak-9P model eventually serving in the Korean war. It was a version built expressly for combat at medium-low altitude which proved to have excellent overall characteristics and to be very competitive with the best aircraft in production at the time.

The Yak-3 project was launched toward the end of 1941, with the aim of building the smallest and lightest fighter on which it was possible to adopt the M-107 engine. However, the program was halted for approximately a year, due to delays in engine tunings, as well as the priority given at the time to the production in large quantities of combat planes already in existence. It was not until August, 1943, that the Yak-3 project was taken up again, despite the fact that the engine which it was planned to adopt was still unavailable. Modified as far as the original was concerned by the adoption of a new wing (with reduced wingspan and surface area, it had already been used on the Yak-1M which went into production during 1942), improved from an aerodynamic and structural point of view, and fitted with a Klimov M-105 engine capable of generating in the region of 1,300 hp, the prototype appeared toward the end of the year, and it immediately began initial tests. The first results were very promising, and during flight testing, the new aircraft showed a notable increase in speed, about 30 mph (50 km/h) at 10,855 ft (3,300 m) compared to the contemporary versions of the Yak-9, as well as an advantage of approximately 25 mph (40 km/h) at the same altitude over its most serious and effective rival, the German Messerschmitt Bf.109 G. However, the series of tests proved to be particularly long, and the first production series aircraft did not go into service until July 16, 1944, with the 91st Air Regiment of the VVS. Nevertheless, once under way, production assumed a great pace. In August alone, the assembly lines completed 100 aircraft, and when they ceased in May 1945, the total amounted to 4,848.

From the point of view of maneuverability, the Yak-3 was an outstanding aircraft, and proved capable of outclassing not only the Bf.109 G, but also the Focke Wulf Fw.190 A (below 19,736 ft - 6,000 m). It was used intensively in ground attack, bomber escort, and interception at low altitude. As well as its long and extensive career in the units of the VVS, many foreign units that had chosen to fight in the Soviet Union also adopted the aircraft. These included the Poles of the 1st Warsaw Fighter Regiment and the French of the Groupe Chasse Normandie-Niemen.

color plate

Yakovlev Yak-3 1st Escadrille Regiment de Chasse Normandie-Niemen 303rd Air Division Soviet Air Force - USSR 1944. The Regiment was composed of French pilots

Aircraft:	Yakovlev Yak-3
Nation:	USSR
Manufacturer:	State Industries
Type:	Fighter
Year:	1944
Engine:	Klimov M-105PF-2, 12-cylinder V, liquid-cooled, 1,300 hp
Wingspan:	30 ft 3 in (9.20 m)
Length:	27 ft 11 in (8.50 m)
Height:	7 ft 11 in (2.42 m)
Weight:	5,871 lb (2,660 kg)
Maximum speed:	412 mph (665 km/h) at 10,197 ft (3,100 m)
Ceiling:	25,197 ft (10,700 m)
Range:	558 miles (900 km)
Armament:	1 × 20 mm cannon; 2 machine guns
Crew:	1

A Yak-3 in service with the French "Normandie-Niemen" squadron.

Formation of Yak-3s in service with the "Normandie-Niemen" squadron, consisting of French volunteers enrolled in the Soviet Air Force. The squadron's aircraft bore the Soviet insignia with the Lorraine Cross painted on their tails. The latter was often accompanied by the French flag painted on the propeller spinner.

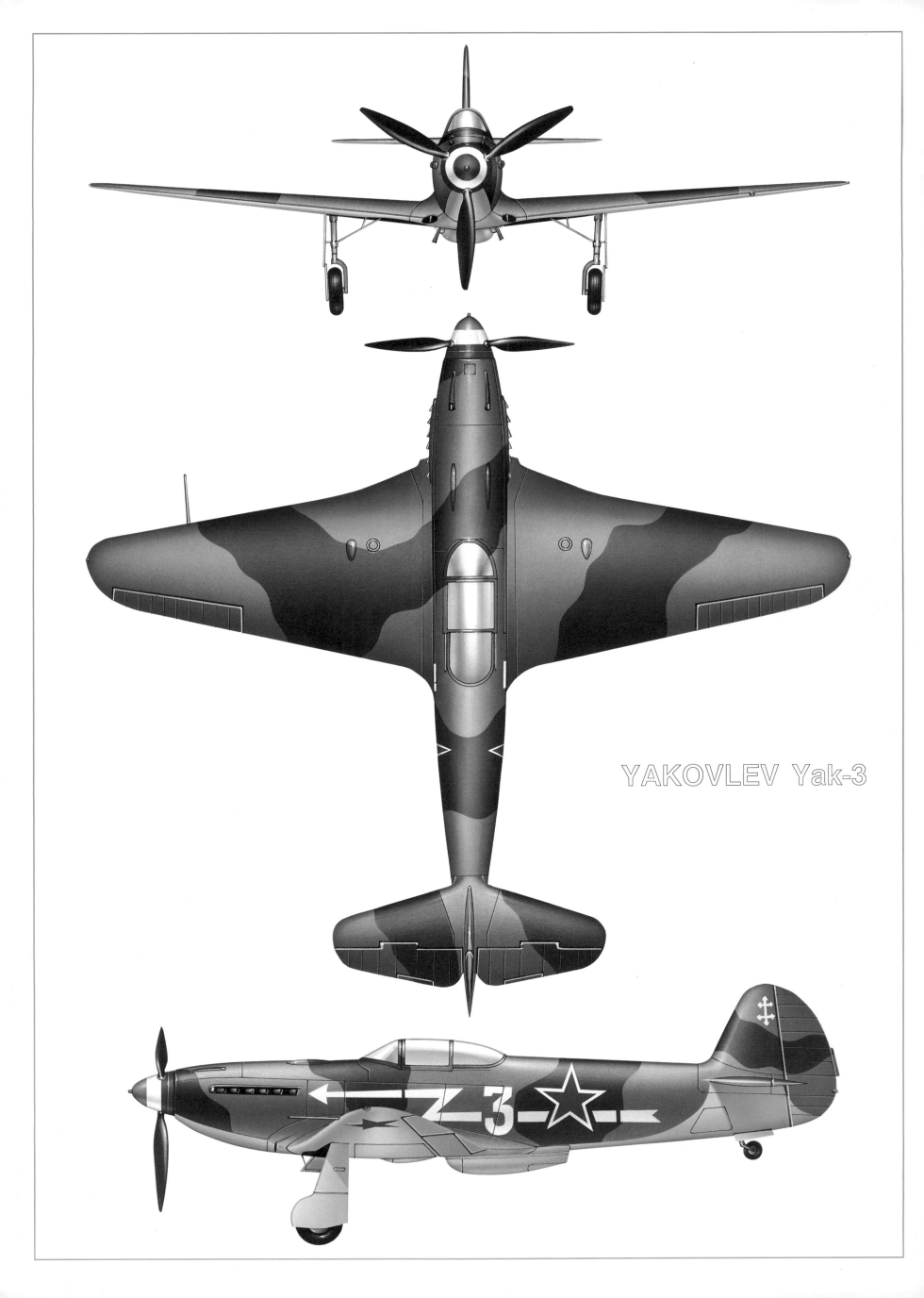

YAKOVLEV Yak-3

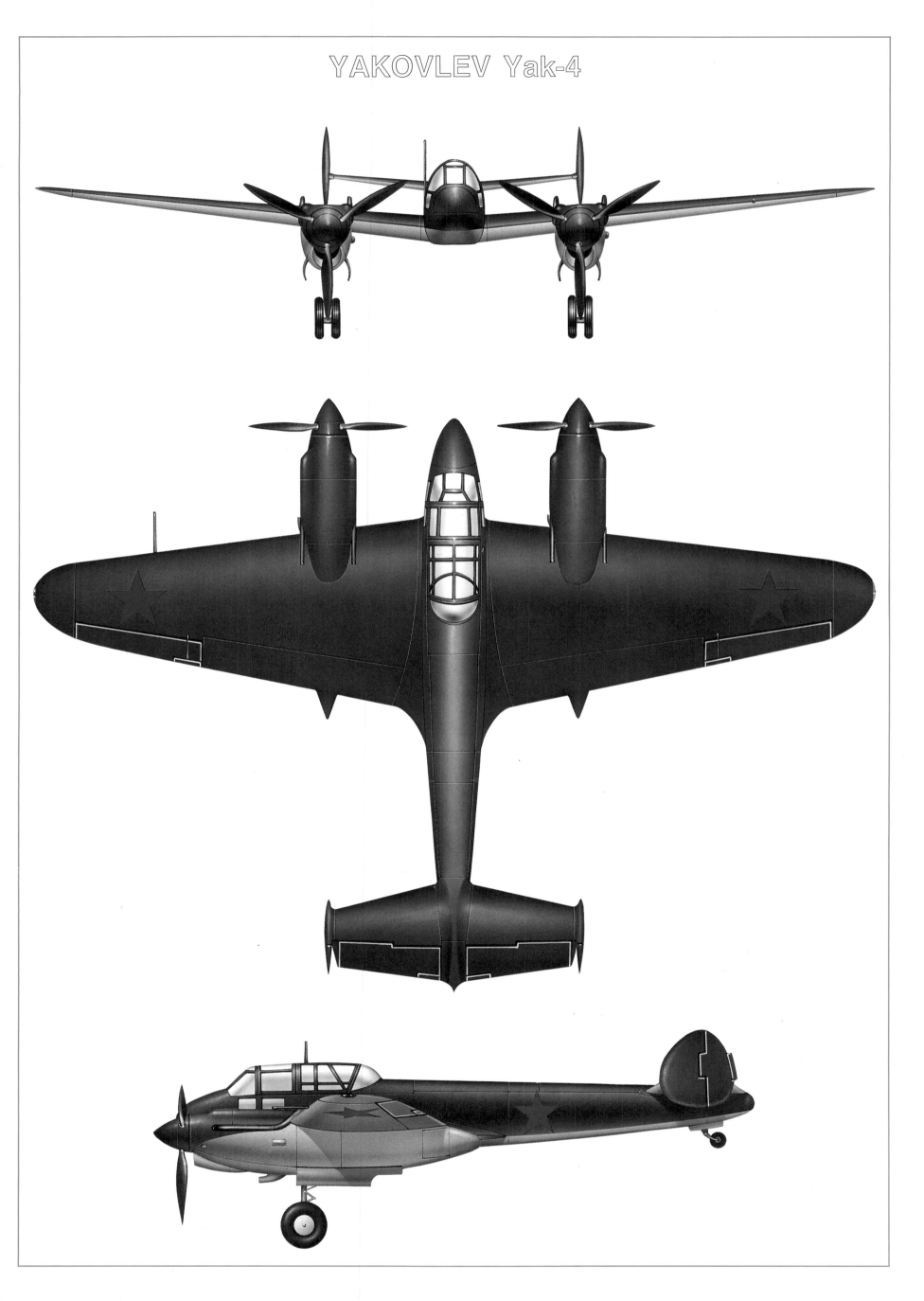

Aleksandr Sergheievic Yakovlev's first military project was initially designated Ya-22 (AIR-22) and appeared at the beginning of 1939. An elegant two-engine monoplane with retractable forward tricycle landing gear and double empennages, it was conceived as a long-range reconnaissance plane. The prototype made its maiden flight on February 22 of the same year, and its overall performance made such a good impression (especially as far as speed was concerned) that it was decided to alter the project in order to construct a light bomber, suitable also for carrying out the role of ground attack.

The two-engine aircraft was redesignated BB-22, although the changes necessary for the new role that had been requested led to a large series of modifications, which occupied the designer for many months. The housing of the two-man crew had to be changed, as well as the position of the armament and the fuel tanks, and an internal bomb hold had to be created. The first BB-22 was completed on the final day of the year and made its maiden flight on January 20, 1940. At the same time, it was decided to construct another two prototypes, one for photographic reconnaissance (R-12), and the other for long-range fighter escort (I-29). During flight tests and operative evaluations, the BB-22 (powered by a pair of Klimov M.103 engines generating 960 hp each) gave excellent proof of its performance, especially as far as its speed was concerned, reaching a maximum speed of 329 mph (530 km/h) at sea level. Moreover, it had a range of 496 miles (800 km) and a service ceiling of 28,947 ft (8,800 m).

During the course of the year the project (officially designated Yak-2) was improved still further. The new version was designated Yak-4 and went into production in the autumn. Compared to the previous version, the housing for the crew and the armor were improved, while the adoption of the more powerful Klimov M.105 engines led to a further improvement in the aircraft's performance and allowed for an increase in the bomb load. In all, approximately

600 two-engine Yakovlevs came off the production lines, most them Yak-4s. However, their operative service did not prove to be particularly satisfactory. The aircraft were very vulnerable, especially when compared with the Ilyushin Il-2s, which were stronger and more protected.

Because of combat experiences the two-engine Yak's career was cut short: production ceased in 1942, and the surviving aircraft were removed from front-line service and relegated to high-altitude reconnaissance missions. They remained operative in this role until the end of the war.

---

color plate
Yakovlev Yak-4 Soviet Air Force - USSR 1942

Aircraft:	Yakovlev Yak-4
Nation:	USSR
Manufacturer:	State Industries
Type:	Attack
Year:	1941
Engine:	2 Klimov M.105R, 12-cylinder V, liquid-cooled, 1,050 hp each
Wingspan:	46 ft (14.00 m)
Length:	30 ft 8 in (9.34 m)
Height:	—
Weight:	11,479 lb (5,200 kg)
Maximum speed:	335 mph (540 km/h) at 16,447 ft (5,000 m)
Ceiling:	31,250 ft (9,500 m)
Range:	745 miles (1,200 km)
Armament:	3 machine guns; 1,329 lb (600 kg) of bombs
Crew:	2

A Yak-4 which was damaged and captured by the German troops during the invasion of Russia.

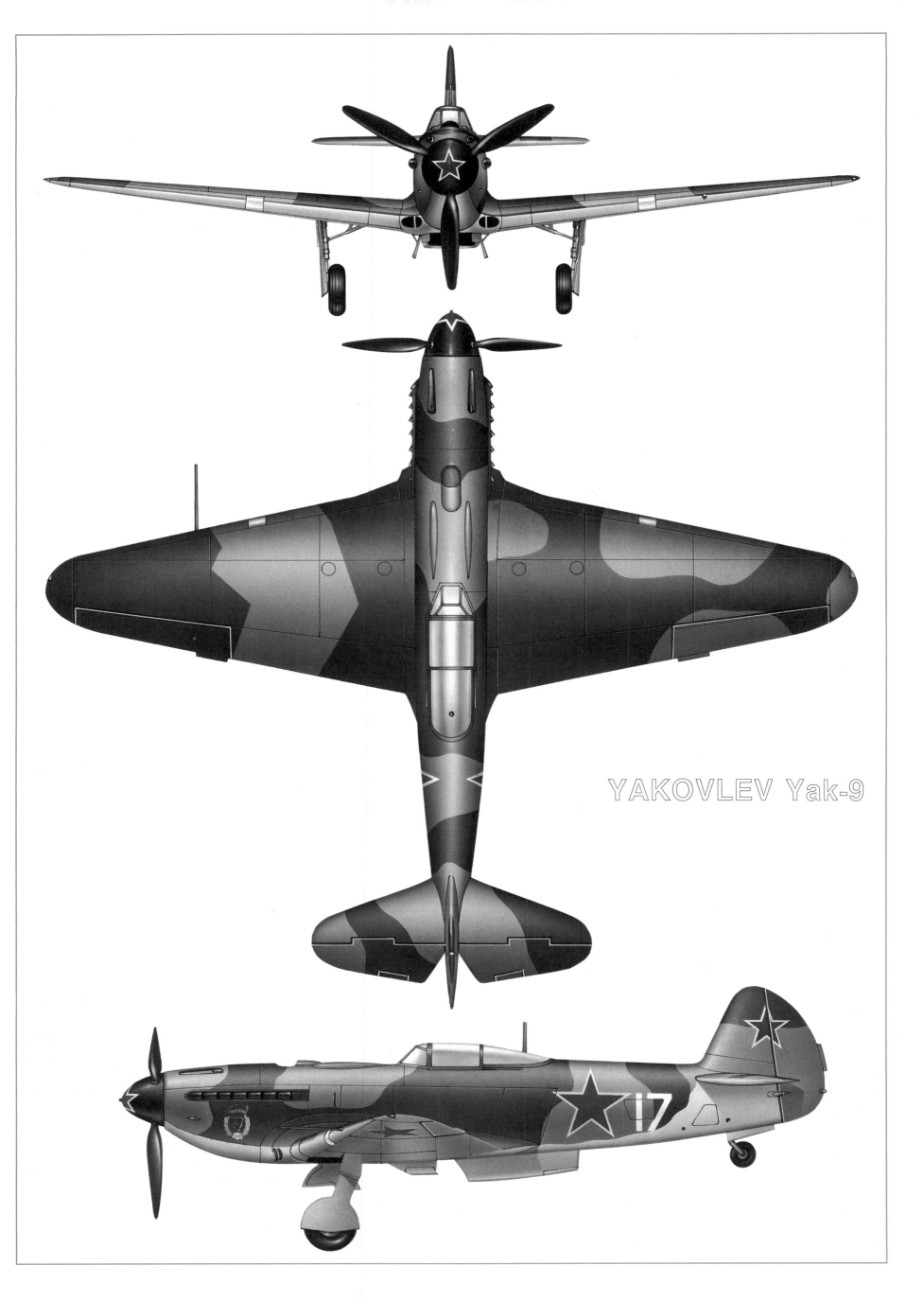

YAKOVLEV Yak-9

The series of Yakovlev fighters, which originated with the Yak-1 of 1941, was one of the most important families of combat planes built by the Soviet Union during World War II. A total of more than 30,000 were built (including 16,769 Yak-9s), and their career lasted well beyond the end of the conflict, continuing until the 1950s. The Yak-9P, the last and best to make use of the airframe, was in fact used during the Korean War.

The Yak-9 was originally a development of the Yak-7 fighter of 1941, of which 6,399 were built. It was from the Yak-7D, an experimental variant, that the new model was derived. The need to build a better series of these aircraft was dictated above all by the need to improve their range. The half-wings were partially redesigned, while the pilot's cockpit was moved slightly farther back, and the position of the radiator in the belly was also altered. Production began in the summer of 1942, and the Yak-9 was delivered to the fighter units in October.

The aircraft's intensive career (which began during the battle of Stalingrad) did not prevent it from being updated, a process that initially regarded its armament. In the Yak-9M version, a 12.7 mm weapon was added to the 20 mm cannon and the original machine guns, while the cargo capacity of the Yak-9B model was exploited to the full, and the aircraft could carry a maximum bomb load of 883 lb (400 kg). These were followed by the Yak-9T; tested in December 1942 and operative from the beginning of the following year, it was suitable for antitank attack.

In the 1943 summer a new variant, the Yak-9D, entered service. It had a more powerful engine and was intended for the role of long-range escort fighter. In this aircraft the increase in range, which eventually surpassed 807 miles (1,300 km), was obtained by reducing the defensive armament until it consisted of a 20 mm cannon and a single 12.7 mm caliber machine gun. A further improvement was made in the Yak-9DD, a version derived from it, in which the range was increased to 1,242 miles (2,200 km). These aircraft were mainly used to escort the formations of American bombers which took off from bases in Great Britain to carry out raids on oil fields in Rumania.

The last variant to be built during the war was the Yak-9U, whose prototype took to the air in December 1943. In this model, Yakovlev substantially renewed the airframe, redesigning its entire basic structure (which became all-metal, like its covering) and remarkably improving its aerodynamic lines. In addition, the span and surface area of the wings was increased, while a more powerful engine, the 1,650 hp Klimov M-107A, was adopted. This improved the performance of the aircraft remarkably, increasing the maximum speed of 372 mph (600 km/h) at 11,482 ft (3,500 m) achiev-ed by the Yak-9D to approximately 434 mph (700 km/h) at 18,092 ft (5,500 m). It was from this aircraft that the last postwar version, the Yak-9P, was subsequently developed.

In addition to its intensive and lengthy career in the units of the VVS, the Yakovlev Yak-9 also equipped numerous foreign units that had chosen to fight in the Soviet Union. These included the Poles of the 1st Warsaw Fighter Regiment and the French of the *Groupe de Chasse Normandie-Niemen*, whose pilots chose the Yak-9 after having tried the American Bell P-39 and the British Hawker Hurricane. After the war, apart from the Soviet Union, the Yak-9 was adopted above all by Bulgaria, Poland, and Yugoslavia.

---

color plate

Yakovlev Yak-9 Guards Fighter Regiment - Soviet Air Force 1944

Aircraft:	Yakovlev Yak-9D
Nation:	USSR
Manufacturer:	State Industries
Type:	Fighter
Year:	1943
Engine:	Klimov M-105PF, 12-cylinder V, liquid-cooled, 1,250 hp
Wingspan:	32 ft 10 in (10.00 m)
Length:	24 ft 11 in (8.50 m)
Height:	9 ft 10 in (3.00 m)
Weight:	6,876 lb (3,115 kg)
Maximum speed:	372 mph (600 km/h) at 11,482 ft (3,500 m)
Ceiling:	32,894 ft (10,000 m)
Range:	825 miles (1,330 km)
Armament:	1 × 20 mm cannon, 1 machine gun
Crew:	1

A formation of Yakovlev Yak-9Ds in flight.

Formation of Yak-9s with their propeller hubs painted in characteristic fashion with the red star.

CONTENTS